PROMOTING NATURE
IN CITIES AND TOWNS
A Practical Guide

PROMOTING NATURE
IN CITIES AND TOWNS
A Practical Guide

By Malcolm Emery for the Ecological Parks Trust

CROOM HELM
London • Sydney • Dover, New Hampshire

Aided by grants from The Nature Conservancy Council, The Carnegie United Kingdom Trust and The Calouste Gulbenkian Foundation and a loan from The World Wildlife Fund

Croom Helm Ltd, Provident House, Burrell Row,
Beckenham, Kent BR3 1AT
Croom Helm Australia Pty Ltd, Suite 4, 6th Floor, 64-76 Kippax Street,
Surry Hills, NSW 2010, Australia
Croom Helm, 51 Washington Street,
Dover, New Hampshire, 03820, USA

British Library Cataloguing in Publication Data

Emery, Malcolm
    Promoting nature in cities and towns: a practical
    guide
    1. Nature conservation — Great Britain   2. Cities
    and towns — Great Britain
    I. Title II. Ecological Parks Trust
    639.9'0941   QH77.G7

    ISBN 0-7099-0966-7
    ISBN 0-7099-0970-5 Pbk

Library of Congress Cataloging in Publication Data applied for

Typeset by Leaper & Gard Ltd, Bristol, England in 9pt Parlament Roman
Printed and bound in Great Britain

Contents

PART ONE: HOW TO START UP NEW SITES

PART TWO: DEVELOPING SITES — ECOLOGICAL PRINCIPLES AND PRACTICES

7

Plates

1A. Oxford ragwort (*Senecio squalidus*), is a typical plant of urban wasteland, so called because it 'escaped' from a botanic garden in Oxford in the early 1900s. Its wind-blown seeds have allowed it to spread throughout the British Isles, along road and rail networks, and it can find root-holds in the most inhospitable and barren places, including cracks in masonry, as in this photograph (source: Nature Photographers)

1. Common spotted orchid (*Dactylorhiza fuchsii*) on a vacant site in Barking, East London. Many unusual and rare wild plants may be found growing in British towns and cities (source: John Tyler)

2. The black redstart (*Phoenicurus ochrurus*) naturally inhabits mountains and cliffs. In the 1940s, these birds increased in Britain when city bomb-sites provided suitable new nesting habitats (source: Bruce Coleman)

3. The Kestrel (*Falco tinnunculus*) thrives in built-up areas, hunting for small birds and mammals amongst the vegetation of road verges and urban open spaces, and nesting in tall trees and buildings (source: Bruce Coleman)

4. Many British wild animals are becoming more common in urban areas, even the shy and secretive badger (source: John Tyler)

5. Natural succession describes the gradual process by which vegetation develops naturally on undisturbed sites, following a general pattern of initial colonisation of bare ground by annual and biennial plants, and their gradual replacement by perennials and woody perennials (shrubs and trees). This photograph illustrates the various stages together on one site (source: Oliver Gilbert)

6. Natural succession in water follows a general pattern of open water being colonised by submerged and floating plants, with emergent plants encroaching inwards from the water's edge. As the root mass of emergent plants clogs and dries out the fringes of the water body, trees such as alders (*Alnus* spp.) and willows (*Salix* spp.) are able to colonise (source: Peter Wakely, Nature Conservancy Council)

7-15 Types of plant communities found on urban sites (see page 124 for a classification of urban plant communities)

7. Open communities on walls, roofs, pavements, etc., dominated by mosses, liverworts, ferns and lichens. This photograph illustrates a carpet of the mosses *Ceratodon purpureus* and *Bryum argenteum* on a tarmac car park. Carpets such as this are important winter feeding habitats for blackbirds which search the moss cushions for seeds and insect pupae (source: David Shimwell)

8. Floating and submerged communities of freshwater plants in ponds, derelict docks, canals, flooded sewage beds, etc. This photograph illustrates Basingstoke canal: floating plants — frog bit (*Hydrocharis morsus-ranae*) and duckweeds (*Lemna* spp.); submerged plants — milfoils (*Myriophyllum* spp.) (source: Peter Wakely, Nature Conservancy Council)

9. Weed communities dominated by annual or biennial plants on newly disturbed vacant sites: for example (A) demolition sites are typically flattened and graded by heavy machinery; (B) such sites soon become covered with colourful flowers, including species with wind-blown seeds, such as dandelions (*Taraxacum officinale*) and ragworts (*Senecio* spp.) and annual or biennial species such as shepherd's purse (*Capsella bursa-pastoris*), yarrow (*Achillea millefolium*) and plantains (*Plantago* spp.) (source: Oliver Gilbert)

10. Water's edge communities of emergent, tall swamp plants, around the margins of rivers, canals, ponds, etc. For example, a pond on a pulverised fuel ash tip with emergent marginal plants including reedmace (*Typha latifolia*), branched burr-reed (*Sparganium erectum*) and common reed (*Phragmites australis*) (source: David Shimwell)

11. Water's edge communities of emergent, short swamp and marsh plants, dominated by grass/reed/perennial herbs/rush and marsh plants. For example, a boggy area of Wimbledon Common, London, dominated by rushes (*Juncus* spp.) and sedges (*Carex* spp.) (source: Philip Masters)

12. Rank, perennial, tall grass and tall herb communities of embankments, uncut road verges, etc. For example, a road embankment in Bristol with pyramidal orchid (*Anacamptis pyramidalis*) growing amongst ox-eye daisies (*Chrysanthemum leucanthemum*), cocksfoot grass (*Dactylis glomerata*) and an abundance of other tall herbs. Note the young ash (*Fraxinus excelsior*) also colonising the embankment (source: Avon Wildlife Trust)

13. Scrub vegetation of thickets, hedges, park borders and vacant sites which have been undisturbed for perhaps 20 years, dominated by woody shrubs less than 5 m in height. For example, gorse (*Ulex europaeus*) and willows (*Salix* spp.) in Washington New Town (source: Philip Masters)

14. Low, perennial, grass and grass-herb communities, maintained either by disturbance, e.g. mowing or trampling; or by unfavourable conditions, e.g. low soil fertility. For example, a periodically mown churchyard in Sheffield with herbs such as daisies (*Bellis perennis*), dandelions (*Taraxacum officinale*), buttercups (*Ranunculus* spp.) and clovers (*Trifolium* spp.) growing amongst short grasses such as common bent (*Agrostis tenuis*) and smooth meadow grass (*Poa pratensis*) (source: Oliver Gilbert)

15. Deciduous and evergreen woodland, greater than 5 m in height, with a more or less closed canopy, and urban 'pasture' woodland, with an open canopy. For example, bluebells (*Endymion non-scriptus*) growing along the edge of a nineteenth-century beech (*Fagus sylvatica*) plantation (source: David Shimwell)

16. Gang-mown short grass, typical of too many British traditional town and city parks. This could aptly be called 'green desert' (source: John Tyler)

17. (A) This disused railway in Birmingham used to be mown regularly. Simply leaving it un-mown for three years has allowed an attractive community of wildflowers to develop, increasing its value for wildlife at the same time (source: Urban Wildlife Group); (B) this sea of colour was achieved by the Rural Preservation Association (now called Landlife), by simply sowing a vacant plot with seeds of wildflowers once common in British cornfields, but now, sadly, less so, for example: corn cockle (*Agrostemma githago*), corn flower (*Centaurea cyanus*), corn marigold (*Chrysanthemum segetum*) and poppy (*Papaver rhoeas*) (source: author)

18 and 19. Habitat creation: the William Curtis Ecological Park, London. A lorry park transformed into an oasis in the inner city (source: Ecological Parks Trust)

20 and 21. Habitat creation: Linnet Lane in Liverpool. A sunny bower for residents to share with wildflowers, birds and butterflies, created in a corner plot (source: Landlife (formerly the Rural Preservation Association))

22 and 23. Habitat creation: the Rural Preservation Association (Landlife) Nature Garden at the Liverpool Garden Festival in 1984. This garden collected two prizes of honour and the Festival Gold Medal (source: Landlife (formerly the Rural Preservation Association))

24. Nature in the city is for people to enjoy: landscape painting at the William Curtis Ecological Park, London (source: Stephen McAndrews)

25. People of all ages, but most particularly children, can benefit from close contact with wildlife. Very young explorers, minibeast hunting in the pond at the William Curtis Ecological Park, London (source: John Davidge)

26. Sheep grazing in a Northampton churchyard. This is a traditional British practice which has gone on for generations, but which now is rarely seen (see page 262) (source: John Tyler)

27. Coppicing. This woodland in Suffolk has been traditionally managed as coppice since the thirteenth century. Note the standard trees left amongst the coppice stools and the standing underwood in the right background (see page 287) (source: Heather Angel)

28. Regenerating hazel (*Corylus avellana*) coppice. At this stage, the coppice is at its best for wild birds, providing nesting and sheltering habitat (source: J. Bateson, Nature Conservancy Council)

29. Pollarding. The pollarded hornbeams (*Carpinus betulus*) are in Epping Forest (source: Heather Angel)

30. Hedge laying. This traditional form of hedgerow management rejuvenates and thickens the hedge, ensuring its longevity as a valuable wildlife habitat (see page 293) (source: author)

Figures

Tables

Acknowledgements

Many thanks to the following:
The Nature Conservancy Council (NCC), for helping to finance the project.
NCC staff, in particular George Barker and Ted Hammond.
Max Nicholson, John Tyler, Stephen McAndrews and Philip Masters for helpful
    criticism and advice throughout the project.
Colette Maude, John Andrews and Lesley MacKinnon for help, and patience,
    while editing the text.
Teresa Sexton for welcome moral support and assistance in organisation and
    liaison.

The following for constructive advice on particular sections:
Don Aldridge — Chapter 8, 'Interpretation' (co-author).
Professor Tony Bradshaw — creation and management of habitats.
Lyndis Cole — site surveying/selection and principles of design.
Dr Ray Gemmell — creation of habitats.
John Knights — legal considerations and constraints.
Jan McHarry — forming a local group.
George Peterken and Keith Kirby — woodland.
Peter Thoday — gardening for the handicapped.

Sincere thanks to the helpful staff of the various kindred groups and
organisations visited during work on the project.

Foreword

The paradox, not to say scandal, of so many inner-city citizens being deprived of ready access to open spaces and to nature, while so many thousands of acres in their neighbourhoods stand vacant and derelict, has won more and more attention during the past decade. Energetic individuals and groups have started projects for greening the cities and for turning to good use a number of suitable empty sites. Their efforts, however, have shown up the many obstacles and complications which still stand in the way of really widespread and successful remedial measures.

The difficulties fall into four main groups. First, it is not easy to find out whose permission is needed to use a given site, or on what terms it can be secured, if at all, and for how long. Second, each site has its constraints on public use, whether through dangerous features, access limitations or topographic and ecological handicaps. Third, given that a way can be found round such difficulties it is still necessary to devise and carry out a complex management plan in order to realise the potential of the site and to safeguard against a variety of troubles. Last but not least the project has to be harmonised with and embraced by the local community and by relevant interest groups such as schools, youth organisations, civic and environmental groups and the disabled.

For this the right organisation is essential, which in turn requires a conveniently available digest of the state of the art in creating city nature parks and similar urban green spaces. The Ecological Parks Trust, with its own considerable practical experience over the past eight years and its many contacts with others in the field, has undertaken this task with the support of the Nature Conservancy Council, the Carnegie United Kingdom Trust, the Gulbenkian Foundation and others. This practical guide, written and researched for the Trust by Mr Malcolm Emery, one of its own former wardens, is, it may be hoped, only the beginning of a series of follow-up initiatives, of which the first will be a travelling exhibition conveying the same message in an alternative form (the Carnegie United Kingdom Trust's contribution). Simultaneously, the Trust's Research Group, also supported by the Nature Conservancy Council, is embarking on a comprehensive series of ecological and social science studies of urban ecology and conservation which is designed to expand and deepen the knowledge on which a future edition of this guide will be able to draw, in combination with developments being made by such kindred bodies as the British Trust for Conservation Volunteers, the Groundwork Trust and the Royal Society for Nature Conservation.

At the same time the Trust is expanding its own research and experimental programme, especially at the new Rotherhithe Ecological Park, made available to it by the London Docklands Development Corporation, and is exploring the possibility of establishing a formal training course for those intending to establish or manage city nature parks and similar projects. In these and other ways the Trust will pursue its mission to elaborate and reinforce a sound basis for a variety of projects throughout the country, to enable city-dwellers to enjoy immediate and rewarding access to nature. As many already understand, there are few such effective, low-cost and creative devices for enhancing the opportunities for a better life for those living in inner cities.

Max Nicholson
Chairman
Ecological Parks Trust

PART ONE
How To Start Up New Sites

1 Introduction — Why Urban Nature Conservation?

During the past decade in Great Britain, the number of self-help groups actively involved in the conservation of wildlife in our towns and cities has gradually increased. Urban dwellers are becoming more and more aware of and sympathetic to the wealth of plant and animal life around them. Local authorities have begun to consider the ecology of wild plant and animal communities in their development policies for cities and more and more authorities are appointing ecologists to look after the wildlife of the urban landscape. There is an increasing awareness of the need to conserve nature in cities which reaches into the classroom, the public consciousness and right across the professions from landscape architect and planner to park manager. So why do all these people consider urban nature conservation to be worthwhile?

1.1 Personal benefits

In the late nineteenth and early twentieth centuries, the Industrial Revolution caused millions of people to move into urban areas, taking them away from the daily contact with natural scenery and wildlife which their ancestors had experienced for a hundred generations before. Today, over 80 per cent of the British population live in towns and cities. Studies have shown that urban dwellers, and in particular inner-city dwellers cannot, or do not, easily gain access to the countryside or even the urban fringe. There is an urgent need for more natural greenspace in our cities to provide the urban population with refreshment from the complexities and rigours of urban life.

A recent study (Tartaglia-Kershaw 1982) examined how people in Sheffield used a piece of woodland and found that it provided some important benefits to local residents. The public saw the wood as a resource providing continuity; links with past childhoods. The woodland influenced residents' development of identity with place and community, stimulating feelings of security and a desire to stay in the area.

Other studies involving individual interviews and group discussions have shown how and in what way urban dwellers benefit from contact with natural wildlife areas. The projects studied appealed to people with widely varied interests, ages and personalities. Involvement in the projects led to feelings of pride and achievement, learning new skills, increased awareness of local history, getting to know people better, developing a team and community spirit and increased levels of responsibility in individuals. People enjoyed the physical exercise and general feelings of freedom. They were able to 'escape' from the city environment, to retreat peacefully and repair battered emotions and to 'get back to nature' and appreciate its richness and variety. Long-term effects of involvement with the projects included increased community interest and co-operation between teenagers, increased confidence, a feeling amongst adults of setting down roots and often significant changes in life-style (sometimes even changes in choice of career) towards areas of public service or environmental improvement. When involved with informal greenspace, children exhibited high levels of inventiveness in play. There is very little to fire a child's imagination in formal parks; their natural urges for adventure often seek expression on wasteland sites.

The enterprise of self-help groups is seen as healthy, particularly where public service, rather than profit, is the prime motivation. Energy, enthusiasm, self-motivation, commitment and initiative are all part and parcel of the urban nature conservation movement as it tries to revitalise community facilities by nurturing wildlife in our towns and cities. Stimulating people to care more for wildlife increases the care they show for one another.

1.2 Educational benefits

First-hand experience is always the best way to learn, regardless of age. By creating areas of natural greenspace in the city, students of all ages can come into intimate contact with wild plants and animals, rather than having to read about them in books.

By observing living organisms in their wild habitats, rather than in the glass case or cage of the zoo, museum or classroom, students can begin to appreciate the beauties and complexities of growth, behaviour, competition between species, and changes in time as night follows day and seasons progress. By learning about and appreciating the richness of nature, young and old alike may be able to realise its value and develop a desire to conserve it, not only in their own area, but in the countryside and wherever else they go.

City children may be able to visit the countryside once or twice a year, on conducted school trips to rural field study centres. One of the problems with this arrangement is the time it takes some children to adjust to new environments. By the time some children have calmed down and adjusted to the novelty of the field centre, so that they are ready to learn, the field trip may be nearly over. Inner-city nature, being so much more accessible, allows teachers and children to visit sites more regularly, at less expense. The children then have the time gradually to learn about and become familiar with the natural environment, and to observe its important seasonal changes throughout the year.

1.3 Environmental benefits — wasteland as a resource

Our towns and cities are in a constant state of change as development and decay proceed apace. These processes generate wasteland. In 1976 the Civic Trust estimated that over 100,000 hectares of urban wasteland existed in Great Britain and the figures will be much the same today. The size of wasteland sites will vary from areas less than 1 hectare, commonly found in the inner city, to areas over 10 hectares around such installations as power stations on the city fringes. Long stretches of derelict railway lines and embankments, disused mineral workings, areas which are too waterlogged or precipitous to build upon; there are many reasons for urban sites being left as waste. Some sites may only be temporarily vacant, for example gap sites where buildings have been demolished and new buildings are eventually to be built. Others may be vacant for many years, because development is out of the question. All these sites have the potential to be used as a resource for urban dwellers, so long as they can be made safe (e.g. free from toxic wastes, etc.). If ignored for long enough, waste sites will be colonised by wild plants and animals. By adopting a site and capitalising on this natural process of colonisation, we can help it along and create safe oases of greenery where before lay an ugly, derelict piece of urban decay. These oases can enrich the quality of the local environment. Trees and bushes can act as barriers from the noise, dirt and clamour of the city, and the sound of humming bees and bird song can be a pleasing substitute for the roar of traffic.

1.4 Benefits to wildlife

Traditional nature conservation in Britain has tended to concentrate on the countryside, creating nature reserves and protecting rare species and disappearing habitats. Today, the struggle to protect the plants and animals of our countryside continues against increasing pressure, for example from intensive agriculture. Modern high technology has provided farmers with larger machinery and sophisticated agrochemicals to increase agricultural productivity. As a consequence, many of our hedgerows are being lost as they are being ripped out to make larger fields for the larger agricultural machines. Even where hedgerows survive, new techniques using tractor-mounted hedge-cutting machines mean that the numbers of hedgerow trees are decreasing at an alarming rate. Ancient, flower-rich hay meadows are being ploughed, re-seeded and fertilised to produce swards made up of just one or two grass species. Deciduous woodlands are being cleared for agriculture. Ponds are filled in and wetlands are being drained.

Probably the most powerful and far-reaching pressure against wildlife in our countryside is that produced by the extensive use of pesticides and powerful synthetic fertilisers. Insecticides and herbicides deplete the countryside of the plants and invertebrates which form the base of the complex food webs in the communities of wild creatures. Fertilisers enter and pollute our waterways as they are washed into them from the surrounding fields.

Compare this picture to the situation in our towns and cities. Over the past few decades, our cities have become much cleaner. Domestic and industrial pollution have decreased. The attitude of the urban population has changed as people have become increasingly aware of the need for clean air and water and increasingly sympathetic to wild creatures. Not surprisingly, therefore, the number of wild plants and animals living in our towns and cities has increased, while much of the countryside continues to experience a general decline.

Table 1.1 illustrates how comparatively rich different urban environments are for wildlife according to the levels of disturbance or management to which they are subjected. A new grouping of urban environment types not mentioned in the table is the specially created environments, such as city nature parks, ecological parks and wildlife gardens, which are now becoming more numerous in our cities, thanks to city schools and wildlife groups. These would commonly fall into the same category as 'suburban areas' (third column). Many urban environments are surprisingly rich in wildlife. For example, in Bristol, the density of foxes is one of the highest recorded in a city anywhere in the world. Other mammals such as badgers, hedgehogs and woodmice continue to increase in urban areas. Blackbird population densities in urban and suburban areas tend to be higher than those in rural areas. Apart from the animals most readily seen in cities, such as pigeons, starlings, sparrows and the like, a host of unusual species are to be found. In a garden in south-east London, over 700 species of beetle have been identified (Davis 1978) and in another garden in Leicester, over 17,000 species of plants and animals, including 330 butterfly and moth species and 345 flowering plants (Owen and Owen 1983). Unusual sites

Table 1.1 Classification of artificial environments of urban and industrial origin according to their relative biotic diversity and the degree of disturbance or management to which they are subjected

	Relative Biotic Diversity		
Disturbance/ management	*Low*	*Medium*	*High*
Low	Grossly polluted areas	Old, disused mineral workings (except those in column 3)	Older chalk and limestone; colliery subsidence flashes
Medium		Urban waste land; grounds of power stations and hospitals, etc.; urban waterways and reservoirs; rubbish dumps	Flooded gravel pits (with recreational use); railway land; old-fashioned sewage farms; larger parks and golf courses, etc.
High	Active quarries and mines; urban centres and dense housing; heavy industrial areas, refineries, etc.; stations, ports, depots, etc.; urban roads	Formal parks; sports fields and airfields; allotments	Suburban areas

Source: from Davis (1976).

such as the many dumps of calcareous and other alkali industrial waste in the north-west of England are now covered in orchid-rich plant communities containing many rare species (Gemmell 1982). Newly disturbed urban sites where excavation or demolition or dumping of soil occurs tend to develop 'ruderal' vegetation (vegetation of disturbed soils) which includes many species, once common arable weeds, but which are now becoming rare in the age of agricultural herbicides.

The wildlife of towns and cities does not, however, have it all its own way. Ground-nesting birds suffer from predation by cats and dogs. High population densities mean that many people will use wild areas if they have access and so trampling and disturbance will tend to exclude sensitive plants and animals in many situations. It is possible to reach a compromise by providing sanctuary areas on our city sites for these creatures, while providing the public with facilities for observing them without disturbing or harming them. The extremes of rubbish dumping on one hand and excessive tidiness on the other can both be detrimental to wildlife. Clearing up litter and leaving some of our park grassland unmown can both help wild plants and animals.

1.5 Economic benefits

The contributions which urban nature conservation can make to improving the living environment for town and city dwellers can have economic spin-offs. The rate at which people move away from an area should decrease if it becomes more pleasant to live there. Another feature of nature conservation is that it is labour-intensive. Kidd and Scott's 1982 study of urban nature conservation and youth unemployment suggests that many of our young unemployed can benefit significantly from involvement in urban nature conservation projects.

There are many opportunities for encouraging wildlife in a host of different situations in towns and cities. Local authorities, professional planners and landscape architects, land managers, voluntary organisations and, above all, the individual inhabitants of our towns and cities could and should collaborate to conserve and create areas for wildlife and then to use and enjoy them.

1.6 References

Baines, C. (1982) 'Urban wildlife — conservation and re-creation', *Natural World*, Spring 1982:16-17, Royal Society for Nature Conservation

—— (1984) 'Landscape in practice', *Landscape Design*, 2:27-8

Batten, L.A. (1973) 'Population dynamics of suburban blackbirds', *Bird Study*, **20**:251-8

Benson, J.F. (1981) 'Animal communities in an urban environment', *Landscape Research*, **6**:8-11

Bradshaw, A.D. (1982) 'The biology of land reclamation in urban areas' in R. Bornkamm, J.A. Lee and M.H. Seaward (eds.), *Urban Ecology*, Blackwell, pp. 293-303

Bradshaw, A.D. and Chadwick, M.J. (1980) *The Restoration of Land*, Blackwell

Burrows, J. (1978) 'Vacant urban land — a continuing crisis', *The Planner*, Jan., pp. 7-9

Davis, B.N.K. (1976) 'Wildlife, urbanisation and industry', *Biological Conservation*, **10**(4):249-91

—— (1978) 'Urbanisation and the diversity of insects', *Symposium of the Royal Entomological Society*, **9**:126-38

Dutton, R.A. and Bradshaw, A.D. (1982) *Land Reclamation in Cities*, HMSO, London

Ecological Parks Trust (1981) *New Life for Old Space. A guide to handbooks and leaflets covering the principles and methods of converting small urban sites into nature areas in Britain*, EPT, London

Gemmell, R.P. (1982) 'The origin and botanical importance of industrial habitats' in R. Bornkamm, J.A. Lee and M.H. Seaward (eds.), *Urban Ecology*, Blackwell, pp. 30-40

Greenwood, E.F. and Gemmell, R.G. (1978) 'Derelict industrial land as a habitat for rare plants in S. Lancs. (V.C. 59) and W. Lancs (V.C. 60)', *Watsonia*, **12**:33-40

Greenwood, R. (1983) 'Gorse Covert, Warrington — creating a more natural landscape', *Landscape Design*, **143**:35-8

Harris, S.S. (1977) 'Urban foxes — the adaptation of a large predator to city life', Section D, 139th Annual Meeting, British Association for the Advancement of Science, Birmingham

Kelcey, J.G. (1975) 'Industrial development and wildlife conservation', *Environmental Conservation*, **2**(2):99-108

Kidd, S. and Scott, R. (1982) *Urban Nature Conservation and Youth Unemployment*, Nature Conservancy Council

Mabey, R. (1974) *Unofficial Countryside*, Collins, London

Mostyn, B.J. (1979) 'Personal benefits and satisfactions derived from participation in urban wildlife projects', Social and Community Planning Research/Nature Conservancy Council

Murton, R. and Harrington, C. (1982) 'Recreation at the urban fringe: Conflict or conciliation?', Dept. Geography, University College, London. Paper for Royal Geographical Society Conference, 22 April 1982

Nature Conservancy Council (1979) *Nature Conservation in Urban Areas: Challenge and Opportunity*, NCC

Owen, J. and Owen, D.F. (1975) 'Suburban gardens; England's most important nature reserve?', *Environmental Conservation*, **2**:53-9

—— (1983) 'The most neglected wildlife habitat of all', *New Scientist*, 6 Jan., pp. 9-11

Ratcliffe, D.A. (ed.) (1977) *A Nature Conservation Review*, 2 vols., Cambridge University Press

Tartaglia-Kershaw, M. (1982) 'The recreational and aesthetic significance of urban woodland', *Landscape Research*, Dec., pp. 22-5

Teagle, W.G. (1978) *The Endless Village*, Nature Conservancy Council

Tregay, R. and Gustavsson, R. (1983) *Oakwood's New Landscape. Designing for nature in the residential environment*, Warrington and Runcorn Development Corporation

Woodward P. and Berger, R. (1984) *Planning with Nature. A guide for all who help shape the environment of our towns*, Urban Wildlife Group, Birmingham

2 How to Begin. Establishing a (Local) Wildlife Group

2.1 Why form a group

(a) Within a community, each individual has personal abilities, experience and ideas. A group can pool this wealth of local knowledge and achieve far more, working together, than individuals can, working in isolation. The workload may be properly shared.
(b) The group acts as a focal point for people to meet their neighbours and develop a feeling of community spirit.
(c) Local government and professional organisations will be more responsive to and co-operative towards a well-organised group than to an equally large number of disorganised people.
(d) A recognised group will be more able to generate material and financial support from both the public and private sectors.

The nucleus for a group usually consists of a small number of people with shared interests in urban wildlife. It may appear to such a small group, with their special interests, that they are largely alone in the community. This has often proved not to be the case. For example, local issues, such as the impending loss of a popular piece of woodland to industrial development, may precipitate a public enquiry. During crises such as this, the ranks of active urban wildlife enthusiasts may swell suddenly. Sadly, in many cases, public enthusiasm comes too late to stop the development. It would therefore seem logical for any small groups of enthusiasts to form larger, more organised, wildlife groups. These would then be better prepared to stop such destruction of important sites, or to argue for changes in local authority policies.

Such groups may also perform many other functions of benefit to the local community. The Nature Conservancy Council publication *Urban Nature Conservation and Youth Employment* describes urban nature conservation as a combination of three complementary elements:

a) The preservation and management of existing wildlife and habitats in urban areas.
b) The creation of new habitats which can accommodate the needs of both wildlife and urban people.
c) The education of urban dwellers regarding the existence of nature in towns and cities; the potential to accommodate a wider diversity of species; its importance; and the role they can play in conserving, developing and enjoying the wildlife resources on their own doorsteps.

2.2 Getting the ball rolling

Your first consideration when starting a group is whether or not there are others in the area already doing what you intend to do. The following is a list of organisations that may know of groups, or may have some operating in the area (see Appendix 15 for addresses):

(a) Government organisations

Countryside Commission — the government organisation responsible for amenity and access, primarily in rural and urban fringe areas.

Nature Conservancy Council — the governmental conservation body with officers responsible for nature conservation, rural and urban, in each region of the country.

(b) Environmental/conservation/community organisations

British Association of Settlements and Social Action Centres — a confederation of organisations committed to initiating and developing work to tackle some of the problems of individuals and groups in urban communities.

British Trust for Conservation Volunteers — a national organisation with many regional conservation corps bases.

Civic Trust — a general conservation and amenity organisation with regional branches, e.g. Civic Trust for the North-West.

Council for Urban Studies Centres — a central group, based at the Town and Country Planning Association (London) serving urban studies centres in towns and cities throughout the country.

Ecological Parks Trust — an organisation, based in London, but offering advice nationally on the development of derelict urban sites for nature study, etc.

Friends of the Earth — a national environmental lobby group with regional groups throughout the country.

National Federation of City Farms — an umbrella organisation for urban farms in many British cities.

The Royal Society for Nature Conservation (RSNC) — an umbrella organisation for the County Naturalists' Trusts.

Urban Wildlife Group, Birmingham — also offering advice nationally on derelict/dormant land reclamation.

The local groups from such organisations may also be able to provide addresses for others in the area, such as local wildlife groups, resource centres, conservation volunteers and local natural history societies.

Don't depend on these organisations completely to tell you what is already happening in your area. Replies to enquiries may take a long time to come and you may spend a very long time writing letters. Ask around your local area yourselves. Local youth clubs, social centres, libraries, museums, the local police station, council social services department, citizen's advice bureau, schools and colleges — any such local organisations may be able to tell you of other projects nearby.

Having located any other groups, you need to find out from them what their functions are, and to what extent their proposed activities complement or duplicate yours. It will then be easier to judge whether your plans are worthwhile. By talking to others in private you will be able to test your plans and ideas for your group, seek advice on any worries and gain a second opinion. After such consultation, a newly-formed group will probably gain the support and expertise of the others, and would benefit from association with them.

At this stage it is also essential to contact local councillors and local authority officers to explain the proposals for forming your group. Local authorities are involved in community affairs at many levels, such as social welfare, education, planning, parks and recreation. Your group needs to gain their respect and stands to benefit a great deal from mutual support and co-operation. The planning department may have available detailed information from past surveys of the area. The local council, apart from facilitating proposed group activities, may provide material and financial assistance for projects involving environmental education, or improvements to the local environment (see also section 2.6.1 for continued relations with local authorities). The borough housing department may have a slum-clearance plan for the area, and may be able to help you locate and use (through some form of rent) temporarily vacant sites.

2.3 Suggestions for an efficient group structure

An efficient group structure will take time to develop, but a well-organised, established group will usually have a committee, with particularly important areas allocated to various teams and sub-committees. These may be created or dissolved as necessary. The committee itself may be elected annually from the general membership and is usually responsible for overall policy, financial matters and relations with local authorities and other bodies.

Sub-committees and teams not only dissipate the workload, but also allow many more members to become actively involved in group affairs. Each sub-committee normally has a representative on the group committee. In this way, all activities may be efficiently carried out and co-ordinated.

If the general membership know that such committees and teams exist, and who their members are, then important information can move more efficiently along the group 'grapevine' from anyone individual to the team or committee most able to use the information. A useful booklet for anyone working on a committee is Clarke (1978).

It is very important to keep the group structure flexible; objectives must never be thwarted by too rigid a structure. It is equally important to avoid putting all the power in the hands of a few people, and responsibility, therefore, should be shared among as many group officers and members as possible. Such shared responsibility is in itself useful for the morale of the entire membership, allowing more people to feel involved and knitting your group together.

If your group finds its structure of sub-committees and teams becoming bulky and unwieldy, then it may be getting too large. Small groups are usually more efficient because of closer communication between members. Such close links break down if groups are too large, making it advisable to form more than one group, each, for example, dealing with separate sections of a large neighbourhood and working in co-operation with each other, but independently self-sufficient if necessary. While you will probably need to start quite informally, a proper legal constitution should be adopted as soon as practicable (see Appendix 1).

2.3.1 Group officers

Your key officers are the chairperson (co-ordinator) and secretary, and they will tend to work harder than other members. The chairperson is, in effect, the group leader and representative in any liaison with other groups, organisations and local authorities. The chairperson, therefore, needs to be a local resident who knows the area well and is known and respected by the community.

The secretary needs to be informed of all group activities, deal with all correspondence, be responsible for the maintenance of records and take initiatives within your group's strategy. The secretary usually handles the day-to-day administration of the group and will, therefore, need to be a good organiser.

In active groups, the chairperson and secretary will often need the help of a vice-chairperson and assistant secretary. This allows work to be carried on in their absence, and enables the workload to be split, possibly releasing the secretary from having to take minutes at meetings, etc.

The group treasurer should, ideally, have business experience and financial ability, but anyone with commonsense who is capable of keeping accurate records should be able to perform adequately the duties of treasurer. The London Voluntary Service Council produce a useful guide for treasurers entitled *Basic Book-Keeping for Community Groups*, written by Jim Smith. Members, subscribers and donors should be able to see what is happening to group funds, which makes it necessary to keep detailed accounts of all expenditure and income and to produce an annual analysis for all to see.

If your group has a bank account, the chairperson, secretary and treasurer may become signatories for cheques drawn on the account. A common arrangement is to require two signatures on a cheque before it becomes valid. The details of such are quite simple and the local bank will be only too happy to explain them and make the necessary arrangements. The treasurer usually holds the cheque book and so another signatory has to countersign the treasurer's signature on every cheque. This, and the many other responsibilities of the main officers, should be shared as far as possible with the other committee members. (See section 2.9 for further information concerning group finances.)

2.3.2 Sub-committees and teams

The strategies of your group and the issues of concern during any particular period will determine the types of sub-committees and teams needed. In some cases, a committee may never grow larger than one or two people with responsibility for particular areas, e.g. publicity officer(s) or membership officer(s). Possible examples include the following.

Membership sub-committee — responsible for recruitment, provision of membership cards, etc., records of all members past and present, arranging educational and social events, and keeping members informed of group activities and policy decisions, etc.

Publicity sub-committee — producing a regular newsletter, publicity materials and press statements, liaising with designers, printers and the media, maintaining lists of sites for posters and organisations to notify of activities, ensuring that the group is mentioned in lists published by the local authorities and newsletters of other voluntary organisations, and representing the interests of the membership.

Projects sub-committees and teams — responsible for knowing all parts of the area well, surveying and cataloguing sites within the area, preparing and arranging group projects such as: environmental improvements, site management and school projects.

Technical sub-committees and teams — dealing with, for example, legal matters, planning applications, landscape design, ecological surveying and management techniques, soil science, etc.

Education sub-committee — dealing with the many aspects of environmental education.

Fund-raising sub-committee — organising fund-raising events and applying for financial aid from charities, government, the local authority and other organisations.

The group membership will contain individuals with many varied talents, local knowledge, and the willingness to contribute to one or more sub-committees and teams. It is useful to pinpoint the abilities of individuals by asking new members what they are able and prepared to do. A questionnaire may serve this purpose, containing questions such as:

— What is your profession?
— What are your interests, hobbies and skills?
— What qualifications do you have?
— What special knowledge or experience do you have?
— Which of the following activities would you be interested in contributing to: tree planting, site clearance, other muddy outdoor activities, nature study, ecological surveys, organising events, producing publicity materials, producing newsletters, educational activities, any others?

Wildlife groups may often have a core of dedicated naturalists with unfortunately limited experience in other fields. Professionals such as artists, architects, planners, landscape designers, lawyers, builders, accountants, teachers, salespeople, businesspeople, contractors, health workers and many others may all be able to provide crucial specialist support. It may often be necessary to consult such specialists and it is far better that they are part of your group, active, ideally, in one or more of the sub-committees or teams. If their knowledge is passed on to as many members as possible, the experience and strength of your group will grow, the need for outside professional help will be reduced and the potential benefits to any new member will be increased. A useful reference to the functions of committees is Clarke (1978).

2.3.3 Working with volunteers

Volunteers are a great asset and deserve thanks, concern and respect. In an agreement between a group and volunteers everyone needs to be clear about what each can expect from the other. The use of volunteers in a manner that causes suspicions of 'cheap labour' or 'gap filling' is likely to cause resentment. Both the volunteer and your group must benefit from the arrangement.

It may be useful for potential volunteers to fill in a simple sheet giving details such as: previous voluntary work experience, skills, interests, times available, and any other relevant information. If it is also ensured that volunteers are well acquainted with all the details of group activities and objects, the danger of misunderstandings arising is lessened. New volunteers need to be introduced and prepared for the work they will be doing, no matter how simple; an individual or number of people should take responsibility for any briefing, training or support they may need. For example, it is usually worthwhile showing volunteers how important their work is and the value of learning from each other's experiences. Make sure that there is someone to whom they can make enquiries, criticisms, or even suggestions for improvements.

Volunteers must not end up out of pocket. Expenses should be taken into account and allowances made to volunteers from your group budget. In case expenses and allowances affect volunteers' entitlement to social security benefits, the local office of the Department of Health and Social Security should be consulted; they produce a leaflet (NI 240/Mar. 82) on *Voluntary Work and Social Security Benefits.*

It is always advisable for groups to take out insurance policies to cover volunteer activities (see section 3.3 for further details).

An extremely useful guide to the do's and don'ts of working with volunteers is Pettigrew (1985) which covers most aspects of involving volunteers in the environment, including sections outlining why volunteers are recruited, how to recruit and keep them, necessary organisation, equipment and cost considerations.

2.4 Communication

A well organised group structure and calendar of meetings and events provides the basis for good lines of communication within the group and the local community, 'tapping in' to the local grapevine and providing opportunities for feedback.

2.4.1 Newsletters

A newsletter is important because it can keep the membership fully informed of the group's activities; it is advisable to try and produce one three or four times a year. This allows a reliable calendar of events to be compiled and enclosed, enough time between newsletters for contributions to be prepared and is often enough for readers to be kept up to date with any changes in the group, such as new addresses and appointments. It may be necessary from time to time to produce emergency newssheets, such as when sudden crises, new developments or surprise opportunities occur.

Your newsletter should incorporate the following points:

— a large and varied selection of short articles, with items of interest to as wide a readership as possible;
— invitations welcoming contributions to the newsletter;
— an updated list of group officers, with addresses and telephone numbers for further contact;
— a calendar of upcoming events;
— an invitation and application form for membership;
— whenever possible, some form of comments form or questionnaire to stimulate members to air their views (and encourage community feedback).

The return address would normally be that of the newsletter editor or team. The latter are usually part of the publicity sub-committee or team, and will need to be prepared to receive and deal with a lot of correspondence and phone calls. The following is a general summary of the work involved in newsletter production.

(a) Clerical — handling the mailing list and any subscriptions. Mailing out or delivering each issue. Ensuring contributors get their reports and articles in on time. Typing up contributions so that they can be copied easily.
(b) Editorial — deciding what to put in or leave over for the next newsletter. Checking dates and venues, etc. Organising page layouts, illustrations, etc.

and fitting contributions together (shortening where necessary).

Production of a newsletter is a typical instance where an individual, or small number of people, may find themselves with more work than they can handle. Anyone finding themselves unable to cope should be able to inform fellow members, who ought to respond by helping out as much as possible. People consistently left to work on their own will quickly become disillusioned when the going gets tough and may, quite understandably, desert the group.

The same principle applies to any other reasons for discontentment within the group. Anyone who has a complaint should not keep it to themselves, allowing resentment to build up. Views should be aired at the earliest opportunity, in open discussion, so that disagreements may be resolved rapidly and group activities can proceed. Although this may seem a hard principle, it is probably better than the alternative of prolonged, hidden ill-feeling between members.

2.4.2 Other tools of communication

Photographs are an invaluable way of recording and communicating your group's achievements. These may be used in slide shows and exhibitions or printed in local newspaper articles, newsletters and leaflets. Black and white film produces the best results when black and white printing is required; colour film does not convert to black and white print very well.

Video film is becoming a very popular communication tool among community groups, and is ideal for recording special events. It is easy to use and, although the equipment itself is expensive, it may be borrowed from one of the following: a local university, polytechnic, college, school, adult education institute, education department or other local authority department, community centre, arts centre, youth club, resource centre or organisations such as the Arts Council or the Regional Arts Association. Alternatively, if more funds are available, it may be possible to hire equipment for the event.

An information stall in the local street market is another useful way of keeping the community informed of your group's activities. Newsletters, leaflets, posters and other items of wildlife interest may be displayed. The stall will provide an opportunity for members to chat personally with people about local affairs, while finding out their views at first hand and enhancing local knowledge of your group's existence.

If you get the opportunity to put on *an exhibition*, for example in a local hall, library or school, it is important to avoid presenting merely an unrelated mixture of descriptive pictures and literature. If possible, the exhibition should follow a theme: perhaps the history of wildlife in the area; or important recent local developments; or, for example, if the exhibit is in a school, a theme of environmental education. The best way of communicating in an exhibition is to interpret and cater correctly for the interests of visitors. People will be more interested in an exhibit with a story to tell than in a collection of unrelated pieces of information.

Illustrated talks and lectures are a useful and entertaining way of passing on detailed information about particular special subjects, events or projects. It is always of benefit to a group if members are able and prepared to visit others to give such talks. When, on the other hand, guest speakers attend group events or a member gives a talk, it is useful for another member to take notes, and having checked with the speaker that the noted information is correct, to put them in the next group newsletter for the benefit of those who were unable to attend.

2.5 Meetings

There are general principles which will apply to all meetings. The following are some useful points to remember:

(a) *Purpose.* Make sure you know why you are calling the meeting.
(b) *Duration.* No meeting should go on for much more than one hour without a break. Either give people a breather and a cup of coffee, or try to get the main points of a meeting over within the first hour and discuss less crucial matters in the pub afterwards.
(c) *Atmosphere.* Try to arrange seating and lighting so that people are comfortable. A circle of chairs with the chairperson at a natural focal point is much better than rows of seats facing forward to a platform.
(d) *Agenda.* Work out some form of agenda in advance of the meeting, and get it agreed by the meeting before you start.
(e) *Chairing the meeting.* The task of the chairperson demands sensitivity and good-natured firmness. The following are examples of what is involved, based on recommendations from the Friends of the Earth (1984):
— Ensuring that the agenda is workable and that everyone understands it.
— Making sure everyone knows who everyone else is from the start and welcoming newcomers, speakers, etc.
— Asking the right people to speak on each agenda item and explaining to the meeting what is hoped to be achieved by discussing that item.
— Make sure that one person speaks at a time and that all who wish to, have a say, as far as possible.
— Encouraging the quieter people at the meeting and maintaining a balance so that the more vociferous individuals do not take over the meeting.
— Allocating sufficient time to each part of the agenda. It may be necessary, for example, to announce that after two more contributions on an item, the meeting will have to move on to discussing the next subject.
— Avoiding needless repetition of points which may best be, or may already have been, covered under an item elsewhere on the agenda.
— Thanking people for attending and making helpful contributions to the meeting.

2.5.1 Preparation of the first public meeting

From the very beginning, it is advisable to spread the workload as much as possible, particularly as the number of people involved in the preparation for the first public meeting will probably be small.

Aims and objectives

The small nucleus of enthusiasts should meet and discuss their ideas for the future, so that broad proposals for the group's aims and objectives may be put down on paper. These may then form the fabric of the publicity and of the agenda for the first public meeting.

The venue

Although it will be difficult to judge how many people will come to the meeting, the bigger the hall the better, within reason. If funds are not available for the hire of a hall, premises may be available (for free or at reduced rates) via:

local schools or colleges, church halls, community centres, pubs or hotels, boy scouts, women's institutes or other existing groups. Quakers Friends Meeting Houses are popular venues. They will usually be prepared to display literature about your group on a permanent basis.

The meeting place should be familiar to local people and accessible to everyone, situated close to the centre of the community with public transport nearby and preferably with facilities for OAPs and people in wheelchairs, etc.

A sensible time to start a meeting is about 7.30pm-8.00pm in the week, allowing people time to eat after work, or around 2.00pm at weekends.

Provision of refreshments and attractions such as audio-visual shows serve as added stimuli, attracting more people to attend.

Publicity

Publicity is absolutely essential for the success of the first public meeting. All publicity should take the form of simple and concise statements of what the meeting will be about, i.e. the proposed formation of a local wildlife group and the reasons, with the date, time and place of the meeting and, ideally, some suggestions of how people may help and benefit by attending. It is also essential, even at this early stage, to provide a reliable address and telephone number for further enquiries.

Two to three weeks before the meeting, posters in bright colours and bold lettering may be displayed in prominent positions, for example:

local authority/council offices	bingo halls	banks
	shops	libraries
local houses	colleges	clinics
schools	clubs	community centres
churches	launderettes	

Local high street branches of building societies often accept more elaborate displays in their windows, if such material is available.

The posters may be followed up by house-to-house distribution of leaflets a few days before the meeting. Photocopied sheets should be sufficient at this stage, as long as the text in the leaflet is clear, concise and easy to read. A local school, college or business person may be prepared to provide free, or at least cheap, photocopying. Write an invitation to existing groups, e.g. amenity societies. They probably will not attend but often they can have a lot of power/ dignitaries associated with them that can be useful.

It is always worth going out and talking to locals at every opportunity, to find out what they think about your group's plans. Personal contact is a far more effective way of winning people over than even the glossiest publicity material.

Local newspapers and radio stations are usually willing to publicise community events. In both cases, it is best to write a short, simple letter to the news editor, outlining the venue for the meeting, the aims and objectives of your group, and providing an address for interested readers or listeners to contact. This letter should be sent at least three weeks before the event. Then, two weeks before, if there has been no acknowledgement or reply to the letter, phone and check if the item has been accepted.

It is important at this early stage to set up good working relations with the local media, as they could well rank among your greatest allies in the long term. There are many local 'free' newspapers, usually distributed to all households in the area, and displaying, on the whole, a strong interest in community activities. If you cultivate a friendship with them, or one of their journalists, you may be able to provide articles for the newspaper and they may be able to forewarn you of forthcoming events in the local area. If it proves difficult to find local names and addresses for the media, these may be found in *Benn's Press Directory*, which should be available at the local library.

2.5.2 The first public meeting

Even though the first public meeting will be informal, more will be achieved in the time available if it is structured. It is, therefore, useful to have an agenda on paper. Copies may be handed to people as they arrive, so that everyone can follow the proceedings and take them away afterwards to show others. A typical agenda may comprise the following:

(a) A short welcome and thanks to those present.
(b) A short introduction outlining broad aims and objectives and introducing the small nucleus of founder members/organisers.
(c) A list of discussion points, e.g.:
  — Why such a wildlife group is needed.
  — What other groups are there in the area?
  — If so, how can your new group co-operate with them?
  — What are the local residents' views about their environment?
  — How can your group help children, teenagers, families, old people, the disabled, schools, etc. in the community?
  — Are there any sites in the area which are worth conserving or may be developed as nature areas?
  — Any suggestions for projects such as clean-up campaigns, or environmental education activities, etc.
  — Have local residents ever been unable to have a say in local authority affairs and will the group enable them to do so in the future?
  — Conclusions, if any.
(d) Election of group officers (optional at this stage).
    At the first public meeting, it may be useful to elect a 'steering group' whose job it is to produce a group constitution for the next meeting, at which time officers will be elected to form the group committee. Key officers, the secretary, chairperson and treasurer, are normally proposed from the floor and elected by a vote, should there be more than one person proposed. Some groups delay election of officers, preferring to wait and see which people are really interested, in case the committee is weakened by unreliable individuals who may lose enthusiasm and disappear. The committee should be a fairly balanced group of keen supporters and should comprise around 8-12 members, allowing broad representation without becoming too unwieldy. The time for elections is best discussed and decided upon at the first public meeting.
(e) Any other items: ideas and discussion points from the floor.
(f) The next meeting: its time, date, place and agenda.

Points to remember at the meeting

— If attendance is low, do not be discouraged. If the meeting is successful, those present will spread the word and numbers should subsequently improve. As the local community becomes more aware and believes your activities to be important, they will become more supportive.
— Do not allow individuals to monopolise the meeting; others will rapidly get bored.

— Pass a sheet around during the meeting, asking people for their names and addresses for future contact.
— At the end of the meeting, it may be acceptable to make a collection to cover costs (e.g. the hall and refreshments) and to start off the group's funds.
— With all meetings, it is very important to have accurate records of all decisions and, as far as possible, all the important discussion points leading up to them. These then provide a reliable source of back-reference, for example, should someone wish to check the details of a proposed plan of action. One way to record details of a meeting is by means of a tape recording, transcribing the important details afterwards. If this is not possible, notes should be taken of all the key points arising. As each topic is covered, these notes, or 'minutes', may be read out so that everyone is quite clear about what decisions have been reached and what has been recorded. Minutes may be sent to those concerned before each subsequent meeting, so that they may confirm records of a previous meeting as accurate.

2.5.3 Group meetings

If the group meetings are arranged to occur regularly, they will be easier to plan and publicise, enabling the membership to keep track of their dates.

Group committee meetings

Ideally, group committee meetings should be held each month, either on a fixed day, such as the first Friday of the month, or on a fixed date, such as the 10th of the month. The first group committee meting will probably be informal and without an agenda. There will be plenty to discuss, such as the conclusions drawn at the first public meeting, the aims, objectives and organisation of your group, and your constitution. One of the members present should take notes of conclusions reached, courses of action decided upon and those volunteering to take them, etc. These minutes may then be used as a basis for the matters on the agenda for the second group committee meeting. Subsequent meetings may be conducted according to an agenda similar to the following:

— apologies from members unable to attend;
— minutes from the previous meeting;
— matters arising from the minutes.

These should only take a few minutes and to achieve the most in the time available, lengthy discussion should centre upon 'matters to be discussed'. These should be listed under separate headings in the agenda:

— any other business i.e. matters not included in the agenda so far;
— date, time and place of the next meeting.

The secretary or the secretary's assistant normally takes minutes at the meeting. Under the heading of agenda, written-up minutes usually begin with the date, time and place, and then the names of all present with details of the proceedings. A week before each meeting, the secretary circulates its agenda. Minutes from the previous meeting are also circulated, allowing members to check them and prepare any contributions they wish to make. Members wishing to discuss particular matters at a committee meeting should inform the secretary, ideally at least two weeks before the meeting, in time for them to be included in the agenda.

Sub-committee and team meetings

These may also be arranged to occur regularly, the frequency depending necessarily upon the urgency of work programmes during any particular period. For example, technical and projects sub-committees and teams may normally meet each month. If, however, your group is setting up a wildlife area, you may need to meet once a fortnight, in order to keep track of such factors as site clearance work, negotiations with the local authority and planning procedures. Again, for the sake of efficiency, sub-committee and team meetings should be well organised. Agendas and minutes will provide invaluable records of all transactions. Representatives can then report to the group committee and provide short reports of such transactions at the latter's meetings.

Meetings with the membership and general public

It is unfortunate that groups commonly contain a core of active members, making up a small percentage of the total group membership, but doing a large proportion of the work. Try to avoid alienating these active members from the rest of the group membership and the local community. Meetings with the membership and general public are, therefore, of great value in this respect, and their main functions can be summarised as follows:

— To maintain close contact between active group members, the membership and the local community.
— To allow group officers to report back to the membership and the community on how group activities are developing.
— To test local reactions to your group's aims and objectives and to formulate plans for the future, taking into account the wishes and suggestions of the local community.
— To ensure that the local residents feel a part of your activities.
— To stimulate inactive group members into action and to attract new members.
— To publicise current group activities.
— To provide information on urban wildlife which may be useful or of educational value to the general public.

To fulfil any of these functions, public meetings need to be as informal, pleasant and interesting as possible. The easiest way to achieve this is to blend group business with some of the social and educational events so that the public and members may be informed and entertained at the same time.

Indoor and outdoor events

The following is a list of examples:

Indoor events:
Informative and educational
    talks and lectures
Slide shows and film shows
Discussions and workshops
Quizzes and competitions
Discos and children's parties
Cheese and wine and other social
    events
Exhibitions
Fund-raising events

Outdoor events:
Nature walks and outdoor study
Visits to other sites and organisations
Social excursions
Stands at local carnivals and fetes
Bonfires and barbecues
Tasks, for example, planting, seed
    collection, digging, tidying, grass
    cutting, scrub bashing, building
    paths, steps, walls, etc.

Many people prefer getting involved in practical work rather than talking at meetings. Outdoor tasks are extremely important in involving such people, while showing that the group is capable of more than just talking and forming committees. A well-organised event programme is essential in helping to maintain community interest and group spirits, providing enjoyment as an effective reward for the endeavours of active members and volunteers and providing healthy publicity for your group. If possible, the events should be arranged, in terms of booking halls and arranging speakers, etc., at least six months in advance, to allow time for the events to be well-publicised. Your group should be able to look forward over a six to twelve month calendar and see what events, meetings and tasks lie ahead. A useful reference for organising events is Hoyland *et al.* (1983).

2.6 External relations

In order to function effectively, an urban wildlife group has to be fully aware of and up to date with the activities of other similar organisations in its area, and has to work in harmony with them. Then, links can be formed, and your group may benefit from any specialised advice or support they may offer. 'Do as you would be done by': all external relations should follow this principle. It is good practice when receiving assistance from another group or organisation to be fully prepared to return the favour. Also, it is important not to make the mistake of omitting to acknowledge help; proper acknowledgement and thanks should always be given to any groups, individuals or organisations for their assistance.

2.6.1 Relations with local authorities

Although your wildlife group should not be party political, you will need to understand the local authority structure and how it works. Try to identify potentially sympathetic members of local authority departments and ensure that they are kept informed of your views and activities. It is good practice to invite local councillors and local authority officers to be members of group committees as an aid to better liaison.

It may be, for example, that one of the reasons for forming your group in the first place was a feeling that the local authority had not been doing enough for the local community, or was not giving the environment enough consideration. Even in such a situation, where you may originally have been formed as a 'pressure group', it is important to maintain good relations with the local authority. To keep up with current developments, local authority minutes and agendas may be obtained by annual subscription.

The elected members of the local council have the responsibility of making decisions for the community which elected them. Where an urban wildlife group is concerned with such decisions, it may become usefully involved by offering constructive proposals, advice and assistance to the council members. The local authority will be more likely to welcome reasoned, practical advice from a community group during the decision-making process, than public confrontation after a decision has been made. The following are some ways in which a wildlife group may be able to help a local authority:

(a) **Voluntary manual work** — rubbish clearing and litter picking on small derelict sites;
— developing unused sites as nature areas for the local community;

— cleaning out ponds, canals and other waterways;
— tree planting, etc. and other environmental projects.

(b) Liaison and research — conducting surveys of the area, for example, open spaces for wildlife, amenity, recreation and environmental improvements;
— exchanging information between the authority and the community;
— encouraging public participation, rather than disruption, in local authority matters.

2.6.2 Relations with other wildlife and amenity groups

Section 2.2 gives a list of examples of other groups which may be active in the area and Appendix 15 gives full addresses for further enquiry. Always remember that it takes time and money for a group to answer an enquiry, so enclose an s.a.e. and even make a small donation, or offer to pay, where appropriate. A newly-formed wildlife group stands to benefit greatly from the existence of such groups, but only if co-operation and good communication links are established. This can be achieved:

(a) informally, by mutual exchange of newsletters and other information; or
(b) formally, by mutual affiliation and co-opting representatives on to one another's committees; or
(c) by combining both of the above approaches.

Benefits of links with other groups include:

— shared contacts and facilities (both locally and nationally);
— extra input of skills, knowledge and experience;
— opportunities to organise larger projects.

2.6.3 Relations with academic and professional institutions

Your wildlife group, with its other associated, affiliated or friendly groups, will have access to a wide range of skills and knowledge, some of it quite technical. However, academic and professional institutions and organisations will probably often be able to provide further detailed technical information, as well as facilities and equipment. The following are some examples.

Local junior and secondary schools   Even if the staff are not experienced wildlife enthusiasts, they may be interested in wildlife group projects with schoolchildren and may be prepared to contribute advice on teaching methods or to provide materials and facilities. Schools may also welcome group members to give talks to the children about the local wildlife and your group's activities. A special school membership may be a useful way of keeping in touch with local schools. Newssheets could be provided, along with the group newsletter, to post on notice boards for both the staff and pupils to read. The new requirements for fieldwork as part of the revised curriculum for Biological Studies in the General Certificate of Secondary Education call for much closer collaboration between schools and environmental groups.

Colleges, polytechnics and universities   Students and staff of any local college, particularly those working in departments of biological science, will probably be interested in the work of a local wildlife group. They may even be prepared to get involved. Unlike the staff, students are often only in the community for the duration of their college courses. While in the community, however, some students may be interested in projects such as biological surveys of the area, environmental improvements and other research projects, especially students of biology, botany, zoology, ecology, geography, environmental science, soil science, horticulture, landscape design and sociology. Members of staff are also well worth persuading to get involved with the group, if only as guest speakers or advisers. As with all educational institutions, staff and students may themselves benefit from wildlife group activities by gaining opportunities for research and study in the field.

Museums and libraries   Sympathetic museum curators and librarians are valuable allies to any community group with the special resources and information they are able to provide.

Professional institutions and organisations   Your group may do its best to build up its own store of knowledge and materials and be independent of outside professional help, but from time to time, outside help will become necessary. This may range from legal advice from a lawyer or a citizens' advice bureau, to the loan of buckets and wheelbarrows from a local builder. The basic principle of obtaining help from the professionals is the 'scrounge principle'. There is no stigma attached to scrounging if the cause is a worthy one. Usually, people are readily prepared to help out if they see that their contributions are being put to good use, with proper acknowledgement and thanks. As wide a range of professional institutions and organisations as possible should be included in the list of group contacts. It is difficult to predict at any time what type of urgent professional assistance your group might need.

2.7 Keeping records

The following is a list of the types of records worth keeping:

— Agendas and minutes from all meetings.
— All letters: incoming, copies of replies and other outgoing letters.
— Accounts of all income and expenditure.
— Minutes and reports from all sub-committees and teams.
— Any written project work, educational work, species lists, etc. from surveys.
— Membership records.
— Copies of newsletters and all publicity material.
— A collection of newspaper cuttings, etc. of the group's activities.
— Pictorial records.
— Lists of contacts, volunteers, benefactors, etc.

A good file of records is useful in the short term for reference purposes and may be of historic value in years to come. Filing cabinets are usually reliable and fireproof, but unless the group is able to find an unwanted old cabinet, they are extremely expensive. Box files are a cheap alternative and are small enough for a group member to keep at home. They can be emptied and re-used at the end of the year with their original contents stored elsewhere. The secretary usually manages current files, but when old files begin to pile up, it may be possible to get permission from a local library or the local authority to use some of their storage space. Wherever possible, important records should be duplicated in case the originals are lost.

2.8 Group organisation

Too rigid an administrative framework can be as counter-productive for your group as no framework at all. It is extremely important to begin discussing and drawing up both a sensible strategy and structure as soon as possible. The two go together and are interdependent. Possible factors to consider include the following:

— The needs of the local community.
— The resources of your group and how they can contribute to those needs.
— Group aims, objectives and priorities, and the main areas upon which activities may most usefully be centred.
— If and how group officers are to be elected (chairperson, secretary, treasurer) to form a group committee.
— What the duties and responsibilities of group officers will be.
— How long officers will serve before coming up for re-election.
— If and how special teams are to be formed (are they needed for fund-raising, technical matters, projects, etc.).
— How group membership will be organised (cost and reductions for children, families, groups, senior citizens, etc.).
— The rights of members.
— Adoption of charitable status, formation of a friendly society, etc. Will the group be able to achieve all its objectives as an informal group, or will you need to become a legally constituted organisation? See Chapter 3 for further details of the legal considerations involved.

2.9 Finance and fund-raising

Finance and fund-raising are constant tasks for all voluntary groups and so the literature on the subject is extensive. Blume (1977) and Mullin (1976) are recommended as comprehensive books on the subject.

The following is a list of key points to remember when trying to raise funds for your group:

(a) Fund-raising, as with all group activities, should be *enjoyable* as well as profitable, otherwise most willing fund-raising volunteers will rapidly lose enthusiasm for their work.
(b) Fund-raising efforts are generally more successful if you have specific *projects* which donors can understand. If you ask for funds merely to help the 'group' it will be much less effective than a request, for example, for funds to help to construct a pond or to make a children's nature area.
(c) The success of fund-raising events invariably involves *chance*. Unforeseen accidents can happen. Events may be rained off, or key volunteers may have to drop out at the last minute. Do not be over-ambitious, do not finalise your plans too far in advance and try to avoid committing too much expenditure before you have actually raised any money.
(d) *Budget carefully.* Write down all the likely costs for a fund-raising event (costs may include hire charges, printing, postage and phone calls, transport, staff fees and volunteers' expenses). Don't forget hidden expenses, such as stationery, insurance, and other obscure expenditures. They all add to the expense. Balance likely costs against likely receipts and only proceed when you feel safe that the event will produce funds.
(e) Although final arrangements for fund-raising events are best left until as

late as possible, with as much *flexibility* as possible, to allow for any unforeseen setbacks, certain time-consuming tasks, for example addressing envelopes, may be dealt with far in advance. Also, insufficient notice of a time and place will prejudice levels of attendance.

(f) *Personal contacts* are always worthwhile, whether organising an event or applying to large donor organisations for grant aid. Celebrities and local dignitaries can help to boost events. Company directors or trustees of charitable trusts can, if skilfully enlisted, lend valuable support to applications for grants made to their organisations.

(g) *Keep accurate records* of names and addresses of all donors:

(i) to minimise the risk of asking for money twice and annoying the donors. Where large-scale mailings requesting small amounts of money are concerned, it is usual, just in case of error, to apologise in advance on the mailing if more than one has been sent. Address lists are notoriously difficult to keep up to date;

(ii) if you know from your records that a donor has given funds before, you can ask again and thank them for their continued support;

(iii) records enable new staff to see who has already donated, and their correct names and addresses, avoiding further mistakes.

(h) Finally, *tailor* fund-raising events and grant applications to the interests of the donors. This may involve putting on events which are appropriate for the locality, or applying to an organisation for funds to support specific projects in which you would expect that organisation to be interested.

2.9.1 Applying to charitable trusts

The main source of information on trusts is the *Directory of Grant-Making Trusts* (ed. Skinner), which is published by the Charities Aid Foundation and revised annually. The directory lists details of over 2,000 trusts giving grants of over £500. The directory is expensive but your local library should have a copy. *Always* use an up-to-date edition, as officers and addresses change from year to year. Your local authority should also have a copy of the *Central Register of Charities* containing details of all charities (over 10,000), whether fund-raising or grant-making. You may be able to find charities prepared to make grants smaller than £500 in this directory.

Before applying:
— Check that the trust has interests in projects similar to your own.
— Find out as much about the trust as possible. Most trusts have full details of their activities in their annual reports.
— If the trust has a clerk or secretary, ask them for an application form or their preferred method of application and a copy of their annual report.
— If a trustee is well-enough known, ask them how you may frame your application and ask for their personal support, bearing in mind that some trustees are initially unwelcoming to such approaches unless they are very tactfully made.

When applying:
— Tailor your application to the interests of the trust.
— Clearly outline your aims, objects and the history of your group.
— Describe the project(s) for which funds are needed.
— Emphasise the need for, value of and the pioneering aspects of the project(s).
— Explain what is being done to raise funds in other ways.

— Provide realistic estimates of project costs and an honest summary of your financial position (annual budgets and accounts).
— State whether you need prime funding for capital expenditure in the near future, or whether it is for long-term revenue to keep the project going.

Further advice and information on applying to charitable trusts may be obtained from the following (see Appendix 15 for addresses):

Charities Aid Foundation
Charities Information Bureau
Charity Commission
Northern Ireland Department of Finance (charities branch)
Scottish Council of Social Service

2.9.2 Grants from local and central government

Section 2.9.10 lists sources of such statutory funds. Before applying for such grants carefully research your group's eligibility for grant aid and get all the information needed to support your application.

2.9.3 Applying to industrial and commercial organisations

Applications to organisations are governed by rules of thumb similar to those given above for charities. Applications should be tailored to relate to the sphere of the organisation's activities. Personal contact with a company director or other officer may help your application, particularly if you are able to persuade them to lend their personal support.

2.9.4 Covenants and legacies*

Figure 2.1 illustrates (A) an example of a format for a deed of covenant, and (B) a format for a legacy. Both are governed by legislation and strict rules apply. Further information is available from the Inland Revenue. The Charities Aid Foundation can administer covenants for charities for a small fee. This can be worthwhile as the legal and paper work involved can be daunting.

2.9.5 Fund-raising locally

Local fund-raising is an excellent way of involving the public, local businesses, local authority officials, etc. with the group. Maintaining good relations with people is extremely important.

2.9.6 House-to-house and street collections

These must be authorised by the appropriate licensing authority, usually the local chief of police. Returns, showing the funds raised and the accounts, must be made by law to the licensing authority (see also section 3.1.6).

2.9.7 Events

Time events so that they do not clash with those of other local groups. Always

---

*Posthumous donations, often as part of will and testament of the deceased.

Figure 2.1

(A) Example of a format for a deed of covenant

(Charity's Name and Registered Number)
DEED OF COVENANT

I ....

of ....

hereby covenant with ....

of ....

(hereinafter called the Charity) that for a period of .... years from the date hereof (or during the remainder of my life, which ever period shall be the shorter) will pay to the Charity on the .... day of .... (month) such a sum as after the deduction of income tax will amount to ....

Signed, sealed and delivered

Signature ....   Date ....

In the presence of: ....

Signature of witness ....

Address of witness ....

BANKER'S ORDER

To .... (Name of Bank)

Please pay the sum of .... on the .... day of .... 19.., to ... (Charity's name and address) and thereafter make like payments on the same date for .... years, making a total of .... payments.

Account no: ....   Name and address of donor: ....

Signature ....   Date ....

(B) Example of a format for a legacy BY BEQUEST

I hereby bequeath the sum of .... pounds to ..... (Charity's name and address) and declare that the receipt of the Honorary Secretary or Treasurer shall be a good discharge for the same.

Source: Blume (1977).

estimate costs carefully and avoid large overheads. Events may include the following:

Jumble sales
Fetes (outdoor) and bazaars (indoor)
Craft fairs
Discos/dances
Open house/garden
Coffee mornings/wine and cheese parties
Barbecues/bonfires with firework displays
Sponsored events, e.g. walking, swimming, slimming, community work, giving up smoking, etc.

Ways in which funds may be raised at these events include:

modest charges for entrance;
bring and buy/home-made produce stalls;
refreshments;
tombola/raffles/lotteries (see section 3.1.6 for 'legal considerations and constraints');
stalls selling bric-a-brac, books, records, bottles and cans, food, toys, plants, etc.

2.9.8 Re-cycling

Moderate amounts of money can be made from re-cycling paper and board. Local paper merchants may be able to co-operate in this respect.

2.9.9 Trading

It is perfectly legal for your group to trade. If, however, you are a charity, trading must not become your primary object, or you may lose your charitable status.

2.9.10 Recommended sources of advice and further information

See Appendix 15 for addresses of organisations mentioned.

General publications

Bates, S. (1981) *Fundraising and Grant Aid for Voluntary Organisations — a guide to the literature*, National Council for Voluntary Organisations, 45 pages. A list of useful publications with notes on their contents indexed under subjects (NCVO, 1982, also publish a 3-page selective bibliography on fund-raising)

Blume, H. (1977) *Fund-Raising. A comprehensive handbook*, Routledge & Kegan Paul, 188 pages. A comprehensive guide to all aspects of fund-raising, essential for voluntary groups

Courtney, R. (1983) *The Northern Ireland Fund-Raising Handbook*, Belfast, Simon Community

'Grapevine', BBC TV (1980, rev. 1982) *Fund-Raising*. 21-page pamphlet in the 'Grapevine' series

Mullin, R. (1976) *The Fund-Raising Handbook*, Mowbrays. A comprehensive and practical handbook covering all aspects of fund-raising

National Council for Voluntary Organisations (1981) *Lotteries and Gaming, Voluntary Organisations and the Law*. This outlines sections of the 1968 Gaming Act which affect fund-raising methods often used by voluntary organisations

National Federation of Community Organisations (1982) *The Community Organisations Survival Kit*, Blackrose, 39 pages. A useful concise guide to all aspects of finance and fund-raising

Scottish Council of Social Service (1982) *Grant Making Trusts and Organisations in Scotland*. A directory

Smith, J. (1979) *Basic Book-Keeping for Community Groups*, London Voluntary Service Council, 31 pages. A useful guide to handling money, accounts, balance sheets, cash analysis, the auditor, etc.

Grant aid

National Council for Voluntary Organisations (1980) *Sources of Statutory Money:*

a guide for voluntary organisations, Bedford Square Press, 21 pages. Lists non-governmental bodies who are authorised to give grants to voluntary organisations. Also lists the acts which authorise local authorities to grant aid to voluntary organisations and shows how to apply for a grant

—— (1983) *Government Grants — a guide for voluntary organisations,* Bedford Square Press, 56 pages. A more comprehensive guide than the 1980 version above, covering grants from central government, the EEC and local authorities and 'quangos' such as the Commission for Racial Equality

Skinner, E. (ed.) (annual) *Directory of Grant-Making Trusts,* Charities Aid Foundation. A comprehensive directory of trusts giving grants over £500, updated annually. This book is expensive, but should be available in your local library

Urban aid

In England, local authorities apply to the Department of the Environment each year for grants to support projects contributing to social need and alleviating urban deprivation. Priority is given to capital projects and those which aim to stimulate local economic development and improve the environment, although projects run by voluntary organisations are strongly encouraged.

The Inner City Unit of the local council will explain the current or imminent grants available, give advice on how to apply and supply the necessary application forms. For further information, contact the National Council for Voluntary Organisations Inner Cities Unit.

In Wales and Scotland local authorities apply annually to the Welsh Office and Scottish Office respectively, so voluntary groups still approach the Inner City Unit of the local council. For further information on urban aid in Wales, contact the Wales Council for Voluntary Action.

For groups in Scotland, the Scottish Community Education Council (SCEC) publish a very useful 37-page booklet *Urban Aid Explained.* For further information contact SCEC.

Grants in the field of ecology/nature conservation. Examples:

Countryside Commission — Grants

Department of Education and Science — Grants for educational research or the provision of educational services.

Nature Conservancy Council — Grants for:

 (i) the establishment, maintenance and management of nature reserves in Great Britain;

 (ii) the provision of advice and dissemination of knowledge about nature conservation;

 (iii) the commissioning, support or carrying out of relevant research; and such other things as are conducive or incidental to the performance of these functions.

Contact any of these organisations for further information and application forms.

2.10 *References*

Benn's Business Information Services, *Benn's Press Directory* (updated annually), 2 vols.

Clarke, C. (1978) *Working on a Committee,* Community Projects Foundation

Fletcher, D.E. (ed.) (1976) *Amenity Society Know-how,* Civic Trust for the North-West, pp. 7-22

Friends of the Earth (1984) *Campaign Manual.* Available from FoE HQ

'Grapevine' (1981) *How to Form a Group,* BBC TV, London

Hoyland, J. *et al.* (1983) *Community Festivals Handbook,* Community Projects Foundation

London Voluntary Service Council (1981) *Voluntary but not Amateur,* 1981-2 edn

National Council for Voluntary Organisations (NCVO) (1983) 'Who Can Help Voluntary Organisations', Info. Leaflet 13 (1st rev.)

—— (1981) 'Improving Effectiveness in Voluntary Organisations', Report of the Charles Handy Working Party

Nature Conservancy Council (1982) *Urban Nature Conservation and Youth Employment*

Pettigrew, W. (1985) *Involving Volunteers in the Environment,* The Volunteer Centre

Rose, C. and Pye-Smith, C. (1982) 'Getting Organised', *Wildlife,* June, pp. 214-19

Skinner, E. (ed.) (annual) *Directory of Grant-Making Trusts,* Charities Aid Foundation

Smith, J. (1979) *Basic Book-Keeping for Community Groups,* London Voluntary Service Council

Wales Council for Voluntary Action (1983) 'Working with Volunteers', Information Sheet No. 5

2.11 Useful organisations

When writing to these organisations for advice, enclose an s.a.e. Some organisations just do not have the resources to cover mailing costs. (See Appendix 15 for addresses.)

British Association of Settlements and Social Action Centres (BASSAC)

British Trust for Conservation Volunteers (BTCV) Regional Offices

Civic Trust regional branches

Community Projects Foundation

Council for Urban Studies Centres (CUSC)

Countryside Commission

Ecological Parks Trust (EPT)

Friends of the Earth (FoE)

National Federation of City Farms

Nature Conservancy Council (NCC) (publications)

NCC regional offices

Royal Society for Nature Conservation (RSNC) (and the County Naturalists Trusts)

Wales Council for Voluntary Action

3 Legal Considerations and Constraints

This chapter only intends to provide a rudimentary understanding of the main areas where a local group may need to face legal considerations and how the group may seek legal advice. It does *not* form a statement of the law.* From the beginning, the group is well advised to secure help from specialists, e.g. members with professional knowledge, such as law students, lawyers, etc., or a local citizens' advice bureau or law centre. (See section 3.5 for sources of legal advice.) However, all representatives acting for your group need to be aware of the legal consequences of their activities. A valuable source of reference is *Voluntary but not Amateur*, a guide to the law for voluntary organisations and community groups, published by the London Voluntary Service Council (see Appendix 15 for address). Much of the information in this section is based on the LVSC publication.

3.1 The establishment of local groups

A properly established local group needs to be aware of its legal responsibilities, for its own protection and the protection of all those affected by its activities. As your group develops, new responsibilities will arise, as the following sections should illustrate.

3.1.1 The constitution

A constitution is a detailed document describing aims, objectives, structure, capabilities, and the rules under which your group will operate. The constitution serves to avoid confusion and often proves useful as a 'silent referee' in disputes.

Some points to remember while preparing the group constitution:

Look for a model   Try to locate any other groups who already have constitutions and who carry out activities similar to those you are planning. This can make the job of drawing up an appropriately detailed constitution much easier.

Name   Your group may use any name which is not misleading or likely to cause confusion with any other group or organisation, but a brief, memorable name for the group is a good idea.

Objects   This clause outlines all the areas of your group's concerns. All its activities should come within the limits of the objects clause, otherwise they will be unauthorised. If your group wishes to apply for charitable status, all its

---

*Please note that all the statements in this chapter are simply for guidance in understanding what legal matters may be encountered in this field. In no case should they be relied upon as authoritative statements of the law.

declared objects must be charitable and fall into one or more of the following categories: relief of poverty, advancement of education and religion, certain other purposes beneficial to the community. These are the four heads of charity recognised by law. If only some objects are charitable, your group has to inform the Charity Commission of any changes to the constitution, particularly changes in objects. (See section 3.1.3 for further information on charitable status.)

Powers (i.e. the means by which your group may achieve its objects)   So that all possible means may be covered, it is worthwhile inserting a general clause, for example: 'the group shall have the power to do all things necessary for the fulfilment of its objects.'

Membership   Whatever the special types of membership agreed upon, they should be clearly outlined in the constitution.

Subscription   This clause should cover the method by which subscriptions are determined and the procedures to be followed when members lapse in paying their subscriptions.

Indemnity   A clause needs to be included so that members are not liable for any loss suffered by your group (unless wilfully caused by the member) and are entitled to reimbursement for any expenses incurred while working for your group.

Meetings   This clause should outline the types of meetings, who may attend and vote, who may convene meetings, the notice to be given to members beforehand and the quorum required before the meeting's proceedings are valid.

Group committee   This clause covers the officers to be appointed, the methods of appointing and removing committee members, the powers of the committee, committee meeting procedures and the numbers required to form a quorum.

Finance   This clause should include the period that the financial year will run, the responsibilities of the treasurer, e.g. bank account records and annual accounts, and how audits will be carried out. There should also be a statement that funds raised are only put to group use.

Trustees   Unless your group is a company limited by guarantee, it is not legally able to hold property or to enter into contractual or other legal relationships in its own name. To do this, trustees have to be appointed so that any property or investments, etc. can be held in their names.

This clause should outline methods for appointing and removing trustees and any special powers to be conferred on them.

Alterations to the constitution   Alterations are usually made at annual general meetings or, in special cases, at extraordinary general meetings. This clause should include the notice required to hold the meeting, the majority required for alterations to be made and, in the case of a registered charity, a statement that no alterations are to be made which will cause your group to lose its charitable status.

Dissolution   This clause should outline the procedures to be followed if and when your group decides to dissolve, for financial or other reasons. This decision usually requires a majority at a group committee meeting, followed by a majority at an extraordinary general meeting. In the case of a registered charity, the Charity Commission governs the disposal of any group assets. Generally, these must go to a similar charity.

Before the constitution is finally drafted, it is worthwhile checking with a professional in case there are any glaring omissions in the clauses which may put the group and its membership at risk. If none of the members has the necessary expertise, it may be worth contacting a local law centre, council for voluntary service, community worker, solicitor or some other professional with knowledge of legal matters. It is extremely important that the final document is sound in its coverage of group activities.

Appendix 1 is an example of a constitution used by the Ecological Parks Trust (EPT), a London-based organisation, operating nationally. EPT is a charity, so its constitution has been approved as satisfying the requirements of the Charity Commission (see section 3.1.3 for further details of charitable status).

This constitution follows the format required for a charitable company, limited by guarantee. Some sections in the constitution have been underlined. These are the sections which you may change if you were to adopt this format for your group constitution. Otherwise, you could adopt the remaining sections as they stand.

Some of the many other sources of model constitutions are as follows (see Appendix 15 for addresses).

Age Concern — Greater London	Model constitution for a pensioners' club
Civic Trust	Draft constitution for an amenity society
London Adventure Playgrounds Association	Model constitution for an adventure playground group
London Tenants Organisation	Model constitution for a tenants' association
London Union of Youth Clubs	Model constitution for a youth club
London Voluntary Service Council	Model constitution for a council for voluntary service
National Council for Voluntary Organisations	Specimen constitution for an unincorporated organisation having a membership
	Specimen deed for a charitable trust
	Specimen memorandum and articles of association for a charitable company limited by guarantee
National Federation of Community Organisations	Draft constitution for a community association

3.1.2 Group organisation

Section 2.5 outlines how a local group may be organised and section 3.1.1 describes a constitution. A newly-formed local group needs a basic set of 'rules', stating at least its name, objectives, membership and running procedures. This helps to ensure smooth conduct and can avoid disputes at a later date. However, as activities expand to include the handling of large sums of money, the responsibility for managing sites or projects and even possibly the employment of staff, the constitution will need to be improved to incorporate protection (a legal format) for any legal responsibilities your group may have to take on. There are a range of options for a legal format open to local groups. The major options are:

Unincorporated organisations:
  Unincorporated association, society or club
  Friendly society

Incorporated organisations:
  Industrial and Provident Society (IPS)
  Company
  Trust

The major difference between unincorporated and incorporated organisations is that the latter has a corporate legal existence of its own. While it is only able to act on behalf of its members, an incorporated organisation has legal rights and duties in its own right. An unincorporated organisation has no separate legal existence, and any property acquired, or any legal action taken, must be the responsibility of trustees, appointed by the organisation.

Unincorporated associations, societies and clubs

A newly-formed local wildlife group will commonly fall into this category. The group constitution provides for a membership from which a management committee of elected, co-opted or otherwise appointed individuals may be drawn. These individuals may then personally enter into contracts on behalf of the group and act as group 'trustees'. If the group wishes to hold property, open a bank account, take out legal proceedings, insurance or enter into any other legal contracts, the 'trustees' will need to lend their names to any legal papers and in doing so, take full legal responsibility. So long as activities are local and on a small scale, this arrangement may be highly satisfactory.

Legal Responsibilities of Members of Committees of Unincorporated Voluntary Organisations, Guidance Note 1, 1981 is a useful set of guidelines produced free of charge by The National Council for Voluntary Organisation (NCVO).

Unincorporated associations, societies and clubs have the advantage that they are independent, self-regulating and are usually cheap to set up. However, independence brings with it the lack of external statutory authority to provide legal support and control when needed. The following sections outline some of the costs and benefits for a group registering with such statutory authorities.

Friendly societies

Registration under the Friendly Societies Act of 1974 gives a group some legal advantages and protection. For example, when a group trustee dies, retires or is replaced, any property held in his/her name passes to the succeeding trustees, avoiding the legal costs of conveying the property. If a legal dispute arises within the group, the Registry's office also offers cheap arbitration services. These advantages, plus the relatively simple structure required for a Friendly Society's organisation, may be suitable for a local group which has expanded its activities to include holding property and handling substantial finances.

A group with charitable objects may register as a Friendly Society and become an 'exempt charity'. It gains the advantage of recognition as a charity without the need to register with the Charity Commissioners (see also section 3.1.3 for further information on charitable status).

To register, the group must have at least seven members, a registered office and an acceptable constitution. It must appoint trustees, send an annual return to the Chief Registrar of Friendly Societies and must have its assets and liabilities valued by a qualified actuary every five years.

Further information, application forms and copies of model rules may be obtained from the Chief Registrar at the Registry of Friendly Societies (see Appendix 15 for address). In September 1985, the cost of registration was £220 plus £36 per annum for registering of annual returns.

If the group decides to accept the costs of registration and the 'intrusions' of the Chief Registrar into group affairs, it may be worthwhile considering an alternative type of registration which will provide both corporate status (a legal identity for the group) and limited liability to its members.

Incorporated organisations

An incorporated organisation is a legal 'person'. It can sue and be sued, own property in its own name, go into liquidation and change its constitution. It is 'owned' by its members and is operated by its committee, or directors, who are elected and removable by the members. The organisation does not require trustees to take legal responsibility on its behalf and members have very limited personal liability. In a financial crisis or if the group is liquidated (wound up), individual members may have to pay a nominal sum, for example £1, towards outstanding debts (except in the case of a member who has acted fraudulently in the conduct of group affairs).

To acquire corporate status, a group needs to register under one of two Acts; the Industrial and Provident Societies Act 1965 or the Companies Acts 1948-1981.

Industrial and Provident Societies (IPS)

A group may register as an Industrial and Provident Society if it is a society for carrying on an industry, business or trade and is either a bona fide co-operative society or is intended to be conducted for the benefit of the community.

The group must be democratically run, be non-profit making, have at least seven members, have accounts audited, submit an annual return and have an approved name, generally with 'Limited' after it. Groups registering as Industrial and Provident Societies with charitable purposes may become 'exempt charities'. In this case, the group should send a draft set of rules to the Charity Division of the Inland Revenue to obtain their guidance on whether they would accept the group as charitable for tax purposes (see also section 3.1.3 on charitable status).

The Chief Registrar of Friendly Societies also oversees the activities of Industrial and Provident Societies. Application forms and Form 617 (explaining how the criteria of the IPS Act are to be applied) are obtainable from the Chief Registrar (see Appendix 15 for address). In September 1985, the cost of registration was £300, or £140, if the Society adopts the 'modern rules', as specified by the Registry of Friendly Societies.

Companies

A group may register under the Companies Acts of 1948-1981 to become one of two forms of limited company; a company limited by shares (a commercial association) or a company limited by guarantee (an association whose aim is to further some political or social cause). In a company limited by shares, liability for the debts of the company is limited to the face value of the paid-up shares held by the shareholders. In a company limited by guarantee, there are no shareholders, but the members, who must be at least two in number, agree to guarantee to pay any debts of the company up to a limit of usually £1 or £5 each. These members then elect directors to run the company. Company constitutions consist of a Memorandum (containing objects) and Articles of Association (rules).

The Companies Acts provide a ready-made comprehensive constitution with details of mechanisms for controlling disputes, provisions for holding meetings, voting rights, altering the constitution, etc.

A group may alter this constitution, within reason, to fit their particular requirements, with the advice of a lawyer or solicitor.

To register, a group must have an approved name and constitution and the solicitor or director involved in the formation of the company must submit a statutory declaration in compliance with Companies Acts requirements. All documents should be sent to the Registrar of Companies in Cardiff or, for groups in Scotland, the Registrar of Companies in Edinburgh (see Appendix 15 for addresses).

In September 1985, the cost of registration was £50, increasing to as much as £250 with legal fees. The National Council for Voluntary Organisations produces useful leaflets entitled *The Companies Acts 1948 to 1981: Articles of association and specimen memorandum for a charitable company limited by guarantee (1983)* free of charge.

Trust

A charitable company limited by guarantee may also become a trust or vice-versa. Although easy to work in practice a trust created with a proper Memorandum and Articles is complex to create and impossible to describe in detail here. Those interested should refer to Appendix 1 giving the full text as agreed by the Charity Commissioners and the Inland Revenue for the Ecological Parks Trust. The National Council for Voluntary Organisations (NCVO) produce a *Specimen deed for a charitable trust,* free of charge.

3.1.3 Charitable status

To become a registered charity, a group needs to register under the Charities Act 1960. A charity is an organisation established for 'charitable purposes' in the strict legal sense, and can include either unincorporated or incorporated organisations.

Groups registered as charities are responsible to the Charity Commission (see Appendix 15 for address). Responsibilities lie with the group 'trustees'. In the case of a trust deed, the trustees are those named in the deed or appointed under it. In the case of an unincorporated association, they are holding trustees or the committee members. In the case of an incorporated association, they are the directors (even if they are not called directors). Table 3.1 summarises the obligations of trustees as set out by the Charity Commission.

The problem with unincorporated organisations, societies, clubs and charitable trusts is the *unlimited personal liability* to which those equivalent to their trustees are exposed. In some cases, such organisations may put their investments and property in the name of the Official Custodian for Charities. Income from such investments is remitted gross, and some of the disadvantages of 'trustees' being at personal risk are overcome. The Charity Commission publishes information on this arrangement in: *Leaflet OCI: The*

Table 3.1 Some obligations of trustees as set out by the Charity Commission

(i)   They must administer the charity properly in accordance with the documented purposes of the charity.

(ii)   They must manage and protect the charity's property, land and investments, e.g. they should insure property for reinstatement value. Trustees may be personally liable for any shortfall between the insured value and the full reinstatement cost [see section 3.3 for further information on insurance].

(iii)   They must take personal responsibility for their actions, although they act jointly with other trustees, and not on their own.

(iv)   Decisions concerning the charity must be taken by trustees acting together. They may, however, consult experts.

(v)   They must keep the number of trustees up to effective working strength.

(vi)   They cannot receive any payment from the charity's property or income, except reasonable expenses.

(vii)   They must ensure that only the charity beneficiaries qualified to benefit do so. [The Charity Commissioners have the power to discharge trustees and officers of a charity in cases of misconduct or mismanagement. See Table 3.2.]

(viii) They must apply to the Charity Commission if they wish to change the objects of the charity in any way.

(ix)   They must keep proper accounts and submit them to the Charity Commissioners.

(x)   Trustees may be held personally liable for debts brought about by poor management. However, provided management activities have been handled reasonably and the advice of the Charity Commissioners sought and properly acted upon, no liability will result.

Source: adapted from LVSC, *Voluntary but not Amateur* (1981).

Official Custodian for Charities: charity funds and *Leaflet OC2: The Official Custodian for Charities: charity land.*

Of the incorporated organisations, Industrial and Provident Societies do not have to register with the Charity Commission and companies limited by guarantee, rather than by shares, are the only form of company acceptable for registration as charities.

Even small groups of friends working together in the evenings may register as a charity, so long as they satisfy the Charity Commission in England and Wales, or the Inland Revenue in Scotland and Northern Ireland, that the purposes or objects of the group (as described in the objects clause of the group constitution) fall *exclusively* under one or more of the following heads of charity:

(i) The relief of poverty or the direct or indirect help of 'distressed gentlefolk'.
    Unlike the other three heads which must provide benefit to the public at large, 'poverty' charities will be accepted for registration even if they are directly or indirectly benefiting only a small group of connected people. This can cover the poor, sick, handicapped or mentally ill.

(ii) The advancement of education, the provision of (nonpolitical) education, in or out of schools.
    This can cover, for example: promotion of science; commercial education; teaching the principles of 'discipline, loyalty and good citizenship'; promotion of physical education; provision of facilities such as libraries, projectors, courses, etc. to enable teaching to be more effective; or even theatre which is cultural, classical or an education in the arts (rather than mere entertainment). Overall, groups' educational objects must benefit the

community to be acceptable. Propaganda for political groups or parties is unacceptable, but education about political principles or politics in the academic sense may be.

(iii) The advancement of religion — the promotion and maintenance of religious faiths.

This can cover any monotheistic faith (believing in one God), though established religions may find registration easier. This must be an out-going benefit to the public if a religious group is to be a charity. Enclosed religious societies will not qualify as charities. Their objects must include the instruction and education of the public.

(iv) Other purposes beneficial to the community — only those purposes bene-ficial to the community (or a large part of it) in a way recognised by law. This includes community benefits such as: moral welfare; protection of lives or property; relief from taxes; recreation; art and commerce; and animal charities (only if they benefit the *human* public).

If a group's objects fall *entirely* under one or more of these heads, they may wish to register as a charity. In deciding whether or not to register, the group needs to weigh the advantages and disadvantages of charitable status.

The advantages of becoming a charity

Becoming a registered charity improves your group's public image. Local traders and the general public will be more responsive to appeals for free goods, donations or help. Many existing sources of finance are themselves charities and, therefore, unable to fund non-charitable groups. Even those able to fund non-charitable groups often choose not to, as a rule of thumb, because of the large number of applications they commonly receive. One of the main advantages of becoming a charity lies in the field of taxation. Both the charity and the donor may benefit from tax exemption. The taxes concerned are as follows:

Corporation Tax — on company profits.

Income Tax — when an individual or company covenants to pay a fixed sum to a charity for a minimum period of four years, the charity recovers at the basic rate of income tax paid by the donor. If the donors pay income tax at higher-than-basic rates they can themselves claim tax relief, while seeing their money go to a charity of their choice, rather than to the state. For example, if a person with a tax rate of 50 per cent covenants £100, the charity gets £143 (recovering the basic tax rate) and the donor gets £28 tax relief, so it costs the donor only £72 to give £143 to charity.

Stamp Duty — usually 2 per cent of the market value of property when trans-ferred — a charity may obtain an exemption stamp, releasing it from obligations to pay this duty.

Rates — charities are entitled to mandatory rate relief of at least 50 per cent on premises occupied (excluding water rates). Local authorities have the discretion to give up to 100 per cent rate relief.

Capital Transfer Tax — charities are exempt from paying this tax, normally levied on gifts and property passing on death.

Capital Gains Tax — charities are exempt from paying this tax, normally levied on capital profits on property disposals.

Value Added Tax — on sales of goods and services (although the majority of charities do not receive relief). Further information may be obtained from the local VAT Inspector at the Customs and Excise.

Development Land Tax — this tax is usually chargeable when the development value of land is realised, but does not apply to charities.

The disadvantages of becoming a charity

The most commonly experienced disadvantage is the limitation the law places on certain forms of political and campaigning activities. The law allows a degree of political activity if it is in pursuit of the charity's objects. However, a body which intends to indulge in political propaganda, or to press for changes in the law in some way, may well be acting outside charitable limits.

Another possible disadvantage is the control which the Charity Commissioners (in England and Wales) and the Inland Revenue (in Scotland and Northern Ireland) exercise over the activities of a charity. Your group may be restricted because its objects must be *exclusively* charitable in the legal sense. Your group's ability to alter its objects is similarly restricted, and the Commission (or Inland Revenue) may conduct inquiries into group activities. Table 3.2 summarises the main powers and duties of Charity Commissioners.

Table 3.2 The main powers and duties of Charity Commissioners

(i)   To provide the services of a permanent Trustee, known as the Official Custodian of Charities, to hold funds and land on behalf of charities.
(ii)   To establish and maintain a register of charities which the public may consult. The register lists the purposes of the charity, where to get in touch and, if known, the income available.
(iii)   To decide which organisations are charitable in law and to remove from the register any organisations not considered charitable, as well as any charities which cease to exist or operate.
(iv)   To institute inquiries into charities where necessary, for example where mismanagement is suspected.
(v)   To receive accounts of charities and place them on registration files for public inspection.
(vi)   To supply local authorities with copies of such entries in the register of charities as are needed for a local index [groups wishing to locate their nearest local index may either enquire with the Charity Commission or their local authority].
(vii)   To receive reports and recommendations from local authorities as a result of local reviews.
(viii)   To make orders in exercise of the same jurisdiction as the High Court to:
          (a) establish schemes for the administration of charities;
          (b) appoint and remove charity trustees;
          (c) vest or transfer property.

Note: The Charity Commissioners publish an Annual Report which can be a useful guide to their current priorities and thinking.

Source: adapted from NCVO Information Sheet No. 20.

Procedure for registration as a charity

Legally, an organisation may be a charity without being registered but, if it is not registered, the important tax reliefs and other benefits available to charities may be — and often are — refused by the relevant authorities.

If a group feels that charitable status would be useful, then it is advantageous to consider registration while drawing up a group constitution, before group activities have been publicised. A draft constitution (two copies) may be sent to the Charity Commission for their comment before it is adopted by your group (or the Charity Division of the Inland Revenue for groups in Scotland or Northern Ireland). It helps here to use as a model a constitution which has already been agreed by the Charity Commissioners with a minimum of indicated exceptions, and to tell them this (see Appendix 1).

If the relevant authority agrees that the constitution is suitable, then the group may formally adopt it and register as a charity.

If your group has to establish a constitution before charitable status has been obtained, it is essential that the constitution allows amendment to be made for the purposes of achieving charitable status.

Your group may simplify registration procedures by adopting one of the Charity Commission's model clauses.

Applications should be made to the Charity Commissioners for England and Wales; Southern Office or Northern Office (see Appendix 15 for addresses).

If the Charity Commission will not accept your group, it is possible either to request an interview with the Commission or to ask a solicitor with experience in charity law to argue your group's case. If your group and the Commission cannot reach an agreement, it is possible to appeal to the Chancery Division of the High Court, then to the Court of Appeal and finally (with consent) to the House of Lords. Normally, with proper caution, politeness and sound legal advice, your group should never find itself drawn in to such an unnecessary situation.

Groups in Scotland do not come under the Charity Commission but the Inland Revenue Claims Branch in Edinburgh (see Appendix 15 for address). Your group should send a draft constitution and a copy of accounts to the local Inspector of Taxes. Once this has the Inspector's approval, a certified true copy of the group constitution is sent to the Inspector, as finally approved. Soon after, your group should receive a letter from the Inland Revenue in Edinburgh establishing its charitable status and providing a charity reference number. There is no register of charities in Scotland. Advice on charitable registration may be obtained from the Scottish Council of Social Service (see Appendix 15 for address).

Groups in Northern Ireland are also outside the remit of the Charity Commission. They should submit constitutions and accounts to the Charities Division, Inland Revenue Claims Branch. The Charities Branch of the Northern Ireland Department of Finance (see Appendix 15 for addresses) was given many similar functions (but not registration) to those of the Charity Commission though with restricted powers. They can, for example, give advice to prospective and established charities.

Charities in Northern Ireland are exempt from rates. To claim exemption, your group should apply to the Rating Division of the Northern Ireland Department of Finance (see Appendix 15 for address) for exemption under section 41c of the Rates (Northern Ireland) Order 1977.

Further useful organisations for groups considering applying for charitable status include the following (see Appendix 15 for addresses).

The Charities Aid Foundation — a charity set up to promote the flow of funds to charities. Publishes an annual *Directory of Grant-Making Trusts*, which is usually available in public libraries and is invaluable for any charity looking for financial assistance.

The Charities Information Bureau — a centre for advice and information, serving Birmingham and the West Midlands only.

The Charity Trading Advisory Group — gives advice to charities, with minimal charges for services, and publishes *Charity Trading Handbook.*

Voluntary Aid; London Society of Chartered Accountants — a society which acts as a clearing house, matching requests from charities with volunteer accountants, experienced in working for charities. Outside London, addresses for similar societies of chartered accountants may be obtained from the Institute of Chartered Accountants in England and Wales.

3.1.4 Responsibilities for public activities

In organising any public activity, your group needs to be aware of its responsibilities to safeguard its membership and the general public and generally to abide by the law.

Public liability

If injury, loss or damage results from the negligence of:

(a) the group (or its trustees);
(b) any employees;
(c) possibly any voluntary worker;

then the group (or its trustees) can be held legally responsible. Pure accidents, where the group or its member concerned cannot be held responsible, do not establish legal liability (see section 3.3 for public liability insurance). Where a group organises a range of different indoor and outdoor activities, e.g. excursions or rubbish clearance work, it is well worth having some routine procedure for reporting even minor accidents, so that the basic facts are recorded at the time. There is a legal requirement that one person should be made responsible for first aid (preferably someone with proper training). The following are some examples of safety considerations which should be kept in mind.

(a) Wherever activities take place, a reliable first aid kit should be available. The Order of St John (St John's Ambulance Brigade) supply catalogues of first-aid kits recommended for different users (see Appendix 15 for address).
(b) The group should make sure that the addresses and telephone numbers of the nearest doctor and hospital are known (and available).
(c) *Before* running an activity, premises or sites should be properly checked for any hazards such as missing floorboards in buildings, concealed holes in the ground, toxic substances on sites, live electric cables, unsafe structures, broken glass, jagged metal or major roads and railways nearby.
(d) Participants in activities should be properly protected from any such hazards, e.g. protective gloves for volunteers clearing rubbish, etc.

The Royal Society for the Prevention of Accidents (RoSPA) are a useful source of information on public safety, as they produce guidelines for particular activities such as charity walks, firework displays, etc. (see Appendix 15 for address). The Institute of Biology also produces a set of guidance notes for codes of practice entitled *Safety in Biological Fieldwork* (D. Nichols (ed.) 1983).

'Disclaimer notices' are often seen, for example, in cloakrooms or car parks, disclaiming responsibility for loss or damage. However, a group will never be able to avoid liability for death or personal injury merely by displaying such a notice. The group may only escape liability for, say, articles lost from a cloak-room if it is shown that in all the circumstances, it was fair and reasonable to rely on such a notice.

Wrongful advice

A group giving advice to members of the public may find itself liable if injury, damage or financial loss results from the advice being incorrect. This applies even if the advice is given free of charge (see section 3.3 for professional indemnity insurance).

Even if advice is honestly given, in the belief that it is correct, there is no defence if 'reasonable care' was not taken in giving it. For liability to arise the recipient must have relied on the advice or information in a way that is reasonably foreseeable. If a recipient makes use of advice in an unforeseen and unexpected way, liability will probably not arise.

The group needs to be doubly careful when giving advice if the adviser knows that it will be passed on, for example in a newsletter, or even by word of mouth (although in the latter case, should liability result, the claimant may have difficulty in proving that the advice was given).

Use of vehicles

If a voluntary organisation uses vehicles, it is legally obliged to insure them.

If group employees or voluntary workers use their privately-owned vehicles on group business, the group risks liability for any accidents resulting from negligence on the part of the vehicle owners. The group may take out a 'contingent liability' insurance policy to cover itself for such risks. Vehicle insurance is covered in detail in section 3.3.3. The use of vehicles is understandably an area of high risk to a group organising regular excursions and organisers need to be constantly aware of the insurance requirements for such activities.

Events

The following are examples of the legal responsibilities of groups involved in organising events:

(a) The principle of public liability applies, both for the safety of visitors to group premises and to members of the public involved in group activities elsewhere (see section 3.3.4).

(b) Before holding a meeting in a public place, seek permission from the chief executive's department of the local authority and the police at least 36 hours beforehand (excluding Sundays).

(c) On private premises, a group has the right to refuse admission (without stating a reason) and to ask anyone acting in a disorderly way to leave, on the grounds that a breach of the peace is feared.

(d) If a group wishes to use a loud speaker for non-commercial purposes, it is advisable to check the local by-laws with the chief executive's department of the local authority. Loud speakers are illegal in public places between 9.00pm and 8.00am. At other times, 48 hours' notice must be given to the local police before using them.

(e) A group wishing to admit the public to a dance or party, whether in the street, a marquee or private building may need one or more of various music, dancing, drink and entertainment licences. These are obtainable from either the local authority or licensing justices. Another source of forms and publications is The Solicitors' Law Stationery Society Ltd (see Appendix 15 for address), who produce standard rules for licensed clubs and application forms for licences.

Children out of school

If a group organises activities for children, those supervising the children have the duty to act as a careful parent to see that the activity area is safe and that belongings are secure. These are general principles and, should a parent sue for damages, injury or loss due to negligence, the courts would use these principles to decide the case. The law about disciplining children is very unclear and supervisors are recommended not to use physical force.

In some cases, parents may sign a form consenting to their child going on an outing and paying for it. This is a 'contract' in the legal sense, involving an agreement that something is to be done and some consideration (usually payment of money). The group on behalf of which the contract is made is 'party' to it and is responsible for any breach in it. The individual volunteer or employee who actually breaks the contract may not be legally responsible.

Safety, and hence public liability insurance, are extremely important for any activities involving children (see section 3.3 for further details).

If your group activity involves 'looking after' children up to 16 years old, you may need to register with the social services department of the local authority and comply with requirements regarding staffing, maintenance of premises, etc. The legal considerations for activities involving organised school parties are usually governed by the policies of the school involved. Useful sources of information on children out of school include Madge and Loxley (1982) and Wood *et al.* (1982).

3.1.5 Responsibilities as an employer

Although a newly-formed wildlife group is unlikely to have funds or the need to employ staff, your group may eventually take on, for example, a paid secretary or part-time field workers, as activities expand. The first step for any group considering employing staff is to seek advice. Employers' responsibilities are understandably complex. Therefore, this section merely provides a summary of points to be considered with important sources for further advice and information given throughout.

(i) At the outset, the group needs to be aware of the legal rights of employees. The local Department of Employment can provide details of employees' legal rights (see section 3.7 for useful organisations).

(ii) Advertisements for a post should contain the job title, a brief description of the post, an address for further details, a contact for further enquiries, salary, the place of work, and qualifications definitely needed and the closing date for applications. When deciding upon an acceptable salary, the group should check with the local Wages Inspectorate of the Department of Employment.

(iii) A legal contract of employment comprises a letter of appointment from the employer, a letter of acceptance from the employee and written conditions of service provided by the employer and signed by the employee. Specimen contracts of employment are available from Oyez Publishing Ltd (see Appendix 15 for address) and the London Voluntary Service Council publication *Voluntary but not Amateur* provides a model letter of appointment and model conditions of service.

(iv) Employers with more than five staff must issue a written statement of their policy concerning the health, safety and welfare of employees and should provide necessary instruction, training and supervision. Further information on these requirements may be obtained from the Health and Safety Executive (see Appendix 15 for address).

(v) Employers must take out and maintain suitable insurance to cover against liability for any injury or disease caused to employees (full or part-time) in the course of their employment. An employer must be insured for at least £2 million to cover any one claim and must display the certificate of insurance for the benefit of employees. Further information, general guidance and a copy of the leaflet *Employers' Liability (Compulsory Insurance) Act 1969* are available from the Health and Safety Executive. (See also section 3.3.2 for further details of employers' liability insurance.)

(vi) Employers must deduct income tax (Pay As You Earn: PAYE) from the wages of all employees, whether full or part-time, permanent or temporary, earning above the minimum rate. Further advice and a comprehensive guide to PAYE is available from the Inland Revenue local office. Tax tables are supplied for each week or month in the year, and copies are also available in public libraries and tax offices. Tax and National Insurance contributions must be paid to the Collector of Taxes within 14 days of the end of the month.

(vii) There are three categories of National Insurance which provide benefits for unemployment, sickness, injury at work, maternity, widowhood, retirement and death, in return for regular weekly contributions:
(1) Employed (working for an employer);
(2) Self-employed (working for oneself);
(3) Non-employed [neither (1) nor (2)].
Self-employed and non-employed people are responsible for paying their own contributions.

(viii) Further information and advice on pension schemes is available from the local Department of Health and Social Security and the Social Workers Pension Fund (see Appendix 15 for address).

(ix) Further information and advice on redundancy, industrial relations, employment legislation, employees' rights, etc. is available from the Advisory, Conciliation and Arbitration Service (ACAS). The British Institute of Management publishes management information sheets, for example *The Employment Protection Act — a practical guide for managers,* and the Institute of Personnel Management produces a *Practical Guide to the Employment Protection Act* (see Appendix 15 for addresses).

3.1.6 Fund-raising and group accounts

Finance and fund-raising are dealt with in detail in section 2.9. The following information in this section summarises the legal requirements for groups handling money.

Accounts

Newly-formed wildlife groups are well advised to keep proper books of accounts and to prepare statements of income and expenditure from time to time, say, every three months. Registered charities are required to do this by law, producing an income and expenditure account to cover not more than 15 months, and a balance sheet made up to the end of the accounting period. Funds must be used in accordance with the charity's constitution and conditions of any particular grant, otherwise the Charity Commissioners can require the charity to recover funds used improperly by its trustees.

If your group opens a bank account, the bank should be able to offer advice and any necessary legal documents. It is customary to have two signatories for each cheque, to safeguard against incompetence or fraud (see also section 2.3.1).

Income and expenditure should be itemised and recorded and it is usual for an individual, such as the group treasurer, to authorise and record these details. The treasurer may also check the work of the individual/s doing the accounts. The London Voluntary Service Council produce a useful guide for treasurers entitled *Basic Book-Keeping for Community Groups* written by Jim Smith.

At the end of the financial year, your group may have its accounts audited, and this is best done by a professionally qualified accountant. Depending on the group constitution, accounts of income, expenditure and balance sheets may be prepared for the approval of members, usually at an annual general meeting.

Fund-raising

The main fund-raising activities likely to be affected by legal considerations include: collections for charity, charity shops, amusements with prizes and competitions with prizes, and raffles and lotteries.

It is extremely important to take legal advice before running any fund-raising activities. The local Citizens' Advice Bureau or Law Centre will be able to outline the legal requirements involved.

A charity wishing to make house-to-house or street collections must apply in writing, at least a month in advance, to the licensing authority (usually the chief of police of an area). National charities that have been granted a Home Office Exemption Certificate need not apply. However, all charities should notify local authorities of proposed collections and avoid clashes with other charities. Organisers should generally ensure that collectors are over 16 years old, responsible, and that they follow the regulations of wearing an authorisation badge, bearing both their own signature and that of the organiser. Collectors must also carry a Certificate of Authority signed by the organiser. By law it is necessary to submit a return form to the licensing authority after the collection indicating the amount of money received, the number of boxes used, expenses incurred, etc.

A collection box in a group's own hall, room, shop or office is not illegal. It is also possible to make a collection on private premises under a house-to-house permit.

If a charity runs a shop, trading must not be one of the main objectives unless it is a direct or necessary implementation of the charity's object. Failure to fulfil this requirement may result in loss of charitable status and tax on trading profits.

Value added tax (VAT) is payable when taxable gross annual takings are over £18,000. Further information on the law, tax and VAT is available from the National Council for Voluntary Organisations (NCVO), the VAT Liability Division of the Customs and Excise, and the Charity Trading Advisory Group (see Appendix 15 for addresses).

If your group wishes to hold amusements with prizes to raise funds, for example at a bazaar or fete, all proceeds after expenses must be put to purposes other than private gain and the prizes offered must not be the main attraction inducing people to attend. Competitions with prizes (pool betting) normally involve making forecasts about sporting or other events, with some element of skill involved. This may only be conducted by promoters who are registered with the local authority. Application for a permit, for which there is no charge, and general information on pool betting, should be made to the local offices of the Customs and Excise, or to the headquarters office (see Appendix 15 for address).

The legal requirements for raffles and lotteries vary according to the amounts of money involved. Generally, the law distinguishes between small, private raffles and lotteries and the larger, public lottery.

Small lotteries with prizes costing in total £50, taking place and drawn at bazaars, fetes, etc. do not need to be registered. Few restrictions apply, provided funds do not go to private profit.

Private lotteries, where sales are limited to group members or to people living or working on the premises, have the following legal requirements:

— the promoter must be appointed in writing by the group;
— each ticket should bear the name and address of the promoter, a statement showing to whom sales are restricted, and a standard price;
— prizes must be delivered only to those people to whom the tickets were sold. Tickets must not be sent through the post.

Public lotteries must be registered, either with the local authority or with both the local authority and the Gaming Board (see Appendix 15 for address). These sources will also supply further details of registration costs and legal requirements for public lotteries.

3.2 The use of sites

The acquisition and use of a site brings with it legal responsibilities, both in terms of tenure and the uses to which the site is to be put. It is extremely important not to rush through the various steps involved and, as with all legal matters, any important communications should be in writing, with copies kept in a safe place. While considering adoption of a site, your group needs to consider both terms of tenure and planning and building regulations, in order to avoid overlooking disasters such as unforeseen costs or restrictions on the use of sites.

3.2.1 Tenure

For your group's own protection, no legal documents of tenure should be signed without taking legal advice. A friendly solicitor, a local Law Centre or Citizens' Advice Bureau should be able to help. It is also worthwhile checking with any other local groups which use sites in the area. The three main forms of legal tenure are freehold, lease or licence, obtainable from public or private landowners.

Freehold is the ideal form of tenure, but will probably be too expensive for a small urban group. Acquiring a freehold normally involves proper legal advice, a mortgage and is done through a solicitor.

A *lease* is a less expensive option, entitling your group to exclusive possession of a site for some definite period. Again, the legal meaning of terms in a lease must be clearly understood and legal advice is an absolute necessity. It is important to clarify:

— how long the lease is for;

— whether it is renewable and on what terms;
— how much the rent is, [a (nominal) peppercorn rent may be possible];
— how often the rent will be reviewed.

If your group has a five year lease, you are liable for the rent for the whole period unless there is the right to 'surrender' (give up) or 'assign' (transfer) the lease.

The terms of lease may also include clauses which require the property to be maintained in a reasonable condition. This may mean repair, improvement or the expenditure of group funds. It may be worthwhile having the site and any buildings inspected by a friendly surveyor before signing a lease. You must be clear on any likely running and repair costs. Under certain conditions, tenants leasing a property are protected under the Landlord and Tenant Act 1954.

A *licence* is probably the most common form of tenure used by small groups, allowing them limited rights to use sites but conferring no rights of exclusive possession. Licences are always restricted to a stated time, have a stated limited purpose and cannot be sold to other people or sub-licensed. A licence will usually contain terms of notice for termination but there is no legal protection except the right to 'reasonable notice' and this will depend upon the circumstances. The Landlord and Tenant Act 1954 does not give any protection to groups holding property under licence.

3.2.2 Planning and building regulations

Planning regulations are controlled under Part III of the Town and Country Planning Act 1971 dealing with planning control (usually referred to as 'development control'). This is the responsibility of the local planning authority, which is the metropolitan borough, or the district council, whichever the case may be. In Scotland, district planning authorities are district councils within the area of a regional planning authority. Regional planning authorities deal with regional surveys and structure plans and exercise reserve powers in place of district planning authorities.

If a group wishes to alter the use of buildings and/or land or carry out certain modifications of external appearance, planning permission may be required from the local planning authority.

There are over 23 legal classes of use and a change from one use class to another will require planning permission. A new building will always require planning permission and penalties for failing to comply with planning laws may include demolition or a substantial fine. Special planning restrictions may also apply if a site is in a conservation area or if it contains listed buildings or trees covered by tree preservation orders (see section 3.4.1).

Building regulations are designed to protect the public from shoddy, unhealthy and dangerous buildings. In addition to planning permission, any developer must make a separate application to ensure that proposed building work complies with building regulations. Any plan which does not comply cannot receive planning permission and building inspectors visit each development to ensure conformity. Building regulations are enforced by the district or borough surveyor.

During negotiations for acquiring a site, these regulations need careful consideration. A friendly solicitor may be able to check on the need to apply for permission as part of your group's research before any contracts are exchanged or leases signed.

Further inquiries concerning planning and building regulations should be made at the local planning office inquiry desk (planning inquiries).

Apart from the legal constraints of the Town and Country Planning Acts, there are certain powers which are derived from land ownership and constraints which arise from present and former use of land. The legal owner of a site has the right to constrain any new owner by covenant (i.e. can dictate what a site can and cannot be used for) and any existing occupier may have user rights. Often these can be more powerful even than planning permission in determining the use of a site.

The procedure for obtaining planning permission is quite simple. A planning application is submitted by completing a short form from the local council's planning department, with an attached drawing or map of the site. The planning department's main interest is the legal class of use for the site. However, your group should have a clear understanding of plans for the site's development at this stage, and should be able, if necessary, to show how the site will look when plans have been implemented (see Chapter 5, 'Principles of Design'). Each form will have marked on it the statutory number of days within which the planning department must reply. The process of acceptance can, however, be lengthy and at least three months must be allowed from first inquiry to receiving a decision, though complicated applications can take longer.

For use of buildings or any property that is more than temporary, detailed planning approval will be needed. Such approval requires completion of another form with detailed drawings and specifications. It may be worthwhile gaining the help of an experienced artist, landscape designer, architect or planner to draft such drawings and specifications according to your exact wishes. This will help ensure that the 'appearance' of the detailed planning application will be acceptable to the authority. Table 3.3 gives an example of a landscape and development checklist prepared in the Hampshire County Planning Department.

Table 3.3 Landscape and development checklist

LANDSCAPE AND DEVELOPMENT CHECKLIST

This checklist is a guide to both Developer and Local Planning Authority for the preparation and assessment of the environmental aspects of Planning Applications. For a detailed explanation of the contents, the checklist should be read in conjunction with Landscape and Development Publications: Survey and Analysis, Housing, Industry and Agricultural Buildings, etc., available on request.

PLANNING BACKGROUND
Local Plan Reference, Planning Brief, Conservation Areas, Sites of Special Scientific Interest, General Improvement Areas, Ancient Monuments, Listed Buildings, Tree Preservation Orders, Nature Reserves, Areas of Particular Landscape Importance, Areas of Outstanding Natural Beauty, Height Restrictions Zones, Safeguarding Areas and Areas liable to flooding, Easements and Rights of Way.

SITE SURVEY
Character of the Site eg.
    Urban, Rural, Suburban, Village
Site Boundaries
    Location, type
Geology and Soils
Micro Climate
Landform (contours)
Drainage
    Natural, manmade
Vegetation
Land Use:
    On site, off site
Wildlife
Historic Features
Circulation and Access:
    Pedestrian, vehicular, public transport

Services
Above and below ground
Pollution:
On site, off site
Views
Into site, out of site

ANALYSIS AND DEVELOPMENT BRIEF

Analysis of the Survey Data with the Development Brief will form the basis of the design. Drawings at 1:1250 or 1:500 should be submitted, which should logically determine the following:

Valuable Site Features
Areas of Major Constraints
Landuse Conflicts
Ecological Considerations
Landscape Character
Visual Considerations
Areas to be Developed
Access and Circulation
Phasing and Programming

DEVELOPMENT: ....

LOCATION: ....

REFERENCE NO: ....

SITE PLAN

The Site Plan Proposals should be illustrated at 1:1250 or 1:500 and should record in outline the following information:

Site Works and Protection
Features to be retained
Landscape Structure
Location of Buildings:
Types, materials, colour,
Surfaces
Hard, soft, other,
Road Network
Footpath Network
Cycleways, Bridlepaths etc.
Open Space Network
Contours and Levels

Services:
Existing, proposed
Land Drainage
Boundary Information:
Type, location

DETAILED PROPOSALS

The Detailed Proposals should be illustrated at 1:200 or 1:100 and should record the following information:

Planting Details:
Location, species, size, density, site
preparation
Landscape Structures
Walls
Fences
Gates
Seating and litter bins
Play equipment
Steps and ramps
Levels and drainage falls
Lighting
Signing
Other site features
Services (above and below ground):
Routing, levels, type, markers
Substations
Telephone and post boxes
Bus stops

MANAGEMENT PLAN

The Management Plan should be illustrated at 1:1250 or 1:500

Responsibility:
Public, private
Maintenance Frequency
Grass areas
Ornamental planting
Native planting
Woodland
Water areas
Access:
Public, private, emergency
Uses:
Multi purpose, restricted

Source: Hampshire County Planning
Department.

The checklist may seem complicated, but it is merely designed as a 'reminder' to avoid those seeking planning permission omitting important information. The local authority planning department should have a planning aid section should any difficulties arise in preparing a planning application; appealing against refusal of a planning application or an enforcement notice; obtaining information about town planning matters and making the best use of it; appearing at a public enquiry, etc.

Further sources of information concerning planning include (see Appendix 15 for addresses):

The Royal Town Planning Institute, who publish:

Your Planning Application — when and how to apply for planning permission.

Should I appeal? — appeals against application refusals and other planning decisions.

Can I object? — when and how to comment on planning applications and Development Plan proposals (available on receipt of an s.a.e.).

The Town and Country Planning Association, who publish:

A Citizen's Guide to Town and Country Planning (this should be available in the local library).

The various Community Technical Aid Centres throughout the country.

Where to Find Planning Advice — a list of chartered consultant town planners, which should be available in the local library or council planning department.

Planning Aid (Scotland).

The Department of the Environment (and the Welsh office) — publish a guide to procedure entitled *Local Plans: Public local inquiries*, available at HMSO bookshops.

3.3 Insurance

Any voluntary or community group should be constantly aware of all risks arising from group activities, and where risks are great enough and funds are available, should insure against them. Your group needs to look after its own property, protect its paid or voluntary workers, and run its affairs efficiently enough to minimise the possibility of any claims being made upon it.

Groups wishing to take out insurance may get advice on the best terms of cover for a variety of activities by consulting an insurance broker. Brokers earn their commission from the insurers with whom business is placed, so a group should not have to pay anything for their advice. The law allows only those who are registered to use the title 'insurance brokers' and a list of local registered brokers may be obtained from the British Insurance Brokers Association (see Appendix 15 for address).

There are various essential points to be remembered when dealing with insurance matters:

— The basis of any insurance contract is a proposal form which a group completes and which the insurance company uses to determine the premium (cost) of insuring. All relevant information, no matter how trivial, must be included on this form, as any inaccuracy or omission may make the policy invalid in the event of a claim.

— If your group suffers loss and wishes to claim insurance, the insurance company should be notified *without delay*, preferably in writing, giving full particulars.

— If a claim is made against your group, or one of its representatives, under no circumstances should legal liability be admitted or any attempt be made to negotiate a settlement. This should be left to the insurance company who will have the necessary professional expertise. All correspondence relating to the claim should merely be acknowledged and passed on to the insurance company, so that they can reply on your behalf.

— To avoid unnecessary delay, any correspondence with the insurance company should include the policy number and claim reference.

— The sum insured must be adequate and insurance cover should be checked, at least once a year, to take into account inflation and any newly-acquired risks.
— Your group should be able to act quickly in the event of an accident or loss. It would be inadvisable to wait until the next committee meeting before taking action. It is worthwhile vesting power in a group member to take swift action, perhaps in consultation with a group trustee or committee member.
— Sometimes, the terms on which a group receives grant aid may require specific types of insurance cover.
— Where a group leases a site, or occupies it under licence, the terms of occupancy should specify who is responsible for insurance.

3.3.1 Fire, theft, loss or damage

Fire insurance cover for property may be based either on its market value (the price which the property would fetch on the open market), or reinstatement (the cost of repairing the property to the same condition as it was when new). Fire insurance cover for contents may be indemnity (the property is insured for its present-day value, taking into account wear and tear) or reinstatement (insured to provide new replacements when items are destroyed).

Fire insurance can also be extended to include 'special perils' such as storm, flood, burst pipes, earthquake, riot, explosion and impact damage, as well as loss of revenue (e.g. inability to continue work on fire-damaged premises).

Insurance against theft covers only theft involving forcible entry to, or exit from, a building, and does not cover walk-in thefts. Insurance companies usually survey the security of a property and take into account the nature and value of contents, the character of the neighbourhood and any history of past burglary losses, before agreeing on insurance premiums.

It is possible to cover valuable articles which might be stolen or damaged under an 'All Risks' policy. This type of cover still operates when the articles are not on the list of property insured.

A money policy may be taken out to cover cash, cheques, postal orders, stamps, etc. against loss or theft.

A fidelity guarantee policy may provide cover against loss resulting from fraud or dishonesty on the part of employees, committee members, volunteers or other group members with access to group funds.

Further specific policies may be taken out, for example to cover loss or damage to glass, fittings and equipment liable to breakdown, and goods in transit.

3.3.2 Group liabilities

There are numerous forms of legal liability and a variety of different types of insurance to cover them. Section 3.1.2 on group organisation and section 3.1.3 on charitable status give details of who is legally liable when claims are made against a group, depending on its organisation.

Claims for damages may be made against those legally liable for:

— the injury, ill-health or death of employees, voluntary workers or members of the public;
— loss or damage to property of the above;
— loss or damage caused by giving incorrect information (see section 3.1.4 Responsibilities for public activities, 'wrongful advice').

Available insurance policies generally cover the costs of such claims, as well as the costs of investigating and defending them.

Under the Employers' Liability (Compulsory Insurance) Act 1969, a group with employees is legally obliged to insure them against injury, ill-health or death. The employers must display a copy of the certificate of insurance in a prominent place (see also setion 3.1.5 Responsibilities as an employer). Employers may be liable if it can be shown that they have not carried out their statutory duties, as defined by the 1969 Act, or if negligence can be proved.

A public liability insurance (third party) policy will protect a group against legal liability for injury, ill-health or death of persons other than employees (see also section 3.1.4 Responsibilities for public activities) and for damage to or loss of their property. When taking out such a policy, it is important to choose a sensible amount of cover. If a maximum amount is chosen for any one accident and a successful claim against the group exceeds this amount, the group or its trustees will be legally liable to meet the difference. The advice of an insurance broker or insurance company is therefore of prime importance when choosing the maximum amount of cover, taking into account all of the group's activities and requirements. In the same way, brokers and/or insurers should always be consulted when organising special events, in case additional cover is needed, for example:

— if a group hires premises;
— if a group lets its premises or parts of its premises;
— if other people carry out work on behalf of the group (in case individual volunteers are negligent and claims are brought against them rather than the group).

3.3.3 Vehicles

If your group uses vehicles, you are legally obliged to insure them under the Road Traffic Act 1972. Under any vehicle insurance policy, the insurance company is under legal obligation to pay wherever basic liability for personal injury occurs. However, if you have misled the insurance company over the use of the vehicle, the company may recover the money from your group. It is, therefore, very important that you make it clear in any insurance policy, for what purpose vehicles are to be used. There are three main types of vehicle insurance:

— Third party — providing the minimum cover required by the Act and cover for damage caused to other people's property; accidents on private property; legal fees; passenger liability (in respect of accidents caused by them); and injuries to other people or damage to their property caused by a trailer or caravan while attached to the vehicle.
— Third party, fire and theft — providing third party cover and cover against loss or damage to the vehicle as a result of fire or theft.
— Comprehensive — providing third party, fire and theft cover, and cover against the accidental loss of, or damage to, the vehicle; with a variety of extra additional risks, including for example, windscreen replacement; loss or damage to contents; personal accident cover; medical expenses; etc.

If your group wishes to run minibus trips, it is advisable to take out comprehensive insurance with a personal accident policy for the driver.

With the help of an insurance broker, your group should easily be able to arrange vehicle insurance suited to your needs. Where group employees or volunteers use their own vehicles on group business, there is always the risk that you may suffer claims from accidents arising out of negligence on the part of the vehicle owners, whose persona vehicle insurance will not protect your group from liability. For a small fee, your group may solve this problem by taking out a special 'contingent liability policy'. Volunteers and employees should also ensure that their personal vehicle insurance covers the uses to which their vehicles will be put on group business.

3.3.4 Special events and activities
(See also section 3.1.4 Responsibilities for public activities)

It is possible to take out temporary insurance for special events and policies may be adapted to include a wide range of liability cover, e.g.:

— accidents or loss of property to members of the public;
— loss or damage to display materials;
— the holding and transport of cash;
— goods in transit (unless covered by any removal firms involved).

If people lend materials such as paintings, etc. to your group for special events, it is important to make the risks clear to the lenders, as for example it is not possible to insure against sentimental loss. Cover is strictly limited to the monetary value of items insured.

Your group should always check with their brokers or insurance company that special events are covered for public liability.

One other rather obscure insurance policy which applies to open-air events is 'pluvius' insurance. You may insure against rain restricting or halting an event. Premiums can, however, be expensive and are generally related to the expected revenue of the event. The insurance policy has strict time limits which have to be adhered to. It generally has to be quoted for, agreed and paid for not less than 14 days before the event.

Special activities such as volunteer tasks on sites require both public liability and personal accident insurance cover. The British Trust for Conservation Volunteers offers such cover, through its own policies, to affiliated groups, whilst on conservation tasks. An information sheet describing these policies, or copies of the full policies, are available from BTCV on request (see Appendix 15 for address).

3.4 Wildlife and the law

During any group activities, such as wildlife surveys, excursions, site management tasks, etc., it is important for group members to be aware of the laws affecting wildlife, and for them to educate volunteers, children and other members of the public whenever possible.

The following is a list of statements on wildlife legislation from the Nature Conservancy Council leaflet *Wildlife, the Law and You*.

Birds
Unless you have a licence, it is illegal to:

— Kill, injure, take or possess any wild bird (unless a 'pest' species).
— Employ certain cruel or indiscriminate methods of killing or capturing any wild birds (including pest species).
— Take, damage or destroy any wild bird's nest (while in use) or eggs (except

in the case of pest species, if you are the owner or occupier of the land or have his/her permission).
— Sell or show in a competition any live wild bird (though this does not apply to certain species if bred in captivity and ringed).
— Sell any dead wild bird (apart from some sporting birds).
— Sell the eggs of any British species of wild bird.
— Disturb any specially protected wild bird while it is nesting, or its dependent young.

Further enquiries for information on the complex legislation covering wild birds may be made to the Royal Society for the Protection of Birds (RSPB) (see Appendix 15 for address).

Animals other than birds

Unless you have a licence, it is illegal to:

— Kill, injure, take, possess or sell a specially protected wild animal, though exceptions may be made, for example for the protection of property in an emergency.
— Damage, destroy or obstruct access to any place such an animal uses for shelter, protection or breeding, or disturb the animal while it is there.
— Sell any such animal or any other amphibian or reptile (including frogs, toads, slow worms and grass snakes) or anything derived from it.
— Kill or capture certain mammals (including badgers, pine-martens, dormice, hedgehogs and shrews) by using, among other things, traps, snares, poisons, gas, weapons, or with the aid of artificial lights or sound recordings.
— Employ certain cruel or indiscriminate methods of killing or capturing any wild animal, including the use of self-locking snares, bows and crossbows, explosives (other than firearms) and live decoys. If you set a snare which is allowable under the law, you must inspect it at least once a day.

Further enquiries for information on the complex legislation covering wild animals may be made to the Nature Conservancy Council (see Appendix 15 for address). A licence should always be sought from the NCC to photograph a specially-protected bird while it is on or near its nest, and to photograph a specially-protected animal in its place of shelter.

Plants

Unless you have a licence, it is illegal to:

— Intentionally pick, uproot or destroy any specially protected wild plant or even collect its flowers and seeds.
— Sell these plants or their seeds if taken from the wild.
— Uproot any wild plant intentionally, except on your own land or with permission.

Introduced species

Unless you have a licence, it is illegal to:

— Release or allow to escape into the wild any foreign animal or any of the 42 non-native species which are already established in the wild, for example, mink, grey squirrel, coypu, Mongolian gerbil and several fish, such as the zander.

— Plant or otherwise cause to grow in the wild:
  giant hogweed (*Heracleum mantegazzianum*),
  Japanese knotweed (*Polygonum cuspidatum*),
  giant kelp (*Macrocystis pyrifera*), or
  Japanese seaweed (*Sargassum muticum*).

Introduced foreign species may thrive and spread rapidly because of lack of competition and, like the grey squirrel and coypu, they may cause damage to trees and crops. They may also cause the number of our native species to decline by competing for their food and space.

Fines for committing offences under the current wildlife legislation can be as high as £500.

3.4.1 Trees and the law

Trees and woodlands may be protected from felling either by *tree preservation orders* (TPOs) or *felling licences*. Under the Town and Country Planning Act 1971 and the Town and Country Amenities Act 1974, local planning authorities may place a TPO on any tree, group of trees or woodland in order to conserve the amenity of the area. Your group may apply to the local planning department for a TPO. Such an order takes six weeks to come into effect, during which time, the owner may object. In an emergency, where your group knows a tree is to be felled and wishes to stop it, emergency TPOs may be made and these are valid for six months, while arrangements for a permanent order are made. Once a TPO exists, trees cannot be felled or branches cut without the consent of the planning authority.

There are 5,000 *conservation areas* in Britain where no tree over 7.5 cm diameter at breast height (d.b.h.) or of approximately 1.45 m height, may be felled, lopped or uprooted without giving the local planning authority six weeks' notice. TPOs may also be applied in these conservation areas. It is always worthwhile for a group to check whether or not it lies within a conservation area.

Under the Forestry Act 1967, nobody may fell trees of a certain size or number without a felling licence, granted by the Forestry Commission. The following may be felled without a licence: trees under 7.5 cm d.b.h., coppice or underwood under 15 cm d.b.h., fruit trees and trees in orchards, gardens, churchyards or public open spaces. A licence is not required if less than approx. 22 m³ of timber is to be felled in any calendar quarter. This is equivalent to four trees, each 15-18 m high, with a d.b.h. of 75 cm. Not more than 4.50 m³ of the quarterly allowance can be sold. As with the granting of permission to fell under a TPO, many felling licences are granted on condition that the area is replanted with trees. The fine for felling a protected tree can be £1,000 or more. £1,000 or more.

If a group wishes to assess literally the *monetary value of a tree*, the Tree Council (see Appendix 15 for address) have devised an evaluation method for amenity trees. The method uses six standard factors for a tree, plus any special factors such as historical association or exceptional rarity. For each of these factors, the tree is given a score of 1 to 4 points.

The monetary value of the tree is then estimated by multiplying together the scores for all the factors, with the value of one unit taken as £1 as at September 1974 and raised thereafter to allow for general inflation. Leaflets describing this method in detail are available from The Tree Council. The following table and example illustrate how the method works:

Factor	Points			
	1	2	3	4
1 Size of tree	Small	Medium	Large	Very large
2 Useful life expectancy	10-20 yrs	20-40 yrs	40-100 yrs	100+ yrs
3 Importance of position in landscape	Little	Some	Considerable	Great
4 Presence of other trees	Many	Some	Few	None
5 Relation to the setting	Barely suitable	Fairly suitable	Very suitable	Especially suitable
6 Form	Poor	Fair	Good	Especially good
7 Special factors	None	One	Two	Three

For further explanations of these categories, consult The Tree Council leaflet. Example:

A healthy plane tree, about 50 years old, in a prominent position in the centre of a small town.

		Points
1 Size	large	3
2 Useful life expectancy	40-100	3
3 Importance in landscape	considerable	3
4 Presence of other trees	none	4
5 Relation to setting	very suitable	3
6 Form	good	3
7 Special factors	none	1

Total score $= 3 \times 3 \times 3 \times 4 \times 3 \times 3 \times 1 = 972$ (say £972 before allowing for inflation since 1974).

Although some people would consider the concept of monetary evaluation of a tree to be in 'bad taste', the value of such a method in negotiating to protect trees or in considering them properly in development plans, etc. is clear.

3.4.2 Further reading

Botanical Society of the British Isles (BSBI) (1982) *Code of Conduct for the Conservation of Wild Plants*, British Museum (Natural History), London

British Museum (Natural History) (1975) *Wildlife, the Law and You*, BM (NH) Publication No. 780

Cooper, J.E. and Eley, J.T. (eds.) (1979) *First Aid and Care of Wild Birds*, David and Charles, Newton Abbot. Contains an outline of the law relating to wild birds

Department of the Environment (1978) *Tree Preservation: a guide to procedure*, HMSO

McClintock, D., Perring, F. and Randall, R.E. (1977) *Picking Wild Flowers*, Jarrold, Norwich

Pollard, R.S.W. (1976) *Trees and the Law*, Arboricultural Association

Royal Society for the Protection of Birds *Birdwatchers Code of Conduct*

—— *Wild Birds and the Law*

Town and Country Planning Association *Protecting Trees: a guide to legislation,* Planning Aid Unit

Relevant Acts (copies of which may be purchased from HMSO or through booksellers or may be available at local libraries). Examples:

Animals (Cruel Poisons) Act 1962
Badgers Act 1973
Conservation of Wild Creatures and Wild Plants Act 1975
Control of Pollution Act 1974
Criminal Damage Act 1971
Local Government, Planning and Land Act 1980
Nature Conservancy Council Act 1973
Protection of Animals Acts 1911
Protection of Birds Act 1954-1967
Theft Act 1968
Water Act 1973
Weeds Act 1959
Wildlife and Countryside Act 1981

3.5 Sources of legal advice

Addresses for all the organisations in this section may be found in Appendix 15.

General sources

Citizens' Advice Bureaux (CABs) — approximately 900 in the British Isles, administered by a National Association (NACAB), with 16 area offices, excluding the Northern Ireland Association, the Scottish Association (SACAB) and the Greater London CAB service (GLCABS). Any member of the public can walk into a CAB and ask for free help, information or advice. The bureau will either advise, provide information, act for the persons needing help or refer them to another specialist. For example, if your group needed the help of a solicitor with special expertise, the local CAB would be able to recommend a suitable one and sometimes arrange legal aid.

Interchange (formerly Inter-Action) Advisory Service — provides voluntary organisation/community groups with information through the Contact Advisory Service Coordinator.

Law Centres — approximately 45 in the British Isles, administered by the Law Centres Federation, providing a wide range of free legal advice and representation to people and groups in deprived communities. Services include landlord/tenant problems; planning; legal rights; self-help groups.

National Council for Voluntary Organisations (NCVO) — the legal department of NCVO provides advice and information on the fundamental matters of trust law and practice and administration of voluntary organisations. NCVO also provide citizens advice notes service (CANS); constitutions; employment legislation; fiscal policy; fund-raising; legislation monitoring service; and VAT advice.

3.5.1 Using solicitors

When in need of a solicitor's help, your group may find difficulty in finding one with the necessary first-hand experience in handling self-help groups. There are very few members of the legal profession with a clear understanding of the aims, objectives, priorities and needs of wildlife groups. Other local groups with experience of similar situations, or, as already suggested, a local citizens' advice bureau, may be able to recommend a suitable solicitor. At the first meeting with a prospective solicitor, the group should determine:

— What hourly rates they will charge. Solicitors can be expensive, and their rates can vary, for example, according to their qualifications and rank, and the type of work they have to do for you. However, some solicitors may lower their charges for a voluntary group or charity.
— Approximately how long will they take to carry out the duties your group requires, for example, advising on, or drafting a legal document.
— What priority can they give your work? Ideally, your group's solicitors should be sympathetic and supportive enough to minimise delay when legal matters need urgent attention.

3.6 References

Blume, Hilary (1977) *Fundraising — a comprehensive handbook*, Routledge & Kegan Paul

Council for Environmental Conservation (CoEnCo) (1982) *Wildlife and the Law*

Hamilton, Elizabeth (1981) *Trees and the Law*, Woodland Trust

Lobbenberg, Susan (1981) *Using Urban Wastelands: a guide for community groups*, Bedford Square Press

London Voluntary Service Council (1981) *Voluntary but not Amateur: a guide to the law for voluntary organisations and community groups*, LVSC

Madge, N. and Loxley, J (1982) *Out of School — legal responsibility*, British Association of Settlements and Social Action Centres

National Council for Voluntary Organisations (NCVO) — Useful reports — see Appendix 15 for address

Charities: Constitutional forms and liabilities of trustees, Guidance note no. 2 (1981)

Legal responsibilities of members of committees of unincorporated voluntary organisations, Guidance note 1 (1981)

Specimen constitution for an unincorporated organisation having a membership (1983)

Specimen deed for a charitable trust (1983)

The Companies Act 1948 to 1981: Articles of association and specimen memorandum for a charitable company limited by guarantee (1983)

What is a charity? Charity law and formation of charities, Information sheet no. 20 (1983)

Nature Conservancy Council (1982) *Wildlife, the Law and You*, NCC

Nichols, David (1983) *Safety in Biological Fieldwork* (2nd edn), Institute of Biology

Pedlar, Paula (1983) *Insurance Protection: a guide for voluntary organisations and for voluntary workers*, NCVO, Chameleon Press

Phillips, A. (1982) *Charitable Status. A Practical Handbook* (2nd edn), Inter-Action

Smith, J. (1979) *Basic Book-keeping for Community Groups*, London Voluntary Service Council

The Tree Council (1976) *An Evaluation Method for Amenity Trees,* London
Wood, G., Jenkins, C. and Stedman, M. (1982) *Out of School,* Assistant Masters
    and Mistresses Association

3.7 Useful Organisations *(see Appendix 15 for addresses)*

General

Interchange City Farms Advisory Service
Law Centres Federation
London Voluntary Service Council (LVSC)
National Association of Citizens' Advice Bureaux
National Council for Voluntary Organisations

Group organisation

Registrar of Companies (Scotland)
Registry of Companies (England and Wales)
Registry of Friendly Societies

Charitable status

Charities Aid Foundation
Charity Commissioners for England and Wales
Charities Information Bureau
Charity Trading Advisory Group
Inland Revenue Claims Branch, Charities Division (for groups in Northern
    Ireland, Wales and England)
Inland Revenue Claims Branch (for groups in Scotland)
Institute of Chartered Accountants in England and Wales
Northern Ireland Department of Finance, Charities Branch
Scottish Council of Social Service
Voluntary Aid, London Society of Chartered Accountants

Responsibilities for public activities

Assistant Masters and Mistresses Association
British Association of Settlements and Social Action Centres
The Order of St John (St John's Ambulance Brigade)
The Royal Society for the Prevention of Accidents (RoSPA)
The Solicitors' Law Stationery Society Ltd

Responsibilities as an employer

Advisory, Conciliation and Arbitration Service (ACAS)
British Institute of Management
Health and Safety Executive
Institute of Personnel Management
Oyez Publishing Ltd
Social Workers Pension Fund

Fund-raising and group accounts

Customs and Excise, Headquarters Office
Customs and Excise, VAT Liability
Gaming Board, Lotteries Division

Planning and building regulations

Planning Aid Service for Londoners

Royal Town Planning Institute
Town and Country Planning Association (TCPA), Community Technical Aid
    Centre (CTAC)
Town and Country Planning Association

Insurance

British Insurance Brokers Association

Wildlife and the law

Botanical Society of the British Isles
Council for Environmental Conservation (CoEnCo)
Forestry Commission
Natural History Museum
Nature Conservancy Council
Royal Society for the Protection of Birds
Royal Society for Nature Conservation (RSNC)
The Tree Council
Woodland Trust

4 Site Surveying and Selection

Even if your newly-formed urban wildlife group has a site of its own, it may be worthwhile conducting a survey of the local area to locate vacant plots of land with the most potential as wildlife areas of possible benefit to the community. The task may seem a daunting one, but could nevertheless be attempted. A well-conducted survey should provide a valuable picture of the local area, opportunities to contact local residents with special interests in particular sites and a solid base of knowledge with which to co-ordinate all future group activities. It would, for example, be undesirable for your group to develop a wildlife site (a) if there was a better site nearby or (b) if the community and group membership, not having been consulted, showed little interest or support.

The easiest way of planning and conducting a survey efficiently may be to set up a small sub-committee, possibly as part of the projects sub-committee, to co-ordinate the survey from start to finish.

4.1 Preliminary research

The most useful function of the co-ordinating sub-committee could be to organise and minimise wastage of time and effort on the survey, particularly as your group may only have limited resources at their disposal. In order to do this, the co-ordinators may draw up a strategy similar to that illustrated in Figure 4.1. The key features lie in the preparations before the survey begins. These include the following:

(a) Locate any information already available on the area and draw up a map with all vacant sites marked.
(b) In consultation with the group membership and local community, determine what uses the site(s) will be put to when selected from the survey.
(c) For each chosen use, determine the key site requirements.
(d) Incorporate these requirements into the design of site record sheets and instructions for the volunteers on the survey, so that they can easily pick out potentially suitable sites and eliminate unsuitable ones. As well as being used in the process of selection, the information collected during the survey will be used in preparing planning applications, site designs and the management plans for those chosen. Before designing record sheets, it is necessary to understand first which site characteristics are most important in this respect. Chapter 5, 'Principles of Site Design', explains the importance of various site characteristics in drawing up designs and management plans.

Figure 4.1 Surveying the local area: strategy

Task	Action
1. Publicise the proposed survey and recruit volunteers from membership and local community	Co-ordinating sub-committee
2. Locate other sources of help and information, e.g. maps and surveys already completed, from other organisations and local authorities (Section 4.1.1)	Co-ordinating sub-committee
3. Prepare a map of the survey area, with all known vacant sites marked, and draw up a preliminary list of possible site uses (Section 4.1.2)	Co-ordinating sub-committee
4. Organise a special public meeting and, possibly, an opinion survey for people's ideas to be aired (Section 4.1.2)	Co-ordinating sub-committee
5. At the public meeting, outline the area to be surveyed, discuss and decide upon site uses and site requirements (Section 4.1.2)	Group membership, local community, other organisations, local authority, etc.
6. Design site record sheets, and instruction sheets for volunteers (Section 4.1.3)	Co-ordinating sub-committee
7. Hold briefing session for volunteers (Section 4.2.1) to explain site record sheets and instructions for volunteers	Co-ordinating sub-committee and volunteers
8. Prepare maps for volunteers (Section 4.2.2)	Co-ordinating sub-committee
9. Conduct the area survey (Section 4.2.3)	Co-ordinating sub-committee
10. Provide survey back-up, co-ordinating volunteers, researching site histories, lifespans, ownership, legal considerations, etc. (Section 4.2.4)	Co-ordinating sub-committee
11. Assess survey results and shortlist sites suitable for the group (Section 4.3)	Co-ordinating sub-committee and volunteers
12. Survey chosen sites in more detail (Section 4.4)	Co-ordinating sub-committee and volunteers

4.1.1 Sources of help and information

The following are examples of those to whom enquiries may be made.

Registers of all vacant sites over one acre in extent

Under the powers of the Local Government Planning and Land Act (1980, part x) and by request of the Secretary of State for the Environment in 1982, the Department of the Environment has the responsibility of producing such registers for district and borough councils.

All these councils in England and some in Wales and Scotland should therefore have available to the public on request copies of any registers produced. Alternatively, the Department of the Environment may be able to provide copies. Their head office and library in London has registers for the whole country and their nine regional offices each have copies for their respective region. The 'Land Decade' is also doing research and campaigning for better use of land. They may be contacted at the Land Council (see Appendix 15 for full addresses).

Other local authority help

Even if the local authority do not have a register of vacant sites, there is usually a large range of material, both free and at a charge, available in local authority planning departments. In any event, it is worthwhile securing local authority interest, particularly that of ward councillors and planners, with their detailed knowledge of the area and of current local issues.

It may also be worthwhile contacting the county council planning officer (regional planning officer in Scotland). The county may not be able to give detailed advice, but may prove supportive in other ways, perhaps through the county ecologist or conservation officer, if such posts exist.

If there is a parish, community or neighbourhood council, they may be interested and prepared to help with proposed surveys. (Some spend money on small environmental projects.)

National organisations working in nature conservation

The following national bodies may be active locally and should be informed of any local surveys (see Appendix 15 for addresses).

The Council for the Protection of Rural England Although mainly interested in the countryside, CPRE encourage local surveys of hedgerows and publish a descriptive leaflet 'Hedges — Historical Surveys'. The local CPRE branch and County Trust for Nature Conservation may be interested in any hedges in the area.

The Nature Conservancy Council (NCC), is the official body responsible for the conservation of flora, fauna, geological and physiographic features throughout Great Britain. The Council's staff are based in regional offices as well as at its headquarters in Peterborough (England), Edinburgh (Scotland) and Bangor (Wales).

The Royal Society for Nature Conservation (RSNC) is an 'umbrella' organisation for the County Naturalist's Trusts, co-ordinating their activities throughout the country. They also run 'WATCH', a young people's trust for environmental education. WATCH conducts a nationwide survey of nature in towns through its many regional groups and schools groups. This involves surveys of open greenspace, the results of which are stored at WATCH headquarters near Lincoln.

The Tree Council runs a national tree survey as part of its object of promoting public interest in and care for the nation's trees (see also section 3.4.1 and Appendix 4).

These organisations may have already surveyed the local area, or could have information relevant to the proposed survey. They may be prepared to help your group and provide back-up facilities, etc. Conversely, the results of a local survey may be of use to such organisations themselves. In this situation, they may suggest the use of survey techniques which will produce data in a form suited to their needs. Co-operation is essential, as ever, for the mutual benefit of all concerned.

Local bodies

Local community groups, natural history societies, schools and colleges may also have survey information of their own, or may be interested in helping, perhaps for example as part of a school or college research project. The local reference library or museum are good sources of information on the area, for example, details of local history, current affairs, maps, etc., and are usually aware of any local surveys that have already been conducted.

Good publicity at the outset may bring offers of advice and help. A letter to the local press is worthwhile, describing what the proposed survey will involve, why it is being conducted, and inviting anyone interested to participate. Invitations need not be restricted to your group membership. The survey may well interest members of other groups and individuals with interests other than nature conservation, such as photography, local history and geography. Such new recruits may then choose to become members of the wildlife group as a result of their involvement in the survey.

4.1.2 Site uses and requirements

When deciding what types of site to consider in a survey, it is useful first to determine what the sites are to be used for. This may be best discussed at a well-publicised special meeting involving your group membership, the local community, other groups, schools, colleges and the local authority, etc. It may also be useful to conduct a local opinion poll. This could comprise a question- naire containing a list of possible site uses, asking people to indicate which they considered most important and giving them the opportunity to suggest others. The meeting and opinion poll may also stimulate further interest and offers of help with the site survey itself.

Some possible site uses are:

nature trail
nature reserve
unmanaged wilderness area
managed ecological park/city nature park
school nature area
urban field centre
wildflower garden, e.g. for birds and butterflies
community garden
invalid garden/sensory garden for the blind
urban farm
corner landscape feature
woodland
coppice woodland
tree nursery

The examples in this list are not mutually exclusive. One site may incor- porate a nature trail, unmanaged wilderness area, managed ecological park and community garden. However, splitting site uses up into definable projects simplifies the task of determining the site requirements for each use. Each of the examples in the list of uses (above) has slightly different requirements. Before considering these, there are some general ones for all sites. The following are some examples. Sites should either conform to these requirements or it should be feasible for the group to make them do so:

Accessible — central, near to residential areas, schools, public transport routes, allowing easy access to all age groups (possibly including invalids).
Safe — not polluted or dangerous in any other way (concealed shafts, precipices, unstable steep slopes, etc.). See section 4.4.2 for further information on pollution.
Disused — to the extent that the site's development would add to, rather than detract from, local amenities.
Available — terms of tenure: can the group lease, licence or come to some agreement over tenure of the site, and for how long?
Size — small enough for the group to feel confident that they can develop the site successfully.
Wildlife value — Any sites which already provide havens for wildlife, or which could do so with a little help from you, are of value in an urban environment. It is worthwhile for you to campaign for the conservation of nature in the city and to develop, protect and restore such sites.

A checklist of these and any other considerations should be drawn up, taking into account the majority views of the membership and local community. When considering the different requirements for each of the site uses, your group may find itself faced with a bewildering array of information. Table 4.1 illustrates a possible method of arranging this information for easy reference. A similar table could be drawn up for proposed site uses or, if preferred, personal methods devised of recording the relative importance of different site requirements. The table should then prove useful both to the volunteer surveyors in the field and to the co-ordinators interpreting the survey results.

Considering possible site uses separately, the following are examples of points to consider when identifying site requirements.

Nature trail

Interesting and educational urban nature trails may be set out either on a site or along any pedestrian thoroughfare. If a trail is to be included on a site managed by your group, the main requirements are safe access and a public right of way. Of course, varied habitats, species-richness and the presence of uncommon or rare species all add to the value of a site or route for a nature trail.

Nature reserve

There are three main situations in which sites should be managed as local nature reserves, or as sites of special scientific interest (SSSIs). First, if the site has been relatively undisturbed and retains its original (relic) flora and fauna; second, if very unusual environmental conditions are present, such as those found on some alkali wastes, which have resulted in the development of unusual plant communities, for example, orchid meadows (see Gemmell 1977) and third, if rare species or other types or rare communities, habitats, etc. are present. Further information on SSSIs is available from the Nature Conservancy Council (1983) leaflet.

Nature reserves by definition are set aside primarily for the conservation of nature, but also provide for recreation and education. Public use is often

Table 4.1 Site requirements for particular site uses

	NT	NR	W	EP	SN	WG	CG	IS	CL	AA	CW	TN
REQUIREMENTS												
Minimum area (ha.)	—	1	.5	1	.1	.1	.1	.1	.1	.1	1	.2
Minimum lifespan (yrs)	1	*	1	3	2	2	2	2	1	2	20	3
Buildings on site	—	B	B	B	B	B	B	B	—	—	B	B
Staff on site	B	B	B	B	E	B	—	B	—	—	B	B
AMENITY VALUE												
Parking space	B	B	B	B	B	B	B	B	—	—	B	B
Good (safe) access	B	B	B	B	E	B	B	E	B	B	B	B
Safe for the public	E	B	E	E	E	E	E	E	B	E	B	B
Close to local residents/schools	B	B	B	B	E	B	B	B	B	B	B	B
LEGAL REQUIREMENTS												
Secure against theft	—	B	—	B	B	B	B	B	—	B	B	B
Planning permission and liability insurance	E	E	E	E	E	E	E	E	E	E	E	E
OWNERSHIP/TENURE												
Common land	B	D	B	B	B	B	B	B	B	B	B	B
Public open space	B	D	B	B	B	B	B	B	B	B	B	B
Private land	B	B	B	B	B	B	B	B	B	B	B	B
Group ownership	D	B	D	D	D	D	D	D	D	D	D	D
Group lease/licence	B	B	B	B	B	B	B	B	B	B	B	B
Gentlemen's agreement	B	B	B	B	B	B	B	B	B	B	B	B
SUBSTRATES PRESENT												
Fertile (top) soil	—	—	—	—	—	—	B	B	—	B	B	B
Nutrient-poor subsoil	—	—	—	—	—	—	D	D	—	D	D	D
Concrete/tarmacadam	—	—	—	—	D	D	D	D	D	D	D	D
Rubble/rock	—	—	—	—	D	D	D	D	D	D	D	D
WATER												
Soil water table/water content adequate	B	B	B	B	B	B	B	B	B	B	B	E
Standing/running water present	B	B	B	B	B	B	B	B	B	B	B	B
Water supply (e.g. mains water) available	B	B	B	B	B	B	B	B	B	B	B	E
TOPOGRAPHY												
Flat	—	—	—	—	—	—	—	B	—	—	B	B
Sloping	—	—	—	—	—	—	—	D	—	—	—	D
Irregular	—	B	B	B	B	B	—	D	—	—	—	D
WILDLIFE												
Varied habitats	B	B	B	B	B	B	—	—	B	—	B	—
Species-rich	B	B	B	B	B	B	—	—	B	—	B	—
Rare species present	B	B	D	B	B	B	D	D	D	D	D	D

Key

E = essential
B = beneficial
— = not applicable/unimportant
D = detrimental
* = for as long as possible

Uses

NT = nature trail, NR = nature reserve, W = wilderness, EP = ecological park/city nature park, SN = school nature area, WG = wildflower, bird and butterfly garden, CG = community garden, IS = invalid/sensory garden, CL = corner landscape AA = amenity area, CW = coppice woodland, TN = tree nursery

restricted. Although rare in urban areas, some urban reserves do exist. One example is Moseley Bog in Birmingham (see Appendix 15 for the address of the 'Save Our Bog' campaign): this site has been designated an SSSI by the Nature Conservancy Council. During the survey, your group may discover a site rich in wildlife, and may consider it valuable enough to develop as a nature reserve, with some degree of restriction on public access. In such a situation, local representatives of the Nature Conservancy Council or the County Naturalists Trust can offer advice and verify the site's wildlife value. It may then be easier to plan a course of action for the site's development with optimum benefits to both the site flora and fauna and to the local people.

A nature reserve may be the only case where your group considers buying the site. In all other examples, it is probably more practical to accept that sites will eventually be developed and that the most sensible arrangement for the site tenure will be by agreement, licence or lease.

Unmanaged wilderness area

Many urban sites exist with well-established plant communities on them, ranging from dense banks of weeds to established scrub and woodland. You may consider such a site suitable for adoption without modifying these plant communities, allowing them to develop naturally and permitting unrestricted public access. The main site requirement in this case would be that the site could be made safe for the public.

Managed ecological park/city nature park

An ecological park may be defined as a site, created or modified, and managed to encourage a rich diversity of native plant and animal species. It can provide a refuge for nature in urban areas as well as an amenity for public recreation, nature conservation and field study. For example, a site with little wildlife value but ideally situated for community use can be landscaped, planted and developed using ecological principles. A very wide range of urban sites may be suitable for ecological parks, as the site requirements are as flexible as the park's design. The William Curtis Ecological Park in London was created in 1977 and managed by the Ecological Parks Trust. It was an example of a rich array of habitats, containing a diverse mixture of native species, yet created from an area of 'hoggin and ash', almost totally denuded of vegetation.

Unlike the 'traditional' nature reserve, an ecological park/city nature park may be designed for extensive public use. The minimum area required will depend upon the number of functions the park is to perform. Will the site, for example, have an interpretative centre, a pond, a tree nursery, wildflower garden, wilderness area, grassland area, trees planted, etc.? (See Chapter 5 for further details on the principles of site design.)

School nature area

School nature areas may either be developed within school grounds, or on sites near to schools. Where schoolchildren are involved, safety becomes doubly important. For example, when considering a site near to a school, the number of major roads which link them need considering, along with safety consider-ations concerning the site itself.

Wildflower garden/community garden

The site requirements for gardens vary according to the plants to be grown. Wildflowers may be grown in a variety of substrates, with particular species adapted to low nutrient soils, acid soils, etc., whereas, cultivated plants usually need a substrate of relatively fertile topsoil. Gardens need only be short-term projects, for example to brighten up temporarily vacant dull corners in residential areas or on school grounds.

Invalid garden/sensory garden for the blind

Safe access and site safety are the most important factors in this case. Any site can incorporate these to allow the handicapped to enjoy visiting it with the rest of the general public.

Corner landscape feature

These sites are best situated on or near busy pedestrian routes, where they will be of most benefit and may be kept under surveillance. A wide range of sites, of varying size, life expectancy, topography, etc. may be suitable.

Woodland/coppice/tree nursery

In considering woodland sites, the group needs to determine whether they will be able to manage a site properly and size and life expectancy become important factors. For example, commercial coppicing is generally not feasible on sites less than 5 ha. in area, and usually requires anything from a 5 to a 30 year cycle of management, depending on what the coppice wood is to be used for. Your group may, however, be interested in criteria other than profit, for example, increased habitat diversity, community involvement and the acquisition of wood-craft skills. In this case, much smaller areas of coppice may be feasible. The British Trust for Conservation Volunteers *Woodlands* handbook (1980) gives the following recommendations for area and age of coppice plots:

> For wildlife, a 7 to 15 year rotation is best. Normally, the best flowering of herbaceous plants is in the second and third Spring after coppicing. Ten-year old coppice is about at its best for nesting birds, while after about 20 years it begins to decline for this purpose ... The size of coppice plots may be anything from a minimum of a quarter acre (0.1 hectare) in small woods, to a maximum of about 3 acres (1.2 hectares).

A tree nursery may be constructed on an area as small as 100 sq m (100-150 young trees may be grown on a sq m). Soil quality is important, and a life expectancy of at least three years is necessary for the site (see Chapters 6 and 7 for further information). Useful sources of information on woodlands, coppicing and tree nurseries include: British Trust for Conservation Volunteers, Arboricultural Association, Forestry Commission, Men of the Trees, The Tree Council, Trees for People, Woodland Trust, Department of Agriculture for Northern Ireland Forest Service (see Appendix 15 for addresses).

As it is not possible to 'categorise' all possible site uses, these examples are merely a short list of some possibilities, with examples of some of the considerations which should be made when surveying and assessing sites. Any one site may incorporate a number of these uses given as examples.

The following are recommended sources of information on three areas of site use beyond the scope of this book (see Appendix 15 for addresses).

(i) *Allotments*: The National Society of Allotment and Leisure Gardeners Ltd, the Soil Association, Friends of the Earth and Allotments for the Future.
(ii) *City farms*: The National Federation of City Farms and the Interchange City Farms Advisory Service.
(iii) *Recreation/sports areas*: The National Children's Bureau, National Playing Fields Association, Pre-School Playgroups Association, Child's Play and Handicapped Adventure Playground Association.

4.1.3 Site record sheets and instructions for volunteers

For the sake of efficiency, in the area survey, site record sheets and instructions may only need to contain enough detail to allow volunteer surveyors to *identify* any sites which may be suitable and rapidly eliminate those sites entirely unsuited for the uses proposed by your group. More detailed site surveys may then be conducted on those sites shortlisted out of the many in the area.

The area survey site record sheet

The following is an example of a possible format for a site record sheet.

1. *Date of visit(s)*.
2. *Recorder's name(s)*.
3. *A reference number* for the site, corresponding to a numbered location on a masterplan of the area (held by the co-ordinators).
4. *Site location* — Ordnance Survey grid reference and address of the site (if one exists).
5. *Area* (ha./acres/sq m).
6. *Site owner's* name, address and telephone number.
7. *Contacts* — names, addresses and telephone numbers, e.g. local authority officers or local residents interested in the site.
8. *Details of any other groups* interested in the site.
9. *Former use* of the site and date this ceased (if known).
10. *Lifespan* of the site — e.g. the expected length of time before the site will be lost to development.
11. *Site features* (to be marked as far as possible on map (14)).
    (a) physical — e.g. soils and other substrates; any areas of water; site topography; any areas extremely exposed or heavily shaded;
    (b) biological — e.g. habitats present; mature trees;
    (c) notable species of plants and animals found in each habitat;
    (d) other features — e.g. obstructions such as gas mains and sewers, fencing, buildings, etc.
12. *Access* — for cars, public rights of way, etc.
13. *Notes* — e.g. on the proximity of schools, residential areas, etc., the potential amenity value of the site and any other features considered important.
14. *Sketch map* of the site, showing the site orientation, points of access, important features on site, neighbouring areas of greenspace, screening buildings, etc.

It is doubtful that a volunteer could fill in all the details on such a record sheet just by visiting a site once or twice. The record sheet should nevertheless be as comprehensive as possible. Even though such a sheet may never be entirely completed, there is less chance of important information being left off, merely because the record sheet does not require that information. In this example, information such as the lifespan and details of other groups interested in the site may be added after the necessary enquiries have been made by the survey back-up (see section 4.2.4).

The site record sheets need not follow the format of this example exactly. What is important is that the sheet can accommodate all the information necessary to assess the value of the site to your group and the local community. Volunteers conducting the survey should be aware of those features considered valuable, so that they will be 'on the look-out' for such features when surveying their sites.

The most important function of written instructions for volunteers is to ensure that, as far as possible, they all understand the site record sheets and complete them in the same way. Taking the site record sheet given as an example above, most of its numbered sections are self-explanatory and not open to misinterpretation. However, sections 11 and 14 may need accompanying instructions. Volunteers will undoubtedly encounter a wide range of substrates, habitats and other features. In order to avoid confusion in interpreting completed site record sheets, these features could be recorded in a standard way, combining an agreed set of symbols for the sketch map in section 14 with some standard means of completing section 11.

It may simplify the volunteer's task of recording site features in section 11 if a series of categories are provided, allowing volunteers to 'tick' many site features, rather than writing them out. Figure 4.2 is a simplified system which may be more suitable for the unusual features likely to be encountered on urban sites. Using the system in Figure 4.2, habitats and substrates present on a site may be ticked off in the boxes provided (in each category, blanks are provided for any features not already covered (boxes G, H, 11, 12, 13 and 20)). For example, ferns growing in wall crevices, etc. may be included in box 11. Any notable species found in each habitat may be written in the space below, with the relevant habitat numbers next to them, where applicable. For example, an area of woodland dominated by *Betula* (birch) and *Salix* (willow) species would receive a tick in box 7 D and the species of *Betula* and *Salix* listed below with the number 7 next to each. The most important or extensive habitats may then be illustrated in the sketch map in section 14 of the site record sheet. Figure 4.3 illustrates possible standard symbols for site features on the sketch map.

Figure 4.2 Chart of substrates, habitats and notable species

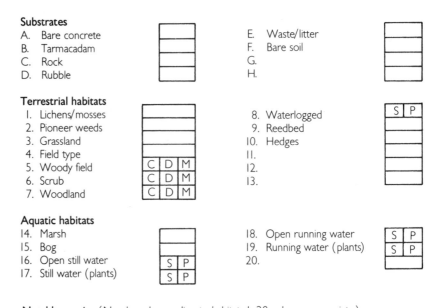

Substrates
A. Bare concrete
B. Tarmacadam
C. Rock
D. Rubble
E. Waste/litter
F. Bare soil
G.
H.

Terrestrial habitats
1. Lichens/mosses
2. Pioneer weeds
3. Grassland
4. Field type
5. Woody field
6. Scrub
7. Woodland
8. Waterlogged
9. Reedbed
10. Hedges
11.
12.
13.

Aquatic habitats
14. Marsh
15. Bog
16. Open still water
17. Still water (plants)
18. Open running water
19. Running water (plants)
20.

Notable species (Numbered according to habitats 1–20, where appropriate.)

Key
S = seasonal, P = permanent, C = coniferous, D = deciduous, M = mixed

Figure 4.3 Examples of possible symbols for sketch maps

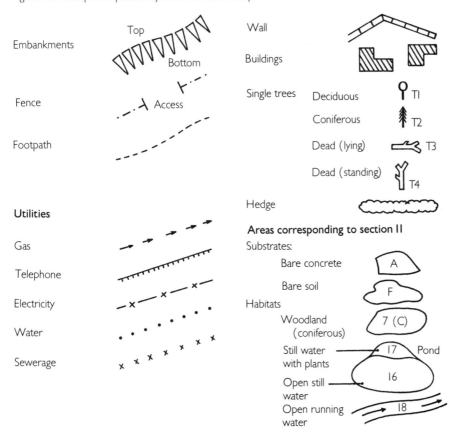

Note: Single trees may be numbered with TI, T2 ... Tn, so that notes may be made about particular trees shown on the map, for example as follows, TI mature elm (*Ulmus glabra*) 10m high, 0.6m diameter, etc. This method of numbering trees is similar to that used by The Tree Council in its National Tree Survey. If your group wishes to contribute to the survey, or check whether their local area has been surveyed, they may contact The Tree Council. Appendix 4 gives more details of the Tree Council's national survey and illustrates the methods used

Volunteers may be provided with instruction sheets explaining how to fill in sections 11 and 14, including more detailed explanations of substrate and habitat types (see Figure 4.2), for example as follows:

A. Bare concrete — flat expanses of concrete, cracked or not, e.g. floors of demolished buildings, concrete paths, etc. at, or below, the surface of the soil.
B. Tarmacadam — flat expanses or heaps of tarmac.
C. Rock — natural rocks or rock outcroppings, *not* man-made.
D. Rubble — flat expanses or heaps of bricks, concrete fragments, mortar, slag, etc.
E. Waste/litter — areas of heavy fly-tipping, alkali/acid waste, coal spoil, gravel, sand, ash, etc.
F. Bare soil — areas of soil of any type, not colonised by plants, with or without stones, bricks, etc.

1. Lichens/mosses — areas where only these groups have colonised.
2. Pioneer weeds — areas freshly colonised by weed (ruderal) species (usually dominated by annuals and biennials).
3. Grassland — open grassland vegetation, with or without herbs; less than 15 cm high.
4. Field type — (rank) tall vegetation dominated by non-woody (usually perennial) plants; 15 cm-2 m high.
5. Low-growing scrub — vegetation dominated by woody perennial plants; deciduous (D), coniferous (C) or mixed (M); canopy 15 cm-2 m high.
6. Scrub — vegetation dominated by woody perennial plants; deciduous (D), coniferous (C) or mixed (M); canopy 2 m-5 m high.
7. Woodland — vegetation dominated by woody perennial plants, deciduous (D), coniferous (C) or mixed (M); canopy over 5 m high.
8. Waterlogged — areas where the soil is so saturated that patches of water are visible; seasonally (S) or permanently (P).
9. Reedbed — waterlogged areas dominated by reeds and/or rushes.
10. Hedges — planted or otherwise, cut or overgrown, linear strips of trees, shrubs and hedgerow herbs, usually running along boundaries.
14. Marsh — 'water's edge' vegetation dominated by marshland plants on waterlogged soil or mud.
15. Bog — wet acid peat, often with *Sphagnum* mosses and other bog species.
16. Open still water — standing water, including stagnant water with algal blooms, uncolonised by higher water plants; (S) seasonal (P) permanent.
17. Still water (plants) — standing water with emergent/submergent water plants; (S) seasonal (P) permanent.
18. Open running water — running water uncolonised by higher water plants; (S) seasonal (P) permanent.
19. Running water (plants) — running water with submergent/emergent plants; (S) seasonal (P) permanent.

NB: Avoid confusing volunteers with terms. For example, ensure that they are familiar with the meanings of 'woody perennial, annual and biennial'. Section 5.1 describes these in detail.

At the time of writing, there is no standard format for an area survey of this kind and the suggestions made in this section are based on methods used by different groups and organisations currently surveying urban areas throughout Great Britain. Figure 4.4 is an example of a sophisticated, very well-designed area survey format used by the City Wildlife Project (CWP) in Leicester. The species lists are based on the flora of the Leicester area and the format is custom-designed for Leicester. Having used this format for some time, the CWP staff are already considering refinements to it.

Figure 4.4 Leicester Habitat Survey Form and survey form key

LEICESTER HABITAT SURVEY
CITY WILDLIFE PROJECT,
31 LONDON ROAD,
LEICESTER. TEL. 552550

RECORDER ☐☐☐☐☐☐☐☐☐☐☐☐☐☐☐ DATE ☐☐☐8☐ TIME ☐☐☐☐–☐☐ hrs
SITE ADDRESS ☐☐☐☐☐☐☐☐☐☐☐☐☐☐☐☐☐☐☐☐☐☐☐☐☐☐☐☐☐☐☐☐☐☐

GRID REF ☐☐☐☐☐ A – Z REF ☐☐☐ AREA ☐☐☐ ha
OWNER ☐☐☐☐☐☐☐☐☐☐☐☐☐☐☐☐☐☐☐☐☐☐☐☐☐☐☐☐☐☐☐☐☐☐

TENANT ☐☐☐☐☐☐☐☐☐☐☐☐☐☐☐☐☐☐☐☐☐☐☐☐
CONDITIONS OF VISIT ☐☐☐☐☐☐☐☐☐☐☐☐☐☐☐☐☐☐☐☐☐☐☐☐☐☐☐☐

SITE DESCRIPTION

NATURAL HISTORY OBSERVATIONS

OTHER SURVEY INFORMATION	
Mammals	
Birds	
Reptiles / Amphibs	
Fish	
Butterflies	
Inverts	
Flora	
Fungi	
Ferns	
Mosses	
Lichens	

SITE HISTORY

P	O	D

SITE NAME		NUMBER

SKETCH

NORTH

⊘

100m
25m

REMINDER

Boundaries
Adj. land use
Access
Scale
North
Paths
Tipping
Topography

	Bareground	Agric./Hort.	Ruderal	Tall Herb	Close Mown	Occas. Managed	Grazed	Unmanaged	Isol. Shrubs	Scrub	Hedgerow	–Cont./Gap.	–Lay/Clip/Unman.	–Height 1 2 3 3+	–Survey	Isol. Trees	Woodland Structure	Aq – Marginal	Aq – Still	Aq – Flowing	Built	Other	Soil Analysis	Surface Type T C Se S G R A Co	Drainage G M P	Land Use	A a / A s / A l / C e / E d / H o / S w / P s / R v / R w / W a / G / R / T i / I. C / S p / N O
A																											
B																											
C																											
D																											
E																											
F																											

LEICESTER HABITAT SURVEY

CITY WILDLIFE PROJECT
31 LONDON ROAD, LEICESTER. TEL: 552550

SITE NAME _____
SITE Nº _____
GRID REF. _____
RECORDER _____
DATE _____ 8

Columns: A B C D E F

TREES & SHRUBS (WOODLAND)

Scientific name	Common name
Acer campestre	(Field Maple)
Acer platanoides	(Norway Maple)
Acer pseudoplatanus	(Sycamore)
Aesculus hippocastanum	(Horse Chestnut)
Alnus glutinosa	(Alder)
Alnus incana	(Grey Alder)
Betula pendula	(Silver Birch)
Betula pubescens	(Downy Birch)
Buddleia davidii	(Buddleia)
Carpinus betulus	(Hornbeam)
Castanea sativa	(Sweet Chestnut)
Chamaecyparis lawsoniana	(Lawson's Cypress)
Corylus avellana	(Hazel)
Cotoneaster spp.	(Cotoneaster)
Crataegus laevigata	(Midland Hawthorn)
Crataegus monogyna	(Hawthorn)
Cytisus scoparius	(Broom)
Fagus sylvatica	(Common Beech)
Fraxinus excelsior	(Ash)
Ilex aquifolium	(Holly)
Juglans regia	(Walnut)
Laburnum anagyroides	(Laburnum)
Larix decidua	(European Larch)
Ligustrum ovalifolium	(Garden Privet)
Ligustrum vulgare	(Wild Privet)
Malus domestica	(Cultivated Apple)
Malus sylvestris	(Crab Apple)
Picea abies	(Norway Spruce)
Pinus sylvestris	(Scots Pine)
Platanus hybrida	(London Plane)
Populus alba	(White Poplar)
Populus canescens	(Grey Poplar)
Populus x canadensis	(Italian Poplar)
Populus nigra v.italica	(Lombardy Poplar)
Populus tremula	(Aspen)
Prunus avium	(Cherry)
Prunus sp.	(Plum)
Prunus spinosa	(Blackthorn)
Pyracantha coccinea	(Firethorn)
Quercus cerris	(Turkey Oak)
Quercus robur	(Pedunculate Oak)
Rhamnus catharticus	(Buckthorn)
Rhododendron spp.	(Rhododendron spp.)
Ribes rubrum	(Red Current)
Ribes uva-crispa	(Gooseberry)
Robinia pseudacacia	(False Acacia)
Rosa canina	(Dog Rose)
Rosa sp.	(Rose)
Salix alba	(White Willow)
Salix babylonica	(Weeping Willow)
Salix caprea	(Goat Willow)
Salix cinerea	(Grey Willow)
Salix fragilis	(Crack Willow)
Salix viminalis	(Osier)
Sambucus nigra	(Elder)
Sorbus aria	(Whitebeam)
Sorbus aucuparia	(Rowan)
Taxus baccata	(Yew)
Tilia x vulgaris	(Common Lime)
Ulex europaeus	(Gorse)
Ulmus procera	(English Elm)
Viburnum opulus	(Guelder Rose)

GRASSES, SEDGES & RUSHES

Scientific name	Common name
Agropyron caninum	(Bearded Couch-grass)
Agropyron repens	(Couch-grass)
Agrostis gigantea	(Black Bent-grass)
Agrostis stolonifera	(Fiorin)
Agrostis tenuis	(Common Bent-grass)
Aira caryophyllea	(Silver Hair-grass)
Aira praecox	(Early Hair-grass)
Alopecurus geniculatus	(Marsh Foxtail)
Alopecurus myosuroides	(Black Twitch)
Alopecurus pratensis	(Meadow Foxtail)
Anisantha sterilis	(Barren Brome)
Anthoxanthum odoratum	(Sweet Vernal-grass)
Arrhenatherum elatius	(Oat-grass)
Avena fatua	(Wild Oat)
Brachypodium sylvaticum	(Slender False-Brome)
Briza media	(Quaking-grass)
Bromus mollis	(Lop-grass)
Carex flacca	(Carnation-grass)
Carex hirta	(Hammer Sedge)
Carex otrubae	(False Fox-Sedge)
Carex riparia	(Great Pond Sedge)
Catapodium rigidum	(Hard Poa)
Cynosurus cristatus	(Crested Dog's Tail)
Dactylis glomerata	(Cock's-foot)
Deschampsia caespitosa	(Tufted Hair-grass)
Festuca arundinacea	(Tall Fescue)
Festuca gigantea	(Tall Brome)
Festuca pratensis	(Meadow Fescue)
Festuca rubra	(Red Fescue)
Glyceria fluitans	(Flote-grass)
Glyceria maxima	(Reed-grass)
Holcus lanatus	(Yorkshire Fog)
Holcus mollis	(Creeping Soft-grass)
Hordeum murinum	(Wall Barley)
Hordeum secalinum	(Meadow Barley)
Juncus articulatus	(Jointed Rush)
Juncus bufonius	(Toad Rush)
Juncus conglomeratus	(Conglomerate Rush)
Juncus effusus	(Soft Rush)
Juncus inflexus	(Hard Rush)
Lolium perenne	(Rye-grass)
Luzula campestris	(Field Woodrush)
Milium effusum	(Wood Millet)
Phalaris arundinacea	(Reed-grass)
Phleum bertolonii	(Cat's-trail)
Phleum pratense	(Timothy)
Phragmites australis	(Reed)
Poa annua	(Annual Poa)
Poa pratensis	(Smooth-stalked Mdw.)
Poa trivialis	(Rough-stalked Mdw.)
Scirpus lacustris	(Bulrush)
Trisetum flavescens	(Yellow Oat)
Typha latifolia	(Great Reedmace)
Vulpia bromoides	(Barren Fescue)
Vulpia myuros	(Rat's Tail Fescue)
Zerna ramosa	(Hairy Brome)

HERBS

Scientific name	Common name
Achillea millefolium	(Yarrow)
Acorus calamus	(Sweet Flag)
Aegopodium podagraria	(Ground Elder)
Aethusa cynapium	(Fool's Parsley)
Alisma plantago-aquatica	(Common W. Plantain)
Alliaria petiolata	(Garlic Mustard)
Anagallis arvensis	(Scarlet Pimpernel)
Anemone nemorosa	(Wood Anemone)
Angelica archangelica	(Garden Angelica)
Angelica sylvestris	(Angelica)
Anthriscus sylvestris	(Cow Parsley)
Antirrhinum majus	(Snapdragon)
Apium nodiflorum	(Fool's Watercress)
Arabidopsis thaliana	(Thale Cress)
Arctium minus	(Lesser Burdock)
Arenaria serpyllifolia	(Thyme-leaved Sandwort)
Armoracia rusticana	(Horseradish)
Artemisia absinthium	(Wormwood)
Artemisia vulgaris	(Mugwort)
Arum maculatum	(Lords and Ladies)
Aster novi-belgii	(Michaelmas Daisy)
Atriplex hastata	(Hastate Orache)
Atriplex patula	(Common Orache)
Atropa bella-donna	(Deadly Nightshade)
Ballota nigra	(Black Horehound)
Barbarea stricta	(Sm. fl. Wintercress)
Barbarea vulgaris	(Common Wintercress)
Bellis perennis	(Daisy)
Berula erecta	(Lesser Water Parsnip)
Brassica napus	(Rape)
Bryonia cretica	(White Bryony)
Callitriche stagnalis	(Starwort)
Caltha palustris	(Marsh Marigold)
Calystegia sepium	(Hedge Bindweed)
Calystegia silvatica	(Great Bindweed)
Capsella bursa-pastoris	(Shepherd's Purse)
Cardamine amara	(Large Bittercress)
Cardamine flexuosa	(Wavy Bittercress)
Cardamine hirsuta	(Hairy Bittercress)
Cardamine pratensis	(Cuckoo Flower)
Cardaria draba	(Hoary Cress)
Carduus acanthoides	(Welted Thistle)
Centaurea nigra	(Black Knapweed)
Cerastium fontanum	(Common Mouse Ear)
Cerastium glomeratum	(Stick. Mouse Ear)
Chaenorhinum minus	(Small Toadflax)
Chamomilla suaveolens	(Pineapple Mayweed)
Chamomilla recutita	(Scented Mayweed)
Chelidonium majus	(Greater Celandine)
Chenopodium album	(Fat Hen)
Chenopodium bonus-henricus	(Good King Henry)
Chenopodium rubrum	(Red Goosefoot)
Circaea lutetiana	(Enchanters Nightshade)
Cirsium arvense	(Creeping Thistle)

HERBS

A	B	C	D	E	F	HERBS
						Cirsium palustre (Marsh Thistle)
						Cirsium vulgare (Spear Thistle)
						Conium maculatum (Hemlock)
						Convolvulus arvensis (Field Bindweed)
						Conyza canadensis (Canadian Fleabane)
						Coronopus squamatus (Swine-cress)
						Crepis biennis (Rough Hawksbeard)
						Crepis capillaris (Smooth Hawksbeard)
						Crepis vesicaria (Beaked Hawksbeard)
						Cymbalaria muralis (Ivy-leaved Toadflax)
						Daucus carota (Wild Carrot)
						Digitalis purpurea (Foxglove)
						Dipsacus fullonum (Teasel)
						Elodea canadensis (Canadian Water Weed)
						Endymion hispanicus (Spanish Bluebell)
						Endymion non-scriptus (Bluebell)
						Epilobium angustifolium (Rosebay Willowherb)
						Epilobium hirsutum (Great Willowherb)
						Epilobium montanum (Broad-leaved Willowherb)
						Epilobium tetragonum (Sq.-st. Willowherb)
						Equisetum arvense (Horse Tail)
						Erophila verna (Common Whitlow Grass)
						Erysimum cheiranthoides (Treacle Mustard)
						Euphorbia helioscopia (Sun Spurge)
						Euphorbia peplus (Petty Spurge)
						Filipendula ulmaria (Meadowsweet)
						Foeniculum vulgare (Fennel)
						Fragaria vesca (Wild Strawberry)
						Fumaria officinalis (Common Fumitory)
						Galanthus nivalis (Snowdrop)
						Galega officinalis (Goat's Rue)
						Galeopsis tetrahit (Common Hemp-Nettle)
						Galinsoga ciliata (Shaggy Soldier)
						Galium aparine (Common Cleavers)
						Galium mollugo (Hedge Bedstraw)
						Galium palustre (Marsh Bedstraw)
						Galium verum (Lady's Bedstraw)
						Geranium dissectum (Cut-leaved Cranesbill)
						Geranium molle (Dovesfoot Cranesbill)
						Geranium pratense (Meadow Cranesbill)
						Geranium pyrenaicum (Hedgerow Cranesbill)
						Geranium robertianum (Herb Robert)
						Geum urbanum (Herb Bennet)
						Glechoma hederacea (Ground Ivy)
						Hedera helix (Ivy)
						Heracleum sphondylium (Hogweed)
						Hieracium aprotum (Few-leaved Hawkweed)
						Hieracium pilosella (Mouse-ear Hawkweed)
						Hieracium umbellatum (Leafy Hawkweed)
						Humulus lupulus (Hop)
						Hypericum maculatum (Imp. St. John's Wort)
						Hypericum perforatum (Per. St. John's Wort)
						Hypochaeris radicata (Common Catsear)
						Impatiens capensis (Orange Balsam)
						Impatiens glandulifera (Himalayan Balsam)
						Iris pseudacorus (Yellow Iris)
						Lactuca serriola (Prickly Lettuce)
						Lamium album (White Dead-Nettle)
						Lamium purpureum (Red Dead-Nettle)
						Lamium maculatum (Spotted Dead-Nettle)
						Lapsana communis (Nipplewort)
						Lathyrus latifolius (Br. Iv. Evl. Pea)
						Lathyrus pratensis (Meadow Vetchling)
						Lemna gibba (Gibbous Duck Weed)
						Lemna minor (Common Duck Weed)
						Lemna polyrrhiza (Great Duck Weed)
						Lemna trisulca (Ivy-leaved Duck Weed)
						Leontodon autumnalis (Autumn Hawkbit)
						Lepidium ruderale (N.L. Pepperwort)

HERBS

A	B	C	D	E	F	HERBS
						Leucanthemum maximum (Shasta Daisy)
						Leucanthemum vulgare (Ox-Eye Daisy)
						Linaria purpurea (Purple Toadflax)
						Linaria vulgaris (Common Toadflax)
						Lonicera periclymenum (Honeysuckle)
						Lotus corniculatus (Birdsfoot Trefoil)
						Lunaria annua (Honesty)
						Lupinus polyphyllus (Garden Lupin)
						Lycopus europaeus (Gipsywort)
						Lysimachia nummularia (Creeping Jenny)
						Malva sylvestris (Common Mallow)
						Matricaria perforata (Scentless Mayweed)
						Medicago lupulina (Black Medick)
						Melilotus officinalis (Ribbed Melilot)
						Mentha aquatica (Water Mint)
						Mentha x piperita (Peppermint)
						Mentha spicata (Spear Mint)
						Mercurialis perennis (Dog's Mercury)
						Mycelis muralis (Wall Lettuce)
						Myosotis arvensis (Field Forgetmenot)
						Myosotis scorpioides (Water Forgetmenot)
						Myosotis sylvatica (Wood Forgetmenot)
						Myosoton aquaticum (Water Chickweed)
						Myriophyllum sp. (Milfoil)
						Narcissus pseudonarcissus (Daffodil)
						Nepeta cataria (Catmint)
						Nuphar lutea (Yellow Water-Lily)
						Oenanthe crocata (Hem. Wt. Dropwort)
						Oenothera erythrosepala (Lg. Fl. Ev. Primrose)
						Ononis spinosa (Spiny Rest-Harrow)
						Oxalis acetosella (Wood Sorrel)
						Papaver rhoeas (Common Poppy)
						Papaver somniferum (Opium Poppy)
						Pastinaca sativa (Wild Parsnip)
						Pentaglottis sempervirens (Green Alkanet)
						Petasites hybridus (Butterbur)
						Petroselinum crispum (Wild Parsley)
						Picris echioides (Bristly Oxtongue)
						Pimpinella saxifraga (Burnet Saxifrage)
						Plantago lanceolata (Ribwort Plantain)
						Plantago major (Greater Plantain)
						Polygonum amphibium (Amphibious Bistort)
						Polygonum arenastrum (Knotgrass)
						Polygonum aviculare (Knotgrass)
						Polygonum cuspidatum (Japanese Knotweed)
						Polygonum hydropiper (Water-Pepper)
						Polygonum persicaria (Redshank)
						Potamogeton natans (Broad-leaved Pond Weed)
						Potamogeton sp. (Pond Weed)
						Potentilla anserina (Silverweed)
						Potentilla erecta (Tormentil)
						Potentilla reptans (Creeping Cinquefoil)
						Primula vulgaris (Primrose)
						Prunella vulgaris (Self-Heal)
						Pulicaria dysenterica (Common Fleabane)
						Ranunculus acris (Meadow Buttercup)
						Ranunculus aquatillis (Water Crowfoot)
						Ranunculus bulbosus (Bulbous Buttercup)
						Ranunculus ficaria (Lesser Celandine)
						Ranunculus repens (Creeping Buttercup)
						Ranunculus sceleratus (C.L. Buttercup)
						Raphanus raphanistrum (Wild Radish)
						Reseda lutea (Wild Mignonette)
						Reseda luteola (Weld)
						Rorippa amphibia (Great Yellowcress)
						Rorippa sylvestris (Creeping Yellowcress)
						Rubus fruticosus (Bramble)
						Rubus idaeus (Raspberry)
						Rumex acetosa (Common Sorrel)

HERBS

A	B	C	D	E	F	HERBS
						Rumex acetosella (Sheep's Sorrel)
						Rumex conglomeratus (Clustered Dock)
						Rumex crispus (Curled Dock)
						Rumex hydrolapathum (Water Dock)
						Rumex obtusifolius (Broad leaved Dock)
						Sagittaria sagittifolia (Arrowhead)
						Sanguisorba officinalis (Great Burnet)
						Scrophularia auriculata (Water Figwort)
						Scrophularia nodosa (Common Figwort)
						Scutellaria galericulata (Skullcap)
						Sedum acre (Biting Stonecrop)
						Sedum anglicum (English Stonecrop)
						Senecio erucifolius (Hoary Ragwort)
						Senecio jacobaea (Common Ragwort)
						Senecio squalidus (Oxford Ragwort)
						Senecio viscosus (Sticky Groundsel)
						Senecio vulgaris (Groundsel)
						Silene alba (White Campion)
						Silene dioica (Red Campion)
						Silene vulgaris (Bladder Campion)
						Sinapis arvensis (Charlock)
						Sisymbrium officinale (Hedge Mustard)
						Solanum dulcamara (Bittersweet)
						Solanum nigrum (Black Nightshade)
						Solidago canadensis (Canadian Golden-Rod)
						Sonchus arvensis (Perennial Sow-Thistle)
						Sonchus asper (Prickly Sow-Thistle)
						Sonchus oleraceus (Smooth Sow-Thistle)
						Sparganium erectum (Branched Bur-reed)
						Stachys palustris (Marsh Woundwort)
						Stachys sylvatica (Hedge Woundwort)
						Stellaria graminea (Lesser Stitchwort)
						Stellaria holostea (Greater Stitchwort)
						Stellaria media (Common Chickweed)
						Symphytum officinale (Common Comfrey)
						Symphytum x uplandicum (Russian Comfrey)
						Tamus communis (Black Bryony)
						Tanacetum parthenium (Feverfew)
						Tanacetum vulgare (Tansy)
						Taraxacum sp. (Dandelion)
						Thlaspi arvense (Field Pennycress)
						Torilis japonica (Upright-Hedge Parsley)
						Tragopogon pratensis (Goat's Beard)
						Trifolium arvense (Haresfoot Clover)
						Trifolium campestre (Hop Trefoil)
						Trifolium dubium (Lesser Trefoil)
						Trifolium pratense (Red Clover)
						Trifolium repens (White Clover)
						Tussilago farfara (Coltsfoot)
						Urtica dioica (Stinging Nettle)
						Verbascum thapsus (Great Mullein)
						Veronica beccabunga (Brooklime)
						Veronica chamaedrys (Germander Speedwell)
						Veronica filiformis (Creeping Speedwell)
						Veronica hederifolia (Ivy-leaved Speedwell)
						Veronica persica (Common Field Speedwell)
						Veronica serpyllifolia (Thyme-leaved Speedwell)
						Vicia cracca (Tufted Vetch)
						Vicia hirsuta (Hairy Tare)
						Vicia sativa (Common Vetch)
						Vicia sepium (Bush Vetch)
						Vinca minor (Lesser Periwinkle)
						Viola arvensis (Field Pansy)
						Viola riviniana (Common Dog Violet)
						Viola tricolor (Wild Pansy)

HABITAT SURVEY FORM KEY

Site name
Local name used whenever possible. An appropriate name is adopted if no other exists to help identify the site.

Site code
This has three components: e.g. 21-B6-12 = Map No.-Square No.-Site No.

(i) Map number— Refers to the O.S. composite map constructed by Leicester City Council Planning Department (scale 1:2500).

(ii) Square number — Refers to the ½km square within the composite map. The letter refers to the vertical co-ordinate while the number refers to the horizontal co-ordinate.

(iii) Site number — Each site on the composite map is given a number, specific to that map. If a site extends into one or more adjacent maps then it is numbered on the map in which most of the site occurs. An asterisk indicates such an overlap, e.g. 25-A3-69*.

Scale
The sketch of the site is drawn to the scale which best fits the space available. One of three scales is used and is shown on the right-hand side of the sketch. On the site sketch, 4cm may thus represent 25, 50 or 100 m; the inappropriate scale being deleted. However, if the 50-m scale is used, then both the other figures are deleted and '50m' is written in.

Direction
North is indicated by an arrow within the printed circle.

Sketch
Each site may contain one or more 'parcels'. A parcel consists of a particular habitat type defined by plant communities or structure. Sometimes a topographical feature, e.g. a steep embankment, may be the parcel boundary especially as it is likely to have a different flora to adjacent parcels.

A letter identifies the parcel: A, B, C, D, E or F. If extra parcels are needed (e.g. G, H) then an additional habitat form will be used and the new letters must be inserted in place of the A-F denotations. Various symbols and colours are used to describe map features.

Colour coding of habitats
The major habitat groupings are shown by the following system:

Brown	Woodland, copses, lines of trees, single trees
Dark green	Unmanaged grassland, pasture, tall herb communities
Light green	Close mown grass
Orange	Hedgerow, scrub, isolated shrubs
Yellow	Arable farmland
Yellow stripes	Allotments
Purple stripes	Areas of tipping
Blue	Aquatic systems
Dark green stripes over blue	Emergent aquatic vegetation
Grey stripes over dark green	Bare ground

(a) *Boundaries* (in black)

————————	Site boundary	∧∧∧∧∧∧∧	Wall
— — — — — —	Parcel boundary	⊔⊔⊔⊔⊔⊔⊔⊔⊔	Metal railings
		———⟨———	Open
		××××××××	Mesh
		════════	Wooden fence
		⊖ ⊖ ⊖ ⊖ ⊖	Fence of posts and wire

(b) *Access* (in red) indicating points of access into the site

———————>> Vehicular ⎫ surfaced   — — —>> Vehicular ⎫ unsurfaced
————————> Pedestrian ⎭   — — — —> Pedestrian ⎭

————⟋———— Open access
——+———‖—— Stile and gate

(c) *Paths and roads* (in red)

════════════ Vehicular ⎫ surfaced   ====== Vehicular ⎫ unsurfaced
———————————— Pedestrian ⎭   — — — — — — Pedestrian ⎭

Note: A path or road is considered to be surfaced if it has been deliberately covered with a
  material to strengthen and formalise the route.

(d) *Topography*

Slopes are indicated by triangles. Their dimension and angles represent the angle and
  height of the slope.

Top ▼▼▼ is longer and more gently sloping than ▼ ▼ ▼

(e) *Adjacent land use*

The appropriate encircled abbreviation describes the land use category around the site
e.g. (Wa) — wasteground. (See 'land use' notes for details of abbreviations.)

(f) *Tipped material* (in purple)

Rubbish dumps, piles of rubble, etc. are represented by stripes for large areas or the
letter 'T' for a small area.

Reminder

Features to be noted on the sketch map are listed in the box. Each is ticked as the surveyor
notes their presence or absence, recording them on the sketch as appropriate.

Habitat table

Columns in the table represent habitat types, land uses and environmental factors. For each
parcel (lettered on left-hand side) a tick, letter or number indicates these details where
present. Where columns offer alternatives e.g. (A)griculture/(H)orticulture. One of the
encircled letters is entered in the space below, i.e. A or H.

1. Bare ground: no plants or extremely sparse vegetation.
2. Agricultural: where livestock or arable land occur.
    Horticultural: allotments, tree nurseries, garden centres.
3. Ruderal: early colonising vegetation such as legumes and crucifers.
4. Tall herb: where such plants (e.g. nettles, willowherb) occur as continuous ground
    cover, but are not dominated by grasses.
5. Close mown: grass 10cm high.
6. Occasionally managed: mown or cut infrequently.
7. Grazed: by farm animals or pets including geese. Some areas may be grazed by wild
    rabbits.
8. Unmanaged: grassland areas which may include various herbs and isolated shrubs.
9. Isolated shrubs: shrubs or trees <8m which do not form a continuous canopy.
10. Scrub: shrubs and trees (<8m high) forming a closed canopy. Isolated trees may occur
    within this habitat.
11. Hedgerow: former or remnant hedges may be included if still recognisable as such.
12. Hedgerow — (C)ontinuous/(G)appy: refers to the current state of the hedge,
    whether an unbroken length or with gaps.
13. Hedgerow — (L)ayed/(C)lipped/(U)nmanaged: refers to the management regime
    which the hedge has received.
14. Hedgerow height — 1, 2, 3, 3+: the height in metres.
15. Hedgerow survey: tick if detailed survey information available.
16. Isolated trees: >8m tall and not forming continuous canopy with other trees.
17. Woodland: consists of trees >8m tall, forming a closed canopy, which may or may not
    have a shrub and ground layer.

(S)tructure: if the structure is recorded on the vegetation checklist, then S replaces the tick used simply to denote woodland presence. This then involves recording canopy, shrubs and ground layers separately. C, S, G must be written in place of D, E, F on the checklist.

18. Aquatic — marginal: wetland/marsh habitat. This may include muddy banks which are submerged for only part of the year.
19. Aquatic — still: ponds, lakes, reservoirs, ditches.
20. Aquatic — flowing: rivers, streams, canals.
21. Built: man-made, buildings, structures and artefacts including roads, pylons, foundations, walls, etc.
22. Other: any habitat or feature which will not fit easily into one of the above. This should be elaborated in the 'Site description'.
23. Soil analysis: tick if further information is available on file.
24. Surface type: note type of substrate including that of aquatic habitats where possible.

T	— topsoil	S	— sand	Co	— concrete
C	— clay	G	— gravel	A	— ash
Se	— sediment	R	— rubble	O	— other

25. Drainage — a rating based on a visual appraisal of the site using topography, location, surface type and plant composition as indicators:
    (G)ood: well-drained land, unaffected by waterlogging and lacking any wetland species.
    (M)oderate: land subject to occasional waterlogging without the establishment of a wetland flora.
    (P)oor: land usually by standing or running water, which is subject to flooding and waterlogging. The site will usually support typical wetland plants.
26. Land use:

Aa	— Agriculture: arable, orchards.
As	— Agriculture: livestock.
Al	— Allotments.
Ce	— Cemetery.
Ed	— Educational establishment, e.g. school, colleges.
Ho	— Hospital.
Sw	— Sewage works.
Ps	— Public open space: includes public parks and gardens, riverside walks and amenity areas.
Rv	— Road verge.
Rw	— Railway: includes tracks, sidings, cuttings and embankments.
Wa	— Waste ground: areas formerly occupied by buildings, yards, etc.
G	— Gardens: private or publicly owned.
R	— Residential: private and council housing.
Ti	— Tip.
I.C.	— Industrial/commercial premises.
Sp	— Sport: grounds and pitches owned, leased or rented by clubs and societies.
N	— Navigation: where boats and barges use waterways.
O	— Other: where none of the above categories are applicable, give details in the 'Site description'.

Note:
Prefix with D if the land use no longer exists.

Recorder
Initials of surveyors.

Date
Record the day, month and year.

Time
Show arrival and departure time for each site visit.

Site address
Locate as precisely as possible by giving area of city, nearby streets, landmarks and any other noticeable features.

Grid reference
Eight digits if the site is on more than one map, using that which contains the majority of the site. Take the centre of that section as the reference point.

A-Z reference
Using 'A-Z' street atlas of Leicester and District.

Area
Given in hectares.

Owner
All known details of the owner — including individual, firm or institution name, address and telephone number.

Tenant
Details as above.

Conditions of visit
Whether permission for access was required.

Site description
(a)   General introductory sentence/short paragraph broadly describing the site.
(b)   Briefly describe each parcel habitat and features.
(c)   Land use and evidence of use, e.g. tyre tracks, presence of people and dogs, planted trees, benches, car parks, etc.
(d)   Any comments or reactions from persons met whilst surveying.

Natural history observations
Notes on birds, mammals, insects and other taxa. Any evidence of animal presence such as tracks, remains of prey, droppings, burrows. Record signs of breeding and territoriality, such as: display, nests, young.

Other survey information
Tick category in box if further information is available on the taxa involved.

Site history
Brief description of past changes and developments in land use.

POD
A tick in any of these boxes indicates that proposals to develop the site exist as detailed below:
P   *Proposed* development planned for site. Includes areas designated for change of use in local plans.
O   *Outline* planning approval granted for site.
D   *Detailed* planning permission granted for change of land use. The applicant may have reserved certain areas (e.g. landscaping details) for later approval. Work must commence within five years of approval.

Plant checklist
Abundance scale:
R   — rare: one or a few individuals.
O   — occasional: uncommon.
L   — locally frequent: common in localised areas.
F   — frequent: common and widespread.
A   — abundance: very common, widespread and possibly dominant.

4.2 Conducting the survey of the area

Your group should be ready to carry out the area survey after:

— completing the necessary preliminary research;
— drawing up a map of the survey area with sites marked on it;
— producing site record sheets and written instructions for volunteers;
— recruiting a volunteer team.

The volunteer survey team and the survey co-ordinators need to meet first for a briefing session.

4.2.1 Volunteer briefing and organisation

It is important not to expect too much from individual volunteers. It is essential that they know exactly what is required of them from the beginning and the time-scale to which they will be working. The aims of the briefing session are therefore as follows:

(a) To ensure that each volunteer understands the site record sheets and written instructions and is aware of those site features your group have identified as most important when surveying sites.
(b) To determine how large an area each volunteer, or group of volunteers, can easily cover. A possible approach is to ask the volunteers how large an area they can cope with and then to allocate them areas smaller than those they suggest.
(c) To split the area up between volunteers, or small groups of volunteers. The area could, for example, be split street by street, site by site, or by squares on an Ordnance Survey map (1:2500 scale).
(d) To set up some co-ordinating arrangement. An individual or small group may be nominated to co-ordinate the survey. This will ensure that the volunteers know who to return information to and whom to contact should difficulties arise in the field. Ideally the co-ordinator(s) should be on the telephone and able to receive, collate and file fragmented survey information as it comes in.

At the briefing session stage, conflicting considerations may come into play. On the one hand, your group may wish to restrict the area surveyed, perhaps because you only have a small volunteer force and/or wish to ensure a well-conducted survey without losing detail in the information collected. On the other hand, your group may wish to cover as large an area as possible, whether or not it means 'skimping' on survey detail, so as to avoid missing potentially valuable sites. The chosen option may have to be a compromise between these two opposing considerations.

4.2.2 Maps

The optimum scale of map for recording a site survey in detail is usually 1:1250 or less (80 cm to 1 km) but 1:2500 (40 cm to 1 km) may also be feasible. In the city, photocopies of local streetplans or A-Zs may be most useful to volunteers conducting area surveys in the field, as these are commonly available in the shops in a choice of formats, with widely ranging scales and degrees of detail. However, Ordnance Survey (OS) maps are of a consistently high quality throughout the country and Her Majesty's Stationery Office (HMSO) or your nearest OS agent should be able to sell OS sheets in the 1:1250 and 1:2500 series.

Local authorities, as well as having their own maps of the area, normally possess a licence to reproduce copies of OS maps and may, therefore, be able to provide your group with suitable copies, free of charge. Any OS maps to be used in a group publication may only be reproduced with the permission of: The Director, The Ordnance Survey, Ramsey Road, Maybush, Southampton SD9 4DH. A letter to this address, explaining what the publication is about, will normally result in the necessary authorisation. The local library or museum may also have up-to-date maps of the local area.

To avoid loss of important survey information, it is worthwhile producing copies of all maps for volunteers to use in the field, and duplicates for the co-ordinators to keep in a place of safety. Any information obtained in the field should then be entered onto the duplicate copy as quickly as possible.

4.2.3 Surveying in the field

As with all group activities, safety and legality are important considerations. With volunteers visiting unknown areas, first-aid and safety precautions should be taken wherever possible. Your group, although not legally obliged, may feel morally obliged to provide accident and sickness insurance cover for volunteers. It may be possible for your group to obtain such insurance cover at reasonable rates by affiliating to another group, such as BTCV, or a volunteer bureau, and obtaining cover under their policies (see Chapter 3 for further details of legal considerations and constraints).

If volunteers are to be transported in private vehicles, you should ensure that the driver has full passenger liability cover and that, if a charge is to be made for the journey, the insurance is not invalidated.

Unless volunteers conduct the survey by looking over fences, they will be going on to many publicly and privately owned plots of land. If a site is known to be public, there should be no problem with access (for example, with town parks, public open space, churchyards, etc.). Otherwise, the survey co-ordinators will need to locate the site owners and arrange access (see section 4.2.4 for further details of survey back-up).

If the situation should arise where a volunteer is confronted on a site by an owner or guardian who does not know of the survey, it will be useful for the volunteer to have some form of identification and written details of your group and the project to support their explanation for being there.

With the exception of Ministry of Defence and railway land, to trespass is not a crime. The owner of the land may, however, request a trespasser to leave by a reasonable route and, upon refusal, use reasonable force to eject the tres-passer, and further bring a civil action for damages, if the owner so wishes. There is, however, very little risk of such an extreme situation arising during the survey. It is nevertheless useful to inform volunteers of the importance of politeness.

Volunteers may be provided with clipboards and the following: site record sheets; instruction sheets; maps of their respective survey area (ideally with plastic covers to protect sheets). Preferably, these should be copies, so that any information recorded in the field may be transferred to duplicate copies on file with the survey co-ordinator(s). Every sheet used to record survey details should have a site reference and survey date. It will also help volunteers if they have a telephone number to contact in case of difficulty while conducting the survey.

When surveying the site flora and fauna, good pocket guides are very important tools for the volunteers. Appendix 2 gives some examples of useful guides to plant and animal identification. It should be sufficient, at this stage, to ensure that the site is walked over once in such a way that volunteers are able to plot roughly the boundaries of recognisably distinct stands of vegetation. A compass can be useful for keeping your bearings. Distances can then be simply paced out. On larger sites, a route, moving across the site from one end to the other, and zig-zagging from one side to the other as you go, is probably the most efficient way of covering the ground.

Obviously, some plants and animals are more easily recognised and identified than others. Volunteers will have varying degrees of knowledge. One individual may have a wide knowledge of birds, another of insects, and so on. Whatever the degree of knowledge of a volunteer, the temptation to guess the identity of a plant or animal species must be resisted. It is better to have a list of ten positively identified species than a list of 30 species, most of which are guesses. If the site is shortlisted, then species present can be examined in more detail. Section 4.4.4 deals with surveys of habitats, communities and species in more detail.

It may be worthwhile outlining to the volunteers the law protecting species of plants and animals in Great Britain. The main points are summarised in the NCC pamphlet *Wildlife, the Law and You* as follows:

Killing, injuring, taking or selling specially protected wild animals such as the otter, badger and red squirrel, is against the law;
— disturbing them in their places of shelter is also against the law;
— all wild birds, their nests and eggs are protected (with exceptions for pest and sporting species), and there are special penalties for harming certain rarities;
— specially protected plants must not be uprooted, picked or sold, and uprooting any wild plant is illegal.

Table 4.2 gives lists of protected species.

Table 4.2 Wildlife and the law — protected wild species

Specially protected wild plants

Botanical name	Common name
Alisma gramineum	ribbon-leaved water plantain
Allium sphaerocephalon	round-headed leek
Althaea hirsuta	rough marsh-mallow
Alyssum alyssoides	small Alison
Arenaria norvegica	Norwegian sandwort
Artemisia campestris	field wormwood
Bupleurum baldense	small hare's ear
B. falcatum	sickle-leaved hare's ear
Calamintha sylvatica	wood calamint
Carex depauperata	starved wood sedge
Cephalanthera rubra	red helleborine
Cicerbita alpina	Alpine sow-thistle
Cotoneaster integerrimus	wild cotoneaster
Cyperus fuscus	brown galingale
Cypripedium calceolus	lady's-slipper
Cystopteris dickieana	Dickie's bladder-fern

Damasonium alisma	starfruit
Dianthus gratianopolitanus	Cheddar pink
Diapensia lapponica	diapensia
Epipogium aphyllum	ghost orchid
Eryngium campestre	field eryngo
Euphorbia peplis	purple spurge
Gentiana nivalis	Alpine gentian
G. verna	spring gentian
Gladiolus illyricus	wild gladiolus
Gnaphalium luteoalbum	Jersey cudweed
Himantoglossum hircinum	lizard orchid
Lactuca saligna	least lettuce
Limonium paradoxum	rock sea-lavender ⎫
L. recurvum	rock sea-lavender ⎬ (two rare species)
Liparis loeselii	fen orchid
Lloydia serotina	Snowdon lily
Lychnis alpina	Alpine catchfly
Melampyrum arvense	field cow-wheat
Minuartia stricta	Teesdale sandwort
Ophrys fuciflora	late spider-orchid
O. sphegodes	early spider-orchid
Orchis militaris	military orchid
O. simia	monkey orchid
Orobanche caryophyllacea	bedstraw broomrape
O. loricata	oxtongue broomrape
O. reticulata	thistle broomrape
Petrorhagia nanteulii	chidling pink
Phyllodoce caerulea	blue heath
Polygonatum verticillatum	whorled Solomon's seal
Polygonum maritimum	sea knotgrass
Potentilla rupestris	rock cinquefoil
Pyrus cordata	Plymouth pear
Ranunculus ophioglossifolius	adder's-tongue spearwort
Rhinanthus serotinus	greater yellow-rattle
Saxifraga cernua	drooping saxifrage
S. cespitosa	tufted saxifrage
Scirpus triquetrus	triangular club-rush
Scleranthus perennis	perennial knawel
Stachys alpina	limestone woundwort
S. germanica	downy woundwort
Teucrium scordium	water germander
Trichomanes speciosum	Killarney fern
Veronica spicata	spiked speedwell
Viola persicifolia	fen violet
Woodsia alpina	Alpine woodsia
W. ilvensis	oblong woodsia

Wild birds specially protected at all times

avocet	black-winged stilt
barn owl	bluethroat
bearded tit	brambling
bee-eater	Cetti's warbler
Bewick's swan	chough
bittern	cirl bunting
black-necked grebe	common quail
black redstart	common scoter
black-tailed godwit	corncrake
black tern	crested tit

crossbills (all species)
Dartford warbler
divers (all species)
dotterel
fieldfare
firecrest
garganey
golden eagle
golden oriole
goshawk
green sandpiper
greenshank
Gyr falcon
harriers (all species)
hobby
honey buzzard
hoopoe
Kentish plover
kingfisher
Lapland bunting
Leach's petrel
little bittern
little gull
little ringed plover
little tern
long-tailed duck
marsh warbler
Mediterranean gull
merlin
osprey

peregrine
purple heron
purple sandpiper
red-backed shrike
red kite
red-necked phalarope
redwing
roseate tern
ruff
Savi's warbler
scarlet rosefinch
scaup
serin
shorelark
short-toed treecreeper
Slavonian grebe
snow-bunting
snowy owl
spoonbill
spotted crake
stone curlew
Temminck's stint
velvet scoter
whimbrel
white-tailed eagle
whooper swan
wood lark
wood sandpiper
wryneck

'Pest' species of wild birds

collared dove
crow
feral pigeon
great black-backed gull
herring gull
house sparrow
jackdaw
jay
lesser black-backed gull
magpie
rook
starling
wood pigeon

Wild birds specially protected during
the close season

goldeneye
greylag goose (in the Outer Hebrides,
    Caithness, Sutherland and Wester Ross
    only)
pintail

Other specially protected wild animals

Mammals

bats (all 15 species)
bottle-nosed dolphin
common dolphin
common otter
harbour (or common) porpoise
red squirrel

Reptiles

sand lizard
smooth snake

Amphibians

great crested (or warty) newt
natterjack toad

Fish

burbot

Butterflies

chequered skipper
heath fritillary
large blue
swallowtail

Moths

barberry carpet
black-veined
Essex emerald
New Forest burnet
Reddish buff

Other insects

field cricket
mole cricket
Norfolk aeshna dragonfly
rainbow leaf beetle
wart-biter grasshopper

Spiders

fen raft spider
ladybird spider

Snails

Carthusian snail
glutinous snail
sandbowl snail

The volunteers may minimise the disturbance to wildlife on the sites in various ways during surveying, for example:

(a) When identifying plants, bring the book to the plant and not the plant to the book wherever possible.
(b) Avoid making too much noise or disturbance in areas where birds are nesting, e.g. dense scrub, particularly during the breeding season (March-mid September for most species).
(c) If a nest is discovered, do not move branches aside to get a better look. This may alter the nest surrounding, damage the nest itself and cause the parents to desert it.

If your group wishes to use a site for a tree or wildflower nursery, allotments, gardens, urban farm or other projects requiring particular soil conditions, soil analyses may be necessary. Proper soil analysis is a lengthy and complex procedure and may, therefore, best be carried out only on those sites shortlisted from the area survey. The same applies to detailed analyses of topography, landscape features and wildlife (see section 4.4.2 for further information on soil features, including pollutants).

For the area survey it is best not to waste too much time on fine detail. Ideally, one visit to each site in the summer should allow a rough map and habitat survey to be completed, and should provide enough information for selecting those sites to be shortlisted for more detailed surveys (section 4.4). After 3-5 years, the area survey may then be repeated with the minimum of effort, to keep up with the development of all sites in the area and to identify any new ones.

4.2.4 Survey back-up

Volunteers in the field will probably not be able to find out all there is to know about a site. The survey co-ordinators may be able to help by locating the following information for inclusion on site record sheets:

Who owns the site?

Within the legal system, private owners of property do not have to disclose their names. However, if a site is registered, the owner's name may be on record in HM Land Registry (see Appendix 15 for address). If there are any estate agents' hoardings on the site, they may have the owner's name, but again they are not legally obliged to disclose this information. Volunteers may be able to locate the site owner by asking neighbouring land owners, local people, the police, the fire brigade or the local press.

The local authority may also be able to help. If there are any current planning applications for the site, these may give an indication of the owner, and planning officers will have this information. Alternatively, the borough treasurer (or director of finance) may forward a letter to the owner or leaseholder for your group.

Public (statutory) owners of land have to say if they own a site. These include:

British Waterways Board
British Railways Property Board (Regional Division)
Gas Board
Local Electricity Board
Central Electricity Generating Board
The local, district, metropolitan or county council (some addresses for these bodies are provided in Appendix 15 but it should be possible to locate them in the telephone directory). In the case of land owned by the council, the valuation office or estates department is the section to contact.

Is the site available and for how long?

Having located the owner of a site, the co-ordinators may ask the following questions:

— Is the site available and if not could an agreement be made for temporary use of the site until the owners wished to develop it themselves?
— What is the minimum length of time for which the owner will allow your group to use the site?
— What legal or planning restrictions are there on the use of the site?
— On what terms would the owner consider allowing your group to use the site, e.g. gentleman's agreement, licence, lease, peppercorn rent? (See Chapter 3.2 for legal considerations and constraints relating to site use.)

Site history/former use of the site

Knowledge of the former use of a site is important, as building foundations, underground services, past deposits of wastes or effluents, etc. can all affect the quality of substrate, creating problems with ground preparation, drainage and planting.

Site history is also important when considering the site's wildlife value. As already mentioned in section 4.1.2, the history of a site may show that a site has, for example, remained undisturbed, retaining its original (relic) flora and fauna.

The local library or museum may have historical data on the area and may be able to suggest other sources of information such as local history societies. The district or county council's records office will also contain detailed information on site histories. The library or council records office may have a set of 'Kelly's Directories'. These are produced annually and give details of occupiers, street by street, property by property.

It may be worth contacting the council's environmental health officer to check whether the site has been contaminated.

Generally, the other major sources of historical records include:

— district engineers department;
— maps, Ordnance Survey 1 inch 1801 — (successive editions)
                                     6 inch 1840 — (successive editions)
                                     25 inch 1880 — (successive editions);
— maps, tithe commutation and other special purpose;
— company records, estate maps, railway and dock records, etc. (these may be in the records office);
— personal accounts of employees, site owners, local inhabitants.

4.3 Interpreting area survey results

If a large number of sites have been covered by the survey, the task of short-listing those most suited to your group's requirements may be extremely difficult. You may wish to adopt and develop one or a number of sites and maintain an interest in others for future development, or as suitable sites for development by other local groups.

Shortlisting may be best achieved by a process of elimination. Some sites may be rapidly eliminated, for example, if they are found to be too dangerous, or are due to be built upon, or if the site owners refuse to co-operate. Where such sites are of nature conservation value, try to find solutions to such problems, e.g. try to make dangerous sites safe or persuade unco-operative owners of the value of wildlife in the city, not least to the local community. In order to choose between other sites, it may be worthwhile drawing up a list of priorities, based on the majority wishes of your group membership and the local community. Again, take every opportunity to campaign for the conservation of nature in the city. Too often support from the local authority and local people is not forthcoming, merely because they have not been shown and allowed to consider the benefits of environmental improvements and the encouragement of urban wildlife. If the co-ordinating sub-committee are aware of these wishes, they may draw up the priority list.

At the end of the survey, before sites are shortlisted, a second public meeting would give the opportunity:

(a) for the survey team to report back on the survey findings;
(b) for the membership, local community, local authority, etc. to discuss the group's priorities for shortlisting sites; and possibly
(c) actually to produce a shortlist.

The following is an example of a priority list. (Your group will, of course, need to agree on its own list.) In the example, the site characteristics are listed in order of importance.

Essential site characteristics

1. Available on group's terms (e.g. by lease, licence or gentleman's agreement).
2. Safe, or possible to make safe.
3. Covered for public liability or possible to be made so.
4. Accessible to local people who are sympathetic and who will benefit from the site's development.
5. Expected lifespan of the site acceptable.
6. Expected size of the site acceptable.
7. Free from legal restrictions.

By eliminating sites which do not fulfil requirement 1 and then sites which do not fulfil requirement 2 then requirement 3 and so on, your group should be able rapidly to identify those sites most suited to their needs. By considering features relevant to particular intended site uses, such as the examples in Table 4.1, your group may narrow the field down even further.

Having shortlisted sites from the survey, your group survey team may proceed to examine individual sites in more detail.

4.4 Detailed site surveys

The following section should illustrate how detailed site surveys can throw up information of crucial importance to the development of a site.

The information to be collected may be grouped under the headings: subterranean features; soil features; topography and landscape features; habitats, communities and species.

4.4.1 Subterranean features

These are of particular importance if excavation is to be a possibility during use of the site. If your group intends to excavate a pond, dig foundations, sink posts, etc., it is essential to ensure that no dangerous pipes or cables run beneath the site. The following list summarises such subterranean features and contacts for further information, such as maps, etc.:

Gas pipes

Contact the local regional gas board. There are both standard and high pressure gas mains.

Electricity cables

Contact the local area office of the local electricity board. It may be useful first to locate the nearest electricity sub-station, as this will enable the electricity board to find the appropriate office. There are various types of electricity networks, e.g. cable, local electricity board, central electricity generating board and local electricity board (high voltage).

Telephone cables

Contact the local British Telecom headquarters.

Sewerage pipes/water pipes

Contact the local authority for local sewers and the regional water board for storm drains, deep sewers and water mains.

Wells

Contact the (Hydraulic) Wells Department of the Institute of Geological Sciences in London, tel: 01-589 3444.

Pipelines

Contact the British Pipeline Agency in Hemel Hempstead, tel: (0442) 42200.

In general, site owners should also have details of any utilities running beneath their sites. The planning department of the local authority should also have general details of this kind, as well as information peculiar to the region. For example, London has 'Blue' and 'Red' areas relating to the routes of

London Transport's underground system. In blue areas, excavations may be carried out to a depth of 3m, but in red areas, no digging is allowed.

4.4.2 Soil features

Individual volunteers will not usually be able to conduct proper soil surveys and analyses unaided. A local college or university may be prepared to analyse soil samples and some local authority planning departments have their own laboratories for this purpose. The Ministry of Agriculture, Fisheries and Food (MAFF) Agricultural Development and Advisory Service (ADAS) may also carry out soil analyses for a fee.

If your group wishes to assess soil toxicity for public health and safety considerations, the local authority environmental health officer or pollution control monitoring group may be prepared to help. In certain cases involving public safety, they may be under an obligation to do so. The Department of the Environment also produces useful guidance sheets on the subject, e.g. *Guidance on the assessment and redevelopment of contaminated land* (1983); *Notes on the redevelopment of gas works sites* (1983); *Notes on sewage works and farms* (1983); and *Notes on scrap yards and similar sites* (1983) (see Appendix 15 for address). In the case of assessing soil nutrient status, however, the local authority may not be prepared to help and your group may find a local college or university more cooperative.

The main interacting physical and chemical characteristics of soils contributing to their nutrient status may be grouped as follows:

Physical properties   — soil moisture/soil water tension;
    — soil water table levels;
    — soil composition/structure.

Chemical properties   — acidity/alkalinity (pH);
    — available nitrogen;
    — available phosphorus;
    — available potassium;
    — other major nutrients;
    — trace elements.

Measurement of these characteristics can give a useful estimate of soil quality — a very important factor when deciding whether to plant particular trees or develop particular plant communities on a site.

Soil moisture/soil water tension

Soil moisture changes over time with such factors as rainfall, and in space due to differences in soil composition and packing. To avoid the problem of changes over time, soil field capacity is used as a measure of the water-holding ability of soil. Field capacity is the amount of water retained in soil after all the gravitational water has drained away.

Soil water tension is a measure of the pressure required to remove water from the soil. This pressure is measured in bars. After rainfall, soil may be saturated and soil moisture tension approaches zero bars. At this point, only slight pressure is needed to remove water and, if allowed, it will drain away freely from large pore spaces in the soil. After approximately 48 hours, all this gravitational water has drained away, leaving capillary water held in smaller pore spaces. This point corresponds to the soil field capacity and marks the maximum amount of water the soil can hold for any length of time. Soil moisture tension at this point is approximately 0.05 bars and soil water is easily removed by evaporation, capillary action and the roots of plants. As capillary water is removed, tension rises until, at 15 bars, plants are unable to remove any more water and may wilt. 15 bars is hence termed 'wilting point'. Water held in the soil at tensions of above 15 bars is termed hygroscopic water and is unavailable to plants.

Soil water table levels

The soil water table refers to the top of a zone of saturation in the soil. Saturated soil lacks the air necessary for the survival of many plants, as their roots need to 'breathe'. Most soil animals also need air and will die in water-logged soil. The soil water table level depends upon the amount of water entering the soil and the rate at which it drains away. Soil water tables rarely occur in free-draining soils but are common where drainage is impeded, either:

— where impervious layers occur below the soil, or where the soil is in a low-lying area from which water cannot escape (in these situations, the impedance is said to be due to groundwater conditions and the soils which develop are called groundwater gleys); or
— where impervious layers occur within the soil profile, such as clay horizons, ironpans and compacted layers. (These soils are called surface water gleys or stagnogleys.)

In soils where the water table is high, planting any species not adapted to saturated soils will be a waste of time. If their roots cannot survive without air, they will not be able to penetrate the saturated zone.

Many urban sites do not have soil water tables and loss of soil water may be more of a problem than soil saturation.

Soil composition/structure

Soils are generally made up of proportions of sand, silt, clay (inorganic matter) and humus (organic matter). Figure 4.5 illustrates a method of classifying soil types by the proportions of sand, silt and clay they contain (see also Appendix 3 for a simple analysis of soil clay/silt/sand content by texture).

Undisturbed soils generally form distinguishable layers called 'horizons'. The upper 25 cm of soil is termed the 'A horizon' and is generally the growing region containing most of the soil animals, and organic matter, crucial for the nutrition of plants growing on the surface. Figure 4.6 illustrates a way used to represent soil horizons as a soil profile and what a soil profile might look like in a well-formed soil, under grassland or broad-leaf woodland.

Soil acidity/alkalinity (pH)

Soil pH is a measure of the ratio of hydrogen (H^+) to hydroxyl (OH^-) ions in soil water and attached to soil particles. The more H^+ ions, the more acid the soil, and vice versa. The pH scale runs from 0-14. Up to about pH 6 indicates an acid soil, 6-7 is a neutral soil and above 7 is an alkaline soil. In very low pH (below 4) and very high pH (above 8) conditions, the uptake of nutrients is affected. On urban sites, the most likely nutrient to be affected by pH is phosphorus, which is not available to plants below pH 5.5 and over pH 7.5. However, low pH (4-5.5) and high pH (7-7.9) soils may support very interesting natural plant communities.

Different plants thrive at different pH levels, with widely differing tolerance ranges about these optimum levels. Any plant in soil with a pH outside its

Figure 4.5 The mineral component of the soil

Soil textural triangle; this demonstrates the classification of soil types according to their relative percentages of sand, clay and silt

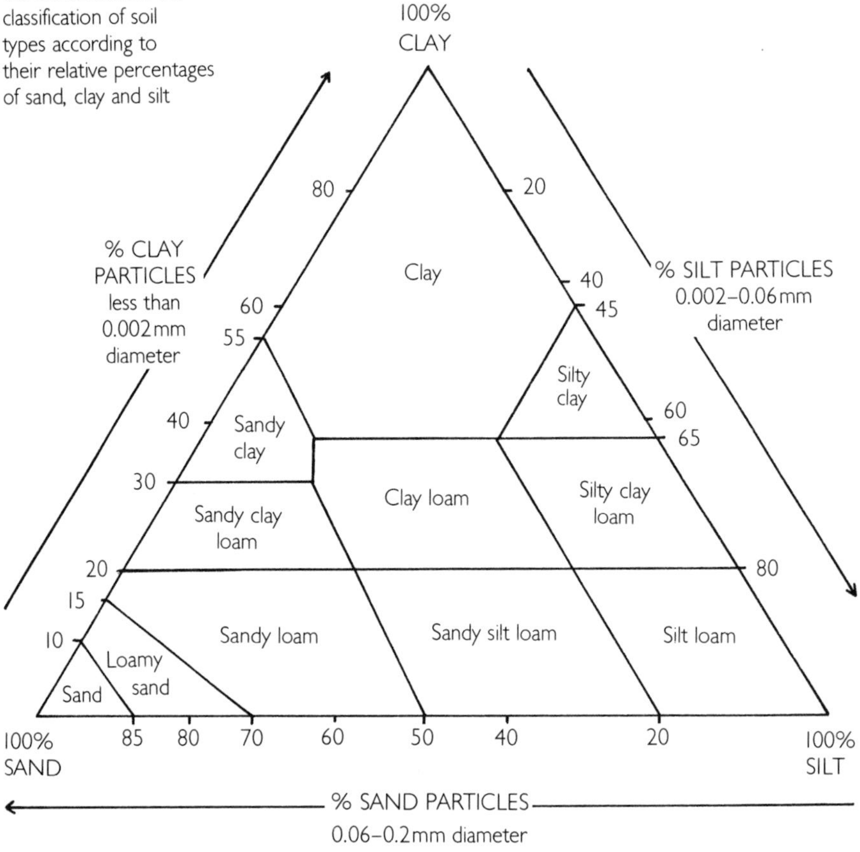
100%
CLAY
% CLAY
PARTICLES
less than
0.002 mm
diameter
% SILT PARTICLES
0.002–0.06 mm
diameter
100%
SAND
100%
SILT
% SAND PARTICLES
0.06–0.2 mm diameter
80
60
55
40
30
20
15
10
20
40
45
60
65
80
85
80
70
60
50
40
20
Clay
Sandy
clay
Silty
clay
Clay loam
Sandy clay
loam
Silty clay
loam
Sandy loam
Sandy silt loam
Silt loam
Loamy
sand
Sand

Source: adapted from Hodgson (1974).

tolerance range will die. In a similar way, soil animals and microflora need favourable pH conditions to survive.

Available nitrogen

Nitrogen (N) is only available to plants in the form of nitrate (NO_3^-). This is the most important plant nutrient for growth. It is removed from the air by free living soil bacteria, e.g. *Azobacter* and bacteria such as *Rhizobium* which live in the root nodules of some plants, e.g. legumes such as clover and trees such as alder and these can subsequently cause an increase in soil nitrogen for other species. Soil microbes also produce nitrates during the decomposition of organic matter. Increase in soil acidity lowers the availability of nitrate ions to plants and nitrate is easily washed from the soil. Therefore, in well-drained acid soils, available nitrate is very low. Nitrogen gives dark green colour to leaves, promotes rapid growth, and increases the yields of leaf, fruit and seeds. A plentiful supply of nitrogen can reduce the number of plant species in grassland and semi-natural communities, since it allows vigorous species such as

Figure 4.6   The soil profile

	Aoo	Fresh organic matter in an undecomposed state
Recognisable structure: F layer	Ao	Organic matter in various stages of decomposition
Mixed (amorphous) structureless: H layer		
Nutrients lost through leaching	Al	Organic matter rich horizon
(Horizons of eluviation)	A2	Horizon of maximum leaching
	A3	Transitional horizon
Nutrients deposited	Bl	Transitional horizon
(Horizons of illuviation)	B2	Horizon of maximum deposition
	B3	Transitional horizon
	C	Weathered parent rock material
	D	Underlying stratum, where different from parent rock material

Well-formed soil

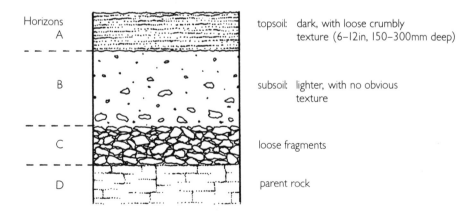

Horizons
A — topsoil: dark, with loose crumbly texture (6–12in, 150–300mm deep)

B — subsoil: lighter, with no obvious texture

C — loose fragments

D — parent rock

The top layer, the 6–12in (150–300mm) of surface is generally known as topsoil. It is made up of soil crumbs formed from rock particles (inorganic matter) which range in size from coarse sand (2–0.2mm) to clay particles (less than 0.002mm) bound together by organic matter (humus) from the breakdown of plant and animal remains. Between the crumbs, the spaces are filled with air and/ or water: the size and amount of these air spaces are critical in determining the soil's capacity to hold moisture

nettles and thistles to grow rapidly at the expense of slower-growing ones. Nitrate deficiency slows plant growth, causing yellowy leaves with brown curling edges. Nitrogen deficiency is the most common. Excess nitrate can lead to effects such as very dark growth of leaves, at the expense of flowers and fruits, increased susceptibility to fungal attack, brittle foliage and weak stems.

Available phosphorus

In most soils, the main source of phosphorus (P) is from weathering of minerals such as calcium phosphate and iron and aluminium phosphate. Decomposing organic material also releases phosphates and in very peaty or sandy soils this may be the main source. Phosphorus is only available to plants in the form of phosphates.

Phosphorus gives a vigorous start to plant growth, stimulating early root formation and growth, hastening maturity and encouraging flower and seed formation. It can help to increase resistance to winter frost and disease and may increase the vitamin content of plants. Unsatisfactory plant growth is more often due to a shortage of phosphorus than of any other plant food, and cultivated soils are often deficient in this element.

Phosphate deficiency is revealed by purple leaves, stems and branches, slow growth, late maturity and low yields of grain, fruit and seed.

Available potassium (potash)

Potassium (K) is important in carbohydrate transport within the plant, helping form strong stems and aiding disease resistance. It improves flower and fruit colour, provides starches, sugar and oils, and decreases the plants' need for water. It is essential to cell division and growth, it helps plants to utilise nitrogen, balances the effects of too much nitrogen or calcium and reduces boron deficiency. Potassium deficiency causes mottling, streaking and curling of leaves, early leaf fall and poor root development.

Excess potassium results in an increase in the water content of plants, making them more susceptible to drought and frost damage.

Other major soil nutrients important to plants include calcium (Ca), magnesium (Mg) and sulphur (S). Very small quantities of the following *trace elements* are also essential for plant growth: manganese (Mn), copper (Cu), zinc (Zn), boron (B), molybdenum (Mb) and chlorine (Cl). Soil with a good content of organic matter is unlikely to be deficient in trace elements.

These groups describe very simply the main characteristics of soils in general. There are many text books on soils and soil science, but for further information from the surveyors' point of view, the most useful reference is the *Soil Survey Field Handbook*, edited by J.M. Hodgson (1974). David Briggs' (1977) book on soils is also a useful source of information. These titles should be obtainable from a local library.

Soil analysis techniques are not absolutely accurate and provide good estimations rather than reliable measurements, even when carried out in a laboratory. Another problem arises with the extreme variability of soil conditions. Every characteristic may vary from one area of a site to another, therefore soil samples may need to be taken from different points across a site in an attempt to 'pick up on' any variation. Appendix 3 illustrates how soil samples may be taken, and describes how your group may carry out simple soil analyses in the field.

Soils on urban sites are unusual, as they often serve as a base for buildings and streets, and as a deposit for solid and liquid wastes. City soils are often modified, varying in their penetrability for roots, water, heat, air and plant nutrients on the one hand, and in filter length (i.e. distance to groundwater) as well as filter quality (i.e. water permeability, absorption or degradation of pollutants) on the other.

The use of groundwater generally lowers the water table in urban areas. The construction of buildings and streets has often compressed and mixed soil and covered it with construction materials, usually meaning a concentration of bricks and mortar, increasing alkalinity, and discarded refuse, enriching soil nutrients. Compressed soil tends to be deficient in air and tends to lose material by erosion in run-off after heavy rain. Street soils are often enriched by nutrients and made alkaline through refuse and construction materials and, at the same time, are subject to pollutants (especially lead) and de-icing salt. Brick waste and subsoil from urban demolition is unlikely to be deficient in phosphorus or potassium, but will be low in nitrogen.

If, for one reason or another, your group is unable to carry out soil analysis it may be possible in some cases to make assumptions without testing the soil. For example, Dutton and Bradshaw (1982) suggest that in normal urban housing clearance areas, the material will be so consistently deficient in nitrogen, somewhat deficient in available phosphorus, and not deficient in anything else, that site development may safely proceed with these assumptions in mind. On the other hand, if tipping of industrial waste is suspected during the history of a site, many complex and extreme conditions of soil nutrient status and toxicity may apply. Gemmell (1977) outlines these conditions in his *Colonisation of Industrial Wasteland*.

It is important to obtain 'base-line' information on soil conditions if your group intends to change the soil in any way and monitor these changes. Without base-line values to compare with, subsequent examinations of the soil will be useless as indicators of change in soil conditions.

4.4.3 Topography and landscape features

If a site has been subject to planning applications in the past, detailed maps of site topography may have been drawn up. In any case, it is worth checking with the local authority planning department.

If no such plans already exist, and your group wishes to map the topography of a site in detail, the planning department of the local authority, or geography department of a local college or university, may be prepared to provide expertise and equipment, such as theodolites, ranging poles, tape measures, etc. Topography can be important, for example, should your group need to know the gradient of a slope for drainage and soil stability considerations, or should they wish to measure the relative levels of different areas of the site when deciding where to site features such as a pond or tree nursery.

Landscape features can be extremely important in urban sites, particularly in their effects on the site conditions for plant growth. Buildings can shade areas at particular times of day, shelter areas from prevailing winds (and hence, often, from rain) as well as increasing temperatures by reflecting solar radiation and storing heat. Therefore, the positioning of buildings on and around a site should be carefully considered, because of their possible effects on the site vegetation.

Mature trees and shelter belts, including walls and fences, should be given similar consideration.

4.4.4 Habitats, communities and species

In section 4.1.3 and Figure 4.2 an outline of a possible simple method for surveying habitats and species is given. When examining sites in more detail, this simple method may be supplemented with further details of the size and distribution of particular habitat types, the types of plant communities in these habitats, and more comprehensive lists of plant and animal species present.

This increase in detail can be particularly important in assessing the wildlife value of certain areas of a site and in deciding which areas, if any, are to be built upon, cultivated or otherwise altered, with minimum damage to the wildlife value of the site as a whole.

It will be easier to collect survey information if volunteers have time to visit sites repeatedly at different times of the year. For example, in winter, when vegetation has died back, certain site features may appear which had been obscured by greenery during the other seasons. Different plant species come into leaf and flower at different times of the year, so repeated visits in the growing season will make plant identification easier. Seasonal features, such as spring and autumn waterlogging, may be missed if only summer visits are made to a site. Many site features will change through the seasons, and a year-round view of a site will give a better idea of a site's potential.

Wild plants found growing on a site will be there because they can tolerate the prevailing site conditions. Detailed examination of vegetation can give some indication of the soil conditions over a site. Every species of plant has its own optimum level and tolerance range to such soil factors as nutrient availability, pH and moisture. By referring to a good plant atlas, such as Fitter (1978), you should be able to determine the optimum conditions and tolerance ranges for any species recorded on the site. In any particular plant community, there are usually a few species which dominate the community by virtue of their size, numbers or habits. Such 'dominant' species are generally reliable indicators of prevailing site conditions. They also often dictate the conditions under which their associated neighbour species have to live. Any trends in optimum conditions amongst groups of species in particular areas (e.g. if most species are found to prefer rich loam or wet acid soils) will generally be reliable indications that such conditions are present in those areas. Table 4.3 gives examples of species found on urban wasteland which can indicate particular soil conditions.

In the area survey, you may have mapped the boundaries between distinct habitats or plant communities, e.g. rubble areas, grassland, scrub, marshy areas, etc. However, the mixtures of plants (and animals) present in each of these areas will probably not be distributed evenly over them. For example, closer examination of the grassland may show different parts to be dominated by different grasses forming recognisably different grassland communities. As far as possible, the boundaries between such different communities should be mapped. The different types may not have clear boundaries between them, rather zones of gradual change from one species mixture to another. These zones of transition or 'ecotones' are often valuable in themselves as they commonly support a rich and diverse mixture of animals and plants from both of the adjoining communities as well as species which will only appear in the transition zone.

Rather than just producing as large a species list as possible for the whole site, make a map of the mosaic of recognisably different communities and then record the species in each separately. In each species list note which species dominate the community, any species which are noticeably limited to the transition zones, etc. In this way, you will be able gradually to build up a

Table 4.3 Some indicator species of urban wasteland

ACID

Agrostis tenuis (common bent grass)
Betula pendula (birch)
Deschampsia flexuosa (wavy hair
    grass)
Holcus mollis (creeping soft grass)
Luzula campestris (field wood-rush)
Pteridium aquilinum (bracken)
Rumex acetosella (sheep's sorrel)
Sonchus spp. (sow thistles)

WET

Agrostis canina (velvet bent grass)
Alnus glutinosa (alder)
Deschampsia caespitosa (tufted hair
    grass)
Equisetum spp. (horsetails)
Filipendula ulmaria (meadowsweet)
Juncus spp. (rush)
Ranunculus repens (creeping buttercup)

NEUTRAL AND ALKALINE

Low fertility[1]

Achillea millefolium (yarrow)
Anthriscus sylvestris (cow parsley)
Bellis perennis (daisy)
Centaurea nigra (knapweed)
Dactylis glomerata (cocksfoot)
Heracleum sphondylium (hogweed)
Hordeum murinum (wall barley)
Lotus corniculatus (bird's-foot trefoil)[2]
Medicago lupulina (black medick)[2]
Plantago spp. (plantain)
Poa annua (annual meadow grass)
Reseda lutea (wild mignonette)
Senecio squalidus (Oxford ragwort)
Silene vulgaris (bladder campion)
Taraxacum officinale (dandelion)
Trifolium pratense (red clover)[2]
T. repens (white clover)[2]
Tussilago farfara (coltsfoot)

Higher fertility[1]

Agropyron repens (couch grass)
Agrostis stolonifera (creeping bent grass)
Artemisia vulgaris (mugwort)
Capsella bursa-pastoris (shepherd's purse)
Cirsium vulgare (thistle)
Lamium purpureum (dead-nettle)
Lolium perenne (rye grass)
Phleum pratense (timothy)
Rubus fruticosus (bramble)
Rumex obtusifolius (dock)
Silene alba (white campion)
Urtica dioica (common nettle)

SPECIES KNOWN TO BE TOLERANT TO HEAVY METALS

Agrostis tenuis (bent grass)
Agrostis stolonifera (creeping bent grass)
Festuca ovina (sheep's fescue)
F. rubra (red fescue)
Minuartia verna (spring sandwort)
Silene vulgaris (bladder campion)

Notes:
1. Considerable degree of overlap between these groups: main indicator of fertility is vigour of
those species present.
2. Low fertility soil may only be lacking in nitrogen; if so, legumes should be growing vigorously
and having effects on associated species.

Source: Dutton and Bradshaw (1982); Bradshaw and Chadwick (1980); Owen (1978).

detailed picture of the relative richness of different areas of the site vegetation. Any locally uncommon or rare species which occur only once or twice or in a restricted corner of the site are best recorded with their location marked on a map of the site. Recording in this way provides much clearer base-line information for further ecological surveys and research and for future design and management decisions, such as deciding which areas, if any, are best left and which can be changed or developed. Detailed examination of habitats, communities and species is, therefore, covered further in section 5.1.4.

4.5 References

Bradshaw, A.D. and Chadwick, M.J. (1980) *The Restoration of Land*, Blackwell, Studies in Ecology, vol. 6

Briggs, David (1977) *Soils*, Butterworths

British Trust for Conservation Volunteers (1980) *Woodlands. A Practical Conservation Handbook* (compiled by A. Brooks and A. Follis), BTCV

Burnham, C.P. (1980) 'The soils of England and Wales', *Field Studies*, **5**:349-63

Department of the Environment (1983) Interdepartmental Committee on the Redevelopment of Contaminated Land:
  'Guidance on the assessment and redevelopment of contaminated land'
  'Notes on the redevelopment of landfill sites'
  'Notes on the redevelopment of gas works sites'
  'Notes on sewage works and farms'
  'Notes on scrap yards and similar sites'

Dutton, R.A. and Bradshaw, A.D. (1982) *Land Reclamation in Cities*, HMSO, London

Fitter, A. (1978) *An Atlas of the Wild Flowers of Britain and Northern Europe*, Collins

Gemmell, R.P. (1977) *Colonisation of Industrial Wasteland*, Arnold, Studies in Biology, no. 80

Hodgson, J.M. (ed.) (1974) *Soil Survey Field Handbook*, The Soil Survey of England and Wales, Soil Survey of England and Wales, Harpenden, Technical Monograph No. 5

Lewis, T. and Taylor, L.R. (1974) *Introduction to Experimental Ecology* (5th printing), Academic Press

Lomax, P. (1982) 'Ecological Park Project; site survey report', Leicester Urban Studies Centre

Nature Conservancy Council (1982) *Wildlife, the Law and You*
—— (1983) *The Selection of Sites of Special Scientific Interest (SSSIs)*

Owen, D. (1978) *Towns and Gardens: The Natural History of Britain and Northern Europe*, Hodder & Stoughton

4.6 Useful organisations

The following is a list of other organisations who may be able to provide specialist advice to a group carrying out detailed site surveys (see Appendix 15 for addresses).

Amateur Entomologists' Society (insects)
Arboricultural Association (trees)
Botanical Society of the British Isles
Botanical Society of Edinburgh

British Bryological Society (mosses)
British Butterfly Conservation Society
British Deer Society
British Entomological and Natural History Society
British Herpetological Society (reptiles and amphibians)
British Lichen Society
British Mycological Society (fungi)
British Naturalists Association
British Pteridological Society (ferns and their allies)
British Trust for Ornithology (birds)
Conchological Society of Great Britain and Northern Ireland (slugs and snails)
Field Studies Council
Freshwater Biological Association
Mammal Society
Men of the Trees
Royal Entomological Society (insects)
Royal Society for the Protection of Birds
Scottish Field Studies Association
Soil Association
Wildflower Society

5 Principles of Site Design

When your group has chosen a site to develop as a wildlife area for the benefit of the local community, some form of site design is needed. Indeed, it will be desirable to check that a practical site design can be proposed before the choice of a site is finalised. In the short term, sensible proposals will be required to obtain the owner's consent and the necessary planning permission to use the site. In the long term, your group will need to develop the site in a way which will benefit both wildlife and the people using it. A good site design should allow your group to achieve these ends and ensure that the management involved is within the resources of the group.

The design will effectively be a compromise between a natural area and a public park or garden. Considering these two extremes separately, management of natural areas requires an understanding and respect of natural processes so that wildlife may be conserved. The traditional design and management of public parks and gardens involves the construction of artificial systems, such as lawns, shrubberies, flower beds with alien species, etc. Management of such systems involves a constant battle against natural processes including the application of fertilisers, the destruction of 'weeds', mowing of lawns and pruning.

This section outlines practical, cost-effective principles of site design which avoid the use of such artificial systems and minimise conflict between public use and the needs of wildlife, by working with nature rather than against it. The section can only be an outline, to enable groups to help themselves. Throughout the design process, the advice of experienced professionals is essential if mistakes are to be avoided (see section 5.4, sources of advice and further information).

5.1 Ecological principles

The word ecology comes from the Greek 'oikos' (household) and 'logos' (study). In the natural sense, this means that ecology is the study of the homes of living organisms, or more accurately their relationships to their neighbours and surroundings in the natural environment. By understanding these relationships, the designer is able to use them as tools for design.

When first examining a site, the designer needs to know what is living on the site, how and why. A survey of the site will identify different habitats and different plant and animal communities (mixtures of species) present in them, but to find out how and why requires an understanding of the complex interactions between the species present and their environmental conditions.

To understand, it is necessary to think both at the level of the individual organism and of the community as a whole.

5.1.1 The individual

When a seed falls to the ground, it requires certain conditions of light, moisture, temperature, soil conditions and nutrients in order to germinate, grow into a mature plant and produce more seed. Each of the 1,800 or so species of wild plants in Great Britain requires its own particular combination of such conditions to thrive. In addition to coping with such environmental conditions, a plant may have to compete with its neighbours for its requirements, be they light above ground or water and nutrients below ground.

For each requirement, a plant has an optimum level and tolerance ranges on either side of this optimum. In optimum conditions, a plant will be strong and healthy and more able to compete with its neighbours, but as one or more of its requirements approaches the limits of its tolerance, the plant will tend to be stunted, less able to produce offspring, and will eventually die.

As well as being a slave to its surroundings, each plant influences the conditions around it. For example, as it grows a plant uses sunlight to produce carbohydrates, by means of photosynthesis. It removes water and nutrients from the soil as it does so. As the plant loses its leaves and when it dies, it returns the carbohydrates and other nutrients it contains, back to the soil. Some plants also fix atmospheric nitrogen with the aid of nodules on their roots, adding to the available nitrogen in the soil as their dead parts decay.

An animal is subject to similar laws of nature to those governing a plant. It has certain requirements and tolerance ranges in terms of food (from plants or other animals), water, warmth, space, etc. It competes with its neighbours in order to satisfy its requirements and successfully produce offspring, and it influences its environment by consuming material and recycling it as it excretes waste materials and eventually dies.

Ecological principles of design involve considering individual animals and plants as active, growing, multiplying organisms, interacting with their surroundings; not just as inanimate pieces in the 'jigsaw' of site design. Because animals and plants are active, the communities they make up are in a constant state of change.

5.1.2 The community

The plant and animal communities present on a site may range from weedy patches on otherwise bare ground to dense scrub and woodland. All are complex, constantly changing mixtures of interacting individuals and the natural processes controlling them are still only poorly understood. However, simple patterns have been recognised in the development of communities which can be extremely useful when employing natural processes in site design and management.

Colonisation and natural succession

These patterns may be divided into *colonisation* (by those species able to reach the site) and *natural succession* (the gradual replacement of certain species by others as the plant and animal communities develop). Recolonisation of disturbed habitats (e.g. demolition sites) is termed secondary natural succession. When bare patches of ground are created and left undisturbed, colonisation by plants depends upon a supply of seed, either from the *seed bank* (those seeds present in the ground) or from the *seed rain* (those seeds blown or transported on to the site). On urban sites, the seed bank may include alien species from garden waste, etc. Similarly, the seed rain may include alien species from nearby parks and gardens. The number of native species in the seed rain will become less, the more isolated the site is from open countryside or other natural expanses of vegetation.

The success of the first colonising species depends upon their ability to sur-

Table 5.1 Some materials on urban sites and the ranges of some of their properties which colonising plants may encounter

Materials	Texture and structure	Water supply	Available nitrogen	Available phosphorus	Available potassium	pH	Toxic materials
	≪ < o > ≫	≪ < o > ≫	≪ < o > ≫	≪ < o > ≫	≪ < o > ≫	≪ < o > ≫	≪ < o > ≫
Colliery spoil							
Fly ash							
Heavy metal wastes							
China clay wastes							
Acid rocks							
Calcareous (alkaline) rocks							
Sand and gravel							
Urban wastes							
Roadsides							
Demolition rubble							

Key   Ranges : ≪ < o > ≫ | a | b | c | d | e |

a = severe deficiency
b = moderate deficiency
c = adequate
d = moderate excess
e = severe excess

e.g. pH

= severe to moderate acidity

Toxic materials

= acceptable to moderate excess

Source: adapted from Bradshaw and Chadwick (1980).

vive the climatic and soil conditions present. Table 5.1 gives examples of the conditions common to a range of materials found on urban sites. Thereafter, as natural succession proceeds, colonising species have to contend with such conditions in competition with other species which have already colonised the site.

Newly-colonised ground is commonly covered with a 'ruderal' type of plant community ('ruderal' describes vegetation of disturbed soils). Most ruderal species are annual or biennial. Annual plants complete their life cycle in one year, growing from seed, flowering, setting seed and dying in one season. Biennials take two years to complete their life cycle, producing seedlings in the first year, and setting seed and dying in the second. These short-lived species depend upon their ability to produce many seeds quickly to ensure their success, and so they are well adapted as early colonisers of open, disturbed and poorly vegetated ground. Some ruderal species not only produce many seeds with highly efficient means of dispersal, their seeds can also remain dormant in the soil for very long periods, only germinating when disturbance creates gaps in the vegetation cover for them to colonise.

As natural succession proceeds, and soil structure and fertility improves, the ruderal community changes gradually to a community dominated by perennial herbs and grasses. Unlike annuals and biennials, these perennials continue to grow and increase in size from year to year. Old leaves and stems die down each autumn and new shoots come up from the roots each spring. Perennials invest more in growth than in seed production. This not only means they are slower to colonise, but once established, they are more able to compete for nutrients than are annuals and biennials.

Eventually, the perennial herbs and grasses are succeeded by larger, deeper-rooting woody perennials, such as shrubs and trees, more able to compete for the light, water and available nutrients than the perennial herbs and grasses. The plant community beneath the shrubs and trees gradually becomes dominated by shade-tolerant species.

Table 5.2 lists a few examples of annuals, biennials and perennials commonly found in natural succession on vacant urban sites.

As the plant communities develop, so will the animal communities which depend upon them. Complex communities of soil animals build up around the tangled root mass of the vegetation, feeding on roots, dead plant and animal matter (and each other) and enhancing the development of the soil structure and fertility. Grazing animals feed on the plants, affecting the survival of individuals and the structure of the plant community.

The process of colonisation by animals is very different from that for plants. Animals are generally more mobile and able quickly to seek out suitable habitats, selecting those most satisfactory to them. Animals such as birds and flying insects are unlikely to find tall buildings or roads difficult barriers to successful colonisation of urban sites. On the other hand, molluscs (slugs and snails) or any other invertebrates unable to fly will be slow in negotiating such barriers. Earth worms may be completely unable to do so.

Habitats which prove satisfactory to many species may attract intense competition between colonising animals, while others, perhaps only lacking in a single essential element, may be left vacant.

The rate of natural succession of vegetation and the mixtures of plants involved is governed by a combination of the following factors:

The supply of new species, carried as seed by wind, water, animals and man. As already described, the lack of nearby seed sources can restrict the number of species arriving on a site. On urban sites, species with light, wind-blown seeds gain an advantage over others in this respect. Common examples include rosebay willowherb (*Chamaenerion angustifolium*), coltsfoot (*Tussilago farfara*), Oxford ragwort (*Senecio squalidus*), goat willow (*Salix caprea*) and even species of orchid, with their microscopic wind-borne seeds (see Gemmell 1978).

Competition. This has been described above, with perennial species out-competing annuals and biennials during the natural succession process. Competition between individuals increases as the vegetation becomes more dense, the victors in the competitive struggle being those individuals more able to obtain light, water and nutrients.

Stress, for example, lack of soil fertility. Although this is enhanced as natural succession proceeds, when the initial soil fertility is low, species with higher nutrient requirements take longer to establish. Extremes of soil acidity can lower the availability of nutrients to plants and so slow succession down. Lack of soil moisture can cause severe stress to plants, as can waterlogging, causing increased soil acidity and starving the plant roots of oxygen. Stress from toxic

Table 5.2 Examples of annual, biennial and perennial species

ANNUALS (AND BIENNIALS)

Anagallis arvensis (scarlet pimpernel)
Bromus (Anisanthe) sterilis (barren brome grass)
Chenopodium album (fat hen)
Matricaria maritima (scentless mayweed (annual to biennial))
Poa annua (annual meadow grass)
Reseda lutea (wild mignonette (biennial to perennial))
Senecio squalidus (Oxford ragwort*)
Senecio vulgaris (groundsel)
Sisymbrium officinale (hedge mustard (annual to biennial))
Urtica urens (small nettle)
Verbascum thapsus (great mullein (biennial))

PERENNIAL HERBS AND GRASSES

Agropyron repens (couch grass)
Agrostis stolonifera (creeping bent grass)
Chamaenerion angustifolium (rosebay willowherb*)
Cirsium arvense (creeping thistle)
Hieracium spp. (hawkweeds)
Lotus corniculatus (bird's-foot trefoil)
Malva sylvestris (common mallow)
Pastinaca sativa (wild parsnip)
Rumex obtusifolius (broad-leaved dock)
Tussilago farfara (coltsfoot)
Urtica dioica (common nettle)

WOODY PERENNIALS (SHRUBS AND TREES)

Alnus glutinosa (alder)
Betula pubescens (silver birch)
Buddleja davidii (butterfly bush*) .
Corylus avellana (hazel)
Fagus sylvatica (beech)
Fraxinus excelsior (ash)
Hedera helix (ivy)
Quercus robur (oak)
Rosa canina (dog rose)
Rubus fruticosus (bramble (blackberry))
Salix caprea (goat willow)

---

* Alien species which commonly occur in natural succession on vacant urban sites.
(See also Figure 6.2 'Natural succession to woodland — the increase in structural diversity'.)

materials, such as heavy metals, can limit the number of species involved in natural succession to a very small number of tolerant plants. Other stress factors common on urban sites include soil compaction, which can resist root penetration, atmospheric pollution and polluted water supply which may prevent sensitive species from surviving.

Disturbance, by animals and man. Continued disturbance of the soil can restrain succession (causing an 'arrested' succession) and only allow a ruderal plant community to develop. Similarly, grazing or cutting the vegetation (and removing cut material) can result in an arrested succession of open grassland. Even removal of cut material lowers the natural rate of nutrient build-up in the soil, thus slowing down succession. Grazers, however, tend to be selective in the material they remove, leaving less palatable species. Add to this the effect of their excretions and the overall effect of grazers is 'patchy' nutrient depletion and nutrient enhancement. Section 7.1 deals with habitat management in relation to natural succession.

5.1.3 Competition, stress and disturbance

These are the three main categories of habitat conditions which influence the survival of established plants. Appendix 5 (from Grime 1979) illustrates a convenient way of representing the relative importance of these three habitat conditions and the vegetation types adapted to contend with them.

Table 5.3 lists some characteristics of competitive, stress-tolerant plants and plants tolerant of disturbance (ruderals).

The implications of the combined effects of competition, stress and disturbance may be summarised as follows:

— In extreme conditions of stress and disturbance, the diversity of plants will be low, and in order to increase this diversity, the amount of stress and disturbance will need to be lessened.
— As conditions of stress and disturbance become less extreme, the arrival and establishment (or the introduction) of new species becomes more effective as a means of increasing species diversity, because of the wider range of species able to tolerate the conditions present.
— In conditions of extreme competition (i.e. in dense vegetation, usually a nutrient-rich soil, dominated by a small number of large, robust species), careful removal of the dominant plants, or carefully increasing stress or disturbance, are means of increasing species diversity, by reducing competition and allowing a wider range of species to survive.

5.1.4 Site survey and analysis in the design process

The following are a sequence of steps in the site survey procedure which will be important to the site design, taking into consideration some of the important natural processes described in sections 5.1.1, 5.1.2 and 5.1.3.

— *Identify different habitats on the site*; e.g. damp hollows, mounds, shaded areas, areas of rubble, etc. and any noticeably different areas of vegetation growing on them, e.g. short herbs, tall grassland with herbs, dense scrub, trees.

— *Distinguish, as far as possible, between these areas and examine each separately,* possibly outlining each area on a site drawing (see Figure 4.2, section 4.1.3, for a possible classification of different habitat types).

— *For each area, identify the most numerous (dominant) species present.* By referring to reliable wildflower guides (see Appendix 2 for examples) *note the characteristics of each species,* for example, its habit (annual, biennial, perennial), its requirements for growth (soil fertility, acidity, moisture, etc.) and any other details (e.g. shade tolerance, ability to fix atmospheric nitrogen.). Fitter's (1978) *Atlas of Wild Flowers* is particularly useful for this. Five or six species per area

Table 5.3 Some characteristics of competitive, stress-tolerant and ruderal plants

Characteristic	Competitive	Stress-tolerant	Ruderal
1. Life forms	Herbs, shrubs, trees	Lichens, herbs, shrubs and trees	Herbs
2. Plant structure	High, dense leaf canopy; extensive sideways spread above and below ground	Extremely wide range of growth forms	Small stature with limited sideways spread
3. Leaf form	Robust, not commonly resistant to desiccation	Often small or leathery, or needle-like	Various, not commonly resistant to desiccation
4. Lifespan of plant	Long or relatively short	Long–very long	Very short
5. Lifespan of leaves and roots	Relatively short	Long	Short
6. Flowering frequency	Established plants usually flower annually	Flowering intermittent, over a long life history	High frequency of flowering
7. Overwintering (perennation)	Dormant buds and seeds	Stress-tolerant leaves and roots	Dormant seeds
8. Regeneration by:	V S W Bs	V B W	S W Bs
9. Maximum growth-rate	Rapid	Slow	Rapid
10. Response to stress	Rapid vegetative growth	Slow vegetative growth	Rapid decrease in vegetative growth, and increase in flower production
11. Resistance to changes in temperature and moisture supply	Weakly developed	Strongly developed	Weakly developed
12. Storage of nutrients	Commonly stored in vegetative structure for next season's growth	Storage systems in leaves, stems and/or roots	Confined to seeds
13. Litter (dead leaves, etc.)	Copious, often persistent	Sparse, sometimes persistent	Sparse, not usually persistent
14. Palatability to (unspecialised) herbivores	Various	Low	Various, often high

Key to 8 (regenerative strategies)

V = vegetative expansion
S = seasonal regeneration in vegetation gaps
W = numerous, small wind-dispersed seeds or spores
Bs = persistent seed bank
B = persistent seedling bank

Source: adapted from Grime (1979).

should be sufficient, but the more the better.

It should be possible at this stage to build up a picture of the plant community types present and the successional stages they have reached.

— *Examine the environmental conditions present in each area/community*, and *look out for overall differences between them*, for example, are some areas more fertile/wet/acid/compacted/polluted/rocky/shaded/well drained/exposed and so on than others?

The environmental conditions present and any differences between them for each area, may help to explain the different species mixes in the plant communities present. Table 5.4 gives examples of vegetation types found in different urban habitats and Table 5.5 gives examples of industrial habitats).

Table 5.4 A summary of vegetation types on urban sites with examples of species

1. Pioneer, open communities of rocks, walls, roofs, pavements and other metalled or trodden surfaces, dominated by mosses, liverworts or other specially adapted rock plants.

1A. Carpets of mosses and flat liverworts; flowering plants absent or sparse and of low vitality, e.g.

Bryum argentium (moss)
Marchantia polymorpha (liverwort)

1B. Lichen-dominated communities of asbestos roofs and concrete, e.g.

Acarospora fuscata
Physcia caesia
Lecanora muralis (lichens)

1C. Isolated stands of ferns and flowering plants in crevices and on ledges, e.g.

Pteridium aquilinum (bracken)
Dryopteris filix-mas (male fern)
Parietaria judaica (pellitary of the wall)
Cymbalaria muralis (ivy-leaved toadflax)

2. Floating and submerged communities of freshwater plants in lakes, ponds, reservoirs, subsidence flashes, derelict docks, canals, flooded sewage beds, etc.

2A. Communities of free-floating, surface and submerged plants of static or slow-moving waters, e.g.

Hydrocharis morsus-ranae (frog-bit)
Lemna spp. (duckweeds)

2B. Communities of floating, surface and submerged plants of static or slow-moving waters (rooted in the mud under the water), e.g.

Potamogeton spp. (pondweeds)
Myriophyllum spp. (water milfoils)

2C. Communities of mosses and liverworts on periodically or permanently submerged rocks and walls of rivers, ponds, pools and canals, e.g.

Brachythecium rivulare (moss)
Lunularia cruciata (liverwort)

2D. Bog communities, dominated by *Sphagnum* mosses and other bog species, more or less floating and on wet, acid peat.

---

3. Ruderal weed communities dominated by annual or biennial plants, on disturbed or newly-created vacant sites.

3A. Open communities of low-growing annuals of gardens, ornamental park borders, roadsides and refuse tips, e.g.

Senecio vulgaris (groundsel)
Capsella bursa-pastoris (shepherd's purse)
Euphorbia helioscopia (sun spurge)
Papaver rhoeas (poppy)

3B. Communities dominated by plants able to withstand extremes of heat and dryness — in derelict brick-rubble, cinder and fuel-ash tips, etc., e.g.

Plantago lanceolata (ribbed plantain)
Achillea millefolium (yarrow)
Melilotus officinalis (ribbed melilot)

3C. Communities on nutrient-rich muds and silts around reservoirs, sewage beds and periodically flooded sites, e.g.

Cardamine pratensis (cuckoo flower)
Myosotis scorpioides (water forget-me-not)

---

4. 'Water's edge' communities of emergent, tall, swamp plants — around the margins of rivers, canals, ponds and lakes.

4A. Reedbeds dominated by *Phragmites australis* (common reed).

4B. Grass- and bulrush-swamp communities, e.g.

Typha latifolia (reedmace)
Sparganium erectum (bur-reed)

4C. Tall marsh communities, dominated by medium-size sedge species (70-150 cm tall), e.g.

Carex paniculata (greater tussock sedge)

---

5. 'Water's edge' communities of emergent, short, swamp and marsh plants (usually less than 70 cm tall), dominated by grass/reed/perennial herb/rush marsh plant species.

5A. Miscellaneous low-growing, emergent, species-poor swamps, e.g.

Nasturtium officinale (watercress)

5B. Rush marshes dominated by species of *Juncus*, e.g.

Juncus effusus (soft rush)

5C. Sedge marshes, dominated by species of *Carex*, e.g.,

Carex nigra (common sedge)

---

6. Rank, perennial, tall-grass and tall-herb (usually taller than 70 cm) communities of embankments, un-cut road verges, abandoned sewage beds and damp swamp and marsh margins; usually on sites which have been left undisturbed and unmanaged for more than two years.

6A. Communities dominated by tall, coarse grasses and umbellifers, e.g.

Arrhenatherum elatius (tall (false) oat grass)
Anthriscus sylvestris ((umbellifer) cow parsley)
Dactylis glomerata (cocksfoot)

6B. Communities dominated by tall (gregarious) native herbs, e.g.

Artemisia absinthum (wormwood)
A. vulgaris (mugwort)
Sysimbrium officinale (hedge mustard)

6C. Communities dominated by introduced plant species, many of garden origin, e.g.

Reynoutria japonica (Japanese knotweed)
Lupinus arboreus (lupin)
Chamaenerion angustifolium (rosebay willowherb)
Impatiens glandulifera (Indian balsam (riversides, damp sites in woods, etc.))

---

7. Low, perennial grass and grass-herb communities; maintained either by disturbance, e.g. mowing or regular public use (trampling), or by unfavourable conditions, e.g. low fertility.

7A. Grasslands on a variety of natural and semi-natural soils, for example on commons and unmanaged parkland, dominated by one or several low-growing (less than 70 cm tall) fine-leaved grass species, e.g.

Agrostis tenuis (common bent grass)
Poa pratensis (smooth meadow grass)
Festuca rubra (red fescue)

7B. Managed, mown grasslands and weedy, perennial herb-grass communities of mainly man-made land, such as landscaped lawns, recreation areas, games pitches, etc., in which rye-grass and/or white clover predominate, e.g.

Lolium perenne (perennial rye grass)
Trifolium pratense (white clover)
Bellis perennis (daisy)

7C. Communities dominated by either introduced or native low-growing (less than 70 cm tall), gregarious, stoloniferous or rhizomatous herbs. These often replace tall herbs (6B) in natural succession where conditions of disturbance or stress occur, e.g.

Plantago major (great plantain)
Medicago lupulina (black medick)
Ranunculus repens (creeping buttercup)
Poa annua (annual meadow grass)
Matricaria matricaroides (pineapple weed (Asia))

---

8. Scrub vegetation of thickets, hedges, ornamental park borders and vacant sites which have been undisturbed, perhaps for over 20 years. Dominated by woody shrub species, less than 5 m in height.

8A. Dwarf scrub dominated by heath-like species less than 70 cm tall (usually on exposed, acid, low fertility soil), e.g.

Calluna vulgaris (heather)
Erica tetralix (cross-leaved heath)

8B. Gorse (*Ulex* spp.) and broom (*Sarothamnus scoparius*) thickets on acidic soils.

8C. Bramble (*Rubus fruticosus* agg.) patches in a variety of habitats.

8D. Mixed woodland-edge scrub and hedgerows dominated by hawthorn (*Crataegus* spp.), elder (*Sambucus nigra*), hazel (*Corylus avellana*) and a variety of other native shrub species, on dry or moist soils of moderate fertility.

8E. Birch (*Betula* spp.), willow (*Salix* spp.), alder (*Alnus glutinosa*) and poplar (*Populus* spp.) scrub of damp soils, either naturally developed or planted.

8F. Scrub of introduced, evergreen and deciduous shrubs, either in managed ornamental situations or naturalised in waste places, e.g.

> *Buddleja davidii* ((China) buddleja, butterfly bush (common on wasteland))
> *Rhododendron ponticum* ((Portugal) rhododendron (popular ornamental))

---

9.   Deciduous and evergreen woodland, greater than 5 m in height with a more or less closed canopy, and urban 'pasture' woodland with an open canopy. These areas will usually have taken over 50 years to develop.

9A. Oak (*Quercus* spp.) woodlands on relatively dry, acidic soils.

9B. Beech (*Fagus sylvatica*) plantation woodlands (native on shallow, calcareous soils).

9C. Mixed or pure sycamore (*Acer pseudoplatanus*), elm (*Ulmus* spp.), ash (*Fraxinus excelsior*) woodlands, copses and coverts on a variety of soil types.

9D. Willow (*Salix* spp.), alder (*Alnus glutinosa*) and birch (*Betula* spp.) woodlands of damp, peaty or silty soils with a high water table.

9E. Ornamental plantation woodlands (in parks and gardens) and avenues (in streets, etc.) in which the predominant trees are introduced deciduous species, hybrids or cultivars, e.g.

> *Platanus acerifolia* (London plane)
> *Tilia* hybrids (limes)
> *Chamaecyparis* spp. (cypresses)

9F. Coniferous plantations of both deciduous and evergreen species (for commercial timber), e.g.

> *Pinus sylvestris* (Scots pine (evergreen conifer))
> *Larix* spp. (larches (deciduous conifers))

9G. Managed urban pasture woodland, comprises expanses of mown grass (7B) with clumps of native or introduced, standard trees, for example in parks, e.g.

> *Quercus cerris* (Turkey oak)
> *Aesculus* spp. (chestnuts)
> *Fraxinus excelsior* (ash)

Source: adapted from Shimwell (1983).

Table 5.5 Industrial habitats

Industrial origin	Types of habitat
Solvay and Leblanc wastes, blast furnace slag, lime wastes, calcareous mine spoils, fuel ash and coal washery wastes	Calcareous, species-rich grasslands and scrub with a rich flora of chalk, limestone and dune-slack plants
Clay, marl, sand and gravel pits and associated spoil heaps	Species-rich damp grassland, marsh bog, reedbeds, scrub and aquatic habitats. Inner slopes and spoil heaps support acidic grasslands, heath and scrub
Limestone quarries, chalk pits and their spoil heaps	Calcareous, species-rich grasslands and scrub of limestone and chalk downland species. Woodland in old quarries. Cliff flora of ferns and rock plants. Damp grassland, scrub, marsh, reedbeds and aquatic habitats on quarry floors
Gritstone and other acidic, hard-rock quarries	Heath, acidic grassland, scrub and woodland. Ferns and rock plants on cliffs. Marsh, bog, reedbeds, scrub, woodland and aquatic habitats on quarry floors
Railway land including trackway, railway sidings, cuttings and embankments	Lime flora on calcareous ballast of trackways and in cuttings through chalk and limestone. Damp grassland, marsh and scrub in cuttings. Species-rich grassland, acidic flora, scrub and woodland on embankments
Mill-ponds, reservoirs, filter-beds, canals, mill-races, subsidence flashes, sewage works and waterlogged land	Damp grasslands, marsh, willow scrub, reedbeds and aquatic habitats with rich emergent and submerged vegetation. Many are important for waterfowl and aquatic fauna

Source: from Gemmell *et al.* (1983).

— *Identify neighbouring sites which may have acted as sources for colonisation.* Such neighbouring areas may either continue to help the development of the site vegetation, by enriching it with new wild species, or cause management problems, by allowing colonisation by undesirable aliens, such as sycamore and other cultivated and exotic plants common in parks and gardens.

— *Investigate the site's history* in order to support and understand better the conclusions drawn so far. Some sites, particularly those near to the built-up urban fringe, may be isolated fragments of countryside which have not themselves ever been built upon. The length of time since isolation occurred, the degree of disturbance to the site since, and the uses to which the site was put before and after being isolated will affect the site vegetation and may help to explain its present condition. On sites which were originally built over and then cleared, the length of time the site, or portions of the site, have lain undisturbed may give an estimate of *the rate at which succession has continued* to produce the vegetation present. This may also give some idea of how the vegetation will change if left unmanaged.

For example, if the site has lain undisturbed for 2-3 years and a rich area of ruderal herbs and grasses has developed, this area, if left alone, may continue to change to a community dominated by perennial herbs and grasses within 5-15 years and woody perennials within 15-40 years. If, however, there are bare patches of soil, or ruderal herb communities present which have hardly changed for 20 years, there may be some explanation in the site history, such as harsh or toxic soil conditions, continued disturbance, or the site may be so isolated that new species are unable to locate it and succession is unable to continue.

If, for example, woodland is present, knowledge of the site's history may explain whether it has been planted or has developed naturally. (Natural woodland usually has a better developed mixture of woodland herbs and shrubs in amongst the trees.)

5.1.5 Management implications of design

Consider the management requirements for each habitat/area of vegetation present. The site design needs to take these into account, and ensure that the work involved in maintaining the site will be within the resources of your group. Wherever possible, the design should incorporate what is already on the site, rather than imposing an artificial landscape over it. This approach not only works out cheaper, but also minimises the damage to any wildlife present and maintains the 'character' of the area. Naturally-occurring communities already present on a site will normally reflect the character of their surroundings. They will have developed from local sources of seed, will comprise species adapted to the environmental conditions present, and will have developed an associated local fauna. Management approaches for the different areas on the site will involve varying combinations of non-intervention, conservation, modification and creation of habitats and communities.

anagement principles and techniques are dealt with in more detail in Chapter 7, but the reasons for adopting these approaches and their consequences may be summarised as follows.

Non-intervention   This is obviously the cheapest approach, but care must be taken when adopting it. The designer (and your group) must be quite sure that any area left unmanaged will not lose its desired characteristics or cause management problems in other areas as it develops naturally.

Conservation of habitats   This approach may be adopted if a particular area is considered valuable in its present state, possibly because the vegetation is rich in desirable or rare species. Many nature reserves are managed in this way to conserve rare or threatened species, communities and habitats.

On an urban site, for example, the designer may wish to conserve a valuable area of wildflower meadow which is in danger of being invaded by scrub. Conservation management in this case may consist of transplanting out the invading shrub and tree saplings and annual mowing of the meadow after the flowers have set their seed. The 'value' of the meadow needs to be compared to the cost and time involved in managing it, so that if a conservation management approach is adopted, your group will be able to follow it through. If in doubt about the wildlife value of a particular area seek out professional advice, for example from the Nature Conservancy Council or the County Trust for Nature Conservation (see Appendix 15 for addresses).

Modification of habitats   The conservation management example above is a form of modification, conserving wildflower meadow by restraining natural succession to scrub. Another form of modification would be to enhance the rate of natural succession by careful planting of extra wild species into a species-poor community. In this case, species would need to be chosen to suit the environmental conditions and the type of community present. Introduction of new species into natural communities runs two main risks. First, the introductions may not survive; second, they may thrive and overrun the community. However, the correct choice can result in a species-rich community which retains the natural character of the site.

An example of modification would be the use of nitrogen-fixing herbs on sites with soil low in nitrates (see Table 5.6). The presence of such species could increase the nitrate levels in the soil, allow species with higher nutrient requirements to survive, and generally enhance the rate of natural succession.

Table 5.6 Some nitrogen-fixing perennial species often found colonising urban sites

		soil[1] preference
Alnus glutinosa	black alder	ANC
Coronilla varia	crown vetch	NC
Lathyrus sylvestris	narrow-leaved ever-lasting pea	NC
Lotus corniculatus	bird's-foot trefoil	NC
Lupinus arboreus	tree lupin[2]	ANC
Medicago sativa	lucerne[2]	NC
Melilotus alba	white melilot[2]	ANC
M. officinalis	ribbed melilot[2]	ANC
Ononis repens	alsike clover[2]	ANC
Trifolium pratense	red clover	NC
T. repens	white clover	NC
Ulex europaeus	gorse	ANC

Notes:

1. All these species thrive on soils low in nitrates (hence less fertile) because of their ability to fix atmospheric nitrogen (and commonly to out-compete other species not able to do so).

   A ⸺ acid soils (pH less than 5.5);
   C ⸺ calcareous (alkaline) soils (pH 5.6 or above);
   N ⸺ neutral soils (pH approx. 5.5).

2. Introduced and cultivated species which have 'escaped' into the wild (some cultivated hybrids of red and white clover may also appear on urban sites).

However, there is always the possibility that, for a time, such species will overrun the community themselves, or the build-up of soil nutrients may allow other vigorous species to take over, for example thistles, nettles and other weeds of fertile soils.

In this situation, the vegetation may need further modification, for example by cutting and removing cuttings to lower the rate of nutrient enhancement.

Creation of habitats   Habitat creation 'from scratch' will be a common component in the design of urban sites. For example, a bare patch of soil in school grounds, or a small newly-cleared site in the heart of a residential area may be worth developing as nature areas because of their locations. Chapter 6 deals in detail with the principles and methods involved.

With this approach, it is up to the designer to mimic the processes of nature and change areas of bare ground into self-sustaining, desirable, semi-natural communities. The term 'semi-natural communities' is used because it is not possible to construct precise replicas of natural communities. For example, ancient woodlands in Great Britain are protected by such organisations as the Nature Conservancy Council because once destroyed, they are not possible to re-create. The fine balance and complexity of the plant community in ancient woodlands has taken many hundreds of years to develop. The more the designer understands the natural processes involved, the more he or she will be able to fit semi-natural communities to the environmental conditions present, and the better the design will be.

Size considerations When planning to create or maintain more than one habitat on a site, it is important to consider the possibilities of one habitat affecting another. If, for example, a grassland area with wildflowers borders an area colonised by shrubs, it is probable that shrub seedlings will begin to invade the grassland. This 'edge effect' can be a real management headache on a small site, particularly if the site design incorporates too many small, different areas of vegetation, likely to merge with one another unless constantly managed. On a one hectare site, for example, it may be practical in management terms to have only three or four different types of vegetation at the most.

The size of habitats on a site is an important factor in terms of their stability, the management they require and the intensity of public intrusion they are able to withstand. In Chapter 6, the importance of habitat size in the creation of habitats is discussed in more detail (woodland, grassland and pond habitats are considered separately).

At the beginning of the design process, the designer needs to be clear about the sources of labour which will be available to manage the site vegetation.

On small-scale sites of around 100 sq m–1 ha, voluntary groups should be able to provide the personal management and care necessary to maintain a variety of habitats. Such groups will be highly flexible and able to carry out labour-intensive tasks on a small scale.

On larger sites of around 3 ha and over, any habitat creation from scratch will require landscape contractors or local authority direct labour teams, for example, to move earth, carry out large-scale planting and subsequently manage the site. Such labour forces tend to be highly inflexible, dependent upon expensive machinery and tied to the economics of time and money. In this situation, the designer may have to accept that creation will be costly. However, by creating low-maintenance semi-natural landscape, e.g. meadow grasslands of 1 ha or over, woodland and scrub blocks of 2 ha or over or, if possible, water bodies and associated reed beds of at least 3,000 sq m in total extent, the designer can greatly lower the amount of costly management required.

Natural plant communities established at this scale should have a degree of biological stability and should, as a whole, withstand public pressure with very little maintenance. Voluntary groups may be able to enhance such large-scale habitats by small-scale planting and management to put finishing touches to the large-scale landscaping.

In certain situations, union difficulties can arise where professional landscape contractors and direct labour teams work on the same project as do volunteers (particularly on areas which would normally be managed by the local authority). Another possible problem on such large areas of natural communities is that of management skills. Although levels of maintenance will be low for stable natural communities, the maintenance will require an understanding of the natural dynamics of those communities and will involve different skills to those normally involved in the management of traditional parks and gardens.

On sites of intermediate size (around 1-3 ha), both voluntary and professional labour sources may be used. On these sites, a balance is needed between the two.

A site developed by a professional labour force, for intensive use as public open space, will probably need to incorporate simple, resilient, low-maintenance habitats, e.g. scrub/woodland, with a fringe of close-cut grassland maintained for extensive recreation.

A site developed by a voluntary group may incorporate a variety of habitats on a similar, but slightly larger scale than on the 100 sq m-1 ha sites already mentioned. In this case, the extra costs of management may be beyond the means of your group. However, local authority funding and community management may provide a solution to this problem.

By using the principles outlined in this section your group should be able to prepare a summary of the environmental features, habitats and communities present on a site, decide how these areas will be used in the site design and anticipate the management requirements involved.

5.2 Principles covering site use

If the site is to benefit the public, they need to be able to use it to its maximum potential. At the same time, it is in everyone's interest that the planned site uses cause as little damage or disturbance as possible to the plants and animals present.

It is necessary to strike a balance between:

— a site designed for wildlife, to the exclusion of the public; and
— a site with too many clashing public uses which eventually destroy the wildlife value.

It may, therefore, be necessary to sacrifice some of the desired uses for the site to ensure its long-term success.

The site design needs to consider:

— The general appearance of landscape features in relation to the surroundings. Its uses need to fit the character of the area and not to clash with the surroundings or appear unsightly to the public.
— The fragility of natural habitats on the site, the effects different uses will have upon them and their suitability for different uses.
— Visitor access, circulation and movement. The movements of visitors need to be controlled for their convenience and safety and to protect fragile habitats on the site.

5.2.1 Site form and appearance

The design should, as far as possible, provide visual relief from the hard urban landscape. In overall appearance, the site needs to fit into the landscape. Interesting landforms, geological, architectural and archeological features may exist on the site or around it. Such features on the site may be considered with the natural communities present and incorporated into the design.

Viewpoints can also be important in the site design and any views of local landmarks or other attractive or interesting features may be important when siting viewpoints or when planting trees, etc. In the same way that vegetation can obscure undesirable views, it can obscure desirable features, unless the designer thinks ahead.

The more attractive the site, the stronger the public's 'belief' in it will be. The attractiveness of large areas of wild grassland, for example on city commons, relates to their size and feeling of space. However, a wild grassland block on a 0.1ha inner-urban vacant site may appear much less visually interesting (just as dull as the short grass of a lawn). On a large site, the odd patch of undesirable plants may pass unnoticed, but on a small site, these may become obvious eyesores.

Design on a small site should, therefore, aim for a diverse mixture of mini-habitats to provide ecological and structural diversity and a pleasing visual effect. Such habitats will need careful planning and management, to prevent one habitat from merging with another, and to minimise the wear and tear of public access. On large sites (from 3ha upwards) the design may involve broad zones and blocks of different vegetation types which slowly merge with one another.

In traditionally-landscaped parks and gardens, plant communities are commonly divided by harsh lines, for example, between grass and pavement, geometric shrubberies and grass, water and water's edge, trees and lawns.

In nature, plant communities merge and overlap with each other to produce species-rich mixed communities (called 'ecotones'), e.g. around woodland edges and glades or in the transition zone between scrub and grassland.

The ecological approach to landscape design uses the ecotone principle to produce species-rich 'soft edges' between neighbouring plant communities. To some people, this may appear untidy. For example, a scrub-grassland edge may appear to be little more than a neglected weed patch. A single cut from a mower to define some form of 'tidy' edge can usually satisfy such views.

5.2.2 Choice of habitats for particular uses

All types of natural vegetation have some nature conservation value. The main requirements of any areas of vegetation to be used for nature conservation are that they are, as far as possible:

— natural, in terms of the mixtures of native species they contain;
— relatively undisturbed, in terms of their 'sanctuary' value for wildlife;
— stable, so that the species being conserved continue to thrive.

Education is an extremely important part of nature conservation and students of all ages should, therefore, be able to study as many different vegetation types as possible. The designer's task is to allow them access to do so with the minimum of damage to the wildlife present.

5.2.3 Zonation, rotation of access and path layout

Zonation

In the overall site design, zonation may be used to separate those habitats needing the minimum of disturbance from those areas where public use is intensive, by putting a 'buffer' zone between them (see Figure 5.1).

This lessens the risk of people who choose only to use the recreation areas accidentally damaging or disturbing the site wildlife. Visitors wishing only to relax in pleasing surroundings may choose to use the buffer zones, particularly if hard landscape in the form of seats, picnic areas, etc. are included in the design and their surroundings are sufficiently attractive.

Areas to be used for intensive recreation (the more resilient habitats and plant communities) should be situated near to the site entrance(s) or on, or near, the site's main public thoroughfare(s).

Figure 5.1 Simple zonation of habitats for different uses

	Resilient habitat	'Buffer zone'	Natural habitat
Use	E.g. close-cut grassland for intensive recreation	Habitat of medium resilience, e.g. for passive recreation	Nature conservation, passive recreation and study
Disturbance	Very disturbed	Moderately disturbed	Minimal disturbance
Wildlife value	Low wildlife value	Medium wildlife value	High wildlife value
Vegetation structure	Uniform	Visually more aesthetically pleasing and structurally diverse	Species-rich; structurally complex
Management	Traditional management, e.g. regular mowing. Few, selected resilient species	Mixture of traditional management and management for wildlife, e.g. additional wild species encouraged. Less intensive mowing	Management for wildlife, e.g. conservation, modification and creation of plant and animal habitats and communities

Source: adapted from Corder, M. and Brooker, R. (1981) *Natural Economy*, Kirklees Metropolitan Council.

More easily-damaged habitats are best situated where casual visitors are least likely to wander.

In this way, careful siting and zoning can lower the level of accidental damage to habitats without resorting to disagreeable 'keep out' and 'keep off' signs.

Rotation of access

The fragility of habitats and the shyness of some animals can vary considerably throughout the year. For example, on a wildflower meadow in spring, before many blooms have appeared, the many young seedlings and shoots present may not be obvious. Accidental trampling at this early stage may destroy the plants before they are able to flower. Later in the season, when mature flowering plants are easily visible, the visitor will be more able to avoid walking on them.

Spring and autumn are also times of heavy rainfall and certain areas of the site may become periodically waterlogged. Apart from getting their feet wet, visitors walking across such areas can cause severe damage to the 'mat' of vegetation, more so than they would if the soil was drier and more resilient.

In areas suitable for nesting birds, such as hedgerows, scrub thickets and dense woodland, the breeding/nesting season (March-mid-September) is a sensitive period. Excessive noise or public intrusion into the area may dissuade birds from building their nests, or cause them to desert.

In these three examples, there is a definite need to channel visitors away from the areas during 'sensitive' times of the year. This principle of rotation of access may be applied to all habitats in the site design, wherever visitor pressure threatens to damage any in particular. If, for example, constant public access to a meadow threatens to destroy the vegetation cover, it may be practical to split the meadow into two or more portions, only allowing access to one while allowing other portions to recover. Visitors will still be able to visit and enjoy the meadow, without destroying it in doing so.

Path layout

When designing the path layout, it is important that the public should have access to as many habitats on the site as possible. On the one hand, it is undesirable that habitats should be destroyed by excessive public use, but on the other, wildlife areas in the city are for the public's benefit. Combined with careful zonation and rotation of access, a carefully aligned path network can allow visitors access and protect the site wildlife at the same time.

Visitors will tend to keep to clearly marked paths, particularly if the path surface is safe and easy to walk on. For example, visitors will generally adopt a simple mown strip across a flower meadow as a pathway. However, if a path layout consists of too regular a grid of straight lines, users may stray off the paths and make short cuts. This is a common problem on formally-landscaped public open spaces, with the corners of lawns trampled bare and new paths being worn across mown grass, and even flowerbeds. Such informal pathways may be termed 'desire lines', as they link points of public interest and commonly follow the easiest routes between them.

The desire line principle may be very useful in site design. If your group acquires a site which has been vacant and open to casual public use, various desire lines may be already apparent in the form of paths worn through the site vegetation. In this case, it would be advisable to consider carefully these lines as the basis for a path network.

The site's development may remove some points of interest and add new ones. If its design is going to alter the site at all, it may be worth leaving the routing of paths for a while. This will allow visitors to use the site, enabling you subsequently to pick out the most popular routes they take. These may then form the basis for a path network.

It is not generally advisable to rush the layout of paths or to spend large amounts of time and money at the beginning, putting down permanent surfaces. Rather, it is better to begin with a temporary path network and alter it to suit the behaviour of visitors.

If visitors will be following paths with no guides or directions, a system of loops leading back to the beginning may be the most suitable arrangement, particularly on large or densely-wooded sites, where visitors may lose sight of their starting point. If the paths are not loops, but lead into vegetation terminating somewhere out of sight of the starting point, visitors may choose to wander off the path into the vegetation, rather than retracing their steps.

Another useful function of a network of loops is that they may be routed around any habitats your group wish to maintain as undisturbed areas, e.g. nesting areas for wild birds or vegetation easily destroyed by trampling. Such habitats may be ruined if paths criss-cross them, breaking them up into fragments. Carefully sited viewpoints on a loop pathway can allow casual visitors to see as much of the habitats as they would if they were wandering freely through them, but without causing as much disturbance or damage.

On wetland sites, raised walkways with non-slip surfaces are a common (and rather expensive) solution to the problem of public access. These allow safe access to boggy and otherwise hazardous areas and help to protect the wetland wildlife from trampling and other disturbance.

A useful way of keeping visitors to the paths in woodland is to employ natural barriers. For example, if cut branches (possibly brashings from path clearance work) are piled alongside paths and bramble is allowed to grow over them, only the more adventurous visitor will try to cross such a dense thicket. The bramble is a more attractive alternative to fencing. It will not obscure the view from the path, it will bear flowers and fruit, and will provide a haven for small animals.

In enclosed areas of vegetation, for example scrub or woodlands, paths may be made more interesting if they wind through the vegetation. Straight, monotonous pathways provide fewer surprises, and there is always something different around the corner when the visitor cannot see too far ahead.

A prime consideration in laying out paths is that of public safety. Paths should avoid dangerous areas, such as precipices; steep slopes should incorporate durable steps; path surfaces should be free of jagged obstructions and objects; slippery surfaces should be avoided and the possible effects of path erosion should be considered in pathway design. Sources of further information on path construction methods include the British Trust for Conservation Volunteers handbook on footpaths (Agate 1983) and the Countryside Commission for Scotland, who publish information sheets on the subject from their information centre in Battleby, Perth (see Appendix 15 for address).

5.3 Economics of design with nature

This section outlines some of the areas where substantial savings in time, energy and money, may be made by using an ecological rather than a traditional approach to landscape design and management.

The overall cost of ecological design and management will depend upon the amount of work needed to change site conditions so that semi-natural, self-sustaining communities can develop. This can vary considerably from one site to another. The ecological approach does not, therefore, provide a cheap alternative to traditional landscape in all cases. On some sites where it is needed, the initial establishment of pioneer vegetation may be costly, but generally, as a well-designed nature-like landscape develops, the mixture of plants and animals in it (the ecosystem) becomes more stable, requiring less human intervention.

The following examples help to illustrate this point.

Ground preparation

In order to change site conditions to fit the site design, traditional methods commonly involve extensive alteration of the ground surface. Waterlogged areas may be drained; unwanted ponds and ditches filled in; the ground surface may be levelled and extensive soil preparation may be carried out. All these preparations commonly employ heavy machinery.

Ecological methods can remove the need for such expensive preparation by, as far as possible, fitting the design to the site topography, soil and water conditions already present. In some situations where vegetation is to be established on a flat site, diversity in relief may be created by making mounds or hollows. However, this is more an option than an expensive necessity.

Imported soil

Should soil need to be imported on to a site, traditional methods commonly require fertile topsoil to provide the nutrients for fast establishment and survival of exotic and cultivated species.

Ecological methods require the opposite. Imported soil of low fertility is more desirable. This provides a growing medium for a wide range of wild plants which commonly occur in the early stages of natural colonisation and succession. These plant communities can then undergo natural succession enriching the soil in nutrients as they develop (see section 5.1.2). Thus, subsoil, brick rubble and even cinders, are cheaper options for import. For example, in 1977, approximately 4,000 cu m of excavated subsoil and demolition spoil were used to cover hard core during the creation of the William Curtis Ecological Park (see Cole 1980). This has proved an ideal growing medium during the Park's natural development. The cost of importing was £100, compared to an estimated cost of £12,000 for an equivalent volume of topsoil.

Choice of species (wherever planting is necessary)

The main considerations in choice of species for traditional landscape design are the tastes of designers or their clients. Exotic and cultivated species mixes are traditionally employed to produce visual effect (with particular blends of colour and texture); structural effect (with blends of shape and size); and functional effects (durability, etc.). Such mixes commonly require intensive management to maintain their appearance and the nutrient conditions they require.

The main considerations in species choice for ecological design are the suitability of each species for the conditions into which it is placed. Native species mixes are employed which form, as far as possible, balanced, self-sustaining nature-like communities, suited to the environmental conditions present.

The economic consequences of these two different approaches to species choice are first, that native species are generally cheaper to obtain than are exotic or cultivated species. Second, the ecological mixtures require much less intensive management than traditional mixtures (so long as the ecological design successfully 'fits' the environmental conditions present and involves the correct mixture of species). Third, these native species will tend to have higher survival rates than exotics. (Chapter 6 covers the choice of species for the creation of habitats in more detail.)

Planting methods and species survival

Where traditional planting methods neglect to consider ecological requirements, poor species survival can result. Tree planting provides a good example. Traditional methods sometimes involve planting standards (2.5-3 m high), to provide 'instant' landscape, often with very little after-care. Standards need supporting with stakes until their roots have taken strong hold. Movement by the wind can damage roots as well as shoots. The ties holding trees to stakes require maintenance. Broken ties can result in damage to both the tree roots and stems as the wind rocks the plant. If a metal tree guard has been used, wind-induced movement can lead to the stem chafing against the guard; the tree may be ring-barked and may die as a result.

Wherever possible, ecological methods should avoid the use of standards and instead use transplants (0.2-0.45 m), whips (0.5-1.0 m) or feathered whips (1.5-2.5 m). The reasons for this choice may be summarised as follows:

— Increased survival: the roots of the smaller trees are more able to withstand the shock of transplanting than those of standards. (This is partly due to the sheer size of the root mass required on a standard tree and the subsequent difficulty in avoiding root damage during transplanting.)
— Reduced expense: the smaller trees are cheaper to buy and require less support than standards, lessening costs for additional stakes and ties.

(Correct methods of tree planting and maintenance are covered in more detail in Chapters 6 and 7.)

For example, in 1982 one Parks Department in Britain, using traditional methods, had tree and shrub planting costs of upwards of £6 per sq m of area planted. However, the Warrington and Runcorn Development Corporation (WRDC) equivalent planting costs (inclusive of ground preparation) averaged between 60p and £1.50 per sq m (excluding maintenance). This was achieved by using native species rather than exotics, a greater number of whips and transplants, as opposed to standard trees, and often planting into prepared subsoil rather than importing costly topsoil. Over 50 per cent of the WRDC budget for woodland planting went into careful ground preparation and maintenance to ensure survival. A survival rate of at least 95 per cent was achieved, compared to survival rates in some local authority plantings of 40 per cent, or even as low as 25 per cent, when traditional methods were used. With savings such as these, WRDC was able to set up public consultation and Ranger services, encouraging environmental education, contributing to the success of their semi-natural landscapes and cutting down the rates of vandalism which many local authorities find so costly (see Bradley 1982).

Soil fertility

The traditional landscape approach commonly depends upon continual tedious application of expensive manures and fertilisers to maintain the health of the vegetation. In many situations, such application of fertiliser promotes the growth of unwanted vigorous weeds and results in increased costs for their removal.

The ecological approach, by attempting to develop a vegetation cover suited to the soil conditions, can avoid such costly dependence.

In extremely poor nutrient conditions, where some degree of increased fertility is required, an example of an ecological method of enhancing fertility is the use of nitrogen-fixing species to increase the available nitrates in the soil for other plants. For example, once established in grassland, clover can supply about 100 kg of nitrogen per ha per year to the sward. To provide this quantity of nitrogen, it would be necessary to apply annually at least 600 kg per ha of a complete fertiliser containing 15 per cent nitrogen.

Weeds

Traditional landscape design and management commonly involves intensive weeding, to maintain the health *and* appearance of the vegetation. Expensive chemical weedkillers are a popular alternative to labour-intensive weeding methods in the continual drive to produce a 'weed-free landscape'.

An ecological approach lessens the need to remove weeds. In most ecologically designed and managed habitats, the species commonly considered as weeds in traditional landscape form part of the natural vegetation and will not be as vigorously invasive as they would be in, for example, an artificially prepared, fertilised flowerbed.

In the few situations where unwanted 'weeds' do occur, an ecological management approach would be to weed by hand, or mechanically. Apart from being expensive, weedkillers can be harmful to other species (and people). The Royal Society for the Protection of Birds (RSPB) leaflet 'Pesticides and the Gardener' outlines some of the risks involved to wildlife when using herbicides and insecticides.

Pests

Pesticides are commonly used in traditional landscape in much the same way as herbicides in an attempt to produce 'pest-free' landscape. Again, an ecological approach means that species considered as pests in traditional landscape form part of the natural animal community associated with the vegetation. Expensive pesticides become undesirable, rather than necessary.

Long-term management (see also Chapter 7)

The general features of traditional management may be summarised as follows:

— The vegetation is made up of unstable, artificial mixtures of plants (often including exotic and cultivated species) which need intensive, continued management, to maintain their appearance and the conditions necessary for their survival.
— Modern management methods involve less manpower and more high cost/ high technology methods (for example, using machinery designed for uniform operations on a large scale, with artificial fertilisers and pesticides).
— The designer can normally leave the responsibility of maintenance to 'gardening and park-keeping' staff, with basic horticultural skills (e.g. planting, weeding, mowing, pruning, etc.).

In comparison, ecological management may be summarised as follows:

— As far as possible, the vegetation is made up of stable, self-sustaining, nature-like mixtures of native plants, suited to the conditions present and requiring only low levels of management.
— Management methods involve more manpower (manual labour operations on a small scale) with an overall saving by using little or no high technology machinery, fertilisers or pesticides.

— The same team, including the designer, needs to be continuously responsible for management ensuring that the vegetation develops in a stable way. Management staff, therefore, need to be aware of overall management objectives and to have some understanding of the natural dynamics (ecology) of the landscape.

5.4 Sources of advice and further information

The following are annotated lists of local sources, national organisations and regionally-based organisations (see Appendix 15 for addresses).

Local sources

County Naturalists' Trust (or Trust for Nature Conservation): members or officers of the Trust may be able to advise on the nature conservation value of a site.

Local authority landscape departments: landscape designers, landscape architects and planners in the department may be able to lend their advice, criticisms and skills to a site design.

Local colleges or universities (and colleges of horticulture or agriculture): lecturers, researchers or students from departments of botany, environmental sciences, landscape, etc. may be interested in helping with a site design.

Local council land reclamation unit or ecology unit e.g. Lancashire County Council Joint Reclamation Team: some local authorities employ specialists to handle derelict land reclamation, etc. and such professionals may give valuable advice on landscape management, etc.

National organisations

Allotments for the Future: for advice on the design and management of urban allotments.

Arboricultural Association: for advice on design and management of tree plantings, choice of species for different situations, etc.

Association of Community Technical Aid Centres (ACTAC): for the addresses of the many affiliated technical aid centres located around the country providing advice on technical matters including design and management.

British Butterfly Conservation Society (BBCS): for advice on butterfly gardening, food plants, etc.

British Trust for Conservation Volunteers (Headquarters for publications, various Regional Ofices for volunteer groups): for advice on many aspects of practical conservation management. BTCV handbooks are of a consistent high quality.

Countryside Commission (advisory services): for information on landscape management (*see also Countryside Commission for Scotland*). The Commission also sponsor the regionally based Groundwork Trusts.

Ecological Parks Trust: for advice on low cost ecological design, creation and management of urban sites for nature conservation, recreation and study.

Environmental Advisory Unit, University of Liverpool, Department of Botany: for advice on various methods of reclamation of derelict land.

Friends of the Earth: a nature conservation organisation with various regional groups involved in urban projects.

Handicapped Adventure Playground Association: for advice on the design and construction of playgrounds for the handicapped.

Landscape Institute: publishes an annual directory of landscape practices situated throughout the country. Charges for advice, etc. will vary from practice to practice and individual practitioners may be prepared to give advice either at a reduced rate, or free of charge. The Institute can also help clients select a suitable practice for their particular requirements, on receipt of a letter of enquiry.

National Federation of City Farms: for addresses of the many affiliated farms throughout the country and advice on city farm design and management methods.

National Playing Fields Association: for advice on the design and management of recreation areas.

National Society of Allotments and Leisure Gardeners Ltd: for horticultural advice.

Nature Conservancy Council (NCC) (Interpretative Branch for literature, Regional Offices for advice): for advice on the nature conservation value of a site and any wildlife consideration in site designs.

Royal Society for Nature Conservation (RSNC): umbrella organisation for the County Naturalists' Trusts (Trust for Nature Conservation).

Royal Society for the Protection of Birds (RSPB): for information on bird gardens, habitats for birds, etc.

Society for Horticultural Therapy: for advice on the design and management of gardens for the handicapped.

Soil Association: for information on soil and its management.

Woodland Trust: for advice on tree planting and maintenance, woodland design and management for nature.

Regionally-based organisations

Coventry Countryside Project: set up after the Coventry Wildlife Survey completed its work on sites in and around the city

Department of the Environment for Northern Ireland, Nature Reserves Committee

Environmental Resource Centre (Edinburgh)

Glasgow Urban Wildlife group

Green Cure Trust (Bristol)

Groundwork Trusts (Merseyside)

'IMPACT': the Greater Manchester Clean-Up Campaign

'Landlife' (formerly Rural Preservation Association (RPA)): Regional Offices in Merseyside, Leeds, Southampton, Greater Manchester, Lancaster and Ireland

Leicester City Wildlife Project

London Adventure Playgrounds Association

London Wildlife Trust

Swansea City Council Environment Dept., Conservator of the Lower Swansea Valley

Urban Wildlife Group (Birmingham)

5.5 References

Agate, E. (1983) *Footpaths: A practical conservation handbook*, British Trust for Conservation Volunteers

Bradley, Christine (1982) 'An ecological approach' in Ruff, Alan R. and Tregay, Robert (eds.), *An Ecological Approach to Urban Landscape Design*, Dept. of Town and Country Planning, University of Manchester, Occasional Paper No. 8, p. 36

Bradshaw, A.D. and Chadwick, M.J. (1980) *The Restoration of Land*, Blackwell, Studies in Ecology, Vol. 6

Brooks, A. (1977) *Dry Stone Walling: A practical conservation handbook*, British Trust for Conservation Volunteers

——(1980) *Hedging: A practical conservation handbook* (rev. ed), British Trust for Conservation Volunteers

Cole, L. (1980) *The Creation of the William Curtis Ecological Park*, Ecological Parks Trust

——(1982) 'Does size matter?' in Ruff, A.R. and Tregay, R. (eds.), *An Ecological Approach to Landscape Design*, Dept. of Town and Country Planning, University of Manchester, Occasional Paper No. 8, p. 70

Countryside Commission for Scotland, Battleby Display Centre, Information sheets (and Information sheets [plants]) — *Plants and Planting Methods for the Countryside*, continually updated

Dutton, R.A. and Bradshaw, A.D. (1982) *Land Reclamation in Cities*, HMSO, London

Gemmell, R.P. and Greenwood, E.F. (1978) 'Derelict industrial land as a habitat for rare plants', *Watsonia*, **12**:33-40

Gemmell, R.P., Connell, R.K. and Crombie, S.A. (1983) 'Conservation and creation of habitats on industrial land' in *Reclamation 83* (Proceedings, International Land Reclamation Conference, Grays, Essex, 26-29 April)

Grime, J.P. (1974) 'Vegetation classification by reference to strategies', *Nature*, **250**:25-31

——(1979) 'succession and competitive exclusion' in Wright, S.E. and Buckley, G.P. (eds.), *Ecology and Design in Amenity Land Management*, Proceedings Conference, Wye College, Kent, pp. 57-70

Ruff, Alan R. (1979) 'The use of ecological principles in design solutions in urban open space' in Wright, S.E. and Buckley, G.P. (eds.),*Ecology and Design in Amenity Land Management*, Proceedings Conference, Wye College, Kent, pp. 205-15

Shimwell, D. (1983) 'Conspectus of urban vegetation types' (unpublished), prepared for the Groundwork Trust

Tandy, C.R.V. (1975) *Landscape of Industry*, Leonard Hill Books

PART TWO
Developing Sites — Ecological Principles and Practices

6 Creation of habitats

Natural habitats contain extremely complex communities of native plants and animals. Chapter 5 describes how these communities constantly change, as new species replace others in the process of natural succession. A mature natural community, such as ancient oak woodland, takes hundreds of years to develop its unique and diverse mixtures of plants and animals. It is only possible in the short term to create simplified imitations. Hence, terms like 'naturalistic' or 'nature-like' are found in the literature on habitat creation. However, these attempts at mimicking nature produce habitats with much more diversity and wildlife value than the traditional parks and gardens of our towns and cities.

In this chapter, habitats are split for convenience into four separate headings: grassland/meadow; scrub/woodland; freshwater; and 'mini-habitats' (such as insect/bird gardens, etc.).

It is very important to record all details of projects undertaken, including changes over time. Such information will be extremely useful for future projects and just as much can be learned from failures as from successes.

Management of these habitat types is covered in detail in Chapter 7. However, it is important to remember that consideration of their management requirements is needed before habitat creation begins. Allowance should be made for both the immediate after-care of newly created habitats and their long-term requirements. If there are nearby areas of vegetation from which seeds may reach a site, then any habitats created may change according to the effects of this 'seed rain', and as the vegetation itself matures. Unmanaged open herb/grassland can mature to dense herb/grassland, with a decrease in the number of species present. Scrub species can invade and the scrub can itself mature to produce woodland eventually. In a similar way, natural succession can alter wetland habitats such as ponds. Such changes may be acceptable on a particular site. It all depends on what the designers want in the long term.

6.1 Grassland/meadow

The features of grasslands created for traditional public parks and gardens, tennis lawns, football pitches, etc. may be summarised as follows:

— Seed mixtures of productive, fast-growing grasses, in particular, rye grass (*Lolium* spp.), are sown on specially prepared, fertile soils. The grassland produced is resistant to trampling, but species-poor, because the vigorous grasses out-compete other less-vigorous herbaceous species.
— Management is intensive, involving a maintained balance of soil moisture and high fertility, and regular mowing.
— The resultant monotonous, short-turf grassland is satisfactory for intensive public use, but has very little benefit for wildlife, and can be expensive to

maintain. For groups wishing to establish such areas of turf, a useful reference is Johnson's (see Appendix 14 for address) *Turfgrass Seeds Handbook — for professionals involved in the creation and maintenance of turf.* In order to create species-rich grassland and meadow which, although less resistant to wear and tear, will be more attractive and more valuable for wildlife, a completely different approach is taken.

6.1.1 Ground preparation

The basic requirement for the establishment of species-rich grassland is poor soil, for example, low nitrogen, dryness or acid conditions. In these conditions, a large number of species may be established on a small area, because species able to tolerate stress tend to be poor competitors. Unfertilised clay, sand or peat are suitable, as, for example, are the ground conditions on many urban demolition sites. On areas of higher fertility, for example disused gardens and allotments, vigorous, competitive perennials such as docks (*Rumex* spp.), creeping thistle (*Cirsium arvense*) and couch grass (*Agropyron repens*) may be a problem. These may be cleared by weeding, or if manual weeding is impractical, by the use of herbicides such as glyphosate (proprietary name: 'Tumbleweed') two to four weeks before cultivation begins (see Appendix 12 for further recommendations concrning herbicides). However, removal of perennials may still leave fertile soil into which they may easily return.

A shorter-term solution to the problem of fertile soil (or any other undesirable ground) conditions may be to cover the ground with a layer of, for example, subsoil. This would probably have to be over 100 mm deep to mask the effect of the layers beneath. Alternatively, it may be worth removing the topsoil completely and selling it. The exposed subsoil, or replacement subsoil, could then be prepared as a growing medium.

Expensive soil improvements such as fertiliser treatment and land drainage should be avoided. Surface tilling will be necessary. Particularly impervious materials such as compacted clay subsoil may need roughly breaking up. This may be done in autumn, so that the frost can get to it, then by raking, harrowing and rolling, a rough tilth may be prepared for seeding in the spring. Deep ripping should not be necessary, and may even be undesirable, as it may encourage deep root penetration and more vigorous growth. The seedbed should be fine and firm, but not too deep.

Large stones and boulders need removing before preparing the area. If left, they may become concealed by the vegetation, and damage to grass-cutting equipment may result. Any large stones brought to the surface during raking or harrowing may be removed after sowing seeds. The slight compaction caused by trampling feet treads in the seed and can help successful germination.

If only a small proportion of the area is compacted, it may be worth leaving it to provide extra variation in the site conditions, so that the diversity of the vegetation will also increase. The same principle applies to other small areas, for example with different conditions of fertility or moisture. On flat sites, greater variation may be achieved by landscape modelling: moving earth to create mounds, hollows and shallow slopes; altering the ground moisture, for example by diverting watercourses; and by altering the depth of the growing medium.

Importing ground materials is another option for creating variation, and in some cases may be a necessity. Any imported soil should be low in nutrients, in particular, available nitrogen. Clay may be imported to impede drainage. Sand, gravel, peat, subsoils, brick rubble and cinder may be combined in different mixtures to produce a variety of ground conditions. Alkaline wastes may be mixed in to produce conditions for calcareous species-rich grassland or merely to lower excessive ground acidity (common, for example, on ash). See Table 5.1 for further details of the qualities of different ground materials.

6.1.2 Choice of species

Species need to be chosen to suit site conditions of, for example, soil fertility, moisture, pH and light.

Grasses

In most cases, an *Agrostis/Festuca* grass mix will be satisfactory. Choice of other species will depend upon conditions of light, soil moisture, fertility and pH. Other factors such as resistance to trampling and the grass height may also be important considerations depending upon the degree of public use expected and the desired height of the sward.

Table 6.1 is given as a starting point only in selecting grass species. There are well over 100 common grass species in Great Britain, each with different

Table 6.1 Examples of grasses and their suitability for different conditions

Species	DA	DL	GL	W	RGW	RGD	RGG	HF	LF	RT	H	SH
Agrostis stolonifera (creeping bent grass)	*	*		*					*	M	L	
A. tenuis (bent grass; brown top)	*	*	*			*			*	L	L	
Alopecurus pratensis (meadow foxtail)	*	*	*				*		*	H	L	*
Anthoxanthum odoratum (sweet vernal grass)	*				*				*	L	M	
Cynosurus cristatus (crested dog's tail)		*			*				*	H	L	
Deschampsia flexuosa (wavy hair grass)	*			*	*				*	L	M	
Festuca arundinacea (tall fescue)			*	*	*			*	*	M	H	
F. longifolia (hard fescue)	*	*				*			*	L	L	
F. ovina (sheep's fescue)	*	*				*			*	L	L	
F. pratensis (meadow fescue)			*				*	*		M	M	
F. rubra commutata (Chewings red fescue)	*	*				*			*	M	M	
F. rubra rubra (creeping red fescue)	*	*				*			*	L	M	
F. tenuifolia (fine-leaved fescue)	*	*				*			*	L	L	
Holcus lanatus (Yorkshire fog)			*				*	*		L	H	
Lolium perenne (perennial rye grass)			*				*	*		H	M	
Phleum pratense (Timothy)			*				*	*		L	H	
Poa annua (annual meadow grass)			*	*	*			*	*	M	M	*
P. nemoralis (wood meadow grass)	*	*				*			*	M	L	
P. pratensis (smooth-stalked meadow grass)			*				*	*		H	M	
P. trivialis (rough-stalked meadow grass)			*	*	*			*	*	M	M	*

DA	= dry acid	RGG	= rough grass on good loam
DL	= dry limestone	HF	= high fertiliser response
GL	= good loam	LF	= low fertiliser response
W	= wet	RT	= resistance to trampling (low, medium and high)
RGW	= rough grass on wet sites	H	= height (low, medium and high)
RGD	= rough grass on dry sites	SH	= shade

Source: Philip Masters, (unpublished) personal communication.

requirements and adaptations. Hubbard (1968) and Fitter and Fitter (1984) are useful references for British grasses. The Countryside Commission Advisory Booklet No. 13, *Grassland Establishment in Countryside Recreation Areas*, lists details of grass species, their varieties and recommended mixes for different uses and site conditions. The Nature Conservancy Council publication, *Creating Attractive Grasslands using Native Plant Species* (Wells *et al.* 1981), suggests grass/wildflower mixtures for different conditions. The availability of native seed mixes from commercial suppliers continues to improve, along with the quality of advisory literature they provide. Table 6.2 lists these and other further sources of information on grass seed mixes for different situations.

Table 6.2 Sources of further information for recommended species of herbs and grasses for planting

Reference	Groups covered	Number of species listed	Additional notes included
Herbs (flowering plants including some grasses)			
Agate 1983, pp. 141-4	(a) Grasses and (b) herbs resistant to trampling	(a) 21(N) (b) 32(N)	Height, habit, habitat, reproduction, comments
pp. 145-7	Plants for slope stabilisation, screens and barriers	42(N)	Type, habitat, use, comments
Botanical Society of the British Isles 1982	Flowers	25(N)	Soil type
Bradshaw and Chadwick 1980	Legumes	19(N,I)	Soil, climate
Corder and Brooker 1981, pp. 67-72	Herbs	95(N)	Urban habitats, height, colour, flower, remarks, period
Countryside Commission 1980, pp. 19-21, 24	Legumes and their varieties Flowers for acid soils Flowers for calcareous soils	8(N,I) 11(C) 13(N) 18(N)	Soil types, pH, etc. — —
Jefferies 1981, p. 40	Legumes	20(N,I)	Soil pH, nutrients, water
Ruff A. 1979, pp. 65-8 pp. 103-31	Herbs Herbs	44(N) 256(N)	Ground and light conditions Qualities, suitability, soil type, remarks, etc.
p. 132	Tubers and bulbs	11(N)	Suitability, height, colour, soil
p. 132	Salt plants	12(N)	Suitability, height, colour, etc.
Wilson 1981 p. 142	Plants for and on walls	34(N,I,C)	—
Grasses, rushes and sedges			
Botanical Society of the British Isles 1982	Grasses	11(N)	Soil type

Reference	Groups covered	Number of species listed	Additional notes included
Bradshaw and Chadwick 1980	Grasses	15(N,I)	Fertility, pH, moisture, temperature, cultivars
Countryside Commission 1980, pp. 10-18	Grasses and their varieties	16(N) 60(C)	Soil, climate, management, etc.
Ruff 1979, p. 68 pp. 140-1	Grasses Grasses Rushes Sedges	17(N) 11(N) 3(N) 4(N)	Suitability, qualities, height, competition, propagation, soil type, remarks

Reference	Groups	Mixtures for:
Lists of species mixes		
Bradshaw and Chadwick 1980, p. 193	Grasses and legumes	Hydroseeding on china clay wastes (for pasture)
p. 239	Grasses and legumes	Pasture on pulverised fuel ash
p. 266	Grasses and legumes	Roadsides (British standard and less aggressive mixes for neutral and acid soils)
Countryside Commission 1980, pp. 33-42	Grasses and legumes Different (4-6 species) mixes are given for acid, neutral and calcerous soils	Informal recreation areas Areas of visual importance Grassed car parks Camp sites Picnic areas Under trees Sand dunes Damaged footpaths
Dutton and Bradshaw 1982, p. 45	Grasses	Rapid establishment, hard-wearing, requiring cutting and fertilising Slow establishment, less wear resistant, lower maintenance requirement Acid soils, as a background for wildflower mixes
Moffat 1976	Grasses	Road verges, subsoil sites/mounds Steep slopes on clay subsoil/poor soil Steep slopes on good soil Hard-wearing mix on good soil Heavy and wet soils Light, dry soils Damp areas
Wells *et al.* 1981	Grasses and grassland herbs	Heavy clay soils (grass/short herbs; grass/tall herbs) Chalk/limestone soils (grass/short herbs; grass/ tall herbs) Alluvial soils (grass/short herbs; grass/tall herbs)

Notes: C = cultivated varieties; N = native; I = introduced.
See section 6.1.8 for full references.

Wildflowers

Table 6.3 gives examples of common, easily propagated, native wildflower species and the types of grassland in which they grow. As with Table 6.1, the list is not exhaustive and it is worthwhile referring to wildflower guides, lists of recommendations (such as those listed in Table 6.2) and the advisory literature of reputable seed suppliers (see Appendix 14 for examples). Non-competitive species, with low nutrient requirements are the most suitable, and a wide variety of such species may be found to suit most soil conditions.

Table 6.3 Examples of flowers for grassland

Species	Grassland types						
	AG	AW	CG	CW	DG	NG	SG
Achillea millefolium (yarrow)	*	*	*	*		*	
Agrimonia eupatoria (agrimony)			*	*			
Ajuga reptans (bugle)			*	*		*	*
Allium ursinum (ramsons)			*	*		*	*
Angelica sylvestris (angelica)					*	*	*
Anthriscus sylvestris (cow parsley)			*	*		*	
Arctium minus (burdock)				*		*	*
Artemisia vulgaris (mugwort)				*		*	
Campanula rotundifolia (harebell)	*	*	*	*			
Cardamine pratensis (cuckoo flower)					*	*	
Carduus nutans (musk thistle)			*	*			
Carlina vulgaris (carline thistle)			*	*			
Centaurea nigra (hardheads)	*	*	*	*		*	
C. scabiosa (greater knapweed)			*	*			
Chelidonium majus (greater celandine)						*	
Chrysanthemum leucanthemum (oxeye daisy)			*	*		*	
C. vulgare (tansy)			*	*		*	
Digitalis purpurea (foxglove)	*	*					*
Diplotaxis muralis (wall rocket)				*			
D. tenuifolia (perennial wall rocket)				*			
Dipsacus fullonum (teasel)			*	*		*	
Eupatorium cannabinum (hemp agrimony)			*	*	*		*
Filipendula ulmaria (meadowsweet)			*	*	*	*	
Fumaria officinalis (common fumitory)			*	*		*	
Galium verum (lady's bedstraw)	*	*	*	*		*	
Geranium pratense (meadow cranesbill)			*	*		*	
G. robertianum (herb Robert)	*	*	*	*		*	*
G. sylvaticum (wood cranesbill)	*	*			*	*	*
Geum urbanum (herb Bennett)			*	*		*	*
Heracleum sphondylium (hogweed)			*	*		*	
Hypericum perforatum (perforate St John's wort)	*	*	*	*		*	
Jasione montana (sheep's bit scabious)	*	*					
Knautia arvensis (field scabious)			*	*		*	
Lathyrus pratensis (meadow vetchling)			*	*		*	
Linaria vulgaris (yellow toadflax)			*	*			
Lotus corniculatus (bird's-foot trefoil)	*	*	*	*		*	
L. uliginosus (large bird's-foot)					*	*	
Lychnis flos-cuculi (ragged robin)					*	*	
Malva sylvestris (common mallow)			*	*			

Species	AG	AW	CG	CW	DG	NG	SG
Myosotis arvensis (field forget-me-not)	*	*	*	*		*	
Origanum vulgare (marjoram)			*	*			
Papaver rhoeas (field poppy)						*	
Polygala vulgaris (common milkwort)	*	*				*	
Potentilla erecta (common tormentil)	*	*					
Primula veris (cowslip)	*		*		*	*	*
P. vulgaris (primrose)						*	*
Ranunculus acris (meadow buttercup)	*	*	*	*		*	
R. bulbosus (bulbous buttercup)			*			*	
R. repens (creeping buttercup)	*	*	*		*	*	
R. sceleratus (celery-leaved buttercup)					*	*	
Reseda lutea (wild mignonette)				*			
R. luteola (dyer's rocket)				*			
Rhinanthus minor (yellow rattle)	*	*				*	
Sanguisorba officinalis (great burnet)					*	*	
Silene alba (white campion)				*			
S. dioica (red campion)						*	*
S. vulgaris (bladder campion)				*			
Smyrnium olustratum (Alexanders)			*	*		*	
Succisa pratensis (Devil's bit scabious)						*	
Teucrium scorodonia (wood sage)	*	*				*	*
Verbascum thapsus (mullein)			*	*		*	
Veronica chamaedrys (germander speedwell)			*	*		*	
V. persica (common field speedwell)			*	*		*	
Vicia cracca (tufted vetch)			*	*		*	
V. sepium (bush vetch)			*	*		*	*
Viola odorata (sweet violet)			*	*		*	*
V. riviniana (common dog violet)	*	*	*	*		*	*
V. tricolor (wild pansy)			*	*		*	

Key

AG = acid grassland
AW = acid wasteland
CG = calcareous grassland
CW = calcareous wasteland
DG = damp grassland
NG = neutral grassland
SG = shaded grassland

Source: Philip Masters, (unpublished) personal communication.

6.1.3 Sources of seed

There are two basic options: a group may collect seed of common local species, or seed may be bought from commercial suppliers.

Seed collection

One advantage of collecting seed from locally common plants is that the plants will probably be adapted to local soils and climatic conditions, as well as representative of local vegetation types. The examples in Table 6.3 are species with large or easily collectable seed heads.

Table 4.2 lists 61 specially protected wild plants. These are so rare that picking them, or even collecting their seed, has been made an offence, punishable on conviction by a fine not exceeding £1,000.

The Nature Conservancy Council have developed the following guidelines for selecting species for seed collection (see Wells *et al.* 1981).

— The species should be regular members of the grassland community.
— They should not be rare.
— They should be relatively abundant in a variety of grasslands and preferably have a wide distribution in the British Isles.
— They should be perennial, preferably long-lived and with an effective means of vegetative spread.
— A high proportion of the species used should have colourful flowers, and these should be attractive to insects.
— Highly competitive and invasive species, known to form single-species stands in the wild, should be avoided, e.g. tor-grass (*Brachypodium pinnatum*).
— The seed should have a high percentage germination over a range of temperatures and should not have dormancy problems or special requirements.

Table 6.4 lists the months in which Wells *et al.* (1981) were able to collect ripe seed from wild populations of 116 grassland species in central England. The table suggests that August and September are the best months to collect seed. However, ripening periods for most species last only a few days.

Table 6.4 Months in which ripe seed is available from wild populations of 116 grassland species in Central England

MAY

Taraxacum officinale

JUNE

Taraxacum officinale

JULY

Anthriscus sylvestris	*Hordeum secalinum*
Arrhenatherum elatius	*Hypochoeris radicata*
Briza media	*Leontodon hispidus*
Bromus erectus	*Luzula campestris*
B. racemosus	*Lychnis flos-cuculi*
Carex flacca	*Medicago lupulina*
C. hirta	*Plantago lanceolata*
Chrysanthemum leucanthemum	*Polygala calcarea*
Cynosurus cristatus	*Ranunculus bulbosus*
Dactylis glomerata	*Rhinanthus minor*
Deschampsia cespitosa	*Rumex acetosa*
Euphrasia nemorosa	*Sanguisorba officinalis*
Festuca arundinacea	*Senecio integrifolius*
Fritillaria meleagris	*Taraxacum officinale*
Helianthemum chamaecistus	*Tragopogon pratensis*
Hieracium pilosella	*Trisetum flavescens*
Holcus lanatus	*Viola hirta*

AUGUST

Agrostis stolonifera
Alopecurus pratensis
Anthyllis vulneraria
Briza media
Bromus erectus
Carex flacca
C. hirta
C. spicata
Centauria nigra
C. scabiosa
Centaurium erythraea
Cerastium holosteoides
Cirsium acaule
Conopodium majus
Crepis capillaris
Dactylis glomerata
Filipendula vulgaris
Gentianella amarella
Geranium dissectum
G. pratense
Helianthemum chamaecistus
Helictrotrichon pratense
Heracleum sphondylium
Holcus lanatus
Hordeum secalinum
Knautia arvensis
Koeleria cristata
Lathyrus pratensis
Leontodon hispidus
Lotus corniculatus
Luzula campestris
Lychnis flos-cuculi

Medicago lupulina
M. sativa
Melandrium album
Melilotus altissima
Onobrychis viciifolia
Ononis spinosa
Phalaris arundinacea
Picris hieracioides
Plantago lanceolata
P. media
Poterium sanguisorba
Primula veris
Prunella vulgaris
Ranunculus bulbosus
Rhinanthus minor
Rumex acetosa
Sanguisorba officinalis
Scabiosa columbaria
Sieglingia decumbens
Stellaria graminea
Succisa pratensis
Thymus drucei
T. pulegioides
Tragopogon pratensis
Trifolium campestre
T. pratense
Trisetum flavescens
Veronica chamaedrys
V. officinalis
Vicia angustifolia
V. cracca
Viola hirta

SEPTEMBER

Agrimonia eupatoria
Agropyron repens
Angelica sylvestris
Anthoxanthum odoratum
Asperula cynanchia
Astralagus danicus
Betonica officinalis
Blackstonia perfoliata
Campanula glomerata
C. rotundifolia
Carlina vulgaris
Centaurea scabiosa
Cirsium acaule
Clinopodium vulgare
Crepis capillaris
Daucus carota
Festuca rubra
Filipendula vulgaris
Galium verum
Gentianella amarella
Heracleum sphondylium
Hippocrepis comosa

Leontodon autumnalis
L. hispidus
Linum catharticum
Lotus corniculatus
L. uliginosus
Molinia caerulea
Onobrychis viciifolia
Ononis spinosa
Pastinaca sativa
Phleum pratense
Picris hieracioides
Pimpinella saxifraga
Plantago lanceolata
P. media
Poterium sanguisorba
Primula veris
Prunella vulgaris
Ranunculus acris
Reseda lutea
R. luteola
Sanguisorba officinalis
Scabiosa columbaria

Serratula tintoria
Sieglingia decumbens
Silaum silaus
Stellaria graminea
Succisa pratensis

Thymus pulegioides
Tragopogon pratensis
Trifolium pratense
Vicia hirsuta

OCTOBER

Achillea millefolium
A. ptarmica
Carlina vulgaris
Daucus carota
Galium verum
Gentianella amarella
Leontodon autumnalis
Lotus uliginosus

Pimpinella saxifraga
Potentilla erecta
Poterium sanguisorba
Ranunculus acris
Scabiosa columbaria
Silaum silaus
Succisa pratensis

NOVEMBER

Galium verum

Pimpinella saxifraga

Source: Wells *et al.* (1981).

In a single meadow, individual plants of the same species will ripen on different days and the seeds on each plant will not necessarily all be ripe at the same time.

The best time to collect seeds is just before they fall from the parent plant. If collected too early, the seeds may not be viable (i.e. will not have the energy to germinate) or may even become dormant. If the collectors get to the plants too late, the seed may have already fallen.

This variation in ripening times presents collectors with a dilemma. One way to avoid wasting time and effort on badly-timed collecting expeditions is to plan ahead, as in the following examples:

— During spring and early summer, examine local areas of vegetation as often as possible and identify any substantial populations of plants suitable for seed collection later in the year.
— Draw up a list of these plants and their locations.
— By reference to wildflower books (e.g. Phillips 1977 and Table 6.4 in this section) find out when each species finishes flowering and starts to produce seed. (Note: flowering and seeding times also vary across the country and from year to year.)
— Construct a harvesting calendar, for all the locations, with each species and its location marked, e.g.

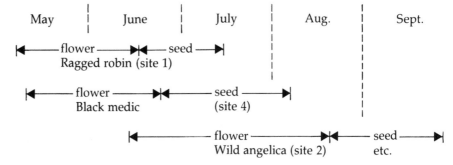

— Using the calendar as a guide, revisit the plants early at the onset of seeding, keeping an eye on them until their periods of maximum ripeness, when collecting will be most successful.
— If possible, check the proposed harvesting timetable with, for example, local naturalists, the County Trust for Nature Conservation or the nearest branch of the Nature Conservancy Council, as they may have constructive advice to offer.

The alternative to forward planning is to gather together as many willing volunteers as possible on a dry day in July, August or September and take 'pot luck' on what will be found.

The following are basic rules of seed collection in the field:

— Seek the permission of the land owner before collecting.
— Try to collect dry seed and do not use containers, such as plastic bags, which will cause the seeds to 'sweat'. Boxes, trays, bottles, hessian or stout paper bags are more suitable. (If wet seed is collected, it should be spread to dry as soon as possible; damp seed may become mouldy or may germinate prematurely.)
— Even in areas where most of the plants are full of ripe seed, avoid collecting more than one-fifth of the total present for any one species. In this way, there is little likelihood of harming that species' survival in the next growing season.
— Try wherever possible to shake seeds from the plants into the collecting containers. This increases the proportion of fully-ripe seed collected, avoids damaging the plants and allows later collections to be made. Wells *et al.* (1981) give further recommendations for particular species.
— Avoid collecting seeds of different species in the same container.
— Keep a record of the collector's name, those species collected, where, when and in what quantities. Copies of such records (along with details of where the seed is to be used) should be sent to the Regional Data Bank. This will either be a local museum natural history section, or a local regional recorder for the Biological Records Centre (see Appendix 15 for the BRC address).

This method of collecting seed from individual plants by hand is time-consuming, but it does allow maximum control over species choice. Hand collection is ideal for small-scale projects and your group may choose exactly what is to be planted out, gradually building up a stock of small amounts of seed for a wide variety of species. Another possibility is to pick selectively at different times during the flowering season. It may be possible to select different strains with different flowering periods. The following are three alternative methods to collecting wildflower seed by hand:

Hay bales from species-rich meadows will contain mixtures of seeds from the species growing there, although some will have been lost during bailing and handling.

Mechanical cutting   Various small mechanical mowers with grass boxes are currently available, e.g. Flymo, Hayter, Suffolk (see Appendix 14 for addresses). These cut, and collect, cuttings *and seed* at the same time. It may be possible to hire or borrow such a machine and harvest seeds wholesale from a local site. Cutting a species-rich meadow in this way (after flowering) and removing the cuttings will also benefit the meadow itself. Section 7.3.2 discusses this in more detail.

The chopped hay or cuttings may then be spread over the prepared seeding area and the cuttings will act as a mulch while the seeds germinate.

Vacuum cleaners   It may be worthwhile experimenting with vacuum cleaners as a method of wholesale collection of ripe seed, e.g. Allen garden sweepers, Bob Andrews Ltd, Bartrop Ltd and Helpmate (see Appendix 14 for addresses). Various researchers have found this method successful (e.g. Prof. A. Bradshaw used an industrial vacuum cleaner to collect large quantities of seed from ripe heather). A car vacuum cleaner running off a battery may be an ideal alternative for seed collection on a smaller scale.

These mechanical methods may make it possible to collect more seed than could be collected by hand, but they do lower the degree of control over species choice. If, for example, the collection area contains odd plants of vigorous, undesirable species, it will be difficult to avoid their seeds being collected along with seeds of the other, more desirable species present.

Seed handling and storage

As soon as possible after collection, harvested plant material should be spread out thinly on trays, or hung in coarse hessian (or other fabric) bags, to dry slowly. Drying areas are best kept warm and well ventilated. Coarse plant material should be removed from the seeds, as far as possible, to allow them to dry naturally, and to remove harmful insect pests. Seeds of 'squashy' fruits should be cleaned from the fruit as quickly as possible.

Seed generally requires around 2-4 weeks to dry properly. Once dry, seed may be sealed in airtight containers (e.g. screw-top bottles) and stored for long periods in a refrigerator at around 2°C. If no such equipment is available, most seeds will survive quite adequately, just kept cool and dry, for example in a bedroom drawer. Containers should be clearly labelled as follows:

— name of species;
— collection location (and the habitat from which it came);
— collection date;
— collector's name.

This will avoid unnecessary mistakes when choosing which seed to sow and when. These methods should enable most seeds to be stored for roughly five years. Wells *et al.* (1981) give further recommendations for particular species.

Final points to remember concerning moisture and temperature of stored seed:

— Too rapid drying can cause the seed's outer layer to shrink and become impervious to water.
— Storage at temperatures of 0°C or below may cause ice crystals to form inside the seeds. This will destroy seed tissue, effectively 'killing' the seed.

For those interested in long-term seed storage, further sources of information on storage include the Royal Botanic Gardens, Kew Seed Bank (Wakehurst Place) and the University Botanic Garden, Cambridge (see Appendix 15 for addresses).

Seed viability

The ability of seeds to germinate can be an extremely important factor, worth investigating once they have been collected. It can be disheartening to collect and store seed, only to find that it fails to germinate when sown. Research into the viability of the many species of wildflower seed is still limited (references on the subject include Wells *et al.* (1981), Gorer (1978), Grime *et al.* (1981) and Roberts (1972)). However, simple tests may be carried out in the home. For example, seeds are placed on moist tissue paper in dishes or jam jars with lids. If the paper is kept moist, at room temperature, in good light conditions, most seeds should germinate within a month. To estimate the percentage germination a large number of seeds should be used, for example, for each species, five jars/dishes with 20 seeds in each. When the seeds germinate, root tips and/or shoot tips can be seen protruding through the seed coats. Continually check the jars/dishes every few days either for a set period of time (e.g. 1-2 months) or until the seeds have all germinated. In this way, a lot can be learned about how the seeds may behave when sown, and how valuable the species is for future use.

There are many reasons, apart from seed death, which may cause seed germination to be poor. The two most common reasons are hard seed coats and cold requirements. Problems with hard seed coats can be overcome by rubbing seeds between sheets of coarse sand paper. Alternatively, seeds may be put in a jar or tin, lined with sand paper and shaken for 5-10 minutes (seed scarification). Most legume seeds require this treatment. Seeds with cold requirements can be made to germinate after refrigeration (6 weeks at 1-4°C) or by sowing in autumn, to allow winter frosts to break their dormancy. Refrigeration can be very useful if your group wishes to delay sowing species with cold requirements and add them to a spring-sown species mixture. Table 6.5 lists examples.

Table 6.5 Species whose seeds may require special treatment before sowing

(a) Germination enhanced by scarification prior to sowing

Anthyllis vulneraria	kidney vetch
Erodium cicutarium	common storksbill
Geranium spp.	cranesbills, storksbills
Helianthemum nummularium	common rockrose
Hippocrepis comosa	horse shoe vetch
Lathyrus spp.	vetchlings, everlasting peas
Lotus spp.	trefoils
Medicago lupulina	black medick
Melilotus spp.	melilots
Onobrychis viciifolia	sainfoin
Sanguisorba minor	salad burnet
Sarothamnus scoparius	broom
Trifolium spp.	clovers
Vicia spp.	vetches

(b) Germination enhanced by cold treatment (6 weeks at 0-4°C) or by sowing in autumn

Campanula glomerata	clustered bellflower
Daucus carota	wild carrot
Pimpinella saxifraga	burnet saxifrage
Primula veris	cowslip
Reseda luteola	dyer's rocket, weld
Sanguisorba officinalis	great burnet

(c) Germination enhanced by moist storage at 5°C (numbers in parentheses indicate duration of treatment in months)

Aegopodium podagraria (12)	ground elder
Agrimonia eupatoria (3)	common agrimony
Alchemilla vestita (19)	Alpine lady's mantle
Anagallis arvensis (13)	scarlet pimpernel
Angelica sylvestris (3)	field angelica
Anthriscus sylvestris (3)	cow parsley
Arum maculatum (6)	cuckoo pint
Caltha palustris (3)	marsh marigold
Capsella bursa-pastoris (10)	shepherd's purse
Campanula latifolia (1)	large campanula
Carex laevigata (5)	smooth sedge
C. nigra (1)	common sedge
C. panicea (18)	carnation grass
Chaenorrhinum minus (1)	small toadflax
Chelidonium majus (3)	greater celandine
Conopodium majus (9)	pignut
Eleocharis palustris (19)	common spike-rush
Galium aparine (1)	goosegrass
Impatiens parviflora (4)	small balsam
Lamiastrum galeobdolon (6)	yellow archangel
Linum catharticum (2)	purging flax
Lonicera periclymenum (4)	honeysuckle
Lycopus europaeus (9)	gipsy-wort
Mentha aquatica (1)	water mint
M. arvensis (18)	corn mint
Myrrhis odorata (1)	sweet cicely
Odontites verna (3)	red rattle
Papaver dubium (2)	long-headed poppy
P. rhoeas (3)	field poppy
Pimpinella major (11)	greater burnet saxifrage
P. saxifraga (2)	burnet saxifrage
Pinguicula vulgaris (2)	common butterwort
Primula veris (6)	cowslip
Rhinanthus minor (3)	yellow rattle
Saponaria officinalis (2)	soapwort
Silaum silaus (10)	pepper saxifrage
Smyrnium olustratum (11)	Alexanders
Solanum dulcamara (6)	woody nightshade
Sparganium emersum (1)	unbranched bur-reed
Stachys sylvatica (8)	hedge woundwort
Torilis japonica (8)	upright hedge parsley
Trollius europaeus (8)	globe flower
Verbena officinalis (3)	vervain
Viola arvensis (3)	field pansy
V. hirta (14)	hairy violet
V. lutea (5)	mountain pansy
V. palustris (3)	marsh violet
V. riviniana (3)	common violet

Source: Wells *et al.* (1981); Grimes *et al.* (1981).

Buying seed

The commercial availability of wildflower seed continues to increase. More growers are stocking seeds, either as single species, or in specially-prepared mixes for different site conditions. (Appendix 6 lists some examples from British Seed Houses and John Chambers seed suppliers, see Appendix 14 for addresses.) Many growers are now improving the quality of their supplies, for example by using Nature Conservancy Council recommendations when preparing their wildflower seed mixes.

Appendix 14 lists examples of reputable firms selling wildflower seeds. The seed suppliers are split into those providing seeds of *named* origin, either native to Britain or foreign; and those providing seed of *un-named* origin, sometimes foreign.

This can be very important, depending upon the aims of the group buying the seed. If seeds are to be used to create areas of vegetation for nature conservation, then foreign varieties of native species are undesirable. Such aliens commonly have different growth types and behave differently from native varieties. However, they can hybridise. Hybrids may spread through the vegetation, disrupting its natural characteristics and destroying any natural balance your group may be trying to achieve. Seeds of the same species from another country can produce plants with unexpected vigour, competitiveness, different growth form, shade tolerance, etc. If in any doubt whether such hybridisation is undesirable on your site, the safest option is to choose seed which is purely of British origin. It will be too late to do anything about it once the seed is planted and hybrids have appeared in the newly-created vegetation.

In general, it is possible to buy the following:

— Individual species of grasses and wildflowers. Buying a selection of individual species allows complete freedom of plant choice to suit the planting area. Grass seed is much cheaper than wildflower seed (prices in 1985 averaged around £2-3 per kg).
— Specially-prepared seed mixtures of only grasses, wildflowers, or the two combined (e.g. Appendix 6). It is not generally possible for suppliers to alter these mixtures to suit the buyer's needs, for example, when the mix doesn't quite suit the conditions of the area to be planted, or if the buyer wishes undesirable alien species to be omitted from a mixture. It is, therefore, extremely important to check the source of seed for each species in a mixture and to ensure that the latter fits planting site requirements before buying.
— Nurse species. Westerwolds rye grass (*Lolium multiflorum*) is a nurse species, available from many of the suppliers in Appendix 14. It is an annual grass which if sown in spring with a seed mixture, will germinate quickly and provide an open but protective canopy for the other species within weeks of sowing. The rye grass is then mown down to 8-10 cm within ten weeks of spring sowing, or before growth exceeds 25 cm. This mowing prevents the rye grass from producing seed and, by the next season (by virtue of its being an annual), it should have disappeared from the sward. Wells *et al.* (1981) recommend a sowing rate for the rye grass of 46 kg per ha or less. *Note*: A word of caution. Some practitioners advise against the use of Westerwolds because of the risks involved, should you fail to mow it at the right time. By allowing it to set seed, you may find it more difficult to eradicate from the sward. When considering buying seed, it is worthwhile writing to as many suppliers as possible and comparing the costs and qualities of mixes they have to offer, or phoning the companies and talking to a representative.

Seed merchants, such as those listed in Appendix 14, often publish useful advisory literature with their wildflower seed catalogues. These can cover ground preparation, seed storage, germination, propagation, sowing and aftercare.

Depending on a group's finances, and the suitability of available mixes, the following options are available (in order of increasing expense):

— a cheap grass mix and locally-collected wildflower seed;
— grass mix and nurse species and locally-collected wildflower seed;
— grass mix and wildflower mix*;
— grass mix and nurse species and wildflower mix*.

Locally-collected grass seed is rarely worth the trouble. In many cases, commercial seed is so cheap that local collection should not be necessary. It may be better to concentrate volunteer effort on wildflower seed collection.

When ordering seed mixes, write on the order form: 'no substitutions will be accepted without prior notification.' Otherwise, suppliers may sometimes substitute one species for another, without telling you, if it is out of stock.

On large-scale seeding projects (e.g. over 2 ha) requiring quantities of seed in the region of 50 kg or over (for example, local authority plantings, etc.), suppliers will provide mixes tailored to customer requirements. However, their stocks of wildflower seeds are limited when dealing in such quantities. Local authorities and professional landscape designers commonly order seed by means of a 'tender document' with a format similar to the following (the letters A, B, etc. to be replaced by the names of the chosen varieties):

Provide a seeds mixture composed by weight of:
x% red fescue: certified seed of A, B or C
y% smooth meadow grass: certified seed of D, E or F, etc.

(The following paragraph may also be included to ensure quality and reliability.)

The seed shall be thoroughly mixed including a seed dressing as appropriate and delivered in 50 kg (or as required) units. In addition to a percentage analysis of the mixture as a whole, a dated seed test analysis from an Official Seed Testing Station giving the percentage purity and germination and the corresponding certification number for each constituent of the mixture shall accompany each delivery.

6.1.4 Sowing the seed

Recommended sowing periods vary throughout Great Britain. The following are rough guidelines for different regions in the British Isles:

South West: March-May and Sept.-Dec.
South East: Sept.-Nov.
West of Pennines and North West: July-Nov. and April
East of Pennines and North East: July-Nov.

Ideally, the sowing area should have been prepared and left to settle for sowing (autumn preparation for spring sowing, or spring/summer preparation for late summer/autumn sowing; see section 6.1.1 for ground preparation.) Just before sowing, the area should be cleared of weeds, lightly raked and rolled

---

*In order to save money on these two options, wildflower mixes may be bought and sown in smaller quantities that those recommended by the supplier, and supplemented in the mix by locally-collected seed.

until a fine, firm, even tilth is achieved. Seed may be mixed with an equal quantity of sand, sawdust or peat to ensure a more even distribution, and to make it easier to see where the seed has fallen.

To ensure an even distribution of each species, it is important to keep the seeds well mixed in their container, as smaller seeds will tend to accumulate at the bottom unless the mix is periodically 'stirred up.'

Wells *et al.* (1981) and the literature of seed suppliers give useful recommendations for sowing rates, generally measured in kg of seed per ha.

On smaller sites, the seed is generally spread by hand. After sowing, it is important to incorporate the seed into the top few cm of the soil by raking or harrowing. Hand-raking and stone picking involve slight trampling which helps seeds to make contact with the soil. On light soils, a light roller can perform the same function and aid germination. For successful germination, the seeded area needs to be kept moist, but well drained. If the area becomes too dry, or too waterlogged, establishment will be poor (see Figure 6.1).

If sowing to create species-rich grassland, it is advisable to sow wildflower seed together with the grass seed. Wildflower seed sown after grass has established will be less successful.

6.1.5 Immediate after-care

The sown area should be carefully watched during the weeks following sowing, both to ensure that the seedbed doesn't dry out and to note the growth of any undesirable perennial 'weeds'. As far as possible, any weeds, such as *Sinapsis arvensis* (charlock), should be removed by hand weeding, or spot application of a weedkiller, e.g. glyphosate (see Appendix 12 for further discussion on the use of herbicides). After around 6-8 weeks, the vegetation should be made up of:

— the nurse crop (if sown) or weeds, 10-20 cm tall;
— sown grasses, 4-8 cm tall;
— broad-leaved flowering plant seedlings, less than 2 cm tall.

At this stage, the area should be cut with a rotary mower or Allen scythe at a height of about 8-10 cm, and again, about every two months for the first growing season. Cuttings should be removed each time. Cutting should remove the nurse crop (if sown), reduce competition from weeds and allow species-rich grassland to establish, ready for the next growing season (see Chapter 7 for further details of long-term management).

6.1.6 Propagation of wild plants

A useful way of multiplying quantities of locally-collected seed is to set up a wildflower nursery. Growing your own seed also lessens the need to collect excessive amounts from local wild populations.

The nursery may be either indoor or outdoor. The literature on cultivating wildflowers in this way is very limited and there is ample scope for experimentation. Examples of groups already running their own wildflower nurseries include the Urban Wildlife Group in Birmingham, Landlife (formerly the Rural Preservation Association) in Liverpool and Tower Hamlets Environment Trust in London (see Appendix 15 for addresses).

Outdoor seedbeds

For successful propagation the seedbed should be cultivated to a fine tilth and

Figure 6.1 Ground preparation and sowing seed

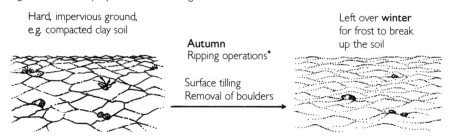

Hard, impervious ground,
e.g. compacted clay soil

Autumn
Ripping operations*

Surface tilling
Removal of boulders

Left over **winter**
for frost to break
up the soil

*Deep ripping should not be necessary, and may even be undesirable, as it may encourage deep root penetration and more vigorous growth

Spring

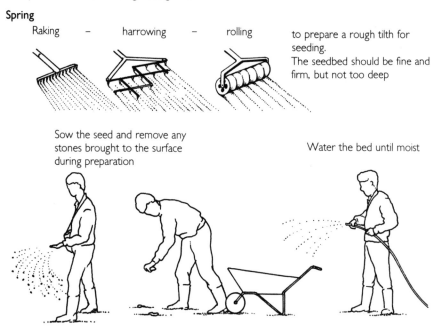

Raking – harrowing – rolling

to prepare a rough tilth for seeding.
The seedbed should be fine and firm, but not too deep

Sow the seed and remove any stones brought to the surface during preparation

Water the bed until moist

To hand-sow seed evenly, make two passes over the area, the second at right angles to the first

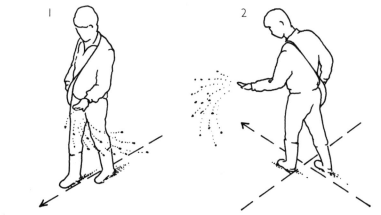

1

2

If the area begins to dry out, water periodically to keep soil moist and to aid germination

perennial weeds should be eliminated, e.g. using glyphosate 2-4 weeks before cultivation (see Appendix 12 for recommendations for herbicide use). Seeds are sown in rows wide enough apart for access and easy inter-row weeding. Sow by hand into shallow furrows and gently spread a thin layer of soil over the seed. Also add water to ensure good contact between seed and soil.

In their experiments using these methods, Wells *et al.* (1981) found that most seeds sown in autumn germinated adequately throughout winter. Seeds requiring cold treatment germinated in the following spring. During the following season, very few flowers/seeds were produced; plants put on a lot of vegetative growth and required thinning. Seed from all species was generally available two years after sowing.

Transplanting

This is a means of speeding up the growth of plants and the production of seeds. One method is to sow seeds in trays of sterilised seed compost in a glasshouse kept at 15°C, in January and February. The trays are kept moist and in March and April, the seedlings are pricked out into peat pots filled with John Innes No. 1 commercial compost. Yoghurt cartons or plastic cups will do, as long as the plastic is not transparent and drainage holes are made in the bottom of each pot. As the plants grow, they are gradually hardened off and planted out in early May. A cheaper alternative is to sow seed as above, but to sow in April without heat, under glass, for example using a cold frame. Many species grown in this way will produce flowers and seeds in the same year, and subsequent seed production far exceeds that for plants growing in the wild.

6.1.7 Turf transplants

Gilbert (1982) experimented with this technique as an alternative to sowing wildflower seeds. Old pieces of 5-10 cm-thick turf of various sizes were successfully transplanted from a calcareous grassland onto disused limestone workings. The landscape team of the Warrington and Runcorn Development Corporation had similar successes (see Tregay and Gustavsson 1983). The benefits of such an approach in creating species-rich grassland may be summarised as follows:

— Once transplanted, the turves act as seed sources for the surrounding area, as well as centres from which species in the turf can spread out vegetatively.
— The contrast between the dense turf growth and the openness of the surrounding vegetation during the years after transplanting adds to the diversity of the grassland area.
— Species suited to the site, but with seed that is either very difficult to collect or to germinate, may be introduced easily and should be able to establish.
— Along with the turf plant species, animals (invertebrates) common to the particular grassland type are introduced into the area, contributing to the natural system by, for example, enhancing soil development and humus production.

Transplanting turf would be more expensive than sowing wildflower seed on a large scale, but could be extremely useful in the creation of semi-natural grassland habitats on a small scale. Turves placed on slopes may cause problems; for example, if rainfall run-off washes around them, erosion may occur.

It is important to obtain the land-owner's permission when digging up turves; not doing so constitutes an offence under the 1981 Wildlife and Countryside Act.

Wathern and Gilbert's experiments (1978) also suggested that topsoil rich in the seeds of desirable species, such as soil from old meadows and steep unmown grass banks, may be used to enrich a newly-created grassland site. It has already been suggested earlier in this section (6.1.1) that nutrient-rich topsoil can promote the growth of undesirable vigorous species. Any topsoil used as a source of desirable seeds should, therefore, be spread sparingly. If the ground onto which the seed-rich topsoil is scattered is low in nutrients, there should be very few problems with vigorous weeds. The thin layer of topsoil should have little effect on ground conditions and should merely act as a germinating medium for the seeds it contains.

6.1.8 References

Agate, E. (1983) *Footpaths: A practical conservation handbook,* British Trust for Conservation Volunteers

Botanical Society of the British Isles (1982) *Growing Wild Flowers from Seed,* available from BSBI

Bradshaw, A.D. and Chadwick, M.J. (1980) *The Restoration of Land,* Blackwell Scientific, Studies in Ecology, Vol. 6

Corder, M. and Brooker, R. (1981) *Natural Economy. An Ecological Approach to Planting and Management Techniques in Urban Areas,* Kirklees Metropolitan Council

Countryside Commission (1980) *Grassland Establishment in Countryside Recreation Areas,* Advisory Series No. 13

Duffey, E. *et al.* (1974) *Grassland Ecology and Wildlife Management,* Chapman & Hall, London

Dutton, R.A. and Bradshaw, A.D. (1982) *Land Reclamation in Cities,* HMSO, London

Fitter, R. and Fitter, A. (1984) *Guide to the Grasses, Sedges, Rushes and Ferns of Britain and Northern Europe,* Collins

Gilbert, O.L. (1982) 'Turf transplants increase species diversity', *Landscape Design,* November, p. 37

Gorer, R. (1978) *Growing Plants from Seed,* Faber & Faber, London

Grime, J.P., Mason, G., Curtis, A.V., Rodman, J., Band, S.R., Mowforth, M.A.G., Neal, A.M. and Shaw, S. (1981), 'A comparative study of germination characteristics in a local flora', *Journal of Ecology,* **69**:1017-59

Hubbard, C.E. (1968) *Grasses* (2nd edn), Penguin

Jefferies, R.A. (1981) 'Legumes for the reclamation of derelict and disturbed land', *Landscape Design,* May, pp. 39-41

Johnsons Seeds (1980) *Turfgrass Seeds Handbook,* W.W. Johnson and Son Ltd

Moffatt, J.D. (1976) 'Grass seed mixes for different situations and functions (non-toxic sites)', Ecological Information paper, Warrington and Runcorn Development Corporation

Phillips, R. (1977) *Wildflowers of Britain,* Pan

Roberts, E.G. (ed.) (1972) *Viability of Seeds,* Chapman & Hall, London

Robinson, S. (1982) *Grassing of Temporary Vacant Sites,* Workshop Report No. 1, National Turfgrass Council

Ruff, A.R. (1979) *Holland and the Ecological Landscape,* Deanwater Press

Tregay, R. and Gustavsson, R. (1983) *Oakwood's New Landscape. Designing for Nature in the Residential Environment,* Warrington and Runcorn Development Corporation

Wathern, P. and Gilbert, O.L. (1978) 'Artificial diversification of grassland with native herbs', *Journal of Environmental Management*, **7**:29-42

Wells, T., Bell, S. and Frost, A. (1981) *Creating Attractive Grasslands using Native Plant Species*, Nature Conservancy Council

Wilson, R. (1981) *The Back Garden Wildlife Sanctuary Book*, Penguin

6.1.9 Useful organisations (see Appendix 15 for addresses)

Biological Records Centre (maintain records of seed collections)
Ecological Parks Trust
Landlife (formerly Rural Preservation Association) (wildflower nursery)
Royal Botanic Gardens, Kew Seed Bank (seed storage)
Tower Hamlets Environment Trust (THET) (wildflower nursery)
University Botanic Garden, Cambridge (seed storage)
University of Sheffield, NERC Unit of Comparative Plant Ecology
Urban Wildlife Group (wildflower nursery)

6.2 Scrub/woodland

Section 5.1.2 illustrates how herbs and grassland form part of our natural vegetation and how, by the process of natural succession, such vegetation is gradually replaced by invading woody (shrub and tree) species to produce scrub, and eventually woodland. Natural areas of scrub in Great Britain may be defined as vegetation where the cover by woody species (mainly shrubs) exceeds that of herbs and grasses (the shrubs and trees being less than 7 m high). The scrub develops into woodland as certain tree species exceed 7 m and form a canopy over the shrubs and herbs (see figure 6.2(A)). These definitions depend somewhat on the species. For example, an area of hawthorn bushes over 8 m tall would still often be classed as scrub and an area of young oak trees averaging 4 m in height may be classed as woodland. Figure 6.2(B) (from Duffey *et al.* 1974) gives simplified examples of common pathways of scrub successions in this country.

The aim in woodland habitat creation is to manipulate this natural process of succession rather than waiting the many years it may take for shrubs and trees to invade naturally. It is possible to speed up the process by planting natural mixes of tree and shrub species to provide the following:

— Increased natural and structural diversity. Figure 6.2(A) illustrates simply how the structural diversity of vegetation increases during natural succession to woodland.
— Valuable cover for wildlife. Scrub/woodland provides nesting cover for birds and protection for many other animals including species such as butterflies and other insects which venture out into grassland/herb habitats to feed on leaves, nectar and pollen, etc.
— An educational resource. Areas of scrub and woodland may be provided to illustrate the effects of succession and lack of management on natural plant communities, and to provide widely ranging types of plant and animal communities for study.
— Physical screening. Scrub, and to a greater extent, woodland, can provide barriers or filters against noise, wind dust and airborne pollutants. Thickets or hedges of scrub may be used to hide ugly landscape features and to channel public movement and/or protect fragile areas of vegetation.

Figure 6.2 (A) Natural succession to woodland — the increase in structural diversity

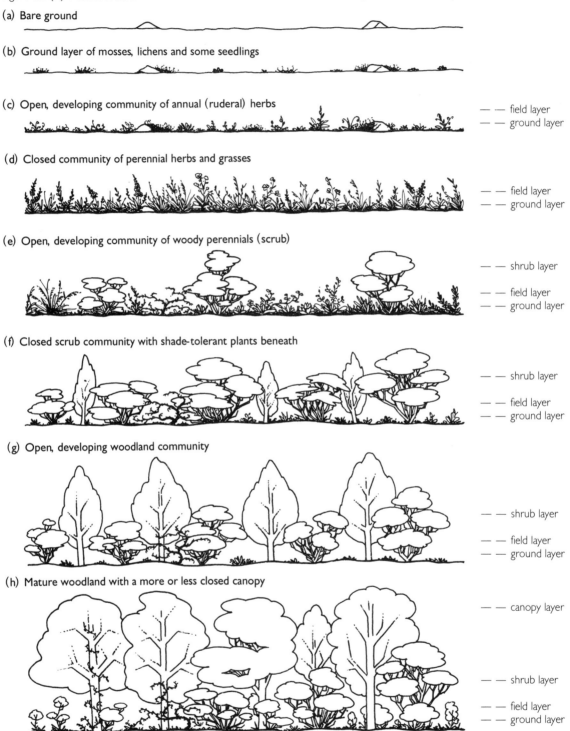

(a) Bare ground

(b) Ground layer of mosses, lichens and some seedlings

(c) Open, developing community of annual (ruderal) herbs

— — field layer
— — ground layer

(d) Closed community of perennial herbs and grasses

— — field layer
— — ground layer

(e) Open, developing community of woody perennials (scrub)

— — shrub layer

— — field layer
— — ground layer

(f) Closed scrub community with shade-tolerant plants beneath

— — shrub layer

— — field layer
— — ground layer

(g) Open, developing woodland community

— — shrub layer

— — field layer
— — ground layer

(h) Mature woodland with a more or less closed canopy

— — canopy layer

— — shrub layer

— — field layer
— — ground layer

The heights of layers are generally: ground layer, up to 0.1m; field layer up to 2m; shrub layer up to 5m; and canopy layer up to 15m or more

Figure 6.2(B) Possible pathways of scrub–woodland succession

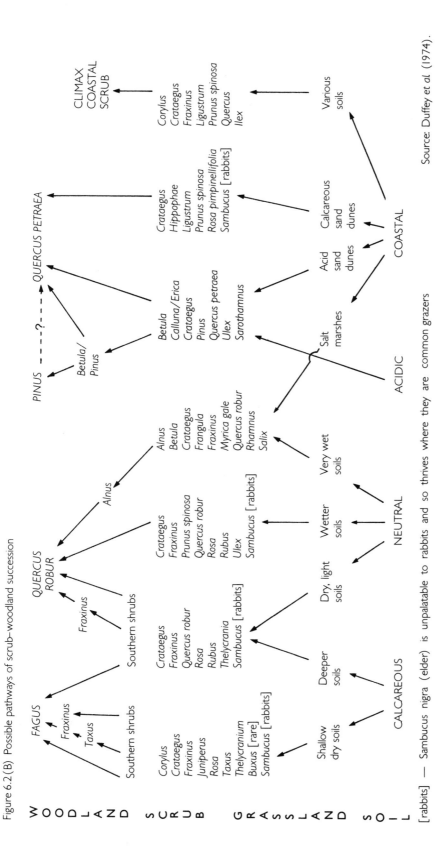

Source: *Duffey et al.* (1974).

[rabbits] — *Sambucus nigra* (elder) is unpalatable to rabbits and so thrives where they are common grazers

When planning the creation of scrub or woodland, your group must consider the time needed for such habitats to mature and the feasibility of managing them while they do so. Rich scrub habitats may be developed over a few years (e.g. 5-6), but true woodland takes many years to begin to mature (at least 30). Therefore, before implementing a planting scheme, your group should have a legal right to use the site for a satisfactory length of time and should be fairly sure that the manpower will be available to carry out any necessary management activities (see section 7.4).

The following are extremely valuable comprehensive sources of information on shrubs, trees and their management: Beckett and Beckett (1979); Brooks (1980); Edlin (1975); Evans (1984).

6.2.1 Ground preparation

Shrubs and trees generally need well-drained, well-aerated, moderately fertile soil if planting is to be successful. When creating scrub/woodland habitat, whole areas of ground may be prepared, or individual pits for each plant.

Opinions differ on the advisability of using either of these two approaches. Ploughing and rotavating whole areas destroys the soil profile and any vegetation cover present, but produces conditions free of weed competition for 2-3 years. Leaving the soil profile intact and inserting individual plants may be desirable, particularly in grassland where the grass may stop competitive weeds from competing with the young trees and shrubs, or where the grassland/herb species themselves need to be conserved. In certain situations, however, vigorous grass growth can cause young trees to suffer quite severely from competition for light and nutrients.

Ploughed or rotavated plantations are sometimes undersown with low-maintenance, slow-growing grass mixtures which are said to have several effects:

— the grass keeps down the water loss during periods of drought;
— on shales or rubble, the surface heating and dryness (a common problem on urban sites) which often kills young trees and shrubs, is reduced;
— small trees and shrubs are less obvious to vandals.

Strongly-growing perennial herbs, legumes and grasses compete with and sometimes kill newly planted trees and shrubs. If planting is to be successful, it may be necessary to maintain an area 0.6-1 m square around the new plantings clear of such vegetation. This is often done by scraping the area clear with a mattock (screefing), or by laying mulch mats around the tree bases (e.g. black polythene). This and other management requirements should be borne in mind when deciding how large an area to plant (see section 7.4) for further details of management requirements).

Planting beds

Planting beds may be prepared if an instant community of young trees and shrubs is required. For ease of maintenance, an area 2.5-6 m wide is recommended. The area is dug over or rotated to a depth of about 230 mm. To aid drainage and to make a bed more effective, it may be cultivated into a slight dome, about 230 mm higher in the centre than at the edges. If there are vigorous perennial weeds present, such as dock (*Rumex obtusifolius*), thistle (*Cirsium arvense*) or couch grass (*Agropyron repens*), it is advisable to work the bed over in late spring/early summer and leave it to settle for 3-4 months. Weeds may be destroyed during this period, either by cultivation, or by cutting, raking and spraying with a non-selective systemic contact herbicide in late summer (see Appendix 12 for further details concerning use of herbicides). The area will be subsequently free of harmful, competitive weeds when planting takes place in the autumn and early winter.

Although shrubs and trees generally require higher levels of soil nutrients than herbs or grasses, it is not advisable to use topsoil for planting. This promotes the growth of vigorous weeds. Subsoil, or even crushed brick rubble, will have lower nutrient levels, but more importantly, a greatly reduced content of vigorous weed seeds.

Fertilisers should generally be used when planting to give the young shrubs and trees a better chance of establishing. Fertilisers high in nitrogen (N) are not commonly used, as weeds tend to take them up more than the trees. This is dealt with in detail in section 6.2.5.

6.2.2 Choice of species

When creating scrub/woodland habitats, the same principle applies (as with any other vegetation type) of selecting species which will survive amongst neighbouring species and tolerate the environmental conditions present.

Tables 6.6 and 6.7 are simple guides to the different shrub and tree species which may be used in different situations;
Appendix 7 lists characteristics of tree and shrub species separately; Appendix 8 lists scrub mixtures for different ground conditions; and Appendix 9 lists woodland planting mixtures for different ground conditions. Table 6.8 gives sources of further information on tree and shrub species recommended for planting.

Native species and natural associations

The mixtures in Appendices 7-9 are based on *natural associations,* and this can be important when creating scrub/woodland habitats for wildlife.

Natural associations of shrubs and trees have the following advantages over arbitrary mixes suited only to the environmental conditions present:

— the species may have a better chance of surviving together in the habitat;
— the scrub/woodland conditions produced will be more suitable for later additions of associated herbs, grasses and ferns, etc. between and beneath the shrubs and trees;
— the conditions produced will be more suitable for animals associated with such a habitat to colonise successfully the planted area. Many animals require varying combinations of grassland, scrub and woodland species as food, and for shelter during different periods in their life cycles.

The species mixtures in Appendices 7-9 are quite large and complicated, and are only meant as a guide to the sort of mixtures one should aim eventually to create. In the initial stages of creating woodland/scrub habitats, it may be simpler and more practical to plant the main constituent species of the mixture and add more species later.

The landscape team of the Warrington and Runcorn Development Corporation use simple native species mixes for their large-scale plantings around housing developments, etc. (see Table 6.9). The team know how to manage successfully these simple mixes and will develop them as their design team gains management experience and widens its knowledge of vegetation structure.

Table 6.6 Native trees and shrubs found naturally on major soil types

	A	B	C	D	E	F	G	H	I	J	K
TREES											
Alder			*	+							
Ash	*	+	*	*			*			*	
Beech							*	*			
Birch: hairy				+		+				+	+
Birch: silver		+			+	*					+
Cherry: bird		+		+						+	
Cherry: wild	+		+					+	+		
Crab apple	+	+									
Field maple	+		+				+				
Guelder rose	+	+		+			+				
Hawthorn: common	+	+	+	+							
Hawthorn: Midland	+		+								
Hazel	*	+	*	+			+			+	
Holly	+								+	+	
Hornbeam	+								+		
Mountain ash					+	+					
Oak: pedunculate	*	*	*	*	*	*	*				
Oak: sessile		+			+	+				+	
Sallow											*
Small-leaved lime			+								
Whitebeam								+	+		
Willow: goat			+	+							+
Willow: white			+	+							+
Wych elm		+	+	+			+			+	
Yew								+	+	+	
WOODLAND EDGE/SCRUB											
Blackthorn	+	+	+	+							
Dog rose	+	+	+	+			+	+	+	+	
Dogwood	+		+				+	+	+		
Elder	+	+	+	+							
Field maple	+		+				+	+	+		
Goat willow	+	+	+								
Guelder rose	+	+					+				
Hawthorn: common	+	+	+	+			+	+	+	+	
Hazel	+	+	+	+			+	+	+	+	
Privet	+							+	+		
Sallow	+	+	+								+
Spindle	+		+				+	+	+		
Wayfaring tree								+	+		

Key   A — Southern well-drained soil, B — Northern well-drained soils, C — Southern wet heavy soils, D — Northern wet heavy soils, E — Southern dry sandy soils, F — Northern dry sandy soils, G — Southern limy clays, H — Southern shallow limy soils, I — Southern deep limestone soils, J — Northern and Western limy soils, K — Southern wet/waterlogged sites

Notes:

* — dominant; + — present.

Source: Philip Masters, (unpublished) personal communication.

Table 6.7 Plants most suitable for urban conditions

TREES

	1	2	3	4	5	6	7	8	9	10	11	12	13
Alder: common		*	*			*	*					*	
Ash	*							*	*				
Beech	*						*						
Birch: hairy		*						*	*				
Birch: silver				*			*	*	*	*	*	*	
Blackthorn	*	*		*			*	*					
Broom										*	*	*	
Cherry: bird	*												
Cherry: gean	*												
Crab apple	*												
Hornbeam	*								*				
Horse chestnut	*												
Lime: large-leaf	*					*							
Lime: small-leaf	*												
Maple: field	*						*						
Mountain ash	*						*				*		
Oak: pedunculate	*	*	*	*									
Oak: sessile	*					*							
Poplar: white		*					*						
Whitebeam: common							*	*	*				
Whitebeam: Swedish				*			*	*	*				

WOODLAND EDGE/SCRUB

	1	2	3	4	5	6	7	8	9	10	11	12	13
Dogwood: native	*						*						
Elder		*		*		*	*	*	*		*	*	
Guelder rose	*	*		*			*	*	*				
Hawthorn: Midland	*	*		*			*	*	*				
Hawthorn: native	*	*					*	*	*		*		
Hazel	*						*	*					
Holly	*							*	*				
Honeysuckle	*	*		*			*						
Ivy	*			*		*	*	*					
Osier: common	*	*	*				*						
Privet: native	*						*						
Rose: Burnet	*						*	*	*		*		
Rose: dog	*	*		*			*	*	*		*	*	
Sallow: common	*	*	*	*			*						
Willow: dwarf	*							*					
Willow: goat	*	*	*	*		*	*						
Willow: white	*	*	*										

Key 1 = well-drained loam; 2 = poorly-drained clay/silt; 3 = waterlogged clay/silt; 4 = poor clay; 5 = subsoil only; 6 = rubble; 7 = rubble/soil mix; 8 = exposed sites; 9 = atmospheric pollution; 10 = unburnt shale; 11 = burnt shale/very dry soil; 12 = ash; 13 = lime waste

Note: Many of the plants will grow in a wider range of conditions than those listed, e.g. almost all of them will do well on a good loam. The table gives the sites where they can be used to best advantage.

Source: Philip Masters, (unpublished) personal communication.

Table 6.8 Sources of further information for recommended species of trees and shrubs for planting

Reference	Groups covered	Number of species listed	Additional notes included
Arboricultural Association Leaflet No. 5 (see Villier)	Trees for:		Height, soil tolerance, climatic tolerance
	Clay soils	150 (N,I,C)	
	Deep acid soils	200	
	Dry soil on sand/gravel	60	
	Shallow soil on chalk	150	
	Deep soil on chalk	150	
	Damp sites	30	
	Cold exposed areas	50	
	Industrial areas	150	
	Maritime exposure	70	
	Mildest areas of Great Britain	60	
	Upright trees	50	
	Pendulous trees	50	
	Globular-shaped trees	9	
	Conspicuous leaves	40	
	Coloured leaves	50	
	Autumn colour and fruits	90	
	Coloured stems	30	
	Shelter-belt and screen trees	50	
	Tolerant of shade	20	
	Trees for beekeepers	18	
Beckett and Beckett 1979	Native trees and shrubs	58 (N)	20 categories including: soil, climate, habit, height, colour, vigour, wildlife value, propagation
Bradshaw and Chadwick 1980, p. 99	Trees	33 (N,I)	Fertility, pH, moisture, climate
Brooks 1980b	Native trees and shrubs	52 (N)	Size and growth, tolerance and preferred conditions, management notes, comments
Carter 1982	Trees and shrubs	45 (N)	Soil preference, height, propagation, associated wildlife, productive use, firewood value, tolerances
Gorder and Brooker 1981	Shrubs:		Height, flowers, fruit, remarks
	1m	19 (N,I)	
	1-2m	21 (N,I)	
	2m	17 (N,I)	
	Small-medium trees	18 (N,I)	
	Large trees	16 (N,I)	
	Introduced trees and shrubs	15 (I)	

Dutton and Bradshaw 1982	Trees for urban sites Shrubs for urban sites	12 16	(N,I) (N,I)	Comments on soil types
Forestry Commission 1982	Trees	63	(N,I,C)	Species for towns, ages at maturity, soil, notes
Hamilton 1983	Trees mature height: 15m 16-25m 26-35m 36-45m Woodland shrubs	 9 10 9 4 10	 (N) (N) (N) (N) (N)	Comments on soil types
Ministry of Agriculture, Fisheries and Food 1980	Trees and shrubs for hedgerows	11	(N)	Characteristics, sites
Nature Conservancy Council 1980	Trees for wildlife	16	(N)	Comments on wildlife value
Royal Society for Nature Conservation	Trees	25	(N)	Soil preferences, heights, growth rates, propagation, tolerances
Ruff 1979	Wood vegetation Shrubs >0.5m Shrubs <0.5m	29 39 15	(N) (N) (N)	Soil type, remarks
Urban Wildlife Group 1984	Shrubs Climbers Evergreen ground cover Small trees Large trees	12 3 4 8 8	(N) (N) (N) (N) (N)	Notes on their uses in gardens
Wilson 1980	Garden trees	36	(N,I)	Height, maturity, soils, notes

Lists of tree and shrub species mixes

Brooks 1980a	Trees and shrubs	Hedgerows (on different soils and in different conditions)
Dutton and Bradshaw 1982	Ecological associations of trees and shrubs for woodland	Principal species Filler species Pioneer species Edge species
Tregay and Gustavsson 1983	Trees and shrubs	Woodland Tall edge/scrub, with or without open tree canopy Low edge/low scrub Strong/average/good light Shade/heavy shade
Wilson 1981	Trees and shrubs	Hedgerows

Yoxon 1977 Native tree and shrub Oak woods
associations for woodland Oak woods on sandy clays and
gravel
Midland oak woods on heavy
clay soils
Woodlands on dry sandy soil
Ash-oak woodlands on
calcareous soils
Hertfordshire sessile oak
woods on gravel and sands
Lowland oak woodland on
drained calcareous soils
Wet woodlands

Note: C = cultivated varieties; N = native; I = introduced.
See section 6.2.9 for full references.

Table 6.9 Warrington structure planting species mixes

'WOODLAND' MIX

1m centres; group-planted with trees at 10-50 per group and shrubs at 5-10 per group; *Alnus* and *Corylus* planted randomly with occasional group

25.0%	*Corylus avellana*
25.0	*Quercus robur*
20.0	*Alnus glutinosa*
12.5	*Fraxinus excelsior*
5.0	*Ilex aquifolium*
5.0	*Prunus avium*
2.5	*Pinus sylvestris*
2.5	*Sambucus nigra*
2.5	*Ulmus glabra*

TALL EDGE/HEDGEROW MIX

1m or 0.75m centres; group-planted at 5-50 per group; *Lonicera* planted randomly; frequently forms edge to planting; percentage of *Crataegus* increased when used as hedge

42.5%	*Crataegus monogyna*
17.5	*Corylus avellana*
15.0	*Prunus spinosa*
10.0	*Alnus glutinosa*
5.0	*Acer campestre*
5.0	*Sambucus nigra*
2.5	*Lonicera periclymenum*
2.5	*Salix caprea*

SCRUB MIX

0.75m or 0.5m centres; main species group-planted at 5-30 per group; additional shrubs and trees randomly planted when included; forms blocks detached from other planting mixes

75-100% { *Crataegus monogyna*
Prunus spinosa
Rosa canina
Ulex europaeus }

0-15% { *Corylus avellana*
Ilex aquifolium
Sambucus nigra
Viburnum opulus }

0-10% Tree species

LIGHT-DEMANDING MIX

1m centres; all species group-planted at 5-100 per group; may occasionally form edge to plantation; mostly group-coppiced on rotation

22.5%	*Corylus avellana*
17.5	*Alnus glutinosa*
17.5	*Betula pendula*
12.5	*Sorbus aucuparia*
10.0	*Acer campestre*
7.5	*Sambucus nigra*
5.0	*Ilex aquifolium*
5.0	*Populus tremula*
2.5	*Pinus sylvestris*

LOW EDGE MIX

0.75m or 0.5m centres; all species group-
planted at 5-30 per group; percentages
and combinations may vary widely
depending upon effect required; small-
scale variation important

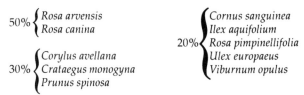

50% { *Rosa arvensis*
     { *Rosa canina*

30% { *Corylus avellana*
     { *Crataegus monogyna*
     { *Prunus spinosa*

20% { *Cornus sanguinea*
     { *Ilex aquifolium*
     { *Rosa pimpinellifolia*
     { *Ulex europaeus*
     { *Viburnum opulus*

GENERAL NOTES

1. 1m centres, etc. refers to the distance between the stem of each tree and its nearest neighbour.
2. Mixes are for guide only but adaptations should reflect local conditions and function.
3. Single species mixes may be included in any location to add further diversity.
4. Planting centres are dependent upon time available for establishment and importance of barrier function for edge mixes.
5. Size of planting groups will vary to increase variety and in relation to percentage of species included in mix.
6. *Rubus fruticosus* not planted as will rapidly colonise suitable areas.
7. Planting percentages do not represent ultimate composition of mixes.
8. Above mixes cannot show full complexity of 'natural' planting but do illustrate basic plant associations which provide potential for successful development.

Source: Greenwood and Moffatt (1982).

Wherever possible, *use what is there*. If a site has patches of scrub and young trees which have established naturally, it will be easier to incorporate these patches into the site design and to extend them with new plantings, than to create new ones elsewhere. The species present in naturally-colonised stands should represent the scrub/woodland character of the area and will be good indicators of the types of species which may be successfully planted alongside them.

Those tree and shrub species which have been present in British native flora for longer periods throughout recent geological history (e.g. since the first of the four Ice Ages) now tend to support richer communities of animals dependent upon them for food.

Tables 6.10 and 6.11 give some indication of the value of native tree and shrub species for wildlife. Such species are also a habitat and food source for many other invertebrates, for birds and small mammals. Many plants thrive best under native trees and shrubs because they provide the right conditions of light, humidity, leaf litter, etc.

Alien species can destroy such conditions. An oak woodland invaded by rhododendron, or an ash woodland invaded by sycamore, soon suffer losses of field and ground layer plants (and their attendant wildlife), as they are shaded out by the invaders.

Problems with urban trees

Size can be a problem with some native tree species. Oak, lime, beech, horn-beam and ash in their wild forms are very large trees at maturity. They can cause nuisance by blocking light/views from windows, etc. and by interfering with overhead telegraph wires and electric power cables. Many city streets have lines of badly lopped limes and poplars which would be too big if allowed to grow properly. To fell a large tree in a built-up area is very expensive. It may be possible to obtain smaller-growing or 'fastigiate' (trees whose branches grow up almost vertically) forms of these species from a major nursery (see section 6.2.3).

Poplar and willow species present special problems on clay soils near to buildings. Their high water demands are met by wide-spreading and shallow roots. In periods of alternate drought and rain, these give rise to contractions and expansions in the clay which can cause the collapse of walls. Their roots are very successful at blocking and rupturing drains. They can penetrate a drain and extend along it for 10 m or more. Such trees should not be planted within 20 m of buildings or underground water pipes.

Table 6.10 (a) The number of insect species known to be associated with various trees in Britain; (b) a re-analysis including insect and mite species

Trees	(a)	(b)
Quercus robur and *Q. petraea* (oak)	284	423
Salix 5 spp. (willows)	266	450
Betula 2 spp. (birches)	229	334
Crataegus monogyna (hawthorn)	149	209
Prunus spinosa (sloe)	109	153
Populus 4 spp. (poplars)	97	189
Pinus sylvestris (Scots pine) E	91	172
Alnus glutinosa (alder)	90	141
Ulmus 2 spp. (elms)	82	124
Malus sylvestris (crab apple)	—	118
Corylus avellana (hazel)	73	106
Fagus sylvatica (beech)	64	98
Fraxinus excelsior (ash)	41	68
Picea abies (spruce) *	37	70
Tilia 2 spp. (lime)	31	57
Sorbus aucuparia (mountain ash)	28	58
Carpinus betulus (hornbeam)	28	51
Acer campestre (field maple)	26	51
Larix decidua (larch) *	17	38
Abies spp. (fir) * E	16	—
Acer pseudoplatanus (sycamore) *	15	43
Juniperus communis (juniper) E	—	32
Ilex aquifolium (holly) E	7	10
Castanea sativa (sweet chestnut) *	5	11
Aesculus hippocastanum (horse chestnut) *	4	9
Juglans regia (walnut) *	3	7
Quercus ilex (holm oak) * E	2	5
Taxus baccata (yew) E	1	6
Robinia pseudoacacia (false acacia) *	1	2
Platanus × *hybrida* (plane) *	0	—

Notes:
* = introduced species; E = evergreen species; — = not examined by researchers.

Although these figures indicate clearly the higher wildlife value of some species over others, the figures are not to be taken literally. For example, some of the insect species are uncommon in Great Britain and are not likely to occur in urban habitats.

Source: (a) Southwood (1961); (b) Kennedy and Southwood (1984).

1.A. Nature abhors a vacuum. Oxford ragwort (Senecio squalidus)

1. Rare plants, such as the common spotted orchid (Dactylorhiza fuchsii), may be found in towns and cities

2. Black redstarts (Phoenicurus ochruros), often breed on derelict, vacant city sites

3. *Kestrels* (Falco tinnunculus)*, can often be seen hovering over urban wasteland and road verges in search of their prey*

4. Wild animals, such as this badger, are becoming more common in urban areas

5. The various stages of natural succession together on one site

6. *Natural succession in water*

7.*Open moss communities*

8. *Floating and submerged communities of freshwater plants*

Tree roots can present other hazards below ground, including the disruption of gas mains and electric cables.

Seeds falling from trees into cracks in masonry can cause damage when they germinate. Falling leaves can accumulate, blocking gutters and drains and making public footpaths slippery during wet autumn periods.

Ill-sited hedges, bushes or trees may obscure sight-lines, for example, at road junctions, or their branches may obscure light from street lamps, rendering public footpaths unsafe at night.

Tree branches can snap under heavy snow or in high winds. Elms used to be notorious for this. Poplars can also become unsafe in this way, as they often mature and die from the inside out. A mature poplar may appear healthy, but may have brittle heartwood, making it prone to collapse at any time.

6.2.3 Sources of trees and shrubs

The following is a list of possible sources.

Local commercial nurseries. Local suppliers should be listed in the telephone directory Yellow Pages under 'Nurserymen or seedsmen'.

The local authority. Some local authorities' parks departments may be prepared to supply free trees and shrubs from their own nurseries. (However, do not accept alien or poor quality stock, just because it is free.)

Forestry Commission. The local Forestry Commission district officer or the county or district forester can give advice about getting planting stock.

Horticulture Week (Gardeners' Chronicle, Horticultural Trade Journal). These are invaluable journals in which the larger nurserymen and growers advertise.

Table 6.11 Insect species associated with genera of woody plants (insects also feeding on up to seven other genera included)

Crataegus spp.	hawthorn	230
Prunus spp.	blackthorn/cherry	157
Malus spp.	apple	133
Corylus avellana	hazel	107
Rosa spp.	rose	107
Rubus spp.	bramble, etc.	107
Ulex spp.	gorse E	52
Lonicera periclymenum	honeysuckle	48
Acer spp.	maple, sycamore	41
Sorbus spp.	whitebeam/mountain ash	36
Ligustrum vulgare	privet E	35
Juniperus communis	juniper E	27
Rhamnus catharticus	buckthorn	27
Euonymus europaeus	spindle	19
Sambucus nigra	elder	19
Clematis vitalba	travellers' joy	18
Cornus sanguinea	dogwood	18
Viburnum spp.	guelder rose/wayfaring tree	17
Ilex aquifolium	holly E	13
Taxus baccata	yew E	6
Buxus sempervirens	box E	4

Note: E = evergreen species.
Source: Duffey *et al.* (1974).

Horticultural Trades Association Handbook and Buyer's Guide. This is a useful annual guide to reputable sources of planting stock.

Donations from other non-commercial sources, e.g. sympathetic land-owners, other local groups, etc. As already mentioned, only gifts of good quality stock should be accepted. Also, if your group has to travel to another site, dig up the stock, and transport it back, costs may rise above those for an equivalent amount of commercial stock, delivered to the site.

Buying trees and shrubs

When buying stock from commercial suppliers, it is best to order well in advance of use. Many customers reserve trees early in the year and stocks of well-grown plants may be in short supply by late September/October.

In order to avoid possible error, clearly specify the species required, if possible with its botanical name, e.g. pedunculate oak (*Quercus robur*). If a nursery mistakenly supplied the wrong type of oak, it may not become obvious until the planted tree comes into leaf. The quality of stock is more important than its price. It does not pay to buy cheap material. It is advisable to secure the help of a suitably qualified/experienced horticulturalist or arboriculturalist to inspect the stock before purchase. Good, well-grown plants should be sturdy, with a healthy leading shoot, and should have been moved within two years, ensuring a compact and fibrous root system.

The true origin of each stock is called its provenance. If a tree is grown in England from seed collected in Norway, its provenance is Norway. Trees purchased from nurseries are seldom of local provenance and are often foreign in origin.

Most tree species offered for sale are now required, under EEC regulations, to have been raised from certified seed (i.e. derived from selected parent trees or stands of accepted quality).

The following species come within these regulations (N = native species):

Silver fir (*Abies alba*); European larch (*Larix decidua*); Japanese larch (*Larix leptolepsis*); Norway spruce (*Picea abies*); Sitka spruce (*Picea sitchensis*); Austrian and Corsican Pine (*Pinus strobus*); Douglas fir (*Pseudotsuga taxifolia*); red oak (*Quercus borealis*); pedunculate oak (*Quercus robur*) N; sessile oak (*Quercus petraea*) N; beech (*Fagus sylvatica*) N; and poplars (*Populus* spp.) N.

Further details may be found in the Forestry Commission publication *The Marketing of Forest Tree Seed and Plants* — free from their Edinburgh office (see Appendix 15 for address).

All other species are free of such controls. If your group is unable to locate a reputable local nursery, the local authority (or County Council) tree specialist should be able to recommend suppliers (see section 6.2.6 for further details on the choice of tree and shrub types and sizes, and their handling during transportation and prior to planting).

The following are examples of 1983 price ranges for commercially available trees (Hamilton 1983); the prices still held in 1985. (See also Figure 6.7 and section 6.2.6. for details of different size groups.)

— transplants (below 90 cm tall) 5-50p each;
— whips (90 cm-2.4 m) 30p-£2 each;
— standards (2.4-4.8 m) £1.50-£12.50 each;
— advanced nursery stock (approx. 6 m) £40 each.

Buying seed

There is much current interest in the seed industry in the use of tree and shrub seeds in landscaping and reclamation to produce natural vegetation cover. The commercial availability of seed from trees and shrubs of British provenance should therefore increase in time. Appendix 14 lists three suppliers recommended by the Forestry Commission (who can also supply seed), one of which — British Seed Houses — also supply tree and shrub seed of named provenance, some of which is native.

It is most important to avoid seed of non-British provenance for nature conservation planting schemes. Some foreign seed may be of doubtful quality and of a different genetic type. There are no quarantine regulations governing the importation of tree *seed* into the British Isles. Seeds from trees of provenance to the north of the planting site are preferable, since they are liable to grow better than seeds from the warmer south. Where possible, a preferable alternative to buying seed is to collect it from local sources.

Collecting seed

Collecting seed locally has the advantage that the young trees and shrubs produced will be of the same genetic type as other local trees of the same species. This can be very important if the aim of growing is to enhance the natural richness of the area. It is important, particularly in urban areas, to ensure that trees from which seed is to be collected are not of foreign stock.

Seeds from larger trees may be difficult to collect as they are so high up. Only a few species, such as oak and beech, have seeds so large that it is worth collecting them after they have fallen. One solution is to keep in touch with local forestry workers (e.g. the parks department or other local managers of mature woodland) and look out for trees being felled or lopped when seed is ripe, or even to ask that felling/lopping be delayed until ripening. Seed may then be collected from fallen branches.

In order to collect seed in the tree tops, special safety equipment is required. Examples are the 'tree bicycle' for climbing trunks and possibly a scrambling net to enable pickers to reach outer branches. These are used by large commercial concerns and the Forestry Commission to collect seed annually from selected parent trees. However, skilled professional staff are needed to use such equipment. Using ladders can be very dangerous if proper care is not taken. Ladders must be firmly anchored at top and bottom, always with helpers on the ground to steady them and ideally roped to the tree at the top.

Seeds may be reached from the ground by using a long pole with a hook on the end to bend down branches, or by cutting off seed-bearing twigs with long-handled pruning tools.

Points to remember when collecting

— Secure the permission of the landowner before collecting any seed.
— Trees may be stunted because of past management or because of genetic defects. Seed gathered from stunted trees is likely to produce more stunted trees; if healthy offspring are desired, then seed should only be collected from healthy trees. However, for the purposes of nature conservation, variety of form can be more important than good timber production.
— Seed needs to be kept dry, so, ideally, collect in dry weather; and use open-weave canvas, hessian or paper bags.
— Keep different species in separate bags, and label all bags and storage containers clearly with: the botanical name of the species, date and place of collection, and any notes on the habitat, etc. which may be relevant to the future performance of seeds when planted.

— Where possible, collect seed from trees growing in similar conditions to those which the seeds will encounter when you plant them out.
— Ensure that adequate preparation for storing, germinating, planting, etc. is arranged *before* venturing out to collect seed. It will be disheartening if time is wasted collecting seed which dies through lack of forward planning (see section 6.2.4 for further details on seed storage and germination).

Table 6.13 in section 6.2.4 gives further information on seed collection, storage and sowing methods for some tree and shrub species.

Collecting trees and shrubs

Tree and shrub seedlings and saplings may be obtained from nearby sites, particularly where they would otherwise die or be destroyed. The following are points to bear in mind when collecting.

— Digging up of any plant without the permission of the landowner is illegal.
— Indiscriminate removal of plants from, for example, woodland, can be harmful to the habitat.
— Unlike nursery-raised seedlings and saplings, wild plants have had no special treatment to promote successful transplanting and will be less reliable.

Vegetative propagation

An alternative to collecting tree and shrub seeds is to collect vegetative parts and propagate them. This approach may be useful, for example, when desirable local parent plants do not bear viable seed, or when exact replicas or 'clones' of such parent plants are wanted.

Table 6.12 lists some species which may be propagated and the methods used. The three methods are:

— Cuttings: the removal of shoots for rooting.
— Layering: bending a side shoot and pegging it to the ground so that it roots and can be removed for transplanting.
— Suckers or stooling: at intervals, certain shallow-rooting trees send up upright shoots; these may be removed and transplanted.

Figure 6.3 illustrates how these methods are carried out. In general, vegetative propagation requires great skill. Horticulturalists have developed methods which include the three already mentioned, along with grafting and many sophisticated techniques involving rooting media, controlled temperature, humidity and synthetic growth hormones.

Sheat (1957) gives a comprehensive guide to the best methods, and Brooks (1980b) gives further useful information on the methods outlined in Figure 6.3. Transplanting methods are covered in detail in section 6.2.6.

6.2.4 'Growing your own'

The choice of growing your own, or buying ready-grown plants, will depend very much on what your group wants from the exercise. Buying plants from reputable suppliers is a convenient and reliable way of obtaining materials for quick creation of habitats. Collecting and storing seeds; seed treatment and germination; vegetative propagation; and nurturing seedlings through to the transplanting stage, may involve a lot of work. However, if one object is to learn from these activities, growing your own is an ideal way for volunteers, children, naturalists and others to get involved, gain practical experience and derive some creative enjoyment. Valuable sources of further information include: Aldhous (1975), Liebscher (1978) and Edlin (1975).

Table 6.12 Methods of vegetative propagation for different tree and shrub species

Species	Cuttings	Layering	Suckers or stooling
Alnus glutinosa (alder)	+		
Buxus sempervirens (box)	+		+
Cornus sanguinea (dogwood)	+		+
Corylus avellana (hazel)	+	+	+
Frangula alnus (alder buckthorn)			+
Hedera helix (ivy)	+		
Hippophae rhamnoides (sea buckthorn)			+
Ilex aquifolium (holly)	+		
Juniperus communis (juniper)	+		
Ligustrum vulgare (privet)	+	+	+
Lonicera periclymenum (honeysuckle)	+	+	
Malus sylvestris (crab apple)			+
Populus alba (white poplar)			+
P. canescens (grey poplar)	+		+
P. nigra (black poplar)	+		+
P. tremula (aspen)	+		+
Prunus avium (wild cherry)		+	+
P. padus (bird cherry)		+	+
P. spinosa (blackthorn)		+	+
Pyrus pyraster (wild pear)			+
Rhamnus catharticus (buckthorn)	+	+	+
Rubus idaeus (raspberry)			+
Rosa canina (dog rose)	+	+	+
Salix spp. (willows)	+		
Sambucus nigra (elder)	+		
Sorbus torminalis (wild service)			+
Taxus baccata (yew)	+		
Tilia cordata (small-leaved lime)			+
T. platyphyllos (large-leaved lime)		+	+
Ulmus procera (common elm)			+
Viburnum lantana (wayfaring tree)	+	+	+
V. opulus (guelder rose)	+	+	

Source: Carter (1982); Brooks (1980b); Liebscher (1978).

Figure 6.3 Vegetative propagation

(A) Cuttings — taken in late autumn or early winter. Always use a sharp knife

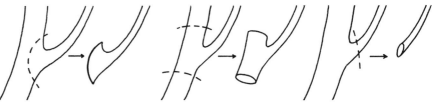

Heeled cuttings (Avoid damaging parent plant or take from branches which have already been pruned)

Unheeled cutting (e.g. poplar and willows)

Previous year's growth   Succulent new growth

Cut into sections with at least two nodes to a section

Discard

200–230mm long

Store in moist sand or a rooting medium (25% coarse sand, 25% grit, 50% acid peat) in a cool place, or heel in until planting. Temperatures around 5°C (41°F) should stop buds from bursting before roots have formed

Plant out from early January to March. Avoid frosty ground

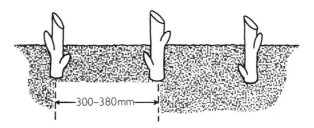

←—300–380mm—→

Firm around the stems and water well

(B) Layering — carried out in autumn or early winter

(a) Coppice, e.g. hazel
(see section 7.4.6)

(b) Young/springy stems,
e.g. dog rose

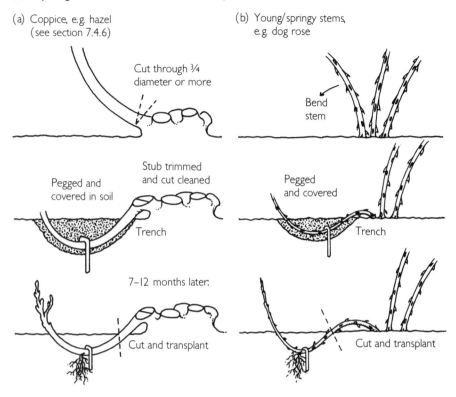

Cut through ¾
diameter or more

Bend
stem

Stub trimmed
and cut cleaned

Pegged and
covered in soil

Pegged
and covered

Trench

Trench

7–12 months later.

Cut and transplant

Cut and transplant

(C) Suckers, e.g. common elm

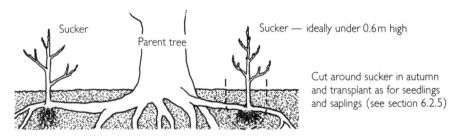

Sucker

Parent tree

Sucker — ideally under 0.6m high

Cut around sucker in autumn
and transplant as for seedlings
and saplings (see section 6.2.5)

(D) Stooling (or 'crown thinning') for species which do not normally sucker, but which will
coppice (see section 7.4.6), e.g. hazel

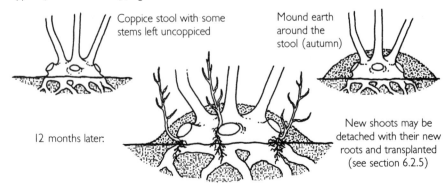

Coppice stool with some
stems left uncoppiced

Mound earth
around the
stool (autumn)

12 months later.

New shoots may be
detached with their new
roots and transplanted
(see section 6.2.5)

Table 6.13 gives details of collection and storage methods for some trees and shrubs. The following categories (a)-(d) refer to the second column in the table.

Table 6.13 Collection, storage and sowing of seeds of different tree and shrub species

Species	Collection	Storage	Comments	
			Collection	Sowing (average germination per cent, where known)
Acer campestre (field maple)	Sept-Oct	c18	Some seed most years. Can be sown immediately	2nd spring; 40g/sq m
Aesculus hippocastanum (horse chestnut)	Sept/Oct/Nov	c6	Non-native. Can be sown immediately, or:—	Mar-May; 1 kg/sq m (75)
Alnus glutinosa (alder)	Sept/Oct/Nov	b	Pick cones shortly before they ripen	Damp, *not* waterlogged soil; 10mm deep; 10g/sq m (35)
Betula spp. (birches)	Jul/Aug/Sept	a or c6	Pick catkins shortly before. Can be sown immediately, or:—	Mar-Apr; 5g/sq m (40)
Carpinus betulus (hornbeam)	Aug/Sept/Nov	c18	Pick ripe seed before seed heads break up. Plant germinated seeds immediately	2nd spring; 5-10mm deep; 60g/sq m (45)
Castanea sativa (sweet chestnut)	May/Jun/July	d	Non-native. Warm summer is needed to ripen nuts	Mar-Apr; 0.75kg/sq m (75)
Cornus sanguinea (dogwood)	Sept/Oct	c6	Can be stratified whole	Mar-Apr; 5-10mm deep
Corylus avellana (hazel)	Sept/Oct	c3-4	May be picked from the ground or when husks begin to brown	Apr; singly, 25-40mm apart; up to 50mm deep; 0.5kg/sq m (80)
Crataegus spp. (hawthorns)	Sept/Oct/Nov	c18	Pick fully ripe berries. Can be stratified whole	2nd spring; 5mm deep; 100g/sq m
Euonymus europaeus (spindle)	Sept/Oct/Nov	c6	Pick when capsules have split to reveal seeds	Mar-Apr; 20g/sq m; good soil needed (80)
Fagus sylvatica (beech)	Aug/Oct/Nov	d	Free from husks before sowing. Sow immediately, or:—	Mar-Apr; 0.25kg/sq m (60)
Fraxinus excelsior (ash)	Sept/Oct/Nov	c16-18	Aug for sowing immediately or Oct for stratifying. Seeds must be dry when collected	2nd spring; 60g/sq m (70)
Ilex aquifolium (holly)	Nov/Dec/Jan	c16 or a	Pick when ripe. Wash and dry to store, or stratify whole	2nd spring; 5-10mm deep; 30g/sq m (80)
Larix decidua (larch)	Nov/Dec/Jan	b	Non-native	Apr-May; 15g/sq m (30)
Ligustrum vulgare (privet)	-/July/-	c9	Pick berries when ripe and remove seed	Apr; 5-10mm deep

Malus sylvestris (crab apple)	Sept/Oct	c2	Pick from tree. Avoid rotten or scabby fruit	Jan; 10-25mm deep; in sunny position
Pinus sylvestris (Scots pine)	Nov/Jan/Feb	b	Collect cones before they open	Apr-May; 100g/sq m (70)
Populus tremula (aspen)	Apr-May	none	Collect catkins when white down appears. Sow immediately	Apr-May; difficult to grow (consult Gray 1953)
Prunus avium/padus (cherries)	July/Sept/Oct	c4	Pick ripe berries before birds do. Sow immediately, or dry and store in open containers:—	Mar-Apr; 150g/sq m (80)
P. spinosa (blackthorn)	-/Oct/-	c6 or 18	Pick ripe berries	1st/2nd spring; 25-30mm deep
Quercus spp. (oaks)	Sept/Oct/Nov	d	Collect from ground. Free acorns from cups	Mar-Apr; singly; 1kg/sq m (80)
Rhamnus catharticus (buckthorn)	Sept/Oct	c6	Pick fully ripe berries	Mar-Apr
Rosa canina (dog rose)	-/Sept/-	c7	Remove seeds from hips	Apr; 5-10mm deep
Sambucus nigra (elder)	Aug/Sept	c6 or 18	Collect as soon as ripe	1st/2nd spring; 5mm deep
Sarothamnus scoparius (broom)	-/Aug/-	a	Pick pods when black. Pop open by hand	Mar-Apr; 8g/sq m (80)
Sorbus aria (whitebeam)	Aug/Sept/Oct	c6-24	Pick fully ripe berries	5mm deep; 50g/sq m
S. aucuparia (rowan)	July/Aug/Sept	c6-24	Pick fully ripe berries. Store in open container	5mm deep; 50g/sq m (70)
Taxus baccata (yew)	Sept/Oct/Nov	c16	Pick berries from tree. Seed and foliage (not berries) deadly poisonous	2nd spring; 10g/sq m
Tilia spp. (limes) small-leaved/(*large-leaved)	-/Oct/-	c18	May be collected from the ground	2nd spring; up to 50mm deep, 25-40mm apart; 50g/sq m (*200g/sq m) (70)
Ulex europaeus (gorse)	Oct/Nov	a	Pick pods when black. Pop open by hand	8g/sq m
Ulmus glabra (wych elm)	May-Jun	none	Fertile seed rare. Pick when wings lose pigment. Sow immediately	May-Jun; 15g/sq m (40)
Viburnum lantana (wayfaring tree)	-/Aug/-	c3	Collect soon after fruiting	Nov; 5-10mm deep
V. opulus (guelder rose)	Sept/Oct	c12	Collect soon after fruiting	Sept-Oct; 5-10mm deep

Note: Column 3 'Storage', gives the type of storage (a)-(d) — see main text for details, and the number of months.
Source: Aldhous (1975); Devon Trust for Nature Conservation (1981): Liebscher (1978); Yoxon (1977).

(a) Small seeds should be dried in a well-ventilated place and turned from time to time until they reach a constant weight. Remove any mouldy seed and store the rest in sealed containers in a cool place; seeds may last for several years at 2°-5°C (36°F-41°F) if kept dry. Broom and gorse seeds will need their dormancy breaking before sowing. Put a volume of seed in a bowl, pour five times that volume of boiling water over it and leave to cool.

(b) Cones (e.g. alder, larch, Scots pine) may be opened by warming, and seeds removed by shaking the cones in a coarse sieve. Seeds are then stored as in (a).

(c) Separate seed from fleshy fruits by soaking in warm water and gently mashing; the seeds should sink and the flesh should float. Alternatively, store the fruit in open-weave sacks until spring and then separate. Separation is not essential for hawthorn or holly.

To avoid poor germination, seeds in this category need stratifying before sowing. The numbers in column 3 of Table 6.13 represent the periods of stratification needed (in months). So, for example, dogwood (*Cornus sanguinea*) seed needs stratifying for six months from September/October, to be ready for planting out in the following March or April. Field maple (*Acer campestre*) seed needs 18 months, and the seed will not be planted out until the following spring. The seeds of such species are dormant when picked.

The aim of stratification is to break this dormancy by keeping the seeds moist (not wet) and cool. They take up moisture, dormancy is broken, and the seeds swell until they split. At this stage, the seed embryos will be well enough developed for germination to begin.

Figure 6.4 Vertical cross-section of a stratification pit

Internal widths and depth of pit = 750 x 750 x 750mm

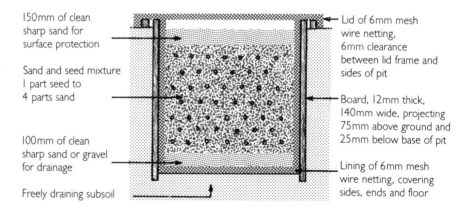

150mm of clean sharp sand for surface protection

Sand and seed mixture 1 part seed to 4 parts sand

100mm of clean sharp sand or gravel for drainage

Freely draining subsoil

Lid of 6mm mesh wire netting, 6mm clearance between lid frame and sides of pit

Board, 12mm thick, 140mm wide, projecting 75mm above ground and 25mm below base of pit

Lining of 6mm mesh wire netting, covering sides, ends and floor

Notes:
(a) All woodwork should be treated with a copper-based preservative. Creosote must not be used, as it may harm seeds close to the boards
(b) Corner posts of the pit may be made from hard wood or angle iron driven well in. Boards must extend into the corners, those on the ends of the pit lapping the ends of the boards on the sides

Source: Aldhous (1975).

Methods of stratification vary according to the amount of seed to be handled. The amount of seed should be estimated before stratification, either as the number of seeds or their weight. This information is important when working out what areas of seedbeds need preparing when the seeds are ready for planting out. Mix the seed with four times its weight of sand, to ensure that each seed is separated from its neighbours. Small amounts may be stored in plastic bags in a refrigerator, or mouse-proof boxes in a cool shed (and kept moist).

Larger quantities may be put in large earthenware pots with drainage holes in stratification pits (see Figure 6.4).

The seed is ready for sowing when root tips (radicles) are visible in the splits in the seed coats, and a few have begun to emerge.

An alternative to stratification is to cultivate an area of ground in September/October and sow seed as soon as it is collected; seed will either germinate in the following spring or the second spring. This method has the disadvantage of the extra work involved in weeding the area and the loss of seed to mice and other seed-eaters.

(d) If acorns are sown immediately, cover with 75-100 mm of soil and remove this in March. Acorns (and hazel nuts) may also be sown directly into a sward by randomly dropping them into grass and pressing into the soil with your shoe. If seeds must be stored, spread out and turn the seed from time to time; for example, turn oak once or twice a week, and turn beech daily for the first two weeks, then once or twice a week. After December, once a month is sufficient. Seeds must be kept moist and plump, but must not be allowed to become mouldy.

Seedbeds

To get the best germination results, the soil for the seeds needs to fulfil the following requirements.

A fine tilth   Heavy soils need rough digging in autumn and leaving until spring so the winter frosts can break them up. Sandy soils rarely require this treatment. Heavy soil can cause future damage to seedling roots during transplanting, while lighter soils are more likely to dry out. The best soil is a light loam.

Deep   Deeper soils retain more moisture in dry weather. Dig to 100 mm on heath or woodland soil, and 200 mm on grassland.

Well-consolidated   This ensures that soil moisture can reach the surface layers by capillary action, lessening the degree of drying out in warm dry weather. A firm seedbed also maximises the contact between seed and soil.

Well drained   Waterlogging can literally drown some seeds and permanently damp conditions can encourage fungal rots which kill off seedlings.

Free from extremes of temperature   Avoid frost hollows and east-facing slopes (where morning sun may cause serious damage after a frosty night).

Weed free   The most harmful weeds are perennials, such as *Agropyron repens* (couch grass) whose creeping rhizomes can snare up the delicate seedling roots and wreak havoc when either are removed.

Moderately fertile and not too acid

The details for seedbed preparation are given in Figure 6.5. Press the seeds into the bed, either with the back of a spade, or a plank, or a roller. Cover small seeds with coarse sand, to a depth about 1.5 times the seed length. Large seeds are covered with 2.5-4 cm of nursery soil.

If no ground is available for seedbeds, trees may be grown in containers. Seeds are started off in seed trays or 'Dunemann boxes' (see Figure 6.5), filled, ideally, with a growing medium of well-rotted leaf litter or a half-half mix of litter and peat, or litter and pulverised bark. Conifer seeds need some conifer litter in the growing medium; this contains mycorrhizal fungi which the conifer roots need in order to obtain nutrients. Small numbers of seeds may be germinated in plastic bags, hung on a wall, or singly in yoghurt pots. Whether sown in seedbeds or containers, the seeds and seedlings must be kept moist,

Figure 6.5 (A) Seedbed preparation; (B) preparation of Dunemann boxes

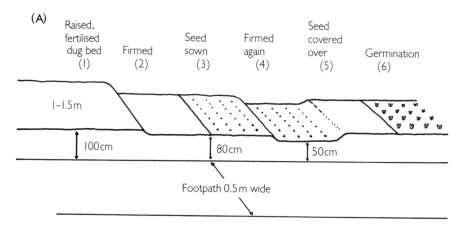

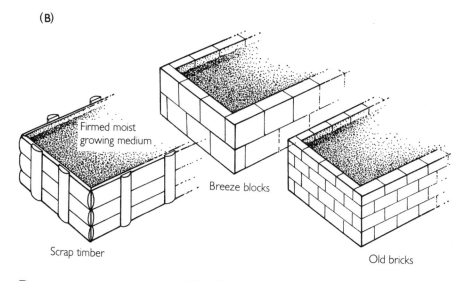

The growing medium is prepared as in (2)–(6) for seedbed preparation

weed-free, well-shaded, and protected from seed-eaters, e.g. by fine mesh netting 6-12 mm gauge.

If seeds fail to germinate when expected, it is worth waiting for a year, in case they germinate in the following season. Percentage germination can vary enormously. If you wish to test seed viability, Aldhous (1975) and Liebscher (1979) give methods. These methods, however, involve the destruction of 100 or more seeds. It may be better to sow the seed and be patient. Table 6.13, under 'sowing comments', includes some examples in parentheses of the average percentage germinations to be expected. One- or two-year-old seedlings are then transplanted, usually between October and April, avoiding periods of frost (mid-winter transplanting is particularly harmful to holly). Repeated transplanting stimulates the seedlings to produce sturdy, dense fibrous root masses.

The new growing medium should be a neutral, fertile, mineral, weed-free soil, which allows the seedlings to become sturdy, with well-developed roots, giving them a better chance of survival when planted out.

Containers for transplanted seedlings need to be at least 250 mm deep, and 250 mm in diameter. Examples of containers include:

— 4-5 litre plastic bottles, with their tops removed and drainage holes punched in the bottom;
— terracotta flower pots;
— for seedlings of larger seeds: old buckets with drainage holes;
— polythene grow-bags (remove these before planting out seedlings);
— peat or fibre pots. These are designed to be left on. When the transplants are planted out, the pots rot away. One benefit of transplants in containers is that, once they have developed into sturdy individuals, they can be planted out with the minimum damage to their roots.

Seedling beds need digging in the October-November preceding transplanting. An organic manure dug in approximately two weeks before, and a final recultivation on the day should produce a good bed for the transplants.

The transfer to the new bed should be carried out as quickly as possible, and roots should never be exposed to direct sunlight or left to dry out. The more roots and fine rootlets on the transplants, the better they will grow, so lift them carefully with a fork and tease off the soil before transferring them.

Transplants may be lined out either in separate holes, or, with larger numbers, along trenches large enough to accommodate the roots without crushing or twisting them. Table 6.14 outlines recommended lining-out densities.

Transplants must be firm enough in the ground not to be uprooted by a gentle, steady pull. They should not stay for more than two years in one spot, but should be moved to fresh soil.

The transplant beds may be kept weed-free by frequent light hoeing.

The tree nursery

The most effective way of 'growing your own' trees and shrubs is to set up a tree nursery, usually involving a long-term commitment — several years if the nursery is to be successful. This demands the following requirements:

— A piece of land which will be secure for at least five or six years (an area of 10 m² may produce up to 100 trees each year).
— A supply of water.
— A team of people who hopefully will ensure that the nursery is looked after.

Table 6.14 Recommended lining-out densities for different sizes of transplants

Average height expected at lifting (mm)	Spacing at lining out (mm)	Number of plants per sq m
less than 200	40 × 200	129
200-400	50 × 200	97
400-600	75 × 200	65
over 600	100 × 200	50

Note: 200mm is the space between lines of transplants 40mm apart. Plants to be lifted after one growing season may be transplanted at a closer spacing than if they are expected to remain in the bed for two growing seasons. Seedlings less than 40mm tall are too small to be handled easily. If more than 40 per cent of all seedlings in a bed are less than 40mm tall, the whole bed is better left to grow on for a second year.

Your group may have already grown some trees, or a local school may wish to get involved.
— A source of materials for fencing, tools for maintenance, and funds for sundry items such as manure, fertilisers, mulches, etc.

Figure 6.6 illustrates a plan for a small tree nursery based on British Trust for Conservation Volunteers recommendations. Such a nursery could be set up on an allotment, at the edge of school playing fields, in a corner of someone's garden, or anywhere where the site could be looked after.

There are already many successful small tree nurseries in Great Britain being run by voluntary groups, schools, etc. In general, the work involved is a little, all year round — ideal for continual community involvement without over-working people. From your group's point of view, a tree nursery provides a ready source of material for sundry planting projects, without depending upon commercial suppliers and their deliveries.

Direct seeding

In recent years, certain professional landscape practitioners have carried out research into the creation of woodland habitat by seeding tree and shrub species directly. Professional interest in the method stems from the following considerations:

— It may work on sites where planting has been impractical, is too costly or has failed.
— It has proved successful on topsoils, subsoils and mineral wastes.
— Some species, e.g. oak (*Quercus* spp.) which are difficult to establish by planting, are very successful when seeded directly.
— The whole initial process of establishing woodland can be carried out in one operation.
— Direct seeding is generally cheaper than planting for amenity woodlands.

Preparation of seed for sowing is covered earlier in this section. Ground preparation is necessary for direct seeding and the following points need consideration.

Soil   Seeds need moisture to germinate successfully. Seed is sown deeper in lighter soils as moisture retention is less than in heavier soils. Seed may not be sown on waterlogged soils.

Figure 6.6 Tree nursery — 3m². This drawing shows the nursery in early summer. A nursery of this size, if well-managed, can produce 100 trees each year

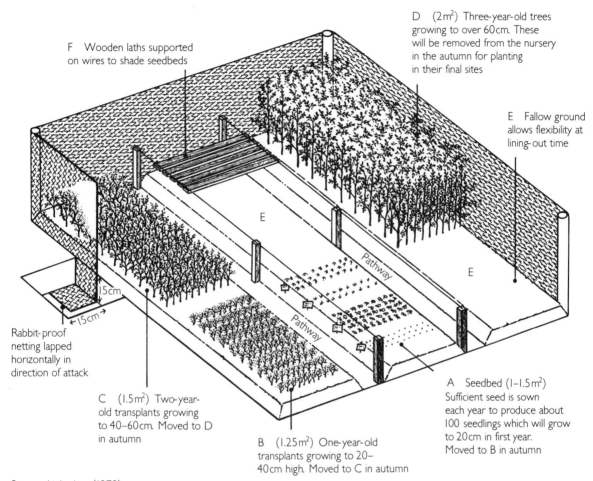

D (2m²) Three-year-old trees growing to over 60cm. These will be removed from the nursery in the autumn for planting in their final sites

F Wooden laths supported on wires to shade seedbeds

E Fallow ground allows flexibility at lining-out time

Rabbit-proof netting lapped horizontally in direction of attack

C (1.5m²) Two-year-old transplants growing to 40–60cm. Moved to D in autumn

B (1.25m²) One-year-old transplants growing to 20–40cm high. Moved to C in autumn

A Seedbed (1–1.5m²) Sufficient seed is sown each year to produce about 100 seedlings which will grow to 20cm in first year. Moved to B in autumn

Source: Liebscher (1978).

Aspect and exposure Higher seed rates may be needed on exposed sites, or nurse crops may be used to protect young seedlings.

Climate Where dry springs are a problem, e.g. in the east, autumn sowing is preferable and, if unavoidable, spring sowing should be as early as possible.

Predators A covering of soil or mulch must be used to protect the seed from predators. An example of a mulch which has been used successfully is chopped straw, mixed with bitumen at a rate of approximately 600g per sq m. Many other organic and inorganic mulches may be tried, if they are economic.

Preparation of the ground for seeding should remove herbaceous species which would otherwise compete with the germinating woody seedlings. Glyphosate may be used to kill the existing vegetation before seeding (see Appendix 12 for further recommendations concerning herbicides).

If used, nurse crops are sown with the tree seeds. These should:

(a) provide a suitable environment for seeds to germinate and seedlings to grow; in some cases, they can act as a substitute for a mulch;

(b) reduce the germination of vigorous weeds and their ability to compete with the woody seedlings;

(c) Bind the soil together. This may be particularly important if woody species are seeded on to slopes liable to erode in wet weather.

Wheat, sown at a rate of 50 kg per ha, has proved a useful nurse crop. It fulfils the conditions above and, being an annual, dies back around July and August, allowing the woody seedlings a burst of autumn growth.

The herbicide propyzamide does not harm woody species and has been used to keep herbaceous weeds down between seedlings (see Appendix 12 for further recommendations concerning herbicides).

References: La Dell (1983), and A. Luke, Cambridge Direct Tree Seeding Ltd (see Appendix 15 for address).

The possibilities for planting mixtures of seeds and young trees are discussed further in section 6.2.6.

Table 6.15 Main nutrients in common manures and fertilisers

	Nitrogen	Phosphate	Potassium	Comment
	(Figures represent per cent in dry matter)			
Manures				
Farmyard manure	0.6	0.3	0.7	
Horse manure	0.7	0.5	0.6	
Straw	0.5	0.2	0.9	
Municipal composts	0.5	0.25	0.1	
Spent mushroom compost	0.6	0.5	0.9	
Sawdust	0.2	—	—	
Peat	0.5	0.07	0.04	
Poultry manure:				
Deep litter	1.7	1.8	1.3	
Broiler	2.4	2.2	1.4	
Dried	4.2	4.3	1.6	
Pigeon manure	3.4	1.4	1.2	
Sewage sludge:				
Digested	1.1	1.0	0.1	
Activated	5-6	2.9	0.6	
Pulverised refuse	0.59	0.40	0.32	
Seaweed	0.6	0.3	1.0	
Hop waste	2.5-3.5	1.0	—	
Fertilisers				
Hoof and horn	7-16	—	—	
Meat and bone meal (slow)	5-10	18	0.2	High calcium
Fishmeal	6-10	5.9	0.8	High calcium
Dried blood (quick)	13	0.8	—	
Feathers	3-13	—	—	
Leather dust	5-12	—	—	
Wood ash (quick-acting)	—	—	1.7	
Leaf mould	0.4	0.2	0.3	
Shoddy (industrial waste)	2-15	—	—	

Inorganic fertilisers

Nutrient	Fertilisers (Percentage available nutrient in brackets)
Nitrogen (N)	Nitrate of soda (16.5)
	Nitrate of ammonia (Nitrochalk) (25)
	'Nitroshell' (34.5)
	'Nitram' (34.5)
	'Nitro 26' (26)
	Sulphate of ammonia (21)
Phosphate (P)	Superphosphate Granular (19)
	Powder (18)
	Calcium phosphate
	Rock phosphate
	Triple superphosphate (47)
Potassium (K)	Nitrate of potash (40-45)
	Muriate of potash (48)
Magnesium (Mg)	Epsom salts
	Magnesium limestone (11% total Mg)
	Kieserite (16% total Mg)
	Magam (Magnesium ammonium phosphate) slow release
Compound fertilisers	Growmore (7:7:7)
	Osmacote (18:11:10) (very expensive)
	Enmag (5.5:20.5:9)

Source: after MAFF, 'Organic Manures' (1975).

6.2.5 Fertilisers

Table 6.15 shows the nutrient contents of some organic and inorganic fertilisers. An important point to remember when planning the use of fertilisers on new plantings is the risk involved in using high nitrogen mixtures. Nitrogen tends to benefit weeds more than the young trees, as the weeds often take it up more quickly and consequently can suppress the trees by their vigorous growth.

The best organic fertilisers are farmyard and stable manures, but these may be expensive. It may be possible to get sawdust, pigeon manure or sewage sludge for little or no cost other than transport. They should all be worked in directly by hand or rotavation, at rates around 25 tonnes per hectare.

The amounts of nutrients in synthetic inorganic fertilisers are precisely measured. These nutrients are available to the plant more quickly than those in organic fertilisers. Availability is measured in units, a unit being 500 g. For example, on a standard 50 kg bag of compound fertiliser, the amount of available nitrogen (N), phosphorus (P) and potassium (K) would be marked as 15:15:15 units 7.5 kg of each). The bag should also have recommended application rates marked. Slow release inorganic fertilisers are available, but these are expensive and organic fertilisers are better in this respect, particularly as they also contain organic matter that improves the soil structure.

When dealing in large quantities over a long period, inorganic fertilisers are preferable, but the following points should be kept in mind.

— Some materials may be contaminated, e.g. sewage sludge by heavy metals and/or unwanted weeds, mushroom compost by pesticides.
— Straw on its own and in farmyard manure, and sawdust and other wood

wastes, will cause nitrogen to become unavailable to plants in the early stages of decomposition. This will be released in the later stages. If the materials are applied raw, plant growth will be poor and leaves may turn yellow. Addition of a nitrogen fertiliser should solve this problem.

Ideally, these materials should be allowed to stand for six months to one year before being applied, so nitrogen is not taken up when they are used.

A very good reference on the subject is Hills (1975) *Fertility without Fertilisers* which covers in detail compost, leaf mould, peat, manure, municipal compost, sewage sludge and green manures.

6.2.6 Planting out

There are four main causes of casualties to young trees and shrubs during planting out, namely:

— physical damage;
— moisture loss;
— frost;
— lack of nutrients.

Advance planning can minimise the effects of these. The following are points to remember, summarising the information contained in the rest of this section:

(a) Be prepared to plant out at the right time of year.
(b) Have a plan prepared for the number of plants, their planting patterns, mixtures and spacings to be used.
(c) Ensure that there is enough space for the number of trees and shrubs to be planted and that the manpower is available to do the work.
(d) Ensure that facilities are available for the temporary storage of live plants, in case of hold-ups, such as unexpected harsh frost or lack of manpower.
(e) Arrange transport and handling properly so that plants suffer the minimum stress in the process.
(f) Employ the correct planting methods.

When to plant

Deciduous, broad-leaved species should be planted when dormant, between leaf fall in late autumn, up to a few weeks before the new leaves emerge in spring. Periods of dormancy will vary from place to place and from year to year, and the trees already growing locally may be used as a guide for this.

Planting in frosty conditions should be avoided, particularly with evergreens. It is, therefore, extremely risky to plant during the period of harsh frosts between late December and early February.

There is little chance of a species such as holly surviving if planted in mid-winter. March is commonly a period of cold, drying winds and should also be avoided. Moisture loss in such conditions can result in high casualty rates, particularly with birch and beech.

The optimum time for planting out is mid-October to early December, when soils are warm and moist. Deciduous trees and shrubs planted during this period can begin to establish their roots before their leaves emerge. Spring plantings may not have time to develop their roots to enable them to take up water successfully before the leaves emerge. This, combined with the March winds, can stress the plants and lead to their death.

Figure 6.7 Types of plant material for young trees

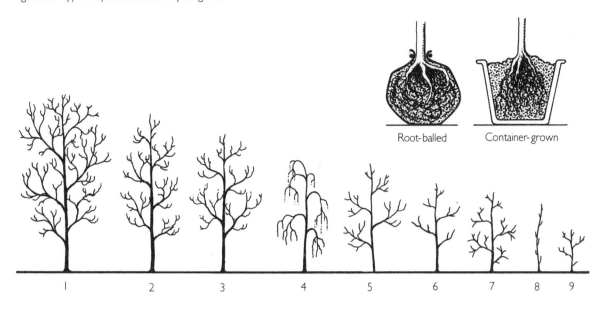

Root-balled   Container-grown

1.	Extra heavy nursery standard	4.5–5m (13'–18')
2.	Tall standard	1.8–2m (6'–6'8")
3.	Standard	1.7–1.8m (5'8"–6')
4.	Weeping standard	1.7–1.8m (5'8"–6')
5.	Half standard	1.1–1.6m (3'6"–5'2")
6.	Quarter standard	0.3–0.75m (1'–2'6")
7.	Feathered trees	all sizes
8.	Whip	450–900mm (1'6"–3')
9.	Transplant	150–600mm (6"–2')

Container-grown species may be planted out at any time of year, although autumn is still best. They are more able to survive as their roots suffer much less damage and disturbance.

Frost damage is less likely in built-up areas because of the higher temperatures around buildings, but in open spaces frost damage may occur in hollows where cold air can collect. Ash, beech, oak, larch and spruces are very frost tender and should not be planted in such hollows, while birch, poplar, pines and willows are frost hardy.

Advance planning of planting spacings, mixtures and patterns

Section 6.2.2 gives a simple guide to the choice of species for different site conditions. Having decided which species to use, you need to plan carefully what sizes of young tree and shrub to use and in what patterns they will be planted. Figure 6.7 illustrates different size groupings of young trees.

Standards (trees with clear, branchless stems) Extra-heavy nursery and tall standards are best handled by landscape contractors, as they will have the heavy duty machinery necessary for handling them. In general, the bigger a plant is, the more difficult it is to establish. Standards are grown by a system of undercutting and transplanting to produce a tight mass of roots; they are normally available bare-rooted. In this condition the roots dry out very easily and are often damaged during lifting and transplanting. Standards are also available root-balled, with most of the fibrous root system intact, or container-grown with a good, tight root-ball. These may be more than twice as expensive as bare-rooted but are more likely to put on good growth soon after planting, and can be planted up to a month after the end of the normal planting season.

Feathers   Feathers are young trees grown without pruning of side branches, and are available from transplant size upwards, but above 900 mm. They are difficult to handle, being bulky, with many branches which can easily be damaged, but are particularly useful in giving a variety of structure to new planting.

Whips   Whips are young trees with a single slender stem 450-900 mm tall. They are more expensive than transplants (about five times the price for hard-woods) but considerably bigger. They are small enough, however, to avoid the disadvantages of standards.

Transplants   A transplant is a young tree, 150-600 mm high, which has been grown in a seedbed, then transferred to a transplant line. The formula commonly used by suppliers, 1 + 2, means that the plant has spent one year in a seedbed and two years in a transplant line. The transplants should not spend more than two years in a transplant line, so the formula 1 + 2 + 2 is possible for five-year-old transplants.

Your choice of which sizes to plant out will be affected by how long you are prepared to wait for the vegetation to grow to a desired height. Traditionally, standard trees have been planted to produce an immediate effect. They are, however, expensive (for the price of one standard you could buy 150 small trees), difficult to handle, require stake supports and are very easily damaged during handling and planting. A lot of money may be tied up in a few standard trees which often fail, if they are not vandalised first.

Two-year-old feathered seedlings or whips are cheaper, much easier to handle and can survive planting out without the need for stakes and ties. Within 2-3 years of planting, these smaller trees can overtake staked standards planted at the same time, becoming sturdier and looking more natural.

The density of plantings can also vary. Table 6.9 in section 6.2.2, for example, shows the dense spacings used by the Warrington and Runcorn Development Corporation. ('1 m centres' means that the distance between the stem of each tree and its nearest neighbour is about 1 metre.) With trees planted this closely, after a few years individual trees need to be removed ('thinning') or cut back to ground level ('coppicing') to avoid overcrowding. This sort of management requires some skill and an understanding of the natural structure desired in the maturing plantation (see section 7.4 for further details of woodland/scrub management).

Planting at close centres (0.9 m for whips and transplants and 0.45 m for shrubs) does have some advantages.

(a) A barrier is formed quickly and the surrounding vegetation is rapidly suppressed.
(b) Plants protect and force each other to grow taller than in a less dense planting. A dense thicket is formed, similar to the way woodlands grow up naturally.
(c) The general public may find dense plantings visually more acceptable.

When deciding upon planting densities, these advantages must be weighed

Figure 6.8 Examples of possible simple planting patterns

(A) Grid-planted mixture for a northern oakwood on a poor site

```
B   B   S   S   S   S   M   M
B   B   S   S   S   S   M   M
A   A   O   O   O   O   S   S
A   A   O   O   O   O   S   S
A   A   O   O   S   S   A   A
A   A   O   O   S   S   A   A
C   C   A   A   Bi  Bi  O   O
C   C   A   A   Bi  Bi  O   O
```

Alder (A)   16 (nurse)
Bird cherry (B)   4
Mountain ash (M)   4
Oak (O)   16
Scots pine (S)   16 (nurse)
Silver birch (Bi)   4

(B) Quincunx-planted woodland edge mixture of shrubs

```
C       H       H       C
    R       R       R
C       H       H       C
    R       R       R
C       H       H       C
    R       R       R
C       H       H       C
```

Hawthorn (C)

Hazel (H)

Rose (R)

(C) Staggered row planting for copses or shelterbeds

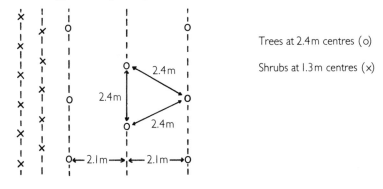

Trees at 2.4m centres (o)

Shrubs at 1.3m centres (x)

(D) Asymmetrical stagger

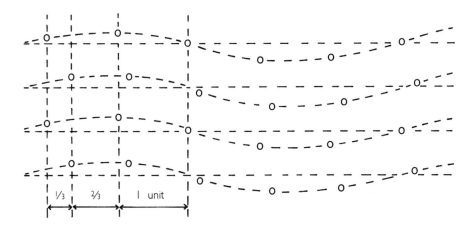

against the costs and practicalities of future thinning operations (in this case, after five years or so).

In general, trees should not be planted closer than 1.8m centres. Even at this spacing, thinning may be necessary 15 years after planting. The Woodland Trust has found that 0.9-1.2m tall trees planted 3.6m apart will create a wooded effect within a few years. This spacing is equivalent to 750 trees per ha and thinning is only necessary at a later stage, perhaps 25 years after planting.

Figure 6.8 gives examples of simple approaches to planting patterns. The simplest pattern is a regular grid (A). An alternative is the 'quincunx', with a plant in the middle of each square (B), whilst (C) illustrates how even spacings may be achieved using staggered rows. You may choose to use more natural, less regular planting patterns, but be careful not to let the plan get too complicated, as it can easily go wrong with inexperienced workers.

Figure 6.9 gives an example of a possible plan for planting a new copse or wood with a nature-like structure of trees and shrubs. The figure illustrates how the wood may look when planting is completed. It is not, however, a good idea to plant such a wood all at once. The planting sequence is best arranged to follow the natural sequence of woodland development, usually shrubs → pioneers → climax.

First, plant the whole area with shrubs: shade-tolerant species in the centre, and light-tolerant edge species in a band around the boundary.

Then, fast-growing pioneer tree species may be planted, spaced out between the established shrubs. These will then grow up in 10-15 years to form a canopy, producing a vegetation structure similar to that of immature pioneer woodland/scrub.

This sort of vegetation creates conditions ideal for seedling growth of the slower-growing, longer-lived climax tree species. If these are now planted amongst the pioneers and shrubs, they will be protected from exposure and high light levels (common causes of failure for seedlings of such species planted out in the open). There are exceptions, however, to this rule. Check the light requirements of the species being planted. For example, some climax species, like oak, are not very shade-tolerant; beech and lime are perhaps the most shade-tolerant.

Pioneers can act as a nurse crop and eventually form an understorey as the climax species overtop them. The use of fast-growing nurse tree species to protect climax species is widespread in forestry practice. Non-native commercial species such as Japanese larch or Norway spruce may be used and removed as a commercial crop once the climax species have established. Native nurse species such as alder need not be removed, but may be coppiced (see section 7.4.6 for further details of coppicing). The local authority or Forestry Commission (See appendix 15 for address) may provide advice on suitable nurses for your area.

In Figure 6.9, the single-species group plantings are recommended because they grow better this way and will provide more stable areas of vegetation which associated communities of plants and animals may colonise.

Should management become a problem, such single-species group-type plantings are also more resilient when unmanaged than, for example, randomly-mixed species. If a stand of randomly-mixed species is left unmanaged, usually only the vigorous species will survive and the woodland structure will become species-poor.

The following is a summary of points to bear in mind when drawing up plans for planting patterns.

— Arrange species to produce a balanced blend of foliage and flowers.

Figure 6.9 An example of a possible nature-like planting

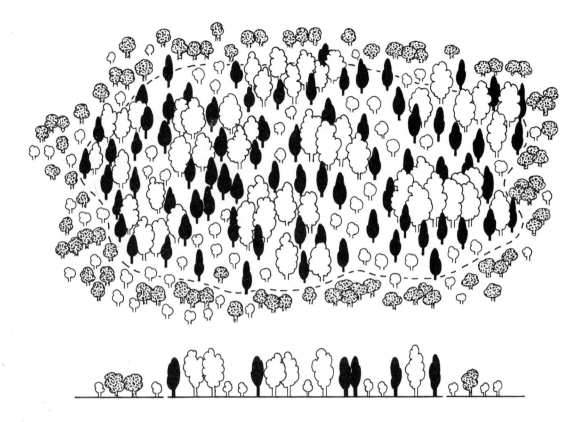

Key

 Shrubs. Planted in blocks of 10–25 of one species, at 1.5m centres, e.g. shade-tolerant species: bird cherry, hazel, holly, wild privet, hawthorn*, spindle, sweet briar. Edge species: blackthorn, gorse, broom, field maple*, dog rose.

 Pioneer (edge) tree species. Planted in groups (4,8,16, etc.) at 4–5m centres, e.g. field maple*, mountain ash, whitebeam, wild cherry, ash*, birch*, alder*.

 Nurse tree species. Planted between the climax species at 4–5m centres, e.g. birch*, alder*, conifers such as larch, pine, spruce.

 'Climax' tree species. Planted in groups (4,8,16, etc.) at 4–5m centres, e.g. oak, ash*, beech, hornbeam, Scots pine.

Note: * = species which fall into more than one category.

— Avoid planting too many different species to produce an unattractive hotchpotch.
— Consider the size and shape of plants at maturity, as well as the time it will take them to mature.
— Consider how seasonal changes will alter the appearance of the plantings.
— Try to avoid planting in straight lines and square blocks. Design layouts which suit the landscape.
— Consider the wildlife value of each species.

— If possible, avoid planting standards for instant effect when shrubs and whips would be more likely to survive.
— Remember the need for access to services, for machinery, for maintenance, etc.
— Consider what the labour and cost requirements will be for weeding, thinning and other management needed to maintain the planted mixtures.

Species to avoid

Vigorous species which may exclude other desirable species: e.g. in some situations, the native bramble (*Rubus fruticosus*) or non-natives such as sycamore (*Acer pseudoplatanus*), *Rhododendron ponticum* and *Aucuba japonica*.

Other species to avoid are plants associated with diseases, such as barberry (*Berberis vulgaris*) — the winter host plant of the destructive wheat rust (fungus), and some species such as mezereon (*Daphne mezereum*) and the wild pear (*Pyrus cordata*) which are unlikely to survive in general planting schemes, as they require very specialised habitats.

Handling and transporting stock

The two main causes of tree death during transportation are physical root damage and desiccation. The time between lifting (digging up) trees and re-planting should be kept to a minimum. All the time roots are out of the ground there is a risk of water loss. If ordering trees, arrange for delivery to be as near the planting date as possible. Lifting can be more damaging to some species than others. Oak, for example, has a tap root which is easily damaged, resulting in poor survival after planting out. Small trees are lifted using a fork which is less liable to cut their roots than a spade. During transport (e.g. in a closed van), young plants are always stacked with bundles of roots inwards and stems outwards, to minimise moisture loss. If storage is necessary, bare-rooted trees and shrubs may be stored in heeling-in trenches (see Figure 6.10(A)) sufficiently deep to minimise frost damage to the roots. Bundles of whips and shrubs should be loosened if stored for more than a few days, otherwise plants in the centres will die. A layer of straw over the plants will give extra protection from frost.

If trees have been transported in plastic bags or baled in hessian (see Figure 6.10(B)) to retain moisture, it is better not to disturb them until they are needed for planting. Trees in their winter dormant state may be stored in plastic bags for several weeks, but must *always* be shaded and kept in a well-ventilated place. Plastic can absorb heat from direct sunlight and overheating can kill the plants.

Container-grown plants in plastic containers can be stood in a trench or standards laid at an angle in a heeling-in trench. Again, plastic containers should be shielded from sunlight. Remember to remove all containers and root wrappings before planting.

Planting methods

Immediately before planting an area, 600-900 mm around the tree should be cleared of weeds. (See section 6.2.1 for further details of ground preparation.)

Large trees   The drawbacks of choosing to plant larger feathered trees or standards have already been discussed in this section. However, if larger trees are to be used, they are planted in pits. In average conditions, the pit dimensions are as follows:

A

B

9. (A) Newly-disturbed vacant sites are (B) soon dominated by colourful communities of annual and biennial weeds

10. Water's edge communities of emergent, tall swamp plants

11. Water's edge communities of emergent, short swamp and marsh plants

12. *Rank, perennial, tall grass and tall herb communities on embankments, uncut road verges, etc.*

13. *Scrub vegetation, undisturbed for perhaps 20 years, dominated by woody shrubs less than 5m in height*

14. *Low, perennial grass and grass-herb communities, maintained either by disturbance or unfavourable conditions*

15. *Deciduous and evergreen woodland, over 5m in height, and urban 'pasture' woodland*

The playing of
ball games
in this area
is forbidden

16. *A 'green desert' of gang-mown short grass*

A

B

17. *What can be done: (A) by leaving an area un-mown; and (B) by simply sowing a vacant plot with wildflower seeds*

18. and 19. Habitat creation: the William Curtis Ecological Park, London, transformed from a lorry park into an inner-city oasis

Figure 6.10 Tree storage and transportation

(A) Heeling-in trench

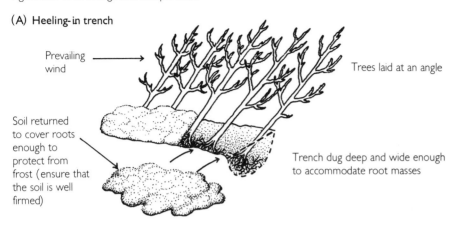

Prevailing wind

Trees laid at an angle

Soil returned to cover roots enough to protect from frost (ensure that the soil is well firmed)

Trench dug deep and wide enough to accommodate root masses

(B) Transportation

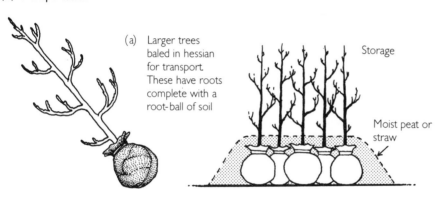

(a) Larger trees baled in hessian for transport. These have roots complete with a root-ball of soil

Storage

Moist peat or straw

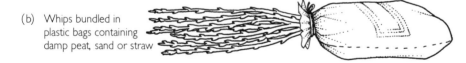

(b) Whips bundled in plastic bags containing damp peat, sand or straw

(C) Container-grown trees

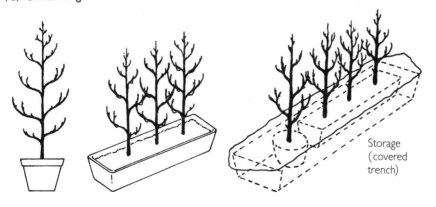

Storage (covered trench)

Figure 6.11 Pit-planting larger trees

(A) Digging the pit

A benched pit on a slope

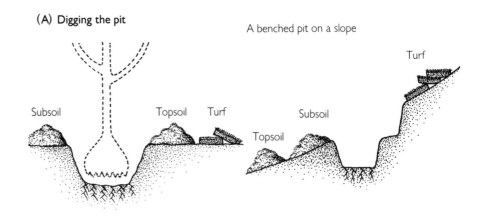

Subsoil   Topsoil   Turf

Turf

Subsoil

Topsoil

(B) Putting in the stake (Ref.: BTCV 1980 Handtools)

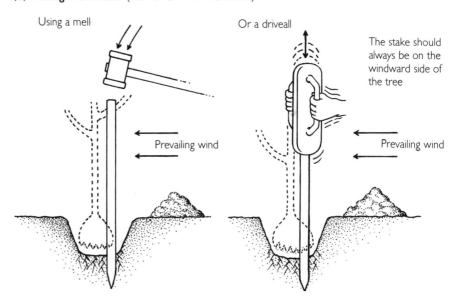

Using a mell

Or a driveall

The stake should always be on the windward side of the tree

Prevailing wind

Prevailing wind

(C) Putting in the tree

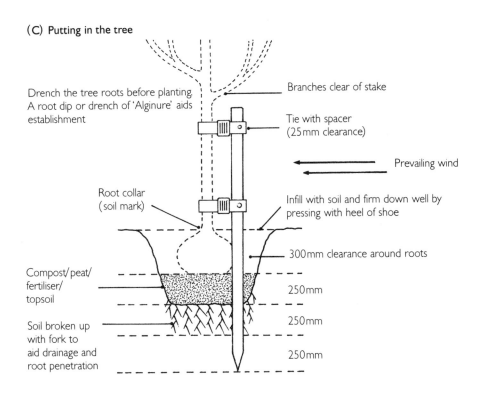

Drench the tree roots before planting. A root dip or drench of 'Alginure' aids establishment

Branches clear of stake

Tie with spacer (25mm clearance)

Prevailing wind

Root collar (soil mark)

Infill with soil and firm down well by pressing with heel of shoe

300mm clearance around roots

Compost/peat/ fertiliser/ topsoil

250mm

250mm

Soil broken up with fork to aid drainage and root penetration

250mm

Soak around the planted tree with one or two buckets (8–16 litres) of water and spread a layer of coarse bark mulch around it (taking care not to pile the mulch up against the tree itself). The coarse mulch aids moisture retention and restricts weed growth. Plastic mulch mats, weighted with stones or coarse gravel, perform the same function

(D) On heavy wet soil   On a light dry soil

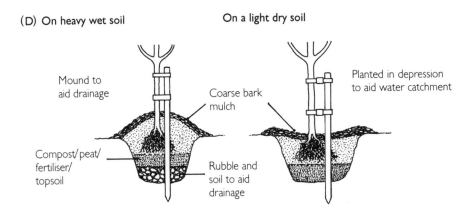

Mound to aid drainage

Coarse bark mulch

Planted in depression to aid water catchment

Compost/peat/ fertiliser/ topsoil

Rubble and soil to aid drainage

(E) Ties (different gauges are available for different-sized trees)

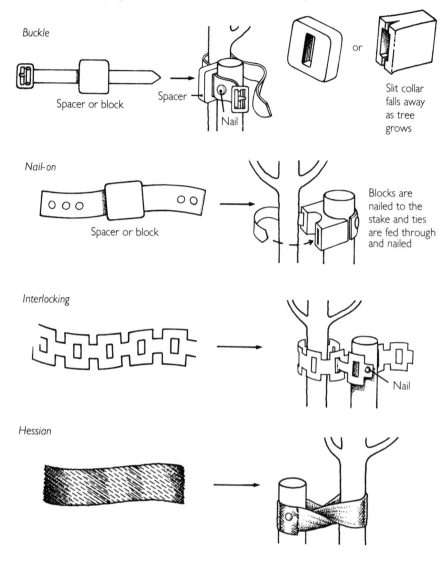

Buckle

Spacer or block

Spacer

Nail

or

Slit collar
falls away
as tree
grows

Nail-on

Spacer or block

Blocks are
nailed to the
stake and ties
are fed through
and nailed

Interlocking

Nail

Hessian

(F) Alternative methods of staking

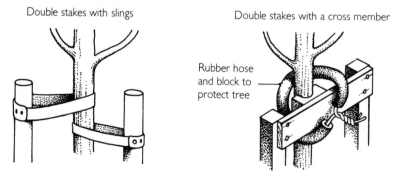

Double stakes with slings

Double stakes with a cross member

Rubber hose
and block to
protect tree

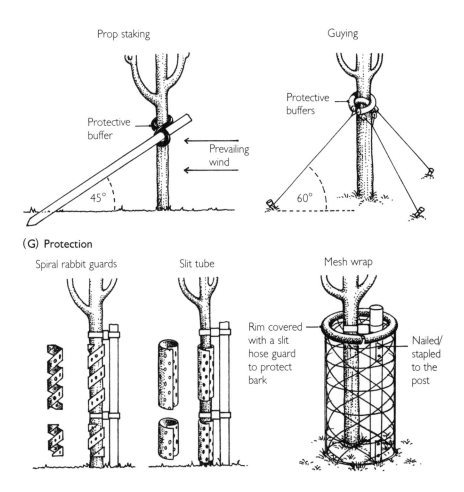

Prop staking

Guying

Protective buffer

Prevailing wind

45°

Protective buffers

60°

(G) Protection

Spiral rabbit guards

Slit tube

Mesh wrap

Rim covered with a slit hose guard to protect bark

Nailed/ stapled to the post

Small feathered trees (about 1 m high): 0.5 m wide × 300 mm deep
Large feathered trees and standards (1-2 m high): 1 m wide × 600 mm deep
Extra-heavy, transplanted nursery stock (2-5 m high): 1.5 m wide × 600 mm deep

If in doubt, a good rule of thumb is to allow 300 mm clearance all round the tree root-ball and 250 mm below (see Figure 6.11(C)).

The following are guidelines for the preparation of planting pits. When digging the pits, always keep the topsoil and subsoil in separate piles.

(a) On stiff clay or sites where a lot of heavy machinery has been used, the pit will soon become waterlogged unless it has some form of drainage. It should be linked to existing drains or the bottom of the pit excavated below 600 mm and filled with a rubble/soil mix.
(b) Position a stake slightly off centre so that it will be facing the prevailing wind, and using a drivall (see Figure 6.11(B)) (wearing safety helmets) drive the stake through the bottom of the pit for at least 600 mm. Alternatively, use a mell (see Figure 6.11(B)).
(c) If planting on grassland, put the cut turf upside down at the bottom of the pit. Otherwise, spread a 60 mm layer of compost or peat and fertiliser at the bottom.

(d) The material used to refill the pit depends on the existing soil. If it is a good loam, simply replace. If it is poor or clayey, mix in about a third by volume of peat and bonemeal mixed with half to a third of the rubble/clay. Mix in coarse sand on a wet site. The tree roots need to be able to cross the barrier between the pit soil and the surrounding substrate. If the changes in soil conditions across this barrier are too extreme, the roots will merely extend round and round the pit.

(e) Collect the tree from storage, remove container or plastic sacking if root-balled (do not remove loose-weave hessian packing, since this will break down easily). Do not disturb the root-ball, and make sure that the roots do not dry out. Trim cleanly any damaged roots. Plant at the soil mark (see Figure 6.11(C)) and if the roots are heavily developed on one side put them windward.

While one worker holds the tree in the correct position with the roots at the right height, the other fills in the pit, shaking the tree from time to time, to make sure that there are no air spaces left. Firm in the soil with gentle treading as the hole is being filled and firm up heavily when planting is completed.

(f) Loop a tree tie around the tree at about 500 mm from the top of the stake and 300-600 mm from the bottom and nail to the stake. The stake should not extend into the branches, and additional ties should be used if necessary to keep the tree firm and away from the stake.

(g) Spread a 150 mm layer of coarse bark mulch around the tree, being careful not to pile it up against the tree itself.

(h) The final step is to fit a tree guard. Plastic sleeves are available as spirals or slit tubes 600-700 mm long. They are suitable as guards against rabbit damage (see Figure 6.11(F)). Another form of plastic tubing is the 'Tuley Tube', constructed from transparent plastic. They physically protect young trees against grazing, simplify weeding and act as mini 'greenhouses', increasing early growth of the trees.

Wire mesh   In intensively-used areas wire mesh guards are necessary. They are available ready-made, between 500-1500 mm in height and 200-600 mm in diameter. They come either in halves or one piece and are best fixed together with hog rings. Loop the hog rings round the wires at 150 mm spacing and close them by squeezing tight with pliers.

There should be padding around the top to stop bark chafing if the tie comes loose. Either wrap hessian strips around it or fit a slit strip of plastic hose pipe as shown in Figure 6.11(G).

Stakes   Stakes for standards should be about 2.5-3 m long and treated with a preservative; 50 × 50 mm planed softwood stakes are commonly used, but round larch and sweet chestnut are equally as good. The stake must be stout enough to provide a firm anchor for the tree: it is a false economy to buy anything other than sound timber.

Ties (see Figure 6.11(E))   Ties can be the rubber buckle type which can be adjusted by letting out the buckle, or made on site from nail-on strips of hessian. An alternative is to use old inner tube, car seat belts or nylon tights: anything which is both strong and flexible will do. Whatever is used, there must be a buffer between the stake and the tree to prevent chafing of the bark. Never use rope, cord, or anything likely to cut the bark. Ties are available from forestry and horticultural suppliers and made by S.H. Rainbow (Green Bros.), Hailsham, Sussex.

On slopes, the pits should be benched, as in Figure 6.11(A). If planting a species into soil which is a little too heavy and wet, it is good practice to plant on slightly raised mounds, or conversely, where the soil is slightly too light and dry, planting in slight depressions may prove successful (Figure 6.11(D)).

Failure to maintain ties, stakes or guards can lead to the death of the tree. Ties wear out and even treated stakes can rot at the base after a few years. When this happens, the tree, which has not been supported by its own roots but rather by the stake, is liable to be severely rocked by the wind. This causes root damage and the tree may die, snap off or fall over completely. If a mesh guard is used, a tree with broken ties can sway in the wind and rapidly ring-bark itself on the guard.

Small trees and shrubs   Smaller trees offer a variety of other planting methods as well as pit-planting, notably notch planting and turf planting (see figure 6.12).

Schlich and Mansfield spades are commonly used for such work as they are straight, with strong handles and have bulges at the top of the blade which help to make space for the transplant. A garden spade, if used carefully, and grubbing mattock, can also be used.

Notch and turf planting are satisfactory methods on uncultivated areas with species which have shallow, spreading roots, but deeper rooting species with tap roots will require small pits, particularly on heavy, clayey soils.

6.2.7 Immediate after-care

Drenching the soil with water immediately after planting settles the soil, improving the trees' chances of survival. Heavy pruning is also recommended (see Figure 6.13). By pruning back tree side shoots, upright growth is stimulated. Cutting shrubs right back to a few cm encourages bushy growth. Plants that have been pruned have stronger roots in the spring and less of a problem with water loss through the leaves.

To minimise the possibility of fungal infections, all cut surfaces and wounds due to accidental splitting should be coated with a tree wound paint, for example Arbrex 805, as soon as possible. A delay of half an hour can be enough to allow fungal spores to infect the wounds.

If the planting is in an area of established vegetation, weeds may be a problem for the trees. Weeds should have been cleared from around the planting areas during the summer before planting.

However, the disturbance caused to the soil during planting may stimulate weed seed in the soil to germinate. A coarse mulch of chopped bark or a mulch mat (black plastic or roof felt) can prevent this problem. The mats can blow away and so are best held down with stones or coarse gravel. Fine mulches are less effective, as they can absorb moisture themselves and act as a growing medium for wind-blown seeds.

Residual, pre-emergent herbicides such as Simazine or Venzar are also sometimes used for this purpose. These are applied to the soil immediately after planting. (See Appendix 12 for further considerations of the use of herbicides.)

The survival of the plantings depends upon an adequate supply of water, light and nutrients and protection from severe competition from surrounding weeds. The long-term management methods reflect these needs and they are discussed further in section 7.4.

Figure 6.12 Planting smaller trees and shrubs. In all cases, drench with at least ½ a bucket of water (4 litres) immediately after planting

(A) Notch planting

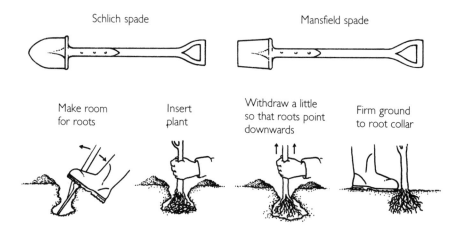

Schlich spade Mansfield spade

Make room for roots Insert plant Withdraw a little so that roots point downwards Firm ground to root collar

(B) Different notching methods

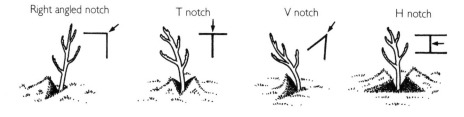

Right angled notch T notch V notch H notch

(C) On ploughed soil (usual ploughing distance 1.5m) depending on soil water conditions:

A = ridge top planting on wet soils
B = furrow side
C = furrow bottom on dry soils

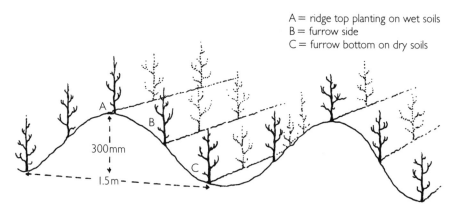

300mm

1.5m

(D) Planting in turf (with shallow surface rooting species)

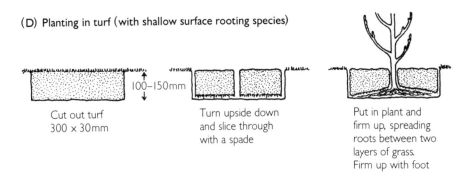

100–150mm

Cut out turf
300 x 30mm

Turn upside down
and slice through
with a spade

Put in plant and
firm up, spreading
roots between two
layers of grass.
Firm up with foot

(E) Pit-planting (best for large whips on clayey soils)

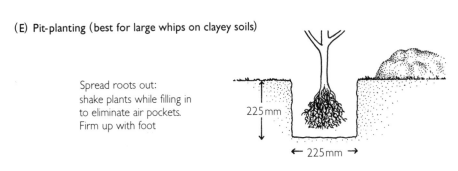

Spread roots out:
shake plants while filling in
to eliminate air pockets.
Firm up with foot

225mm

← 225mm →

(F) Planting in peaty ground and stony ground

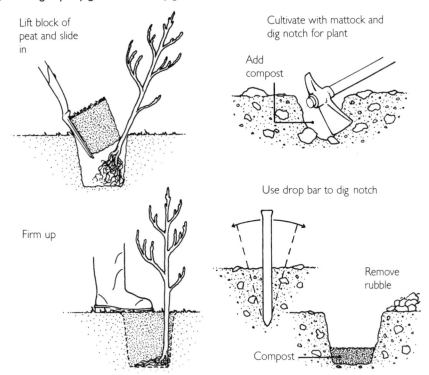

Lift block of
peat and slide
in

Cultivate with mattock and
dig notch for plant

Add
compost

Firm up

Use drop bar to dig notch

Remove
rubble

Compost

Figure 6.13 Winter pruning after autumn planting

Pruning side shoots promotes upward growth

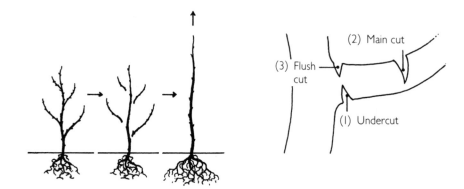

(2) Main cut

(3) Flush cut

(1) Undercut

Cutting back shrubs promotes bushiness

Mulches and mulch mats

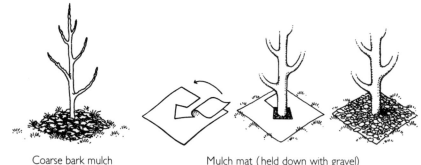

Coarse bark mulch   Mulch mat (held down with gravel)

Woodland grasses, flowers and climbers

The introduction of understorey plants is best attempted after the trees and shrubs have formed a continuous canopy, since woodland understorey plants are adapted to moist shady conditions. If they are planted before the canopy closes, they may fail because of excess light, heat and drying effects of the sun, combined with severe competition from other plants. The introduction of woodland understorey plants is, therefore, covered in section 7.4.1 as one of the management approaches for diversifying the woodland for wildlife.

6.2.8 Hedges

In cities, hedges are useful as people-proof barriers. Generally, robust, fast-growing plants are required: beech and hornbeam, for example, are best kept for garden hedges. Hawthorn, blackthorn and hazel are the best native plants. Holly, guelder rose, privet and, on appropriate sites, dogwood, wayfaring tree, field maple and crab apple can be planted in small numbers, to add visual and wildlife variety to a hedge. Hedges of native plants are cheaper, better for wildlife and often more attractive than those of plants such as cypresses or privet.

An example of an 'average' species mixture for a hedge, suggested by Baines and Smart (1984) is as follows:

	Per cent
Crataegus spp. (hawthorn)	60
Acer campestre (field maple)	20
Viburnum opulus (guelder rose)	5
Rosa canina (dog rose)	5
Ilex aquifolium (holly)	5
Ligustrum vulgare (wild privet)	5

Look at existing hedgerows in the area and draw up a similar species mixture, based on those species which do well.

Brooks (1980a) should be consulted for a detailed account of the establishment and early care of hedges. It is unlikely that a ditch or bank will be wanted for an urban hedge, but it is an advantage to plant on a low mound 225-300 mm high. The soil can be prepared by ploughing or rotavating along the intended line to a depth of 300-350 mm or by double digging. The aim in all cases is to prepare a well tilled soil at least 300 mm deep. Plants should be set 200-450 mm apart. A very dense hedge can be established by planting at 100 mm centres.

Planting a hedge

(a) Mark out a line with twine, making a cut in the ground with your spade along its entire length and dig out a trench the depth of your spade and 300-400 mm wide.
(b) Position the plants at the correct intervals.
(c) Backfill with your spade, straightening and firming each plant as you go.
(d) A single worker repeats the process for the second row, two workers plant a row each.

Alternative method of planting a hedge

(a) Line out and dig a trench as before but only dig out 600 mm of trench at one end.
(b) A second worker holds a plant in position, while the digger piles soil from further along the line on the plant. This is continued along the line placing each plant in the section of trench opened up when the preceding plant is backfilled.
(c) It can be done one row at a time or both rows together.

Protecting and managing a newly-planted hedge

Young hedges need protecting from rabbits, which are surprisingly common in urban/urban-fringe areas, and a rabbit-proof fence may be necessary. Where rabbits are not a problem, people may be. It is not easy to see the young plants in a hedge in its first few winters, and they are very easily trampled down unknowingly. A fence with two strands of plain wire can be used to mark the line, but where vandalism is likely, this should not be done. Some authorities recommend cutting the hedge back to 50-75 mm to encourage growth. However, in open areas it is probably better not to cut back, but to trim lightly each year until the hedge has reached the desired height.

Figure 6.14 Planting a hedge

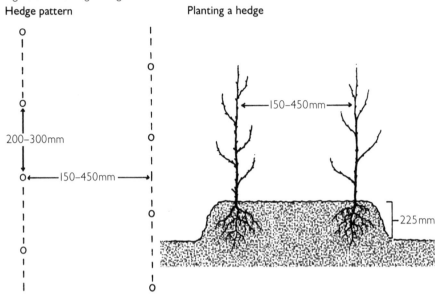

Hedge pattern   Planting a hedge

The Ministry of Agriculture, Fisheries and Food leaflet *Planting Farm Hedges* gives notes on the species most often used and simple guidelines to planting methods. The notes in Brooks' *Hedging* (1980a) are more detailed and cover the types of species best suited to different soil conditions. Cameron (1984) is an interesting summary of current knowledge of the biology and history of hedges in Britain.

6.2.9 References

Aldhous, J.R. (1972; reprinted 1975) *Nursery Practice*, Forestry Commission Bulletin 43, HMSO

Baines, C. and Smart, J. (1984) *A Guide to Habitat Creation*, Greater London Council, Ecology Handbook No. 2

Beckett, K. and Beckett G. (1979) *Planting Native Trees and Shrubs*, Jarrold

Blatchford, O.N. (ed.) (1978) *Forestry Practice*, Forestry Commission Bulletin 14, HMSO

Bradshaw, A.D. and Chadwick, M.J. (1980) *The Restoration of Land*, Blackwell, Studies in Ecology, Vol. 6.

British Trust for Conservation Volunteers (1980) *Handtools* (compiled by A. Follis)

Brooks, A. (1980a) (revision) *Hedging*, BTCV

—— (1980b) *Woodlands. A practical conservation handbook*, BTCV

Cameron, R.A.D. (1984) 'The biology and history of hedges: exploring the connections', *Biologist*, **31**(4):203-8

Carter, E. (1982) *A Guide to Planting Trees and Shrubs for Wildlife and the Landscape*, Farming and Wildlife Advisory Group (FWAG)

Corder, M. and Brooker, R. (1981) *Natural Economy. An ecological approach to planting and management techniques in urban areas*, Kirklees Metropolitan Council

Countryside Commission for Scotland (1980) *Plants and Planting Methods for the Countryside*, Battleby Display Centre

Devon Trust for Nature Conservation (1981) *Growing Trees and Shrubs from Seed*, Bulletin No. 3

Duffey, E. *et al.* (1974) *Grassland Ecology and Wildlife Management*, Chapman & Hall, London

Dutton, R.A. and Bradshaw, A.D. (1982) *Land Reclamation in Cities*, HMSO

Edlin, H.L. (1975) *Guide to Tree Planting and Cultivation*, Collins

Evans, J. (1984) *Broadleaved Silviculture*, Forestry Commission Bulletin No. 62

Forestry Commission (1982) *The Marketing of Forest Tree Seeds and Plants*, HMSO

Gray, W.G. (1953) *The Raising of Aspen from Seed*, Forestry Commission Record No. 2, HMSO

Greenwood, R. and Moffatt, D. (1982) 'Implementation techniques for more natural landscapes' in Ruff, A. and Tregay, R. *An Ecological Approach to Urban Landscape Design*, Occasional Paper No. 8, Department of Town and Country Planning, University of Manchester

Hamilton, E. (1983) *Tree Planting: 1, 2, 3, 4*, Woodland Trust Newsletters 9, 10, 11, 13

James, N.D.G. (1966) *The Forester's Companion*, Blackwell

Kennedy, C.E.J. and Southwood, T.R.E. (1984) 'The number of species of insects associated with British trees. A re-analysis', *J. Anim. Ecol*, **53**:455-78

La Dell, T. (1983) 'An introduction to tree and shrub seeding', *Landscape Design*, **8**:27-31

Liebscher, K.A.R. (1979) *Tree Nurseries*, BTCV

Ministry of Agriculture, Fisheries and Food (MAFF) (1980) *Planting from Hedges*, Advisory Leaflet (ADAS) 763

Nature Conservancy Council (1980) *Treeplanting*, Nature Conservation Guides series

Ranson, C. (1979) *Planting Coppice for Firewood*, Nature Conservancy Council

Royal Society for Nature Conservation. (n.d.) *Tree Planting and Wildlife*, leaflet

Ruff, A.R. (1979) *Holland and the Ecological Landscape*, Deanwater Press

Sheat, W.G. (1957) *Propagation of Trees, Shrubs and Conifers*, Macmillan

Southwood, T.R.E. (1961) 'The number of species of insect associated with various trees', *J. Anim. Ecol*, **30**:1-8

Tregay, R. and Gustavsson, R. (1983) *Oakwood's New Landscape. Designing for Nature in the Residential Environment*, Warrington and Runcorn Development Corporation

Urban Wildlife Group (1984) *Trees and Shrubs for Wildlife*, information leaflet

Villier, H. (undated) *A Tree for Every Site: A select list of trees and shrubs*, Arboricultural Association leaflet No. 5

Yoxon, M. (ed.) (1977) *Creative Ecology, Part 1*. Ecological Studies in Milton Keynes, No. 18, Milton Keynes Development Corporation

6.2.10 Useful organisations (see Appendix 15 for addresses)

Arboricultural Association (incorporating the Association of British Tree Surgeons and Arborists)

Department of Agriculture for Northern Ireland: Forest Service

Forestry Commission: Forest Research Station and Northern Research Station

Men of the Trees

Town Trees Trust

The Tree Council

Trees for People

Woodland Trust

6.3 Freshwater

As well as the natural expanses of freshwater in Great Britain, such as lakes, pools, streams and rivers, many have been created by man. In medieval times, ponds were constructed to breed fish for food and as water supply for human settlements. From the eighteenth century onwards especially, extensive lakes were constructed in private estates and parks. More recently, gravel workings and reservoir construction have created further great expanses of water as our cities have expanded. However, small ponds, reedbeds, marshes and wet meadows in Britain have been severely depleted. This is due to the advent of piped water supplies, the decline of horses as working animals and grants for filling in farm ponds and draining waterlogged areas.

Rich communities of plants and animals can exist in and around even a small pond. A pond can, therefore, be a useful educational resource, as well as a rich habitat for wildlife and an attractive addition to the landscape. Ponds constructed for these reasons will require management.

If neglected, they may stagnate, as nutrients build up in the water (eutrophication). The water plants eventually die or the vegetation may undergo succession as illustrated in Figure 6.15.

This section deals with the methods for creating new ponds, and section 7.5.3 covers their management, as well as the improvement and management of existing areas of freshwater.

6.3.1 Siting a new pond

The most important requirement for a new pond is an adequate supply of unpolluted water. Natural sources of water are preferable to tap water. The water in British mains is treated with chemicals such as chlorine and may have accumulated soluble salts which make it nutrient-rich. A water supply rich in such nutrients can cause problems. It provides ideal conditions for species of algae such as *Cladophora* which undergo 'blooms', either filling the water with a dense cloud of algal cells or forming mats on the surface. Such blooms can cut off the light for submerged water plants and eventually kill them. If not removed, the bloom can eventually lead to the pond becoming stagnant.

Section 6.3.4 outlines methods of using existing watercourses and high groundwater levels, but if such conditions are not present on a site, other sources of water will need to be found. The rainfall catchment area for a pond will be increased by siting it on low, flat ground where water will naturally collect. The rainfall run-off from the surrounding soil may be channelled into the pond by laying or diverting land drains. Rain-water may also be piped from the roofs of nearby buildings. Run-off from nearby parkland, roads or car parks may be polluted (see section 6.3.5). Pollutants such as dirt particles and oil may be removed by incorporating a silt/oil trap into the pool inflow (see Figure 6.16 for two of the many designs currently available). However, direct surface run-off from nearby surfaces such as roads or car parks will not be easily controlled and ponds should be sited well away from such features. During long dry spells, polluted dust accumulates on these hard surfaces. A sudden rainstorm can wash large quantities of the accumulated pollutants into the pond, causing a very severe 'pollutant shock' to the system.

Water plants need an adequate supply of sunlight and ponds situated in heavy shade may become stagnant. Trees can cause problems with falling leaves clogging up the pond, and the shade they cause during the summer. Any trees should, therefore, be on the north side of the pond.

It is important that the pond is visible and not tucked away in an area prone

Figure 6.15 Natural succession in open water: (A) nutrient-poor; (B) nutrient-rich

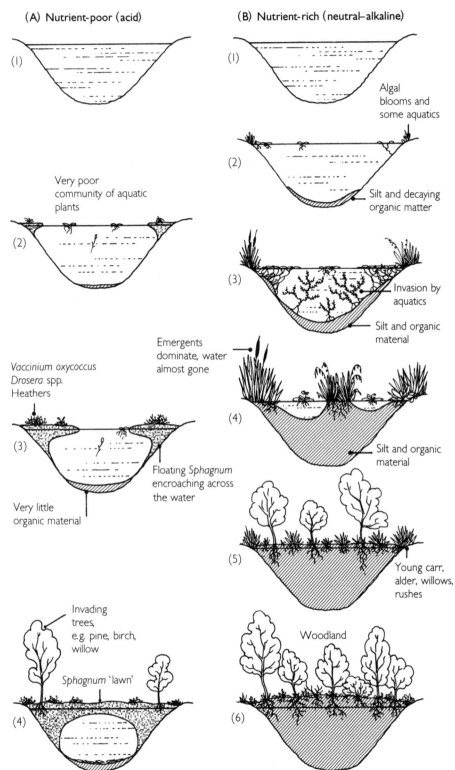

(A) Nutrient-poor (acid)

(1)

Very poor
community of aquatic
plants

(2)

Vaccinium oxycoccus
Drosera spp.
Heathers

(3)

Very little
organic material

Floating *Sphagnum*
encroaching across
the water

Invading
trees,
e.g. pine, birch,
willow

Sphagnum 'lawn'

(4)

(B) Nutrient-rich (neutral–alkaline)

(1)

Algal
blooms and
some aquatics

(2)

Silt and decaying
organic matter

(3)

Invasion by
aquatics

Silt and organic
material

Emergents
dominate, water
almost gone

(4)

Silt and organic
material

(5)

Young carr,
alder, willows,
rushes

(6)

Woodland

Figure 6.16 Silt/oil traps

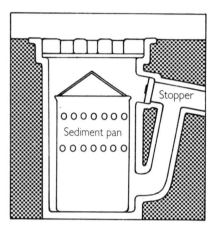

Silt trap. Sediments are periodically removed by lifting out and emptying the sediment pan

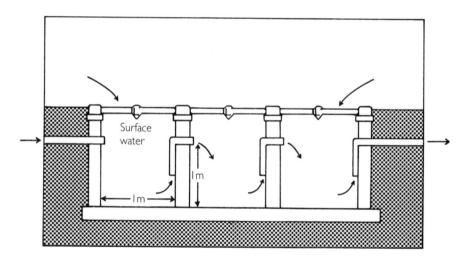

Petroil and oil trap. This works on the principle that petrol and oil float on water and are, therefore, unable to pass through the submerged tank outlets

to vandalism. Being able to see the pond is also an important safety feature, particularly where it is likely to be visited by unsupervised young children.

When siting the pond, be careful not to overlook the habitats already present. These may be more valuable or interesting than would result from the pond's construction. Be careful also not to drain valuable wetland habitats for the sake of a little extra water in the pond.

The bigger the pond, the more stable will be the plant and animal communities which develop. A pond less than 5 × 5m across will usually be too small. A water depth up to 1-1.5m is necessary if clear water is to be easily maintained. This gives an idea of the minimum amount of ground area and depth required.

Inner-city sites often have services running beneath them such as storm drains and water pipes, gas and electricity supplies. Great care should be taken to avoid these during excavation. Ponds constructed over land drains have a mysterious tendency to lose water (see section 4.4.1 for further information on locating underground services). On some inner-city sites, excavation is often made difficult, for example where rubble or concrete foundations lie beneath the soil. In certain situations, for example where subsoil is being imported onto the site, it may be possible to 'build up' the bowl of the pond, rather than excavating it (or to use a combination of both).

Water is an attractive target for fly-tipping as it can hide the rubbish. Siting the pond away from vehicular access and in a visible position lessens this problem.

Try not to waste the spoil excavated for the pond. For example, use it to make a useful landscape feature or, if valuable topsoil is removed, it may be sold.

6.3.2 The pond shape

By varying the shape of the pond margins, banks and bottom, you will allow a richer mixture of plant and animal communities to develop in and around it and the pond will look more natural (see Figure 6.17).

Banks with slopes around 1:20 will allow a wide fringe of marginal vegetation to develop quickly. Steeper slopes of around 1:3 will allow a narrower fringe to develop more slowly. The areas of deeper and shallower water created by varying the contours of the pond bottom will similarly suit a range of different vegetation types. Winter freezing and summer overheating can be lethal to many forms of life in shallower water and areas deeper than 0.75 m can provide havens against such temperature extremes, as well as zones of escape, should the pond begin to dry up during a drought.

Ensuring that such deeper areas are all connected will avoid the possibility during drought that particular pockets of water become isolated from other deeper ones.

On larger ponds, islands are a desirable feature, as their isolation can allow species to thrive which are more susceptible to disturbance.

Artificial marshes may be created at the edge of a pond by extending the waterproof lining over a shelf and laying on it weed-free subsoil and peat or marshland soil.

Practical and safety considerations must prevail when varying slopes and water depth. A slope gradient greater than 1:3 is too steep for flexible pond liners because the soil needed to cover them (as protection against sunlight) will not stay in place. This is less of a problem below 1 m depth in the water as sunlight is filtered and less harmful to the liner.

Steep banks falling straight into deep water should be avoided wherever there is risk of unsupervised children gaining access. For safety's sake, gradually shelve or gently slope the pond banks down to provide deep water (1-1.5 m) so that the only way children can get into it is by wading out. Similarly, sudden increases in depth in the pond bottom are to be avoided.

6.3.3 Marking out, levelling and lining requirements

To minimise the chances of wasted effort, for example excavating too deeply, a detailed plan is useful before excavating the pond. Figure 6.17 gives an example of a pond with an approximate water surface area of $12\,m \times 12\,m = 144\,m^2$, with a small marsh, approximately $15\,m^2$ in area.

This pond would be marked out on the ground with stakes joined together with string (* in the figure).

Figure 6.17 Plan for a pond: (A) overhead view; (B) in section

(A)

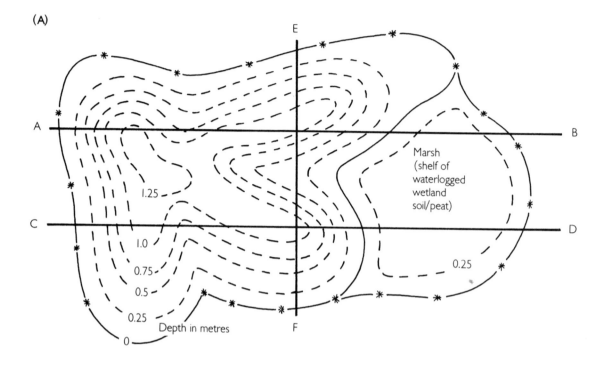

Marsh
(shelf of
waterlogged
wetland
soil/peat)

1.25

1.0

0.75

0.5

0.25

0

0.25

Depth in metres

(B)

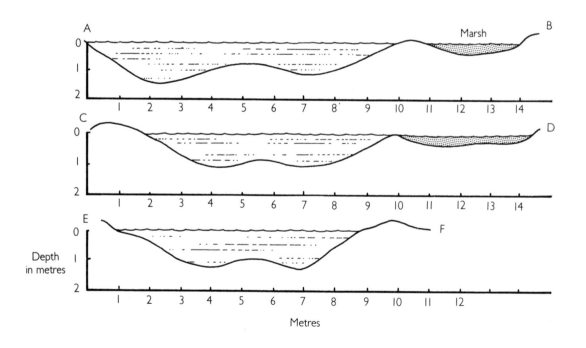

Marsh

Depth
in metres

Metres

Figure 6.18 A simple water level

Equipment: A length of garden hose, at least 5 m longer than the pool is wide, and two pieces of open-ended transparent tubing to fit on each end

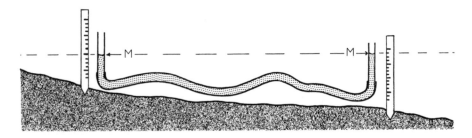

M = Meniscus — when the hose is filled with water until visible in both transparent tubes, the water will always settle at its own level. No matter how the hose lies in the hole, the height of the water in the tube will be the same at both ends, so that an imaginary line running between will always be horizontal. The height of the water in each tube may be compared to marked stakes, set in the ground at the edges of the hole, to gauge the level of the ground or pond banks.

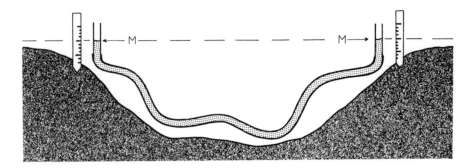

The stakes may also be used to gauge the levelness of the ground. If each stake is marked with 10 mm (1 cm) divisions a simple water level may be used before and after excavation (see Figure 6.18). The perimeter can then be lowered or built up as required.

If the pond is to be lined, you will need to estimate the area of the pond bottom. To do this on site, run a tape measure down one side of the excavation, along the bottom and up the other side, to estimate its length. Then repeat the process for its width. If a flexible liner is to be used, add 1 m to each measurement to allow for overlap at the edges. The exercise can be carried out on paper using a scale plan as in Figure 6.17(B) and estimating the length of the contoured bottom, using a piece of string or flexible wire.

For example, in Figure 6.17, the approximate length and width of the pond bottom are 16 m (E-F) and 15.5 m (A-B) respectively. Therefore, a flexible liner 17 × 16.5 m would be needed.

Considering the amount of clay that would be required for puddling (see section 6.3.4 on using clay for pond construction):

length = 16 m   width = 15.5 m
(allow a 1 m safety margin each way again)
17 × 16.5 = 280.5 m².

For a puddled clay lining 250 mm thick (which is equivalent to 1.3 × 250 mm = 335 mm raw clay), the amount of raw clay required is: 280.5 × 0.335 = 93.96 cu m.

6.3.4 Methods of creating new ponds

The BTCV handbook *Waterways and Wetlands*, compiled by Brooks (1981), is an extremely detailed source of further information on these methods, and is a valuable reference for anyone considering developing freshwater features.

Using existing watercourses

If a stream or river passes through a site, either an on-stream or an off-stream pond may be feasible (see Figure 6.19). In these cases, it is necessary to obtain the approval of the local water authority and to allow professional engineers to handle the design of the pond. The creation of the pond will alter the dynamics of the watercourse and a poor design may result in problems with flooding, for example, should a sluice or dam collapse. Under Section 23 of the Water Resources Act 1963, a licence is required by any person who wishes to abstract water from an inland water (i.e. river, stream, etc.) or from underground strata. A licence under Section 36 of that Act is also required if any person wishes to construct impounding works in an inland water, and an 'on-stream' pond involving the construction of a dam would normally fall into that category.

Applications for such licences under the Act should be made to your local water authority. There is commonly a requirement to advertise applications for several weeks in local newspapers in order to give people who think they might be affected a chance to make representations. Copies of applications and any other relevant documents have to be on deposit with the authority for inspection by members of the public during a period specified in the public notice.

Figure 6.19 Examples of (A) on-stream and (B) off-stream ponds

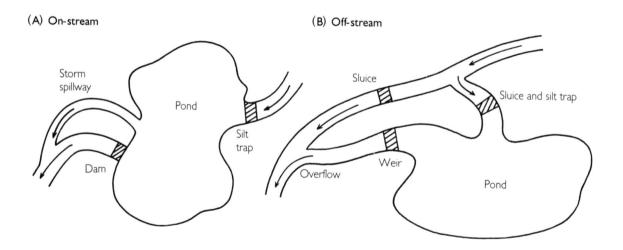

(A) On-stream

Storm spillway

Pond

Silt trap

Dam

(B) Off-stream

Sluice

Sluice and silt trap

Overflow

Weir

Pond

Silt traps are to remove suspended dirt and oil, etc. These are cleaned out from time to time. Sluices are adjustable barriers to control water levels. The weir is a stationary barrier set at the desired pond water level

There may also be land drainage aspects which also require consideration, and possibly consent, under the provisions of the Land Drainage Act 1976. Brooks (1981) summarises some of the technical difficulties of constructing on-stream and off-stream ponds.

Using existing conditions of high water table or soil impermeability

Direct indicators of such conditions include springs, seepage lines and wet patches. It is worthwhile checking after heavy rain when the soil has begun to dry and to look out for patches where groundwater continues to reach the surface. Wet patches may be due to 'top-ponding', where the top layer of soil is impermeable, often because of compaction. In some cases of top-ponding, however, breaking through the compacted layer will cause the water to drain away.

Certain plants are indicators of spring waterlogging. For example, rushes (*Juncus* spp.), horsetails (*Equisetum* spp.), meadowsweet (*Filipendula ulmaria*) and alder (*Alnus glutinosa*) grow naturally where the soil is wet most of the time.

The most reliable method of checking the soil water table is to dig one or more test pits, at least 1 m deep and to observe the presence/absence and level of water in the soil over the course of at least a year. The pits should be straight-sided holes, covered to avoid rain filling them and affecting the water level. If the pits show adequate levels of water throughout the year and if an impermeable subsoil is present, a pond may be constructed by stripping off the topsoil, digging out a hollow and using the material from the hollow to form a shallow sloping bank around the pond, as in Figure 6.20. The bank effectively enlarges the immediate catchment area for rainfall running into the pond.

On many inner-urban sites, streams do not occur and groundwater levels are much too low to be tapped. This is often because of the huge amounts of water extracted for human use and because of the presence of materials such as ancient building foundations and demolition rubble, etc. lying over the natural substrate.

Using clay

Probably the oldest examples of the use of clay in Great Britain are 'dew ponds' (see Figure 6.21). The ancient skills of siting and constructing them properly have almost been lost over the years. It is known, however, that they are generally situated where annual rainfall is around 1000 mm and annual evaporation 450 mm.

Figure 6.20 Use of high water table/impermeable bottom

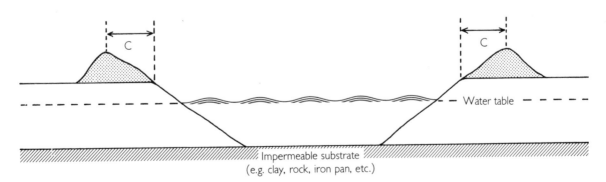

Impermeable substrate
(e.g. clay, rock, iron pan, etc.)

C = increased catchment area for runoff from rainfall

Figure 6.21 A dew pond

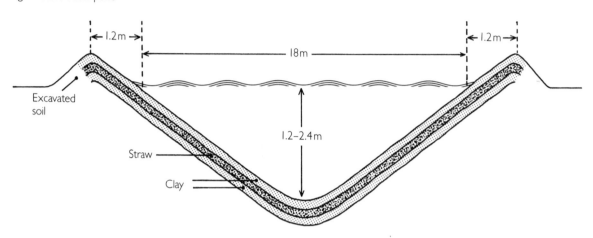

Clay was also used to line man-made lakes in Victorian parks and many miles of canals where they were constructed over permeable soils.

The traditional method of working the clay is 'puddling'. Raw clay has cracks and air spaces in it. It is spread onto the prepared, smooth, stone-free surface to be sealed and 'puddled' by wetting and gradually treading or pummelling until the air is removed and the layer of clay becomes solid and plastic. As long as the clay is kept moist, it will remain impermeable to water. However, if allowed to dry out for anything more than a few days, puddled clay may develop severe cracks which may only be repaired by extensive re-puddling. This can be a real problem where water levels are liable to fluctuate, therefore a puddled clay lining is probably impractical for a pond with an unreliable supply of water.

Other considerations concerning the use of puddled clay include:

Cost If a local landowner has a supply of unwanted clay, it may cost very little to import, but it is more often the case, because of the sheer bulk of material needed, that the cost of transporting the clay is very high.

Labour Traditionally, herds of stock (cows or sheep) were driven over the clay to puddle it. The modern equivalent could be a group of volunteers or school children in wellington boots. Alternatively, where the substrate is firm, a tractor may be driven backwards and forwards over the clay. Whatever the method, the work should be completed in a relatively short time, but not rushed. An adequate labour force is, therefore, essential, normally one worker for each sq m to be puddled.

The whole area should be puddled with a few cm of clay and then the whole process repeated with more layers added until the desired thickness is achieved. Ponds need to have linings at least 200 mm thick. At least 300 mm depth of raw clay should be used to allow for the compression caused by the puddling.

The raw clay is added a shovelful at a time. A little water is added (not too much) and the moistened clay is trodden into a solid layer, with neighbouring workers treading their areas together. The sloping sides and pond bottom are puddled with the same thickness of clay, ensuring that there are no projections

Table 6.16 Rough costs (1985) for flexible pond liners

Liner	Gauge	Approximate cost per sq m (£)
Polythene	1500 (375 micrometres)	2.00-2.50
(Mastic tape)	(50mm wide)	1.50-2.00 (per m)
PVC (laminated)	0.35mm	2.50-3.00
Butyl rubber		
(pure)	0.76mm	5.50-6.00
(EPD/butyl)	0.76mm	4.50-5.50
Rawmat		5.00-6.00

and that the substrate is firm and not liable to slip.

If work has to stop, the clay must be kept moist or even flooded temporarily, until work can continue. Avoid frosty weather as the clay can crack and lift as the water in it freezes.

A puddled clay pond should be durable enough for school parties to pond-dip, etc. and will be immune to leaks as long as the clay is thick enough and is always covered with water. Watering cattle and horses may damage a puddled clay lining, but sheep or goats may actually improve it as they tread the clay.

Using flexible pond liners

Sheets of polythene, PVC and butyl rubber are becoming very popular, cheap pond-lining materials.

Each type of material has slightly different qualities. All need covering with soil to lessen the degrading effect sunlight has on them (clear or light-coloured polythene is the most susceptible). Polythene sheets may be joined together with specially designed mastic tape. PVC and butyl sheets need to be heat-welded together by the manufacturers.

Table 6.16 gives examples of costs for different gauges of liners. The increase in cost from polythene to PVC and butyl is matched by an increase in tough-ness and durability. These factors need careful consideration when choosing a flexible lining material.

All three types of liner are laid using the same procedure. The excavated pond must have a smooth surface with all sharp stones removed. Sharp variations in the slope of pond banks or in the shape of the pond bottom should be avoided. This becomes more important the deeper the pond and hence the higher the pressure of water on the liner.

The base and sides need to be firm. Loose soil may shift and stress the liner once it is in place and filled with water. Banks with gradients higher than 1:3 are not recommended, as the soil covering needed to protect the sheeting from sunlight will not stay in place on steeper slopes.

The excavation needs to be 150-200mm deeper than the final depth to accommodate the liner and its protective layers.

Figure 6.22 illustrates the principle of protecting the liner from above and below to prevent puncture.

First, 50mm of sand is spread over the surface of the excavation. Stone-free

Figure 6.22 Laying a flexible pond liner

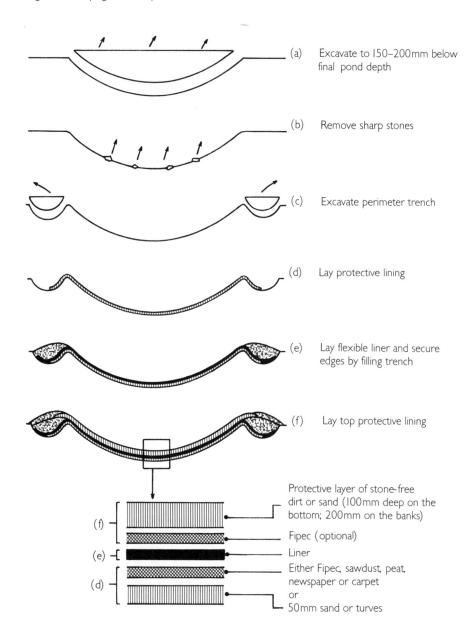

(a) Excavate to 150–200mm below final pond depth

(b) Remove sharp stones

(c) Excavate perimeter trench

(d) Lay protective lining

(e) Lay flexible liner and secure edges by filling trench

(f) Lay top protective lining

(f) — Protective layer of stone-free dirt or sand (100mm deep on the bottom; 200mm on the banks)

— Fipec (optional)

(e) — Liner

(d) — Either Fipec, sawdust, peat, newspaper or carpet

or

— 50mm sand or turves

peat, fine ash, sawdust, old newspapers or pieces of carpet are possible alternatives. It is possible to buy specially made fibre matting for this purpose (proprietary name 'Fipec', available from Butyl Products, see Appendix 14 for address).

Once the excavation is thus properly padded, the liner may be laid. To secure the edges properly, a trench, one spade width and depth, is dug around the pond so that the liner may be properly secured around the edges. The liner is then laid so that it lies loosely in the excavation with its edges lying in the trench. In warm weather, polythene and PVC expand, so extra slack is needed

20. and 21. Habitat creation: Linnet Lane, Liverpool, a sunny bower created on a corner plot

22. and 23. Habitat creation: gold medal garden at the 1984 Liverpool Garden Festival

24. *City nature is for people to enjoy: landscape painting at the William Curtis Ecological Park*

25. *People of all ages, especially children, can benefit from close contact with wildlife*

26. *Traditional sheep grazing in a Northampton graveyard*

27. *Traditional management by coppicing in this Suffolk woodland dates back to the thirteenth century*

28. *Regenerating hazel* (Corylus avellana) *coppice*

29. *Pollarded trees in Epping Forest*

30. *Hedglaying, a traditional form of hedgerow management*

to allow for shrinkage when the sheets cool. Both materials may be folded to accommodate irregularities in the pond shape. Butyl must not be folded. If you have to tape polythene sheets together, overlap sheets by 150 mm, clean the overlaps and join using mastic tape at least 75 mm wide. Moving a board along under the sheets as you tape will provide a solid surface on which to press the sheets together.

The liner is then covered with a 100 mm layer of stone-free soil as a protection against sunlight. If extra protection is needed against heavy use of the pond, for example if it is to be used by schoolchildren, another layer of Fipec matting, between the liner and the soil, will lessen the danger of puncture. Where people (children) are expected to paddle, or pond-dip, etc., a layer of smooth river gravel will provide added protection as well as a microhabitat for invertebrates. Do not use other materials such as newspapers or carpet for this purpose as they may contain toxic solvents, etc. When filling the pool with water, use a plastic sheet wherever water pours into the pond, to prevent scouring (washing soil away).

Don't use permeable soil or sand to cover the edges of the liner. A clayey soil is preferable. Porous soil may act as a 'wick' causing water to percolate over the edge of the liner by capillary action.

Bentonite clay

Bentonite is a fine-powdered clay manufactured to line reservoirs, etc. It is marketed as 'Volclay' and is very expensive. It is mixed with the soil lining of an excavated pond/pool and, upon contact with water, swells to 15 times its volume to form an impermeable lining similar to puddled clay, but with the advantage that it is not so liable to cracking when it dries out. Rates of application vary according to the type of soil and the suppliers will advise if a ½kg soil sample is sent to them for analysis.

Bentonite is only really suitable for large-scale projects which are well financed. The clay is not suitable for small, shallow ponds as it swells too much and may severely reduce the depth of the pond.

Further information on Bentonite clay may be obtained from the suppliers, Rawell Marketing Ltd (see Appendix 14 for address) or by referring to Brooks (1981). Rawell also manufacture a membrane impregnated with Bentonite clay, marketed as 'Rawmat'. This is a new product at the time of writing, but it may prove an ideal material for lining small ponds.

Concrete

Many town gardens and school grounds contain small concrete ponds. A garden pond 1.8 m^2 and 150 mm deep requires a concrete base 100 mm thick and sides 150 mm thick. A larger pond 3 m^2 and 0.6 m deep requires both the base and sides to be at least 150 mm thick (Brooks 1981). Ponds much larger than this need the skills of professional contractors or structural or civil engineers to calculate lining requirements.

A great deal of skill is required to construct a waterproof concrete pond lining. As the concrete is being laid, new concrete will only bond with the previous batch if laid within 2-4 hours. Slabs over 3 m^2 require joints to allow the concrete to expand and contract as temperature changes. Joints are strips of metal or PVC which bridge the joint and have a number of ribs or ridges to minimise seepage.

Concrete ponds with sloping sides are less liable to be damaged by the pond freezing, as the ice will push upwards rather than against the pond wall. Concrete should never be laid in frosty conditions as the water in the concrete mixture may freeze and destroy the structure of the material.

Cement contains chemicals toxic to aquatic life, so a new concrete pond must be refilled and emptied several times for at least one month. Each time, scrub the concrete to remove surface deposits. After this, when the water is clear, bottom gravel and plants and animals may be introduced.

Further information on the construction of concrete ponds may be found in Brooks (1981), Franck (1972) and Shirley (1980), or by enquiring with the Cement and Concrete Association (see Appendix 15 for address).

Glass fibre

Ready-made rigid glass fibre pool linings can be purchased, but are very expensive and usually much too small for anything other than a pond for a garden or school quadrangle. Steep-sided pools are not recommended; a pond with shallow sloping sides and plenty of ledges is more appropriate. The ledges can hold soil in which water plants may be established. The hole for the liner must be well padded with firm compacted sand to fit exactly the contours of the glass fibre, and the lining should be as level as possible when in place.

Whatever method is used to construct the pond, try to have it completed and filled with water by early spring, as this is the best time.

6.3.5 Problems associated with urban water features

Pollution   Pollutants include run-off from car parks, roads, paved areas, etc. This can contain particles of brick and mortar, concrete, ash, bitumen, rubber and metal, oil, petrol, heavy metals such as lead from exhaust fumes and animal (especially dog) faeces.

Bacteria from faeces are a direct health risk. Oil and petrol, apart from being toxic, form a layer over plants and still water which prevents the passage of oxygen essential for animals to breathe. Suspended solids in the water cause problems by preventing sunlight reaching submerged plants, and settling out as silt. Heavy metals can build up in the water to levels dangerous to plants and animals. In certain situations, industrial waste causes additional problems, for example, water from coal and iron workings is often heavily polluted with iron, so that the water is rust-coloured.

Small ponds in parks and on golf courses, etc. are frequently polluted by fertilisers washed off adjacent land.

These are all problems to be borne in mind and, as far as possible, avoided when siting a new pond.

Safety   While people accept canals, rivers, streams and other long-established water features in the city, there is often a hostile reaction to the creation of new ponds because of the alleged risk to children. No pond can be completely safe, so it requires proper consideration of safety in the pond design and siting and sensible public relations to ensure that the project is a success.

6.3.6 Introduction of plants and animals

A newly-created pond will effectively be a sterile expanse of water. If it is tap water, it will probably contain chlorine (Cl) and dissolved salts (products of its treatment and recycling). It takes at least 48 hours for the chlorine to evaporate from the water, so the introduction of plants should not be undertaken for at least 2-3 days after filling the pond. On a site where your pond depends upon a supply of tap water, it is useful to construct a separate, small 'feeder' pond, into which tap water may be fed directly. This is left for a few days, so that the chlorine can evaporate. Then, the water may be allowed to pass into the main pond. The presence of dissolved salts creates nutrient conditions ideal for algae, and in a very short time the water may turn green with algal blooms. This will remain a problem as long as the water is nutrient-rich, but the establishment of healthy plant and animal communities can alleviate the problem and bring the pond into a 'balanced' state with excess nutrients being taken up by the plants and recycled through the plant and animal community.

Water plants

Local naturalists, the County Trust or the local officer of the Nature Conservancy Council should be able to help and advise on local sources of plants.

Wild plants from local waterways and wetlands are by far the best source. They should be representative of the local flora and suited to local ground, water and climatic conditions. Always find out who owns the water and gain their permission before removing plant material. The local authority parks and recreation department or the local water authority may know of waterway clearance work nearby and you may be able to rescue valuable plant material before it is destroyed.

In general, plants with rhizomes are best transplanted rather than grown from seed. Rhizomes are best gathered in the spring at the end of the plants' dormant period when they are beginning to shoot. Dig up the rhizomes with a spade and be sure to keep them in moist mud while in transit. The mud may also contain root fragments and seeds of other desirable species. Many submerged and emergent aquatic plants without rhizomes can be transplanted as cuttings if they are pushed into the mud (or weighted down on to it), but roots should be dug up wherever possible.

Some species may be introduced by scattering seed collected locally (or bought from a reputable supplier).

There is an extensive literature on the different plant species suitable for ponds (see Table 6.17). Suppliers of pond plants generally produce literature on the qualities and requirements of different species and it is becoming easier to find native aquatic plants on sale in water gardens and nurseries in this country. The following are a few examples of useful native aquatic plants, their valuable qualities and methods for transplanting them (all of these species provide food for wildfowl).

Submerged aquatics   These are very important as they provide food and shelter as well as oxygenating the water for aquatic animals. The increased oxygen levels help microscopic zooplankton to survive. These and other small aquatic animals feed on the algae responsible for algal blooms. If the pond has a layer of mud on the bottom, submerged aquatics may be transplanted into water up to 2 m deep, either by weighing down or by tying in a hessian bag full of soil. In shallower water, these may be placed where you wish the plants to establish, but in deeper water, it may be necessary gently to throw the weighted bundles of plants into the water.

Examples of species include:

— *Myriophyllum spicatum* (spiked water milfoil). An attractive species whose fine whorled leaves cast little shadow. Prefers base-rich conditions.
— *Potamogeton crispus* (curled pondweed) prefers base-neutral conditions, water 0.1-0.5 m deep, and is tolerant of disturbance.
— *Potamogeton perfoliatus* (perfoliate pondweed) prefers clean water.
— *Potamogeton gramineus* (various-leaved pondweed) has some tolerance to pollution.

— *Potamogeton pectinatus* (fennel pondweed) will tolerate pollution and turbid
  water, growing in depths of up to 0.5 m. Prefers base-rich conditions and is
  tolerant of disturbance.
— *Ranunculus aquatilis* agg. (common water crowfoot) bears attractive flowers.
  Prefers base-rich conditions and clean water, 0.1-0.5 m deep.
— *Sagittaria sagittifolia* (arrowhead) prefers base-rich conditions, water 0.1-
  0.5 m deep and is tolerant of disturbance.

Table 6.17 Sources of further information for recommended aquatic plant species

Reference	Groups covered	Number of species listed	Additional notes included
Baines and Smart 1984	Wetland plants	44 (N)	
Brooks 1981	Water plants:		Height, nutrients, environmental conditions, management notes and comments
	Free-floating	7 (N,I)	
	Submerged, rooted	29 (N,I)	
	Floating-leaved, rooted	7 (N)	
	Emergent	18 (N,I)	
	Marginal	34 (N,I)	
Corder and Brooker 1981	Aquatic plants:		Habitat and distribution
	Submerged, rooted	9 (N)	
	Free-floating	2 (N)	
	Floating-leaved, rooted	5 (N)	
	Emergent	9 (N)	
	Marginal	10 (N)	
Ecological Parks Trust 1981	Water plants	14 (N)	Soil, water depth, comments
Genders 1976	Pond plants:		Height, colour, habit, when in bloom, etc.
	Oxygenating	6 (N,I)	
	Floating	3 (N)	
	Surface flowering	14 (N,C)	
	Marginal	19 (N)	
Kelcey 1977	Water plants:		Type of water, nutrient status, depth, flow, value for water fowl, comments
	Submerged	9 (N)	
	Floating-leaved	7 (N)	
	Emergent/marginal	32 (N)	
Masters and Lancaster 1980	Water plants	11 (N)	
Ruff 1979	Water and marginal plants	36 (N)	Qualities, competition, propagation, observations
Wilson 1981	Pond plants:		
	Oxygenating	13 (N,I)	
	Free-floating	11 (N,I)	
	Rooted, floating-leaved	5 (N,I)	
	Marginal	30 (N,I)	

Key: C = cultivated varieties; N = native; I = introduced.

See section 6.3.7 for full references.

When transplanting submerged aquatics try to select more than one species and plant them in areas where clear water is not needed. Many species are highly invasive in the absence of competition from others, so it is better to establish a number of desirable species in separate blocks at the beginning so that they colonise neighbouring areas of the pond.

Otherwise, when you try to establish a new species, it may fail to compete with the vigorous, well-established species already present. A mosaic of different species with their different growth forms will provide different habitats and food for a variety of different animals.

Floating-leaved rooted aquatics   These also bear submerged leaves which help to oxygenate the water and the undersides of the floating leaves form another microhabitat for pond animals. These species may be transplanted in the same way as submerged aquatics into water up to 2 m deep.

Examples of species include:

— *Nymphaea alba* (white water lily) prefers clean water.
— *Nuphar lutea* (yellow water lily) prefers base-neutral conditions and is tolerant of disturbance.
— *Nymphoides peltata* (fringed water lily) — all the lilies bear very attractive flowers.
— *Potamogeton natans* (broad-leaved pondweed) prefers water 0.5-1.0 m deep and is tolerant of disturbance.

Again, try to introduce more than one species to avoid one becoming dominant. The floating leaves will cast shade and affect the survival of submerged species beneath. Try to achieve a mixture of blocks of floating-leaved aquatics with blocks of submerged aquatics in between.

Emergent aquatics   These species tend to thrive around the pond margins at depths around 100 mm to 0.5 m. Once established, they help to stabilise and protect the pond banks and provide shelter in shallow water for fish and other pond animals.

Examples of species include:

— *Equisetum fluviatile* (water horsetail) prefers clean water 0.1-0.5 m deep.
— *Ranunculus flammula* (lesser spearwort) tolerates shade, bears attractive yellow flowers and prefers base-neutral conditions.
— *Nasturtium officinale* (watercress) prefers base-rich conditions and zone from dry land to depth of 0.1 m.
— *Polygonum amphibium* (amphibious bistort) tolerates fluctuating water levels and drying out. Prefers zone from dry land to depth of 0.1 m.
— *Alisma plantago-aquatica* (water plantain) is tolerant of disturbance and prefers zone from dry land to 0.1 m depth.
— *Butomus umbellatus* (flowering rush) prefers base-rich conditions and will extend to a depth of 0.5 m.
— *Sparganium erectum* (bur-reed) is tolerant of disturbance and will extend to a depth of 0.5 m.
— *Typha latifolia* (reedmace) is tolerant of pollution and silting, but very invasive in water up to 0.1 m in depth.
— *Typha angustifolia* (lesser reedmace) is not tolerant of pollution, but less invasive than *T. latifolia*.
— *Phragmites australis* (common reed) is tolerant of drying, invasive, often becoming dominant in reed swamps.

— *Phalaris arundinacea* (reed canary grass) tolerates fluctuating water levels, strengthens banks.

Plant emergent species in blocks and avoid invasive species on small ponds. If invasive species are planted, choose areas where management may be most easily carried out, e.g. by removal or cutting. Keep in mind the size of mature plants when transplanting.

Marginal plants   These species colonise the wet mud at the water's edge, spreading out into the water and back on to the waterlogged land.
Examples of species include:

— *Caltha palustris* (marsh marigold) has attractive yellow flowers, prefers base-neutral conditions and is tolerant of shade.
— *Veronica beccabunga* (brooklime) prefers base-neutral conditions.
— *Menyanthes trifoliata* (bogbean) has floating stems, with attractive flowers, which will grow out from the margins across the water. It prefers clean water 0.1-0.5 m deep.
— *Myosotis scorpioides* (water forget-me-not) tolerates fluctuating water levels and stabilises banks.
— *Mentha aquatica* (water mint) tolerates fluctuating water levels, is shade-tolerant and stabilises banks.
— *Juncus* spp. (rushes) are, in the case of some species, resistant to wave action, e.g. common spike rush.
— *Iris pseudacorus* (yellow flag) tolerates summer drying, has very attractive flowers and stabilises banks.
— *Carex* spp. (sedges) are, in *some* cases, well adapted to marginal, marshy soils.

The acidity of the pond water may affect the survival of introduced plants, as illustrated in Table 6.18.

Table 6.18 Examples of water plants and the pH of water they can colonise

Water acidity/alkalinity	pH	Species
Extremely acid	1.8-4.5	*Juncus bulbosus* (bulbous rush) *Sparganium angustifolium* (floating bur-reed)
Acid	4.5-6.5	*Nymphaea candida* (small water lily) *Potamogeton graminaeus* (various-leaved pondweed)
Slightly acid-neutral-slightly alkaline	6.0-7.5	*Callitriche palustris* (water starwort) *Potamogeton filiformis* (slender-leaved pondweed) *Potamogeton berchtoldii* (small pondweed)
Alternately alkaline	6.0-9.0	*Myriophyllum verticillatum* (whorled water-milfoil) *Stratiotes aloides* (water soldier) *Wolffia arrhiza* (rootless duckweed)
Alkaline throughout the year	7.0-10.0	*Ceratophyllum submersum* (hornwort) *Lemna gibba* (fat duckweed) *Trapa natans* (water chestnut)

Source: Kabisch (1982).

New plantings on shorelines exposed to winds and wave action may need protecting until they are established. This can be done either by placing floating logs, firmly anchored offshore, or by covering the mud with staked netting before planting. Once the vegetation has established, the logs may be removed and/or the netting will be covered by the vegetation. (Use netting which will rot down.)

Waterside trees   Overhanging trees can cause problems, shading out marginal and floating-leaved plants and filling the pond with leaves; but trees can also be beneficial. For example, a shelter belt 20m or so on the windward side of an exposed pond can act as a windbreak. Trees planted closer can cause air turbulence and help to oxygenate shallow ponds. If close to the water, trees should be planted on the north side. Tree roots can cause damage to pond linings and can block drains (see also section 6.2.2). Never plant trees on earth dams. Avoid siting trees where they may cause problems later. Examples of tree species common on Slightides and waterlogged ground include:

Alder	*Alnus glutinosa*
Willows, e.g.	
bay willow	*Salix pentandra*
white willow	*S. alba*
crack willow	*S. fragilis*
almond willow	*S. triandra*
common osier	*S. viminalis*
common sallow	*S. cinerea*
black poplar	*Populus nigra*

(Keep in mind the size of species at maturity, e.g. black poplar: up to 35 m).

See section 6.2.6 for further information on planting methods for these tree species. Willows are most easily planted as cuttings.

Waterside shrubs   The presence of shrubs adds to the cover provided by marginal plants for the nests and chicks of waterbirds.

Water animals

Imported pond plants will usually have eggs laid in and on their leaves and stems. The mud imported with the plants will contain a variety of pond animals. If you know of a local waterway which is rich in plant and animal life, it is worthwhile collecting some of the mud from it and 'innoculating' your pond with it. It is important to get a healthy invertebrate community established before introducing fish.

Table 6.19 lists several species of freshwater mussels and pond snails which can be collected and transferred to new water bodies. These are useful species as they can help to keep the pond 'clean'. The snails graze on the algae coating the mud and plants and the mussels filter out plankton from the water.

Many water animals will find their own way to the pond. Water beetles, dragonflies, damselflies, mayflies, caddisflies, stoneflies and many others can fly between ponds as adults. Waterbirds visiting ponds can sometimes inadvertently carry the eggs of some species on their legs.

Once the invertebrate community is well established it may be possible to stock larger ponds with fish. Before fish can be moved from other local water bodies, a licence is required from the water authority.

Section 7.5 deals with the management of freshwater and includes methods of enhancing the value of a pond.

Table 6.19 Examples of pond animals which feed on algae

Snails These graze on filamentous and mat-forming algae

Ancylus lacustris	lake limpet
Aplecta hypnorum	moss bladder snail
Limnaea pereger	wandering snail
L. stagnalis	great pond snail
L. trunculata	dwarf pond snail
Planorbis complanatus	flat ramshorn
P. planorbis	ramshorn

Mussels These feed on planktonic plants and animals which make the water cloudy

Anodonta cygnea	swan mussel
Sphaerium corneum	horny orb-shell
Unio pictorum	painter's mussel

Small herbivorous crustaceans These feed on floating algae, fairy shrimps and water fleas

Bosmina spp.
Cyclops spp.
Cypris spp.
Daphnia spp.

6.3.7 References

Baines, C. and Smart, J. (1984) *A Guide to Habitat Creation*, Greater London Council Ecology Handbook No. 2

Bowen, U. (1977) *How to Make a Small Pond*, Berks., Bucks. and Oxon Naturalists' Trust (also available from BTCV as part of their Conservation Projects Pack, 1980)

Brooks, A. (1981, rev. edn) *Waterways and Wetlands: A Practical Conservation Handbook*, British Trust for Conservation Volunteers

Corder, M. and Brooker, R. (1981) *Natural Economy. An Ecological Approach to Planning and Management Techniques in Urban Areas*, Kirklees Metropolitan Council

Ecological Parks Trust (1981) Information leaflets: 'Stocking an Artificial Pond'; 'Creation and Development of the Pond at the William Curtis Ecological Park'

Franck, N. (1972) *Concrete in Garden Making*, Cement and Concrete Association

Genders, R. (1976) *Wildlife in the Garden*, Faber

Haslam, S.M., Sinker, C.A. and Wolsely, P.A. (1975) *British Water Plants*, Field Studies 4(2), Field Studies Council (available as an offprint)

Kabisch K. (1984) *Ponds and Pools — Oases in the Landscape*, Croom Helm, London

Kelcey, J.G. (1977) 'Water plants' in Yoxon, M. (ed.), *Ecological Studies in Milton Keynes. No. 18. Creative Ecology part 1. Section 5*, Milton Keynes Development Corporation

—— (1978) 'Creative Ecology part 2: Selected aquatic habitats', *Landscape Design*, **121**:36-8

Macan, T.T. (1963) *Freshwater Ecology*, Longmans, Green

—— (1973) *Ponds and Lakes*, Allen & Unwin, London

Macan, T.T. and Worthington E.B. (1972) *Life in Lakes and Rivers* (3rd edn), Collins, New Naturalist

Masters, P. and Lancaster, I. (1980) *Wildlife Areas for Schools*, Durham Trust for Nature Conservation

Newbold, C., Purseglove, J. and Holmes, N. (1983) *Nature Conservation and River Engineering*, Nature Conservancy Council

Ruff, A.R. (1979) *Holland and the Ecological Landscapes*, Deanwater Press Ltd

Shirley, D.E. (1980) *An Introduction to Concrete. Notes for Students*, Cement and Concrete Association

Wilson, R. (1981) *The Back Garden Wildlife Sanctuary Book*, Penguin

Witton, B.A. (1979) *Rivers, Lakes and Marshes*, Hodder & Stoughton, London

6.3.8 Useful organisations (see Appendix 15 for addresses)

Freshwater Biological Association — A research organisation which produces very useful identification guides to aquatic life.

Institute of Terrestrial Ecology (Wetlands Section) — A research organisation which produces identification guides. They also survey a proportion of ponds and lakes appearing on 1:250,000 OS maps to check on their condition.

The Local Water Authority — Apart from the range of technical expertise within your local authority, they commonly have permissive powers to secure the use of water for recreational purposes, and may be able to give financial assistance in the creation of lakes and ponds where they would provide an amenity for the general public as well as a haven for wildlife.

6.4 Wildlife gardens and 'mini-habitats'

Sections 6.1, 6.2 and 6.3 emphasise the use of natural mixtures of plants to produce nature-like habitats, the aim being to provide living space for self-sustaining communities of wild plants and animals. Volunteers of all ages can be involved in such habitat creation projects and can gain pleasure from watching their work 'bear fruit' as the communities develop.

On a smaller scale, for example in a small corner of a site, a school quadrangle, a private garden, or even a window box, there is not enough room to create such habitats. However, these small areas can be 'gardened' for wildlife, providing opportunities for personal involvement with nature, complementing larger habitats in the area and adding to local resources for wildlife. The work of one enthusiast in a garden in Leicestershire illustrates just how rich the wildlife of a garden can be. Jenny Owen (1983) has identified over 1,700 species in her 700 sq m garden, over a period of eleven years. These include 345 species of flowering plants, 21 species of fungi (toadstools, etc.), 330 species of butterflies and moths (*Lepidoptera*), 114 species of flies (*Diptera*), 50 bird species and five mammal species.

A window box or flower border in a sunny sheltered position, if planted with the right flowers, can provide nectar and pollen for insects throughout the spring and summer, and seeds for birds in autumn. Small trees and shrubs may be planted to provide berries for birds. A lawn may be converted into areas of long and short grass and wildflower meadow. In the limited space of, say, a school quad or small garden, fences and walls may be used to support climbing plants, or even be replaced with hedges. The possibilities for the wildlife gardener are endless. Without necessarily re-creating nature-like habitats, small areas can be made into feeding and watering places for animals passing through. In our towns and cities, many bird species already depend on our bird tables and nest boxes, and many insect species (for example, butterflies and moths) on the pollen and nectar from garden plants.

If your group designs and manages a larger nature area, a small corner put aside as a wildlife garden can be of enormous benefit, particularly to schoolchildren. The children can easily manage the garden and can learn practical skills such as soil preparation, seeding, transplanting, making paths and rockeries, bird tables and nest boxes, etc. Willing hands are needed to look after the plants and the garden needs protecting in some way from the intrusions of litter and the activities of vandals. Larger areas of wilderness, grassland, woodland, etc. may survive a certain amount of recreation, play, or even deliberate damage, but a small wildlife garden could be destroyed in a very short time by such activities.

6.4.1 Food plants

Appendix 10 gives a list of wild plants with notes on their food value for wildlife, and Table 6.20 lists further sources of information. The literature on food plants for insects and birds is very extensive and it should not be difficult to find more than enough recommended species to choose from. You may decide only to use native species, but many garden plants provide rich supplies of pollen, nectar and fruit and can boost the food value of the garden. Sunflowers (*Helianthus* spp.) are a good example with their huge flower heads brimming first with nectar and then with seeds.

Table 6.20 Sources of further information for recommended food plants for birds and insects

Reference	Groups covered	Number of species listed	Additional notes included
British Butterfly Conservation Society (n.d.)	Herbs for nectar	18 (N)	Butterfly species
Cribb 1982	Nectar plants	24 (N) 37 (N)	Butterfly species
Genders 1976	Wall plants to attract birds	39 (N,I,C)	Height, when in bloom, colour, berries and fruits
	Shrubs and trees for birds	35 (N,I,C)	
	Hedging species for birds	32 (N,I,C)	
	Butterfly caterpillar food plants	60 (N,I,C)	Butterfly species
	Nectar plants:		
	Garden flowers	24 (N,C)	When in bloom
	Wildflowers	20 (N)	Butterfly species
	Night-scented flowers for moths	25 (N,I,C)	When in bloom
	Flowers for bees	64 (N,I,C)	Height
Kelcey 1977	Insect garden plants:		
	Herbs	19 (C), 17 (N)	
	Shrubs	20 (C), 6 (N)	
Masters and Lancaster 1980	Trees for wildlife in the North East	13 (N)	
	Trees for poor soils	5 (N,I)	
	Alien trees	5 (I,C)	
	Shrubs for wildlife in the North East	7 (N)	

	Shrubs for birds and insects	10 (I,C)	
	Herbs for wildlife	9 (N)	
	Garden plants	12 (I,C)	
Phillips 1977	Food plants for moth and butterfly caterpillars:		
	Trees	12 (N)	Moths and butterflies which
	Shrubs	10 (N)	feed on them
	Herbs	31 (N)	
	Flowers for insects	27 (N,I)	
	Seeds and berries for birds	25 (N,I)	
	Pollen and nectar for bees and butterflies:		
	Herbs	85 (N,I)	Arranged in calendar format
	Trees and shrubs	45 (N,I)	
Wilson 1981	Bird food plants; shrubs and herbs	30 (N,I,C)	
	Butterfly food plants	20 (N,I,C)	Natural history of butterfly
	Plants for butterflies:		species
	'Cottage garden'	41 (N,I,C)	
	Night-scented for moths	16 (N,I,C)	
	Annual, biennial and perennial food plants for bees	46 (N,I,C)	
Yarrow 1973	Shrubs	24 (N,I)	Birds, butterflies, bees, other
	Herbs	33 (N,I)	insects. Remarks on habitat, etc.
Yarrow 1978	Shrubs	24 (N,I)	Birds, butterflies, bees, other
	Herbs	33 (N,I)	insects. Remarks on habitat, etc.
	Water plants for wildfowl	28 (N,I)	Habitat, etc.

Key: N = native; I = introduced; C = cultivated varieties.

See section 6.4.7 for full references.

6.4.2 Features of a wildlife garden

Paving and hard surfaces   'Chequer-board' gardens are an easy way of establishing growing plots (Figure 6.23(A)) in areas of paving, allowing easy access without undue disturbance to the plants.

Walls   Darlington (1981) is a comprehensive description of the ecology of the animals and plants living on walls. Old and crumbling walls, provided they are not too dangerous, may be suitable for ivy (*Hedera helix*) to grow over. Ivy can cause problems since it takes moisture from the mortar, so it should not be used against the walls of buildings. The nooks and crannies in an old wall and the ivy growing over it provide a habitat for insects, birds and small mammals throughout the year. As the masonry decays, the mortar breaks down and soil collects in cracks, thus other plants are able to colonise the wall.

Walls with sound masonry are ideal for other climbing plants. Many of the more attractive climbers will only do well on a well-sheltered south-facing wall. North- and west-facing walls receive considerably less sunshine than south- and east-facing. Some of the hardiest climbers are:

— *Hydrangea petiolaris*
— *Lonicera periclymenum*   (Honeysuckle)
— *Parthenocissus cinquefolia* (Virginia creeper)
— *P. tricuspidata*   (Boston ivy)
— *Polygonum baldschuanicum* (Russian vine)

In the south of England, where there is some lime in the soil, old man's beard (*Clematis vitalba*) and white bryony (*Brionia dioica*) are native climbers worth planting. Plants bearing brightly coloured fruits include:

— *Celastrus scandens*
— *Cotoneaster horizontalis*
— *Pyracantha atalantioides* ⎫
— *P. rogersiana*   ⎬   evergreens
                 ⎭

Figure 6.23 (A) A 'chequerboard' garden on a paved area; (B) frames for climbers

(A) Paving stones

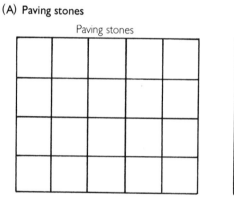

(B) Wall or fence

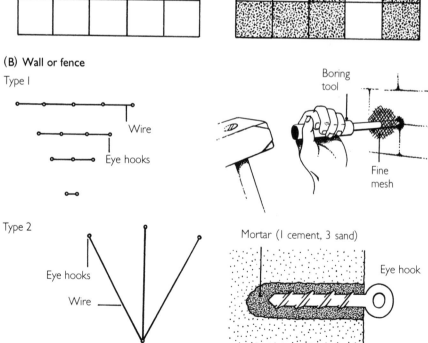

Check that the wall is sound in the area you wish the climbers to spread. Repair the mortar around any loose bricks, etc. Virginia creeper and Boston ivy will not usually need any support. Firethorn (*Pyracantha*), cotoneaster and plants with very strong stems are usually best trained against a set of parallel wires about 300 mm apart, starting 600 mm from the ground. These are fastened either to masonry nails or galvanised eye hooks (see Figure 6.23(B), type 1).

Masonry nails are fixed by hammering into the mortar between the bricks until they are firm. *Always swing your arm from the side, not in front of you,* so that if the nail bounces back, you will not be hit. Protective goggles or a piece of fine mesh screening will protect you from flying chips. The nails should stand 50 mm proud from the wall.

To fix eye hooks, punch a hole on the wall using a lump hammer and wall boring or tubular boring tool. Fill the hole with mortar (1 part cement:3 parts sand) and push in the eye hook when it has partially dried (see Figure 6.23(B)).

Honeysuckle, clematis, etc. may be supported on a simpler system such as the triangular frame in Figure 6.23(B), type 2.

Planting climbers

Prepare a planting pit as for a shrub or standard tree (see section 6.2.6), the pit being 300 mm wider than the root-ball, and at least 150 mm from the wall. Put 75 mm of well-rotted compost or peat and balanced fertiliser into the pit. Mix the compost or peat with the topsoil (1:1); position the plant and refill, firming in by foot. Train the plant stems on to the trellis; water in and lay 75-100 mm of mulch around the plant. Climbers may be planted in this way and trained over open fences and trellis, but a close-boarded wooden fence will need a wire frame to support the plant stems.

Rubble   Piles of rubble or rocks provide cover for small animals and, if soil collects between them, rockery plants such as stonecrop (*Sedum* spp.) may be grown on them. If you have unwanted piles of rocks or rubble it may be worthwhile using them to build a dry-stone wall similar to those found on uplands. Crevices between the stones in the wall provide ideal nesting sites for species such as the wren or the pied wagtail. Brooks (1977) is the most comprehensive reference available on dry-stone walling.

The survival of plants and animals on vertical surfaces such as walls, fences and rockeries is significantly affected by aspect. A south-facing surface is in the sun for large parts of the day and can heat up and dry out considerably. A north-facing surface remains cool and shaded in comparison and plants and animals are generally more able to colonise it.

Heaps   Piles of rotting wood, leaf litter, compost, etc. provide ideal habitats for many species of fungi and invertebrates, as well as cover for small mammals. Undisturbed layers of leaf litter and humus on the ground are very important for over-wintering invertebrates.

Flower beds and shrubberies   The plant species in Appendix 10 are predominantly native species; Appendix 11 gives examples of cultivated garden plants also rich in food for wildlife. In general, wildflowers and garden plants may be grown in the same flower bed. Mixtures may be planned to provide food throughout the year, or in the traditional way, to give a show of colour with their food value as an additional bonus. Beds of annuals may be grown on poor soil, clearing away the dead stems every autumn to ensure that the nutrient content of the soil stays low and that the seeds can germinate next spring in the absence of any severe competition. On richer soils, beds of perennials are more appropriate. However, avoid planting vigorous invasive species such as nettle (*Urtica dioica*) or creeping thistle (*Cirsium vulgare*). These are best grown in areas of rough grassland in a corner where their spread will not cause problems.

If there is room for shrubs or small trees, they may be used to create vertical structure in the vegetation. Where a leafy canopy is formed, shade-tolerant herb and shrub species may be planted beneath (see also section 6.2). A high canopy is attractive to songbirds, shrubs provide shelter and nesting sites, and the flowers beneath are a habitat for ground-nesting and ground-foraging birds, small mammals and other woodland creatures.

Hedges   Section 6.2.8 provides further information on planting hedges. A hedge made up of a mixture of species is a richer habitat for wildlife than the traditional garden hedge of just one species.

Grassland   Section 6.1 deals with grassland creation and section 7.3 describes its management for wildlife. Even a small patch of lawn may be adapted for wildlife. Traditional short turf lawns are popular foraging grounds for starlings, thrushes and blackbirds, particularly where they are open and the birds are not menaced by nearby borders where cats may lurk. Lawns are commonly mown to a height of 35-40 mm every 7-10 days. A lawn may still be kept neat by raising the mower blades to around 75 mm, or by using a scythe to cut at this height. Scything is much less harmful than mowing to animals living on the plant stems. Marginal areas may be left uncut and developed as flower meadows. Long grass is a valuable source of food for a great variety of butterflies, moths and other insects. It provides a habitat for small mammals and the grass seed is a nutritious food for many bird species. Predators such as the kestrel and the weasel will hunt in long grass in preference to short turf. Figure 7.2 in section 7.3.2 illustrates how different wildflowers may be encouraged by the use of different cutting regimes. Remember to remove cuttings, but try to leave them lying for several days, to allow animals to move off them and back down into the stubble.

Water   All animals need water. Even a small tub or bird bath will enhance the value of your wildlife garden by attracting birds to drink and bathe. If there is room for a small pond, aquatic insects and amphibians may also be able to thrive. The common frog, for example, is becoming increasingly dependent on garden ponds as the small pools in the countryside are being neglected or filled in. Section 6.3 covers the creation of a pond and section 7.5.3 describes its management.

6.4.3 Bird tables and nest boxes

Figure 6.24 (A)-(F) illustrates some ideas for nest boxes. They should be sited facing away from the prevailing wind, rain and sun. Space them well apart; for example, four boxes will probably be the maximum for a small garden. Some birds are territorial, and will fight with others of the same species for space. For this reason, a variety of boxes for different species is worthwhile in a small garden. In some instances, birds and butterflies 'do not mix'. Open-fronted nest boxes (Figure 6.24(C)) are ideally suited to the needs of the spotted flycatcher. An adult flycatcher can easily take over 200 butterflies in a day from a successful butterfly garden, so it is a good idea to site such nest boxes as far away from the butterfly garden as possible.

Figure 6.24 Nest boxes

(A) Standard box

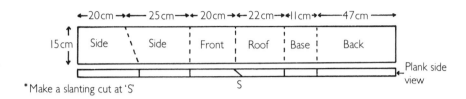

←20cm→ ←— 25cm —→ ←— 20cm —→ ←—22cm—→ ←11cm→ ←——47cm——→

15cm | Side | Side | Front | Roof | Base | Back

Plank side view

*Make a slanting cut at 'S'   S

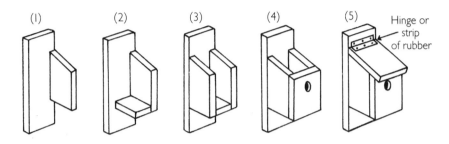

(1)   (2)   (3)   (4)   (5)   Hinge or strip of rubber

Entrance holes 25mm in diameter allow smaller birds to enter. Holes 30mm in diameter allow sparrows and starlings to enter. 50mm diameter is appropriate for larger birds such as jackdaws and great spotted woodpeckers

(B) 'Log' box

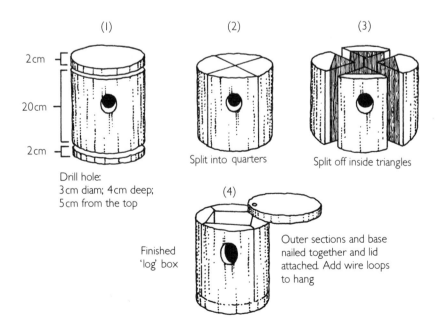

(1)   (2)   (3)

2cm

20cm

2cm

Drill hole:
3cm diam; 4cm deep;
5cm from the top

Split into quarters

Split off inside triangles

(4)

Finished 'log' box

Outer sections and base nailed together and lid attached. Add wire loops to hang

(C) Open-front box (e.g. for robins, wagtails, spotted flycatchers)

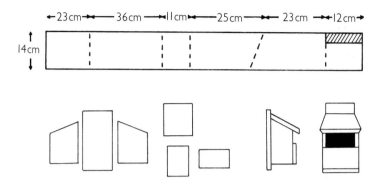

(D) Wedge-shaped nest box for treecreepers (tits may also use this box)

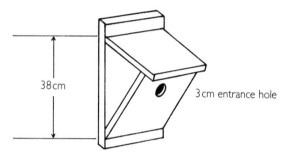

38cm

3cm entrance hole

(E) Funnel (drainpipe) nest box for owls

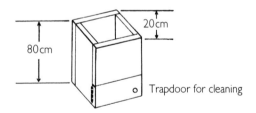

80cm

20cm

Trapdoor for cleaning

(F) Nest box for swifts

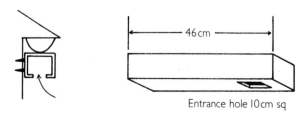

46cm

Entrance hole 10cm sq

Make sure that the boxes are positioned in safe places and have lids secured against the intrusions of cats. Hardwood boxes are less likely to have their entrance holes enlarged by grey squirrels (predators of eggs and chicks!). A box situated where a tree, shrub or wall plant hides it from view is more likely to be used, so a compromise, with the box just visible from a window or other distant vantage point is the ideal, allowing observation of their activities without disturbing them. Different species prefer to nest at different heights above the ground. A good book on British birds, for example Hayman and Burton's 1978 book *The Bird Life of Britain*, will give information on their nesting habits. A local naturalist or your County Naturalists Trust should be able to provide details of the different species in your area, or those likely to be attracted to nest in your garden. With this information, choose types of boxes and plan their positioning to suit the birds' requirements and your chances of success will be increased.

It is important to clean out nest boxes once the birds have left. Insecticide dusts will kill parasitic mites and fleas, but great care must be taken while using them. (See Appendix 12 for further information on insecticides.)

Useful references for bird boxes include Flegg and Glue (1971) and Genders (1976). The Royal Society for the Protection of Birds (RSPB) (see Appendix 15 for address) produces comprehensive guidelines on the subject.

The RSPB also provide useful information on bird tables. Figure 6.25 illustrates an example of a free-standing table. Birds should only be fed during autumn and winter and then food should be put out every day. They will become dependent on the food and a break in supply can mean the death of small birds in a very short time. In cold weather, they can easily lose over one-third of their body weight just in keeping warm. Therefore, during very cold

Figure 6.25 Bird tables

A simple, hanging feeding tray

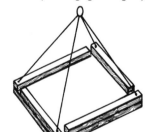

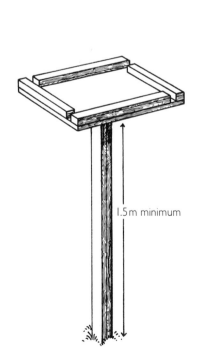

1.5 m minimum

A seed hopper with internal divider for different food to be dispensed on either side of the table

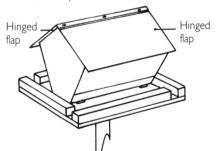

Hinged flap

Hinged flap

spells, food put out both in the mornings and evenings will help small birds to survive. Continually replace water when it freezes and keep the table free of mouldy food and bird droppings.

Foods harmful to birds include: salted peanuts, salted meats, desiccated coconut or other dehydrated foods. Bread is not really harmful, but is of little nutritional value to the birds. Artificial food should not be put out in spring, as it can be lethal to young nestlings.

Nutritious foods include: kitchen scraps such as fat, meaty bones, cheese, etc., fresh fruit, (unsalted) nuts and raisins. Specially prepared bird food may be bought from pet shops (check with the RSPB for recommended suppliers). Useful references on the subject include Soper (1977) and Wilson (1981).

6.4.4 Bat boxes

All 15 species of bats in Britain are undergoing decline and one of the contributory factors is a lack of suitable sites for roosting, hibernating and rearing young. Figure 6.26 illustrates a bat box suitable for this purpose. Avoid using wood coated with preservatives or paint as these discourage and often poison the bats.

Boxes are best sited on the south-east side of a tree or building, at least 3 m above the ground. Regular inspection is recommended to check whether the box is occupied. If you find bats, try to identify them, but with the minimum of disturbance. Disturbance during hibernation (November–March) can be lethal, and the mothers need to be left alone to rear their young during June and July. Further information on bats and their conservation is available from the Nature Conservancy Council, the Fauna and Flora Preservation Society, the Royal Society for Nature Conservation publication *Focus on Bats* and the Institute of Terrestrial Ecology Research Station at Monks Wood (See Appendix 15 for addresses). Researchers at Monks Wood are studying the ecology of bats in Britain and any information on the location of bat colonies should be sent to them. Bats are now specially protected by law under the Wildlife and Countryside Act (see section 3.4 for further details). Stebbings and Walsh (1985) give a very good guide to the proper construction, siting and care of roosting and hibernation boxes for bats.

Figure 6.26 Bat roosting box

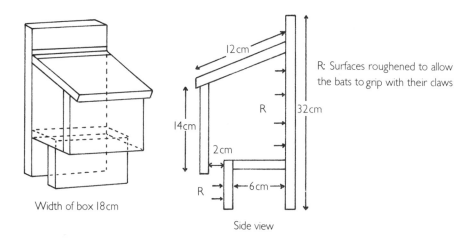

R: Surfaces roughened to allow the bats to grip with their claws

Width of box 18cm

Side view

6.4.5 Hedgehogs

Hedgehogs are well-established in our cities and thrive in many suburban gardens, urban parks, cemeteries and other open greenspaces. Although hedgehogs require a healthy diet of invertebrates such as slugs, snails, earthworms and insects, they will happily lap up saucers of milk and bread offered by friendly householders. Each hedgehog commonly hunts over quite a large area, so several may visit a small garden on separate nights and may easily be mistaken for the same animal.

If your wildlife garden is rich in invertebrates, and there are hedgehogs in the area, it is likely that you will be visited regularly. The following are garden features which may be dangerous to hedgehogs:

Slug pellets   If used, these should be placed in a tube or under a heavy object where hedgehogs cannot reach them. Dead, contaminated slugs should be removed daily.

Pits or vertical-sided holes   Provide ramps or other means for hedgehogs to climb out.

Litter   Including cans and jars in which foraging hedgehogs can get trapped.

Figure 6.27 Hedgehog house

(A) Dimensions of the box

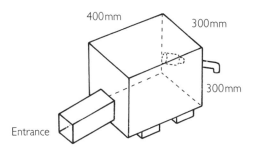

(B) Section of the completed house

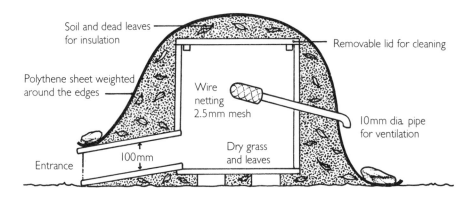

Hedgehogs need plenty of stored fat to survive the winter hibernation period. If you find a hedgehog in the garden in autumn and it weighs less than 450 g, it will probably be a young hedgehog, born late in the season, and will have little chance of survival. You can help by feeding with animal protein such as minced meat, raw liver, dog food (not fish-based), scrambled egg and a constant supply of fresh water. Once it weighs over 500-680 g, you may choose a warm, dry day to release the animal.

Figure 6.27 illustrates another way of helping hedgehogs, by providing a shelter from the extremes of winter. A useful reference on the natural history of the hedgehog is Morris (1983).

6.4.6 Gardens for the handicapped

Wildlife gardens have a great deal of educational value. They also have great potential in the field of horticultural therapy for the handicapped. Cultivating plants and observing the wildlife attracted to the garden is good 'reality' training and can stimulate handicapped persons' interest in the world around them. The dexterity required to cultivate the plants, etc. aids in training injured or infirm muscles, teaches eye-to-hand co-ordination, etc., while providing the simple pleasure of creating something vital and colourful.

Valuable sources of further information and help with gardens for the handicapped include the Society for Horticultural Therapy and Rural Training, who publish the *Growth Point* magazine, and the Federation for the Promotion of Horticulture for the Disabled (see Appendix 15 for addresses). The Oxfordshire Health Authority provide a useful guide to gardening equipment for the disabled in their publication *Leisure and Gardening* (Wilshere 1983). The information is based on work carried out at the Mary Marlborough Lodge, Nuffield Orthopaedic Centre, Oxford, and includes a wide selection of tools and various cultivation methods for the disabled. Examples of tool categories include: tools which can be operated from a sitting position without bending the back and one-handed tools, not requiring a strong grip.

Another useful publication covering a wide range of outdoor activities for handicapped people is Cotton (1981). This book is based on work at the Churchtown Farm Field Studies Centre in Cornwall, which is owned and maintained by the Spastics Society. It covers hundreds of outdoor activities, from environmental education in the city to the seashore and mountain life on the Eiger!

The Countryside Commission also publish a booklet on informal recreation for disabled people (Countryside Commission 1981; rev. 1982) which provides details of design and construction methods for paths, handrails, signboards, seats, tables, etc. and other ways of improving access onto sites for the disabled.

Elliott (1978) provides an easily understandable guide to the use of gardening to educate and give pleasure to handicapped children. This book is a mine of ideas and information on the practical and educational aspects of the subject.

These are just a few of the many publications on the subject. Section 6.4.7 lists other references and section 6.4.8 lists organisations who may be able to provide further advice. Probably the best way to begin designing a site for use by the handicapped is to go and visit handicapped people in the area and any centres already catering for them. You will only really be able to find out what is needed if you talk to the potential users first.

Some general points to remember about gardens for the handicapped.

(a) There are many types of handicap   It is wrong simply to group handicapped people together without recognising the important differences between disabilities and between individuals. A handicap, whether mild or severe, is merely a feature, like hair colour. The handicapped are the same as everybody else, except that there will be some things they are unable to do. There are obvious differences between the physically and the mentally handicapped and it is extremely difficult to design a site for use by both groups at the same time with any degree of success.

(b) Good access is essential   Do not design a garden for the handicapped in a place where they cannot reach it. To a person using a walking frame or stick, or confined to a wheelchair, 100 m between points of interest or, for example to the nearest toilet, is a very long way. Toilets need also to be suitably designed for wheelchair users. Parking points for vehicles need to be as near to the site as possible. Make sure that there are no obstacles such as high kerbs, steps or narrow passages between the parking or access points and the site. If you need to protect the site by locking it up, make sure that the key is not kept miles away and that, when a disabled person does get hold of the key, they are able to open the gate easily. Narrow gateways, heavy gates, stiff hinges and locks can sometimes be unsurmountable barriers.

(c) The site may be for passive use   An example of a site for passive use would be an area of a park or public open space designed for all the general public, including the handicapped, to enjoy. In this situation, avoid making it seem that the area is for handicapped people only. Rather, enhance the landscape to make it attractive for everyone, while incorporating features allowing easy access and suitable seating arrangements so that people find the area comfortable to be in. Examples of suitable features include:

— Seats which are high enough for the less physically able. Low benches can be extremely difficult to get on and off of. The provision of arm rests also makes getting up out of a seat much easier. Instead of providing plain benches arranged singly or in straight lines, set them in patterns at points of interest on the site so that families or social groups can sit together. Allow sufficient space *between* seats for wheelchair users so that they are not physically excluded from sitting with a group. Ensure that any tables on the site allow for a person in a wheelchair to sit at them.
— Scented gardens for the blind. Don't mix or confuse different scents. Plant individual species in patches so that people can enjoy their individual perfumes. Some plants release their scent when brushed against, and would therefore be ideal growing around and against seating. Don't allow plants to grow across pathways, particularly at eye level, where they may not be detected by a walking stick and so may hit people in the face.
— Access to the vegetation. Low-growing plants may be made more accessible by raising borders (or lowering paths) so that people less able to bend down, or those confined to wheelchairs, can easily smell the scents of the plants and appreciate their form and texture. Try to be subtle in designing raised beds; for example, rather than having expanses of concrete or brick walls, try natural stone with rock plants growing in it.

Any method of bringing plants within reach enhances the value of a site for the enjoyment of the handicapped. However, ensure that in doing so, you do not put the public at risk. Avoid plants with thorns, spines, stinging hairs, etc. or any plants which are poisonous. This is particularly important with children, the mentally handicapped and the mentally ill. Table 6.21 gives examples of the more poisonous wild and cultivated species to be found in this country. Tigwell (1980) and the MENCAP Rural Advisory Service, pamphlet no. 4 gives further details of the symptoms associated with poisoning by these plants.

(d) Sites may be for active use　As already described, horticultural therapy can be very valuable in rehabilitating and improving the quality of life for the

Table 6.21 Examples of the more poisonous plants to be found in Britain

Plant	Toxicity	Most poisonous parts
Aconitum napellus (monkshood)	F	R, L
Aesculus hippocastanum (horse chestnut)	P	Fr
Aethusa cynapium (fool's parsley)	F	A
Aquilegia vulgaris (columbine)	F	A
Arum maculatum (cuckoo pint)	P	S
Atropa belladonna (deadly nightshade)	F	A
Bryonia dioica (white bryony)	P	A
Circuta maculata (water hemlock)	F	A
Conium maculatum (hemlock)	F	A
Convallaria majalis (lily of the valley)	P	Fl
Daphne mezerium (mezereon)	P	B, Fr
Datura stromonium (thorn apple)	F	S
Delphinium ambiguum (larkspur, delphinium)	F	S
Digitalis purpurea (foxglove)	P	A
Helleborus foetidus (hellebores)	F	A
H. niger	F	A
H. viridis	F	A
Hyscyamus niger (henbane)	P	A
Ipomoea purpurea (morning glory)	H	A
Laburnum anagyroides (laburnum)	F	S, B
Lupinus spp. (lupins)	P	S
Nerium oleander (oleander)	F	A
Nicotinia spp. (tobaccos)	F	A
Rheum rhaponticum (rhubarb)	F	L (leaves only)
Ricinus communis (caster oil plant)	F	A
Solanum tuberosum (potato)	F	L
Tamus communis (black bryony)	F	R
Taxus baccata (yew)	F	A (except red flesh around the seed)

Key: Toxicity (if eaten)　　　　　　　　　　Most poisonous parts

　　F　= fatal (even in small doses)　　　　B　= bark
　　P　= poisonous (can be fatal, especially in　　R　= roots
　　　　children)　　　　　　　　　　　　L　= leaves
　　H　= halucinogenic (can cause brain damage)　Fr　= fruit
　　　　　　　　　　　　　　　　　　　　Fl　= flowers
　　　　　　　　　　　　　　　　　　　　S　= seeds
　　　　　　　　　　　　　　　　　　　　A　= all the plant is equally toxic

Note: Some species of British fungi are very poisonous. If you suspect that anyone has eaten poisonous plant or fungal material, make them vomit as quickly as possible, even if no apparent illness is immediately obvious. Some poisons have a delayed effect and so symptoms of poisoning may not be apparent for several hours. Take the victim, and a sample of the material eaten, to a doctor, or hospital casualty department, as quickly as possible.

Source: Tigwell (1980).

handicapped. A garden for handicapped people to use for practical cultivation purposes really needs to be private, in a protected site and not overlooked by passers-by. The disabled gardeners need to feel relaxed while working, without feeling that they are being watched. Such gardens, therefore, are more appropriate for private gardens, sheltered homes and similar institutions. Further information on tools, raised planting beds, etc. and horticultural methods may be found in Elliott (1978), Wilshere (1983) and Rowson and Thoday (1981).

(e) Don't forget to consult the users This point cannot be stated too often. Too many gardens have already been made for handicapped people without consulting the individuals who were expected to use them. Such sites may never be used, for a whole range of different reasons, such as inaccessibility or inappropriate design. Find out who in the neighbourhood of the site may use it. If there are aged, infirm or handicapped people in the area who want to use the site, involve them in its design. It is very difficult, especially for professional designers of sound health, to see things through the eyes of the handicapped person.

6.4.7 References (including gardens for the handicapped)

Allan, P.B.M. (1979) *Larval Foodplants*, Watkins and Doncaster, Hawkhurst, Kent

Avon Wildlife Trust (1982) *Gardening for Butterflies*, Avon Wildlife Trust

British Butterfly Conservation Society (BBCS) (n.d.) 'Butterflies for your garden', A4 leaflet

Brooks, A. (1977) *Dry Stone Walling. A practical conservation handbook*, British Trust for Conservation Volunteers

Chinery, M. (1978) *The Natural History of the Garden*, Fontana

Clouston, B. (ed.) (1978) *Landscape Design with Plants*, Heinemann

Cribb, P.W. (1982) *How to Encourage Butterflies to Live in Your Garden*, Amateur Entomologists' Society, Conservation Committee

Curry, D.A. (n.d.) *Planning an Outdoor Studies Area in the School Grounds*, Devon County Educational TV Service

Darlington, A. (1981) *Ecology of Walls*, Heinemann Educational

Flegg, J.J.M. and Glue, D.E. (1971) *Nest Boxes*, British Trust for Ornithology, Tring (BTO Field Guide No.3)

Genders, R. (1976) *Wildlife in the Garden*, Faber

Glue, D. (1982) *The Garden Bird Book*, Macmillan

Hayman, P. and Burton, P. (1978) *The Birdlife of Britain*, Mitchell Beazley

Hills, L.D. (1975) *Fertility without Fertilisers*, Henry Doubleday Research Association

Inner London Education Authority, Nature Study Scheme (1983) 'Plants for wildlife gardening', A4 leaflet

Kelcey, J. (1977) 'Insect garden species list' in Yoxon, M. *Ecological Studies in Milton Keynes 18*, pp. 31-2, Milton Keynes Development Corporation

Masters, P. and Lancaster, I. (1980) *Wildlife Areas for Schools*, Durham County Conservation Trust

Morris, P. (1983) *Hedgehogs*, Whittet Books

Oates, M. (1985) *Garden Plants for Butterflies*, Brian Masterton, Fareham

Owen, J. (1983) *Garden Life*, Chatto & Windus

Newman, L.H. (1967) *Create a Butterfly Garden*, Worlds Work Ltd, John Baker

Phillips, J. (1977) 'Plants for insects and birds' in Yoxon, M. *Ecological Studies in Milton Keynes 18*, Section 4, pp. 36-45, Milton Keynes Development Corporation

Rothschild, M. (1983) *The Butterfly Gardener*, Michael Joseph

Royal Society for Nature Conservation (n.d.) *Focus on Bats — A Guide to Their Conservation and Control*, RSNC, Lincoln

Ruff, A. (1979) *Holland and the Ecological Landscape*, Deanwater Press

Soper, T. (1977) *The Bird Table Book in Colour* (4th edn), David & Charles

Stevenson, V. (1985) *The Wild Garden*, Windward

Urban Wildlife Group (1984) *Trees and Shrubs for Wildlife*

Wilson, R. (1981) *The Back Garden Wildlife Sanctuary Book*, Penguin (paperback); 1979 Astragal Books (hardback)

Yarrow, A.E. (1973) 'Planting design and management for wildlife interest', *Landscape Design*, **102**:14-16

—— (1978) 'Planting design and management for wildlife' in Clouston, B. (ed.), *Landscape Design with Plants*, Heinemann

Gardens for the disabled

Cotton, M. (1981) *Out of Doors with Handicapped People*, Souvenir Press

Countryside Commission, (1981; rev. edn 1982) *Informal Countryside Recreation for Disabled People*, CC Advisory Series No. 15

Elliott, P. (1978) *The Garden and the Handicapped Child*, Disabled Living Foundation

Rowson, N.J. and Thoday, P.R. (1981) *Raised Planters for the Disabled*, University of Bath

Tigwell, E.M. (1980) 'Poisonous plants to be avoided in gardens for the disabled' in Federation for the Promotion of Horticulture for the Disabled, Proceedings, 1980 Conference

Upton, A.J. and Thoday, P.R. (1980) *A Bibliography of Horticulture and Out-Door Amenities for the Handicapped and Disadvantaged*, University of Bath, Horticulture Group

Wilshere, E.R. (1983) *Leisure and Gardening*, Oxfordshire Health Authority, Equipment for the Disabled Series

6.4.8 Useful organisations (see Appendix 15 for addresses)

Amateur Entomologists' Society, Conservation Committee

British Butterfly Conservation Society

British Trust for Ornithology

Council for Environmental Education

Horticultural Trades Association

Institute of Terrestrial Ecology, Monks Wood

Royal Society for Nature Conservation (also *Watch*)

Royal Society for the Protection of Birds (also Young Ornithologists Club)

Gardens for the disabled

Advisory Committee for Blind Gardeners, Southern and Western Regional Association for the Blind. Seminars and advisory pamphlets

Centre on Environment for the Handicapped

Churchtown Farm Field Study Centre

Disabled Living Foundation

Federation for the Promotion of Horticulture for the Disabled. Conferences and publish conference proceedings, handbooks, a directory and bibliography on the subject

Gardens for the Disabled Trust. Advice, practical help and grants

Horticultural Therapy Training Centre, Warwickshire College of Agriculture. Study days, staff training courses, demonstration garden, tools and equipment

Mary Marlborough Lodge, Nuffield Orthopaedic Centre. Advice, study days

MENCAP, Rural Advisory Service. Advice, training courses and advisory pamphlets

Society for Horticultural Therapy and Rural Training. Advice, land-use volunteer team, information and resource centre, *Growth Point* magazine

Society for Promotion of Rehabilitation in Gardening (SPRIG)

Spastics Society

University of Bath, Horticulture Group

7 Long-term management

Whether you take on a site with established vegetation, or whether you create habitats on a vacant site, the plant and animal communities will need careful management in the long term, bearing the following general points in mind.

(a) Aim to maximise the site's contribution to the wildlife of the area, increase the diversity of species wherever feasible and manage the site to stop areas becoming species-poor.
(b) As an aid to (a) above, management can include rejuvenation of some habitats from time to time by small-scale disturbance over limited areas. For example, by clearing openings in woodland, thinning of scrub, removal of pond vegetation and cutting grassland.
(c) Seasonal work should be organised to cause minimum disturbance for wildlife. In most cases, work is carried out in late autumn, winter and early spring.
(d) Wherever possible, on small areas, manual rather than mechanical techniques should be used. (This also encourages more community involvement.)
(e) Chemicals should only be used where other forms of vegetation manipulation are not possible or practical.
(f) Management should aim at a compromise between visitor use and protection of the site wildlife; for example, by means of rotational access, zonation, etc.

The long-term management of a site is a very important consideration in the initial design process. Points (a)-(f) are, therefore, also considered in Chapter 5, 'Principles of Site Design'.

To ensure that the wildlife visiting, colonising and living on a site is able to thrive from season to season, it is vital that long-term management is not too disruptive. Continuity from year to year is essential. When planning the long-term management of a site, therefore, think as far ahead as possible and try to arrange for management work to follow a regular annual pattern. This principle is explained further for each habitat in sections 7.3-7.5.

7.1 Management in relation to natural succession

Section 5.1.2 describes the process of natural succession — the gradual replacement of species with new ones as vegetation develops. Primary colonisers of bare soil, rubble or open water are succeeded by more robust, competitive species. Unless succession is halted by disturbance, lack of resources (e.g. nutrients) or of colonising species, woodland eventually develops.

By examining carefully (a) the conditions present on a site, (b) the mixtures of plant species present and (c) the plant species you might expect to colonise the site from areas nearby, it is possible to predict roughly how natural succession may proceed if uninterrupted. Armed with this knowledge, you then have the choice of allowing new types of vegetation to develop naturally, or interfering by either stopping the vegetation's natural development or enhancing it.

Figure 7.1 illustrates the effects of some general management practices on natural succession (A) on land and (B) in water. The practices in the figure all tend to halt succession, but the opposite is also possible. For example, seeding

Figure 7.1 Natural succession and the effects of management

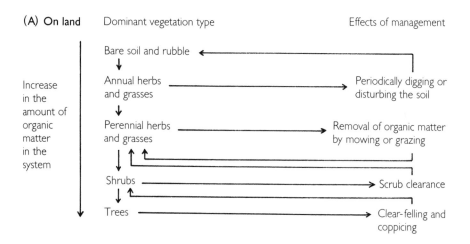

(A) On land

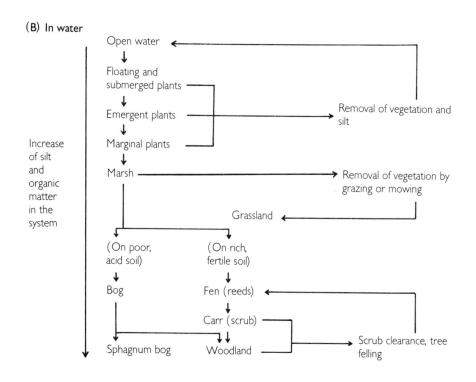

(B) In water

areas of annual herbs and grasses with perennial species will speed up the rate of succession, as would the planting of shrubs among perennial herbs and grasses.

Remember that natural succession can work for or against you. On a very isolated site, where only a sparse supply of seeds can colonise naturally, a knowledge of natural succession enables you to introduce an 'innoculum' of the correct species so that natural succession will do the rest (see Chapter 6 on habitat creation). In established vegetation, however, it is normally only possible to stop natural succession proceeding by continued management. Sections 7.3-7.5 covers some of the management techniques involved under the headings grassland/meadow, scrub/woodland and freshwater/ponds.

7.2 The management plan

Good base-line information and well thought out forward planning are essential if a site is to be managed successfully in the long term.

Chapters 4 and 5 respectively, describe site surveying and site design and illustrate how the two stages should take into account future management needs. Survey information, design and management proposals make up the material for a management plan. This is, in effect, a volume of relevant site information which shows others, such as local authority officials or potential donors of money and materials, that you know what you are doing. Anyone working on the site should be able to use it for reference. By producing a detailed plan you will lessen the possibility of confusion over what is to be done, when and why. Without such a plan, there will be constant changes in methods and intentions as people leave and new people get involved with a site. The format of a management plan will vary in complexity according to the site's size, its uses and many other considerations, but there is a basic logical structure which may be employed, involving three stages:

(1) detailed descriptive information on the site and its history;
(2) evaluation and objectives for management and the reasoning behind them;
(3) ways and means of achieving objectives, work programmes, etc. — often termed 'Prescription'.

Table 7.1 illustrates a possible format for a plan for an inner-urban site. The format is adapted from one proposed for use by County Naturalists' Trusts on their reserves (Stedman 1979; Wood and Warren 1978). It is meant as a general guide. Your plan may need to include extra sections, for example a complete design section with subsequent management requirements. Do not be over-elaborate. The most useful type of plan is one which is readily understood and which gives easy access to the most important information a manager needs. A plan prepared and stored with a loose-leaf format is the most managable and is easy to up-date and amend. Each section should begin on a fresh page, and dates when sections are written or revised should always be included to avoid confusion. It will be easier for new people to understand the plan if maps, appendices and references are included with each appropriate section, rather than in a separate section at the end. An index and amendments sheet, with dates, at the front of the plan will make it easier to tell which sections were completed/amended and when.

The plan may take several years to prepare, with various management/ project groups completing different sections. It is always worthwhile to locate someone in a local Naturalists' Trust or the regional branch of the Nature Con-

Table 7.1 Example of a management plan format for an inner-urban site

A	**DESCRIPTION**

A.1	General
	    Location and size
	    Details of tenure and access
	    National grid reference (your reference) and OS map coverage
	    List of people involved with the site (addresses, tel. nos.)

A.2	Environmental
	    Physical (climate, water, rocks, soil, substrate, etc.)
	    Biological (plants, animals, communities)
	    Cultural (archaeology, past uses, past management, public interest)
	    Ecological relationships

A.3	Reference materials
	    Relevant published and unpublished materials
	    Maps (e.g. geological, historical)
	    Photographs

B	**EVALUATION**

B.1	Reasons for establishment — story of the site's acquisition
	    Interested parties (groups) involved and their objects as groups
	    (if any) from group constitutions

B.2	Evaluation
	    For nature conservation
	    For education and for research
	    For recreation/amenity

B.3	Features relevant to site management
	    Ecological trends
	    Man-induced trends
	    External factors affecting the site
	    Legal constraints
	    Obligations (non-legal)

B.4	Management objectives
	    Broad — short/long term
	    Detailed — short/long term

C	**PRESCRIPTION**

C.1	Projects
	    Register of projects
	    Descriptions of projects
	    Project groups

C.2	Work schedule (to include relevant project groups)
	    Priorities
	    Work programme, e.g. for five years
	    Annual timetable

D	**REFERENCE MATERIALS**
	Costs and sources of finance and other resources

servancy Council who has knowledge of management plans. You will almost certainly begin work on the site with only a partial plan, but as work proceeds, it will become evident what is needed, you will be able to compile or discover more information, and the plan will gradually become more detailed. A shortened form, or outline, of the plan is always useful to show to local councillors or other officials to give them an idea of your aims and methods of achieving them.

Considering the sections in Table 7.1 in more detail:

A. DESCRIPTION. This section may largely be made up of survey information (see Chapter 4 'Site Selection and Surveying').

In *A.1 the general description*, the most useful scale Ordnance Survey maps for site detail are from 1:1250 to 1:2500. The local authority planning department, or the local Ordnance Survey (OS) agent, should be able to provide maps of this scale range. Details of tenure should include the conditions under which the site is leased or licenced for use, etc. Access should include permission (if any) required for entry on to the site, access points, holders of keys, etc. The people involved with the site may include local residents or teachers, management committee members, volunteers and local authority officials.

It is better to put all names, addresses and telephone numbers in one section rather than scatter them throughout the plan. This makes it easier to accommodate the sporadic changes that are needed to keep up to date. In other sections, if necessary, make references back to this section for contacts or further information, etc.

A.2 the environmental description contains the raw base-line data for future management. If you are going to create or manage habitats on a site, it is crucial that managers understand the conditions present.

Physical factors include:

Climate — rainfall, temperature, prevailing winds and their seasonal fluctuations.
Water (hydrology/hydrography) — soil water content, areas of water, drainage patterns and their seasonal fluctuations.
Rocks — the underlying rock-type, e.g. alkaline limestone or acid granite.
Soil/substrata — nutrient status, structure, acidity, etc.

These will all affect the types of plant, and animal, communities able to survive on the site.

Biological factors include:

Plants — a list of all species present, with records of those dominating the habitats, any indicator species and any notably unusual or rare species.
Animals — as for plants, covering mammals, birds, reptiles, amphibians, fish and invertebrates.
Communities — any recognisable mixtures, e.g. wet grassland or oak/ash woodland.

A vegetation map should be included to illustrate the extent of different recognisable communities and the locations of notably unusual or rare species.

Cultural factors include:

> Archaeology — known or suspected evidence of ancient use or occupation of the site.
> Past uses — any known uses up to the time you acquired the site, e.g. recreation, industry, dumping, etc.
> Past management — any known management up to the time you acquired the site, e.g. grazing, mowing, coppicing, application of fertilisers, etc.
> Public interest — any current or potential interest in the site, e.g. local rights of access, landscape, amenity, recreation, education, research, nature conservation, etc.

Ecological relationships. This considers the general inter-relationships between the preceding three sections, and their effects on the ecology of the site. This will include:

> Rock and soil types associated with particular types of vegetation, e.g. a legume-rich grassland on nitrogen-poor substrates.
> Climate and aspect, e.g. prevailing winds may cause desiccation and stunting of shrubs and trees, or high rainfall may cause nutrients to be leached from the soil.
> Land use, e.g. grazing may have created open, short grassland. Tipping of alkali wastes may have allowed the development of a community of calcareous species.
> Adjacent habitats, e.g. seeds from nearby areas of vegetation may be brought to the site by the wind, or by animals (and people) visiting the site.

A.3 Reference materials should include anything which will enhance the general description of the site. If any reference materials apply to just one of the sections above, then it is better to include them with that section. The most useful photographs for reference are annual and seasonal comparisons. If you select defined viewpoints, and take photographs from them from season to season and year to year, you will have a ready-made pictorial progress report. One way of ensuring that subsequent photographs will be taken of exactly the same area is to choose views where permanent fatures are part of the picture, e.g. rocks, walls, edges of buildings,etc. If a sketch is made of the positions of such features in the very first photograph, with a note of where the photographer was standing, then subsequent photographs can locate, from the sketch, that point and frame the features as in the original.

B. EVALUATION. This section needs to be drawn up by all interested parties, so that their wishes may be taken into account. Unlike 'A. DESCRIPTION' which is broadly permanent base-line information on the site and its history, this section may need to be amended as local needs and opinions change. Constraints of one kind or another are also likely to vary with time.

B.1 Reasons for establishment. This should describe why the site was acquired. The main influence will be the objects of the individuals and groups involved, and these need to be stated. A formally constituted group will have an objects clause in their constitution. Inclusion of this clause here in the plan should make it clear to anyone reading it what the group's interests are and, hence, why they are developing the site.

B.2 Evaluation. This relates directly to B.1 above. The value judgements of different groups and individuals will depend upon their interests and points of view. These may be wholly pro-nature conservation, education, community services, etc., or a combination of these and others. Whatever the combinations of interests, you need to determine the value of the site and its various features to the local community as well as to wildlife.

Evaluation for nature conservation. Sites of high nature conservation status are rare in urban areas. In the unlikely event that your site is valuable (or you think it may be) contact your local County Naturalists' Trust or the regional office of the Nature Conservancy Council (see Appendix 15 for addresses). These organisations are responsible for county nature reserves, local nature reserves (LNRs), national nature reserves (NNRs) and sites of special scientific interest (SSSIs). They employ methods of assessing a site's nature conservation value at international, national, regional and local levels. The main criteria used are:

— size of the site;
— diversity of habitats, communities and species;
— naturalness of communities;
— rarity of habitats, communities and species;
— fragility of habitats and communities;
— typicality (representative of habitat or community/type within an ecological range;
— recorded site history;
— position in an ecological/geographical unit.

This approach may be adapted for an inner-urban site which is not to be managed as a 'nature reserve'. The value of individual communities should be assessed bearing in mind the extent to which the public will use the site. If you are creating habitats on a site, you will also need to take this into account (see Chapter 5, 'Principles of Design'). For example, the size of the site is important as it sets limits on the number of different plant and animal communities it can support which you will have the resources to manage and which will withstand public pressure. Fragile habitats and communities, such as scrub for nesting birds or wet meadow for wildflowers, are only really feasible if you can maintain them while, at the same time, allowing public access.

Evaluation for education. This requires liaison between your group and the local educational community (teachers, advisers, local education authority inspectors, Her Majesty's Inspectors [HMIs], etc.).
    You may intend to warden the site and you may have naturalists within your group. By combining the expertise of such individuals with that in the local educational community, you should be able to assess how the site may be used as a field study area. Field study need not be limited to natural history and ecology, but may include creative writing, maths, history, geography, etc. The site will be of most value to local schools if it represents a resource otherwise absent in the area.

Evaluation for recreation/amenity. This requires liaison with the local community and their representatives (e.g. community groups and local authority staff, such as officers in the parks/leisure department) to determine what is already available in the area and how your site can complement it. Provision of interpretative materials bridges the gap between recreation/amenity and education. It is worthwhile assessing the value of such materials at this point, e.g. leaflets, notice boards, nature trails, etc.

Evaluation for research. Local colleges or research organisations may be interested in the site. Possible areas of research may include:

— ecological (urban soil conditions, species adaptation to urban environments, colonisation, etc.);
— social (needs of the local community and the benefits they derive from the site, etc.);
— landscape design and management.

B.3 Features relevant to site management. This section should consider any-thing which will affect site management. Such factors need to be taken into account before formulating management objectives.

Ecological trends. These include any natural processes such as natural succession and seasonal waterlogging.

Man-induced trends. These include disturbance, erosion, soil compaction and wear to the vegetation caused by public use.

External factors. These include local pollution, local developments (housing, industry, roads) and the effects of neighbouring areas of vegetation and any-thing outside the site which will affect it.

Legal constraints. You may be constrained in what you do on a site by the terms of tenure. Other possible constraints include those under the Wildlife and Countryside Act, the Occupier's Liability Act and the Health and Safety at Work Act (see chapter 3 for further details of legal considerations and con-straints).

Obligations (non-legal). These may best be summarised here as 'good neighbour policy'. You also have obligations to all the people involved with and using the site.

B.4 Management objectives. The information in the site description and evalu-ation allows you to draw up realistic management objectives. Initially, your objectives may be rather broad. For example, in the short term, making the site safe (repairing fencing, clearing rubbish, etc.) or in the long term, enhancing the site and access (extending an area of woodland by planting, developing a path network, creating a pond, providing facilities, etc.). As work continues, these objectives may be refined and re-drafted in more detail. In the plan, the objectives may be categorised, e.g. under:

— habitat management;
— provision of facilities;
— education;
— interpretation;
— research, etc.

C. PRESCRIPTION. This section outlines the practical application of your management objectives. The most effective way of doing this is to break the proposed work down into recognisable projects, related to particular areas of the site or to particular objectives.

C.1 Projects. Construct a project register so that, at any one time, the total management required is summarised and easy to see. Each project in the register should be described by summarising essential features, e.g.

— objectives of the project;

— time period to completion;
— methods to be used;
— manpower required;
— materials and equipment required;
— costs and sources of funds;
— any legal and other constraints.

If you are lucky enough to have a substantial number of supporters, volunteers and experienced individuals interested in one or more projects, it is also worthwhile organising project groups and outlining their structure in this section of the plan.

C.2 Work schedule. This largely comprises a series of time-sheets or calendars for work. Where there are a number of projects to be conducted and a shortage of manpower, it is necessary to leave less important work until later. You therefore need defined priorities to facilitate choosing which projects to postpone, e.g.

Priority 1. to meet legal obligations and safety requirements.
Priority 2. to maintain the wildlife value of the site and its value to local people.
Priority 3. to enhance the site's value for wildlife and local people.

The work programme is an outline of all work and may be a projection for several years ahead. The annual timetable allows the group (and project groups) to see what work has to be done and when during each year. It may include notes of project priorities, the number of working-days involved and names of any volunteers taking on responsibility for particular projects.

D. REFERENCE MATERIALS. Any references not included with relevant sections in the plan should be kept in this section. They may include aerial photographs, lists of contacts, sources of finance and other resources. You may choose to put all bulky tables or species lists, etc. at the back of the management plan so that they do not clutter up the text of the plan itself.

7.2.1 Monitoring and re-appraisal

It is very important to keep records of what work is carried out and how site vegetation develops. Without such records, you run the risk of:

(a) continuing work towards objectives doomed to failure;
(b) achieving successes without knowing how you did;
(c) overlooking changes in the site conditions which will affect the success of your management proposals.

By monitoring what work is done, you will be able to gauge the feasibility of individual objectives. Problems may arise, such as a shortage of manpower, or ground conditions which are too dry for a proposed habitat creation project. By referring to the records, you should be able to re-draft the objectives in the management plan to allow for the problem.

Monitoring may be carried out in a number of ways. For example, a diary or log book of day-to-day activities may be kept. Annual surveys may be carried out to up-date the initial species lists in the management plan. Similarly, annual and seasonal photographic comparisons may be made (as outlined in A.3 in this section). Any significant work activities may be recorded on 'event record cards' which are stored easily and retrieved for reference (Peterken 1969).

More detailed monitoring of the vegetation's development may be achieved by marking out permanent quadrats within habitats, e.g. on grassland, or permanent transects (lines of quadrats) across one or more habitats.

7.2.2 Management of individual habitats

Although sections 7.3-7.5 treat different habitats separately, all habitats interact with each other in nature. Sharp dividing lines between natural habitats are rare. Boundaries such as the water's edge or woodland edge tend to contain rich mixtures of species from habitats on either side of the boundary, along with species adapted to living in the transition zone itself.

When drawing up management plans for a series of habitats on a single site, remember the potential richness of the boundaries between them. Aim to create and maintain zones of gradual transition between them, for example: woodland–woodland edge–scrub–tall grass and herbs, or open water–floating and submerged aquatics–emergent and marginal aquatics–marsh–wet grassland and carr (wetland scrub).

7.3 Grassland/meadow management

Natural, and semi-natural, grasslands in Great Britain may be considered in three separate groups according to soil type:

Calcareous grasslands develop on basic soils with a high calcium carbonate content, usually over limestone or chalk.
Acidic grasslands occur on soils of low pH, e.g. over granite, millstone grit, acid greensand, etc.
Neutral grasslands occur on soils such as clays or loams, which are neither very basic or acidic.

Except for those on some of the rich riverside (alluvial) loams, semi-natural grasslands are termed low-productivity grasslands. High-productivity grasslands are those which have been agriculturally 'improved' by the addition of fertilisers. The addition of major nutrients leads to a decrease in floral diversity as slower-growing species are excluded by vigorous species, such as *Lolium perenne* (perennial rye grass). It is common practice in agriculture to cultivate, fertilise and reseed pasture with highly-productive cultivated varieties of *L. perenne* for grazing dairy cattle or producing silage, etc. Legumes such as *Trifolium* spp. (clovers) and *Medicago sativa* (lucerne) are often included to increase the nitrogen levels in the sward. Species-poor, high-productivity grassland is totally unsuitable for the conservation of wildlife. Throughout this section, management is aimed at maintaining the productivity of grassland at a low level, avoiding vigorous grass species such as *L. perenne*.

In the wild, there are two natural influences which maintain open grassland. The first is fire, a management tool which is much too dangerous for use on inner-urban sites. The second, more important, influence is grazing by wild animals. Grass species have evolved varying abilities to withstand defoliation. The most delicate plant tissues are the growing tissues (or meristems). In most plants, meristems are situated at nodes on the stem and at stem tips. Grass meristems are at the leaf bases at ground level, below the reach of grazers or fire. Some grassland flowers have similar mechanisms of protection against defoliation damage. Many species have rosettes of leaves, the young ones in the centre of the plant, at ground level, protected from grazing by their position and often by the presence of defensive hairs, etc. After grazing or burning, grasses regenerate and can produce branches (or tillers) at ground level; the degree of tillering varies between species. To aid regeneration, grasses and sedges have ready supplies of carbohydrate and starch reserves in the root and shoot bases. In many of the grassland (broad-leaved) wildflower species, long tap roots and underground storage organs serve the same purpose.

Different types of natural grassland, whether they be moorland or chalky downland, owe their species composition to the regimes of grazing and/or fire imposed upon them, combined with the influence of soil and climatic conditions. Similarly, the richness of our ancient traditional hay meadows, with their diverse arrays of wildflowers, is a result of unaltered cutting regimes as the hay was harvested late every summer for generation after generation. The meadows were then grazed commonly by cattle or sheep during the autumn and winter. The hay-meadow plants became established because they were able to flower and seed before the harvest. The removal of the hay each year, and autumn grazing, ensured that leaf litter and nutrients did not build up in the sward, thus preventing the invasion and domination of the sward by more vigorous competitive and nutrient-demanding species.

Continuity in management is very important if species are to establish and thrive. A variety of different management regimes on a site will only increase the species diversity if each regime is continued from year to year. Certain areas, such as picnic spots, play areas and footpaths, may need to be maintained for intensive visitor use, something which would involve frequent cutting to produce new growth, and tillering to withstand trampling. On less intensively-used areas, however, a mosaic of strips or patches of long and short grass may be maintained to encourage different plants (and the animals which depend upon them for food and shelter). For example, short grass (20-50 mm) favours rosette-leaved species such as:

Bellis perennis (daisy)
Plantago spp. (plantains)

and low creeping plants such as:

Potentilla reptans (creeping cinquefoil)
Veronica spp. (speedwells)
Sagina procumbens (procumbent pearlwort)
Medicago lupulina (black medick)
Lotus corniculatus (bird's-foot trefoil)
Trifolium spp. (clovers)
Ajuga reptans (bugle)
Prunella vulgaris (self heal)
Achillea millefolium (yarrow)

This type of sward is best achieved by grazing, although mowing can produce satisfactory results. Open areas of short grass provide feeding grounds for birds such as crows, rooks, starlings, blackbirds, thrushes and robins. They are often seen searching out the earthworms, leatherjackets, beetle larvae and other invertebrates which live in and beneath the turf.

Long grass is much richer in invertebrates than short-cut turf, and provides cover for ground-nesting birds and small herbivorous mammals such as mice and voles. It is, also, a rich hunting ground for insect eaters such as the dunnock, shrew and hedgehog, and carnivores such as the kestrel, weasel, stoat and the fox.

Spring flowers of grassland include:

Primula vulgaris (primrose)
Cardamine pratensis (cuckoo flower)
Primula veris (cowslip)
Fritillaria meleagris (fritillary) — now a very rare plant in Great Britain
Ranunculus acris (buttercup)
Ajuga reptans (bugle)

Taller, summer flowers of grassland include:

Geranium pratense (meadow cranesbill)
Papaver rhoeas (field poppy)
Daucus carota (wild carrot)
Reseda luteola (wild mignonette)
Knautia arvensis (field scabious)
Tragopogon pratensis (goat's beard)
Centaurea nigra (hardheads)
Linaria vulgaris (toadflax)
Verbascum thapsus (mullein)
Cichorium intybus (chicory)

7.3.1 Management by grazing

In the unlikely event of your having a pet pony, cow, goat, sheep, rabbits, geese, etc. you may consider grazing as a possible management tool for grassland. The effects of grazing, however, on the floristic composition of grassland are very complex (and, therefore, difficult to control) as the following points illustrate:

— Generally, grazers select the more nutritious plants, and parts of plants, from the pasture, avoiding the tougher, older ones. When stocking rates are low and each animal has plenty of choice, the more palatable species can quickly disappear from the grassland.
— When stocking rates are high, the animals cannot afford to be so choosy over what they eat. In this situation, the most abundant species in the grassland are likely to make the biggest contribution to their diet. This is a means of controlling coarse, competitive grasses should they begin to dominate a pasture.
— Different animals graze the sward down to different heights. Grazers' preferences also change throughout the year as the nutritional value of the plants and the dietary needs of the animals vary.
— Animals tend to trample the vegetation as they feed, near to gateways and water troughs in particular. Where trampling is heavy, resistant species such as *Polygonum aviculare* (knotgrass), *Matricaria matricarioides* (pineapple weed) and *Coronopus squamatus* (swine cress) tend to colonise. Elsewhere, the bare patches of soil created by trampling commonly allow annuals and perennials to germinate from seed.
— Animal urine tends to contain most of the nitrogen and potassium which is recycled into the soil. Animal droppings contain high levels of phosphorus and calcium. Patches of dung and urine tend not to be grazed for anything from four weeks to 18 months which results in 'soiled' patches developing

tall herbage containing vigorous, nutrient-demanding species such as *Cirsium arvense* (creeping thistle) and *Urtica dioica* (stinging nettle). The poorer the nutrient content of the soil, the more marked these nutrient-rich patches become.
— Generally, less palatable wildflower species, e.g. *Senecio* spp. (ragworts) and *Ranunculus* spp. (buttercups), will increase in grazed pasture.
— Summer grazing is the most harmful to wildflowers, and the insects which depend on them. Autumn and winter grazing is preferable and, wherever possible, a system of rotational grazing is best (e.g. grazing any one area once every three or four years). On large nature parks (say over 10 ha) grazing is a useful grassland management tool for wildlife, as it maintains floristic diversity and creates a mosaic of micro-environments which is beneficial to a wide variety of grassland plants and animals. Useful references on the subject include Williams *et al.* (1974) and Lowday and Wells (1977).

Surprisingly, grazing animals are becoming a more common sight in our towns and cities. There is a growth of city farms, and horses and ponies are increasingly popular. The National Federation of City Farms (see Appendix 15 for address) is an invaluable source of information and advice on animal husbandry and agriculture. On small urban sites, grazing animals may be interesting for visitors and their children, but, from a management point of view, cutting or mowing are simpler methods of managing grass swards, not requiring the degree of commitment and responsibility involved in animal husbandry.

7.3.2 Management by cutting

Cutting differs from grazing as a management tool in the following ways:

Selectivity   The manager has no control over what grazers will eat within a pasture; the grazers exercise their own choice. The 'bite' of a mowing machine is much less selective than that of a grazing animal, but the manager has full control over which areas will be cut and to what height. (A hand scythe or powered 'strimmer' may also be used to cut very small areas or particular single-species stands.)

Nutrient enhancement   Cutting does not result in the patches of dung and urine caused by livestock. Nutrients, however, will be returned to the sward wherever cuttings are left to rot down. On very nutrient-poor grassland, this may not be significant. Nevertheless, it is advisable to remove all grass cuttings, but leave them for at least two days before doing so, to allow invertebrates to migrate back into the stubble.

Trampling   Soil compaction and physical damage to the sward is much less severe on cut areas than it is on grazed pastures.

Figure 7.2 illustrates some cutting regimes which may be used to create different types of grassland. In all of these, cuttings should be raked up and removed.

7.2(A) illustrates how unmanaged grassland develops throughout one season, achieving, in this example, a height of 0.75 m by July and gradually dying back after seed set in September. If allowed to continue, this grassland might undergo natural succession to scrub over a few years.

Figure 7.2 Grassland cutting regimes (always remove cuttings)

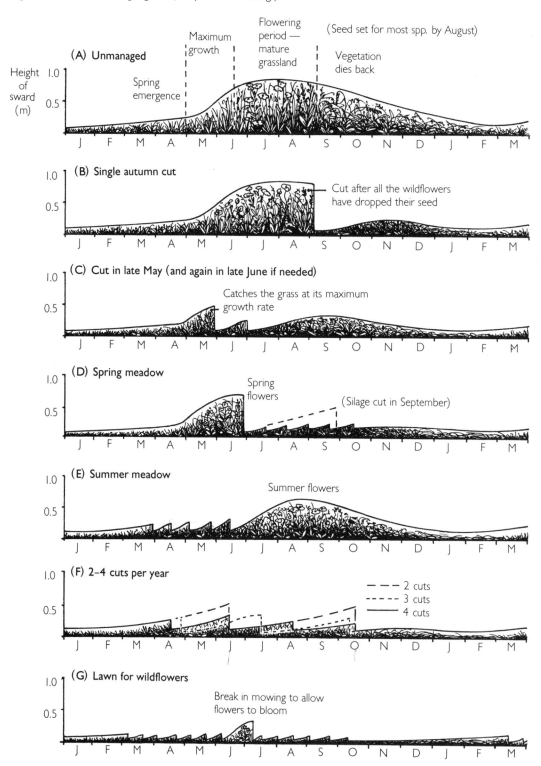

(A) Unmanaged

Height of sward (m)

Spring emergence

Maximum growth

Flowering period — mature grassland

(Seed set for most spp. by August)

Vegetation dies back

(B) Single autumn cut

Cut after all the wildflowers have dropped their seed

(C) Cut in late May (and again in late June if needed)

Catches the grass at its maximum growth rate

(D) Spring meadow

Spring flowers

(Silage cut in September)

(E) Summer meadow

Summer flowers

(F) 2–4 cuts per year

– – – 2 cuts
- - - 3 cuts
—— 4 cuts

(G) Lawn for wildflowers

Break in mowing to allow flowers to bloom

7.2(B) illustrates how a single cut after seed set (August/September, or later) allows the grassland to regenerate in the following year. This is the bare minimum of management needed to arrest succession at the tall grassland stage.

7.2(C) is a cutting regime designed to knock out vigorous coarse grasses from a sward by cutting back to 50 mm during their maximum growth period (late May) and, if necessary, again in late June. (In the north of Britain, cutting should be carried out a week or so later.) Cutting at these times also prevents the coarse grasses from setting seed. This regime should keep the sward at a height of around 300 mm. Once coarse grasses have been eliminated, say from an area designated for wildflower meadow, it should be possible to switch to a meadow cutting regime.

7.2(D) illustrates a cutting regime for spring meadow. This is a traditional method used to produce a hay crop in late June. It favours spring flowers, as they are able to set seed before the harvest. The first cut is to 50 mm. For the rest of the season, the sward is either cut regularly to 100 mm, grazed, or left until September and cut for silage.

7.2(E) is a regime which favours summer flowers. Regular cutting to 50 mm between March and early June helps to knock out vigorous coarse grasses on the same principle as 7.2(C) above.

7.2(F) is a regime commonly used in country parks to maintain areas for moderate recreational use (e.g. picnic or play areas). The regime produces a sward 70-150 mm high. Cutting is at:

2-monthly intervals for four cuts;
3-monthly intervals for three cuts;
or 4-monthly intervals for two cuts, from April to October.

This regime is aimed primarily at maintaining a sward of a certain resilience; however, so long as the cutting is carried out at the same time each year, those wildflowers able to bloom and set seed between cuts will be favoured.

7.2(G) illustrates a typical mowing regime for a wildflower lawn. The grass is cut every 10-14 days to a height of about 25 mm, and a 4-5 week gap is left in the mowing around May or June to allow flowers to bloom and set seed.

These examples are merely to illustrate the effects of particular cutting regimes. Variations of these regimes can add to the diversity of your grassland, so long as continuity is maintained. For example, portions of an area under a particular regime may be allowed to recover or rejuvenate for a few years (in a similar way to the rotational grazing mentioned earlier).

Cutting tools

In medium or long grass, where properly supervised volunteers can do the work, hand scythes may be used on a small scale, leaving whole cut stems intact and suitable for hay. Small garden mowers tend to be either the rotary or cylinder type. Rotary mowers, either with wheels or hover mowers of the 'Flymo' design, are suitable for short to medium height grass, but will get clogged in long grass, say taller than 500 mm. Cylinder mowers are only really suitable for even, short turf. Rotary and cylinder mowers slice the plant stems up and are not suitable for hay making. Both types of machine may be fitted with collection boxes, with the exception of hover mowers, which may be fitted with collection bags. Power strimmers are useful for very small-scale cutting, such as that around concealed stonework or the bases of trees (being careful not to damage the tree bark), or to cut the tops off coarse grasses before they set seed and spread. On a larger scale, long grass may be cut for hay using a power scythe. Tractor-drawn flail mowers can cope with any height of sward, but tend to chop the stems up. Gang mowers are cylinder mowers designed for cutting even, short turf on a large scale.

Reciprocating power scythes such as the Allen scythe are the only small cutting machinery suitable for cutting long grass for hay. Hay may be gathered green or left to dry. If left to dry, the hay needs to be turned once or twice. On large areas, tractor-mounted hay rakes may be used or, on a smaller scale, volunteers. Turning hay while it dries encourages ripe grass and wildflower seed to fall back into the stubble.

If large areas of drying hay are going to pose a fire hazard, Forage harvesters may be used to cut and collect the grass for silage or to bale it as green hay.

Smaller machinery may be hired from agricultural or gardening contractors or you may be able to borrow a mower from a friendly gardener. Agricultural contractors may be able to offer reasonable rates on the hire of larger-scale machinery, or may be able to do the work for you. A cheaper possibility is to ask the help of the local authority.

Look around for a smallholder, farmer, stable or city farm (see Appendix 15 for the address of the National Federation of City Farms). If such people are offered hay or silage free of charge, they may be prepared to come and harvest it themselves. The local authority parks department may be able to put you in touch with possible customers.

7.3.3 Weeding

The concept of 'weeds' should not really apply to wildflower meadow. You may, however, wish to remove problem species such as *Rumex* spp. (docks), *Chamaenerion angustifolium* (rosebay willowherb) or *Cirsium* spp. (thistles), invasive tree and shrub seedlings such as *Acer pseudoplatanus* (sycamore) or *Salix caprea* (goat willow). Mowing should eradicate such species. Alternatively, you may employ hand-pulling or cutting down individual plants, followed by spot treatment of the cut stems with a systematic herbicide gel such as glyphosate (proprietary name, 'Tumbleweed', 'Roundup' or 'Spasor'). See Appendix 12 for further recommendations on the use of herbicides.

7.3.4 Introducing new species to established grassland

Cutting or grazing can lower nutrient levels, eliminate vigorous species and make conditions more favourable for new plants to colonise grassland. If, how-ever, your grassland is species-poor and isolated from sources of seed, such as nearby areas of natural vegetation, the introduction of new species may be the only way to increase the richness of the grassland.

Choose species suited to the site conditions, that is:

— species which normally grow in the type of grassland mixture and soil con-ditions present, e.g. dry neutral grassland or wet acid grassland;
— species which will flower and seed under the mowing/grazing regime employed on the area.

The success of introductions depends upon their ability to establish in the sward. Seeds sown straight on to the grassland are unlikely to do so. They will be unable to develop the necessary roots as the plants present will already have taken up most of the available space in the soil. The older the grassland, the more completely the space will be taken up. Seed is best sown into gaps in the sward. Raking or harrowing breaks up the mat of vegetation, removing dead material and creating gaps. If this is done in late summer (July/August), then seeds sown in autumn (September) will have a chance to take root and establish before the next spring's flush of growth. The older the grassland, the more dense the root mass will be in the soil rendering raking and harrowing less effective.

Herbicides are an alternative method of opening up a dense grassland sward. These should only be used where physical methods are not possible. Propyzamide (proprietary name, 'Kerb 50W') and Dalapon-based herbicides are selective contact poisons which will kill grasses and leave broad-leaved plants. Glyphosate-based herbicides such as 'Tumbleweed' are non-selective translocated poisons which penetrate into the plant roots and kill the whole plant. See Appendix 12 for further details concerning the use of herbicides.

An alternative to seeding into gaps in the turf is to introduce new species as ready-grown plants. These are more likely to survive if planted in the autumn as this allows their roots to establish before the spring flush of growth. Grow the plants in pots or seed trays and plant each species in groups with individual seedlings spaced 300-500 mm apart. This is particularly important if each plant needs pollen from another in order to produce seed.

If you know of another similar piece of grassland to your own which is about to be lost or damaged, it may be worthwhile collecting turves and transplanting them. The turves will contain not only plants and seeds, but a whole complex community of soil animals which will spread out into the sward.

7.4 Woodland/scrub management

Unmanaged scrub will usually undergo natural succession to woodland, while young unmanaged woodland will eventually develop into closed canopy woodland. Under a closed canopy, the conditions of dense shade restrict the number of species able to survive beneath. Conservation management of scrub and woodland usually aims to maintain both types of habitat, with as diverse an array of species mixtures as possible within them.

This section outlines first, methods of managing newly planted scrub and woodland, and second, how to manage these habitats once they are established.

7.4.1 Newly-planted woodland/scrub

It is necessary to keep back weeds and grass around newly planted whips and transplants for at least the first two years after planting. The main object is to keep the young tree, and in particular, its leading shoot, free of weeds and grasses falling on it in the autumn. It is usual to use a sickle (reaping hook, bagging hook) and short stick; vegetation is held back with the stick and cut with the sickle. Cutting back weeds in this way reduces the ability of their roots to compete for nutrients with those of the young tree. If weed growth is too vigorous, this root competition can help to stunt, and even kill, young saplings. However, if weed growth is not too vigorous, simply trampling down the vegetation around each tree can be just as effective, and only vegetation likely to fall on the new trees need be cleared. Watering, if feasible, is a management priority during the first few years, particularly on arid urban sites.

During very dry summer spells, a bucket of water a day for each young tree may be necessary to keep trees from dying.

Beating up (replacing dead saplings)

At the end of the summer following planting, check each plant to see if it has established. If more than one in ten has died, plant replacements in the coming season.

When the deaths are mainly of one species, it is worth seeking advice (from the Forestry Commission or local authority) on why this is so, and replace with another species if appropriate. It is not worthwhile beating up in the second season, since the replacements will not catch up and are suppressed by their neighbours.

The ability of woodland herbs to colonise a newly planted urban wood will be extremely limited. Even in countryside plantations, many species colonise very slowly and some plants will never come in to a plantation. It is, therefore, worthwhile introducing woodland herbs.

When the tree canopy has begun to close, usually 2-3 years after planting, the young trees and shrubs should have begun to provide some of the shading and shelter which woodland herbs commonly require. This also helps to exclude shade-intolerant species which might compete against woodland species and stop them establishing. Suitable species are listed in Table 7.2.

Table 7.2 Suitable species of woodland herbs to introduce into young woodland/scrub

Propagation

Wildflowers

	—	//	*Aconitum vulparia* (P)	wolf's bane
		//	*Adoxa moschatellina*	Moschatel
	—		*Alliaria petiolata* (WE)	garlic mustard
B	—	//	*Allium ursinum*	wild garlic
		//	*Anemone nemorosa*	wood anemone
		//	*Arum maculatum* (P)	lords and ladies
	—		*Cardamine flexuosa*	wavy bitter cress
		//	*Circaea lutetiana*	enchanter's nightshade
		//	*Convallaria majalis*	lily of the valley
	—		*Corydalis claviculata*	climbing corydalis
	—		*Digitalis purpurea* (WE)	foxglove
B			*Endymion non-scriptus*	bluebell
	—		*Euphorbia amygdaloides*	wood spurge
B			*Galanthus nivalis* (WE)	snowdrop
	—		*Galium sylvaticum*	wood bedstraw
	—		*Geranium robertianum* (WE)	herb Robert
		//	*Lamium album*	white deadnettle
		//	*L. galeobdolon*	yellow archangel
		//	*Mercurialis perennis*	dog's mercury
B			*Narcissus pseudonarcissus* (WE)	wild daffodil
		//	*Oxalis acetosella*	wood sorrel
		//	*Polygonatum multiflorum*	Solomon's seal
//	—		*Primula vulgaris*	primrose
	—		*Ranunculus auricomus*	Goldilocks' buttercup
	—		*R. ficaria*	lesser celandine
	—		*Sanicula europaea*	sanicle
	—		*Silene dioica*	red campion
		//	*Stachys sylvatica* (WE)	hedge woundwort
		//	*Stellaria nemorum*	wood stitchwort
	—		*Teucrium scorodonia*	wood sage
		//	*Veronica montana*	wood speedwell
		//	*Viola riviniana*	dog violet

Grasses, rushes and sedges
- — *Brachypodium sylvaticum*   wood false brome
- — // *Carex pendula*   great pendulous sedge
- — *Deschampsia flexuosa*   wavy hair grass
- — *Luzula sylvatica*   greater wood-rush
- // — *Melica uniflora*   wood melic grass
- // — *Milium effusum*   wood millet grass

Climbing plants
- // *Bryonia dioica* (P)   white bryony
- // *Clematis vitalba* *   old man's beard
- // *Lonicera periclymenum*   honeysuckle
- // *Rubus fruticosus* agg. **   bramble

Key

WE = woodland edge species; P = very poisonous.

* *C. vitalba* is a very vigorous species which may smother the trees if introduced too early.

** *R. fruticosus* can also be very vigorous. If there is some already present, do not introduce any more.

Propagation symbols

// plant turves, or by splitting root masses

— sow seed (leaf mould compost and light shading help germination)

B plant bulbs or tubers

Source: adapted from Ruff (1979).

The success of the introductions will be enhanced by using a woodland mulch. This will help to suppress weeds, and the woodland herbs planted into it should thrive. Suitable mulches include leaf sweepings, shredded wood waste and, of course, leaf litter from other woods. The latter may already contain seeds of woodland herbs.

If collecting seeds or turves from other woods, make sure you have the owner's permission beforehand. Avoid undue damage to the collection area. Only collect a small proportion of turf or seed from each area or population of plants. For example, try to estimate the amount of seed present and never take more than 20 per cent. (Section 6.1.3 covers seed collection and buying seed in more detail.)

Cleaning

About 8-10 years after planting at 2m centres (earlier after planting at 1m centres), the plantation reaches the thicket stage, when branches have become interlaced. Cleaning is normally carried out at this point.

Three steps are taken:

(a) Cutting out trees and shrubs that have invaded the plantation and are suppressing planted species. In a commercial forestry plantation all invading species are cut out, but in amenity/conservation planting this need not be done if they do not interfere with the growth of the planted species. In some cases, the invading species may themselves be of high conservation value.

(b) Climbers, for example honeysuckle and ivy, should be cleared only if they are suppressing trees.

(c) Wolf trees, i.e. those that have grown quickly and have developed an oversized top, should be cut out. Alder is quite likely to shoot ahead of other planting. Where it is suppressing growth, it should be cut back. If there is sufficient light it will regenerate as a shrub layer within the plantation. In conservation planting there is less need to control wolf trees unless they are of species which are to be cut out later anyway.

Thinning

A 1 ha plantation intended to form an oak wood will be planted with 3,500 trees (assuming a 2 m spacing originally), and should have 75 at maturity. Thinning, therefore, is essential. Volunteers can certainly carry out thinning, but the selection of trees to be removed is a highly skilled operation, particularly when there is a mixture of species and a varied structure is wanted.

The objectives of thinning are:

(a) To reduce the number of trees so that those remaining have sufficient growing space and do not have excessive root competition.
(b) To remove harmful, e.g. wolf, diseased and dying trees.
(c) To ensure the right distribution of mature trees.

In general, thinning starts when trees are 9 m high, but growth rates vary from site to site. In typical conservation planting which may include alder and conifer nurses and hardwoods, thinning may start at 10-15 years with some of the alders and conifers, with substantial thinning in favour of the hardwoods at 15-25 years. Where planting is at very close centres (less than 1 m) thinning may be necessary after 5-10 years.

The work is best done with a bow saw. It is unlikely that a mechanical scrub cutter (clearance saw) will be worth using. Ideally, the cleared trees should be cut up and left to rot on the floor of the plantation to aid soil formation. However, this can be unrealistic on urban sites where the fire risk may be great, or where local residents complain about 'untidiness'.

Two types of thinning are practiced:

Low or regular thinning is the removal of damaged or suppressed trees to ensure that mature trees come from the fastest-growing and strongest of those planted. It is the commonly-used method in Great Britain for forestry plantations but of less use in conservation/amenity.

Crown or irregular thinning is when dominant trees are thinned in favour of the best plants, and slower-growing trees are retained so that there is a variety of heights. This is the method of most use in conservation.

By definition, irregular thinning does not conform to any simple pattern or set of rules. The result of successful irregular thinning should satisfy the objectives (a)-(c) mentioned above and produce a pleasing wide variety of trees of different size and species. The thinning operations should proceed slowly and carefully; skill comes with long experience as the worker learns to anticipate roughly how trees will grow amongst their neighbours.

The worker needs to look at each tree and its neighbours to decide whether it is likely to develop satisfactorily during the coming thinning cycle, or whether it should be cut back or taken out.

To plan the thinning and spacings of trees left after thinning you need to anticipate the growth rates of the trees and the size and shapes they will attain at maturity. Table 7.3 gives the heights and spreads of some common trees at maturity. If you have been able to observe the progress of trees for some years, you should also be able to judge how fast they are growing.

Table 7.3 Heights and spreads of common trees. These are often attained by mature individuals in reasonable conditions, open-grown or widely spaced. Roots can spread much further than the crown

Height range	Relatively broad crown	'Normal' spread	Relatively narrow crown
(metres)	spread ultimately greater than height	spread between 2/3 and equal to height	spread less than 2/3 height
6-15	Goat willow Hawthorn White poplar	Bird cherry Rowan Whitebeam	Juniper Aspen Holly
16-25	Crack willow White willow Yew Gean (wild cherry)	Hornbeam Large-leaved lime	Alder Birches
26-35	Pedunculate oak Wych elm Beech	Ash Small-leaved lime Sessile oak	Scots pine European larch

Source: Countryside Commission for Scotland (1982).

Use of brushings — habitats for wildlife

Brushwood and timber from cleaning and thinning may be left in piles to provide cover for nesting birds and small mammals, as well as habitats for fungi and invertebrates dependent upon rotting wood. In the absence of the mature, dead and dying trees which woodland hole-nesting birds normally use, appropriate nest boxes may also be erected (see section 6.4.3 for further details). Bat boxes may be erected for the same purpose (see section 6.4.4).

7.4.2 Established woodland/scrub

Established woodland is a very complex habitat to manage for wildlife; woodland processes are very slow and it can take many years for significant changes to occur in the woodland structure. It is, therefore, important (and there is time) to survey the woodland properly (see Chapter 4) before embarking on any management. The soil and climatic conditions, the mixtures of species present and the effects man has had on the woodland's history will all be important factors to consider while drawing up an appropriate management plan (see section 7.2).

Three essential reference texts for anyone planning the management of a piece of established woodland are Brooks (1980), Kirby (1984) and Peterken (1981). Brooks is a comprehensive guide to the principles and methods of woodland management, written for use by nature conservation volunteers. Kirby gives an up-to-date account of the conservation management of broadleaved woodland and how this relates to current forestry practice. Peterken is an equally comprehensive guide to the origins and ecology of British woodlands, the types of woodland in Britain, their distributions throughout the country and the principles of woodland nature conservation.

Man's effects on British woodlands

During the period 5000-3000 BC, the British Isles were clothed with primeval forests. By around 3500 BC, Neolithic man had cleared significant areas. By the time of the Norman conquest woodland covered perhaps 15 per cent of England and this has been reduced to around 7 per cent today. By the thirteenth century (the middle or medieval ages), English woods were being managed, with Welsh woods following a little later and most Scottish Highland forests being affected by the time of the seventeenth century. Truly natural (primeval) woodland is extremely rare or, possibly, non-existent in the British Isles. All existing woodlands have been affected by man in some way.

They are, therefore, classified as either semi-natural woodlands (originating from natural woodland regeneration) or plantation woodlands (planted). They can also be divided into, primary or secondary woodland. 'Primary' describes a woodland which is likely to have occupied a site since the time of the primeval forests. 'Secondary' woodland grows on land which was formerly cleared and used for other purposes.

Using these distinctions, Peterken (1981) splits existing woodlands into four categories:

(A) Primary (Ancient*) Semi-Natural, e.g. traditionally managed woods dating from 1600 or before, ancient high forest (mainly the 'native' pinewoods of Highland Scotland), and ancient woods on inaccessible sites such as ravines and cliffs.
(B) Secondary (Recent) Semi-Natural, e.g. scrub and woodland developing naturally on formerly unwooded ground (post 1600).
(C) Primary (Ancient) Plantation, e.g. ancient semi-natural woodland (A) which has been cleared and re-planted before 1600 with an even-aged stand of broad-leaves or conifers.
(D) Secondary (Recent) Plantation, e.g. stands of broad-leaves or conifers planted, since 1600, on formerly unwooded ground.

These categories are not completely distinct and some woods will fall on borderlines between them, for example, a neglected plantation (D) will tend to revert to secondary semi-natural woodland (B).

In general, the older and more natural a woodland, the greater its nature conservation value. Thus, in the above categories (A) is the most valuable. Ancient semi-natural woodlands contain many features deriving directly from the primeval forests. Because of the extremely long time they have had to develop, the communities of plants and animals they contain have become diverse in structure and species numbers. They often contain rare species which have little ability to colonise new sites. As such woodlands tend to be isolated, these rare species can easily become locally extinct should the woodland be damaged. The soils of ancient semi-natural woodlands are relatively undisturbed, protected over the centuries by the trees. As a result, the soil structure tends to be well-developed, with a distinct soil profile, characteristic of original forest soils. The seed bank and communities of soil organisms present tend also to be extremely rich and diverse. The richness and unique features of ancient semi-natural woodland cannot be recreated once they are destroyed.

In category (B) above, secondary woodland which has developed for at least 150 years by natural succession also has high nature conservation value, by virtue of its richness in structure and species present.

Peterken has classified ancient, semi-natural woodlands according to the

---

*Ancient woodland may also be old secondary. For example, a woodland which has grown up on a fourteenth-century site.

mixtures of species they contain; Table 7.4 is a summary of the different groups in his classification. Detailed descriptions of soils, trees, shrubs and herb species common to each group are given by Peterken (1981), and shorter descriptions by Brooks (1980).

Table 7.4 Woodland stand types in British ancient, semi-natural woodland

1. ASH-WYCH ELM WOODLAND
   1A. Calcareous ash-wych elm woods
       a. Southern variant   b. Northern variant
   1B. Wet ash-wych elm woods
       a. Heavy soil variant   b. Light soil variant
   1C. Calcareous ash-wych elm woods on dry and/or heavy soils
       a. Eastern variant   b. Sessile oak variant
   1D. Western valley ash-wych elm woods

2. ASH-MAPLE WOODLAND
   2A. Wet ash-maple woods
       a. Typical wet ash-maple woods   b. Wet maple woods
   2B. Ash-maple woods on light soils
       a. Variant on poorly-drained soils   b. Variant on freely-drained soils
   2C. Dry ash-maple woods

3. HAZEL-ASH WOODLAND
   3A. Acid pedunculate oak-hazel-ash woods
       a. Heavy soil form   b. Light soil form
   3B. Southern calcareous hazel-ash woods
   3C. Northern calcareous hazel-ash woods
   3D. Acid sessile oak-hazel-ash woods

4. ASH-LIME WOODLAND
   4A. Acid birch-ash-lime woods
   4B. Maple-ash-lime woods
       a. Lowland variant   b. Western variant
   4C. Sessile oak-ash-lime woods

5. OAK-LIME WOODLAND
   5A. Acid pedunculate oak-lime woods
   5B. Acid sessile oak-lime woods

6. BIRCH-OAK WOODLAND
   6A. Upland sessile oakwoods
       a. Upland birch-sessile   b. Upland hazel-sessile
          oakwoods   oakwoods
   6B. Upland pedunculate oakwoods
       a. Upland birch-pedunculate   b. Upland hazel-pedunculate
          oakwoods   oakwoods
   6C. Lowland sessile oakwoods
       a. Lowland birch-sessile   b. Lowland hazel-sessile
          oakwoods   oakwoods
   6D. Lowland pedunculate oakwoods
       a. Lowland birch-pedunculate   b. Lowland hazel-pedunculate
          oakwoods   oakwoods

7. ALDER WOODLAND
   7A. Valley alderwoods on mineral soils
       a. Acid valley alderwoods   b. Valley alderwoods on neutral-
                                          alkaline soils

7B. Wet valley alderwoods
    a. Sump alderwoods   b. Base-rich springline alderwoods
    c. Base-poor springline alderwoods
7C. Plateau alderwoods
7D. Slope alderwoods
7E. Bird-cherry alderwoods
    a. Lowland variant   b. Upland variant

8. BEECH WOODLAND
  8A. Acid sessile oak-beechwoods
  8B. Acid pedunculate oak-beechwoods
  8C. Calcareous pedunculate oak-ash-beechwoods
     a. Dry lime-wych elm variant   b. Moist wych elm variant
     c. Maple variant
  8D. Acid pedunculate oak-ash-beechwoods
  8E. Sessile oak-ash-beechwoods
     a. Acid variant   b. Calcareous variant

9. HORNBEAM WOODLAND
  9A. Pedunculate oak-hornbeam woods
     a. Birch-hazel variant   b. Ash-maple variant
  9B. Sessile oak-hornbeam woods
     a. Acid sessile oak-hornbeam   b. Calcareous sessile oak-
       woods   hornbeam woods

10. SUCKERING ELM WOODLAND
  10A. Invasive elm woods
  10B. Valley elm woods

11. PINE WOODLAND
  11A. Acid birch-pinewoods
  11B. Acid oak-pinewoods

12. BIRCH WOODLAND
  12A. Rowan-birch woods
  12B. Hazel-birch woods

Source: Peterken (1981). Peterken gives maps of the distributions of these woodland types in Britain, describes the soil types on which they occur and mixtures of woody and herb species characteristic of each type

Coppice woodlands

Most ancient woods have been managed as coppice for most of the last one thousand years, leaving a legacy of semi-natural woodlands upon which our knowledge of the natural climax vegetation of Britain is founded. And yet, the coppice system hardly rates a mention in modern forestry literature, and the surviving coppice woods are mostly dismissed as 'scrub' by foresters. — Peterken (1981)

Coppicing involves the periodic cutting back of trees to ground level, causing them to send up multiple stems from the cut 'stools'. These stools can live for many hundreds of years; much longer than they would have as trees left to grow to maturity. The regular removal of stems effectively lengthens the life of the stool.

Casual coppicing may have begun in Neolithic times with young trees being cut for poles and firewood, etc. The practice has since been refined to involve planned cycles of rotational coppicing. At its simplest, the coppicing would involve cutting all the wood in a compartment back to ground level. New compartments are cut each year until the cycle begins again with the harvest of the newly-formed stems in the first compartment.

Lengths of coppice rotations vary according to the size of stem to be harvested and the site conditions affecting growth rates of the wood. For very light wood, required for wicker baskets, woven hurdles, pea sticks, etc., a cycle of up to 12 years is appropriate, 12-15 years for firewood, fencepoles, etc. and 15-30+ years for heavier poles. Traditionally, coppiced species include:

Acer campestre	field maple
Alnus glutinosa	alder
Betulus spp.	birch
Carpinus betulus	hornbeam
Castanea sativa	sweet chestnut
Corylus avellana	hazel
Fagus sylvatica	beech
Fraxinus excelsior	ash
Quercus petraea	sessile oak
Salix spp.	willow
Tilia spp.	lime
Ulmus spp.	elm

More complex forms of coppicing include mixed-species coppicing, where different species in the same stand are managed on different rotations, and selection coppicing ('furetage'), where only a proportion of shoots are cut at any one time from each stool (particularly useful with beech as it helps the weak coppice stools to survive).

Since the thirteenth century, a 'coppice with standards' system has commonly been used. Under this, individual 'standard' trees, usually oak, are allowed to grow to provide heavy timber while stands of coppice between them are harvested at frequent intervals for lighter wood. Other canopy species, such as ash, may also be used as standards.

From the seventeenth century onwards, planting became a significant part of the coppicing system. By the late nineteenth century, coppice woods became less profitable and between 1920 and 1950 many coppiced woods ceased to be managed. Today, traditionally coppiced woods are few and far between. Bradfield Woods in Suffolk is one notable example, acquired by the Royal Society for Nature Conservation in 1970. Nature conservation organisations, however, throughout the country are bringing about a revival of coppicing on a small scale; for example, the Essex Naturalists' Trust, Shadwell Wood Nature Reserve (Mummery *et al.* 1978).

Pasture-woodlands

Pasture-woodlands are woods where animals are allowed to graze between the trees. In prehistoric times, cattle, sheep and pigs were allowed to graze and browse within the natural woodland beneath the shade and shelter of the tree canopy. This practice still survives on common land, though enclosure as coppice, and development for other uses, particularly during the nineteenth and twentieth centuries, has made such woodlands scarce. Some remain in modified form as private woods, or as parts of deer parks, forests and chases. Among the surviving forests, only the New Forest contains large areas of pasture-woodland.

The long-term maintenance of woodland pasture depended upon a balance between the extremes of, too many trees depleting the herbage, or too much grazing eventually eliminating the growth of replacement saplings. To maintain this balance, trees were 'pollarded', which involved cutting the trees back to 2-3m above ground level. The pollarded trunks sprout multiple stems, out of the reach of livestock, and can be harvested either for winter fodder or to produce similar products to coppice wood. As with coppicing, pollarding can prolong the life of a tree. Many surviving pollards are 300-500 years old, or more. With pollarded trees living longer, the importance of regeneration from seed to maintain a woodland canopy was reduced. If, under such conditions, grazing pressures were not reduced, the woods turned gradually to grassland under a scattering of mature trees. Temporary reductions in grazing pressure, however, even at long intervals, could allow a new generation of trees to grow up. Ranson (1984) summarises the conservation value of pollards.

Hedges with hedgerow trees, and riverside trees located in pastures, were also generally pollarded and may be regarded as forms of wood pasture. (See Section 7.4.9 for further details of hedgerow management.)

Plantations

By the early seventeenth century, man had begun to experiment with planting, as well as using the natural woodlands. Pure stands were planted for coppice or for the production of heavier timber, and the density of timber species in semi-natural woodlands was often increased by planting. Exotic species were first introduced around 1500 and thereafter. In the early and mid-1800s, many timber trees were introduced from North America. The Industrial Revolution and expanding supplies of imported timber from the Empire caused the financial collapse of many oak and beech plantations, and many thousands of acres of today's 'traditional oakwoods' are the derelict remains of nineteenth-century plantations or semi-natural woodlands (Brooks 1980). By the middle of this century the Forestry Commission (established in 1919) was well on the way to creating the now familiar monotonous forests of even-aged blocks of fast-growing conifers. The Commission has now, fortunately, broadened its practices to take nature conservation and landscape into consideration.

British forestry is broadly definable as 'high forest management', with even-aged stands of timber trees, planted as seedlings which have been grown in a nursery. High forest management systems may be grouped as follows:

(A) Clear-cutting. The clearance of a stand in a single felling with replacement by an even-aged stand (usually by planting). This is the main system used today.

(B) Shelterwood systems. The clearance of a stand in two or more successive fellings ('regeneration fellings'). These are timed to allow natural regeneration (or planted seedling regeneration) to occur between the trees left standing. A temporary two-aged structure, therefore, is common in the shelterwood system.

(C) Selection system. Only selected trees are felled in the woodland, resulting in regeneration (usually natural) throughout the woodland.

In recent decades, substantial areas of former coppice woodland have been converted to high forest management by:

(a) promoting single stems from each of the coppice stools to form mature trees; or
(b) clearing and replanting.

The groupings of woodland mentioned so far are not by any means compre-hensive and only provide a simple general picture of the history of British woodlands. Recommended books on the subject include: Edlin (1970), Godwin (1975), Hoskins (1955), Peterken (1981) and Rackham (1976, 1980).

7.4.3 Surveying woodland

Chapter 4 covers the general principles of site selection and surveying, the latter being particularly important in established woodland. A detailed assess-ment of the 'naturalness' of the wood, its past history, the amount of past management and disturbance are all necessary to allow you to judge how to continue managing the wood to the maximum benefit of its wildlife and the people who will use it.

Past history

You can prove a wood is secondary, but it is impossible to prove it to be primary, or even ancient, because there will be gaps in records during which the wood could have been cleared and restored.

Ancient records and maps are one source of historic information. The County Record Office will usually be able to provide papers indexed by parish or borough, and a selection of local estate maps. The local reference library may also have old local books and maps.

The first Ordnance Survey (OS) maps dating from 1805-73 (one inch to the mile) are an invaluable source of information. On these maps it is possible to distinguish between ancient and secondary woods with some degree of cer-tainty (Peterken 1981). Woods with irregular boundaries lying in a patch of ancient enclosures against a parish boundary are likely to be ancient, especially if they are named after the parish or manor, if they have a name indicating tra-ditional management, if they are linked to a village by 'Wood Lane', etc. Woods with regular shapes and straight sides will tend to be recent, especially if they have names such as 'New Plantation' and if they conform with an enclosure pattern of recent origin.

Many ancient woods were bounded by banks and ditches. If these are found to occur in a wood it is worthwhile surveying them on the ground, pacing out distances, gauging directions with a compass, sketching the extent of boundary banks and ditches and comparing them with a 1:10,000 or 1:25,000 scale OS map. Such surveys are best carried out in winter when visibility and ease of movement in the wood will be better. Bank and ditch maps can complement and reinforce archives, giving a geographical outline to the dates provided by historical records.

Other features of a wood's history relevant to its future management include:

(a) The uses to which the wood has been put, e.g. timber, gamekeeping, amenity, as a nature reserve, etc.
(b) Past and present management regimes in the wood, e.g. high forest, coppice, coppice with standards, wood pasture, etc.
(c) If the wood is neglected, the length of time since management ceased.
(d) Any external factors such as changes in drainage patterns, development of surrounding areas, laying of services such as gas, water and electricity, across the woodland, etc. (These factors will not be under your control, and so, any likely future changes and how they may affect future manage-ment need also to be taken into consideration.)

Other nearby woodlands and their histories are also worth examining, as they may bear some relation to your wood in terms of their management and the mixtures of species they contain.

Present condition of vegetation

Try to identify as many plant and animal species in the wood as possible. Your ability to do this will be limited because groups other than birds, butterflies and flowering plants are generally difficult to identify and are within the realm of the specialist. A good inventory of the flowering plants present in the wood is, however, very useful in identifying the type(s) of woodland habitat present and how it(they) may be managed. Late spring/early summer is usually the best time of year for identifying most woodland plants, though some species may need looking at again later in the summer, for example *Carex* spp. (sedges) and *Hieracium* spp. (hawkweeds). Appendix 2 lists some useful guides to identification. Mitchell (1978) and Edlin (1978) are recommended for trees.

Try to distinguish between different habitats and distinguishable units within the wood, and treat each separately, for example:

— associated habitats, such as permanent glades and rides, aquatic features and woodland edge;
— different soil types;
— topographic features such as slopes of different aspect or steepness, well-drained mounds or waterlogged hollows, etc.

The distribution of species throughout the wood may be mapped. This can be particularly useful in the case of (a) rare, (b) indicator and (c) abundant or dominant species.

(a) Wherever unusual, local or rare species are discovered, simply plot their positions in the wood.
(b) Species indicative of particular soil conditions can be mapped as a short cut to the more laborious job of analysing such conditions, e.g. Peterken (1981) gives *Geum rivale* (water avens) as a useful species for mapping moist, base-rich soils.
(c) Abundant or dominant species are best mapped by recording the position of, for example, every tree, or every patch of an undergrowth species; the time and effort required, however, is huge. Alternatively, estimate the actual distributions of species and sketch them out on a map. This approach will be affected by the surveyor's judgement, but for an initial survey the time saved over precise mapping usually justifies this loss of detail. More accurate maps may be drawn up later, if needed.

The aim of surveying is to build up a 'picture' of the woodland composition and structure. Vegetation maps showing the extent of recognised species compositions or 'stand types' are an extremely useful form of record when drawing up a management plan. There are two ways of preparing such maps:

(a) Surveyors may use classification such as that of Peterken (1981) (summarised in Table 7.4), or the scrub and woodland mixtures in Appendices 8 and 9 from Gemmell, and record the distribution of different stand types in the wood which are recognisable in the classification.
(b) The mixtures of species present in each recognisably different area of the wood may be recorded and areas then grouped together according to their similarities.

The structure of stands can help you to recognise the effects of past management:

(i) *Mature plantations* tend to have straight lines of even-aged trees and straight margins to compartments. There are usually only one or two tree species present. Boundaries between compartments are sharp and not usually associated with changes in soil conditions.

(ii) *Former wood pasture* commonly comprises large trees with wide-spreading branches, surrounded by younger, narrow-crowned trees.

(iii) *Old coppice and coppiced trees* are recognisable by the coppice stools at the tree bases, and the multi-trunked form of many trees.

(iv) *Coppice promoted to high forest* usually retains signs of coppice stools in the form of swellings at the trunk bases. The trunks are the result of single coppice stems having been promoted from each stool.

(v) *Naturally regenerating high forest* tends to have a canopy/understorey/field layer structure similar to that illustrated in Figure 6.2(A). The species present tend to represent those found in other nearby areas of woodland/ scrubland, and their distributions in the wood may be related to such features as soil conditions and local seed sources, etc.

Planted coppice may exhibit features of (i) and (ii). In the same way, neglected plantation may exhibit features of (i) and (v).

Analysis

In order to plan management at a detailed level it is important to evaluate the features present in a woodland. The following are features which enhance the value of a wood for nature conservation:

(a) The wood may be a good representative type of ancient semi-natural woodland in a recognised woodland classification, such as that of Peterken (1981). It will be even more valuable if it is made up of a number of types and the transition zones between them, which will often be rich in species.

(b) The more complex the vertical structure of a stand, the more valuable it is. An uneven canopy with a well-developed understorey and ground flora, provides a wide range of habitats for animals and plants (epiphytes), e.g. mosses, ferns and fungi which grow on the trees.

(c) If a stand of trees contains a mixture of age classes, diversity of structure is ensured for many years.

(d) Overmature and dying trees, and dead wood provide highly valuable habitats for woodland animals, particularly in wood pasture where the timber-utilising invertebrate fauna is rich. Stubbs (1972) outlines the value of dead wood for wildlife.

(e) Associated habitats adding diversity to woodland include:

Open glades and rides. These are valuable as areas where shade-intolerant plant species can survive within the woodland. Very rich 'unimproved' grassland is often found in such woodland habitats. The margins of open glades and rides support woodland-edge plant communities and rich associated communities of invertebrates and higher animals. Such margins are much better for invertebrates if they are irregular and diffuse, with a broad scrub transition zone, rather than sharp and hard. Where rides have been, or are, used regularly, the flora and fauna can be different, the soil structure and drainage having been changed by compaction and disturbance.

Water bodies. Streams, pools and areas of seepage are not only valuable as habitats for wetland species, but also for many moisture-loving woodland species which will thrive around their margins. Animals also benefit from a supply of water within the wood. Pools for aquatic plants and animals need to be permanently unshaded; those overhung with trees will rapidly become choked with leaves and tend to stagnate.

Rock faces and outcrops. These are among the most sheltered habitats in Britain. In the conditions of shade and moisture common to woodlands, they provide valuable habitats for many (sometimes rare) species of mosses, ferns, lichens and invertebrates, etc.

(f) *Shelter.* Exposed woodland on a hill top is likely to support poorer communities of invertebrates than a wood in a sheltered situation, or on a south-facing slope. The more diverse the vegetational structure within a wood, and the larger the wood is, the more shelter there will be within the wood. Rides which are winding, with junctions, will be more sheltered than long straight ones. The latter may become wind-tunnels for prevailing winds.

Adjacent habitats   Nearby habitats, such as other woods, scrub, grassland, etc. can enhance the value of a wood in so far as they help support some of the woodland species. In the case of urban woodlands, nearby derelict land, old railway lines, parkland and even gardens can provide benefits in this respect.

When analysing survey results, you need to look out for valuable features as listed in (a)-(f) above. Any valuable features need to be retained, and any that are within your means to achieve should be incorporated into the management plan for the wood.

7.4.4 Principles of woodland management for nature conservation

Peterken (1981) gives the following basic principles:

(1) *Site grading.* Distinguish between (a) individual woods of high conservation value, (b) woodland areas of high conservation value and (c) other woodlands (see 7.4.3).
(2) *Management priorities.* Give special treatment to special sites and special areas (see (13)-(15) below).
(3) *Clearance.* Minimise clearance. Necessary clearance should avoid sites and areas of high conservation value.
(4) *Afforestation.* Accept afforestation (broad-scale tree planting), except on sites of high conservation value, but not so much that non-woodland habitats are reduced to small islands. Where whole areas are being planted up, retain any habitats already present, such as small stands of trees, scrub, streamside vegetation, etc. which will contribute to the diversity of species, structure and habitats in the woodland.
(5) *Woodland patterns.* Develop (or retain) large blocks of connected woodland, while maintaining a scatter of small woods between large blocks.

These principles apply to the distribution of woodland in an area or region. Even if you only have a small urban woodland to manage, or a few to choose from in your local area, the wood you choose must be considered in the light of the contribution its management can make to the wildlife value of other woodlands in the area.

Principles (6)-(12) apply to aspects of woodland management:

(6) *Change*. Minimise rates of change within woods.

Severe changes such as clear-felling or planting conifers in deciduous woodland can cause complete changes in the plant community. Sensitive species, adapted to the conditions prevailing before the change, are lost and new species colonise (usually fast-colonising species). Changes should, therefore, be gradual, allowing time for slow-colonising, extinction-prone species to establish in the areas of change. In a woodland managed, for example, as coppice, with all stages of the coppice cycle present, change is not harmful because the vegetation is in a 'dynamic steady state' where repeated gradual cycles of change occur.

(7) *Stand maturity*. Encourage maturity by maintaining long (felling) rotations. If this is not possible, retain a scatter of old trees after restocking.

Mature trees provide the woodland canopy, creating the shade and moisture conditions suitable for woodland plants and animals to thrive. Many fungi and animals depend on mature, dying or dead timber and risk extinction when such timber is removed from the wood.

(8) *Native species*. Encourage native species and use non-native species only where necessary.

Species should, preferably, be native to the site and Great Britain, i.e. species should be likely to have occurred naturally in the woodland at some time in the site's past. The longer a species has been a natural component of British woodland, the more animal species will have become dependent upon it and the more value it will have for wildlife (see also Table 6.10(a) and Southwood (1961), Kennedy and Southwood (1984)).

(9) *Diversity*. Encourage diversity of (a) structure, (b) tree and shrub species and (c) habitat in so far as this is compatible with other principles.

The structure, (a), may be diversified by maintaining a small-scale mosaic of different age classes throughout the woodland. This ensures that animals and plants dependent on trees of a particular age class can migrate more easily from one part of the mosaic to another. There will be a limit to the diversity of tree and shrub species, (b), which can be encouraged. The more species in the wood, the smaller the population of each species will be, and the higher the risks of particular species becoming locally extinct. Habitats, (c), may be diversified by maintaining permanent features such as open and sheltered glades, and woodland paths and rides to create stable 'woodland edge' habitats. If maintained, the richness of such habitats increases with age (see 7.4.3).

(10) *Regeneration*. Encourage restocking by natural regeneration or coppice growth. Natural regeneration of native species already present in the woodland tends to produce mixed stands with a structure much more diverse than, for example, plantations. The genetic variety of the young trees will be more natural and their suitability for the environmental conditions present much better than that of planted trees. Where natural regeneration is unsuccessful, a tree nursery on site can prove very useful for starting off seeds collected within the wood, so that seedlings can be planted out.

(11) *Rare species*. Take special measures where they are necessary to maintain populations of rare and local species. Minimising clearance, (3) above, and change (6), helps to conserve poor colonisers, and encouraging

mature timber (7), helps those species dependent upon it. If you have rare species in your wood, the local Naturalists' Trust or branch of the Nature Conservancy Council will be able to advise on measures for their conservation. Even in carefully managed stable habitats, however, the species mixtures tend to undergo natural change, and some populations of rare and local species will become extinct.

(12) *Records.* Retain records of management. For example, records of environmental conditions, and vegetation present before management is carried out, are essential for comparison to records of such features after management. The effects of management can only be properly assessed with both sets of records.

Keep records of actions taken in each compartment of the wood. Keep all surviving records of past management and store them in a readily retrievable form. If you wish to adopt an event-recording method compatible with those of other organisations in the field, the Nature Conservancy Council have developed a method suited to their reserves, and your County Trust for Nature Conservation may also have a similar method. Peterken (1969) outlines useful principles and benefits of event record cards.

The final three principles apply to semi-natural woodlands qualifying as special sites and areas ((2) above).

(13) *Natural woodland.* Manage a proportion of woods on non-intervention lines, in order to restore natural woodland, if possible. For example, a piece of ancient, semi-natural coppice woodland may be allowed to grow up into a canopy woodland of mixed-aged structure with the minimum of intervention, such as exclusion of grazing animals and alien plants, with some singling of coppice stools to accelerate upward growth. (Singling is the cutting back of all but one coppice stem so that the one survivor grows into a tree.) It is important to be sure that the canopy woodland you create will have greater wildlife value than the semi-natural coppice which you are replacing (see (14) below). Allowing planted coppice or other plantations to change to semi-natural mixed-aged stands of canopy woodland, will always improve their wildlife value. (The process can, however, take several hundred years.)

(14) *Traditional management.* Maintain or restore traditional management where this is possible, and appropriate. The form of traditional management of most value to wildlife is mixed coppicing where no planting is involved. The structure of an actively-managed coppice has vertical and horizontal diversity. Since coppicing has been part of woodland management for so many hundreds of years, many diverse plant and animal communities have become adapted to the coppice system. Coppicing for wildlife is covered in detail in section 7.4.6.

Traditional pasture-woodland management is of benefit to the many species dependent upon dead-wood. The large numbers of old and dying trees common to parks and pasture-woodlands provide dead-wood habitats for hole-nesting birds, wood-boring insects, fungi, etc. which are often lacking in managed woods.

To maintain such habitats:

(a) Dead wood should only be removed to ensure public safety.

b) Pasture beneath the tree canopy should be maintained by *light* cutting or grazing, promoting a rich sward of woodland herbs and

grasses (see section 7.3 for general principles).
(c) Scrub encroachment should be suppressed.
(d) Pollarding and controlled regeneration (or planting) should be combined to ensure the eventual replacement of the mature trees. Planted or regenerating tree saplings should be protected from grazing and browsing animals.

(15) *'Modern' management.* Where traditional management is not possible or appropriate, introduce alternative systems of management which retain or enhance the conservation value of special sites and areas. The following are two alternatives to restoring coppice management:

(a) Promote coppice to high forest by leaving it to regenerate, and by singling and thinning. This is most appropriate in mixed natural stands. Careful singling and thinning should aim to produce mixed stands of all the species which were present in the unthinned canopy, and an underwood enriched by fresh coppice growth.
(b) Clear-cut the coppice, and plant species which grow naturally on the site. Planted species should be spaced widely so that they have room to grow up to form a canopy, and the former coppice can then survive as an underwood beneath the plantation. Restocking mature stands by regeneration will be beneficial as it ensures an irregular age structure for canopy species (see (10) above).

The planting alternative is more appropriate to the least natural (e.g. uniform, planted hazel or oak) coppices, and to stands where the stock of stems capable of growing into mature trees is insufficient.

7.4.5 Tree felling

Active management of woodland for nature conservation and public use will invariably involve felling some trees. The following are examples of reasons why.

Public safety   The people using the wood should not be put at unnecessary risk and rotting trees overhanging public footpaths should be felled.

Control of disease   A tightly packed stand of trees dominated by a single species is prone to destruction by disease because of the ease with which it can spread from one tree to another. Removal of some trees and their replacement with other species creates a barrier to the spread of disease and effectively increases the resistance of the stand as a whole. Dutch Elm disease has had disastrous effects in Great Britain and the removal of diseased elms is good management practice.

Diversification of the woodland   Good management for nature conservation hinges on this principle. Trees may be felled:

— to open up a dense canopy and help natural regeneration;
— to make space for new species, planted to increase the woodland structure and species complement;
— to reinstate derelict coppice (see section 7.4.6);
— to create or rehabilitate glades, rides and woodland edge (see section 7.4.7).

Removal of 'problem' species Problem species include any trees or shrubs which restrict or suppress the diversity of the woodland. *Acer pseudoplatanus* (sycamore) is a prime example. It is a very vigorous species with wind-dispersed seed capable of spreading quickly and of rapidly dominating a wood (particularly in recent secondary woodland where available space and resources have not already been taken up by other established species). Sycamore-dominated woods tend to be heavily shaded, resulting in poor regeneration of other species and a restricted flora beneath the canopy. The sycamore leaves produce a deep litter which decomposes slowly and so affects the ground and field layer species. The tree itself supports a limited number of animal species because sycamore has only been present in Great Britain for a relatively short time (thought to be a Roman introduction) and only a few species of animal in this country have evolved to depend upon it. Instead, syca-more trees commonly have a very high biomass of a few species of aphids (greenfly) and generalist invertebrates feeding on them. (A 'generalist' in this case describes a species which can eat a wide variety of foods, rather than being adapted to just one or a few.) Conservation management, therefore, commonly involves felling mature sycamore, uprooting seedlings and saplings, and where roots are too well-established to allow removal, painting cut stumps/stems with a stump killer such as ammonium sulphamate solution (see Appendix 12 for safety recommendations concerning herbicides) applied on to the freshly cut stump.

Other problem species include *Rhododendron* spp. (particularly *R. ponticum*), *Aucubus* spp., *Prunus lusitanica* and *Prunus lauroceraceus* (laurels) and *Symphoricarpos albus* (*rivularis*) (snowberry). These are common in many urban woodlands. Introduced and planted in Great Britain as garden shrubs and for game cover, etc., they have spread where unmanaged. All of them cast a dense shade and deplete the woodland field and ground layers. Their associated fauna is poor for similar reasons to those already outlined for sycamore and they were introduced into Great Britain much more recently, largely by Victorian gardeners. These shrubs tend to be resistant to herbicides so the main means of control is cutting and removal of roots. The principle of removing 'alien' woodland species (species not native to the British flora) need not be taken to extremes, particularly in urban plantation or recent secondary woodland where the wood itself may be more a reflection of man's influences than those of nature. The aims of diversifying the woodland and encouraging native species are important, so vigorous, invasive stands of aliens will need controlling, but isolated individuals may be retained to reflect the actual history of the woodland to the people using it, without detriment to wildlife. As an example, *Robinia pseudoacacia* (false acacia) is an introduced alien species common in woods in London. It casts a light shade, it is not invasive and, though it has a poor associated fauna, its deeply fissured bark provides an ideal microhabitat for invertebrates and hence for feeding birds.

Figure 7.3 illustrates some of the principles of tree felling. Trees to be felled should be carefully selected and marked in late summer and are then best felled between October and March, when the sap has descended to the roots and the trees are easier to cut. Felling and clearance work is the most dangerous aspect of woodland management and volunteers will need proper training in the methods involved and the safe use of tools such as the chain saw, felling axes, billhooks, bowsaws and crosscut saws. Brooks (1980) and Follis (1980) are recommended references for such information. The British Trust for Conservation Volunteers run regular training programmes in tree felling and clearance for local conservation corps and affiliated groups, and their training leaflet on tree felling is an ideal handout for your volunteer workforce.

Figure 7.3 Basic tree felling

Always remember: Only properly trained workers should carry out such work. Think ahead. Work slowly and carefully.

(A) Small trees — An upward cut close to the ground with a billhook, or saw right through with a bowsaw

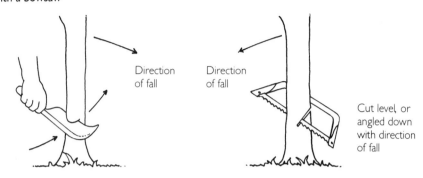

Direction of fall

Direction of fall

Cut level, or angled down with direction of fall

(B) Larger trees (less than 75mm diameter) – Use bowsaw (as above) or notch with a billhook

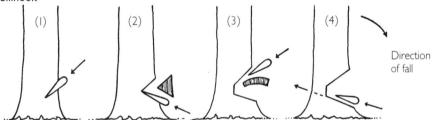

(1)   (2)   (3)   (4)

Direction of fall

(C) Trees greater than 75mm diameter — Undercut to avoid stem splitting (options: b = bowsaw cut, a = axe cut)

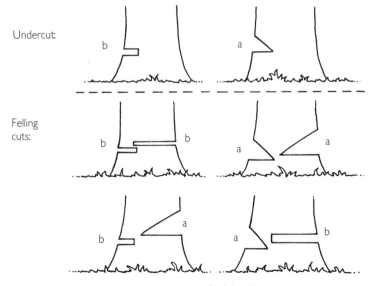

Undercut:

Felling cuts:

Direction of fall in each of these four is towards the left of the diagram

(D) Mature trees — Plan the direction of fall. Viewed from above:

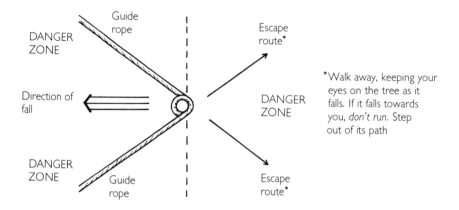

DANGER ZONE

Guide rope

Escape route*

Direction of fall

DANGER ZONE

DANGER ZONE

Guide rope

Escape route*

*Walk away, keeping your eyes on the tree as it falls. If it falls towards you, *don't run.* Step out of its path

Felling procedure:
(1) remove protruding buttresses;
(2) cut a sink (birdsmouth) and then;
(3) make the felling cut

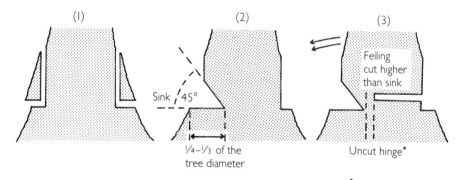

(1)

(2)

(3)

Sink / 45°

Feiling cut higher than sink

¼–⅓ of the tree diameter

Uncut hinge*

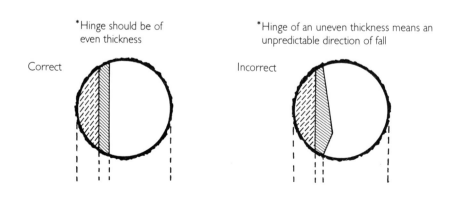

*Hinge should be of even thickness

*Hinge of an uneven thickness means an unpredictable direction of fall

Correct

Incorrect

7.4.6 Coppicing for wildlife

As already described in 7.4.2 and 7.4.4 (principle (14)), coppicing enhances the wildlife value of woodland by providing a gradually changing mosaic of structurally diverse vegetation. A 7-15 year coppice rotation is recommended for wildlife. Generally, the second and third spring after coppicing are the best periods for flowering woodland herbs. After ten years, coppice is at its best for nesting birds, while after about 20 years, its value as a nesting habitat begins to decline. This is because the closed coppice canopy tends to shade out shrubs beneath, opening out what was, before, a dense undergrowth of coppice stems and shrubs.

If the wood you plan to manage is a derelict coppice, your task will be to return it to its original form of management, selecting old stools and young saplings or suckers to cut back. If, as is more common in urban woodland, the wood is plantation or recent secondary woodland, you may be able to begin coppicing some trees straight away, but you may also need to introduce young (e.g. two-year-old) saplings and allow them to grow for 4-7 years before beginning their coppice cycle (see section 6.2.6 for recommendations on planting methods). Whether clearing the underwood and cutting back old coppice or opening up spaces for newly-planted coppice, the initial work will be much harder and labour-intensive than later cutting of coppice will be.

Table 7.5 illustrates the sort of workload involved in coppicing different areas of woodland. Never cut so much that the workforce is unable to clear it

Table 7.5 Workloads involved in coppicing four different woodlands

Site:	Bradfield Woods, Suffolk	Shadwell Wood, Essex	Dales Wood, Essex	Parndon Wood
Labour force	1 full-time, 10 volunteers	Volunteers	2 contractors	1 full-time volunteer
Tools	Chain saw	Chain saw	Chain saw	Hand tools
Area cut (acres)	7	0.5	4	1
Type	25-year-old ash, alder, birch, hazel	50-year-old ash, hazel	50-year-old ash, hazel, maple	60-year-old hornbeam
Man-days spent cutting and sorting	120	c.30	50	50
Produce				
Wood for fashioning	10 tons	1.5 tons	20 tons	6 tons
Poles	5,000	c.100	—	c.100
Firewood or pulpwood	120 tons	13 tons	100 tons pulpwood	25 tons

Note: Volunteer man-days are counted as such — though it might be only 10-4 with a two-hour lunch/pub break: full-time man-day is 8-8.5 hours.
Source: Ranson (1979a).

up on the same day. Tidy the work area as you go, thus minimising the risk of workers tripping up among tangled cut stems lying around.

Forward planning in the short term and long term are essential before you begin to coppice your woodland.

Determine first what total area of your wood is suitable to be managed eventually as coppice. You may then estimate how many plots (coupes) may be planned, according to the length of coppice rotation you have chosen. If, for example, 2 ha of your woodland are suitable for coppicing and you plan a 10-year rotation, then 10 x 0.2 ha plots (with one plot cut each year) may be feasible. An alternative is 5 x 0.4 ha plots (with one plot cut every other year). Such forward plans may need adjusting after the first year's work to ensure that your available labour/volunteer supply can easily cope with the workload. It is better to coppice smaller areas well than to take on too much, rushing the work and creating poorly managed coppice.

Recommended sizes of coppice plots (Brooks 1980) range from 0.1 ha in small woods, to a maximum of 1.2 ha. In many small urban woodlands, this maximum is unlikely to be reached, and plots even smaller than a quarter-acre may be necessary. In a very small wood, it may be possible to space out cutting times even more, e.g. with just three plots, one cut every three years, to produce a nine-year rotation.

The layout of coppice plots needs to be arranged so that, when plots are cut at the end of their growth cycle, the timber can be removed easily and without damage to other plots where young shoots may be growing up. Also try to arrange the rotation so that species can easily move from one plot to another nearby plot with similar habitat conditions. Figure 7.4 illustrates two examples

Figure 7.4 Examples of coppice plot layouts along rides, for a 10-year cycle with one plot cut each year

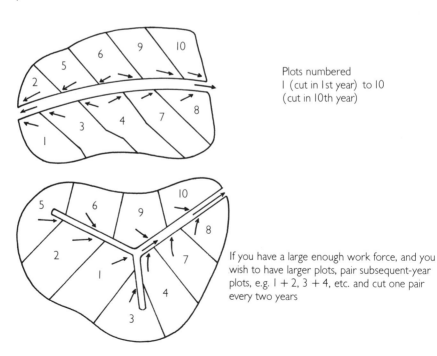

Plots numbered
1 (cut in 1st year) to 10
(cut in 10th year)

If you have a large enough work force, and you wish to have larger plots, pair subsequent-year plots, e.g. 1 + 2, 3 + 4, etc. and cut one pair every two years

Note: ⟶ = routes for removal of timber.

of area crossed by woodland rides and plotted out for 10-year rotation coppice. Each plot would be cut, in a broad front working from the ride, into the woodland, leaving an area clear of coppice stems behind, suitable for the easy removal of timber.

The coppicing calendar

In *late summer* examine the area to be cut. Mark stems (trunks) to be cut, preferably with paint. If you are planning a coppice with standards system, Brooks (1980) recommends leaving about 25 standard trees per ha if the standards are small, and reducing this to 12 per ha when they are larger (say, over 5 m tall). Select standards of a variety of sizes and ages, if possible with at least one mature tree in each coppice plot.

October–March is the best time to cut coppice and to sort out the cut timber on the coppice plot. There is less sap in the stems during this period and the wood is easier to cut. The undergrowth will have died back, so visibility is improved and the amount of disturbance to wildlife is lessened. Figure 7.5 illustrates the principles of felling and cutting to produce a coppice stool. Brooks (1980) includes details of the methods, tools, safety and team-work requirements, etc. of coppicing. Another very valuable reference, written specifically for those

Figure 7.5 Coppicing

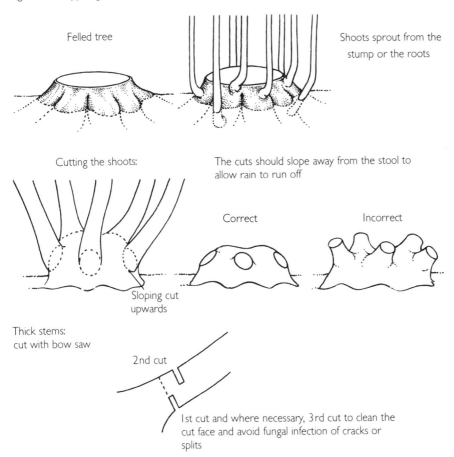

Felled tree

Shoots sprout from the stump or the roots

Cutting the shoots:

The cuts should slope away from the stool to allow rain to run off

Correct

Incorrect

Sloping cut upwards

Thick stems: cut with bow saw

2nd cut

1st cut and where necessary, 3rd cut to clean the cut face and avoid fungal infection of cracks or splits working to re-establish coppice, is Mummery *et al.* (1978). A paper by Ranson (1978) was produced to complement the Mummery *et al.* publication and is also an invaluable source of practical advice on the subject.

The British Trust for Conservation Volunteers run regular training programmes in coppicing for local conservation corps and affiliated groups, and their training leaflet on coppicing is an ideal hand-out for your volunteer workforce.

March-April. As soon as the woodland floor, rides and paths are dry enough, remove any cut timber. If you try to do this when the ground is too wet, you can severely damage the soil structure and ground flora.

For the rest of the year, there is little to be done in coppice woodland except perhaps to protect the regenerating coppice from grazing (unlikely to be a problem in urban woods).

7.4.7 Glades, rides and woodland edge

Glades, rides and woodland edge provide habitat conditions similar to freshly cut coppice, but of a more permanent nature. Generally, conditions are sunny, sheltered and humid. The edges of these habitats are often particularly rich in species. The older the habitat, the more rich the species complement. Glades which are linked to ride systems are generally more useful to wildlife than those which are isolated, as they are easier for plants and animals to colonise. Figure 7.6 illustrates a typical ride/glade or woodland margin. The grassland generally needs only to be cut once a year, between October and March, after

Figure 7.6 Woodland 'edge' habitat

Short
grassland and
wildflowers

Tall grass and herbs,
woody perennials and
shrubs

Woodland

the flowering season, using the principles outlined in section 7.3.2. The centre strip of a ride may need cutting more often, but this is best kept to the minimum required for access. The tall herb/shrub margin is best cut back every 2-3 years. Avoid clearing large strips all at once. Instead, break the strips into units cut each year. This lessens the risk of completely destroying a habitat component which may be crucial, e.g. for the survival of a particular plant or animal species.

Adequate light is essential for glades, so the surrounding woodland trees may need managing for this purpose. If the surrounding trees are mature, the glade will need to be at least 0.2 ha in size. With a 10-15 m margin of shrubs and trees, a 0.1 ha glade is possible. Small glades receive more light throughout the year if they are elongated on a north-south axis.

7.4.8 Scrub management

Scrub represents a stage in the development of vegetation to woodland from open grassland. If you are trying to maintain open grassland, invading scrub may be a management problem. It can, however, be a valuable wildlife habitat in its own right. There are high numbers of plant species associated with scrub in Great Britain, though few of these are rare. Grassland, woodland and marginal species are all commonly represented. If the scrub is undergoing natural succession to woodland, the species mixture and vegetation structure will be in a state of constant change. The rate of change will be affected by climatic and soil conditions and, in some situations, severe environmental conditions may stop scrub succession from continuing to woodland. The following simple stages may be recognised in the development of scrub vegetation (some examples of their value for wildlife are given):

(a) Open grassland with herbs, some small bushes and tree seedlings. This stage provides a feeding habitat for seed-eating birds such as finches.
(b) Closed communities of small (young) bushes and tree seedlings with patches of grass and herbs. This stage provides cover for ground-nesting birds and small mammals.
(c) Open communities of large (mature, fruit-bearing) bushes and trees (less than 7 m high) with smaller woody perennials, some patches of grass and herbs beneath. At this stage, the scrub can be floristically rich, containing both shade-tolerant and shade-intolerant species, and can provide food and shelter for a variety of mammals and other wildlife.
(d) Closed communities of large (mature, fruit-bearing) bushes and trees (less than 7 m high) creating a dense canopy, shading out shade-intolerant species and resulting in an impenetrable thicket. This stage represents a decline in the species-richness of the scrub, though it can provide an ideal nesting and roosting habitat for some birds. Canopy closure can take anything from 25 years on more fertile soils to 50 years on shallow, nutrient-poor soils.

The mixtures of species to be found in naturally generating scrub vary throughout Britain. Duffey *et al.* (1974) describe 15 recognisable scrub types, based mainly on the dominant species. The following is a short summary of these types, listed according to their dominant species and the soil types on which they occur:

A. Scrub on calcareous soils

1. *Corylus avellana* (hazel) scrub is commonly associated with limestone. In

montane areas of north-west Scotland and Derbyshire, as well as maritime areas such as the Burren in Ireland. Other species include: *Betula pubescens* (downy birch), *Fraxinus excelsior* (ash), *Quercus* spp. (oaks), *Prunus padus* (bird cherry) and *Sorbus aucuparia* (mountain ash).

2. *Juniperus communis* (juniper) scrub. *Taxus baccata* (yew) is often present, or where rabbit grazing is a significant factor, *Sambucus nigra* (elder) may be present.

3. *Taxus baccata* (yew) scrub is found on moderately base-rich soils, often forming pure stands.

4. 'Southern mix'. In the South and East of England relatively rich mixtures of scrub occur including *Cornus sanguinea* (dogwood), *Viburnum lantana* (wayfaring tree), *Ligustrum vulgare* (wild privet), *Rhamnus catharticus* (buckthorn), *Euonymus europaeus* (spindle), *Clematis vitalba* (traveller's joy) and *Sorbus aria* (whitebeam).

5. *Buxus sempervirens* (box) scrub commonly forms pure stands, but sometimes includes *Sambucus*, *Taxus* and *Fraxinus*.

6. *Sorbus* (whitebeam) scrub. Whitebeams are never the dominant species, occurring instead mixed with other scrub species on limestone in the West and North of England.

7. *Sambucus nigra* (elder) scrub is common where rabbit grazing occurs, as elder is unpalatable to rabbits.

B. Scrub on neutral soils

8. *Crataegus monogyna* (hawthorn) becomes more dominant in hawthorn scrub on heavy boulder clay soils. Other species include *Rosa* spp. (rose), *Rubus* spp. (bramble), *Prunus spinosa* (blackthorn), *Ulex europaeus* (gorse), *Quercus* spp. (oaks) and *Fraxinus excelsior* (ash).

9. *Prunus spinosa* (blackthorn) scrub is common to neutral-acid soils, often occurring in a mixture with *Crataegus*.

10. *Salix* (willows) and *Alnus glutinosa* (alder) scrub is common to soils with high water tables. Other species include *Salix cinerea* (grey sallow), *Myrica gale* (bog myrtle), *Frangula alnus* (alder buckthorn), *Viburnum opulus* (guelder rose), *Rhamnus catharticus* (buckthorn), *Betula pubescens* (downy birch) and *Fraxinus excelsior* (ash).

C. Scrub on acid soils

11. *Ulex* spp. (gorse) scrub. *Ulex europaea* is very widespread in Great Britain. *U. gallii* is common to the South and West, while *U. minor* occurs in the South-East. On acid grassland, *Ulex* scrub often intergrades with *Crataegus* (see 8 above).

11a. On calcareous heaths, *Ulex* is commonly associated with *Calluna vulgaris* (heather).

D. Maritime (coastal) scrub

12. Cliff tops. The species mixtures present will depend upon the soil type and will be similar to the scrub types already listed, but affected by the added factor of maritime exposure. This exposure and wind-pruning tend to stop natural succession from proceeding to woodland. Generally, species include *Ulex*, *Corylus avellana*, *Prunus spinosa*, *Ligustrum vulgare*, *Rubus* and *Rosa* spp.

    On limestone cliffs, *Juniperus communis* and *Rosa pimpinellifolia* may be present.

13. Sand dunes. Species mixtures depend upon the dune water conditions and base content. *Hippophae rhamnoides* (sea buckthorn) is native to the

eastern coasts and introduced in the West. Associated species include *Salix repens, Sambucus nigra, Prunus spinosa, Ligustrum vulgare, Rosa* and *Rubus* spp. On more acid dune systems, *Hippophae* is less common and scrub succession involves a transition through heathland where *Ulex* may occur.

14. Shingle. Shingle scrub suffers severe maritime exposure and wind-pruning, so dwarfing is a common feature among the scrub plants. Species include *Sarothamnus scoparius* var. *prostratus, Solanum dulcamara* var. *marinum, Prunus spinosa, Ulex europaeus, Sambucus nigra* and *Rubus* spp.

Methods of management

The basic principles of scrub management for wildlife are: (a) to maintain a varied structure in the vegetation and (b) to enhance the number of species present.

Vegetation structure may be manipulated by cutting and clearing. This should be done between January and March to avoid disturbing nesting birds and to allow them time to eat any berries present in autumn and early winter. Cutting every five to six years will only allow scrub vegetation to develop to the stage where a community of small bushes and young trees begins to close. Cutting on a 25 to 30 year rotation allows all stages up to the 'closed community of large bushes and trees' to develop before the next cut. Scrub which regenerates from cleared woody vegetation tends to be denser than before cutting because each cut stump will tend to sprout multiple stems. Young suppressed plants in the field layer and newly-germinated seedlings will add to the density of regenerating stems and a thicket will rapidly result. One way of alleviating this problem is to ensure that stumps are cut sufficiently low to allow mower blades to pass over them. Then, selective mowing can be used to keep back regenerating shoots. Mowing cleared portions for 4-5 years allows grassland to develop and then, if mowing is halted, succession to scrub will recommence by seedlings germinating in the grassland. The resulting scrub will not be as dense as it would have been if left to regenerate immediately after clearance.

If your scrub is very sparse, poor in species, or if regeneration fails, it may be necessary to plant shrubs or seed the area (see section 6.2.6 for planting methods). Once established, young shrubs and trees may be encouraged to thicken out by pruning back their leading and side shoots (see Figure 6.13).

7.4.9 Hedgerow management

The most detailed source of information on hedgerow management is Agate (1984). Other useful leaflets include: Ministry of Agriculture, Fisheries and Food (1982) and Farming and Wildlife Advisory Group (undated). Pollard *et al.* (1974) provide detailed information on the natural history of hedges and their nature conservation value.

Wildlife value

The total number of tree and shrub species to be found in hedges in Great Britain exceeds 30. Over 600 species of wildflowers and other plants are also common to British hedgerows, growing in the hedgebank in the sunny sheltered woodland-edge conditions provided by the trees and shrubs. Hedges provide ideal support for climbing plants such as *Lonicera periclymenum* (honeysuckle), *Rubus* (bramble spp.), *Clematis vitalba* (traveller's joy) and *Calystegia sepium* (hedge bindweed). These can choke the hedgerow shrubs, so from time to time, where hedges need to be stock-proof, it may be necessary to cut back or dig out particularly vigorous climbers where they are adversely affecting the hedge. Where a hedge does not need to form a barrier and value for wildlife is the main requirement of a hedge, such removal of climbers is unlikely to be necessary.

Tall hedges (ideally 1.2-1.8 m high) are good for birds. Species such as the wren, dunnock, garden warbler, blackbird and song thrush will nest more successfully in the upper parts of tall hedges, as they are less prone to predation than they would be if nesting closer to the ground. The more wide and dense the hedge the better. Hawthorn, like other thorny hedgerow shrubs, forms an impenetrable thicket and is particularly attractive to nesting birds. Birds will only nest if there is space for nesting territories and a territory needs to contain enough food for a pair successfully to raise their young.

Hedges tend to come into leaf earlier in the year than woodlands and the rich invertebrate fauna (most of which originates from woodland habitats) rapidly takes advantage of this spring flush of growth. The moist, sheltered conditions in the hedgerow and the plentiful supply of food to be found there provide an ideal habitat for small mammals, amphibians and reptiles. During the winter, the hedge also provides a refuge for hibernation.

Hedge trimming

Trimming is best carried out in winter when disturbance to wildlife will be at a minimum. Even then, overwintering invertebrate populations may be destroyed by trimming, so if you wish to avoid this, trim different sections of the hedge each year, on a rotational basis. It is best to avoid trimming during periods of frost, particularly where thick stems need to be cut or lopped, as the wood may be brittle and the frost may damage exposed tissues, leading to infection.

The only practical way to trim a tall hedge suitable for nesting birds is to produce an 'A' shaped profile by cutting each side of the hedge back with the two faces sloping inwards from the hedge base up to a point at the top. The A-shape ensures optimum exposure to sunlight for each face of the hedge and allows snow to slip off easily in winter.

The more shaded of the two faces of the hedge should be less steep than the unshaded, to help the lower branches on the shaded side to receive more sunlight.

Individual saplings, for example of holly or oak, may be left untrimmed to develop into hedgerow trees, providing more diversity in the hedgerow structure and further potential nesting sites for species such as the wood pigeon, mistle thrush, carrion crow, or even possibly the kestrel, if the trees are able to grow big enough.

Each year, after a hedge is trimmed, the cut stems begin to heal and new shoots appear below the cut tips. Gradually, the plants in an annually-trimmed hedge develop thicker stems and their side branches intertwine with those of their neighbours. As the hedge becomes more dense, bottom and inner branches begin to die back because of the increased shading. Gaps begin to appear at the hedge base after anything from 10 to 20 years. If trimming continues for too many years after this stage, the hedge will probably lose vigour and die back. To avoid this happening, if the hedgerow plants have developed into small trees with thick stems, coppicing will be an effective method of stimulating regrowth. Alternatively, the hedge needs to be left for several years so that it can put up tall stems. The hedge can then be laid.

Hedge laying

Traditionally, hedges were laid for two main reasons:

(i) to make a poor hedge stock-proof; and

(ii) to rejuvenate the hedgerow plants by encouraging them to send up fresh shoots from the bases of the old stems.

Figure 7.7 Hedge laying

(i) Clean the face of the hedge and remove wire, litter, briars, etc.

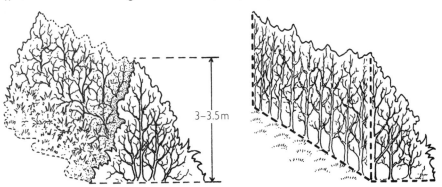

3–3.5 m

(ii) Prepare stakes and binders and place them along the hedge side for easy retrieval as work proceeds

(iii) Cut and pleach

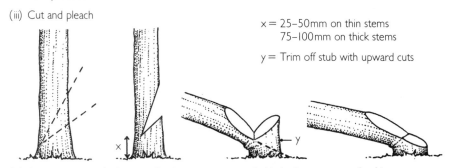

x = 25–50 mm on thin stems
75–100 mm on thick stems

y = Trim off stub with upward cuts

(iv) Stake as you work, driving stakes in a metre or two behind where you are pleaching. Stakes are set 0.5–0.6 m apart

(v) Bind the stakes and then trim off protruding tops

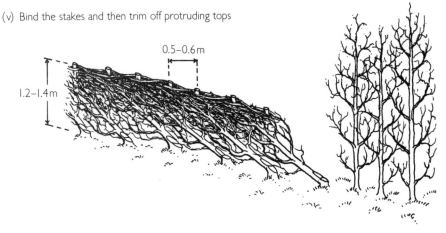

0.5–0.6 m

1.2–1.4 m

(vi) Ensure that all cuts are clean; tidy the laid hedge face, cutting and trimming projecting stems. Make cuts as near to joints as possible, as new shoots will sprout from just below joints

Hedge laying requires practice and a degree of skill to be done properly. There are slightly different traditional styles used in different parts of Great Britain. Agate (1984) provides a detailed guide to laying a 'standard' or Midlands hedge, as well as Welsh and South-Western hedges, and is an invaluable reference for anyone wishing to try it. The British Trust for Conservation Volunteers regularly run training courses in hedge laying and their leaflet on the subject is useful for handing out to volunteers. The following is a short summary of the standard hedge laying procedure:

Ideally, the hedge should have been left to grow to a height of 3-3.5 m before laying. The principle of laying is to cut and push sideways the tall main stems (pleachers) and to intertwine (pleach) their branches. The pleachers are then held in place by stakes. The stakes are usually 35-40 mm top diameter poles, around 1.4-1.8 m long (see Figure 7.7). Traditionally, hazel or ash stakes were cut from the hedge before laying, but ready-made commercial softwood stakes may also be used. To hold down the pleachers, binders ('heathers') are twined around the stake tops. These are lengths of pliable hazel, sweet chestnut, willow, or even clematis, briar or other flexible wood, 2.5-3 m long.

Some hedge layers leave a side branch on stakes cut from the hedge and to use these, rather than binders, to hold down the pleachers. They prefer this method because of their reluctance to leave too much dead wood in the laid hedge.

7.5 Freshwater management

This section deals largely with the management of still water bodies, such as man-made ponds and small pools, subsidence flashes, flooded basements and derelict sewage farm lagoons, common on city sites. The management of flowing water such as streams and rivers is covered in less detail. Brooks (1976, rev. 1981) is an invaluable source of practical information on the management of waterways (including springs, ponds, lakes, streams, rivers, canals and ditches) and wetlands (including swamps, marshes, bogs, fens and wet grasslands). Lewis and Williams (1984) is another extremely detailed and comprehensive guide to the management of rivers for wildlife.

7.5.1 Ecology of ponds and pools

In favourable conditions, even small ponds can develop rich plant and animal communities. In order to manage these communities properly, it helps to understand the requirements of the plants and animals present and how the communities interact and change from season to season. If unmanaged, natural succession will cause a pond to lose its areas of open water as the vegetation develops through a marsh or swamp phase eventually to form wet woodland (as illustrated in Figure 6.15). The basic requirements of aquatic life may be summarised as follows:

Sunlight and carbon dioxide for aquatic plants to carry out photosynthesis
The depth to which sufficient sunlight for plant growth can penetrate the water is called the photic zone. Fluctuations in water level may allow plants to establish below the normal photic zone so long as their leaves can reach up into it. The transmission of light, and hence the depth to which plants can grow, is affected by the colour and turbidity (cloudiness) of the water. Dissolved organic matter can colour water brown, suspended particles of silt can make the water turbid, 'blooms' of algae can shade out rooted plants beneath

them, as can other floating plants such as *Lemna* (duckweeds), *Potamogeton* (pondweeds), *Nymphaea* (water lilies) and any other tall vegetation casting shade over the water. For this reason, tall waterside vegetation, particularly trees and shrubs, needs to be kept back from the water's edge, especially on the south side of the water, as this is the side from which most sunlight comes.

Carbon dioxide is readily soluble in natural waters (about 200 times more soluble than oxygen) and is never in short supply.

Oxygen for plants and animals to breathe (respiration)

Oxygen solubility in water is very poor and available oxygen decreases even more if water is warmed up, because warm water is unable to hold as much oxygen as an equivalent volume of cold water. Oxygen is added to the water by surface aeration (particularly on windy days) and by plant photosynthesis during daylight. It is depleted by plant and animal respiration and by the oxidation of decaying organic matter. Oxygen diffuses very slowly through the water, so, unless the water is mixed or stirred by strong winds, there can be large amounts of oxygen around aquatic vegetation in bright sunlight. For the same reason, oxygen can be severely depleted in shaded areas or where, for example, plant remains are decaying and undergoing oxidation. During the night, a thickly vegetated pond can lose most of its oxygen, and this can only slowly build up again during the day.

Nutrients for plant growth

In a newly-created pond, the amount of nutrients present will depend upon the substrate type and the water quality. An acid substrate in an area of granite rock, for example, will tend to be low in mineral nutrients, as will any soft, acid water. These conditions are commonly found in upland pools on acid rock, predominantly in the North and West of Great Britain. Lowland pools, on the other hand, lying on base-rich soils, with less acid water conditions, will tend to contain more mineral nutrients. Plant growth in fresh water is commonly limited by the availability of essential nutrients, at least during the active growing season. These nutrients include sulphates, phosphates, nitrates and carbonates. In certain situations, these nutrients may be present in excess. Sudden influxes may occur as a result of pollution from sewage, fertiliser run-off and detergents. Some city mains water supplies are re-cycled through water treatment farms and the water re-used. Nutrients such as dissolved salts tend not to be removed completely by water cleansing and so can build up in the mains water.

As water plants take up nutrients and eventually die, organic material gradually falls to the bottom of the pond to decompose, releasing its nutrients into the pond mud. If the mud is disturbed, by uprooting plants or paddling, for example, not only does the water become muddy, but nutrients are stirred and dissolved into the water.

Whatever the cause, if nutrient levels in the water increase too quickly the microscopic plants (algae) with the fastest growth rates gain an advantage over higher plants and can quickly cover the water with dense clouds or 'blooms' of filaments, single cells or gelatinous mats. Although these produce oxygen by photosynthesis, most of it is lost at the water's surface and the dense mat shades any plants beneath. Death and decomposition of shaded plants causes deoxygenation of the lower levels and the plant and animal community collapses. When the algae run out of nutrients, they die and begin to decompose, resulting in stagnation.

Algal blooms can be a real problem in ponds with a nutrient-rich water supply which have not had time to develop a healthy community of higher plants. Where such communities have developed, algae have to compete with the higher plants for nutrients and any blooms which occur tend to be limited to small open areas of the pond where their effects are not too serious. In this balanced situation, the algae cease to be a problem. They are valuable for wildlife as a food source for zooplankton and invertebrate grazers (Pentecost 1982), and form an important component in the web of aquatic life.

Tolerable levels of acidity/alkalinity (pH) and temperature

pH is a useful measure of water acidity/alkalinity and can be easily estimated, perhaps with the help of a local school or college or the local water authority. pH 7.0 is neutral, below 7.0 is acid and above is alkaline. The pH of natural waters ranges from below 4.0 to above 10.0. Low values are found in pools containing strong mineral acids, such as upland pools on granite or bog pools. High values are found in calcareous pools and alkaline pools, on chalk and limestone for example. Different species, particularly animals, are adapted to different ranges of pH, so the mixture of species able to live in a pond may be altered by changes in pH (see Table 6.18 for examples of plants).

In a similar way, different species are adapted to different temperature ranges, with optimum temperatures at which each species functions best. Changes in water temperature are much slower and less extreme than those in the air, but they are till sufficient to cause changes in the mixtures of species present, for example by changing the ability of particular species to compete with their neighbours.

Tolerable levels of pollutants and toxic substances

Once present in still water, most pollutants are very difficult to remove, so it is essential to ensure that they never reach the water in the first place. The main pollutants and toxic substances may be summarised as follows:

(a) Inert suspended matter — this can include inert dust, fine sand, and other fine particles able to be carried by water or suspended in it. When present in large quantities, such substances cause problems with light penetration and can smother submerged plants.

(b) Oils float on water and can spread over very large areas, forming films only a few molecules thick. The films can disrupt gas exchange at the water's surface, but more seriously the oils can kill floating vegetation or aquatic animals coming into contact with them, particularly animals with external gills, or which breathe through their skin. For this reason, run-off from roads or car parks should not be allowed to flow into a pond. If inflow drains for a pond receive water from such areas, the most risky period for the pond is when a heavy rainstorm occurs after a long dry spell. This can result in the pollutants which have accumulated on the road/car park surface being washed suddenly into the drains. It is, there-fore, a good idea to disconnect or divert such drains if a rainstorm threatens after a long dry spell, and only to reconnect them when you are satisfied that the initial polluted 'surge' in the water has passed.

(c) Toxic substances — the many toxic substances produced in urban areas which can find their way into freshwater systems include industrial by-products such as cyanides, arsenical compounds, heavy metals, acids, alkalis and organic substances such as phenols. Some aquatic species are known to show some tolerance to such substances, but even small con-centrations of a toxic substance in the water can significantly change the mixtures of plants and animals present by its harmful effects and side effects on the more sensitive species. For example, as little as 0.1 parts per million of some synthetic detergents can almost halve the rate at which a river takes up oxygen. Concentrations of up to 10 parts per million are not uncommon in urban freshwater bodies (Mellanby 1970).

(d) Pesticides can be a problem whether deliberately or accidentally added to a freshwater body. Run-off from nearby crops, parks or gardens, or spray drift may be avoided only if you have the forewarning and the power to stop its happening. Therefore, accidents can occur. There is no justification, however, for deliberately introducing pesticides to an aquatic system and in particular the increasingly common use of herbicides to control aquatic 'weeds' should be avoided if at all possible.

Compounds such as diquat and dalapon are sometimes used to kill aquatic plants as an alternative to manual clearance. The result is a decaying mass of dead organic matter. In the short term, the effects of this may include a reduction in oxygen supply, an increase in carbon dioxide, a lowering of pH, an increase in bacterial populations, a change in the nutrient status of the water and damage to plant communities and consequently to the communities of animals dependent upon them. Long-term effects may include suppression of growth of new plants and the possible invasion of undesirable herbicide-tolerant new species, such as algae. This would depend to a great extent on the persistence of the herbicide (Newbold 1975).

(e) Organic substances — these include any dead plant or animal material, such as dead leaves from overhanging trees. In urban areas, other significant sources include industrial effluents from sugar mills, breweries and paper mills and, probably the most important, sewage.

Bacterial decomposition of excess amounts of such organic matter can deplete the oxygen essential for aquatic plants and animals. Once decomposition is complete, the mineral nutrients produced can cause algal blooms, particularly if the higher plants have not had time to recover from the initial deoxygenation.

The size and shape of a pond or pool will significantly affect its ecology. For example, the slope of the pond banks will determine the types of plants able to grow around the fringes. Shallow sloping banks will allow wide fringes of marginal vegetation, while steeper slopes will have thinner fringes which develop more slowly. Figure 6.15 illustrates how these fringes extend further into the pond, as rooted plants trap silt and other materials and natural succession proceeds. The rate and pathway of natural succession depends upon the supply of species and the nutrients available to the system. In Figure 6.15 the examples of (A) a nutrient-poor system and (B) a nutrient-rich system illustrate two different possible pathways. The rate of natural succession in a nutrient-poor system is generally slower than that for a nutrient-rich system.

7.5.2 Preliminary surveys of established water bodies (see also
Chapter 4)

As with other habitats, the environmental conditions and associated flora and fauna in and around a water body will change from season to season. Before management can begin, surveys need to be spread over a year at least, involving regular monitoring. Preliminary surveys provide essential information on the physical, chemical and biological features of the water body. This information will then enable you to make more enlightened judgements concerning the management required and will provide a baseline against which the effects of future management and other changes can be compared. The following are key features which will need to be examined (all are interacting factors which can significantly affect each other).

The origin of the water body   Whether it is a natural pond, or man-made. In the latter, this information could be important, for example should the pond lining or dams, etc. need repairing. What is the water source?

Development of the habitat   To what extent are the present conditions a result of past management or of natural succession?

Geology and soils   These are particularly important as they affect the chemical content and pH of the water. Local geology can also influence the rate of run-off in the catchment area of a water body. The less porous the rock and soils of the catchment area, the less likely it is that rainwater will soak away before reaching the pond and the more likely that the pond will receive 'flash' floods of water after storms.

Water quality   This can vary from season to season, particularly if there are fluctuations in water level, so round-the-year measurements of water quality and estimates of the depth and volume (and the effective size of the pond) are useful. A pond with an inflow but no outflow is particularly vulnerable to accumulation of pollutants. If the pond is shallow, with a large surface area:depth ratio, evaporation during the summer can cause pollutants to increase in concentration. It is possible to see oil films and suspended silt clouding the water, but many pollutants are not visible to the naked eye, so it is advisable to have water samples analysed by the local water authority or environmental health department. pH is easy to measure: a local school or college may be able to provide meters or pH indicators. Alternatively, you may buy universal indicator paper and colour cards for testing water within the pH range of 4-10, or narrow-range paper (pH 6-8) from A. Gallenkamp (see Appendix 14 for address).

Appendix 13 illustrates methods of assessing pollution levels in ponds and streams using aquatic invertebrates. Using these methods you can produce a figure for ecosystem diversity to indicate water quality.

If the pond is found to be polluted, try to find the source of the pollutants. Your ability to stop such inputs of pollutants may be limited but it is essential that you are aware of water quality.

Siltation This is a very important cause of water loss in many ponds and pools. Silt can enter a pond as airborne dust or as particles in suspension in the inflow waters. Siltation is enhanced by marginal plants as their stems trap and hold the silt, accelerating its build-up. Dead organic material such as dead aquatic plants or leaves from overhanging vegetation accumulates with the silt and creates a gradually thickening layer of organic ooze. If you find this to be the case in your survey, it is likely that clearing of bottom muck will be a significant part of future management.

Vegetation   It is worthwhile mapping the vegetation in and around the water body. Even a rough map will help to give you an idea of the stage of succession the vegetation has reached, whether certain vigorous species are dominating particular areas, etc. In certain situations, vigorous growth in a particular portion of a water body may be due to a hidden input of nutrients, e.g. seepage of sewage or fertilisers into a pond.

In vegetation mapping, distinguish between the following groups:

— Bankside vegetation (e.g. marsh plants and, in particular, bushes or trees overhanging the water, shading water plants or causing significant inputs of dead leaves and drawing water up through their roots).
— Marginal/emergent vegetation (particularly vigorous species encroaching into the water and contributing to siltation and build-up of organic matter).
— Rooted, floating-leaved aquatics.
— Free-floating aquatics (including algae).
     The last two groupings are important in that the extent to which they cover the water dictates the degree of shading beneath and, obviously, the extent of remaining open water.
— Submerged aquatics. A lack of healthy submerged aquatic plants can severely affect supplies of oxygen necessary for aquatic animals to survive.

Other organisations may already have surveyed the water body, or may be able to help you to do so. Examples include the local regional office of the Nature Conservancy Council, the local County Naturalists' Trust or Natural History Society, local museums and libraries.

Human impact   Apart from the familiar rubbish tipping in urban water bodies (out of sight, out of mind), people may use the pond and the surrounding area. It is important to find out how they use it and to consider this in your management proposals.

7.5.3 Basic management requirements

The basic aim of managing a freshwater body for its associated wildlife, is to try and maintain as diverse a mosaic of habitats and vegetation types as possible, without each becoming too fragmented. By maintaining areas of open water, aquatic and bankside vegetation in balanced proportions from year to year, you can encourage the development of rich associated animal communities. Domination by a few vigorous plant species lowers the diversity of the habitat and its associated animal community. On the other hand, too many plant species crammed into a tiny pond may not have sufficient space or resources for all to survive, with the result that a few of the more vigorous species will probably be the only ones to establish properly.
     There should always be the initial question, 'Is management needed?', and the answer will depend upon the condition of your water body. This question is considered under each of the following sections summarising basic management requirements and the methods used.

Waterway clearance

This covers the removal of rubbish, excess mud, silt and organic matter where necessary.
     Clearance is generally needed where waterways have been physically choked by mud, silt, rubbish or dense vegetation; where water needs deepening to enhance wildlife value; where dumped rubbish or toxic substances in the bottom sediments need to be removed; and where the build-up of mud or silt and invasive emergent vegetation threatens the diversity of the habitat.
     If bottom sediments are highly polluted with toxic materials the only way of restoring wildlife value is to clear out the water body completely and start from scratch.
     If the water body already has valuable plant and animal communities present, it is essential that management causes minimal damage to them. Even in a heavily choked water body, never clear the entire area in one year. At the

most, clear half and allow that to recover before continuing. In the long term, where you are aiming to maintain particular conditions, clearance operations need to be conducted on a small scale and often. Within the area needing to be cleared, identify each area with similar conditions and vegetation type. Ideally, each of these should be split into portions (up to five if possible). Clear one portion each year, so that a rotation is set up. This allows cleared portions to recover, with the help of species re-colonising from neighbouring unharmed portions.

At any time of year, it is impossible to avoid harming some aquatic life during clearance operations. Even in winter when most organisms are dormant, many aquatic animals are present, either hibernating or active in the bottom sediments, so the principle of portioning disturbance is always important.

Most amphibians (frogs, toads and newts) are very mobile and are leaving, or have left, the water by October, and most species spawn from March onwards into the summer. These dates vary with climatic conditions, particularly temperature, so it is always worthwhile finding out the timing of amphibian life cycles in your pond. During the December-February period, over-wintering wildfowl depend upon many inland freshwater bodies and should not be disturbed by management activities.

The least harmful time for clearance operations is usually, therefore, in the late autumn (October-December). Weather may often affect your ability to work, not only because of the deterrent cold, but also because iced-over water bodies can be very dangerous. If you are unable to complete your planned management activities in the late autumn, you may choose to finish the work during the short periods preceding spawning, say, late February. Try, however, to avoid excessive disturbance during the spring-summer growing season.

Excessive disturbance of bottom sediments can be particularly harmful in ponds which are very nutrient-rich (eutrophic), stagnant or undrained. Stirring the nutrient-rich organic sediments into the water can cause algal blooms or lower the water's oxygen content. These effects can be even more marked in hot weather.

Clearance operations can also damage bankside vegetation. Plants will die if smothered in mud. Marshy vegetation or vegetation of waterlogged soils is very vulnerable to damage from trampling. Try to limit access to the water to a few points, situated in the drier bank areas. When removing material from the water, leave it piled in one or two locations on the shore to allow excess water to drain back into the pond. This allows some of the aquatic life to escape before the spoil is taken away.

If the spoil is left near to the water body, make sure that it is far enough away not to be washed back in. Disposal of spoil elsewhere is best arranged with the local authority, or the owner of the land where the spoil is to be dumped, e.g. a local farmer who may use it as fertiliser. Remember that root fragments and rhizomes of vigorous marsh species can cause problems if dumped on marshy or waterlogged soil, as they may regenerate and create a weed problem in the dumping area, particularly if it is farmland.

A valuable source of information for tools and methods is Brooks (1976, rev. 1981).

Vegetation management

The previous section outlined why waterway clearance work should be carried out over limited portions of the water body, on a rotational basis where possible and at times of year when disturbance to wildlife would be at a minimum. Exactly the same principles apply to vegetation management.

Bankside vegetation   This may include wet grassland, herbs, scrub and waterside trees. The main reasons for managing bankside vegetation may be summarised as follows:

— To diversify waterside habitats. You may wish to promote herb-rich flood meadows. Scrub or tall herbs growing right up to the pond edge give access to the water for shy animals. Alternatively, for example, some wildfowl species will find open, low waterside vegetation attractive where they can rest or feed in the mud with a wide field of view and no dense vegetation nearby to conceal predators.
— To control the amount of shading of the water. Dense shade from trees, particularly on the south side of a pool, can exclude many aquatic plants and create areas of poorly oxygenated water.
— To lessen the amount of leaf litter falling into the water. Decaying leaves can smother the aquatic vegetation and use up the available oxygen in the water as they decay.

The management approaches for trees, scrub and grassland are similar to those described in previous sections. If managed properly, waterside trees can be of benefit to aquatic communities. Their roots can stabilise banks. Where they cast light shade over the water, fish may shelter. Mature and hollow trees can provide nesting sites for birds which feed in and around the water. Willows and alder are the most common waterside trees in Great Britain and they are often managed by pollarding during autumn and winter. This gives the trees new vigour, stronger root growth, and helps to prevent them falling and damaging banks or artificial linings. Trees must be kept off dams and well away from canal edges as their roots may break up the water-retaining earthworks and cause leaks. With a small pond, large trees can be detrimental as they draw such huge amounts of water up through their roots. Care must also be taken to ensure that tree roots are kept away from pond liners in case they are punctured. Young willow, alder and other wetland scrub species may be coppiced to provide dense undergrowth at the water's edge.

Reeds, sedge beds and wet grasslands may be managed by mowing or grazing. Grazing between May and October, or cutting mid-June to mid-August, promotes herb-rich wet meadow and restricts scrub invasion. If marshy areas are not cut during these periods, for whatever reason, for example because the ground was too soft and wet, or because you needed to avoid disturbing nesting birds, it may be possible to burn the area in winter to remove old tangled growth. It may also be possible to mow in winter when soft boggy areas are frozen solid.

Brooks (1976, rev. 1981) outlines methods of producing cash crops from reed, sedges (marsh hay) and willow.

Emergent vegetation   This has two main characteristics which often result in a need to control its spread. First, it can extend outwards into the water, trapping organic matter and silt between stems and roots and gradually promoting the development of marsh. Second, a few of the emergent species can often establish complete dominance in the aquatic and reedswamp zones, thus lowering the diversity of the habitat. Examples of such species include: *Sparganium erectum* (bur-reed), *Phragmites communis* (common or Norfolk reed), *Typha latifolia* (greater reedmace), *Glyceria maxima* (reed grass) and *Juncus* spp. (rushes). All these species can spread by means of rhizomes forming mats on or in the mud from which new shoots can sprout. If such species occur naturally in a water body you will have to accept that periodic management (i.e. prevention of their spread) is necessary if they and their associated wildlife are to survive alongside the various other aquatic plants and animal communities. To control their spread, emergent plants may be controlled by either cutting or digging out — digging, though the most laborious, is the more thorough of the two methods.

It is best to work from the outer edge in towards the bank. Digging is difficult in water over 1m deep. The most efficient way to dig out is first to cut around chunks of matted rhizomes, cut under the edges to free them from the bottom, then float the chunk of vegetation to a collection point, either a raft, or punt, or on the bank. Where material is pulled out of the water, work from a few definite locations to minimise trampling. When working on soft mud, use wide planks or galvanised sheeting to avoid sinking. Clear small areas thoroughly, rather than disturbing larger areas and leaving root and shoot fragments to regenerate.

Because digging stirs up so much mud and organic matter, it can lead to rapid nutrient enrichment or deoxygenation of the water, particularly in small, shallow, warm water bodies. Try, therefore, to restrict such operations to the autumn when temperatures are lower, and whenever you carry out a task, try not to disturb the whole water body. Restrict the work to particular small portions in any one year.

Cutting can give temporary control of spread, but it does encourage faster growth with some species. If you want to stop vegetation spreading by cutting alone, it must be done at least once a year. *Phragmites communis* is best cut in July if only one cut a year is feasible. Generally, time of year is unimportant for other species, so time cuts to ensure that wildlife suffers minimal disturbance. If cutting in the spring, cut below the water level to impede aeration of cut shoots. Autumn cuts should be above the water so that winter frosts will restrict shoot regeneration.

Examples of species and their control (remembering that each species is itself valuable for wildlife):

— *Sparganium erectum*. Dig out or cut in August and September.
— *Phragmites communis*. Difficult to eradicate by digging. Dig and pull loose chunks of rhizome mat or cut (as above).
— *Typha latifolia*. Pull out rhizomes where floating or in soft mud, but if they tend to break, dig out. Cutting gives only very temporary control.
— *Glyceria maxima*. Where the rhizome mass is floating in the water or in soft mud, pull out. In more solid silt, dig out in turfs or mow.
— *Juncus* spp. Dig out as turfs or mow.

Floating-leaved (rooted) vegetation   The two main reasons for controlling this type of aquatic vegetation are first, to create areas of open, unshaded water where floating leaves and their stems are clogging a waterway, and second, to restrict the spread of single vigorous species of floating-leaved plants which threaten to take over the waterway.

Nuphar lutea (yellow water lily) and *Nymphaea alba* (white water lily) tend to be very vigorous and often require controlling. Other species such as *Potamogeton natans* (broad-leaved pondweed) and *Sparganium emersum* (unbranched bur-reed) tend to be less vigorous, but may also need to be controlled in certain circumstances. Species tend to spread by rhizomes and sometimes grow too deep to be dug out easily. One method is to use a long-handled cutting tool to chop the deep rhizome mat into managable pieces and then carefully to pull the stems and rhizomes free, floating them away to a collection point. Try to be thorough and to clear small areas properly, minimising the number of discarded rhizome fragments which will reroot.

Cutting is an alternative method for temporary control. In deep water, a chain scythe, or a 'V'-shaped cutter, may be used (see Figure 7.8). The chain

Figure 7.8 Examples of tools suitable for waterway clearance and management of aquatic vegetation

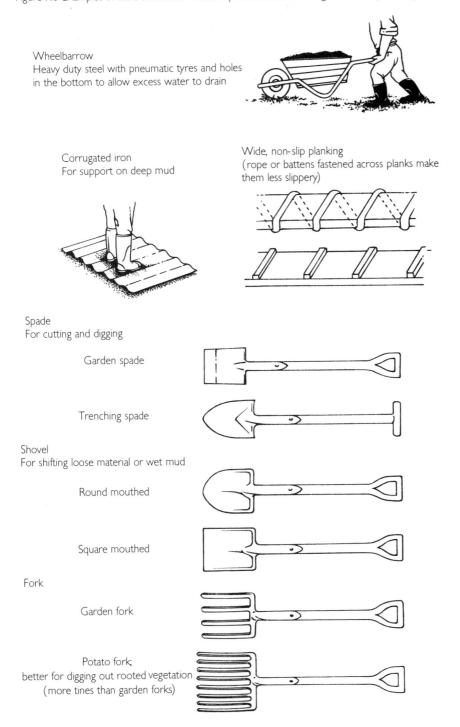

Wheelbarrow
Heavy duty steel with pneumatic tyres and holes in the bottom to allow excess water to drain

Corrugated iron
For support on deep mud

Wide, non-slip planking
(rope or battens fastened across planks make them less slippery)

Spade
For cutting and digging

    Garden spade

    Trenching spade

Shovel
For shifting loose material or wet mud

    Round mouthed

    Square mouthed

Fork

    Garden fork

    Potato fork;
better for digging out rooted vegetation
(more tines than garden forks)

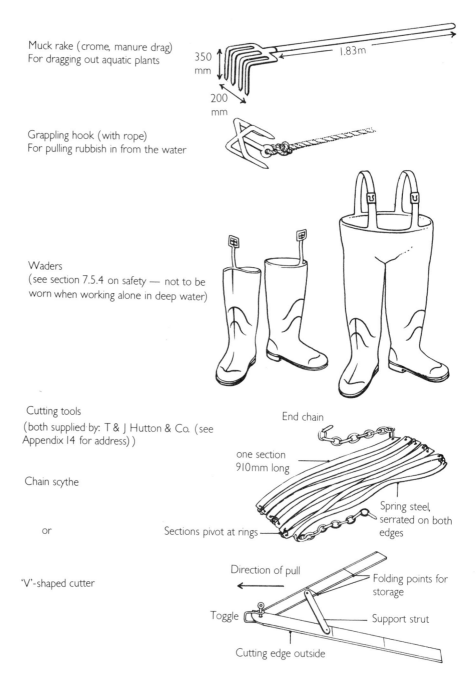

Muck rake (crome, manure drag)
For dragging out aquatic plants

350 mm

1.83m

200 mm

Grappling hook (with rope)
For pulling rubbish in from the water

Waders
(see section 7.5.4 on safety — not to be
worn when working alone in deep water)

Cutting tools
(both supplied by: T & J Hutton & Co. (see
Appendix 14 for address))

Chain scythe

or

'V'-shaped cutter

End chain

one section
910mm long

Sections pivot at rings

Spring steel,
serrated on both
edges

Direction of pull

Folding points for
storage

Toggle

Support strut

Cutting edge outside

scythe may be operated by two people, one on each side of the area being
scythed, and each taking turns to pull the scythe while the other pays out rope.
The 'V'-shaped cutter is pulled through the water, cutting a swathe as it goes.

Submerged, rooted vegetation The main reasons for controlling submerged,
rooted species will be to maintain areas of open water and to restrict the spread
of vigorous species such as *Elodea canadensis* (Canadian pondweed). Other, less
vigorous species which may not need as much control include *Myriophyllum*

spp. (water milfoils), *Hippurus vulgaris* (mare's tail) and the various *Potamogeton* spp. (pondweeds).

Uprooting plants by hoeing is the most effective control method, so long as care is taken to collect fragments of broken rhizomes. Hoeing also stirs up bottom mud, so avoid causing too much disturbance in shallow, warm water. Canadian pondweed may be best raked out using muck rakes in early spring. Another control method is to lay *clean* black polythene over the plants and weight it down with stones. The polythene is left for about a month with non-rhizomatous species and for a full growing season with rhizomatous species. The shading from the polythene kills the vegetation and once the sheeting is removed, the area should stay relatively clear of vegetation for at least a year.

One distinct feature of the polythene sheeting method is that it does not involve the removal of plant material and so the dying plants decay and release nutrients back into the aquatic system. All the other methods described so far do involve removal of vegetation and so may be used as methods of *controlling nutrient levels* in the system. Water plants are effectively a 'nutrient sink'. In a healthy waterway the levels of nutrients entering the system should be compatible with the levels taken up by the various plant and animal communities present. During the process of natural succession, the nutrient content of the system gradually increases as plants begin to fill the water body. By carefully planning a control programme of removal to manipulate the structure of the vegetation, you can also manipulate the nutrient levels in the system, and help to arrest the succession process.

Free-floating vegetation   Of the species of free-floating aquatic plants in Great Britain, two groups have particular significance: *Lemna* spp. (duckweeds) and algae. If your waterway body is smothered in either, vegetation clearance may not be a satisfactory solution to the problem. Both groups indicate high nutrient levels in the water and it is more likely that you will need to locate the source of these excess nutrients and stop it. Although vegetation removal does remove nutrients from the system it may be a waste of time if excess nutrients are continually entering to replace those removed. If the floating mat is a result of a temporary influx of nutrients, then clearing may solve the problem. Other free-floating species include *Ceratophyllum* spp. (hornworts), *Utricularia* spp. (bladderworts), *Stratiotes aloides* (water soldier) and *Hydrocharis morsus-ranae* (frog-bit). These may need clearing from time to time where they are spreading too widely across the water and shading out plants below.

Raking and dragging can clear most floating species. Rakes may be used for scooping out filamentous algae, while floating booms are more suitable to drag out mats of *Lemna* spp. which would tend to pass between the tines of the rakes. Late summer or autumn tend to be the best times for clearance.

General points to remember   Whenever you remove aquatic vegetation leave it on a bank at the water's edge for a while to allow any aquatic animals that can to escape back into the water.

— Consider the effects of management properly beforehand, such as the removal of shading species causing sudden increase in growth from the species they were shading.
— Where clearance operations are extreme, for example when one particular species has had to be removed because it was smothering a pond, recovery of the aquatic vegetation may be poor. The seeds of the smothered species may have decayed. The clearing operations may have been too efficient (desirable species may have also been accidentally cleared) and there may

not be another local source of seed close enough for species to colonise naturally. In this situation the re-introduction of species may be considered. Introductions of species should only be considered if they are known to have occurred naturally in the water body or in the immediate area in the recent past. (See section 6.3.6 for further details on introductions.) Never introduce alien species, such as: *Azolla filiculoides* (water fern), *Elodea canadensis* (Canadian pondweed) or *Acorus calamus* (sweet flag).

— The use of aquatic herbicides in the management of aquatic and bankside vegetation is not recommended. There may be situations where it may seem necessary, where alternative methods are too expensive, for example. The ecological effects of herbicides on aquatic systems, however, are still poorly understood and are even more poorly documented at present. Brooks (1976, rev. 1981) summarises the risks involved in their use and Newbold (1975) reviews knowledge of their effects on aquatic systems (see also Appendix 12 for further recommendations concerning herbicides).

Aquatic animals

So long as you manage a pond to produce a stable mosaic of vegetation types, you need not worry too much about the animal communities. Many of the more mobile species, such as flying insects, will find their own way into the water, and other less mobile species may be easily introduced. The following list is an example of a typical animal community which can exist in a small, healthy, urban pond. The example comes from the William Curtis Ecological Park (London SE1) — a shallow, artificially constructed pond, 20 × 20m in area, with a maximum depth of 1m. Apart from the species deliberately introduced, or accidentally introduced with imported plants and mud, many species have located and colonised the pond of their own accord (source: Ecological Parks Trust, 1985).

William Curtis Ecological Park, London, SE1
Records of Pond Animals 1977-1985
(Report by Fif Robertson)

The pond was filled with water in mid-April 1977. The first plants (with associated invertebrates) were introduced May 1977. Records start 1 July 1977.

CNIDARIA
Hydra viridissima — On water lily pad 1982

FLATWORMS
Dendrocoelum lacteum — Single specimen 31/10/77. Single specimens Oct. 84 and Jan. 85.
Dugesia lugubris — *Dugesia* sp. were commonest flatworms in pond 1979-80. *D. lugubris* most commonly found species 1984.
Unidentified flatworms (probably *D. lacteum*) were regularly attracted to bait for use by schoolgroups 1980-4.

MOLLUSCS
Lymnaea peregra (wandering snail) — Known to be brought in on plants by 31/7/77. Present in small numbers 1980. Population estimated at 3,500 in Oct. 1981.
Lymnaea stagnalis (great pond snail) — 'Large amount' adults and eggs introduced Aug. 1977. Rather scarce until 1978 when population exploded due to feeding on mat of *Cladophora*. Population estimated at 500 in Oct. 1979 after

the death of at least 250, suggesting around 1,000 eating *Cladophora*. Estimated population 1,500-2,000 July 1980 and 4,500 on 6-8 Oct. 1981.

Planorbis planorbis (common ramshorn) — '3 or 4' introduced Aug. 1977, another 12 on 16/12/77. Appeared to have died out by 1978, but occasionally found by school parties 1979. Population estimates at 2,000 by 6-8 Oct. 1981.

Planorbarius corneus (great ramshorn) — First recorded 1981. No further records until Oct. 84 when several found in SE corner of pond. Several more found in SW corner in Jan. 1985, but total population probably not in excess of 100.

Potamopyrgus jenkinsi (Jenkins' spire shell) — 'a few individuals' recorded 1981, none since.

Pisidium sp. (pea mussel) — 'about nine' introduced Aug. 1977. Occasionally found in 1979, and fairly regularly since.

Acroloxus lacustris (lake limpet) — First recorded in small numbers Dec. 1984.

LEECHES

Herpobdella octoculata — Majority of leeches this species 1979 and 1984. May have colonised naturally from the Thames, where it is the commonest species.

Helobdella stagnalis — Present in pond since 1977. A few specimens 1979. Single specimen Dec. 1984.

Theromyzon tessulatum — Single specimen Oct. 1979. Associated with water-birds.

CRUSTACEANS

Asellus aquaticus (water louse) — 'A few' introduced Aug. 1977. Multiplied 1978, 'frequent' 1979. Locally abundant (particularly in decaying vegetation along S shore) 1984 and Jan. 1985.

Gammarus cf pulex (fresh water shrimp) — 'A much larger number' (than *Asellus*), 12-20, introduced Aug. 1977, another 'two dozen' Sept. 1977. Barely survived 1978, more frequent 1979. Later present in small numbers but not very successful.

Daphnia sp. (spp.) (water flea) — Flourishing populations by 1977. Continued flourishing but not identified to species.

Other small crustaceans (*Cladocerans, Ostracods,* possibly *Copepods*) found in the pond but none have been identified to species.

INSECTS

Odonata (dragonflies and damselflies)

Aeshna cyanea (southern hawker dragonfly) — Laying eggs in pond 1979. None since.

Aeshna grandis (brown hawker dragonfly) — Laying eggs in pond 1979. None since.

Aeshna mixta (migrant hawker dragonfly) — Recorded 1980, '81, '83.

Anax imperator (emperor dragonfly) — Seen 1978 (brief visit) 1980, '83, '84.

Sympetrum sanguineum (ruddy darter dragonfly) — One throughout Sept. 1977. None since.

Sympetrum scoticum (black darter dragonfly) — Recorded 1981.

Sympetrum striolatum (common darter dragonfly) — Breeding since 1978, when several male territories, and at least seven females seen laying eggs.

Orthetrum cancellatum (black-tailed skimmer) — Non-breeder 1979. None since.

Coenagrion puella (azure damselfly) — poss. 1978, recorded 1980.

Enallagma cyathigerum (common blue damselfly) — Recorded 1979-81.

Ischnura elegans (blue-tailed damselfly) — Breeding 1978-84.

Hemiptera (bugs)

Unidentified *Corixids* had invaded the pond as early as 11 June 1977, and large populations were evident throughout the pond by July 1977.

Corixa punctata (water boatman) — 1980, common 1984.

Sigara dorsalis (water boatman) — 1980-4. Commonest of *Sigara* spp. in 1984.

Sigara distincta (water boatman) — Several specimens 1984.

Sigara falleni (water boatman) — Two specimens 1984.

Hesperocorixa linnei (water boatman) — Single specimen 1984.

Notonecta glauca (backswimmer) — *Notonecta* sp. present by Aug. 1977. A 'few' introduced 28/9/77. Dominant predator 1978. First identification to species in 1984, but probably common throughout the period 1977-84.

Gerris lacustris (pond skater) — *Gerris* sp. 'occasional' July 1977, vanished in Aug. then reappeared same month. Apparently common ever since. First identification to species 1984.

Ilyocoris cimicoides — 1980, occasional 1984.

Trichoptera (caddisflies)

Limnephilus affinis — Larva in pond 1980. One or two larvae seen since, but not identified and details not recorded.

Diptera (true flies)

Eristalis tenax (rat-tailed maggot) — Larva in pond 1980. Found infrequently each year since..

Other *Dipteran* larvae have been found in the pond but not identified, e.g. *Chironomid* larvae from July 1977, *Tipula* spp. (larvae and exoskeletons) in 1978 and 1979.

Ephemeroptera (mayflies)

Mayfly larvae common in pond from July 1977. Thought to be *Cloeon dipterum* but identification not confirmed.

Coleoptera (beetles)

Agonum marginatum (ground beetle) — 1980.

Bembidion genei (ground beetle) 1980.

Colymbytes fuscus (diving beetle) — Introduced 1980. Recorded 1981-2.

Dytiscus cf marginatus (great diving beetle) — Top predator in pond July 1977. Gone 1978.

Haliplus lineaticollis (crawling water beetle) — 1980.

Hygrobia hermanni (screech beetle) — Larva and adult 1978.

Hygrotus inaequalis (water beetle) — 1980.

Noterus capricornis (water beetle) — 1980.

Noterus clavicornis (water beetle) — 1980.

Platambus maculatus (water beetle) — July 1977.

SPIDERS AND MITES

Pirata cf piraticus (pirate spider) — Quite common on surface of pond amongst emergents 1984.

Water mites are also common in the summer but have not been identified.

FISHES

Gasterosteus aculeatus (three-spined stickleback) — Single pair introduced on 28 Sept. 1977. Large shoals throughout the pond by autumn 1978 but absent from 1979, having been replaced by the ten-spined stickleback.

Pungitius pungitius (ten-spined stickleback) — Introduced some time during

1978, but details of introduction unknown. 'Abundant' in 1979 and 1980 when considered to be the top predator ('shoals of fifty or more cruising about in the shallows'). Continued abundant.

AMPHIBIANS

Triturus vulgaris (smooth newt) — 3 introduced to pond 16/7/77. Unknown number of adults introduced 1980 and June 1981. Failed to become properly established up to this time, probably due to stickleback predation. No discernible breeding 1980-2. Males in breeding condition found in the pond April-June 1983, together with a female in June 1983. Sighted regularly and apparently well-established 1984.

Triturus helveticus (palmate newt) — Introduced 1980 and June 1981. Fate unknown.

Bufo bufo (common toad) — tadpoles introduced March 1978. Half-grown toads found in/near pond at various dates Dec. 1978 to March 1980. A number of adults seen in the pond in 1980, and one chain of toadspawn seen. Later well-established breeders in the deep water at the S end of the pond, with about 50 adults counted in the springs of 1981 and 1982.

Rana temporaria (common frog) — Tadpoles introduced March 1978 but poor success due to dry weather and disturbance by children. Adult frogs and spawn successfully introduced in March 1979. A number of half-grown frogs found through the winter of 1979-80. More spawn introduced in 1980 but some frogs already breeding. More than 70 breeding adults counted in the pond, spring 1982. High survival rate of tadpoles, so park crawling with froglets (e.g. 200 removed from the adjacent lorry park after a heavy rainstorm). 624 supplied to other sites in London during Sept. and Oct. 1982. Breeding in pond from 26 Feb. 1983. 1,282 supplied to other sites in London during March and April 1983, as well as 50 litres of spawn. Apparently no counts of breeding adults in 1984, but still abundant in the park.

BIRDS

Gallinula chloropus (moorhen) — 1977 (no details). Juvenile in Oct. 1979 later caught by cat. Bred amongst *Typha* in 1980 when two out of six chicks survived up to September. Only one live chick seen 1981, dead on 8 August. One of three chicks survived till August in 1982. Two chicks survived in 1983, and the last survivor of the 1984 brood was killed by a cat in September.

Anas platyrhynchos (mallard) — Breeding in park since 1978 or 1979. Generally breed in area of rubble pile, bring young onto pond for two or three days while cats catch most of them, then lead survivors off to the river.

No other birds have bred on the pond. *Other species recorded on and around the pond* since 1977 include: pied and grey wagtails feeding along the water's edge and on the water lily pads; black-headed gulls feeding on sticklebacks in the winters of 1979 and 1980; common sandpiper (1977 and 1978); heron (footprints only 1978 and 1979); tufted duck (1979) and carrion crows seen catching great pond snails from the gravel bank in May 1980 and taking billfuls of matting for their nest in 1982. House sparrows, starlings and blackbirds regularly use the pond for bathing.

The species listed survived in this small pond even though, in a typical year at the Park, over 2,000 schoolchildren used it for pond-dipping and field study.

If you wish to provide nesting habitats for waterbirds, you need to provide at least 90 m of buffer zone between them and sources of disturbance. Some species, such as coot, and the mallard and moorhen mentioned above, are more tolerant of disturbance and more adaptable than most in their choices of nest sites.

Feeding ponds for waterbirds may be as small as 15 × 6 m. Resting ponds should be at least 0.8 ha in area, otherwise roosting birds may be at risk from predation or disturbance. An island, or moored raft, in the middle of a small pond provides protection to water birds. If bare, or covered by short vegetation, waterfowl may use them for resting (many species seem to need to be able to see the water when ashore in order to feel 'secure').

A certain amount of dense cover at the water's edge is also useful, particularly during moulting (beginning in June) when flightless birds need to hide from predators when they come out of the water. Brooks (1976, rev. 1981) and The Game Conservancy (1969) provides further information on the provision of waterway features for wildfowl and other waterbirds.

7.5.4 Safety

Working in water and mud can be dangerous, so safety precautions are extremely important. The risks of drowning should always be borne in mind. Mud can be extremely slippery, so sharp tools should be used with care, or not at all, where volunteers do not have a sure footing or where tool handles are liable to become wet and slippery. Power tools such as chain saws or scrub cutters should not be used where water can damage the machinery or where oil may pollute the water.

The work area must be checked for safety before volunteers enter. Probe bottom mud with a pole and mark any areas with sudden increases in depth. Brightly coloured ranging poles or flags are most suitable for this. Corrugated iron sheets may be used on soft mud for support. Never work on ice over deep water (over 1 m deep). Never work alone in deep water if you are wearing waders. If you stumble and your waders accidentally fill with water, they will be almost impossible to remove without help.

Do not work from a boat unless you are a competent swimmer.

Ensure that volunteers wear satisfactory clothing and, particularly in cold weather, that they have a warm, dry change of clothes with them. Examples of suitable clothing are as follows. When clearing rubbish: thick-soled footwear, old trousers. Avoid handling sharp objects, rather use tools to pull them out with. Never work in bare feet. In cold weather: wetsuit and rubber gloves for insulation. Watch out for symptoms of exposure (cramp or uncontrollable shivering). Generally: wellington boots, waders and rubber gloves (fabric or leather are too slippery when wet). In warm weather: avoid baggy clothing as this is a severe hindrance should you fall in. Simply wear enough clothing to protect your skin from abrasions.

First aid (Brooks 1976, rev. 1981)

A first aid kit is essential and should include at least the following:

Scissors	Cotton wool
Tweezers	25 mm cotton bandage
Packet of needles	100 mm crepe bandage
Matches	Triangular bandage
Large size compressed wound dressings	Eye lotion and eye bath

Box of porous plasters, medium size
Gauze dressings

Antiseptic wipes or mild antiseptic
cream

St John's Ambulance Handbook, or similar book of first aid.

If working regularly in freshwater, volunteers require a valid anti-tetanus vaccination (received within the previous three years), and any cut or wound should be cleaned and treated with antiseptic as quickly as possible. Carcasses of drowned animals should be handled only when absolutely necessary and then with extreme care.

7.5.5 Management of human impact

Bankside vegetation can be severely affected by trampling, so recreational activities such as walking, picnicking, bird-watching, angling, pond-dipping, paddling and swimming can be a real problem around water bodies heavily used by the general public.

Anglers often dig out sloping banks and clear aquatic vegetation to create 'swims' for fishing. Marginal vegetation tends to be most severely trampled where people walk alongside the water, and where people seek access to the water. These access points soon suffer bank erosion where the vegetation cover has broken down. It is likely that animals in the bankside vegetation (particularly mammals and birds) will begin to decline in numbers at much lower intensities of public use than those necessary to cause declines in the numbers of plants.

These problems will always be difficult to resolve, particularly around urban water bodies. However, it is always beneficial to both wildlife and the general public to protect portions of the water's edge from intrusions and disturbance, either as permanent sanctuary areas, or on an annual rotational basis.

The public's enjoyment will not be affected if they can only walk around two-thirds or three-quarters of a water body. The extra wildlife which will be able to survive in the sanctuary portion will greatly enhance the value of the remainder of water body as a recreational resource.

7.6 References

Management plans

Stedman, N. (1979) 'An appraisal of the U.C.L. Management Plan Format for use by a County Trust', University College London, Discussion Papers in Conservation 21

Wood, J.B. and Warren A. (1978) 'A handbook for the preparation of management plans: Conservation Course format, revision 2', University College London, Discussion Papers in Conservation 18

Grassland management

Baines C. and Smart J.(1984) *A Guide to Habitat Creation*, Ecology Handbook No. 2, Greater London Council

Lowday, J.E. and Wells, T.C.E. (1977) *The Management of Grassland and Heathland in Country Parks*, Countryside Commission, CCP 105

Ratcliffe, D. (1977) *A Nature Conservation Review*, Cambridge University Press

Williams, O.B., Wells, T.C.E. and Wells, D.A. (1974) 'Grazing management of Woodwalton Fen; seasonal changes in the diet of cattle and rabbits', *Journal of Applied Ecology*, **11**:499-516

Woodland/scrub management

British Trust for Conservation Volunteers, Training leaflets: 'Coppicing' (1980), 'Tree felling' (1980)

Brooks, A. (1980) *Woodlands: A practical conservation handbook*, British Trust for Conservation Volunteers

Countryside Commission for Scotland (1982) *Plants and Planting Methods for the Countryside*, vol. 1

Edlin, H.L. (1970). *Trees, Woods and Man*, Collins

—— (1973) *Woodland Crafts of Britain*, David & Charles

—— (1978) *The Tree Key*, Warne

Follis, A. (1980) *Hand Tools*, British Trust for Conservation Volunteers

Godwin, H. (1975) *The History of the British Flora* (2nd edn), Cambridge University Press

Hoskins, W.G. (1955) *The Making of the English Landscape*, Hodder & Stoughton

Kennedy, C.E.J. and Southwood, T.R.E. (1984) 'The number of species of insect associated with British trees — a re-analysis', *Journal of Animal Ecology*, **53**:455-78

Kirby, K.J. (1984) 'Forestry operations and broadleaf woodland conservation', Nature Conservancy Council Focus on Nature Conservation No. 8

Lambert, F. (1957) *Tools and Devices for Coppice Crafts*. Young Farmers' Club Booklet 31, republished 1977 by the Centre for Alternative Technology

Langford, J.L. (ed.) (1982) *Woodlands for Wildlife and Timber*, Hereford and Radnor Naturalists' Trust

Mitchell, A. (1978) *A Field Guide to the Trees of Britain and Northern Europe* (2nd edn), Collins

Mummery, C., Tabor, R. and Homewood, N. (1978) *A Guide to the Techniques of Coppice Management*, Essex Naturalists' Trust

Peterken, G.F. (1969) 'An event record for nature reserves', *Quarterly Journal, Devon Trust for Nature Conservation*, **21**:920-8

—— (1972) 'Conservation coppicing and the coppice crafts', *Quarterly Journal, Devon Trust for Nature Conservation*, 4:157-64

—— (1981) *Woodland Conservation and Management*, Chapman & Hall

Rackham, O. (1976) *Trees and Woodlands in the British Landscape*, Dent, London

—— (1980) *Ancient Woodland*, Arnold

Ranson, C. (1978) 'Comments on "A Guide to the Techniques of Coppice Management"', Nature Conservancy Council, duplicated

—— (1979a) 'Coppicing and its produce', Nature Conservancy Council, duplicated

—— (1979b) 'Planting coppice for firewood', Nature Conservancy Council, duplicated

—— (1979c) 'An owner's contract for a wood-merchant to cut underwood in a wood', Nature Conservancy Council, duplicated

—— (1984) *Pollard Trees and Their Conservation*, Nature Conservancy Council

Ruff, A. (1979) *Holland and the Ecological Landscape*, Deanwater Press

Smart, N. and Andrews, J. (1985) *Birds and Broadleaves Handbook: A guide to further the conservation of birds in broadleaved woodland*, Royal Society for the Protection of Birds

Southwood, T.R.E. (1961) 'The number of insect species associated with various trees', *Journal of Animal Ecology*, **30**:1-8

Stubbs, A.E. (1972) 'Wildlife conservation and dead wood', Devon Trust for Nature Conservation, supplement to *Journal*

Scrub management

Duffey, E., Morris, M.G., Sheail, J., Ward, L.K., Wells, D.A. and Wells, T.C.E. (1974) *Grassland Ecology and Wildlife Management*, Chapman & Hall, London

Ward, L.K. (1979) 'Scrub dynamics and management', *Ecology and Design in Amenity Land Management*, Conference Proceedings, Wye College, Kent, pp. 109-27

Hedgerow management

Agate, 1984 (rev. of Brooks, A. 1980), *Hedging: A practical conservation handbook*, (rev. 1975 edn), British Trust for Conservation Volunteers

British Trust for Conservation Volunteers (1980) 'Hedging', training leaflet

Farming and Wildlife Advisory Group (undated) 'A hedgerow code of practice', information leaflet

Ministry of Agriculture, Fisheries and Food (1982) 'Managing farm hedges', advisory leaflet 762

Pollard, E., Hooper, M.D., and Moore, N.W. (1974) *Hedges*, Collins New Naturalist

Freshwater

Anon. (1969) *Wildfowl Management on Inland Waters*, Booklet No. 3, The Game Conservancy

British Trust for Conservation Volunteers (BTCV) (1980) training leaflets: 'Ponds', 'Why dig ponds?'

Brooks, A. (1976, rev. 1981) *Waterways and Wetlands: A practical conservation handbook*, BTCV

Ecological Parks Trust (EPT) (1985) 'WCEP — Records of pond animals 1977-1985', information leaflet compiled by Fif Robinson

Lewis, G. and Williams, G. (1984) *Rivers and Wildlife Handbook: a Guide to Practices which Further the Conservation of Wildlife on Rivers*, Royal Society for the Protection of Birds (RSPB)/Royal Society for Nature Conservation

Liddle, M.J. and Scorgie, H.R.A. (1980) 'The effects of recreation on freshwater plants and animals: a review', *Biological Conservation*, 17:183-206

Mellanby, K. (1970) *Pesticides and Pollution* (2nd imp.), Collins (Fontana New Naturalist)

Mitchell, D.S. (ed.) (1974) *Aquatic Vegetation and its Use and Control*, UNESCO, Paris

Newbold, C. (1975) 'Herbicides in aquatic systems', *Biological Conservation*, 7:97-118

Newbold, C. and Stubbs, A. (1981) 'Wildlife clear-out', *Natural World*, vol. 3 (Winter), Royal Society for Nature Conservation

Pentecost, A. (1982) 'Conservation of freshwaters and their algae',*Ecos*, 3(2):8-11

7.7 Useful organisations (See Appendix 15 for addresses)

British Trust for Conservation Volunteers
Forestry Commission
Freshwater Biological Association
Ministry of Agriculture, Fisheries and Food
National Federation of City Farms
Nature Conservancy Council

8 Interpretation
(co-author, Don Aldridge)

When you have spent a lot of time and effort creating and carefully managing an urban site for wildlife, it can be very disheartening whenever casual visitors to the site are evidently not interested in, do not understand, or even run down what you are doing. Only too often, this happens because of a lack of essential site interpretation.

Site interpretation is *not* just the provision of factual information about the site. Site interpretation may be defined simply as *the art of explaining the significance of a site to those who visit it.*

8.1 Why interpret?

Both on and off the site, the main aim of interpretation is to provoke a desire in people to conserve the site.

You cannot expect members of the public automatically to understand what you are doing with your site. For example, some city dwellers, used to formal parks and gardens, may not readily accept the appearance of nature-like habitats and may consider them 'untidy', particularly after the vegetation dies back in autumn. Some country dwellers visiting the city and finding your site, may accept the wildness and seasonal changes in appearance of the vegetation, but they may consider the site rather feeble and uninteresting compared to the countryside where they live. The country dwellers in this example have failed to understand the extra value of the site arising from its situation — in the city, where such wildlife areas may be a scarce resource.

There is much that you need to explain to casual visitors, to increase their understanding and enjoyment of what your site has to offer.

Get your message over quickly and clearly. Casual visitors appear without warning and may spend less than an hour on the site.

Visitors need to feel welcome and comfortable if you are to gain their full attention. Your message needs to be in the form of an interesting, easily understood and remembered story.

The visitor should be able to identify in some way with the characters of the story. The story should trace the relationships between past and present features of the site and the effects of man (and so, in some way, should fall within the visitor's personal experience). Using this approach, the site interpretation should give a conservation message relevant to the site today.

This need for a clear, short message sets interpretation apart from environmental or conservation education, where students may be prepared in advance, may visit the site by arrangement in organised parties and may carry out follow-up work after their visit. In such a situation, there is more time, for example, for detailed explanations of the site's ecological, social and historical value.

The International Union for Conservation of Nature and Natural Resources (IUCN) defines environmental education as the '*process of recognising values and clarifying concepts in order to develop the skills and attitudes necessary to understand and appreciate the interrelationships amongst man, his culture and his biophysical surroundings*'. Carter (1979) provides a useful, detailed summary of environmental education in an urban setting.

8.2 What do you interpret?

Natural history

Explain the past and present character and value of the site through the interrelationships between its rocks, soils, plants, animals and the people who use(d) it. Try to explain simply the principles of the site's ecology and the value of natural habitats.

History

Explain the site's past in relation to the city environment and social conditions.

Environment

(Environmental features not covered by natural history or history) Explain the present relationships between the site, the local area and local community, etc. Increase the experience of visitors in sensory perception of the environment.

Interpreting these is extremely effective in provoking visitors with little or no interest in natural history to identify with the message and so develop a feeling for the need to conserve the site.

8.3 Who do you interpret to?

Casual visitors will include individuals and groups of all ages and abilities. Special interest groups of known (narrow) age range are probably the easiest to cater for, as you know what they are interested in and have some idea of the level at which to aim the interpretive message. It can be more difficult to reach all the individuals in a group of mixed ages. However, in one case, the family group, the diversity of experience and interests within the group can be a bonus. Face-to-face discussion with a friendly interpreter is an excellent way of getting your message over because individuals can express personal views, ask questions and generally interact, mutually reinforcing their understanding of what you are trying to explain to them. In this and all other interpretive situations, the interpreter needs to know the site well and the quality of information has to be high. Get the facts straight and avoid misleading people just for the sake of answering a question. This is especially important with children.

Don't just simplify the adults' interpretive information for children. Interpreting a site for children requires a fundamentally different approach to that for adults. The following are a few examples to illustrate this point: during the earliest school years, children learn the names of things very quickly. They are usually fascinated by the superlative (the 'biggest', 'longest', 'smallest', 'strongest', etc.). Children commonly are more receptive and have a greater appetite for pure information than adults. Children also tend to be less inhibited than adults and love to discover things through personal examination.

8.4 What sort of message are you conveying?

Consider the site in relation to the city environment as a whole and explain how the site relates to other similar features in the area (if any exist). In doing so, you may pose the questions — how different is the city environment from the countryside and does the site help city dwellers to understand how the two environments relate to each other? Many people take it for granted that the countryside is much richer in wildlife, especially rare species, and will be surprised to find that a good urban site can be as rich, or richer than most ordinary country sites of similar area.

Make it clear why you have put effort into developing the site (e.g. to conserve wildlife in the city, so that people can enjoy intimate contact with it) and explain why you are doing specific things on the site (e.g. not mowing areas of meadow grassland, to encourage wildflowers, insects and birds, etc. or asking visitors not to intrude into sensitive areas so that they help to protect what it is they have come to see).

Explain your goals and objectives for the future and how you are trying to benefit the local people and other site users.

8.5 What interpretive devices should you use?

It is hard to improve on the personal touch in site interpretation. A friendly warden or volunteer, who knows the site well, can chat to visitors, make them feel welcome and answer most individuals' questions. Other interpretive media serve as aids to the interpreter's task, both on the site and elsewhere (e.g. for illustrated talks, interpretive exhibitions and displays, etc.) The following is a list of the main types of media used in interpretation:

(a) Two-dimensional media
> Text, photographs and graphics:
>> in publications;
>> on signs, murals or panels;
>> on wall charts or posters;
>> on nature trail signs or leaflets, etc.

> Projected photographs
> Special effects e.g.:
>> with mirrors and lenses, special lighting, holograms*, stereo*, 3-D viewers, etc. (possibly push-button controlled)

(b) Sound effects
> Repeating messages with displays*
> Listening posts*
> Tapes for use in portable sound guides, etc.*

(c) Three-dimensional media
> Artefacts:
>> rocks, soil samples, pressed and dried plants, animal bones, pellets, droppings, etc. Historical/archaeological materials.

---

*Some of these devices will be too costly and complex for all but the most sophisticated urban parks.

Models and replicas:
Plaster casts, still or mechanical scale models.
Live exhibits:
Your site is a live exhibit in itself, but a small indoor aquarium or vivarium
can be an excellent way for visitors to see animals and plants more clearly.
With such exhibits comes the responsibility for the proper care for the well-being of any animals exhibited.
Viewing devices:
Devices which focus attention on areas of the site, e.g. viewing windows, look-out points, etc.

8.6 Interpretive planning

The previous sections asked the questions 'why interpret, interpret what, to whom, what sort of message and what interpretive devices may be used?' Interpretive planning is a method of answering all these questions in advance, so that you can provide interpretive material properly suited to your site and the people who visit it.

The interpretive plan is similar in structure to the management plan described in section 7.2. If you prepare a written interpretive plan, it is worthwhile incorporating it as a section in the management plan. The following is a simple summary of the steps involved in developing a plan.

The plan may be split into four basic stages: first, to survey the local area and collect relevant information; second, to analyse survey results and prepare an appropriate message; third, to devise a means of putting over a message which is appropriate to the site, the area and potential visitors; and fourth, to implement the plan and manage the interpretive material.

8.6.1 Surveys

People

How do local residents and local authorities perceive the site?

— How many people visit the site? Too few to merit expensive interpretive facilities, or so many that their movements need controlling to relieve pressures on site vegetation, etc.?
— Are the numbers of visitors likely to change in the future? How might interpretive facilities affect this, or how might they need to be changed as visitor numbers change?
— What proportions of the visitor numbers fall into different age groups or ability groups (e.g. non-English speaking)?
— What schools, teachers' colleges, universities, etc. are there in the area? How might they wish to use the site?
— What local specialist societies are there? How might they wish to use the site?

Answering such questions allows you to judge the size of audience you can expect and the types of interest you will need to serve.

The local area and its history

— As your message will be one of positive conservation of the site, you need to celebrate the locality. How does the site relate to its surroundings and local history?

Local facilities

— What other interpretive facilities already exist in the area? How will these affect your planned facility? Can they supplement or replace it?
— What are the local communications media (local newspapers, radio stations, etc.)?
— Can they help in interpreting the site? Will they be keen to carry stories about it?

Site facilities

— What site features are of special interest to user groups?
— Is access to any of these features limited? Does it need to be improved for users, or do you need to explain to users why access should continue to be limited (e.g. to protect sensitive areas of the site)?
— Are there any limitations on access or public safety and should these be improved?
— What services are present (e.g. buildings, electricity, water, toilets, special facilities for children, senior citizens, the handicapped, etc.)?

8.6.2 Survey analysis and formulation of objectives

Taking into account the survey findings, decide what site features to interpret, what message(s) to convey and identify any constraints there may be on what you want to do. The survey will most probably have shown gaps in information on the site and the local area which will need filling if the site is to be interpreted properly.

— Look out for features of the site's history and natural history which are exciting, popular, or in some way are linked with human history in the area.
— What are the constraints imposed by the following?:

  — site management objectives;
  — site size*, access, terrain and visitor safety;
  — legal considerations such as leases or agreements;
  — financial/material resources and manpower.

[*site size is important when you consider the numbers of visitors. A commonly used term for the maximum number of visitors a site can support without suffering undue damage is its 'carrying capacity'. Speight (1973) summarises the ecological effects of visitor pressures. Examples of figures for carrying capacities include 50 people per mile of nature trail per day (Tivy 1972) and 40 people per ha per day in a country park, 'independent of the type of vegetation in the area' (Zetter 1973)].

You should now be able to draw up suitable themes for the messages you wish to convey.

8.6.3 Choosing appropriate media

Examples of media have already been outlined in this section.

— Assess the costs of different media. Apart from manufacturers other local groups and interpretive centres may be able to give some advice. Can grants be obtained for providing leaflets, etc.?
— Are there supplies of electricity, indoor space, etc. available?
— Consider carefully the siting of interpretive displays, so that they attract people to the right features and do not cause damage or disturbance to sensitive areas of the site.
— Take into account the risks of vandalism.
— Consider the reliability of any display equipment, its ease of maintenance and use.
— How much supervision is required?
— How easily can the interpretive facility be changed (or terminated) should site conditions alter unexpectedly?
— Take into account likely audience sizes.
— Can the media be adapted for special groups?

Choose the right media for the messages you wish to convey, whether the facility is indoors or outdoors, and don't mix media to the point where the audience is confused or distracted. Presentations need to be of as high a standard as possible, for example, attractive, with easy-to-read text, etc. Messages should be conveyed at a level and pace appropriate to the interest and knowledge of the target audience (e.g. general public, family groups, young people, specialist groups, etc.). Try to anticipate and have the answers to visitors' questions. This is obviously easier with an interpreter present than with a static display or leaflet. Wherever possible, give the visitor the opportunity to participate, particularly in the case of children. For example, they should be able to ask questions, investigate for themselves, operate equipment, make models, touch, taste, smell, listen, etc. as well as just observing passively.

Pennyfather (1975) is a useful source of further information on different media and interpretive facilities.

8.6.4 Implementation and management

When you finally put the plan into action, compile your interpretive materials and construct the interpretive facility, try to evaluate how successfully you have achieved your overall objectives. The following are examples of some of the most important technical objectives:

(a) gaining visitor interest;
(b) explaining the importance of a site;
(c) helping visitors to 'imagine accurately';
(d) identifying features of interest;
(e) provoking a response of relevance to site conservation;
(f) protecting the visitor and the area.

To check whether the interpretive facilities fulfil your objectives, there are a whole series of possible techniques for continued evaluation, for example:

(a) Direct comments from visitors.
(b) Suggestion boxes.

(c) Careful observation of the behaviour of visitors (the amount of time spent looking at particular sections of a display, listening to commentaries, or the popularity of particular leaflets, etc.). These may be carried out by specialists using quantitative methods of behavioural analysis or sophisticated time-lapse photography techniques. However, an observant volunteer should be able to pick up any serious defects by the resulting uninterested behaviour of visitors.

(d) Visitor questionnaires, preferably with yes/no answers, or with boxes to tick. Be careful not to put off visitors by imposing long and complicated questionnaires on them. Rather, give people the opportunity to fill in questionnaires if they wish to.

Aldridge (1975) gives a comprehensive summary of the sorts of questions you may ask yourselves to evaluate interpretive provisions.

From time to time, displays and leaflets, etc. will need revising and general wear and tear on static provisions will call for repairs. Draw up a time-table for such work in advance. Exhibition panels are commonly taken down for repair every six months or every year. The lifetime of an exhibition will depend upon its information content and may extend from as short a period as one year to as long as ten. Partial up-dating and revision of information may take place annually, with complete revisions every 3-5 years.

8.7 References

Aldridge, D. (1975) *Guide to Countryside Interpretation Part 1. Principles of country-side interpretation and interpretive planning*, Countryside Commission for Scotland, HMSO

Beatty, J.E. (1978) 'Interpretive planning on nature reserves', discussion papers in conservation no. 17, University College London

British Trust for Conservation Volunteers (1984) *D.I.Y. Urban Conservation. A practical guide to improve your surroundings* (information pack)

Carter, G. (1979) *Handbook on Environmental Education in a Totally Urban Setting*, Council of Europe

Conservation Foundation (1982) *The Conservation Annual*

—— (1983) *The Second Conservation Annual*

—— (1985) *The Conservation Review*

King, A. and Clifford, S. (1985) *Holding Your Ground. An action guide to local conservation*, Maurice Temple Smith, London

Pennyfather, K. (1975) *Guide to Countryside Interpretation Part 2. Interpretive media and facilities*, Countryside Commission for Scotland, HMSO

Shell Better Britain Campaign, information packs (updated annually). Produced in partnership with the British Trust for Conservation Volunteers, the Nature Conservancy Council and the Civic Trust

Speight, M.C.D. (1973) 'Outdoor recreation and its ecological effects. A bibliography and review', University College London

Stewart, A. (ed.) (1982) *The Gardening Handbook*, Beacon Publishing

Tilden, F. (1977) (rev. edn) *Interpreting Our Heritage*, University of North Carolina Press

Tivy, J. (1972) 'The concept and determination of carrying capacity of recreational land in the USA', Dept. of Geography, University of Glasgow, Countryside Commission for Scotland Occasional Paper No. 3

Yates, F.N. (1985) *Natural History Teaching Resources*, Ecological Parks Trust

Zetter, J.A. (1973) 'The planning and application of site surveys: The Sherwood

Forest study' in *The Use of Site Surveys in Countryside Recreation Planning and Management*, Countryside Commission, London

Appendix 1 Constitution of the ecological parks trust

THE COMPANIES ACTS 1948 TO 1976

COMPANY LIMITED BY GUARANTEE AND NOT HAVING A SHARE
CAPITAL

MEMORANDUM OF ASSOCIATION

of

ECOLOGICAL PARKS TRUST

1. The Name of the Company (hereinafter called "the Trust") is "The Ecological Parks Trust".

2. The Registered Office of the Trust will be situate in England.

3. The object of the Trust is to advance the education of the public in and to further knowledge of the ecology of urban areas and to develop, conserve, protect and restore the natural resources and animal and plant life of such areas.

In furtherance of and ancillary to this object but not otherwise the Trust has the following powers:—

(a) To acquire permanent or temporary interest in suitable urban land and by promoting the conservation and enhancing the natural history interest in such sites, to develop their full ecological potential.

(b) To provide field studies areas for the benefit of students of all ages and to collaborate with the appropriate voluntary institutions and statutory authorities so as to make the facilities available to as wide a section of the public as possible and in particular, to young persons.

(c) To stimulate public and private interest in care for and education concerning the role of natural fauna and flora in relation to the health, enjoyment, recreation and education of town-dwellers and others of all ages.

(d) To promote research into the ecology of urban areas and to disseminate the results thereof.

(e) To prepare courses of instruction and to encourage the teaching of the natural sciences and field studies in educational establishments.

f) To adopt such means of making known the work and aims of the Trust and to take such steps by personal or written appeals and public meetings to procure subscriptions, donations, entrance fees and other moneys and contributions to the funds of the Trust as may be deemed expedient and apply the same for the purposes of the Trust.

(g) To promote and encourage the objects of the Trust by means of lectures, meetings, broadcasts, exhibitions and publications and such other means as are deemed expedient.

(h) To act in concert, consult or make any arrangements with any local authority, local society, residents association, government agency or the like or with any residents, users or property owners with a view to promoting any of the objects aforesaid.

(i) To establish close links with and render assistance to bodies having objects similar to those of the Trust and to associate or amalgamate with any such companies, societies, associations or bodies.

(j) To make grants, loans and other facilities available to persons or bodies for purposes which in the absolute discretion of the Council are deemed to advance the objects of the Trust, and to subscribe to any local or other charities.

(k) To enter into contracts with suitable agencies in pursuit of the objects of the Trust.

(l) To purchase, lease or otherwise acquire and hold any real or personal property in Great Britain, and any rights or privileges necessary, convenient or desirable for the purposes of the objects of the Trust, and to construct, alter, and maintain any houses or buildings required for such purposes; and to sell, improve, develop, lease, let on hire, mortgage, exchange, dispose of, or otherwise deal with all or any of such property, rights or privileges.

(m) To pay all or any expenses incurred in connection with the promotion, formation and incorporation of the Trust.

(n) To take any gift of property, whether subject to any special trust or not, for any one or more objects of the Trust.

(o) To apply for and acquire and hold any charters, privileges, licences, concessions, patents or other rights, powers or orders from Parliament, the Government, or any local or other authority and to exercise any powers, rights or privileges so obtained.

(p) To make, accept, endorse and execute promissory notes, bills of exchange and other negotiable instruments.

(q) To borrow or raise and secure the payment of money on mortgage of the property of the Trust, or in such manner as the Trust shall think fit.

(r) To raise funds and to invite and receive contributions from any person or persons whatsoever by way of subscription, donation and otherwise provided that the Trust shall not undertake any permanent trading activities in raising funds for its objects.

(s) To invest all moneys not immediately required for the furthering of the objects in or upon such investments securities or property as may be thought fit, subject nevertheless to such conditions (if any) and such consent (if any) as may for the time being be imposed or required by law and subject also as hereinafter provided.

(t) To undertake and execute any trusts which may lawfully be undertaken by the Trust and may be conducive to its objects.

(u) For all or any of the objects of the Trust to employ secretaries, clerks, staff, workmen and professional assistance of all kinds, and to remunerate any person for services rendered, and establish superannuation in schemes contributory or otherwise for salaried officers and servants of the Trust.

(v) To do all such other things as shall further the attainment of the above objects or any of them PROVIDED ALWAYS and it is hereby declared that:

(i) The Trust is established for charitable purposes only in the legal meaning of the phrase and its property and income shall be held and applied for those purposes only, and that all the objects and powers of the Trust set forth in this Memorandum shall be construed as limited by the foregoing terms of this proviso which shall be treated as overriding in effect and as governing all the provisions of this Memorandum notwithstanding anything expressed or implied therein to the contrary.

(ii) In case the Trust shall take or hold any property which may be subject to any trusts, the Trust shall only deal with or invest the same in such manner as allowed by law, having regard to such trusts.

(iii) The Trust's objects shall not extend to the regulation of relations between workers and employers and organisations of workers and employers.

(iv) In case the Trust shall take or hold any property subject to the jurisdiction of the Charity Commissioners for England and Wales, the Trust shall not sell, mortgage, charge or lease the same without such authority, approval or consent as may be required by law, and as regards any such property the Council of Management or Governing Body of the Trust shall be chargeable for any such property that may come into their hands and shall be answerable and accountable for their own acts, receipts, neglects and defaults, and for the due administration of such property in the same manner and to the same extent as they would as such Council of Management or Governing Body have been if no incorporation had been effected, and the incorporation of the Trust shall not diminish or impair any control or authority exercisable by the Chancery Division, or the Charity Commissioners over such Council of Management or Governing Body, but they shall as regards any such property be subject jointly and separately to such control or authority as if the Trust were not incorporated.

4. The income and property of the Trust shall be applied solely towards the promotion of its objects as set forth in this Memorandum of Association, and no portion thereof shall be paid or transferred directly or indirectly, by way of dividend, bonus or otherwise howsoever by way of profit, to the members of the Trust (and no member of its Council of Management or Governing Body shall be appointed to any office of the Trust paid by salary or fees or receive any remuneration or other benefit in money or money's worth from the Trust). Provided that nothing herein contained shall prevent any payment, in good faith by the Trust

(a) of reasonable and proper remuneration to any member, officer or servant of the Trust (not being a Member of the Council of Management or Governing Body) for any services actually rendered to the Trust;

(b) of interest on money lent by any member of the Company (or of its Council of Management or Governing Body) at a rate per annum not exceeding 2 per cent less than the minimum lending rate prescribed for the time being by the Bank of England or 3 per cent whichever is the greater;

(c) of reasonable and proper rent for premises demised or let by any member of the Company (or of its Council of Management or Governing Body);

(d) of fees, remuneration or other benefit in money or money's worth to a company of which a member of the Council of Management or Governing Body may be a member (holding not more than 1/100th part of the capital of that company;) and

(e) to any member of its Council of Management or Governing Body of out-of-pocket expenses.

5. The liability of the members is limited.

6. Every Ordinary Member of the Trust undertakes to contribute to the assets of the Trust in the event of its being wound up while he or she is an Ordinary Member, or within one year after he or she ceases to be an Ordinary Member, for payment of the debts and liabilities of the Trust contracted before he or she ceases to be a member, and of the costs, charges, and expenses of winding up, and for the adjustment of the rights of the contributories among themselves, such amount as may be required, not exceeding One Pound.

7. If upon the winding up or dissolution (except in the case of a reconstruction or amalgamation between Trusts having similar objects) of the Trust, there remains, after the satisfaction of all its debts and liabilities, any property whatsoever, the same shall not be paid to or distributed among the members of the Trust but shall be given or transferred to the Civic Trust or to some other body or bodies having objects similar to the objects of the Trust, and which shall prohibit the distribution of its or their income and property among its or their members to such an extent at least as is imposed on the Trust under or by virtue of Clause 4 hereof, such body or bodies to be determined by the members of the Trust at or before the time of dissolution or in default thereof by a Judge of the High Court of Justice having jurisdiction with regard to charitable funds, and if and so far as effect cannot be given to the aforesaid provision, then to some charitable object.

THE COMPANIES ACTS 1948 TO 1976

COMPANY LIMITED BY GUARANTEE AND NOT HAVING A SHARE CAPITAL

ARTICLES OF ASSOCIATION OF THE ECOLOGICAL PARKS TRUST

INTERPRETATION
1. In these articles:

"The Trust" means The Ecological Parks Trust.
"The Act" means The Companies Act, 1948.

"Ordinary Member" means a member of the Trust for the purposes of the Act.
"The Council" means the Council of Management for the time being of the Trust.
"The Seal" means the common seal of the Trust.
"The Office" means the registered office of the Trust.

"Month" means Calendar month.

"In writing" means written or produced by any substitute for writing, or partly written and partly so produced.

And words importing the singular number only shall include the plural number, and vice versa.

Words importing the masculine gender only shall include the feminine gender; and words importing persons shall include corporations.

Save as aforesaid, any words or expressions defined in the Act, if not inconsistent with the subject or context, shall bear the same meanings in these presents. Reference herein to any provision of the Act shall be a reference to such provision as modified by any statute for the time being in force.

MEMBERS OF THE TRUST

2. The number of Ordinary Members with which the Trust proposes to be registered is 500, but the Council may from time to time register an increase of Ordinary Members.

3. The provisions of Section 110 of the Companies Act, 1948, shall be observed by the Trust, and every applicant for Ordinary Membership of the Trust shall sign a written consent to become an Ordinary Member.

4. The Trust is established for the purposes expressed in the Memorandum of Association.

5. (A) Unless otherwise determined by the Trust in General Meeting there shall be four classes of membership, namely Ordinary Members, Honorary Members, Visitor Members and Student Members. Only the Ordinary Members shall be members for the purposes of the Act.

   (B) The subscribers to the Memorandum of Association shall be the first Ordinary Members of the Trust.

   (C) An applicant for Ordinary Membership shall complete an application form as required by the Trust and shall sign a written consent to become an Ordinary Member. The Council may then admit him to Ordinary Membership on payment of the first annual subscription appropriate to Ordinary Membership. The Council may refuse to admit any applicant to Ordinary Membership without giving any reason.

   (D) An applicant for Visitor or Student Membership shall complete an application form as required by the Trust and on payment of the first annual subscription appropriate to his class of membership the Council may admit him to Visitor or Student Membership (as the case may be). The Council may refuse to admit any applicant to Visitor or Student Membership without giving any reason.

   (E) The Council shall have power to invite persons to become Honorary Members of the Trust and to declare from time to time the privileges to which they shall be entitled provided that the number of Honorary Members of the Trust shall be not more than 6. Honorary Members shall pay no entrance fee or subscription.

6.   The Annual Subscription payable by members shall be such as may from time to time be determined in General Meeting upon the recommendation of the Council.

7.   If the Council shall be of opinion that it is not in the interests of the Trust that any member of any class of membership shall continue to be a member, the Council may convene an Extraordinary General Meeting of the Trust and such member may by Ordinary Resolution be removed from membership, and thereupon his name shall be removed from the Register, and he shall cease to be a member, and shall forfeit his interest and privileges in the Trust.

8.   A member of the Trust shall cease to be a member:

   (a)   If he resigns by giving one month's notice in writing of resignation.
   (b)   If he is removed from membership under Article 7.
   (c)   If he shall be in default for six months in the payment of his annual subscription, provided that the Council may in its discretion reinstate him as a member on payment of all arrears of subscription. For the purposes of this Article all subscriptions shall be deemed to become due on the 1st May in each year save as regards the first subscription of the member which is payable on his admission to the Trust.

9.   Any corporation which becomes a member under Article 5 may appoint, by writing, a person to act on its behalf and may in like manner remove any person so appointed and appoint another in his place, and such person may exercise and enjoy on behalf of such corporation, all the rights and privileges incidental to its membership so long as such membership continues and his appointment is not determined.

10.   No unincorporated society or body may as such, become a member under Article 5 but if any such society or body should desire to obtain the advantages of membership it shall nominate a person to act as its representative, apply in its name for membership and sign the application as its representative and exercise the rights of membership on its behalf. Any such unincorporated society or body may, by writing, remove any person so nominated and nominate another in its place. Every person so nominated may exercise and enjoy on behalf of such unincorporated society or body, all the rights and privileges incidental to its membership so long as such membership continues and his appointment is not determined.

11.   No right or privilege of any member shall be in any way transferable, but all such rights and privileges shall cease upon the member ceasing to be such, whether by death, retirement, termination or otherwise.

GENERAL MEETINGS

12.   (A)   The Trust shall hold a General Meeting in every calendar year as its Annual General Meeting at such time and place as may be determined by the Council, and shall specify the meeting as such in the notices calling it, provided that every General Meeting except the first shall be held not more than fifteen months after the holding of the last preceding meeting, and that so long as the Trust holds its

first Annual General Meeting within eighteen months after its incorporation it need not hold it in the year of its incorporation or in the following year.

(B)   Ordinary Members shall alone be entitled to receive notices of and to vote at General Meetings. <u>Honorary</u>, <u>Visitor</u> and <u>Student</u> Members shall not be entitled to receive notices but may attend and with the leave of the Chairman may speak but not vote at General Meetings.

13.   All General Meetings, other than Annual General Meetings, shall be called Extraordinary General Meetings.

14.   The Council may whenever they think fit convene an Extraordinary General Meeting, and Extraordinary General Meetings shall also be convened on such requisition, or in default may be convened by such requisitionists, as provided by Section 132 of the Act.

NOTICE OF GENERAL MEETINGS

15.   Subject to the provisions of the Act relating to Special Resolutions, twenty-one days' notice at the least of every Annual General Meeting and fourteen days' notice at the least of every other General Meeting (exclusive in every case both of the day on which it is served or deemed to be served and of the day for which it is given), specifying the place, the day and the hour of the meeting and in the case of special business the general nature of that business, shall be given in manner hereinafter mentioned to such persons as are under these presents or under the Act entitled to receive such notices from the Trust; but with the consent of all the members entitled to receive notices thereof, or of such proportion thereof as is prescribed by the Act in the case of meetings other than Annual General Meetings, a meeting may be convened by such notices as those members may think fit.

16.   The accidental omission to give notice of a meeting to, or the non-receipt of such notice by, any person entitled to receive notice thereof shall not invalidate any resolution passed, or proceeding had, at any meeting.

PROCEEDINGS AT GENERAL MEETINGS

17.   All business shall be deemed special that is transacted at an Extraordinary General Meeting, and also all that is transacted at an Annual General Meeting, with the exception of the consideration of the income and expenditure account and balance sheet, and the reports of the Council and of the auditors, the election of members of the Council in the place of those retiring by rotation or otherwise, and the appointment of and the fixing of the remuneration of the auditors.

18.   No business shall be transacted at any General Meeting unless a quorum is present when the meeting proceeds to business. Save as otherwise provided herein, <u>ten</u> Ordinary Members personally present shall be a quorum.

19.   If within half an hour from the time appointed for the holding of a General Meeting a quorum is not present, the meeting if convened on the requisition of members, shall be dissolved. In any other case it shall stand adjourned to the same day in the next week, at the same time and place,

or at such other place as the Chairman shall appoint, and if at such adjourned meeting a quorum is not present within half an hour from the time appointed for holding the meeting the members present shall be a quorum.

20. The Chairman of the Council shall preside as Chairman at every General Meeting, but if there be no such Chairman, or if at any meeting he shall not be present within fifteen minutes after the time appointed for holding the same, or shall be unwilling to preside, the members present shall choose some member of the Council, or if no such member be present, or if all the members of the Council present decline to take the chair, they shall choose some other member of the Trust who shall be present to preside.

21. The Chairman may, with the consent of any meeting at which a quorum is present (and shall if so directed by the meeting) adjourn a meeting from time to time, and from place to place, but no business shall be transacted at any adjourned meeting other than business which might have been transacted at the meeting from which the adjournment took place. Whenever a meeting is adjourned for ten days or more, notice of the adjourned meeting shall be given in the same manner as of an original meeting. Save as aforesaid, the members shall not be entitled to any notice of an adjournment or of the business to be transacted at an adjourned meeting.

22. At all General Meetings a resolution put to the vote of the Meeting shall be decided on a show of hands by a majority of the members present in person and entitled to vote, unless before or upon the declaration of the result of the show of hands a poll be demanded by the Chairman or by at least three Ordinary Members present in person, or by an Ordinary Member or Members present in person and representing one tenth of the total voting rights of all the members having the right to vote at the meeting and unless a poll be so demanded a declaration by the Chairman of the meeting that a resolution has been carried, or has been carried unanimously or by a particular majority, or lost, or not carried by a particular majority, shall be conclusive, and an entry to the effect in the minute book of the Trust shall be conclusive evidence thereof without proof of the number of proportion of the votes recorded in favour of or against that resolution, the demand for a poll may be withdrawn.

23. Subject to the provisions of Article 24, if a poll be demanded in manner aforesaid, it shall be taken at such time and place, and in such manner, as the Chairman of the meeting shall direct, and the result of the poll shall be deemed to be the resolution of the meeting at which the poll was demanded.

24. No poll shall be demanded on the election of a Chairman of a meeting, or on any question of adjournment.

25. In the case of an equality of votes, whether on a show of hands or on a poll, the Chairman of the meeting shall be entitled to a second or casting vote.

26. The demand of a poll shall not prevent the continuance of a meeting for

the transaction of any business other than the question on which a poll has been demanded.

VOTES OF MEMBERS

27. Subject as hereinafter provided, every member shall have one vote.

28. Save as herein expressly provided, no person other than an Ordinary Member duly registered and who shall have paid every subscription and other sum (if any) which shall be due and payable to the Trust in respect of his membership, shall be entitled to be present or to vote on any matter at any General Meeting.

29. No objection shall be raised to the qualification of any voter except at the Meeting or adjourned Meeting at which the vote objected to is given or tendered, and every vote not disallowed at such Meeting shall be valid for all purposes. Any such objections made in due time shall be referred to the Chairman of the Meeting, whose decision shall be final and conclusive.

THE COUNCIL OF MANAGEMENT OF THE TRUST

30. The Council shall consist of a Chairman and up to 20 other Members of the Council of the Trust, all of whom must be Ordinary Members of the Trust, or such other number as may from time to time be determined by the Trust in General Meeting.

31. The first members of the Council shall be such persons as shall be appointed in writing by a majority of the subscribers to the Memorandum of Association.

32. (A) Nominations for vacancies on the Council shall be made in writing and deposited with the Secretary at least six weeks before the Annual General Meeting at which the election will take place.
    (B) A candidate in the election shall be nominated by one member and supported by at least two other members in writing.
    (C) The Secretary shall circulate to all Ordinary Members of the Trust at least 21 days before the Annual General Meeting the Agenda for the Meeting, the names of the candidates properly nominated for the vacancies on the Council and, if so requested, a statement from each candidate of not more than 200 words in support of his nomination.
    (D) Election of members to the Council shall be by secret ballot at the Annual General Meeting. Each Ordinary Member shall have one vote for each vacancy on the Council. Candidates shall be elected to the vacancies on the Council in order of the number of votes cast. In the event of a tie, the Chairman of the meeting shall have a casting vote.

33. Any casual vacancy in the Council may be filled up by the Council, and the Council may from time to time and at any time co-opt additional members of the Council from amongst the Ordinary Members of the Trust up to the prescribed maximum. Any member appointed under this Article shall retire from office at the next Annual General Meeting, but shall be eligible for re-election.

34. The Trust may from time to time in General Meeting increase or reduce the number of members of the Council, and determine in what rotation such increased or reduced number shall go out of office, and may make the appointments necessary for effecting any such increase.

35. Without prejudice to any statutory provision for the time being in force relating to the removal of members of the Council by Ordinary Resolution, the Trust in General Meeting may by Extraordinary Resolution remove any member of the Council before the expiration of his period of office, and may by an Ordinary Resolution appoint another Ordinary Member in his stead; but any person so appointed shall retain his office until the next Annual General Meeting.

ROTATION OF COUNCIL MEMBERS

36. At the first Annual General Meeting of the Trust the whole of the Council shall retire from office, and at the Annual General Meeting in every subsequent year one-third of the Council for the time being shall retire from office, or if the number of such members eligible to retire is not three or a multiple of three, then the number nearest to one-third shall retire from office. At every such Annual General Meeting the Trust shall elect members of the Council in place of those retiring (except in so far as it shall be determined to reduce the number of members of the Council), and in default the retiring member shall, if offering himself for re-election, be deemed to have been re-elected. The officers of the Trust for the ensuing year shall be appointed by the Council at their first meeting after each such Annual General Meeting as aforesaid, and any vacancy in any such office during the course of a year shall be filled by the Council. Any member of the Council who ceases for any cause to be a member of the Trust shall ipso facto vacate office as a member of the Council.

37. The members of the Council to retire in every year shall be those who have been longest in office since their last election, but as between persons who become members of the Council on the same day, those to retire (unless they otherwise agree among themselves) shall be determined by lot. A retiring member of the Council shall be eligible for re-election.

BORROWING POWERS

38. The Council may exercise all the powers of the Trust to borrow or raise money, and to mortgage or charge its undertaking and property, and to issue debentures and other securities, and any such debentures and other securities may be issued at par or at a premium or at a discount.

POWERS OF THE COUNCIL OF MANAGEMENT

39. The business of the Trust shall be managed by the Council who may pay all such expenses of, and preliminary and incidental to, the promotion, formation, establishment and registration of the Trust as they think fit, and may exercise all such powers of the Trust and do on behalf of the Trust all such acts as may be exercised and done by the Trust, and as are not by Statute or by these Articles required to be exercised or done by the Trust in General Meeting, subject nevertheless to these Articles, to the provisions of the Statutes for the time being in force and affecting the Trust, and to such regulations, being not inconsistent with the aforesaid Articles or provisions, as may be prescribed by the Trust in General

Meeting, but no regulation made by the Trust in General Meeting shall invalidate any prior act of the Council which would have been valid if such regulation had not been made.

40. The members for the time being of the Council may act notwithstanding any vacancy in their body; provided always that in case the members of the Council shall at any time be reduced in number to less than the minimum prescribed or in accordance with these Articles, it shall be lawful for them to act as the Council for the purpose of filling up vacancies in their body, or of summoning a General Meeting, but not for any other purpose.

41. The Council may from time to time appoint, for the term of one year, as Honorary Advisors to the Council, persons who by virtue of their office or local standing have an interest in the objects of the Trust, to assist the Council at its meetings.

42. The Council shall appoint and employ all officers and servants as they consider necessary, and shall (subject to the provisions of Clause 4 of the Memorandum of Association) regulate their duties and fix their salaries.

43. All cheques, promissory notes, drafts, bills of exchange and other negotiable or transferable instruments, and all receipts for moneys paid to the Trust shall be signed, drawn, accepted, endorsed or otherwise executed, as the case may be, in such manner as the Council shall from time to time by resolution determine.

DISQUALIFICATION OF COUNCIL MEMBERS
44. The office of Council member shall be vacated if the Council member

(a) Without the consent of the Trust in General Meeting holds any other office of profit under the Trust; or
(b) Becomes bankrupt, or makes any arrangement or composition with his creditors generally; or
(c) Becomes of unsound mind; or
(d) Resigns his office by notice in writing to the Trust; or
(e) Is directly or indirectly interested in any contract with the Trust and fails to declare the nature of his interest. A Council member shall not vote in respect of any contract in which he is interested, and if he does so vote his vote shall not be counted; or
(f) He ceases to be an Ordinary Member of the Trust; or
(g) Is removed from office by a resolution duly passed pursuant to Section 184 of the Companies Act 1948.

PROCEEDINGS OF THE COUNCIL OF MANAGEMENT
45. The Council may meet together for the dispatch of business, adjourn and otherwise regulate their meetings as they think fit, and determine the quorum necessary for the transaction of business. Unless otherwise determined, three shall be a quorum. Questions arising at any meeting shall be decided by a majority of votes. In case of an equality of votes the Chairman shall have a second or casting vote. Honorary Advisors to the Council shall not be counted towards the quorum or be entitled to vote.

46. Seven days' notice (or less with the agreement of any five members of the

Council) at least (inclusive of the day on which the notice is served or deemed to be served but exclusive of the day for which the notice is given) specifying the place, the day and the hour of meeting and including the agenda of the business to be discussed at the meeting shall be given of every meeting of the Council unless in the opinion of the Chairman it shall be expedient to call a meeting on short notice for the discussion of urgent business, in which case the meeting may be called on three days' notice if the notice is sent through the post or on twenty-four hours' notice if the notice is given by telephone or telegraph. It shall not be necessary to give notice of a meeting of the Council to any member for the time being absent from the United Kingdom. On the request of a member of the Council the Secretary shall, at any time, summon a meeting of the Council by notice served upon the several members of the Council.

47. The Council shall from time to time elect a Chairman who shall be entitled to preside at all meetings of the Council at which he shall be present, and may determine for what period he is to hold office, but if no such Chairman be elected, or if at any meeting the Chairman be not present within five minutes after the time appointed for holding the meeting and willing to preside, the members of the Council present shall choose one of their number to be Chairman of the meeting.

48. A meeting of the Council at which a quorum is present shall be competent to exercise all the authorities, under the regulations of the Trust for the time being vested in the Council generally. A member of the Council shall declare his interest in any matter before the Council and may join in discussions on that matter but not vote upon it.

49. No business not included in the agenda mentioned in Article 46 shall be transacted at any meeting of the Council unless in the opinion of the Chairman of the meeting supported by a majority of the other members of the Council present at the meeting such business arises directly out of an item included in the agenda or out of the minutes of the last preceding meeting or is a matter of urgency.

50. A resolution in writing signed by all the members of the Council shall be as effective as if it had been passed at a meeting of the Council duly convened and held.

51. The Council may delegate any of its powers (other than the power to admit or expel members of the Trust) and including in particular its power of management of the Trust to Committees at least one of whose members shall be a member of the Council, as it may think fit. In the exercise of the power so delegated any Committee so formed shall conform to any regulations which may be imposed on it by the Council.

52. All acts bona fide done by any meeting of the Council or of any Committee of the Council or by any person acting as a member of the Council shall, notwithstanding it be afterwards discovered that there was some defect in the appointment of any such member or person acting as aforesaid, or that they or any of them were disqualified, be as valid as if every such person had been duly appointed and was qualified to be a member of the Council.

53. The Council shall cause minutes to be made in books provided for the purpose of all appointments of officers made by the Council and of the proceedings of all meetings of the Trust and of its Council and Committees, and of the names of the members of the Council present at each meeting. Any such minutes of any meeting, if purporting to be signed by the Chairman of such meeting, or by the Chairman of the next succeeding meeting, shall be sufficient evidence without any further proof of the facts therein stated.

SECRETARY

54. Subject to Section 21(5) of the Companies Act 1976 the Secretary shall be appointed by the Council for such time, at such remuneration and upon such conditions consistent with the provisions of Clause 4 of the Memorandum of Association as it may think fit, and any Secretary so appointed may be removed by the Council. The provisions of Section 177 to 179 of the Act shall apply and be observed. The Council may from time to time appoint an assistant or deputy Secretary, and any person so appointed may act in place of the Secretary if there be no Secretary or no Secretary capable of acting.

THE SEAL

55. The Seal shall not be affixed to any instrument except by the authority of a resolution of the Council and shall be so affixed in the presence of at least one member of the Council and of the Secretary or such other person as the Council may from time to time appoint for the purpose, and such member of the Council and Secretary or other person aforesaid shall sign every instrument to which the Seal is so affixed in their presence and in favour of any purchaser or person bona fide dealing with the Trust such signatures shall be conclusive evidence of the fact that the Seal has been properly affixed.

ACCOUNTS

56. The Council shall cause accounting records to be kept in accordance with Section 12 of the Companies Act 1976. Proper books shall be deemed not to be kept if there are not kept such books of account as are necessary to give a true and fair view of the state of the affairs of the Trust and to explain its transactions.

57. The accounting records shall be kept at the Office, or, subject to Section 12(6) & (7) of the Companies Act 1976, at such other place, or places as the Council may think fit, and shall always be open to the inspection of the members of the Council.

58. Subject and without prejudice to the provisions of Article 57 as regards members of the Council, the Trust in General Meeting shall make regulations as to the time and manner of inspection by Ordinary Members of the Trust of the accounts of the Trust and subject to any such conditions and regulations such accounts shall be open to the inspection of Ordinary Members of the Trust.

59. At the Annual General Meeting in every year the Council shall lay before the Trust a proper income and expenditure account for the period since the last preceding account (or in the case of the first account since the incorporation of the Trust) made up to a date not more than four months

before such Meeting and a balance sheet made up as at the same date containing all such particulars with regard to the capital, the assets and the liabilities of the Trust as are required by the Act.

60. Every such balance sheet as aforesaid shall be signed on behalf of the Council by two members of the Council and shall be accompanied by a report of the Council as to the state of the Trust's affairs, and it shall also have attached to it the Auditors' report.

61. A copy of every income and expenditure account, balance sheet and report and of any other documents required by law to be annexed or attached thereto or to accompany the same shall not less than twenty one clear days before the date of the Annual General Meeting, subject nevertheless to the provisions of Section 158(1)(c) of the Act, be sent to the Auditors and to all other persons entitled to receive notices of General Meetings in the manner in which notices are hereinafter directed to be served. The Auditors' report shall also be open to inspection and be read before the Meeting as required by Section 14 of the Companies Act 1967.

AUDIT
62. Once at least in every year the accounts of the Trust shall be examined and the correctness of the income and expenditure account and balance sheet ascertained by one or more properly qualified Auditor or Auditors.

63. Auditors shall be appointed and their duties regulated in accordance with Sections 161 of the 1948 Act Section 14 of the 1967 Act and Sections 13 to 18 of the 1976 Act, the members of the Council being treated as the Directors mentioned in those sections.

NOTICES
64. A notice may be served by the Trust upon any member, either personally or by sending it through the post in a prepaid letter, addressed to such member at his registered address as appearing in the register of members.

65. Any member described in the register of members by an address not within the United Kingdom, who shall from time to time give the Trust an address within the United Kingdom at which notices may be served upon him, shall be entitled to have notices served upon him at such address, but, save as aforesaid only members described in the register of members by an address within the United Kingdom shall be entitled to receive notices from the Trust.

66. Any notice, if served by post, shall be deemed to have been served on the day following that on which the letter containing the same is put into the post, and in proving such service it shall be sufficient to prove that the letter containing the notice was properly addressed and put into the post office as a prepaid letter.

WINDING UP
67. Clause 7 of the Memorandum of Association of the Trust relating to the winding up and dissolution of the Trust shall have effect as if the provisions thereof were repeated in these Articles.

INDEMNITY
68. Subject to Section 205 of the Companies Act 1948 every Member of the Council, Officer and Auditor of the Trust shall be indemnified out of the assets of the Trust against any liability incurred by him as such Member of the Council, Officer or Auditor in defending any proceedings, whether civil or criminal, in which judgement is given in his favour or in which he is acquitted or in connection with any application under Section 448 of the Act in which relief is granted to him by the Court.

Appendix 2 Some useful guides to plant and animal identification

(L) = larger format books

Wildflowers

Clapham, A.R., Tutin, T.G. and Warburg, E.F. (1968) *Excursion Flora of the British Isles*, Cambridge University Press. A concise guide to all common plants in the British Isles, with keys to their identification; not illustrated

Fitter, A. (1978) *An Atlas of the Wild Flowers of Britain and Northern Europe*, Collins. A concise guide to the distributions of wildflowers, with nearly 2,000 distribution maps (L)

Fitter, R., Fitter, A. and Blamie, M. (1978) *The Wild Flowers of Britain and Northern Europe* (3rd edn), Collins. A concise guide, illustrated with colour plates

Keble Martin, W. (1968) *The Concise British Flora in Colour*, Ebury Press. A pictorial reference book, illustrated with colour plates (L)

Lousley, J.E. and Kent, D.H. (1981) *Docks and Knotweeds of the British Isles*, Botanical Society of the British Isles, Handbook No. 3. A complete guide to docks and knotweeds, illustrated with line drawings

Phillips, R. (1977) *Wild Flowers of Britain*, Pan. A photographic guide, with over 1,000 species illustrated in colour (L)

Rose, F. (1981) *The Wild Flower Key (British Isles — N.W. Europe)*, Warne. A guide to the identification of over 1,400 species, with keys to plants not in flower, illustrated with colour plates

Trees and bushes

Edlin, H.L. (1978) *The Tree Key*, Warne. A useful, compact key to British species, illustrated with colour plates

Mitchell, A. (1978) *A Field Guide to the Trees of Britain and Northern Europe* (2nd edn), Collins. A guide to 800 species, illustrated with colour plates and line drawings

Phillips, R. (1978) *Trees in Britain (Europe and North America)*, Pan. A photographic guide, with over 500 species illustrated in colour

Polunin, O. (1977) *Trees and Bushes of Britain and Europe*, Paladin. A concise guide to all the trees and bushes to be found growing wild in Europe, over 1,000 colour plates and photographs

Water plants

Bursche, E.M. (1971) *A Handbook of Water Plants*, Warne. A simple guide to the plants growing in and around ponds, streams, lakes and other freshwater, illustrated with line drawings

Haslam, S., Sinker, C., and Wolsely, P. (1982) *British Water Plants*, Field Studies Council. A key based on the vegetative features of vascular plants growing in freshwater, with notes on their ecology and geographical distribution, illustrated with line drawings (L)

Grasses and sedges

Fitter, R. and Fitter, A. (1984) *Guide to the Grasses, Sedges, Rushes and Ferns of Britain and Northern Europe*, Collins. A comprehensive guide to all species with keys and colour plates

Hubbard, C.E (1968) *Grasses* (2nd edn), Penguin. A complete guide to the grasses of the British Isles, illustrated with line drawings

Jermy, A.C., Chater, A.O. and David, R.W. (1982) *Sedges of the British Isles*, Botanical Society of the British Isles, Handbook No. 1. A complete guide to sedges, illustrated with black and white line drawings

Ferns, mosses and lichens

Dobson, F. (1981) *Lichens. An Illustrated Guide*, Richmond. A guide to almost 500 common species, illustrated with colour and black and white photographs

—— (1979) *Common British Lichens*, Jarrold Nature Series. A useful booklet illustrating 45 species with colour photographs

Hyde, H.A., Wade, A.E. and Harrison, S.G. (1978) *Welsh Ferns, Clubmosses, Quillworts and Horsetails* (6th edn), National Museum of Wales. A useful guide for the British Isles, illustrated with black and white photographs and line drawings

Jahns, H.M. (1983) *Collins Guide to the Ferns, Mosses and Lichens of Britain, Northern and Central Europe*, Collins. A concise guide to over 750 species, illustrated with colour photographs

Phillips, R. (1980) *Grasses, Ferns, Mosses and Lichens*, Pan. A photographic guide with colour illustrations (L)

Smith, A.J.E. (1980) *The Moss Flora of Britain and Ireland*, Cambridge University Press. A key to all British mosses, illustrated with line drawings (requires the use of a microscope to identify species) (L)

Fungi

Kibby, G. (1979) *Mushrooms and Toadstools, a Field Guide*, Oxford University Press. A guide to common species in Great Britain, illustrated with colour plates (identification may require the use of a microscope for spore examination)

Lange, M. and Hora, F.B. (1963) *Collins Guide to Mushrooms and Toadstools*, Collins. A concise guide, illustrated with colour plates (identification may require the use of a microscpe for spore examination)

Phillips, R. (1981) *Mushrooms and other Fungi of Great Britain and Europe*, Pan. A photographic guide to more than 900 species, illustrated in colour (L)

Land invertebrates

Brooks, M. and Knight, C. (1982) *A Complete Guide to British Butterflies*, Jonathan Cape. A comprehensive guide with colour photos of adults, larvae and eggs for every British species (L)

Cameron, R.A.D. and Redfern, M. (1976) *British Land Snails*, synopses of the British Fauna (new series), No. 6, Linnean Society (London), Academic Press. A key to all British species, illustrated with line drawings

Carter, D. (1982) *Butterflies and Moths in Britain and Europe*, Pan. A photographic guide, with over 300 species illustrated in colour (L)

Chinery, M. (1976) *A Field Guide to the Insects of Britain and Northern Europe*, Collins. A comprehensive introductory guide, with over 1,000 illustrations, 778 in colour. Very comprehensive references for keys and further information on the identification of the many groups of British insects. Only a small proportion of the species are found in Britain; therefore check on distribution and in the text

Hammond, C.O. (1977) *The Dragonflies of Great Britain and Ireland*, Curwen. A complete guide, with a key and enlarged colour plates of all British species

Higgins, L.G. and Riley, N.D. (1980) *A Field Guide to the Butterflies of Britain and Europe* (4th edn), Collins. A comprehensive guide to all species, with over 800 colour plates and species distribution maps

Kerney, M.P., Cameron, R.A.D. and Riley, G. (1979) *A Field Guide to the Land Snails of Britain and Europe*, Collins. A comprehensive guide to all species of land snail and slug in N.W. Europe, with colour and black and white illustrations and 392 distribution maps, useful as a check against Cameron

Skinner, B. (1984) *Colour Identification Guide to the Moths of the British Isles. (Macrolepidoptera)*, Viking (Penguin). A comprehensive up-to-date guide with life-size colour photographs of mounted specimens for identification purposes (L)

South, R. (1961) *The Moths of the British Isles* (2 vols.: 1st and 2nd series), Warne. A comprehensive 2-part guide to all species of larger moths (*Macrolepidoptera*), illustrated with colour and black and white plates

Stokoe, W.J. (1979) *The Observer's Book of Butterflies*, Warne. A useful, simple guide to the 69 British species, illustrated with colour plates

Stubbs, A.E. and Falk, S.J. (1983) *British Hoverflies*, British Entomological and Natural History Society. A complete guide with keys to species, illustrated with colour plates (L)

Pond and stream animals

Clegg, J. (1967) *The Observer's Book of Pond Life*, Warne. A compact guide, useful in conjunction with Macan (below), illustrated with colour plates and black and white photographs

Macan, T.T. (1981) *A Guide to Freshwater Invertebrate Animals*, Longman. A useful key, illustrated with accurate line drawings

Maitland, P.S. (1972) *A Key to the Freshwater Fishes of the British Isles*, Freshwater Biological Association, SP7. A key to their identification with notes on distribution and ecology, illustrated with line drawings

Mellanby, H. (1963) *Animal Life in Fresh Water* (6th edn), Chapman & Hall. A guide to all the forms of freshwater invertebrates commonly found in Britain, illustrated with line drawings

Birds, their nests, eggs and young

Ferguson, Lees, J., Willis, I. and Sharrock, J.T.R. (1983) *The Shell Guide to the Birds of Britain and Ireland*, Michael Joseph

Hammond, N. and Everett, M. (1980) *Birds of Britain and Europe*, Pan. A photographic guide to species quite easily seen in Europe, illustrated in colour (L)

Hanzak, J. (1971) *Birds' Eggs and Nests*, Hamlyn. A guide to common British and European species, illustrated with colour plates

Harrison, C. (1975) *A Field Guide to the Nests, Eggs and Nestlings of British and European Birds (with N. Africa and the Middle East)*, Collins. A complete identification guide, with 730 eggs and 145 nestlings illustrated in colour

Hayman, P. (1979) *Birdwatcher's Pocket Guide*, Mitchell Beazley (RSPB). A slim, pocket-size guide to 220 British breeding species, illustrated with colour plates

Hayman P. and Burton, P. (1976) *The Birdlife of Britain*, Mitchell Beazley (RSPB). A comprehensive guide to identification using colour plates and the behaviour of each species (L)

Heinzel, H., Fitter, R. and Parslow, J. (1979) *The Birds of Britain and Europe (with N. Africa and the Middle East)* (4th edn), Collins. A guide to over 1,000 species, with colour illustrations and 825 distribution maps

Hoeher, S. (1974) *Birds' Eggs and Nesting Habitats*, Blandford. A guide to 280 species nesting in the British Isles and/or Central Europe, illustrated with colour photographs

Reade, W. and Hosking, E. (1974) *Nesting Birds, Eggs and Fledgelings* (4th edn), Blandford. A guide to the better known British and European species, illustrated with colour photographs of nesting sites and colour plates of eggs

Mammals

Brink, F.H. van den (1967) *A Field Guide to the Mammals of Britain and Europe*, Collins. A comprehensive guide, illustrated in colour and black and white

Corbet, G.B. and Southern, H.N. (1977) *The Handbook of British Mammals* (2nd edn), Blackwell. An extremely comprehensive guide to all British species, their identification and natural history, illustrated with line drawings, with an extensive reference section

Reptiles and amphibians

Arnold, E.N. and Burton, J.A. (1978) *A Field Guide to the Reptiles and Amphibians of Britain and Europe*, Collins. A comprehensive guide, with illustrations in colour and black and white

Buckley, J. (n.d.) *A Guide to the Identification of British Amphibians and Reptiles*, British Herpetological Society. Inexpensive leaflet covering all native species, illustrated with line drawings

Appendix 3 Soil sampling and some simple field analysis techniques

(i) Sampling

Samples should be taken from the top 15 cm of soil. The amount of sampling necessary will vary according to the size of a site and the evenness in soil type across the site. On a small site with little obvious variation in substrate, six sub-samples of soil may be taken for each hectare, or each site if smaller than one hectare, making a bulk sample, sufficient to fill a 30 × 25 cm plastic bag per ha. This should be enough soil for the usual analysis methods (approximately 250 g dry weight). The sub-samples should be collected at random along a Z or W shaped line across the site.

On larger sites, up to 40 hectares, one sample (comprised of 10 sub-samples) per two hectares should be sufficient.

If a laboratory is helping the group by analysing soil samples for them, sampling is best organised so that soil may be analysed as soon as possible after collection. If samples are placed in plastic bags and tied shut, this will help the soil to remain fresh. Bags should be labelled with sampling date, site name and sample number, and a sketch map of the site should be drawn up with numbered sampling points marked. Other notes may be included on sample bag labels, outlining such features as waterlogging, unusual materials, e.g. coal, subsoil, etc.

(ii) Soil texture (Lewis and Taylor 1974)

It is possible to examine soil texture in the field and to estimate the relative proportions of coarse sand, fine sand, silt and clay in the soil by the following simple method:

First, collect a small amount of soil. Remove any pebbles and crush any lumps until the soil is an even mixture. Moisten the soil until it is sticky or 'plastic'. Then take a small amount and roll and work it between fingers and thumb. Some soils when worked in this way will form a neat 'thread' in much the same way as Plasticine would.

Coarse sand has grains between 0.2 mm and 2 mm diameter. These are large enough to be detected individually by touch and sight. By working coarse sandy soil near to the ear, the sand grains may be heard grating together.

In *fine sand* (0.06-0.2 mm diameter) the grating is less obvious, though individual grains can be detected but not easily distinguished by touch or sight.

Silt (0.002-0.006 mm) feels smooth and soapy, but only very slightly sticky, whereas *clay* (0.002 mm) is characteristically sticky. Dry clays may require a lot of water and manipulation before they develop maximum stickiness.

Soils may be classified into types using the following criteria (see also Figure 4.6).

Sand Soil consisting mostly of coarse and fine sand and containing so little clay that it is loose when dry and not sticky at all when wet. When rubbed, it leaves no film on the fingers.

Sandy loam Soil in which the sand fraction is still quite obvious, which moulds readily when sufficiently moist, but in most cases does not stick appreciably to the fingers. Threads do not form easily.

Loam Soil in which the clay, sand and silt are so blended that it moulds readily when sufficiently moist and sticks to the fingers to some extent. It can be moulded into threads with difficulty, but will not bend into a small ring.

Silt loam Soil that is moderately plastic without being very sticky and in which the smooth soapy feel of the silt is the main feature.

Clay loam The soil is distinctly sticky when sufficiently moist and the presence of sand fractions can only be detected with care.

Silt Soil in which the smooth, soapy feel of silt is dominant.

Sandy clay The soil is plastic and sticky when moistened sufficiently, but the sand fraction is still an obvious feature. Clay and sand are dominant and the intermediate grades of silt and very fine sand are less apparent.

Clay The soil is plastic and sticky when moistened sufficiently and gives a polished surface when rubbed. When moist, the soil can be rolled into threads which will bend into rings. With care, a small proportion of sand can be detected.

Silty clay Soil which is composed almost entirely of very fine material but in which the smooth soapy feel of the silt fraction modifies the stickiness of the clay.

Soil with organic matter present has a good 'crumby' feel when moist.

The following is a simple key for finger assessment of soil texture (from Burnham 1980).

1.　Does the moist soil form a coherent ball?
　　Easily . . . . . (2)
　　With great care . . . . . LOAMY SAND but check using tests 2 and 3
　　No . . . . . SAND

2.　What happens when the ball is pressed between thumb and forefinger?
　　Flattens coherently . . . . . (3)
　　Tends to break up . . . . . SANDY LOAM but check using tests 3 and 4

3.　On slight further moistening can the ball be rolled into a thick cylinder (about 5 mm thick)?
　　Yes . . . . . (5)
　　No . . . . . LOAMY SAND

4.　On slight further moistening can the cylinder be rolled into a thin thread (about 2 mm thick)?
　　Yes . . . . . (5)
　　No . . . . . SANDY LOAM

5.　Can the thread be bent into a horseshoe without cracking, e.g. around the side of the hand?
　　Yes . . . . . (7)
　　No . . . . . (6)

6.　On remoulding with further moisture what is the general 'feel' of the soil?
　　Smooth and pasty . . . . . SILT LOAM
　　Rough and abrasive . . . . . SANDY SILT LOAM

7.　Can a ring of about 25 mm diameter be formed by joining the two ends of the thread without cracking? (If necessary remould with more moisture and begin again.)
　　Yes . . . . . (9)
　　No . . . . . (8)

8.　On remoulding with further moisture what is the general 'feel' of the soil?
　　Very gritty . . . . . SANDY CLAY LOAM
　　Moderately rough . . . . . CLAY LOAM
　　Doughy . . . . . SILTY CLAY LOAM

9.　On remoulding without rewetting can a surface be polished with the thumb?
　　Yes, a high polish like wax with few noticeable particles . . . . . (10)
　　Yes, but gritty particles are very noticeable . . . . . SANDY CLAY
　　No . . . . . (8)

10.   On wetting thoroughly, how strongly does the soil stick one's fingers together?
Very strongly ..... CLAY
Moderately strongly ..... SILTY CLAY

(iii) Soil pH, nitrogen, phosphorus and potassium

The 'Soil Test Kit' made by Sudbury (of Corwen, Clwyd, North Wales LL21 0DR) is a very convenient way of estimating the levels of major nutrients and pH of the soil. Most good gardening and DIY shops will sell Sudbury kits and it may be possible to borrow a kit from a sympathetic local gardener, a local college or the local authority. Kits have full instructions for use, including suggestions for dealing with any deficiencies identified in the soil.

As well as taking measurements over the whole site, it may be worthwhile measuring changes with soil depth, since urban soils are very variable. This type of soil kit, although easy to use, only gives inaccurate estimates of soil nutrients and pH and should be used as a guide, rather than measure, particularly as soil conditions on urban sites may be extreme.

(iv) Soil water table

It is possible to measure the soil water table on site by sinking an open-ended tube into the ground. The tube should be as long as possible, perhaps 50 cm or more and a lid over the tube is necessary to keep out rain. The tube should fill with water to the level of the water table. Any water table present will be affected by rainfall, so it will be worthwhile setting up some form of rain gauge alongside the tube. Measurements of water table levels (using a dip-stick) and rainfall levels may then be compared, preferably with readings taken once or twice a week, for at least a month.

References

Burnham, C.P. (1980) 'The soils of England and Wales', *Field Studies*, **5**:349-63
Lewis, T. and Taylor, L.R. (1974) *Introduction to Experimental Ecology*, Academic Press

Appendix 4 The National Tree Survey

The following is a summary of the information contained in the leaflets: 'Making a Tree Survey' (1972), Council for the Protection of Rural England and 'The National Tree Survey' (1975), The Tree Council.

The Council for the Protection of Rural England developed methods for surveying trees in Great Britain in the early 1970s. These methods were incorporated into The Tree Council's National Tree Survey. The survey was launched in 1975 and aims to establish a national record of the number, species and condition of amenity trees and to reveal sites particularly suitable for future tree planting. The survey is also intended to include trees in hedgerows, shelter belts, groups of trees and small woodlands (up to 1 ha or 2.5 acres) and will provide information for the assistance of local authorities, farmers, foresters and nature conservationists.

It is vital that those participating in the survey should carry out their work accurately and uniformly. Duplication of effort must be avoided and liaison with the district council is essential.

If the group wishes to contribute to the survey, leaflets for volunteers may be obtained from The Tree Council (see Appendix 15 for address). The local district council will provide details of areas not already surveyed, which need surveying, and should be able to help obtain the necessary permission and co-operation of land-owners.

The survey is best carried out by two people working together, and living in or near the chosen area, so that a continual check can be made and changes easily recognised. Spot checks by qualified people should be made. The survey should be undertaken when deciduous trees are in leaf — generally between mid-May and the end of October. It would be advisable to go over the same area at least every 3-5 years and record any changes that have taken place.

The common name of the tree is normally used. Cultivated fruit trees and small mature flowering shrubs are not usually included, if under 2.4 m in height.

Surveyors require the following equipment:

(1) Two grid-system Ordnance Survey maps scale 1:2500 (40 cm to 1 km). One map for use in the field, the duplicate to be returned to the county planning department (if working with their co-operation) or for your own permanent record. It is most important that the map number and survey date is clearly recorded at the top of every page of every record.

(2) Clip board with loose-leaf sheets, preferably with a plastic cover to protect sheets from the weather. The ideal form of recording sheets is loose-leaf ruled paper, previously columned and headed.

(3) Tape measure (preferably of the timber measuring kind).

(4) A book, such as *A Field Guide to the Trees of Britain and Northern Europe* by A.F. Mitchell (Collins), will be useful for identification purposes.

The trees should be recorded under the following code headings and numbered:

Classification	Code
Single trees	T
Areas or linear belts of trees and hedges with significant trees	A
Groups of trees	G
Woods	W
Hedgerows	H

Marking the map (see Figure A4.1)

Single trees = T. These are recorded on the map as a dot in a circle, with the letter code 'T' and its sequential number, e.g. T_1 T_2 T_3 etc.

Areas or linear belts of trees and hedges with significant trees (too many to list singly) = A. These should be marked with dots outlining the area, with the code letter 'A' alongside with the appropriate number.

Groups of trees = G. These are marked by outlining the group with a broken line, with the code letter 'G' and appropriate number alongside. Groups are more than two trees in depth and up to about 60 trees in number.

Woods = W. These are marked by outlining the wooded area with an unbroken line, with the code letter 'W' and the appropriate number. As many species as possible should be named.

Hedgerows = H. Hedgerows without significant trees are marked by a

Figure A4.1 Recording trees, hedges and woodlands on a map

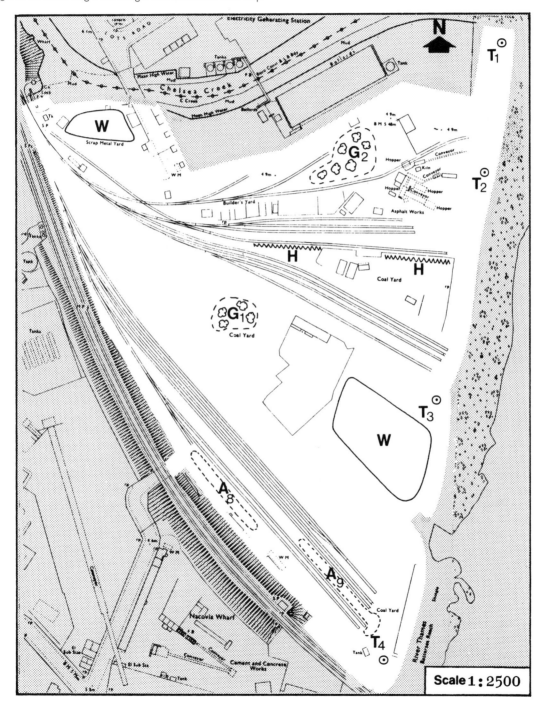

pecked (⋀⋀⋁) line with the code letter 'H' and its number. The main species present in any one hedge should be noted.

Completing the record sheet

The following is an example:
Ordnance Survey map no.:   Date of Survey:
(and grid letters and nos. where given)

Tree no.	Species	Approx. height (m)	Circumference at breast height (mm)	Category	Comments
T4	Oak	10	2,000	A	Beautifully shaped, well-known landmark
T5	Horse chestnut	20	2,200	C	Excessive dead wood; poor leafing. Large cavity at 5m
T6	Elm	18	2,000	D	Almost dead
A10	Hazel hedge with ash, oak and yew trees	8(max.)	1,000(av.)	B	Some promising young oaks
A11	ditto	ditto	ditto	B	Yews becoming dominant
G1	Beech	20(av.)	2,000	A/C	11 mature beeches; 6 in poor condition

Notes on the recording sheet headings:

Species — If you cannot identify the species, put a question mark and try to get a further opinion.

Height — Estimate the height of a tree by simple trigonometry or by multiplying the height of a person standing against it.

Age — The age of most mature trees can be assessed at approximately one year per 25mm circumference.

Circumference — usually measured at a point 1.3m above the ground (breast height).

Category — For the purpose of the survey, trees are divided into four simple categories: A, B, C or D.

A = good specimens of individual or groups of trees, well situated and enhancing their surroundings. These trees must be healthy, well-shaped and showing no sign of die-back or fungal infection. Rare species and trees of special local or historic interest should be noted.

B = normal specimens.

C = poor specimens, e.g. mis-shapen, stunted or with excessive dead wood.

D = dead or dying trees.

Any sign of fungus on or around a tree must cause concern. Abnormally late leafing in the spring or early leaf fall in the autumn indicate decline in a tree's vigour. If in doubt, obtain an expert opinion. It is essential to examine each tree carefully, however difficult the access (for example, heavy growths of ivy can hide serious defects).

Appendix 5 The relative importance of habitat conditions and the vegetation types adapted to contend with them

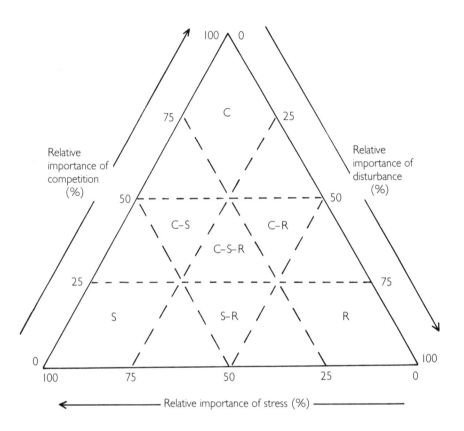

Key to vegetation types

C = competitors
S = stress tolerators
R = ruderals

C–R = competitive — ruderals: adapted to conditions where the impact of stress is low and competition is restricted to a moderate intensity by disturbance
S–R = Stress-tolerant — ruderals: adapted to relatively undisturbed productive habitats experiencing moderate intensities of stress
C–S–R = Competitive — stress-tolerant — ruderals: adapted to habitats in which the level of competition is restricted by moderate intensities of both stress and disturbance

In order to find where a particular species fits into this triangular model, it is necessary to examine its life history and habitat requirements, as well as the degree to which these vary between individuals of the species. The production of such information for all species is understandably a huge task, still to be completed. It is, however, possible to show how the major groups of land plants fit into the triangle:

Major groups of land plants and the conditions of competition, stress and disturbance to which they are adapted. Each triangle should be compared with the total triangle area above.

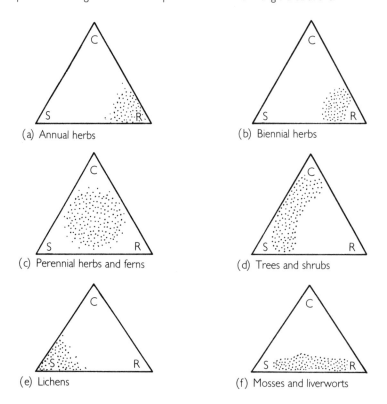

(a) Annual herbs

(b) Biennial herbs

(c) Perennial herbs and ferns

(d) Trees and shrubs

(e) Lichens

(f) Mosses and liverworts

Source: Grime, J.P. (1979) 'Succession and competitive exclusion' in Wright, S.E. and Buckley, G.P. (eds.) *Ecology and Design in Amenity Land Management*, Conference, Wye College, Kent, pp. 57–70

Appendix 6 Examples of commercial seed mixes

(A) British seed houses

W.F.G.5 Mixture for calcareous soils, chalk and limestone areas

Basil, Wild (*Clinopodium vulgare*)
Bedstraw, Lady's (*Galium verum*)
Bellflower, clustered (*Campanula glomerata*)
Bird's-foot-Trefoil, common (*Lotus corniculatus*)
Carrot, Wild (*Daucus carota*)
Cowslip (*Primula veris*)
Daisy, Ox-Eye (*Chrysanthemum leucanthemum*)
Goat's beard (*Tragopogon pratense*)

Harebell (*Campanula rotundifolia*)
Knapweed, Common (*Centaurea nigra*)
Knapweed, Greater (*Centaurea scabiosa*)
Medic, Black (*Medicago lupulina*)
Plantain, Hoary (*Plantago media*)
Sainfoin (*Onobrychis viciifolia*)
Scabious, Small (*Scabiosa columbaria*)
Self Heal (*Prunella vulgaris*)
Thyme, Creeping (*Thymus drucei*)
Vetch, Horseshoe (*Hippocrepis comosa*)
Vetch, Kidney (*Anthyllis vulneraria*)

Dog's-tail, Crested *(Cynosurus cristatus)*
Fescue, Chewing's *(Festuca rubra ssp. commutata)*
Fescue, Creeping Red, Strong *(Festuca rubra ssp. rubra)*

Fescue, Hard *(Festuca longifolia)*
Fescue, Sheep's *(Festuca ovina)*
Sowing Rate: 5.0 g/m² (50kg per ha)

W.F.G.7 Mixture for sowing on dry, free- draining sandy soils

Bedstraw, Lady's *(Galium verum)*
Bird's-foot-Trefoil, Common *(Lotus corniculatus)*
Campion, White *(Silene alba)*
Carrot, Wild *(Daucus carota)*
Daisy, Ox-Eye *(Chrysanthemum leucanthemum)*
Dandelion *(Taraxacum officinale)*
Harebell *(Campanula rotundifolia)*
Hawkbit, Rough *(Leontodon hispidus)*
Medic, Black *(Medicago lupulina)*
Mignonette, Wild *(Reseda lutea)*
Rattle, Yellow *(Rhinanthus minor)*
St John's Wort, Perforate *(Hypericum perforatum)*

Trefoil, Lesser *(Trifolium dubium)*
Vetch, Kidney *(Anthyllis vulneraria)*
Viper's-Bugloss *(Echium vulgare)*
Weld *(Reseda luteola)*
Yarrow *(Achillea millefolium)*
Bent, Browntop *(Agrostis castellana)*
Fescue, Chewing's *(Festuca rubra ssp. commutata)*
Fescue, Creeping Red, Slender *(Festuca rubra ssp. litoralis)*
Fescue, Creeping Red, Strong *(Festuca rubra ssp. rubra)*
Fescue, Hard *(Festuca longifolia)*
Meadow-Grass, Smooth *(Poa pratensis)*
Sowing Rate: 5.0 g/m² (50kg per ha)

W.F.G.6 Mixture for sowing on heavy clay soils

Bedstraw, Lady's *(Galium verum)*
Bird's-foot-Trefoil, Common *(Lotus corniculatus)*
Burnet, Salad *(Poterium sanguisorba)*
Buttercup, Meadow *(Ranunculus acris)*
Campion, White *(Silene alba)*
Carrot, Wild *(Daucus carota)*
Cat's-ear *(Hypochoeris radicata)*
Cowslip *(Primula veris)*
Daisy, Ox-Eye *(Chrysanthemum leucanthemum)*
Dropwort *(Filipendula vulgaris)*
Knapweed, Common *(Centaurea nigra)*
Knapweed, Greater *(Centaurea scabiosa)*
Medic, Black *(Medicago lupulina)*

Plantain, Hoary *(Plantago media)*
Plantain, Ribwort *(Plantago lanceolata)*
Restharrow, Common *(Ononis repens)*
Self Heal *(Prunella vulgaris)*
Vetch, Kidney *(Anthyllis vulneraria)*
Yarrow, *(Achillea millefolium)*
Dog's-tail, Crested *(Cynosurus cristatus)*
Fescue, Chewing's *(Festuca rubra ssp. commutata)*
Fescue, Creeping Red, Strong *(Festuca rubra ssp. rubra)*
Foxtail, Meadow *(Alopecurus pratensis)*
Oat-Grass, Yellow *(Trisetum flavescens)*
Sowing Rate: 5.0 g/m² (50kg per ha)

W.F.G.8 Mixture for sowing on shaded areas — open woodland and hedgerows

Avens, Wood *(Geum urbanum)*
Bluebell *(Endymion non-scriptus)*
Bugle *(Ajuga reptans)*
Campion Red *(Silene dioica)*
Cowslip *(Primula veris)*
Foxglove *(Digitalis purpurea)*
Hedge-Parsley, Upright *(Torillis japonica)*
Herb Robert *(Geranium robertianum)*
Meadow Sweet *(Filipendula ulmaria)*
Mullein, Great *(Verbascum thapsus)*
Primrose *(Primula vulgaris)*
Ragged-Robin *(Lychnis flos-cuculi)*
Ramsons *(Allium ursinum)*
Sage, Wood *(Teucrium scorodonia)*

St John's Wort Hairy *(Hypericum hirsutum)*
Stitchwort, Greater *(Stellaria holostea)*
Traveller's-Joy *(Clematis vitalba)*
Woundwort, Hedge *(Stachys sylvatica)*
Bent, Browntop *(Agrostis castellana)*
Dog's-tail, Crested *(Cynosurus cristatus)*
Fescue, Creeping Red, Slender *(Festuca rubra ssp. litoralis)*
Fescue, Sheep's, fine-leaved *(Festuca rubra ssp. tenuifolia)*
Meadow-Grass, Rough *(Poa trivialis)*
Meadow-Grass, Smooth *(Poa pratensis)*
Meadow-Grass, Wood *(Poa nemoralis)*
Sowing Rate: 5.0 g/m² (50kg per ha)

(B) John Chambers

WILD FLOWER SEED COLLECTION
PACKED IN ILLUSTRATED PACKETS CONTAINING FULL DETAILS

A selection of 53 best known and most easily grown species whose beauty of form and colour makes them ideal subjects for the gardens of Wild Flora lovers.

Marks	No. & Common name	Botanical name	TYPE	HEIGHT Max.cms
∞ = b	2002 Wild flora 'dry' soil wildflower mixture		ABP	90
∞ = b	2004 Wild flora 'wet' soil wildflower mixture		ABP	90
D b	2006 Agrimony	*Agrimonia eupatoria*	P	50
D	2008 Alexanders or black Lovage	*Smyrnium olusatrum*	B	120
D ∞	2010 Bedstraw, lady's	*Galium verum*	P	45
b	2012 Bellflower, clustered	*Campanula glomerata*	P	15
∞	2014 Betony	*Betonica officinalis*	P	45
p ∞ b	2016 Bluebell or wild hyacinth	*Endymion non-scriptus*	P	40
p ∞ = b	2018 Broom	*Sarothamnus scoparius*	S	250
	2020 Burnet, salad or lesser	*Sanguisorba minor (Poterium sanguisorba)*	P	60
∞	2022 Campion, red	*Silene dioica*	P	90
p b	2024 Corncockle	*Agrostemma githago*	A	100
∞ =	2026 Cowslip	*Primula veris*	P	35
D b	2028 Crane's-bill, meadow	*Geranium pratense*	P	60
∞ b	2030 Daisy, ox-eye	*Chrysanthemum leucanthemum*	P	60
D	2032 Elecampane	*Inula helenium*	P	120
b	2034 Feverfew	*Chrysanthemum parthenium*	P	45
p b	2036 Flax	*Linum usitatissimum*	A	60
b	2038 Forget-me-not, field	*Myosotis arvensis*	AB	30
p =	2040 Foxglove	*Digitalis purpurea*	B	120
	2042 Gentian, spring	*Gentiana verna*	P	10
∞	2044 Harebell	*Campanula rotundifolia*	P	30
p	2046 Horned-poppy, yellow	*Glaucium flavum*	BP	60
p ∞ b	2048 Hound's-tongue	*Cynoglossum officinale*	B	60
∞ = b	2050 Mallow, musk	*Malva moschata*	P	80
∞	2052 Marigold, corn	*Chrysanthemum segetum*	A	30
p ∞ = b	2054 Marsh-mallow	*Althea officinalis*	P	100
D b	2056 Meadowsweet	*Filipendula ulmaria*	P	120
= b	2058 Melilot, yellow or ribbed	*Melilotus officinalis*	B	130
p b	2060 Mullein, dark	*Verbascum nigrum*	B	120
D p b	2062 Mullein, great or Aaron's rod	*Verbascum thapsus*	B	200
∞	2064 Oxlip	*Primula elatior*	P	30
∞ = b	2066 Pansy, wild or heartsease	*Viola tricolor*	AP	30
p b	2068 Poppy, field	*Papaver rhoeas*	A	60
	2070 Poppy, welsh	*Meconopsis cambrica*	P	55
p	2072 Pimpernel, scarlet	*Anagallis arvensis*	A	30
∞ =	2074 Primrose	*Primula vulgaris*	P	15
∞ b	2076 Purple-loosestrife	*Lythrum salicaria*	P	100
∞ b	2078 Ragged-robin	*Lychnis flos-cuculi*	P	70
∞ = b	2080 Rock-rose, common	*Helianthemum chamaecistus*	P	25

		No.	English name	Latin name	Type	Height
p ∞ D	b	2082	St John's wort, perforate	*Hypericum perforatum*	P	60
D ∞ =	b	2084	Scabious, devil's-bit	*Succisa pratensis*	P	80
p ∞	b	2086	Soapwort	*Saponaria officinalis*	P	100
		2088	Stitchwort, greater	*Stellaria holostea*	P	50
=	b	2090	Strawberry, wild	*Fragaria vesca*	P	30
Dp	b	2092	Tansy	*Tanacetum vulgare*	P	120
∞	b	2094	Teasel	*Dipsacus fullonum*	B	200
∞ =	b	2096	Trefoil, bird's-foot	*Lotus corniculatus*	P	20
∞		2098	Toadflax, ivy-leaved	*Cymbalaria muralis*	P	60CR
∞	b	2100	Valerian	*Valeriana officinalis*	P	120
∞	b	2102	Vervain	*Verbena officinalis*	P	90
=	b	2104	Violet, sweet	*Viola odorata*	P	15
=	b	2106	Viper's-bugloss	*Echium vulgare*	B	30
∞	b	2108	Wallflower, wild	*Cheiranthus cheiri*	B	23
D ∞	b	2110	Yarrow	*Achillea millefolium*	P	30

Key A = hardy annual; B = biennial; P = perennial; S = shrub; D = dye plant; p = poisonous plant; ∞ = butterfly nectar plant; = = butterfly caterpillar food plant; b = bee plant

Appendix 7 List of trees and shrubs for different conditions

Species	H	W	1	2	3	4	5	6	7	8	9	10	11	12	13	14	15	16	17	18	19	20	21	22	23
Acer campestre (field maple)	15			+			+			+	+														
A. platanoides (Norway maple)*	15-20			+			+																		
A. pseudoplatanus (sycamore)*	25-30			+			+	+		+	+						+	+	+						+
Aesculus hippocastanum (horse chestnut)*	25-30																	+							
Alnus glutinosa (common alder) (N)	20	B,I	+	+	+	+	+	+		+	+	+					+		+			+			+
A. incana (grey alder) (N)*	20			+	+	+	+	+		+	+	+			+			+				+		+	
Atriplex halimus (Mediterranean saltbush)*	—						+																+	+	
Betula pendula (silver birch)	20	I	+	+	+	+	+		+				+	+	+		+	+	+		+	+	+	+	+
B. pubescens (downy birch)	20	I	+	+	+	+	+	+			+			+			+	+	+		+	+	+	+	+
Buddleja davidii (buddleia)*	5				+		+																		+
Buxus sempervirens (box)	7						+													+					
Calluna vulgaris (ling)	0.6					(+)												(+)							
Carpinus betulus (hornbeam)	20-25						(+)			+									+						
Castanea sativa (sweet chestnut)*	25-30														+								+		
Colutea arborescens (bladder senna) (N)*	6				+							+											+			

353

Appendix 7

Species	H	W	1	2	3	4	5	6	7	8	9	10	11	12	13	14	15	16	17	18	19	20	21	22	23
Corylus avellana (hazel)	7	I	+	+			+	+		+	+				+		+	+							
Cotoneaster microphyllus (rock spray)*	1-2						+									+			+						
Crataegus monogyna (hawthorn)	7	B,I	+	+	+	+	+			+	+			+	+			+						+	+	
C. oxyacanthoides (Midland hawthorn)	7	B,I	+	+	+		+			+	+															
Cupressus lawsoniana (Lawson's cypress)*	30-35									+	+				+										
Cytisus scoparius (broom) (N)	1-2	I	+	+	+	+							+		+								+		+
Erica cinerea (bell heather)	0.6						(+)						(+)				(+)								
E. tetralix (cross-leaved heath)	0.6						(+)		(+)		(+)						(+)								
Euonymus europaeus (spindle tree)	3						+				+														
Fagus sylvatica (beech)	30-35			+			+								+	+									
Frangula alnus (alder buckthorn)	3							+				+													
Fraxinus excelsior (ash)	25-30			+			+	+		+	+	+			+		+	+	+		+			+		
Gleditsia triacanthos (honey locust) (N)*	30-40				+								+					+					+		
Hippophae rhamnoides (sea buckthorn)	3-9	B		+		+							+		+	+	+							+	+
Ilex aquifolium (holly)	15	B	+		+													+	+						
Juniperus communis (juniper)	2-4	B	+	+	+	+	+						+	+			+	+							
Larix decidua (European larch)*	30-40		+	+	+	+								+									+		+
L. leptolepsis (Japanese larch)*	25-30		+		+	+			+	+				+									+		+
Ligustrum vulgare (privet)	1-2	B					+	+			+							+	+					+	+
Lonicera periclymenum (honeysuckle)	—					(+)	(+)			(+)	(+)														
Lupinus arboreus (tree lupin) (N)*	3			+			+								+	+								+	+
Malus sylvestris (crab apple)	5-6	B,I									(+)														
Picea abies (Norway spruce)*	30-35		+		+	+			+	+		+		+			+		+						
P. sitchensis (Sitka spruce)*	40-50		+		+	+			+	+		+		+			+	+	+				+	+	+
Pinus sylvestris (Scots pine)	25-30	I	+	+	+	+				+			+	+	+		+	+					+		+
Populus alba (white poplar)*	25-30									+		+			+			+					+	+	+
P. × canadensis (Italian black poplar)*	25-30																	+							
P. canescens (grey poplar)	25-30						+	+		+	+	+													
P. nigra (black poplar)	25-30	I						+			+							+							
P. tacamahaca (balsam poplar)*	25-30						+			+	+	+													
P. tremula (aspen)	20	I	+	+	+	+			+	+		+		+	+		+								+
Potentilla fruticosa (shrubby cinquefoil)	1						+									+									
Prunus avium (wild cherry)	15-25	B		+														+							
P. padus (bird cherry)	10	B					+									+									
P. spinosa (blackthorn)	2-3	I	+	+			+	+		+	+	+			+	+	+								
Quercus cerris (Turkey oak)*	35-40									+	+								+						

Species	H	W	1	2	3	4	5	6	7	8	9	10	11	12	13	14	15	16	17	18	19	20	21	22	23
Q. ilex (holm oak)*	25-30																		+						
Q. petraea (sessile oak)	25-30	B,I		+	+	+									+		+	+	+		+	+			+
Q. robur (pedunculate oak)	25-30	B,I		+	+					+	+						+		+		+	+			+
Rhamnus catharticus (common buckthorn)	5						+	+															+		
Rhododendron ponticum (rhododendron)*	1-3			+		+			+				+	+					+	+					
Robinia pseudoacacia (false acacia) (N)*	25				+								+		+				+			+	+		
Rosa arvensis (field rose)	—	B	+							+															
R. canina (dog rose)	1	B	+	+			+	+		+	+					+	+				+				
R. pimpinellifolia (burnet rose)	0.5			+			+								+	+									
R. villosa (downy rose)	0.5																	+							
Rubus fruticosus (bramble)	1	B	+	+	+	+		+		+	+				+	+	+		+			+			+
Salix alba (white willow)	20-25	B						+				+							+						
S. aurita (eared sallow)*	2											+				+	+								
S. caprea (goat willow)	3-5	I	+	+	+	+	+	+		+	+	+			+	+	+		+			+	+	+	+
S. cinerea (common sallow)	2-3	I	+	+	+	+	+	+		+	+	+			+	+	+		+			+	+	+	+
S. daphnoides (violet willow)*	10											+			+				+						
S. fragilis (crack willow)	20-25	I						+				+							+						
S. pentandra (bay willow)	15							+				+													
S. phylicifolia (tea-leaved willow)*	4				+	+						+				+	+								
S. purpurea (purple willow)	3	I						+				+													
S. repens (creeping willow)	0.4				+	+		+	+			+			+								+	+	
S. triandra (almond willow)	10											+													
S. viminalis (osier)	3-5	I						+				+													
Sambucus nigra (elder)	7	B	+	+	+		+	+		+	+			+	+		+		+			+	+	+	+
Sarothamnus scoparius (broom) (N)	2		(+)	(+)	(+)	(+)							(+)				(+)				(+)	(+)			
S. aria (common whitebeam)	10-15	I		+			+			+			+				+		+		+				
S. aucuparia (rowan)	10-15	B		+	+	+	+						+	+	+	+	+	+	+		+	+			+
S. intermedia (Swedish whitebeam)*	10-15						+										+		+			+			+
S. latifolia (broad-leaved whitebeam)*	10-15						+																		
S. torminalis (wild service tree)	20	B								+					+										
Tamarix gallica (tamarisk)*	3						+						+	+									+		
Taxus baccata (yew)	5-20						+							+					+	+					
Thelycrania sanguinea (dogwood)	3	B					+				+														
Tilia cordata (small-leaved lime)	20-30						+				+					+	+				+				
T. europaea (common lime)	20-30						+			+	+								+						
T. platyphyllos (large-leaved lime)	35-40						+			+	+								+						
Ulex europaeus (gorse) (N)	2-3		+	+	+	+			+	+			+	+	+	+	+					+			+
Ulmus glabra (wych elm)	40	I	+				+			+	+						+	+	+		+				
U. procera (common elm)	40	I								+	+								+						

Species	H	W	1	2	3	4	5	6	7	8	9	10	11	12	13	14	15	16	17	18	19	20	21	22	23
Vaccinium myrtillus (bilberry)	0.6	B,I				(+)			(+)									(+)		(+)					
Viburnum lantana (wayfaring tree)	3	B	+			+	+			+															
V. opulus (guelder rose)	1	B	+			+	+			+	+														

Key to conditions

1.	Pioneering ability	14.	Suitable for cliffs and steep banks
2.	Good natural regeneration	15.	Suitable for rocky and stony places
3.	Tolerance of infertile soil	16.	Tolerance of exposure or altitude
4.	Tolerance of acid soils	17.	Tolerance of smoke pollution
5.	Tolerance of alkaline soils	18.	Tolerance of deep shade
6.	Tolerance of fen peat	19.	Associated with species-rich or well developed ground flora or shrub vegetation
7.	Tolerance of acid peat		
8.	Tolerance of heavy clay soils	20.	Tolerance of colliery waste
9.	Tolerance of calcareous boulder clay	21.	Tolerance of power station ash
10.	Suitable for wet soils	22.	Tolerance of lime wastes, blast furnace slag and calcareous substrates
11.	Suitable for dry soils		
12.	Suitable for shallow soils	23.	Tolerance of refuse tips, quarry spoil demolition rubble, ashes and cinders
13.	Suitable for sand and gravel		

Notes: N = nitrogen fixing; * = introduced; H = height at maturity (in metres); W = wildlife value; B = birds; I = insects

Source: Based on recommendations from Dr R. Gemmell, Ecologist, Joint Reclamation Team, Greater Manchester and Lancashire County Councils (see Appendix 15 for address), with additional information from the following: Beckett, K. and Beckett, G. (1979) *Planting Native Trees and Shrubs*, Jarrold; Carter, E. (1982) *A Guide to Planting Trees and Shrubs for Wildlife and the Landscape*, Farming and Wildlife Advisory Group (FWAG); Phillips, R. (1978) *Trees in Britain, Europe and North America*, Pan; Yoxon, M. (ed.) (1977) *Creative Ecology Part 1*. Ecological Studies in Milton Keynes No. 18, Milton Keynes Development Corporation

Appendix 8 Scrub planting mixtures

Based on recommendations from Dr R. Gemmell, Ecologist, Joint Reclamation Team of the Greater Manchester and Lancashire County Councils (see Appendix 15 for address).

Table A8.1 and the key listed below describe 22 planting mixtures for different types of scrub or shrub cover, based on natural associations of native species. The selection of species and their proportions in each mixture are varied to suit the different soil conditions listed. The mixtures are devised to provide a good diversity of shrub species for amenity and wildlife benefits.

Key to Table A8.1, categories 1 to 22

1. Thicket scrub on acidic and neutral soils
   Soil reaction — neutral to moderately acidic.
   Soil type   — various loams, sands, clays, etc.
2. Thicket scrub on alkaline soils
   Soil reaction — slightly to extremely alkaline with free calcium carbonate present.
   Soil type   — various loams, sands, clays, etc. especially over calcareous materials.

3. Hawthorn scrub on acidic soils
   Soil reaction — neutral to moderately acidic.
   Soil type — wide range of soil types including loams, sands, clays, silt, gravel, alluvium, etc.
4. Hawthorn scrub on clay
   Soil reaction — neutral, slightly acidic or alkaline.
   Soil type — dense clay.
5. Hawthorn scrub on alkaline soils
   Soil reaction — neutral to strongly alkaline with free calcium carbonate present.
   Soil type — wide range of soil types including loams, sands, clays, etc.
6. Birch scrub on upland heath
   Soil reaction — strongly acidic.
   Soil type — thin siliceous, sandy, rocky and peaty soils.
7. Birch scrub on dry acidic soil or lowland heath
   Soil reaction — slightly to strongly acidic.
   Soil type — thin sandy soils, podsols, gravel and stony materials.
8. Birch scrub on neutral soil
   Soil reaction — neutral, slightly acidic or slightly alkaline.
   Soil type — thin soils over rock and infertile subsoils, gravels, stony materials and sands.
9. Birch scrub on alkaline soils
   Soil reaction — alkaline with free calcium carbonate present.
   Soil type — thin calcareous sandy, clay and stony materials.
10. Birch scrub on marshy soil
    Soil reaction — slightly acidic, neutral or alkaline.
    Soil type — various thin and poor soils under wet, poorly drained conditions.
11. Gorse scrub on acidic/heathy soils
    Soil reaction — moderately to extremely acidic.
    Soil type — sandy, gravelly, peaty soils and sandy clays.
12. Gorse scrub on neutral or basic soils
    Soil reaction — neutral or alkaline with some calcium carbonate present.
    Soil type — various soils including sands, gravels, clays, silts, alluvium, etc.
13. Hazel scrub on acidic soils
    Soil reaction — slightly to moderately acidic.
    Soil type — various types including sands, clays, gravels, peaty soils, etc.
14. Hazel scrub on neutral or basic soils
    Soil reaction — neutral or alkaline with calcium carbonate present.
    Soil type — various soils including loams, sands, clays, silts, etc.
15. Hazel scrub on wet or streamside soils
    Soil reaction — slightly acidic, neutral or alkaline.
    Soil type — various including sand, clays, silt, loams, etc.
16. Willow scrub on acidic soils
    Soil reaction — slightly to moderately acidic.
    Soil type — various soils including sands, gravels, clays, silt, stony materials, wastes, etc. under dry or damp conditions.
17. Willow scrub on wet acidic soils
    Soil reaction — slightly to strongly acidic.
    Soil type — various soils including sands, gravels, clays, silt, stony materials, peaty soils and wastes under waterlogged conditions.

18. Willow scrub on neutral or basic soils
    Soil reaction — neutral or alkaline with calcium carbonate present.
    Soil type — various soils including sands, clays, silt, alluvium, wastes, etc. under dry or damp conditions.
19. Willow scrub or wet basic soil
    Soil reaction — neutral to alkaline with calcium carbonate present.
    Soil type — various sands, clays, loams, wastes, etc. under water-logged conditions.
20. Blackthorn scrub on acidic and neutral soils
    Soil reaction — neutral to moderately acidic.
    Soil type — various soils including sands, clays, loams, etc. under dry or damp conditions.
21. Blackthorn scrub on basic soils
    Soil reaction — alkaline with calcium carbonate present.
    Soil type — various loams, sands, clays, etc.
22. Blackthorn scrub on wet soils and by streams
    Soil reaction — slightly acidic, neutral or alkaline.
    Soil type — various loams, sands, clays, silts, etc. under wet conditions or near water table.

Table A8.1 Recommended scrub mixtures. Recommended proportions (%) in 22 scrub mixtures for different conditions

Species	1	2	3	4	5	6	7	8	9	10	11	12	13	14	15	16	17	18	19	20	21	22
Alnus glutinosa (alder)										9												
Betula pendula (silver birch)						10	30	40	30	16						5		4				
B. pubescens (downy birch)							40	10	12	20	40				3		8		6			
Corylus avellana (hazel)	15	8	6	7	4	4	6	6	4	5		2	70	60	70	6	7	6	7	3	3	5
Crataegus monogyna (hawthorn)	15	12	40	45	35		7	6	4			2	5	3		6		3		2	2	
Cytisus scoparius (broom)	10	8	5	4			6	4			7	8										
Euonymus europaeus (spindle tree)					2				2												1	
Frangula alnus (alder buckthorn)			2		1					4							4		2		2	
Ilex aquifolium (holly)	10	10	6	7	6	6	7	4	3						5			4				
Juniperus communis (juniper)						2			1													
Ligustrum vulgare (privet)					2				2								2	2			1	2
Prunus padus (bird cherry)					3								3	4							2	4
P. spinosa (blackthorn)	10	10	7	8	7			4	6	4		7		6	5			7	6	65	65	65
Rhamnus catharticus (common blackthorn)		8			2				2				2				2	2		2		
Rosa spp. (wild roses)	15	10	7	7	7		6	3	4	3	4	6	7	6	4	6	6	5	6	10	6	7
Rubus fruticosus agg. (bramble)	15	10	7	5	5	5	5	5	4	3	4	3	4	3	3	6	5	5	5	7	5	7
Salix aurita (eared sallow)						3									2							
S. caprea (goat willow)			6	5	5	7	5	4	3	3			3	3	2	45	15	40	15	2	2	2
S. cinerea (common sallow)			3	2	2			2	2	6					3	15	50	12	30			2
S. pentandra (bay willow)					1														3			
S. phylicifolia (tea-leaved willow)		2				3																

Species	1	2	3	4	5	6	7	8	9	10	11	12	13	14	15	16	17	18	19	20	21	22
S. purpurea (purple willow)					1				1	2									3			
S. triandra (almond willow)					1					2									3			
S. viminalis (osier)					1																	
Sambucus nigra (elder)			3	3					2	2				3	3			3	4		1	2
Sorbus aucuparia (rowan)						12	8		5	4				7	4							
Taxus baccata (yew)					2																	
Thelycrania sanguinea (dogwood)		8			2				2					2				2			2	
Ulex europaeus (gorse)	10	8	6	4	3	10	8				85	70								8	2	
Viburnum lantana (wayfaring tree)		8			2				2					2				2	2		2	
V. opulus (guelder rose)		3	3		3			3	2	3		2	4	3	3	4	5	3	4	3	2	4

Appendix 9 Woodland planting mixtures

Based on recommendations from Dr R. Gemmell, Ecologist, Joint Reclamation Team of the Greater Manchester and Lancashire County Councils (see Appendix 15 for address).

Table A9.1 and the key listed below describe 27 planting mixtures for different types of woodland, based on natural associations of native tree and shrub species. The selection of species and their proportions in each mixture are varied to suit different soil conditions and different situations (as described in the list). For each mixture, the trees and shrubs are tabulated separately and the shrubs content (as a percentage of trees) is given in the following list. The inclusion of shrubs provides an understorey and structural diversity. The mixtures are devised to allow successional changes to occur so that development requires minimal management.

Key to Table A9.1, categories 1 to 27

1. Pedunculate oakwood on acidic clay soil
   Soil reaction — slightly to moderately acidic.
   Soil type — heavy clay soils or clay subsoil.
   Situation — lowland areas, valley bottoms, low hills and lower slopes of uplands.
   Ground flora — acidic grassland and grass/herb communities rather species-poor.
   Shrub content — high (over 20%).

2. Pedunculate oakwood on neutral loamy soil
   Soil reaction — neutral, slightly acidic or slightly alkaline.
   Soil type — moist soils including deep heavy loams, slightly sandy loams, clayey loams and alluvium.
   Situation — mainly lowland areas and valleys.
   Ground flora — neutral grass/herb communities, moderately species-rich.
   Shrub content — high (over 20%).

3. Pedunculate oakwood on neutral clay soil
   Soil reaction   —   neutral, slightly acidic or slightly alkaline.
   Soil type   —   moist, heavy clays or clayey loams.
   Situation   —   lowland areas, valley bottoms, low hills and lower slopes of uplands.
   Ground flora   —   neutral grass/herb communities, moderately species-rich.
   Shrub content   —   high (over 20%).

4. Pedunculate oakwood on calcareous clay soil
   Soil reaction   —   alkaline with some calcium carbonate present.
   Soil type   —   moist clay soils and heavy clay soils.
   content.
   Situation   —   lowland areas, valley bottoms, low hills and lower slopes of uplands.
   Ground flora   —   calcicolous and neutral grass/herb communities, very species-rich.
   Shrub content   —   high (over 20%).

5. Pedunculate oakwood alkaline loam
   Soil reaction   —   neutral or alkaline.
   Soil type   —   various loamy soils, silts, alluvium, including deep and damp loams.
   Situation   —   mainly lowland areas, valleys and lower slopes.
   Ground flora   —   calcicolous and neutral grass/herb communities, moderately or very species-rich.
   Shrub content   —   high (over 20%).

6. Sessile oakwood on upland heathy soil
   Soil reaction   —   strongly acidic.
   Soil type   —   wet, peaty and shallow siliceous soils.
   Situation   —   upland areas and hillsides under high rainfall.
   Ground flora   —   acidic heath including *Deschampsia flexuosa* (wavy hair grass), *Nardus stricta* (mat grass), *Calluna vulgaris* (common ling), *Vaccinium myrtillus* (bilberry), *Pteridium aquilinum* (bracken), *Molinia caerulea* (purple moor grass), etc.
   Shrub content   —   low (10%).

7. Sessile oakwood on dry acidic soil
   Soil reaction   —   slightly and moderately acidic.
   Soil type   —   dry, light sandy and loamy soils, gravels and sandy clays with good drainage.
   Situation   —   lowland areas under medium rainfall and on dry hillsides.
   Ground flora   —   acidic grassland including *Holcus mollis* (creeping soft grass), *Agrostis tenuis* (browntop bent), *Pteridium aquilinum* (bracken), etc.
   Shrub content   —   high (over 20%).

8. Sessile oakwood on moist, acidic soils
   Soil reaction   —   slightly and moderately acidic.
   Soil type   —   damp, slightly peaty and shallow siliceous soils.
   Situation   —   hilly areas under medium rainfall and at medium altitude.

Ground flora — acidic grassland with some heath species including *Deschampsia flexuosa* (wavy hair grass), *Nardus stricta* (mat grass), *Agrostis tenuis* (browntop bent), *Festuca ovina* (sheep's fescue), *Calluna vulgaris* (common ling) and *Pteridium aquilinum* (bracken).

Shrub content — high (over 20%).

9. Sessile oakwood on wet soil or under high rainfall
   Soil reaction — neutral, slightly acidic or slightly basic.
   Soil type — various, including loams, sands, alluvium, shale, clayey and peaty soils.
   Situation — streamsides, flashes and upland high rainfall areas.
   Ground flora — neutral grass/herb communities, fairly species-rich with rushes and marsh plants often present.
   Shrub content — high (over 20%).

10. Sessile oakwood on neutral soil
    Soil reaction — neutral, slightly acidic or slightly basic.
    Soil type — various soils, particularly damp loams, alluvium, shales, humus-rich soils, but also sandy and clayey conditions.
    Situation — valley bottoms and lowland areas.
    Ground flora — neutral grass/herb communities, moderately species-rich.
    Shrub content — high (over 20%).

11. Mixed oakwood on acidic sandy soils
    Soil reaction — slightly to extremely acidic.
    Soil type — sandy soils, particularly deep soils with good drainage.
    Situation — lowland areas and in valleys.
    Ground flora — acidic grassland and acid heath species including *Holcus mollis* (creeping soft grass), *Agrostis tenuis* (browntop bent), *Deschampsia flexuosa* (wavy hair grass), *Pteridium aquilinum* (bracken) and *Calluna vulgaris* (common ling).
    Shrub content — high (over 20%).

12. Mixed oakwood on neutral sandy soils
    Soil reaction — neutral, slightly alkaline or slightly acidic.
    Soil type — sandy soils, particularly deep soils with good drainage.
    Situation — lowland and valley areas.
    Ground flora — neutral grass/herb communities, variable in composition but may be fairly species-rich in places and species-poor elsewhere.
    Shrub content — medium (15-20%).

13. Beechwood on acidic heathy soils
    Soil reaction — moderately acidic.
    Soil type — sandy, fine gravels and silts, particularly podsols.
    Situation — lowland areas, valley bottoms, lower slopes of hills and valley sides.
    Ground flora — acidic grassland and heath including *Deschampsia flexuosa* (wavy hair grass), *Agrostis tenuis* (browntop bent), *Calluna vulgaris* (common ling), *Pteridium*

aquilinum (bracken), etc.

Shrub content — medium (15-20%).

14. Beechwood on neutral or slightly acidic soils

Soil reaction — neutral or slightly acidic.

Soil type — various loams, particularly deep soils and loams based on silt and alluvium.

Situation — mainly lowland areas, valley bottoms and lower slopes of valley sides.

Ground flora — various neutral and acidic grass/herb communities, sometimes poorly developed but often species-rich.

Shrub content — medium (15-20%).

15. Beechwood on calcareous loam

Soil reaction — alkaline with free calcium carbonate present.

Soil type — various types of loam derived from calcareous materials, including deep and shallow soils, damp and dry conditions.

Situation — lowland areas, valley bottoms and lower slopes.

Ground flora — generally poorly developed because of shading but variable and often species-rich in open areas and when canopy opens out.

Shrub content — medium (15-20%).

16. Ashwood on calcareous soil

Soil reaction — alkaline with free calcium carbonate present.

Soil type — various loams overlying or derived from calcareous materials including shallow soils with various moisture regimes.

Situation — upland and lowland areas under various conditions of exposure and rainfall.

Ground flora — extremely well-developed and very rich in species including many calcicoles.

Shrub content — very high (over 25%).

17. Pinewood on acidic soils

Soil reaction — moderately acidic.

Soil type — various soils, particularly sandy, peaty and siliceous soils.

Situation — upland and lowland areas under high and low rainfall, including exposed sites.

Ground flora — species-poor heathy vegetation of acidic grasses including *Deschampsia flexuosa* (wavy hair grass), *Calluna vulgaris* (common ling) and *Pteridium aquilinum* (bracken).

Shrub content — low (10-15%).

18. Birchwood on upland heath

Soil reaction — markedly acidic.

Soil type — damp, peaty, sandy and siliceous soils.

Situation — hilly areas and moorlands, often with high rainfall.

Ground flora — acidic grasses and heath species, species-poor, with *Deschampsia flexuosa* (wavy hair grass), *Nardus stricta* (mat grass), *Calluna vulgaris* (common ling), etc.

Shrub content — medium (15-20%).

19. Birchwood on dry acidic soils
    Soil reaction   — moderately acidic.
    Soil type   — dry, sandy soils and podsols with good drainage.
    Situation   — lowland areas and hillsides.
    Ground flora   — acidic grassland including *Deschampsia flexuosa* (wavy hair grass), *Agrostis tenuis* (browntop bent), *Festuca ovina* (sheep's fescue), *Calluna vulgaris* (common ling), etc.
    Shrub content   — medium (15-20%).

20. Birchwood on neutral soil
    Soil reaction   — neutral, slightly acidic or slightly alkaline.
    Soil type   — various loams, sands, clays, etc. including dry and moist soils.
    Situation   — lowland and hilly areas including valley bottoms, valley sides, low hills and lower slopes of uplands.
    Ground flora   — well-developed and fairly species-rich but variable.
    Shrub content   — high (over 20%).

21. Birchwood on marshy soil
    Soil reaction   — neutral, slightly alkaline or slightly acidic.
    Soil type   — various loams, sands, silts, alluvium and clays under wet, poorly drained conditions.
    Situation   — upland and lowland areas, especially valley bottoms and near open water.
    Ground flora   — well-developed and often species-rich, with neutral species and rushes, etc.
    Shrub content   — high (over 20%).

22. Birchwood on alkaline soils
    Soil reaction   — alkaline, with free calcium carbonate present.
    Soil type   — various loams, sands, clays, etc. including fen peat.
    Situation   — mostly lowland areas and valley bottoms but on hills and slopes where calcareous materials occur.
    Ground flora   — well-developed and species-rich with calcicolous plants often present.
    Shrub content   — high (over 20%).

23. Alderwood on wet acidic or neutral soils
    Soil reaction   — slightly acidic or neutral.
    Soil type   — various loams, sands, silts, alluvium and clayey soils under wet, poorly drained conditions or marsh.
    Situation   — upland and lowland areas, particularly near ponds, streams, rivers, etc.
    Ground flora   — well-developed and fairly species-rich, with rushes and marsh flora.
    Shrub content   — medium (15-20%).

24. Alderwood on wet alkaline soil
    Soil reaction   — alkaline with free calcium carbonate present.
    Soil type   — various loams, sandy clays, etc. under poorly drained conditions or marsh and including fen peat.
    Situation   — mainly lowland areas and valleys including flushes and by flowing and still water.

Ground flora — well-developed and very species-rich with rushes, marsh flora and calcicoles present.

Shrub content — medium (15-20%).

25. Pioneer birch-alder woodland

Soil reaction — moderately acidic, neutral or alkaline.

Soil type — industrial wastes (colliery spoil, blast furnace slag, quarry wastes, etc.), mineral workings and extremely infertile, wet and stony soils.

Situation — upland and lowland areas under various conditions of exposure and rainfall.

Ground flora — nil, weed flora, naturally colonised acidic, neutral or basic grassland, or planted low or nil maintenance grassland or grass-clover mixtures.

Shrub content — high (over 20%).

26. Pioneer birch-oak woodland

Soil reaction — very acidic, neutral or alkaline.

Soil type — industrial wastes (colliery spoil, blast furnace slag, quarry wastes, etc.), mineral workings and extremely infertile, stony or dry soils).

Situation — upland and lowland areas under various conditions of exposure and rainfall.

Ground flora — nil, weed flora, naturally colonised acidic, neutral or basic grassland, or planted low or nil maintenance grassland or grass-clover mixtures.

Shrub content — high (over 20%).

27. Pioneer birch-oak-alder woodland

Soil reaction — moderately acidic, neutral or alkaline.

Soil type — industrial wastes (colliery spoil, blast furnace slag, quarry wastes, etc.), mineral workings and extremely infertile soils of variable moisture content.

Situation — upland and lowland areas under various conditions of exposure and rainfall.

Ground flora — nil, weed flora, naturally colonised acidic, neutral or basic grassland, or planted low or nil maintenance grassland or grass-clover mixtures.

Shrub content — high (over 20%).

Table A9.1 Recommended woodland mixtures. Recommended proportions (%) in 27 woodland mixtures for different conditions

Trees species	1	2	3	4	5	6	7	8	9	10	11	12	13	14	15	16	17	18	19	20	21	22	23	24	25	26	27
Alnus glutinosa (alder)	8	5	7	5	4		5	10	12	5	4	5	5	5	5	4	4	3	2	4	7	3	60	50	40	4	20
Betula pendula (silver birch)	7	5			6	5	10	5		3	18	5	10	15	5	4	8	25	75	45	20	40	5	6	15	40	25
B. pubescens (downy birch)	7	2	5	6		10	5	10	10		4	8		4	2	6	40			18	45	25	10	10	25	30	20
Carpinus betulus (hornbeam)	6	4	6	5	2		3		3		4		3	4													
Fagus sylvatica (beech)		2		3	2						6		4	25	24	22											
Fraxinus excelsior (ash)	10	15	12	15	20			14	6		6		10	15	55						3	6	4	5	14		
Pinus sylvestris (Scots pine)												4	3	2	2	1		55	2	2							
Populus canescens (grey poplar)		2	3	3	2				3	2			1	2							2	2	1	3	5		

Trees species	1	2	3	4	5	6	7	8	9	10	11	12	13	14	15	16	17	18	19	20	21	22	23	24	25	26	27
P. nigra (black poplar)									3					1	1					1	2	1	3	3			
P. tremula (aspen)	6	4	6	4	4		4	5	7	3	4	5	5	3	4	5	6	4	3	5	3	5	5	3	5	3	5
Prunus avium (wild cherry)		5	4	6	4				4		4		3	5	4					4		3					
Quercus robur (pedunculate oak)	45	45	45	40	40						20	30	10	18	16						4	4	3	3	10	8	10
Q. petraea (sessile oak)						65	55	55	40	55	25	16	20			4	6	10	6	4						10	15
Salix alba (white willow)									3					1	1					1	4	1	3	3			
S. fragilis (crack willow)	4	3	3	2	2				4		3		2		2					1	5	2	3	3			
Sorbus aria (whitebeam)		6		8	3								4	4	3	5	12			4		3					
S. aucuparia (rowan)	7	6		9		20	18	15		4	16	15	10	15	8	8	8	15	16	15	10		10		5	5	5
S. torminalis (wild service tree)		2	3	3	2									1	2												

Shrub species	1	2	3	4	5	6	7	8	9	10	11	12	13	14	15	16	17	18	19	20	21	22	23	24	25	26	27
Acer campestre (field maple)		12	12	8	10				5				4	5	7					3							
Corylus avellana (hazel)	18	12	14	14	12		14	14	16	14	14	12	10	10		6	12	15	10	10	10	10	8	8	10	5	5
Crataegus monogyna (hawthorn)	30	14	20	17	16		24	14	13	16	24	25	18	20	18	18			20	20	6	16	4	5	20	40	35
Cytisus scoparius (broom)						2	3	4									6										
Euonymus europaeus (spindle tree)				2	2									2	2						2						
Frangula alnus (alder buckthorn)									1	2	2	2		2						2	4	2	2	3			
Ilex aquifolium (holly)	7	6	6	5	5		12	10		8	14	8	18	10	8	7	15	10	15	9		9					
Juniperus communis (juniper)													2				5		2								
Ligustrum vulgare (privet)		2		2	2									2	2	2					2	2		3			
Malus sylvestris (crab-apple)	3	3	3	3	3					3		5		3	2												
Prunus padus (bird cherry)		5							6	4				2	7												
P. spinosa (blackthorn)	4	5	5	8	8		3		6	5		10		4	6	12				9	8	9	6	8	10	10	10
Rhamnus catharticus (common buckthorn)				2	2									2	2						2		4				
Rosa spp. (wild roses)	6	5	5	5	5		10	7	5		5	10	8	8	5	5	7		10	8	4	6	5	5			
Rubus fruticosus (bramble)	6	5	5	5	5	20	10	10	6		6	10		8	14	14	10	4		10	10	8	5	8	5	5	
Salix aurita (eared sallow)		2				3	1	2		1							5										
S. caprea (goat willow)	15	8	8	6		6	25	20	15	15	10	15	12	18	14	12		7	45	30	20	12	10	12	18	14	30
S. cinerea (common sallow)	5	4	5	4	4	20		10	22	7	8	5	10	6	5		3	20	20	6	20	5	25	20	30	20	20
S. pentandra (bay willow)		2	2		1				2	1										1	2	1	3	2			
S. purpurea (purple willow)																				1	3	1	3	3			
S. repens (creeping willow)				1	1																						
S. triandra (almond willow)		1		1	1						1									1	3	1	3	2			
S. viminalis (osier)		2	1	2	3				2	2											6	3	8	4			
Sambucus nigra (elder)		4	4	4	4					5		5		3	6	4				5	6	5	6	5			
Taxus baccata (yew)		2	2	1	1						3	2		2	2	2						1					
Thelycrania sanguinea (dogwood)				2	2										2	2							3				
Ulex europaeus (gorse)						30	3	6									15	10	7								
Viburnum lantana (wayfaring tree)				3	2										2	2							2	3			
V. opulus (guelder rose)	6	6	8	5	5			7	5	5				3	3					5	8			4	6		

Appendix 10 List of food plants for a wildlife garden

A. Plants for insects (see also Table 6.11 for numbers of invertebrate species associated with different trees and shrubs)

Plant	Nectar	Notes (B) = butterfly
(i) Shrubs		
Calluna spp. (ling, heather)	Aug-Sept	
Crataegus spp. (hawthorns)	May-June	Food plant for larvae of many moths and other invertebrates
Erica spp. (heaths)	Aug-Sept	
Frangula alnus (alder buckthorn)	May-June	
Hedera helix (ivy)	Sept-Nov	Attracts holly blue (B). Holly leaf miner provides winter food for birds
Ilex aquifolium (holly)	May-Aug	Attracts holly blue (B)
Lonicera periclymenum (honeysuckle)	Jun-Sept	Night-scented for moths
Prunus avium (wild cherry)	Apr-May	
P. spinosa (blackthorn)	Mar-April	Larval food plant for black hairstreak (B) and some moths
Rhamnus catharticus (buckthorn)	May-June	Larval food plant for brimstone (B)
Rubus fruticosus agg. (bramble)	May-Sept	Larval food plant for green hairstreak (B) and many species of invertebrate
Salix spp. (willows and sallows)	March-May	Larval food plants for Camberwell beauty (*S. fragilis*), purple emperor (*S. caprea*) (B) and many moths, e.g. eyed hawk
(ii) Herbs		
Ajuga reptans (bugle)	May-July	
Alliaria petiolata (garlic mustard)	Apr-Jun	Larval food plant for whites and orange tip (B)
Cardamine pratensis (ladies smock)	Apr-Jun	Larval food plant for orange tip (B)
Centaurea spp. (knapweeds)	July-Sept	
Chamaenerion angustifolium (rosebay willowherb)	Jun-Sept	Larval food plant for elephant hawk moth
Cirsium arvense (creeping thistle)	July-Sept	Larval food plant for painted lady (B)
Eupatorium cannabinum (hemp agrimony)	July-Sept	
Fragaria vesca (wild strawberry)	Apr-July	Larval food plant for grizzled skipper (B)
Knautia arvensis (field scabious)	May-Sept	
Lotus corniculatus (bird's-foot trefoil)	May-Sept	Larval food plant for common blue and dingy skipper (B)

Origanum vulgare (marjoram)	July-Sept	
Oenothera biennis (evening primrose)	July-Sept	Night-scented for moths
Primula vulgaris (primrose)	Feb-May	
Prunella vulgaris (self heal)	June-Sept	
Reseda lutea (mignonette)	June-Oct	
Saponaria officinalis (soapwort)	July-Sept	Night-scented for moths
Rumex spp. (docks)	—	Larval food plants for small copper (B)
Silene noctiflora (night scented catchfly)	July-Sept	Night-scented for moths, as are most *Silene* species
Solidago canadensis (goldenrod)	Aug-Oct	
Taraxacum officinale (dandelion)	Mar-Aug	
Thymus drucei (thyme)	June-Aug	
Trifolium spp. (clovers)	May-Oct	Larval food plants for common blue (B)
Urtica dioica (stinging nettle)	—	Larval food plant for small tortoiseshell, peacock, red admiral, painted lady, comma (B)
Vicia spp. (vetches)	—	Larval food plants for blues (B)
Viola spp. (violets)	Apr-July	Larval food plants for fritillaries (B)

(iii) Grasses Examples:

Agrostis tenuis (common bent)	Grasses provide food for the
Anthoxanthum odoratum (sweet vernal grass)	larvae of large skipper, small
Festuca rubra (red fescue)	skipper, wall, meadow brown,
Holcus lanatus (Yorkshire fog)	gatekeeper, small heath, ringlet,
Poa annua (annual meadow grass)	grayling and speckled wood (B)

B. Plants for birds and mammals

Plant	Seed/fruit	Notes (Bi) = birds eat fruit
(i) Trees		
Alnus glutinosa (alder)	Oct-Nov	(Bi)
Betula spp. (birches)	Jul-Aug	(Bi)
Fagus sylvatica (beech)	Sept-Oct	Seed taken by rodents (Bi)
Fraxinus excelsior (ash)	Sept-Oct	Seed taken by rodents (Bi)
Pinus sylvestris (Scots pine)	Nov-Jan	(Bi)
Quercus spp. (oaks)	Sept-Oct	Acorns taken by rodents and jays (Bi)
(ii) Shrubs		
Berberis vulgaris (barberry)	Sept-Oct	(Bi)
Buxus sempervirens (box)	Jun-Aug	Evergreen; good nesting cover and winter-roosting cover
Cornus sanguinea (dogwood)	Sept	Calcareous soils (Bi)
Corylus avellana (hazel)	Sept-Oct	Nuts taken by rodents (Bi)
Crataegus spp. (hawthorns)	Sept	Thorny; good nesting cover; rodents take berries (Bi)

Euonymus europaeus (spindle)	Sept-Oct	Calcareous soils; poisonous (Bi)
Frangula alnus (alder buckthorn)	Aug-Nov	Better on acid soils (Bi)
Ilex aquifolium (holly)	Sept-Dec	Thorny evergreen; good cover and for winter-roosting birds (Bi)
Ligustrum vulgare (privet)	Sept-Oct	Evergreen; calcareous soils (Bi)
Lonicera periclymenum (honeysuckle)	Aug-Sept	(Bi)
Malus sylvestris (crab-apple)	Sept-Oct	(Bi)
Prunus avium (gean)	June-Sept	(Bi)
P. padus (bird cherry)	July-Sept	(Bi)
P. spinosa (blackthorn)	Oct	Thorny; good nesting cover (Bi)
Rhamnus catharticus (buckthorn)	July-Sept	Does well on chalk (Bi)
Rosa spp. (roses)	Aug-Nov	Thorny; good nesting cover (Bi)
Rubus caesius (dewberry)	Aug-Oct	Basic soils (Bi)
R. idaeus (raspberry)	Jul-Oct	(Bi)
R. fruticosus agg. (bramble)	Aug-Oct	Thorny; good nesting cover (Bi)
Sambucus nigra (elder)	Aug-Nov	Nutrient-rich soils (Bi)
Sorbus aria (whitebeam)	Sept-Oct	Mainly light soils, does well on chalk (Bi)
S. aucuparia (rowan)	Aug-Sept	Mainly light soils (Bi)
Taxus baccata (yew)	Aug-Sept	Evergreen; calcareous soils, leaves and fruit poisonous (Bi)
Ulex europaeus (gorse)	Jul-Oct	Thorny; good nesting cover
Viburnum lantana (wayfaring tree)	July-Sept	Not on acid soils (Bi)
V. opulus (guelder rose)	Aug-Nov	Neutral or calcareous soils; rodents take berries (Bi)

(iii) Herbs (many species of the *Compositae* and *Umbelliferae* are useful sources of seed for birds)

Anthriscus sylvestris (cow parsley)	June-Aug	(Bi)
Centaurea spp. (knapweeds)	Aug-Oct	Calcareous soil (Bi)
Cirsium spp. (thistles)	July-Sept	Avoid *C. vulgare* and *C. arvense* in flower beds (Bi)
Daucus carota (wild carrot)	July-Sept	Calcareous grassland (Bi)
Dipsacus fullonum (teasel)	Aug-Sept	Clay soils (Bi)
Heracleum sphondylium (hogweed)	July-Sept	Rough grassland (Bi)
Oenothera biennis (evening primrose)	Aug-Oct	Dry soils (Bi)
Papaver spp. (poppies)	July-Sept	Dry, disturbed soils (Bi)
Rumex spp. (docks)	Aug-Oct	Disturbed soils (Bi)
Urtica dioica (stinging nettle)	July-Nov	Nitrogen-rich soil (Bi)

(iv) Grasses Examples:

Agrostis tenuis (common bent)	July-Sept	Grass seeds provide food for many seed-eating birds such as finches and sparrows
Anthoxanthum odoratum (sweet vernal grass)	Jun-Aug	
Festuca rubra (red fescue)	Jun-Aug	
Holcus lanatus (Yorkshire fog)	July-Sept	

Appendix 11 Garden flowers and shrubs for wildlife

A. Flowering plants (herbs) (for nectar)

Antirrhinum majus	snapdragon
Aster novi-belgii	michaelmas daisy
Aubretia deltoidea	aubretia (rock plant)
Callistephus sinensis	Chinese aster
Centranthus ruber	red valerian
Cheiranthus cheiri	wallflower
Foeniculum vulgare	fennel
Helianthus annuus	sunflower
Heliotropium peruvianum	'cherry pie'
Hesperis matronalis	sweet rocket
Iberis spp.	candytufts
Lupinus polyphyllus	lupin
Nepeta mussinii	catmint
Nicotinia affinis	tobacco plant
Petasites fragrans	winter heliotrope
Reseda odorata	mignonette
Sedum spectabile	ice plant
Solidago virgaurea	golden rod
Tropaeolum spp.	nasturtiums
Verbena bonariensis	vervain

B. Shrubs (for nectar and fruit)

Berberis darwinii	barberry*
Buddleia davidii	butterfly bush
Cotoneaster horizontalis	cotoneaster
Hypericum calcycinum	rose of Sharon
Juniperus virginiana	juniper
Mahonia aquifolium	Oregon grape
Philadelphus spp.	mock orange
Photinia villosa	photinia
Primula veris elatior	polyanthus
Pyracantha angustifolia	firethorn
Ribes sanguineum	flowering currant
Rosa rubiginosa	sweet briar
Symphoricarpus rivularis	snowberry
Syringa vulgaris	lilac

* Barberry may be undesirable in some situations as it is a winter host for a virulent agricultural fungal pest — wheat rust

Appendix 12 Pesticides

There is an extensive literature on the dangers of pesticides (poisons for the control of insects and other 'pests') and there is a bewildering array of such poisons on the market. Most will fall into the following categories:

Insecticides — toxic to insects
Molluscicides — toxic to molluscs (slugs and snails)
Rodenticides — toxic to rodents (mice, rats, etc.)
Bird deterrents — to keep birds away from crops
Fungicides — toxic to fungi
Timber preservatives — toxic to fungi and wood-boring insects
Herbicides (weedkillers) — toxic to plants

Some pesticides are classed as selective, meaning that they are more or less specific, only killing the target species. Others are termed 'broad spectrum', killing many species within a target group.

Understandably, opinions vary on the values and dangers of pesticide use. The main identified dangers are:

— The effects on harmless, non-target species (and people) coming into accidental contact with the pesticides.
— The build-up of toxic residues in the environment and the continual problems of pesticide resistance building up in the pest populations, resulting in a continual need to use higher dose rates and to develop new poisons. (It is an unfortunate fact that the types of organism which usually become pests are the common, resilient species. The less common non-pest species tend to be less common because they are less resilient, so only too often, they are the ones to suffer most where pesticides are used.)

A rather worrying view of the risks involved is given in the Friends of the Earth report on pesticides, which illustrates the dangers, not only to wildlife, but to the public, stemming from over use, poorly trained people handling the poisons, residues in foodstuffs, lack of information on the hazards involved and many other problems. There is general agreement between nature conservationists that most pesticides should never be used on wildlife areas. However, some landscape managers do advocate the use of particular herbicides for the management of weed problems where other methods prove to be impractical. The most common uses are:

— to kill stumps;
— to control perennial weeds in new plantings;
— to remove weed competition where no other means is practical;
— to create completely bare ground for the introduction of new plants.

Herbicides

The Ministry of Agriculture, Fisheries and Food (MAFF) produce a 'List of Approved Products and their Uses', which is revised annually. Roberts (1982) is the other main source of information on weed control. Reference to these will give you an outline of the properties of herbicides on the market and recommendations for their 'safe' use within the law. The following are routine precautions to be taken whenever you use herbicides (or any pesticides):

(a) Read the manufacturer's instructions on the label, particularly the safety precautions.
(b) Apply the chemical at the manufacturer's recommended rates only, and at the times specified. It is very easy to make a mistake when diluting chemicals, so take extra care.
(c) Never transfer chemicals to other containers, especially beer or soft drink bottles, and never use empty containers for other purposes.
(d) Close partly-filled containers tightly and lock them away out of the reach of children and animals.
(e) When working on a site, never leave containers of chemicals unattended. Lock them away safely.
(f) Take great care when pouring concentrated liquids. Always wear protective clothing, including gloves and eye-shield. Clean up spillages immediately.
(g) Clean any protective clothing after use and wash exposed parts of the skin thoroughly.
(h) Do not smoke or eat while using the chemicals, or before washing.
(i) Only prepare the amount of chemical required for the area to be treated. This lessens the problem of disposing of unwanted liquid afterwards.
(j) Safely dispose of all used containers. There should be instructions on the label. Some local authorities will collect empty containers which should have been rinsed and punctured. Unwanted liquids should be well diluted and emptied into a foul sewer. Solid products should be sealed into the container and placed in a dustbin. Aerosol containers must not be punctured or overheated, or they may explode. Burning other containers can be dangerous as the smoke may be toxic. Detailed advice is available from the MAFF leaflet 'Guidelines for the Disposal of Unwanted Pesticides and Containers on Farms and Holdings', available from MAFF or the Health and Safety Executive (see Appendix 15 for addresses).
(k) Avoid spray drift on to neighbouring areas and contamination of waterways. Do not spray on windy days. Where small areas are to be treated, use a spot applicator. For application to single plants, some herbicides are available as gels. Specially designed herbicide gloves, wicks and wipes may be used with gels.
(l) Check spraying equipment, especially nozzles, before use and clean all equipment thoroughly afterwards, at the end of the day.

Every worker/volunteer using herbicides needs to understand, and to follow, these precautions, as well as any special precautions which apply to the chemical being used. Proper training and supervision are essential if accidents are to be avoided. With inexperienced operators, a dye should be added to the chemical mixture, so that sprayed areas are visible.

Types of herbicide

(a) *Contact herbicides* are applied to foliage and kill the above-ground parts of plants. They are, therefore, most effective against annuals. If applied to perennials during their maximum growth period (spring and summer), contact herbicides generally reduce the plants' vigour, but do not kill them.
(b) *Translocated herbicides* enter the plant and are circulated (translocated) to all parts. They are, therefore, commonly used to control perennials.

(c) *Residual herbicides* are absorbed by plant roots. They are commonly applied to the soil to kill plants as they germinate. In high doses they can kill all germinating plants and maintain areas of earth completely bare.

Methods of application

(a) Granules — applied around plants, on to (or in to) the soil.
(b) Sprays — using herbicides in wettable powder or liquid form.
(c) Ultra-low volume (ULV) — using very small volumes of non-diluted herbicide and sprayers specially designed to produce very fine mists. Controlled droplet application (CDA) is an example of ULV where the sprayer regulates the size range of spray droplets. Because the herbicide concentration in the mist droplets is so high and because the droplets are so fine, the slightest wind can cause uncontrollable spray drift, and can result in severe damage to non-target areas. For this reason, ULV should never be used in nature conservation management.
(d) Herbicide glove — e.g. the 'Roguing Glove' produced by Monsanto Chemicals for use with the herbicide glyphosate. Individual plants are killed by squeezing them with the herbicide-soaked glove.
(e) Wipe — e.g. the 'Tumbleweeder' produced by Murphy Chemicals, among others, for use with glyphosate. This is a long, tubular stick containing a herbicide-soaked wick. A cartridge of the chemical is attached to one end and the plants are wiped with the moist wick protruding from the other.

Methods of applying herbicide to limited areas, as in (d) and (e) above, are the only real way of making broad spectrum herbicides selective. Careful dosage and timing of application are also very important in this respect.

Examples of herbicides currently in use (MAFF)

(a) *Alloxydim-sodium* — available as 'Clout' from May and Baker. A soluble powder. Selective, translocated.
    Kills annual grasses and suppresses *Agropyron repens* (couch grass) between broad-leaved plants. Most effective in spring and summer.
    Caution Remains toxic to grasses for at least four weeks.
                Irritating to eyes and skin.

(b) *Ammonium sulphamate* — available as 'Amcide' from Battle, Hayward and Bower. A soluble crystal. Non-selective, translocated, soil-acting.
    Kills fast-growing, vigorous species (especially those requiring high uptake of nitrogen) and tree stumps. Kills not by poisoning, but by poor nutrition. The plants take it up as if it were the nutrient ammonium sulphate. After 8-12 weeks the ammonium sulphamate breaks down in the soil to the harmless nutrient ammonium sulphate.
    Caution Trees may be damaged if their roots extend into soil recently treated with ammonium sulphamate.

(c) *2,4-D* — available either as 'ester' or 'amine' formulations from a number of manufacturers. Selective, translocated.
    Kills broad-leaved plants among grasses.
    Caution Ester formulations are used mainly on grassland and turf. Only amine formulations may be used for weed control near to water. Products for use in turf or near water are marked accordingly. Can be harmful to fish. [Application to water-

courses may lead to illegal pollution. Before using in or near to watercourses, read the MAFF *Guidelines for the Use of Herbicides on Weeds in or near Watercourses and Lakes* and *consult* the appropriate water authority.]

(d) *Glyphosate* — available as liquid solutions (or gels); 'Roundup' from Monsanto (for agricultural use only) or as 'Tumbleweed' from Murphy Chemicals (for use in the garden). Non-selective, translocated.
Gives total weed control. Most effective during the active growing season. Often used to spot-treat individual persistent weeds.
Caution Not to be mixed with other chemicals. Irritating to eyes and skin. Harmful to fish. Dangerous near watercourses. [Application to watercourses may lead to illegal pollution, see above.]

(e) *Simazine and Atrazine* — available as granules ('Weedex S2G' from Ciba–Geigy) or as liquid suspensions (e.g. 'Gesatop 500L' from Ciba–Geigy) or wettable powders (e.g. 'Herbazin 50' from Fisons) from a number of manufacturers. Non-selective, soil-acting herbicide.
Used to prevent germination of plants. Applied either post- or pre-emergence.
Caution Can damage certain trees and shrubs or shallow-sown seeds. Consult the manufacturer's list of such plants before use. At least seven months must elapse after application, before sowing or planting. The label should explain any requirements for the disposal of residues.

Relevant publications

Friends of the Earth (FoE) (1984) *Pesticides — The case of an industry out of control*, A5 leaflet
Her Majesty's Stationery Office (HMSO) *Poisons Rules*
Ministry of Agriculture, Fisheries and Food (MAFF) publications:
Approved Products for Farmers and Growers (annual), available from HMSO
Guidelines for the Disposal of Unwanted Pesticides and Containers on Farms and Holdings, available from MAFF and Health & Safety Executive
Guidelines for the Use of Herbicides on Weeds in or Near Watercourses and Lakes, available from HMSO
Roberts, H.A. (ed.) (1982) *Weed Control Handbook*, Blackwell
Royal Society for the Protection of Birds (RSPB) (1982) *Pesticides and the Gardener*, A4 leaflet

List of suppliers

Battle, Hayward and Bower Ltd, Victoria Chemical Works, Crofton Drive, Allenby Road Industrial Estate, Lincoln LN3 4NP. Tel: Lincoln (0522) 29206/7
Ciba–Geigy Agrochemicals, Whittlesford, Cambridge CB2 4QT. Tel: Cambridge (0223) 833621/7
Fisons PLC, Horticulture Division, Paper Mill Lane, Bramford, Ipswich, Suffolk IP8 4BZ. Tel: Ipswich (0473) 830 492. Technical advice: Levington Research Station, Levington, Ipswich, Suffolk IP10 0NG. Tel: Ipswich (0473) 717811
May and Baker Ltd, Agrochemicals Division, Regent House, Hubert Road, Brentwood, Essex CM14 4TZ. Tel: Brentwood (0277) 230522

Monsanto PLC, Agricultural Division, Thames Tower, Burleys Way, Leicester LE1 3TP. Tel: Leicester (0533) 20864

Murphy Chemical Ltd, Latchmore Court, Brand Street, Hitchin, Herts. SG5 1HZ. Tel: Hitchin (0462) 57272

Appendix 13 Aquatic invertebrates as indicators of water pollution level

Record sheet for a pond

Group 1 factor x 4

		(X)	(Y)
Mayfly nymphs	H		
Caddis larvae	H		
Shrimps			
freshwater	F		
fairy	F		
Polyzoans	F		
Sponges	F		
Stonefly nymphs	C		
Flatworms	C		
Newts/tadpoles	C		
Frogs/tadpoles	C		
Toad/tadpoles	C		

Group 2 factor x 3

		(X)	(Y)
Ramshorn snails	H		
Orb/pea shells	F		
Dragonfly nymphs			
Libellulid	C		
Aeschnid	C		
Damselfly	C		
Greater water boatman	C		
Beetles and larvae			
Greater diving	C		
Lesser diving	C		
Whirligig	C		
Other beetles/larvae	C		
Mites	C		
Fish	C		

Group 3 factor x 2

		(X)	(Y)
Great pond snails	C		
Other pond snails	H		
Moth larvae	H		
Water louse	F		
Alderfly larvae	C		
Lesser water boatman	F		
Water flea			
Cladocerans	F		
Copepods	F		
Ostracods	F		
Leeches	C		
Water bugs			
Water cricket	C		
Pond measurer	C		
Pond skater	C		
Water scorpion	C		
Water stick insect	C		

Group 4 factor x 1

		(X)	(Y)
Worms			
Tubiflex	F		
Stylaria	F		
Others	F		
Fly larvae			
Chironomids red/green	F		
Chironomids gel. sac.	F		
Phantom midge	C		
Dicranota	C		
Cranefly, etc.	F		
Mosquito/gnat	F		
Dixa	F		
Other	F		
Totals			

Record sheet for stream animals

This sheet is used in the same way as that for the pond, to calculate the water quality score.

Group 1 factor x 4

		(X)	(Y)
Shrimps, freshwater	F		
Stonefly nymphs	C		
Mayfly nymphs	H		
Caddis			
silk case (*Agraylea*)	H		
stone cases	H		
tube case (*Limneph.*)	H		
free living	H		
Flatworms	C		

Group 3 factor x 2

		(X)	(Y)
Midge, larvae/blood worms	C		
Wandering snail	H		
Water louse	F		
Alder fly larvae	C		
Leech (*Glossiphonia*)	C		
Leech (*Erpobdella*)	C		
Leech, other species	C		
Beetles and larvae	C		

Group 2 factor x 3

		(X)	(Y)
Limpet	H		
Jenkins' spire shell	H		
Ramshorn snails	H		
Orb or pea shells	F		
Blackfly	F		
Boatmen			
lesser	F		
greater	C		
Pond skater	C		
Red mites	C		
Fish	C		

PO4 mg/litre*			
NO3 mg/litre*			
Conductivity*			

Group 4 factor x 1

		(X)	(Y)
Cranefly larvae	F		
Other fly or gnat larvae	F		
Red worms (*Tubifex*)	F		
Sewage fungus	—		

*A local school or college may be able to help measure these factors.

Key

In the first column (X) use code letters or code numbers for abundance.
These are:

Abundant	A or 10	In the second column (Y) multiply these by the factors. Relative totals
Common	C or 7	give relative score of ecosystem diversity which indicates the water
Frequent	F or 5	quality. This can be called the water quality score.
Occasional	O or 3	
Rare	R or 2	

Note: the numbers are *codes* and not the numbers found. Raw data of actual numbers of individuals cannot be used in the above way, but can be used to give ratios of herbivores (H), filter feeders (F) and carnivores (C). Filter feeders can be arbitrarily split 50/50 between (H) and (C) if desired.

Source: B.V. Cave, Royal Forest of Dean Centre for Environmental Studies, Glos. (Personal communication.)

Appendix 14 Directory of suppliers

Woodlands — forestry equipment

Essex and Chieftain Forge Ltd, Burnside Road, Bathgate, West Lothian. Most forestry equipment

Honey Brothers, New Pond Road, Guildford GU3 1JR. Most forestry equipment

Safety Products Ltd, Holmthorpe Avenue, Redhill, Surrey. Safety gear such as face shields, etc.

S H Rainbow, Summerheath Road, Hailsham, East Sussex. Tubular plastic tree guards and tree ties

Stanton Hope Ltd, 422 Westborough Road, Westcliffe-on-Sea, Essex. Most forestry equipment

Wessenden Products Ltd, Alresford, Hampshire. Spiral plastic tree guards

Wetlands — pond lining materials

Anglo Aquarium Plant Co. Ltd, Wayside, Cattlegate Road, Enfield, London. Tel: 01-363 8548/9. Main distributor of butyl liners for pools

Butylmade Ltd, Lloyds Bank Chambers, High Street, Lingfield, Surrey. Tel: (0342) 834373. Manufacturers of butyl sheeting

Butyl Products Ltd, Radford Crescent, Billericay, Essex. Tel: (02774) 53281. Suppliers of butyl rubber, PVC and Fipec matting

Cement and Concrete Association, Wrexham Springs, Slough SL3 6PL. Tel: (395) 2727

D.I.Y. Plastics Ltd, Suffolk Way, Abingdon, Oxfordshire. Tel: (0235) 3066. Range of pool lining materials

Lotus Water Garden Products, 260/300 Berkhamsted Road, Chesham, Bucks. Tel: (0494) 774451. Lotus PVC liners

Rawell Marketing Ltd, Carr Lane, Holylake, Merseyside L47 4AX. Tel: (051) 632 5771-4. Suppliers of Volclay (bentonite clay) and Rawmat. Water control systems

Robb of St Ives (Water Services) Ltd, East Street, St Ives, Huntingdon PE17 4PB. Tel: (0480) 62150. Membrane installation for reservoirs, lakes, ornamental water, industrial storage, etc.

Sand and gravel — local builders merchants or sand and gravel pits are the best sources for these materials. Ensure that the materials are *not* estuarine. Deposits of salt can destroy the ecological balance of a freshwater pool

Schlegel Lining Technology Ltd, 53 New Street, Chelmsford, Essex CM1 1NG. Tel: (0245) 351005. Suppliers of high-density polythene lining material

Stapeley Water Gardens Ltd, Stapeley, Nantwich, Cheshire. Tel: (0270) 623868. Stapelite butyl pool liners

Stockline Plastics Ltd, Grovepark Mills, Hopehill Road, Glasgow. Tel: (041 332) 9077/9028. Poly-Culture butyl liners

Visqueen Products, ICI Plastics Division, Yarm Road, Stockton-on-Tees, Cleveland TS18 3RD. Tel: (0642) 62288. Suppliers of polythene (phone for list of appointed stockists)

Grassland — mowers

Allen Power Equipment Ltd, The Broadway, Didcot, Oxon. Tel: (0235) 813936.
Also supply sweepers and vacuum cleaners for seed collection

Bartrop (GM) Ltd, Market Place, Highworth, Swindon, Wilts. Tel: (0793)
762400

Bob Andrews Ltd, The Garden Machine Centre, Sunningdale, Berks. Tel: (0990)
21960

Flymo Ltd, Redworth Way, Aycliffe Industrial Estate, Newton Aycliffe, Co.
Durham. Tel: (0325) 315161

Hayters Ltd, Spelbrook, Bishop's Stortford, Herts. CM23 4BU. Tel: (0279)
723444

Helpmate Sweeping Machines, Unit 23, Chiltern Trading Estate, Holmer
Green, Bucks. Tel: (0494) 715544. Also supply sweepers and vacuum
cleaners for seed collection

Suffolk Lawnmowers Ltd, Gipping Works, Stowmarket, Suffolk IP14 1EY. Tel:
(04492) 2183

VICTA (UK) Ltd, Rutterford Road, Daneshill West, Basingstoke, Hants. Tel:
(0256) 50301

Seed suppliers

(A) British seed either collected directly from the wild or harvested from plants
grown from such seed.

John Chambers
15 Westleigh Road
Barton Seagrove
Kettering
Northants. NN15 5AJ
Tel: Kettering (0536) 513748

Emorsgate Seeds
Middle Cottage
Emorsgate
Terrington St Clement
King's Lynn
Norfolk PE34 4NY
Tel: King's Lynn (0553) 829028

Mr Fothergill's Seeds
Regal Lodge
Gazely Road
Kentford
Newmarket
Suffolk CB8 7QB
Tel: (0638) 751161

W.W. Johnson and Sons Ltd
Stells Lane
London Road
Boston
Lincs. PE21 8AD
Tel: (0205) 65051

Kingsfield Tree Nursery
G. & J.E. Peacock
Broadenham Lane
Winsham
Chard
Somerset

Naturescape
Little Orchard
Whatton in the Vale
Notts. NG13 9EP
Tel: Whatton (0949) 51045

Helen McEwen
The Seed Exchange
44 Albion Road
Sutton
Surrey
(please send s.a.e. for catalogue)

Suffolk Herbs
Sawyers Farm
Little Cornard
Sudbury
Suffolk
Tel: Bures (0787) 227247

(B) Tree seed

The Forestry Commission recommend the following suppliers for quality native seeds.

Asmer Seeds Ltd
Ash Street
Leicester
Tel: (0533) 26733

E.F.G. (Nurseries) Ltd
Whitchurch
Shropshire

Tree Seeds of Bamber Bridge
Brindle Road
Bamber Bridge
Preston
Lancashire
Tel: (0772) 311174

(The Commission also supply seed. See Appendix 15 for addresses of Forestry Commission regional offices.)

(C) Suppliers of seed which may or may not be of native British origin.

Augusta Seeds
1-3 Dudley Street
Grimsby
South Humberside DN31 2AW

British Seed Houses Ltd
Bewsey Industrial Estate
Pitt Street
Warrington
Cheshire WA5 5LE
Tel: (0925) 54411

British Seed Houses
Portview Road
Avonmouth
Bristol BS11 9JH
Tel: (0272) 823691

BSH Ltd
No 5 Hanger
Camp Road
Swinderby
Lincs. LN6 9QJ
Tel: (052 286) 714

Gerson & Co (Agricultural) Ltd
Grove Lane
Smethwick
Warley
West Midlands B66 2SE
Tel: (021) 558 3551

Hurst Gunson Cooper Taber Ltd
Avenue Road
Witham
Essex CM8 2DX
Tel: Witham (0376) 3451

Mommersteeg International
Station Road
Finedon
Wellingborough
Northants. NN9 5NT
Tel: Wellingborough (0933) 680 674

Nickersons Seed Specialists Ltd
Field House
Grimsby
Lincs. DN34 45X
Tel: Grimsby (0472) 58021

T. & W. Rimmer
Agricultural Seedsmen
Bickerstaffe Hall
Skelmersdale

Yorkshire
Tel: Skelmersdale (0695) 22023 or 22873

Soil analysis and testing

Chase Compost Seeds Ltd, Bexhall, Saxmundham, Suffolk. Tel: (0728) 21498.
  Home soil test kit
Sudbury Technical Products, London Road, Corwen, Clwyd, Wales. Tel: (0490)
  2502. Sudbury soil test kits and meters
West Meters Ltd, Superdec Buildings, Strand Street, Whitehaven, Cumbria.
  Tel: (0946) 5568. Soil test meters

Hand tools (See also Garden tools for the disabled)

The British Trust for Conservation Volunteers (BTCV), 36 St Mary's Street,
  Wallingford, Oxon. OX10 0EU. Tel: (0491) 39766. Good quality hand tools at
  reduced prices to *affiliated* groups

There are many manufacturers of hand tools and most good hardware shops
should be able to supply all you need.

Garden tools for the disabled

(For further information, contact the Disabled Living Research Unit, Nuffield
Orthopaedic Centre, Headington, Oxford)

Bond Garden Care, QV Sales Ltd, Maidstone Road, Nettleshead, Maidstone,
  Kent ME18 5HP. Grabber hoe and Grabber rake
Odell, Frank and Co. Ltd, Teddington Middlesex. Triggagrip hand tools
Rolcut Ltd, Blatchford Road, Horsham, West Sussex. Tel: (0403) 65997. Seca-
  teurs and shears
Spear and Jackson Ltd, St Paul's Road, Wednesbury, Staffs. WS1 9RA. Tel: (021
  556) 1255. Various tools, including forks and trowels
Standard Manufacturing Co., Rowditch Park, Derby DE1 1ND. Cutting tools,
  pruners, etc.
Stanley Tools Ltd, Woodhouse Mill, Sheffield S13. Forks, hoes, pruners, etc.
Wilkinson Sword Ltd, Sword House, Totteridge Road, High Wycombe, Bucks.
  HP13 6EJ. Tel: (0494) 33300. Forks, hoes, rakes, trowels and various cutting
  tools
Wolf Tools Ltd, Alton Road, Ross-on-Wye, Herefordshire. Tel: (0989) 2905.
  Wide range including spades, hoes, cultivators, powered tools

Wood preservers

(For further information, contact the Countryside Commission for Scotland,
Battleby, Redgorton, Perth PH1 3EW. Tel: (0738) 27921)

B.P. Aquaseal Ltd, Kingsnorth, Hoo, Rochester, Kent. Tel: (0634) 250722
Cementone–Beaver Ltd, Tingwick Road, Buckingham. Tel: (02802) 2561
Cuprinol Ltd, Adderwell, Frome, Somerset. Tel: (0373) 65151
Langlow Products Ltd, P.O. Box 22, Asheridge Road, Chesham, Bucks. Tel:
  (0494) 784866
Rentokil Ltd, Products Division, Felcourt, East Grinstead, West Sussex. Tel:
  (0342) 833022
Solignum Ltd, Thames Road, Crayford, Kent. Tel: (0322) 526966

Timber

Buying timber from a local sawmill or timber yard is generally more economical than going to D.I.Y. shops. It is also worthwhile tailoring your requirements to standard available sizes of timber, avoiding the added cost of cutting it down (or having it cut) to suit your needs.

Hardwoods are usually available in boards of various widths which are machine-planed to standard thicknesses, e.g. 9, 12, 15 or 21 mm. Examples of standard hardwood sections include 21 × 21 mm; 34 × 21 mm; 34 × 34 mm; 46 × 21 mm and 46 × 46 mm.

Softwoods are usually available sawn or planed in boards of standard widths and thicknesses. Sawn timber is cheaper than planed and the planed is obviously slightly smaller than the standard sawn.

Standard sawn board thicknesses: 12, 16, 19, 22 and 25 mm.
Standard sawn board widths: 150, 175, 200 and 225 mm.
Standard planed board thicknesses: 9, 12, 15, 19 and 21 mm.
Standard planed board widths: 150, 175, 200 and 225 mm.
Standard sections (small sawn): 25 × 25 mm; 38 × 25 mm; 38 × 38 mm; 50 × 25 mm and 50 × 50 mm.
If planed, these would be 21 × 21 mm; 34 × 21 mm; 34 × 34 mm; 46 × 21 mm and 45 × 45 mm.
Standard sections (large sawn): 38 × 150 mm; 38 × 225 mm; 50 × 150 mm; 50 × 200 mm; 63 × 200 mm; 75 × 200 mm and 75 × 225 mm.

Check with local dealers to see what standard size timbers they can supply.

Miscellaneous

Alginure Products Ltd, Leyswood House, Groombridge, Tunbridge Wells, Kent TN3 9PH. Tel: Groombridge (089 276) 782. Alginure is a very useful root-dip for enhancing survival when planting trees
A. Gallenkamp, P.O. Box 290, 6 Christopher Street, London EC1. Suppliers of pH indicator paper and other scientific materials and equipment
T. & J. Hutton and Co. Ltd, Phoenix Works, Ridgeway, Nr Sheffield. Suppliers of chain and 'V'-shaped scythes for cutting aquatic vegetation

Appendix 15 Addresses of useful organisations

Advisory Committee for Blind Gardeners, Southern and Western Regional Association for the Blind, 55 Eton Avenue, London NW3 3ET. Tel: 01-586 8079
Advisory Conciliation and Arbitration Service (ACAS), Ayton House, 83-117 Euston Road, London NW1 2RB. Tel: 01-388 3041 (information), 01-388 5100 (general)

Age Concern — Greater London, 54 Knatchbull Road, London SE5. Tel: 01-737 3456

Allotments for the Future, 339a Sherrard Road, Manor Park, London E12 6UH

Amateur Entomologists Society, 355 Hounslow Road, Hanworth, Feltham, Middlesex TW13 5JH

Arboricultural Association, Administration Section (and: Association of British Tree Surgeons and Arborists), Ampfield House, Ampfield, Romsey, Hampshire SO5 9PA. Tel: Braishfield (0794) 68717

Arboricultural Association, Brokerswood House, Brokerswood, Westbury, Wiltshire BA13 4EH

The Assistant Masters and Mistresses Association, 29 Gordon Square, London WC1H 0PX. Tel: 01-388 5861

Association for the Protection of Rural Scotland, 14a Napier Road, Edinburgh EH10 5AY. Tel: (031) 229 1898

Association of Community Technical Aid Centres (ACTAC), Unit B68b, New Enterprise Workshops, South West Brunswick Dock, Liverpool L3 4AR. Tel: (051) 708 7607

Belfast Simon Community, P.O. Box 90, Belfast BT1 1ST

Biological Records Centre, Institute of Terrestrial Ecology, Monks Wood Experimental Station, Abbots Ripton, Huntingdon, Cambs. PE17 2LS. Tel: Abbots Ripton (048 73) 381

Botanical Society of the British Isles, c/o Department of Botany, British Museum (Natural History), Cromwell Road, London SW7 5BD. Tel: 01-589 6323, ext. 701

Botanical Society of Edinburgh, c/o The Royal Botanic Garden, Edinburgh 3

British Arachnological Society (spiders and related species), Stone Rise, 42 Lakeland Park, Keswick, Cumbria CA12 4AT

British Association of Nature Conservationists (BANC), Dept. of Geography, University of Lancaster, Bailrigg, Lancaster LA1 4YR. Tel: (0524) 65201

British Association of Settlements and Social Action Centres (BASSAC), 13 Stockwell Road, London SW9. Tel: 01-733 7428

British Bryological Society, A.R. Perry, Department of Botany, National Museum of Wales, Cardiff CF1 3NP

British Butterfly Conservation Society, Tudor House, Quorn, Loughborough, Leicestershire LE12 8AD. Tel: Loughborough (0509) 42870

British Deer Society, Green Lane, Ufton Nervet, Reading, Berks. RG7 4HA. Tel: (0734) 529 4133. Also: The Mill House, Bishopstraw, Warminster, Wiltshire BA12 9HJ. Tel: (0985) 216608

British Ecological Society, Burlington House, Piccadilly, London W1V 0LQ. Tel: 01-434 2641

British Entomological and Natural History Society, 74 South Audley Street, London W1Y 5FF

British Hedgehog Preservation Society, Knowbury House, Knowbury, Ludlow, Shropshire

British Herpetological Society — see Zoological Society

British Institute of Management, Management House, Parker Street, London WC2. Tel: 01-405 3456

British Insurance Brokers Association, 10 Bevis Marks, London EC3. Tel: 01-623 9043

British Lichen Society, c/o Department of Botany, Natural History Museum, London SW7 5BD

British Mycological Society, Department of Plant Sciences, Wye College, Wye, Ashford, Kent TH25 5AH

British Naturalists Association, Hon. Membership Secretary, 23 Oak Hill Close,

Woodford Green, Essex. Also: 'Willowfield', Boyneswood Road, Four Marks, Alton, Hampshire GU34 5EA and c/o 6 Chancery Lane, The Green, Writtle, Essex CM1 3DY. Tel: (0245) 420 756

British Pteridological Society, 42 Lewisham Road, Smethwick, Warley, West Midlands B66 2BS

British Trust for Conservation Volunteers (BTCV):

Headquarters: 36 St Mary's Street, Wallingford, Oxon. OX10 0EU. Tel: (0491) 39766

North East: Springwell Conservation Centre, Springwell Road, Wrekenton, Gateshead, Tyne and Wear NE9 7AD. Tel: (091) 482 0111

North West: 40 Cannon Street, Preston, Lancs. PR1 3NT. Tel: (0772) 50286

West and North Yorkshire: Hollybush Farm, Broad Lane, Kirkstall, Leeds, Yorkshire. Tel: (0532) 742335

South Yorkshire: Conservation Volunteers Training Centre, Balby Road, Balby, Doncaster DH4 0RH. Tel: (0302) 859522

East Midlands: Conservation Volunteers Training Centre, United Reform Church, Gregory Boulevard, Nottingham. Tel: (0602) 705493/705539

West Midlands: 577 Bristol Road, Selly Oak, Birmingham 29. Tel: (021) 471 2558

Wales: Forest Farm, Forest Farm Road, Whitchurch, Cardiff. Tel: (0222) 626660. Also: Ty Gwydr, Trevelyan Terrace, Bangor, Gwynedd LL57 1AX. Tel: (0248) 354050 and Tyddyn Siarl, Ffordd Eglwys, Llanberis, Gwynedd. Tel: (0286) 872389

East Anglia: Bayfordbury House, Hertford, Herts. SG13 8LO. Tel: (0992) 53067

Thames and Chilterns: 36 St Mary's Street, Wallingford, Oxon. OX10 0EU. Tel: (0491) 39766

South West: Newton Park Estate Yard, Newton St Loe, Bath, Avon. Tel: (02217) 2856

London: 2 Mandela Street (formerly Upper Selous Street), Camden Town, London NW1. Tel: 01-388 3946

South: Hatchlands, East Clandon, Guildford, Surrey GU4 7RT. Tel: (0483) 223294

Northern Ireland: The Pavilion, Cherryvale Park, Ravenhill Road, Belfast BT6 0BZ. Tel: (0232) 645169

Scotland: see Scottish Conservation Projects Trust

British Trust for Ornithology, Beech Grove, Tring, Herts. HP23 5NR. Tel: Tring (044 282) 3461

British Waterfowl Association, 25 Dale Street, Haltwhistle, Northumberland, NE49 9QB. Tel: (0498) 21176

Cambridge Direct Tree Seeding Ltd, 61 Ditton Walk, Cambridge CB5 8QD. Tel: (0223) 60257

Centre for Alternative Technology, Llwyngwern Quarry, Machynlleth Powys, Wales SY20 9AZ. Tel: (0654) 2400

Centre on Environment for the Handicapped, 125 Albert Street, London NW1 7NF. Tel: 01-267 6111

Charities Aid Foundation, 48 Pembury Road, Tonbridge, Kent TN9 2JD. Tel: (0732) 356323

Charities Information Bureau, 161 Corporation Street, Birmingham B4 6PT. Tel: (021) 236 1264

Charity Commissioners for England and Wales:

Southern Office: Charity Commission, 14 Ryder Street, St James's, London SW1Y 6AH. Tel: 01-214 6000

Northern Office (north of a line from the Wash to the Bristol Channel):

Charity Commission, Graeme House, Derby Square, Liverpool L2 7SB. Tel: (051) 227 3191

Central Register: St Albans House, 57/60 Haymarket, London SW1Y 6AH. Tel: 01-214 6000

Charity Trading Advisory Group, 9 Mansfield Place, London NW3 1HS. Tel: 01-794 9835

Child's Play, Francis House, Francis Street, London SW1P 1DE. Tel: 01-828 7364

Churchtown Farm Field Study Centre, Lanlivery, Bodmin, Cornwall PL30 5NN. Tel: (0208) 872148

City Farms Advisory Service — see 'Interchange'

Civic Trust, 17 Carlton House Terrace, London SW1. Tel: 01-930 0914. (Also at this address, the Heritage Education Group and the Town and Country Planning Association)

Civic Trust for the North East, 3 Old Elvet, Durham DH1 3HL. Tel: (0385) 61182

Civic Trust for the North West, Environmental Institute, Greaves School, Bolton Road, Swinton, Manchester M27 2YX. Tel: (061) 794 9314

Civic Trust for Wales, The Welsh Civic Trust, 46 Cardiff Road, Llandaff, Cardiff CF5 2DT. Tel: (0222) 552388

Community Projects Foundation, 60 Highbury Grove, London N5 2AG. Tel: 01-226 5375

Conchological Society of Great Britain and Ireland, 51 Wychwood Avenue, Luton, Bedfordshire LU2 7HT. Tel: Luton (0582) 24801

Conservation Action Project, Peak National Park Study Centre, Losehill Hall, Castleton, Derbyshire S30 2WB. Tel: (0433) 20373

Conservation Foundation, 11a West Halkin Street, London SW1X 8JL. Tel: 01-235 1743

Conservation Society, 12a Guildford Street, Chertsey, Surrey KT16 9BQ. Tel: (09328) 60975

Council for Environmental Conservation (CoEnCo), Zoological Gardens, Regents Park, London NW1 4RY. Tel: 01-722 7111

Council for Environmental Education, University of Reading, School of Education, London Road, Reading RG1 5AQ. Tel: (0734) 875234, ext. 218

Council for Environmental Education — Youth Unit, 45 Shelton Street, London WC2 9HJ. Tel: 01-240 4936

Council for the Protection of Rural England (CPRE), 4 Hobart Place, London SW1 0HY. Tel: 01-235 9481

Council for the Protection of Rural Wales, Ty Gwyn, 31 High Street, Welshpool, Powys SY21 7JP. Tel: (0938) 2525

Council for Urban Studies Centres (CUSC), Streetwork, c/o Notting Dale Urban Studies Centre, 189-191 Freston Road, London W10 6TH. Tel: 01-969 8942

Countryside Commission:

Advisory Services: John Dower House, Crescent Place, Cheltenham, Gloucestershire GL50 3RA. Tel: (0242) 521381

Eastern: Terrington House, 13/15 Hills Road, Cambridge CB2 1NL. Tel: (0223) 354462

Greater London and South East: 25 Savile Row, London W1X 2BT. Tel: 01-734 6010 (Gtr London, Kent, Surrey, Berks., Bucks., Essex, Herts., Oxon., E. Sussex, W. Sussex, Hants., Isle of Wight)

Midlands: Cumberland House, 200 Broad Street, Birmingham B15 1TD. Tel: (021) 632 6503/4 (Shropshire, Staffs., Hereford and Worcs., West Midlands, Warwicks., Derbyshire (except Peaks), Notts., Leics., Northants.)

Northern Office: Warwick House, Grantham Road, Newcastle-upon-Tyne NE2 1QF. Tel: (0632) 328252 (Northumberland, Cumbria, Durham, Tyne and Wear, Cleveland)

North West: 184 Deansgate, Manchester M3 2WB. Tel: (061) 833 0316 (Lancashire, Cheshire, Merseyside, Gtr Manchester and Peak District of Derbyshire)

South West: Bridge House, Sion Place, Clifton Down, Bristol BS8 4AS. Tel: (0272) 739966 (Glos., Avon, Wilts., Somerset, Dorset, Devon, Cornwall)

Wales: 8 Broad Street, Newtown, Powys SY16 2LU. Tel: (0686) 26799

Yorks. and Humberside: 8A Otley Road, Headingley, Leeds LS6 2AD. Tel: (0532) 742935/6 (N., S. and W. Yorks., Humberside)

Countryside Commission for Scotland, Battleby, Redgorton, Perth PH1 3EW. Tel: (0738) 27921

County Naturalists' Trusts (County Trust for Nature Conservation): see Royal Society for Nature Conservation

Coventry Countryside Project, Coventry City Council, Department of Architecture and Planning, Much Park Street, Coventry CV1 5RT. Tel: Coventry (0203) 25555, ext. 2937

Customs and Excise, HQ Office, King's Beau House, Mark Lane, London EC3.

Customs and Excise, VAT Liability, Custom House, Lower Thames Street, London EC4. Tel: 01-626 1515

Department of Agriculture for Northern Ireland: Forest Service, Dundonald House, Upper Newtownards Road, Belfast BT4 3SB. Tel: (0232) 650111

Department of Education and Science, Elizabeth House, York Road, London SE1 7PH. Tel: 01-928 9222

Department of the Environment, Central Directorate of Environmental Protection, Room A3.24, DoE, Romney House, 43 Marsham Street, London SW1 3PY. Tel: 01-212 5464. Also: Wildlife Division, Tollgate House, Houlton Street, Bristol, Avon BS2 9DJ. Tel. (0272) 218811

Department of the Environment (DoE) Northern Ireland, Conservation Branch, Hut 6, Castle Grounds, Stormont, Belfast BT4 3SS. Tel: (0232) 768716

Disabled Living Foundation, 346 Kensington High Street, London W14 8NS. Tel: 01-602 2491

Ecological Parks Trust (EPT), c/o The Linnean Society, Burlington House, Piccadilly, London W1V 0LQ. Tel: 01-734 5170

Environmental Advisory Unit, Department of Botany, University of Liverpool, P.O. Box 147, Liverpool L69 3BX. Tel: (051) 709 6022

Environmental Education Advisers' Association, Pendower Hall Teachers' Centre, West Road, Newcastle-upon-Tyne NE15 6PP

Environmental Resource Centre, Drummond High School, Cochran Terrace, Edinburgh EH7 4PQ. Tel: (031) 557 2135

Farming and Wildlife Advisory Group (FWAG), The Lodge, Sandy, Beds. SG19 2DL. Tel: Sandy (0767) 80551

Fauna and Flora Preservation Society, 8-12 Camden High Street, London NW1 0JH. Tel: 01-387-9656

Federation for the Promotion of Horticulture for the Disabled, Hon. Secretary, Mrs M. Rhodes, Land Management Service, Spastics Society, Thorngrove, Gillingham, Dorset

Field Studies Council (FSC), 62 Wilson Street, London EC2A 2BU. Tel: 01-247 4651

The field centres:

Dale Fort Field Centre, Haverfordwest, Dyfed SA62 3RD

The Draper's Field Centre, Rhyd-y-creuau, Betws-y-coed, Gwynedd LL24 0HB

Flatford Mill Field Centre, East Bergholt, Colchester, Essex CO7 6UL

Juniper Hall Field Centre, Dorking, Surrey RH5 6DA

The Leonard Wills Field Centre, Nettlecombe Court, Williton, Taunton, Somerset TA4 4HT

Malham Tarn Field Centre, Settle, North Yorkshire BD24 9PU

Orielton Field Centre and Oil Pollution Research Unit, Pembroke, Dyfed SA71 5EZ

Preston Montford Field Centre, Montford Bridge, Shrewsbury, Shropshire SY4 1DX (educational enquiries: Information Office)

Slapton Ley Field Centre, Slapton, Kingsbridge, Devon TQ7 2QP

Epping Forest Conservation Centre, High Beach, Loughton, Essex IG10 4AF

Forestry Commission: Headquarters, The Forestry Commission, 231 Corstorphine Road, Edinburgh EH12 7AT. Tel: (031) 334 0303

Research stations:

The Forestry Commission, Forest Research Station, Alice Holt Lodge, Wrecclesham, Farnham, Surrey GU10 4LH. Tel: 042 04 2255

The Forestry Commission, Northern Research Station, Bush Estate, Roslin, Midlothian EH25 9SY. Tel: (031) 445 2176

Conservancy offices:

England:

North West: Dee Hills Park, Chester CH3 5AT. Tel: (0244) 24006

North East: 1A Grosvenor Terrace, York YO3 7BD. Tel: (0904) 20221

East: Block D. Government Buildings, Brooklands Avenue, Cambridge CB2 2DY. Tel: (0223) 58911

New Forest and South East: The Queen's House, Lyndhurst, Hants. SO4 7NH. Tel: (042 128) 2801

South West and Dean Forest: Flowers Hill, Brislington, Bristol BS4 5JY. Tel: (0272) 713471

Scotland:

North: 21 Church Street, Inverness IV1 1EL. Tel: (0463) 32811

South: Greystone Park, 55/57 Moffat Road, Dumfries DG1 1NP

East: 6 Queen's Gate, Aberdeen AB9 2NQ. Tel: (0224) 313361

West: Portcullis House, 21 India Street, Glasgow G2 4PL. Tel: (041) 248 3931

Wales:

North: Victoria House, Victoria Terrace, Aberystwyth SY23 2DA. Tel: (0970) 2367

South: Churchill House, Churchill Way, Cardiff CF1 4TU. Tel: (0222) 40661

Freshwater Biologial Association, The Ferry House, Far Sawrey, Ambleside, Cumbria LA22 0LP. Tel: (09662) 2468

Friends of the Earth (FoE), Headquarters, 377 City Road, London EC1V 1NA. Tel: 01-837 0731. Also: FoE (Scotland), 53 George IV Bridge, Edinburgh EH1 1EJ. Tel: (031) 225 6906

Game Conservancy, Fordingbridge, Hants SP6 1EF. Tel: (0425) 52381

Gaming Board, Lotteries Division, Africa House, 64-78 Kingsway, London WC2B 6BW. Tel: 01-404 5786

Gardens for the Disabled Trust, Headcorn Manor, Headcorn, Kent TN27 8PJ. Tel: (0622) 890360

Geological Society, Burlington House, Piccadilly, London W1V 0JU. Tel: 01-734 2356/2510

Glasgow Environmental Education Urban Projects (GEE-UP), Education Offices, 129 Bath Street, Glasgow G2 2SY. Tel: (041) 204 2900, ext. 2639

Glasgow Urban Wildlife Group, c/o Glasgow Council for Voluntary Services, 234 West Regent Street, Glasgow G2. Tel: (041) 334 5780 (evenings)

'Grapevine', BBC TV, London W12 8QT. Tel: 01-743 8000

Greater London Council Ecology Unit, c/o London Ecology Centre, 45 Shelton Street, London WC2H 9HJ. Tel: 01-379 4324

Greater Manchester Council and Lancashire County Council Joint Reclamation Team, Westward House, King Street, Wigan WN1 1LP. Tel: 0942 48115, ext. 27, Dr R.P. Gemmell (ecologist)

Green Cure Trust, Grosvenor Lodge, Gordon Road, Clifton, Bristol BS8 1AW. Tel: (0272) 30030

Groundwork Trust Headquarters — Operation Groundwork 32/34 Claughton Street, St Helen's WA10 1SN. Tel: St Helen's (0744) 39396. Also: Groundwork North-West Unit, 2nd Floor, 184 Deansgate, Manchester M3 2WB. Tel: (061) 833 9950

Macclesfield Groundwork Trust, Brook Bank House, Wellington Road, Bollington, Macclesfield SK10 5JS. Tel: (0625) 72681

Oldham and Rochdale Groundwork Trust, Bank House, 8 Chapel Street, Shaw, Oldham OL2 8AJ. Tel: (0706) 842212

Rossendale Groundwork Trust, New Hall Hey Farm, New Hall Hey Road, Rawtenstall, Lancs. BB4 6HR. Tel: (0706) 211421

Salford and Trafford Groundwork Trust, 6 Kansas Avenue, Weaste, Salford M5 2GL. Tel: (061) 848 0334

Wigan Groundwork Trust, Alder House, Alder Street, Atherton M29 9DT. Tel: (0942) 891116

Handicapped Adventure Playground Association, Fulham Palace, Bishops Avenue, London SW6. Tel: 01-736 4443

Health and Safety Executive, Baynards House, Chepstow Place, London W2. Tel: 01-229 3456

Henry Doubleday Research Association, Covent Lane, Bocking, Braintree, Essex CM7 6RW. Tel: (0376) 24083

Heritage Education Group, 17 Carlton House Terrace, London SW1

HM Land Registry, 32 Lincoln's Inn Fields, London WC2A 3PH. Tel: 01-405 3588

Horticultural Therapy Training Centre, Warwickshire College of Agriculture, Moreton Morrell, Warwickshire CV35 9BL. Tel: (0926) 651288

Horticultural Trades Association, 19 High Street, Theale, Reading, Berks. RG7 5AH. Tel: (0734) 303132

IMPACT, 39 Northumberland Road, Old Trafford, Manchester M16 9AN. Tel: (061) 872 5583.

Sub-offices:

Room 19, Bredbury Council Offices, George Lane, Bredbury SK1 1DJ. Tel: (061) 494 0466

Room 37, Priory Buildings, 2nd Floor, Union Street, Oldham OL1 1HL. Tel: (061) 620 1620

St George's School, Windsor Street, off Sullivan Way, off Greenhalgh Street, Wigan WN1 3TG. Tel: Wigan (0942) 322576

Inland Revenue Claims Branch, Charities Division, Magdalen House, Stanley Precinct, Bootle, Lancs. L69 9BB. Tel: (051) 992 6363

Inland Revenue Claims Branch (Scotland), Trinity Park House, South Trinity Road, Edinburgh EH5 3SD. Tel: (031) 552 6255

Inland Waterways Amenity Advisory Council, 122 Cleveland Street, London W1P 5DN. Tel: 01-387 7973

Institute of Chartered Accountants in England and Wales, Moorgate Place, London EC2. Tel: 01-628 7060

Institute of Personnel Management, Central House, Upper Woburn Place, London WC1. Tel: 01-387 2944

Institute of Terrestrial Ecology, Monks Wood, Abbots Ripton, Huntingdon, Cambs. Tel: (04873) 381

Institute of Waste Management, 28 Portland Place, London W1N 4DE. Tel: 01-580 5324

Institute of Water Pollution Control, Ledstone House, 53 London Road, Maidstone, Kent ME16 8JH. Tel: (0622) 62034

Interchange City Farms Advisory Service, Community Arts and Resource Centre, 15 Wilkin Street, London NW5 3NX. Tel: 01-267 9421

International Union for Conservation of Nature and Natural Resources (IUCN), 219c Huntingdon Road, Cambs. CB3 0DL. Tel: (0223) 277314 and 277420 (Species Conservation Monitoring Unit) and 277427 (Wildlife Trade Monitoring Unit)

Irish Wildlife Federation, 112 Grafton Street, Dublin 2, Eire. Tel: Dublin (0001) 608346

Joint Committee for the Conservation of British Insects, c/o Dept. of Entomology, Natural History Museum, Cromwell Road, London SW7. Tel: 01-589 6323, ext. 454

Keep Britain Tidy Group, Bostel House, 37 West Street, Brighton, E. Sussex BN1 2RE. Tel: (0273) 23585

Keep Scotland Tidy Campaign, 23 Hill Street, Edinburgh EH2 3JP. Tel: (031) 225 6336

Land Council, 9 Queen Anne's Gate, London SW1H 9BY. Tel: 01-836 5454

Land Decade Education Council, The London Science Centre, 18 Adam Street, London WC2N 6AH

Landlife (formerly Rural Preservation Association), The Old Police Station, Lark Lane, Liverpool L17 8UU. Tel: (051) 728 7011
Branches (no telephone numbers — contact by letter only):
Landlife Lancaster, 25 Gerrard Street, Lancaster
Landlife St Helens, 26 Kiln Lane, Denton Green, St Helens, Manchester
Landlife Leeds, 5 Salisbury Street, Rawdon, Leeds, W. Yorks LS19 6BE
Landlife Manchester, c/o North West Civic Trust, The Environmental Institute, Greave School, Bolton Road, Swinton, Manchester M27 2UX
Landlife Ireland, Calthorne College, Castle Sallagh, Donard, Co. Wicklow, Eire

Landscape Institute, 12 Carlton House Terrace, London SW1Y 5AH. Tel: 01-839 4044

Law Centres Federation (Administration Office), 164 North Gower Street, London NW1. Tel: 01-387 8570

Leicester City Wildlife Project Office, 31 London Road, Leicester. Tel: (0533) 552550

London Adventure Playgrounds Association, 25 Ovington Square, London SW3 1LG. Tel: 01-581 2490

London Tenants Organisation, 17 Victoria Park Square, London E2. Tel: 01-981 1221

London Union of Youth Clubs, 64 Camberwell Road, London SE5 0EN. Tel: 01-701 6366

London Voluntary Service Council, 68 Charlton Street, London NW1. Tel: 01-388 0241

London Wildlife Trust (LWT), 1 Thorpe Close, London W10 5XL. Tel: 01-968 5368

Mammal Society, c/o Linnean Society, Burlington House, Piccadilly, London W1V 0LQ. Tel: 01-387 7050, ext. 415

Mary Marlborough Lodge, Nuffield Orthopaedic Centre, Headington, Oxford OX3 7LD. Tel: (0865) 64811

MENCAP, Rural Advisory Service, Mr D. Carter, 20 High Street, Yatton, Avon BS19 4JA. Tel: (0934) 838560

Men of the Trees, Crawley Down, Crawley, West Sussex RH10 4HL. Tel: (0342) 712536

Ministry of Defence (MoD), Conservation Department, Defence Lands 3, Room 22, Spur 3, B. Block, Government Buildings, Leatherhead Road, Chessington, Surrey. Tel: 01-397 5266

National Association of Citizens Advice Bureaux (NACAB), 110 Drury Lane, London WC2B 5SW. Tel: 01-836 9231

National Association for Environmental Education, Westbourne Teachers' Centre, 17 Westbourne Road, Sheffield S10 2QQ

National Children's Bureau, 8 Wakley Street, London EC1V 7QE. Tel: 01-278 9441

National Council for Voluntary Organisations (NCVO), Information Department, NCVO, 26 Bedford Square, London WC1B 3HU. Tel: 01-636 4066

National Federation of City Farms, c/o Hon. Secretary, 15 Wilkin Street, London NW5 3NG. Tel: 01-267 9421

National Federation of City Farms, The Old Vicarage, 66 Fraser Street, Bedminster, Bristol BS3 4LY. Tel: (0272) 660663

Member farms (not a comprehensive list):

North:
Darnall Community Farm, 66 Mather Road, Sheffield 9. Tel: (0742) 441639
Heeley City Farm, Richards Road, Sheffield S2 3DT. Tel: (0742) 580482

North West:
Liverpool 8, Garden Farm, 4 Madelaine Street, Liverpool L8 8AP. Tel: (051) 708 6097
Rice Lane City Farm, No 1 Lodge, Walton Park Cemetery, Rice Lane, Liverpool L9 1AW. Tel: (051) 521 6790

North East:
Bradford City Farm, Walker Drive, Bradford 8. Tel: (0274) 43500
City Farm Byker, Stepney Bank, Newcastle-upon-Tyne. Tel: (0632) 323698
Meanwood Valley Urban Farm, Sugarwell Road, Meanwood, Leeds 7. Tel: (0532) 629759
Southwick Village Farm, 271 Southwick Road, Southwick, Sunderland, Tyne and Wear. Tel: (0783) 489002

Midlands:
Coventry City Farm, 1 Clarence Street, Hillfields, Coventry CV1 4SS. Tel: (0203) 25323
Newparks Adventure Playground, The Community Centre, St Oswalds Road, Leicester
Stonebridge City Farm, Stonebridge Road, St Anne's, Nottingham NG3 2FR. Tel: (0602) 505113

West Midlands:
Hockley Port City Farm, Hockley Port, All Saints Street, Birmingham, W. Midlands. Tel: (021) 551 6487
Holy Trinity Farm, 57 Stephenson Tower, Station Street, Birmingham. Tel: (021) 643 1990 (after 4 pm)

South West:
Hartcliffe Community Farm Park, Whitehouse Youth Club, Briscoes Avenue, Hartcliffe, Bristol 13. Tel: (0272) 781708

St Werburghs City Farm, Watercress Road, St Werburghs, Bristol 2. Tel: (0272) 428241

Windmill Hill City Farm, Philip Street, Bedminster, Bristol 3. Tel: (0272) 633252

Millbrook City Farm, 4 Church Lane, Highfield, Southampton. Tel: (0703) 555333

London:
Adelaide Community Garden, 46 Blashford, 111 Adelaide Road, London NW3. Tel: 01-586 8310

Culpepper Community Gardens, Nr King of Denmark, Cloudesley Road, London N1 0EJ. Tel: 01-833 3951

Deen Farm, Batsworth Road, off Church Road, Mitcham, London SW19. Tel: 01-648 1561

Elm Farm, Old Gladstone Terrace, Lockington Road, Battersea, London SW8. Tel: 01-627 1130

Kentish Town City Farm, 1 Cressfield Close, London NW5. Tel: 01-482 2861

Newham Wasteland Project, 58 Buxton Road, Stratford, London E15 1QU. Tel: 01-519 2439

Sunnyside Gardens, Crouch Hill Recreation Centre, Hillrise Road, London N19. Tel: 01-263 0293

Vauxhall City Farm, 24 St Oswalds Place, London SW11. Tel: 01-582 4204

East:
New Ark Adventure Playground and Community Gardens, Old Poplar Farm, Oxney Road, Peterborough. Tel: (0733) 40605

Thameside Community Farm Park, Thames Road, Barking, Essex. Tel: 01-594 8449

Wellgate Community Farm, The Old School House, Oaks Centre, Collier Row Road, Romford, Essex RM5 2DD. Tel: 01-590 5980

Northern Ireland:
Glennand Youth and Community Workshop Ltd, Blackstaff Road, Kennedy Way Industrial Estate, Belfast 11. Tel: (0232) 618560

Scotland:
Balbirnie Community Farm, c/o 9 Sorn Green, Glenrothes, Fife KY7 4SF. Tel: (03375) 256

Gorgie City Farm, Gorgie Road, Edinburgh. Tel: (031) 225 3766

Knowetop City Farm, Phoenix Community Education Centre, Quarry Knowe, Castlehill, Dumbarton G82. Tel: (0389) 65885

Lamont Farm Project, Barrhill Road, Erskine, Renfrewshire. Tel: (041) 812 2077

Possil City Farm, Ellesmere Street, Hamiltonhill, Glasgow G22. Tel: (041) 336 8754

Wales:
Cardiff City Farm, 38 Llanmaes Street, Grangetown, Cardiff CF1 7LR. Tel: (0222) 384360

National Federation of Community Organisations, 8-9 Upper Street, London N1 0PQ. Tel: 01-226 0189 (see also University of Bath)

National Playing Fields Association, 25 Ovington Square, London SW3 1LQ. Tel: 01-584 6445

National Society of Allotment and Leisure Gardeners Ltd, 22 High Street, Flitwick, Bedfordshire MK45 1DT. Tel: (05257) 2361

National Trust, 36 Queen Anne's Gate, London SW1H 9AS. Tel: 01-222 9251

National Trust for Scotland, 5 Charlotte Square, Edinburgh EH2 4DU. Tel: (031) 226 5922

Natural History Museum, Cromwell Road, South Kensington, London SW7 5BD. Tel: 01-589 6323

Nature Conservancy Council (NCC), Headquarters and regional office for East Midlands; Northminster House, Northminster Road, Peterborough PE1 1AV. Tel: (0733) 40345

Regional offices:

East Anglia: 60 Bracondale, Norwich, Norfolk NR1 2BE. Tel: Norwich (0603) 20558 (Essex, Norfolk, Suffolk)

North-East: Archbold House, Archbold Terrace, Newcastle-upon-Tyne NE2 1EG. Tel: Newcastle-upon-Tyne (0632) 816316 (Cleveland, Durham, Humberside, N. Yorks., Northumberland, Tyne and Wear)

North-West: South Blackwell, Bowness-on-Windermere, Windermere, Cumbria LA23 3JR. Tel: Windermere (09662) 5286 (Cumbria, Gtr Manchester, Lancs., Merseyside)

South: Foxhold House, Thornford Road, Crookham Common, Newbury, Berks. RG15 8EL. Tel: Headley (063523) 429/439/533 (Berks., Bucks., Hants., I. of Wight, Oxon., Wilts.)

South-East: Zealds, Church Street, Wye, Ashford, Kent TN25 5BW. Tel: Wye (0233) 812525 (E. Sussex, Gtr London, Kent, Surrey, W. Sussex)

South-West: Roughmoor, Bishop's Hull, Taunton, Somerset TA1 5AA. Tel: Taunton (0823) 83211 (Avon, Cornwall, Devon, Dorset, Somerset)

Scotland: Headquarters, 12 Hope Terrace, Edinburgh EH9 2AS. Tel: (031) 447 4784

Wales: Headquarters for Wales: Plas Penrhos, Ffordd Penrhos, Bangor, Gwynedd LL57 2LQ. Tel: Bangor (0248) 355141

NCC Regional Offices in Wales:

Dyfed-Powys: Plas Gogerddan, Aberystwyth, Dyfed SY23 3EB. Tel: Aberystwyth (0970) 828551 (Dyfed [excluding Llanelli Borough], Powys)

South: 44 The Parade, Roath, Cardiff CF2 3AB. Tel: Cardiff (0222) 485111 (Gwent, Mid-Glamorgan, South Glamorgan, West Glamorgan)

Northern Ireland Department of Finance, Charities Branch, Rosepark House, Upper Newtownards Road, Belfast BT4 3NR. Tel: (0232) 184 585

Open Spaces Society, 25a Bell Street, Henley-on-Thames, Oxon. RG9 2BA. Tel: (0491) 573535

The Order of St John (St John's Ambulance Brigade), St John's Gate, London EC1M 4DA. Tel: 01-253 6644

The Ordnance Survey, Ramsey Road, Maybush, Southampton SD9 4DH

Oyez Publishing Ltd, Norwich House, 11-13 Norwich Street, London EC4. Tel: 01-404 5721

Planning Aid Service for Londoners, 26 Portland Place, London W1N 4BE. Tel: 01-580 7277

Pre-School Playgroups Association, Alford House, Aveline Street, London SW11 5DH. Tel: 01-582 8871

Registrar of Companies (Scotland), 102 George Street, Edinburgh. Tel: (031) 225 5774

Registry of Companies, Companies House, Crown Way, Maindy, Cardiff. Tel: (0222) 388588

Registry of Friendly Societies, 17 North Audley Street, London W1Y 2AP. Tel: 01-437 9992

Royal Botanic Gardens, Kew. Tel: 01-940 1171. Also: Seed Bank, Wakehurst Place, Ardingly, Haywards Heath, W. Sussex RH17 6TN. Tel: (0444) 892701

Royal Entomological Society, 41 Queen's Gate, London SW7 5HU. Tel: 01-584 8361

Royal Society for Nature Conservation (RSNC), 22 The Green, Nettleham, Lincoln LN2 2NR. Tel: (0522) 752326

County Naturalists' Trusts:

Avon Wildlife Trust, 209 Redland Road, Bristol BS6 6YU. Tel: Bristol (0272) 36822/3

Bedford and Huntingdon Naturalists' Trust, 38 Mill Street, Bedford MK40 3HD. Tel: Bedford (0234) 64213

Berkshire, Buckinghamshire and Oxon. Naturalists' Trust (BBONT), 3 Church Cowley Road, Rose Hill, Oxford OX4 3JR. Tel: Oxford (0865) 775476

Brecknock Naturalists' Trust, Chapel House, Llechafaen, Brecon, Powys, Wales. Tel: Llanfryach (087 486) 688

Cambridgeshire and Isle of Ely Naturalists' Trust, 1 Brookside, Cambridge CB2 1JF. Tel: Cambridge (0223) 358144

Cheshire Conservation Trust, c/o Marbury Country Park, Northwich, Cheshire CW9 6AT. Tel: Northwich (0606) 781868

Cleveland Nature Conservation Trust, 38 Victoria Road, Hartlepool, Cleveland TS26 8DL. Tel: Hartlepool (0429) 73157

Cornwall Naturalists' Trust, Trendrine, Zennor, St Ives, Cornwall TR26 3BW. Tel: Penzance (0736) 796926

Cumbria Trust for Nature Conservation, Church Street, Ambleside LA22 0BU. Tel: Ambleside (09663) 2476

Derbyshire Naturalists' Trust, Estate Office, Twyford, Barrow-on-Trent, Derby DE7 1HJ. Tel: Burton-on-Trent (0283) 70143

Devon Trust for Nature Conservation, 35 New Bridge Street, Exeter, Devon EX4 3AH. Tel: Exeter (0392) 79244

Dorset Naturalists' Trust, 39 Christchurch Road, Bournemouth, Dorset BH1 3NS. Tel: Bournemouth (0202) 24241

Durham County Conservation Trust, 52 Old Elvet, Durham DN1 3HN. Tel: Durham (0385) 69797

Essex Naturalists' Trust, Fingringhoe Wick Nature Reserve, Fingringhoe, Colchester CO5 7DN. Tel: Rowhedge (020628) 678

Glamorgan Naturalists' Trust, The Glamorgan Nature Centre, Fountain Road, Tondu, Bridgend, Mid Glamorgan CF32 0EH. Tel: (0656) 724100

Gloucestershire Trust for Nature Conservation, Church House, Standish, Stonehouse, Glos. GL10 3EU. Tel: Stonehouse (045 382) 2761

Gwent Trust for Nature Conservation, The Shire Hall, Monmouth, Gwent NP5 3DY. Tel: Monmouth (0600) 5501 (9-1 Mon-Fri only)

Hampshire and Isle of Wight Naturalists' Trust, 8 Market Place, Romsey, Hants. SO5 8NB. Tel: Romsey (0794) 513786

Hereford and Radnor Naturalists' Trust, Community House, 25 Castle Street, Hereford HR1 2NW. Tel: Hereford (0432) 56872

Hertfordshire and Middlesex Trust for Nature Conservation, Grebe House, St Michael's Street, St Albans, Herts. A13 4SN. Tel: St Albans (56) 58901

Kent Trust for Nature Conservation, 125 High Street, Rainham, Kent ME8 8AN. Tel: Medway (0634) 362561

Lancashire Trust for Nature Conservation, Dale House, Dale Head, Slaidburn, Lancs. BB7 4TS. Tel: Slaidburn (02006) 294

Leicestershire and Rutland Trust for Nature Conservation, 1 West Street, Leicester LE1 6UU. Tel: Leicester (0533) 553904

Lincolnshire and South Humberside Trust for Nature Conservation, The Manor House, Alford, Lincs. LN13 9DL. Tel: Alford (05212) 3468

London Wildlife Trust, 1 Thorpe Close, London W10 5XL. Tel: 01-968 5368

Manx Nature Conservation Trust, Bellacross, Andreas, Isle of Man. Tel: Kirk Andreas (062488) 434

Montgomery Trust for Nature Conservation, 18 High Street, Newtown, Powys SY16 2NP. Tel: Newtown (0686) 26678

Norfolk Naturalists' Trust, 72 Cathedral Close, Norwich NR1 4DF. Tel: Norwich (0603) 25540

Northamptonshire Naturalists' Trust, Lings House, Billing Lings, Northampton NN3 4BE. Tel: Northampton (0604) 405285

Northumberland Wildlife Trust, Hancock Museum, Barras Bridge, Newcastle-upon-Tyne NE2 4PT. Tel: Newcastle/Tyne (0632) 320038

North Wales Naturalists' Trust, 154 High Street, Bangor, Gwynedd LL57 1NU. Tel: Bangor (0248) 351541

Nottinghamshire Trust for Nature Conservation, 33 Main Street, Osgathorpe, Loughborough, Leics. LE12 9TA. Tel: Coalville (0530) 222633

Scottish Wildlife Trust, 25 Johnston Terrace, Edinburgh EH1 2NH. Tel: Edinburgh (031) 226 4602

Shropshire Trust for Nature Conservation, Agriculture House, Barker Street, Shrewsbury, Shropshire SY1 1QP. Tel: Shrewsbury (0743) 241691

Somerset Trust for Nature Conservation, Fyne Court, Broomfield, Bridgwater, Somerset TA5 2EQ. Tel: Kingston St Mary (082345) 587/8

Staffordshire Nature Conservation Trust, 3A Newport Road, Stafford ST16 2HH. Tel: Stafford (0785) 44372

Suffolk Trust for Nature Conservation, Park Cottage, Peasenhall, Saxmundham, Suffolk IP17 2NA. Tel: (0728) 3765

Surrey Trust for Nature Conservation, 'Hatchlands', East Clandon, Guildford, Surrey GU4 7RT. Tel: Guildford (0483) 223526

Sussex Trust for Nature Conservation, Woods Mill, Shoreham Road, Henfield, W. Sussex BN5 9SD. Tel: Brighton (0273) 492630

Ulster Trust for Nature Conservation, Barnett's Cottage, Barnett's Demesne, Malone Road, Belfast BT9 5PB. Tel: (0232) 612235

Urban Wildlife Group, 11 Albert Square, Birmingham B4 7UA. Tel: (021) 236 3626

Warwickshire Nature Conservation Trust, 1 Northgate Street, Warwick CV34 4SP. Tel: Warwick (0926) 496848

West Wales Naturalists' Trust, 7 Market Street, Haverfordwest, Dyfed. Tel: Haverfordwest (0437) 5462

Wiltshire Trust for Nature Conservation, 19 High Street, Devizes, Wiltshire. Tel: Devizes (0380) 5670 or 2463

Worcestershire Nature Conservation Trust, The Lodge, Beacon Lane, Rednal, Birmingham. Tel: (021) 453 9477

Yorkshire Naturalists' Trust, 20 Castlegate, York YO1 1RP. Tel: (0904) 59570

The Royal Society for the Prevention of Accidents (RoSPA), Cannon House, The Priory, Queensway, Birmingham B4 6BS. Tel: (021) 233 2461

Royal Society for the Protection of Birds (RSPB), The Lodge, Sandy, Beds. SG19 2DL. Tel: Sandy (0767) 80551. Also: Young Ornithologists' Club (YOC)

RSPB Northern Ireland, Belvoir Park Forest, Belfast BT8 4QT. Tel: (0232) 692547

RSPB Scotland, 17 Regent Terrace, Edinburgh EH7 5BN. Tel: (031) 556 5624/ 9042

RSPB Wales, Frolic Street, Newtown, Powys SY16 1AP. Tel: (0686) 26678

Royal Town Planning Institute, 26 Portland Place, London W1N 4BE. Tel: 01-636 9107. Also: Planning Aid Service for Londoners. Tel: 01-580 7277

Rural Preservation Association (RPA): see Landlife

'Save Our Bog', c/o Mrs J. Fifer, 245 Wake Green Road, Moseley, Birmingham B13 9UZ. Tel: (021) 777 6570

Scottish Civic Trust, 24 George Square, Glasgow G2 1EF. Tel: (041) 221 1466

Scottish Community Education Council, Atholl House, 2 Canning Street, Edinburgh EH3 8EG. Tel: (031) 229 2433

Scottish Conservation Projects Trust: Headquarters, 70 Main Street, Doune, Perthshire FK16 6BW. Tel: (0786) 841479. Also: 54 Waddell Street, Hutcheson Town, Glasgow G5 0LU. Tel: (041) 429 2112

Scottish Council of Social Service, 18-19 Claremont Crescent, Edinburgh EH7 4QQ. Tel: (031) 556 3882

Scottish Field Studies Association, Kindrogan Field Centre, Enochdu, Blairgowrie, Perth PH10 7PG. Tel: (0250) 81286

Sheffield, University of, Unit of Comparative Plant Ecology, Department of Botany, Sheffield S10 2TN. Tel: (0742) 78555

Shell Better Britain Campaign, c/o Nature Conservancy Council PO Box 6, Godwin House, George Street, Huntingdon, Cambs. PE18 6BU. Tel: (0480) 56191

Social Workers Pension Fund, 93/95 Borough High Street, London SE1 1NL. Tel: 01-403 0301

Society for Horticultural Therapy and Rural Training, Goulds Ground, Vallis Way, Frome, Somerset BA11 3DW. Tel: (0373) 64782

Society for Promotion of Rehabilitation in Gardening (SPRIG), c/o College of Occupational Therapists Ltd, 20 Rede Place, Bayswater, London W2 4TU. Tel: 01-229 9738/9

Soil Association, Walnut Tree Manor, Haughley, Stowmarket, Suffolk IP14 3RS. Tel: Haughley (044970) 235/6

Soil Survey of England and Wales, Rothamsted Experimental Station, Harpenden, Herts. AL5 2JQ

The Solicitor's Law Stationery Society Ltd, 237 Long Lane, London EC1. Tel: 01-407 8055

Southwark Wildlife Group, 54 Kingsgrove, London SE15. Tel: 01-732 6984

Spastics Society, 12 Park Crescent, London W1N 4EQ. Tel: 01-636 5020

Swansea City Council, Environment Department, Guildhall, Swansea, West Glamorgan SA14. Tel: (0792) 50821

Thames Polytechnic MSC Urban Ecology Study, Oakfield Lane, Dartford, Kent DA1 2SZ. Tel: (0322) 21328

Town and Country Planning Association, 17 Carlton House Terrace, London SW1. Tel: 01-930 8903/4/5

Town and Country Planning Association, 56 Oxford Street, Manchester M1 6EV. Also: Community Technical Aid Centre, 61 Bloom Street, Manchester M1 3L7. Tel: (061) 236 5195

Town Trees Trust, 11 Gainsborough Gardens, London NW13 1BJ. Tel: 01-794 2764

Tower Hamlets Environment Trust (THET), Brady Centre, 192/6 Hanbury Street, London E1. Tel: 01-247 6265

The Tree Council, Room 101, Agriculture House, Knightsbridge, London SW1X 7NJ. Tel: 01-235 8854

Trees for People, 71 Verulam Road, St Albans, Herts. AL3 4DJ. Tel: (0727) 67196

Trusts for Nature Conservation: see Royal Society for Nature Conservation

University Botanic Garden, Cambridge CB2 1JF. Tel: (0223) 350101

University of Bath, Horticultural Group, School of Biological Sciences, Claverton Down, Bath BA2 7AY. Tel: (0225) 61244 (see also Federation for the Promotion of Horticulture for the Disabled)

University of Sheffield, NERC Unit of Comparative Plant Ecology, Department of Botany, Sheffield S10 2TN

Urban Spaces Scheme, Dept. of Food and Biological Sciences, Polytechnic of North London, Holloway, London N7 8DB. Tel: 01-607 2789

Urban Wildlife Group, 11 Albert Square, Birmingham B4 7VA. Tel: (021) 236 3626

Voluntary Aid, London Society of Chartered Accountants, 38 Finsbury Square, London EC2. Tel: 01-446 2467

Wales Council for Voluntary Action, Llys Ifor, Crescent Road, Caerphilly, Mid Glamorgan CF8 1XL. Tel: (0222) 869224

WATCH (Trust for Environmental Education), 22 The Green, Nettleham, Lincoln LN2 2NR. Tel: (0522) 752326

Wildflower Society, Rams Hill House, Horsmonden, Tonbridge, Kent. Also: 69 Outwoods Road, Loughborough, Leics.

Woodland Trust, Westgate, Grantham, Lincs. NG31 6LL. Tel: Grantham (0476) 74297

World Wildlife Fund UK, Panda House, 11-13 Ockford Road, Godalming, Surrey GU7 1OU. Tel: (048 68) 20551

Youth Environmental Action, 173 Archway Road, London N6. Tel: 01-348 3030

Zoological Society of London, Regents Park, London NW1 4RY. Tel: 01-586 0872

Index